INTRODUCTION TO

POLITICAL
PSYCHOLOGY

INTRODUCTION TO
POLITICAL PSYCHOLOGY

Martha Cottam
Washington State University

Beth Dietz-Uhler
Miami University

Elena Mastors
Washington State University

Thomas Preston
Washington State University

LAWRENCE ERLBAUM ASSOCIATES, PUBLISHERS
2004   Mahwah, New Jersey   London

Senior Editor:	Debra Riegert
Cover Design:	Sean Trane Sciarrone
Textbook Production Manager:	Paul Smolenski
Full-Service Compositor:	TechBooks
Text and Cover Printer:	Hamilton Printing Company

Photos of demonstrations by Otwin Marenin.
Photo of wall of missing persons at ground zero by Steven Stehr.

This book was typeset in 10/12 pt. Times, Italic, Bold, and Bold Italic.
The heads were typeset in Gill Sans Bold.

Lawrence Erlbaum Associates, Inc., Publishers
10 Industrial Avenue
Mahwah, New Jersey 07430
www.erlbaum.com

Library of Congress Cataloging-in-Publication Data
Cottam, Martha L.
    Introduction to political psychology / Martha Cottam . . . [et al.].
        p.   cm.
Includes bibliographical references and index.
    ISBN 0-8058-3770-1 (pbk.: alk. paper)
    1. Political psychology.   I. Title.
JA74.5.C665 2004
320'.01'9—dc22

                                                           2003025976

Books published by Lawrence Erlbaum Associates are printed on acid-free paper, and their bindings are chosen for strength and durability.

Printed in the United States of America
10 9 8 7 6 5

DEDICATION

The authors dedicate this book to Peg Hermann, for her unceasing support for us and for her devotion to the field of political psychology; to Otto Marenin, honorary political psychologist; and to Andrew Mastors-Rao, future political psychologist.

CONTENTS

PREFACE

When colleagues from other disciplines ask us what we specialize in, they are often puzzled when we say political psychology. "What's that?" and "I didn't know there was such a thing" are frequently heard comments. That is primarily because political psychology is not a traditional field in social science, but an interdisciplinary field that attempts to explain political behavior via psychological principles. The field is so interdisciplinary that calling it "political psychology" is misleading because it includes scholars from both political science and psychology, but also from sociology, public administration, criminal justice, anthropology, and many other areas. Also, unlike many fields in the social sciences, political psychology uses multiple methodologies, from experiments to surveys, to qualitative case studies, and beyond. And, if our colleagues from other disciplines have not heard of political psychology, they will soon. Political psychology is an important domain of academic research; students find it fascinating and very often troubling as they are exposed to some of the most shocking examples of political violence; and policy makers would undoubtedly benefit greatly from a better understanding of political psychology. Understanding the psychological causes of political behavior is crucial if we are to affect patterns of behavior that are harmful to humanity and to promote patterns of behavior that are beneficial to humanity.

As the field of political psychology has grown, so has the need for a comprehensive textbook that pulls its many strands of research in political psychology together. This book is a result of the authors' frustration, which was produced by teaching courses in political psychology without such a book. Rather than having students purchase a textbook on psychology, of which they will read only a portion, and a number of books describing political behavior without a psychological explanation of that behavior, we decided to create a text that merges these disciplines. Thus, we present the psychology as it pertains to *political* psychology and explain types of political behavior with political psychological concepts in a single book. We introduce readers to a broad range of political psychology theories and sketch many cases of political activity to illustrate the behavior. Readers do not need a background in psychology or political science to understand the material in this book. However, knowing that our introduction may stimulate a desire for further investigation, we also include suggested readings: Many excellent books and articles that contain rich, nuanced studies of each of the political behaviors we introduce in this book.

Once we embarked upon this project, we quickly discovered that the field of political psychology is much broader than those of us who teach and do research in the area may realize. It ranges from voting behavior to nuclear deterrence, from the politics of race to the politics of genocide. In the pages that follow, many of the patterns of behavior researched by political psychologists are presented, including leadership, group behavior, voting, race, ethnicity, nationalism, political extremists, genocide, and war and deterrence. Because political psychology is so broad, many of us who teach the courses tend to stick to the portions of political psychology we are most familiar with. Consequently, another goal of this book is to educate educators by making it easier to get a background in areas of political psychology that they are unfamiliar with. Specialists in voting behavior, for example, may not know much about geno-cide, but both topics are covered here, and using this book as a primer will enable those who teach political psychology to expand the content of their courses. Students, in turn, will learn the interconnectedness of many patterns of behavior that at first glance seem quite distinct. They will learn, for example, that the same citizens who exercise their political rights in a democracy, by visiting the voting booth on election day, could, under certain circumstances, support an authoritarian dictatorship that forbids political competition and tortures its opposi-tion. Relatedly, we include examples of political behavior from around the world, so students will see that these patterns of behavior are universal—not restricted to people who live in one particular culture or in one type of political system.

Introduction to Political Psychology is designed for upper division undergraduate and grad-uate courses on political psychology, but it has other uses. We introduce readers to many dif-ferent methods of research; hence, it is useful to scholars outside of the classroom. The book also contains material that should be of interest to those in the policy-making community. It presents academic findings in a user-friendly way, and policy makers may be quite surprised to discover the extent to which perceptions, personality, and group dynamics affect the policy-making arena. In a challenge to the commonly held assumption that self-interest drives be-havior, this book shows over and over again, in one context after another, how psychological factors affect our behavior and that of others in ways we rarely recognize at the time the be-haviors take place.

In many respects this is a disturbing book, for it describes some of the saddest events in human history and some of the most horrific things people do to one another for political purposes. But the book also presents many discoveries about how to prevent conflict, how to resolve conflict, and how to recover from it. We hope that after reading this book the reader will begin to comprehend the enormous complexity of human behavior and realize the importance of understanding political psychology's significant role in improving the human condition.

Contents

The book begins with an introductory chapter that discusses what political psychology is and presents some of its history as well as methodological issues. The introduction also presents a representation of the "Political Being," a drawing of the generic political person depicting the mind and heart of people in a political environment. It places components of our thinking and feeling—personality, social identity, values, attitudes, emotion, and cognitive processes—in layers of the mind, with personality being at its core, social identity and values in the next lay-ers, and attitudes, cognitive processes, and emotions closest to the surface. The Being is also depicted in his or her political environment with in-groups and out-groups, representing the importance of group psychology as well as perceptions of political opponents. The Political Being appears throughout the book from chapter to chapter. The relevant portions of the Being and its environment are highlighted at the beginning of each chapter so that the reader begins each chapter with a reminder of the psychological theories and concepts that will be used in the pages to come.

Chapters 2, 3, and 4 introduce the reader to the central psychological theories used in political psychology and some of the most prominent frameworks used in the field as well. This provides students who have little background in psychology an intense introduction to the psychological concepts and theories used in political psychology. It provides students who have little familiarity with politics and political science an introduction to important political concepts as well. All students, whatever their backgrounds, are given a concise introduction to central political psychological frameworks in the first four chapters of the book. These frameworks then reappear repeatedly in the following chapters where patterns of behavior in various contexts are examined in detail. In addition, other frameworks not presented in the preliminary theory chapters are introduced where appropriate. Chapter 2 discusses personality-based theories and frameworks, chapter 3 involves cognitive processes, attitudes, identities, and emotions, and chapter 4 presents group psychology in politics. After chapter 4 the book turns to patterns of behavior. Chapter 5 looks at leadership, specifically presidential leadership in domestic and international politics. Chapter 6 looks at political psychology and the political behavior of the average U.S. citizen, with some comparison with Britain. The chapter looks at arguments concerning the structure and function of attitudes, how people process information and decide for whom to vote, the impact of the media on political attitudes, and the important issues of political tolerance.

Chapters 7, 8, and 9 draw upon psychological findings in studies of social identity, cognitive processes, group dynamics, and emotions in explorations of race and ethnicity, nationalism, and political extremism, respectively. Chapter 7 looks at race in the United States, Brazil and South Africa and then examines ethnic relations and conflicts in several cases across the globe, including Nigeria, Bosnia, and Guatemala. Chapter 8 presents an examination of the impact of nationalism on the behavior of citizens and leaders in both domestic and international politics. The cases used to illustrate the effect of nationalism on domestic politics include conflicts in Northern Ireland, Yugoslavia, Kosovo, Cyprus, Chechnya, the Kurds in Turkey, and German unification. The impact of the political psychology of nationalism on foreign policy behavior is illustrated in this chapter with the cases of World War II and the American war on drugs. Chapter 9 explores behavior normally considered extreme in motivation, intended results, and degree of violence. Included in this chapter are the political psychological causes of white racist organizations, terrorists, state-sponsored repression and torture, and genocide. In addition, chapters 7 through 9 include discussions of conflict prevention and resolution where appropriate. The final chapter, chapter 10, examines the political psychology of nuclear deterrence and conventional warfare.

Learning Tools

Throughout the book a number of learning tools are provided. These include a list of key terms at the end of each chapter and a glossary at the end of the book. Political psychology presents students with a new vocabulary: The list of key terms and glossary assist them in learning and internalizing that new vocabulary. The key terms let students know what they should have learned at the end of each chapter. The glossary provides a quick reference to remind them of the meaning of those terms. Similarly, at the end of each chapter, lists of theories, concepts, and cases introduced in that chapter are included to help students summarize and cross reference the material of that chapter. The summary is designed to assist students in organizing their studies. It also provides students with a tool to assess whether they learned the most important points and concepts in each chapter. Often students have difficulty distinguishing "the forest from the trees," that is, they blend concepts and examples or focus on examples at the expense of central concepts. The summary tells students which concepts and theories are related to which cases. For example, students are introduced to social identity theory and group conflict theories in chapters 3 and 4. In chapter 7, these theories are revisited in the context of race and ethnic conflicts in the United States, Brazil, South Africa, Nigeria, Bosnia, and Guatemala. The summary of chapter 7 explicitly links relevant theories to each case. This, in turn, will assist them in preparation for examinations. Each chapter contains text boxes with interesting related topics for class discussion. The text boxes reflect current and historical events reflecting the impact of political psychology on behavior. Examples include urban street gangs in the United States, the Tulsa race riot of 1921, the plight of a Kurdish teenager in Turkey facing jail for speaking in his native language, Northern Irish disputes about the right to march, and South Africa's President Mbecki's position on AIDS. Many other text boxes such as these contain topics of discussion that help students see a direct connection between the world around them and the political psychology they are learning. Other text boxes, such as those on experimentation, content analysis, and scales used in research, give students insight into how research is done in political psychology. Another learning tool in *Introduction to Political Psychology* is the provision of many tables and illustrative figures that summarize text discussion, thereby giving students the opportunity for quick review and repetition of material. The tables and figures also provide examples of research findings that students find interesting to discuss and debate. For example, in a table in the chapter on leadership (chapter 5), presidents are classified in terms of management style. Previous classifications can be debated and current leaders can also be examined by students as they try their hands at some political psychological analysis. Each chapter also contains a list of suggested readings for those interested in further research in a particular area. This is useful for students writing papers and for those who wish to expand their knowledge of political psychology and the behaviors it produces.

Acknowledgments

This project became much more complex than we anticipated when we embarked upon it. Along the way, we have benefitted from the comments, insights, and ideas of a number of colleagues and students. Among those are Isabel Beck, Libia Billordo, Marilyn Brewer, Miguel Cortes, Stephen Dyson, Bob Hanes, Peg Hermann, Rick Herrmann, Michael Infranco, Bob Jackson, Faith Lutze, Sarkis Mahdasian, Otto Marenin, Dick Moreland, Craig Parks, Claudia Reyes-Quilodran, Ann Rumble, Paul 't Hart, and Michael Young. We would also like to thank our editor, Debra Riegert, who has been incredibly patient. Cynthia Avery, Diane Berger, and Lisa Janowski provided invaluable support and assistance at Washington State University. Finally, we appreciate all of the valuable suggestions from those who reviewed the manuscript including Richard Herrmann (Ohio State University), Leonie Huddy (SUNY, Stony Brook), Michael Milburn (University of Massachusetts, Boston), Joshua Rabinowitz (California State University, Northridge), David Sears (UCLA), and David Winter (University of Michigan).

CHAPTER 1

An Introduction to Political Psychology

Why do people behave the way they do in politics? What causes conflicts such as those in Bosnia, Rwanda, or Northern Ireland? Is racism inevitable? Why do presidents make the decisions they do? Why did 9/11 happen? These and many other questions about politics are of great concern to all of us, whether we are directly affected or are only eyewitnesses through the news. So much political behavior seems to defy explanation and seems incomprehensible, even through hindsight: People start wars that are, in the end, thought of as pointless and futile, such as World War I or the war in Vietnam; civil wars erupt among people who have lived together harmoniously for years, but who then commit hideous acts of barbaric violence against one another, as in the former Yugoslavia, Liberia, or Sierra Leone; groups commit acts of terrorism that kill numerous innocent civilians each year; or a scandal-plagued president cannot resist tempting fate by engaging in an extramarital affair, when he knows full well the extent of the scrutiny by those looking for more scandals. Unless one understands the thoughts and feelings of the people who made the decisions to commit those acts, one cannot fully understand why such things occurred. But an exploration of the psychology—the personalities, thought processes, emotions, and motivations—of people involved in political activity provides a unique and necessary basis for understanding that activity.

This is a book about the psychology of political behavior. In the chapters that follow, we explore many psychological patterns that influence how individuals act in politics. At the outset, we challenge the traditional notion that people in politics act in a rational pursuit of self-interest. This argument concerning rationality is based on a set of assumptions common in political science, but which ignores the many studies done by psychologists. Many people assume that psychology is common sense, because they believe that behavior is rational and predictable. But decades of research by psychologists reveal that behavior is anything but common sense. Although psychologists recognize that much of human behavior is not always rational, human beings, as social perceivers, often operate on the belief that behavior (their own and others) is quite rational. The motivation to expect behavior to be rational is based on two fundamental needs: first, people have a need to make sense of—to *understand*—their world; second, people have a need to *predict* the likely consequences of their own and others' behavior. To the extent that behavior is perceived as rational, these two needs become easier to fulfill.

A more accurate picture of human beings as political actors is one that acknowledges that people are motivated to act in accordance with their own personality characteristics, values, beliefs, and attachments to groups. People are imperfect information processors, struggling mightily to understand the complex world in which they live. People employ logical, but often faulty, perceptions of others when deciding how to act, and they often are unaware of the causes of their own behavior. People often do things that are seemingly contrary to their own interests, values, and beliefs. Nevertheless, by understanding the complexities of political psychology, we can explain behavior that often seems irrational. A few illustrations help us bring this point home. These are examples of behavior that is not at all atypical.

A commonly held belief is that people vote in accordance with self-interest; therefore, people in higher income brackets will vote for the Republican party, and those in lower income brackets will vote for the Democratic party. However, the authors of this book vote for the same candidates and party, despite the fact that their incomes and personal circumstances are vastly different. Is one rational and the others not, or do we share certain values and beliefs that we put above economic self-interest? Another assumption is that people are fully aware of their beliefs and attitudes and that they act in accordance with them, behaving in such a way as to maximize values. But as the following example illustrates, we often act in ways that violate our beliefs and values:

> A friend of ours was sitting on a bench in a crowded shopping mall when he heard running footsteps behind him. Turning, he saw two black men being pursued by a white security guard. The first runner was past him in a flash, but he leapt up in time to tackle the second runner, overpowering him. From the ground, the panting black man angrily announced that he was the store owner. Meanwhile, the thief escaped. Our friend, who is white and devotes his life to helping the oppressed, was mortified. (Fiske & Taylor, 1991, p. 245)

Here, the power of social stereotypes lay unknowingly deep inside the mind of the friend, despite his outward, and no doubt deeply held, values opposed to such stereotyping. This is an example of the power of what psychologists call social categorization, a process wherein we nonconsciously categorize others into groups. On the surface, the act of categorizing people into groups appears logical and rational. The danger, however, lies in the consequences of categorizing people into groups on the basis of characteristics that they might not possess. (The process of social categorization is one that we devote a great deal of attention to in this book.) In the example just given, little harm was done, but the same process can occur on societal levels, and it can produce acts of terrific violence.

Racial discrimination, ethnic cleansing in Bosnia, genocide in Rwanda, are all, in part, outcomes of stereotyping. They are political actions that cannot be understood through conventional political science explanations, yet they are some of the most important and damaging forms of behavior in human societies. Consider the following account:

> The army was determined to stamp out the grass roots support for the guerilllas. A company of one hundred soldiers from Santa Cruz del Quiche' moved into Nebaj the next day and installed a detachment of military police. Within days, leading citizens of the towns began to disappear. Later their bodies were found mutilated and strung up on posts in the town square. (Perera, 1993, p. 71)

Now, consider this example:

> Juliette's family, who were well-off Tutsis, stayed inside their house that first night. The next night, Thursday, when the militia came searching for them, they ran and hid in a banana plantation. On Friday they ran to the school where her uncle . . . was an administrator. Two days later the family decided to go to the place where the Belgian United Nations soldiers were and seek protection from them. But 11 Belgian soldiers had been lined up against a wall and shot the day before, so all the other Belgian soldiers had left. Juliette's family then went to a sports stadium where a lot of other people were sheltering. But here the Interahamwe [militia men] caught up with them and ordered them to another place, an open field where thousands of others had also been rounded up. The

Interahamwe told all the people who were Hutus to go; then they told all the others to sit down and they threw grenades at them. When Juliette became conscious the next morning, she found her mother and brothers dead. Her father was also dead and his body had been hacked to pieces. (Bone, 1999, p. 1)

These two stories depict real life examples of two politically motivated atrocities committed during war, which cannot be explained unless the psychology of the perpetrators is understood. What objective self-interest is served by using a machete to chop up a human being? Why not just quickly kill and be done with it, if the death serves one's interests? These are true stories: The first is from Guatemala during the 1980s and the second from Rwanda roughly 10 years later. These are two very different places, and these acts occurred at different times, yet these two countries have encountered very similar experiences, in terms of brutal acts of violence waged by one group against another. And people in many other countries have similar stories to tell. Political psychology helps explain political behavior along the continuum from everyday political behavior, such as voting, to the most extraordinary kinds of behavior, such as mass terror and violence.

WHAT IS POLITICAL PSYCHOLOGY?

Understanding the psychological underpinnings of these behaviors gives us a different, and arguably a much more complex, understanding of political behavior. Traditional explanations of political behavior often fail to adequately explain some of the most important political decisions and actions people take. Political psychology has emerged as an important field, in both political science and psychology, which enables us to explain many aspects of political behavior, whether they are seemingly pathological actions such as those just described or normal decision-making practices that are sometimes optimal and other times failures. Both psychologists and political scientists have become interested in expanding their knowledge of issues and problems of common interest, such as foreign and domestic policy decision making by elites, conflicts ranging from ethnic violence to wars and genocide, terrorism, the minds of people who are racists, and more peaceful behaviors such as voting behavior, among many other problems and issues traditionally of concern in political science. For example, if we understand the limitations of the abilities of policymakers to recognize the significance of specific pieces of information, then we can institute organizational changes that will help improve our abilities to process information adequately. Likewise, if we can understand the deeper personality elements of the most important of our political leaders, we can comprehend which situations they will handle well and which situations will require more assistance and advice from others. And, if we understand what motivates terrorists to act, we can find ways in which to try to address those motivations and thus counter terrorism.

One goal of political psychology is to establish general laws of behavior that can help explain and predict events that occur in a number of different situations. The approach that political psychologists use to understand and predict behavior is the **scientific method**. This approach relies on four cyclical steps that researchers repeatedly execute as they try to understand and predict behavior. The first step involves *making observations*. This step involves making systematic and unsystematic observations of behavior and events. From these observations, a researcher begins to form hunches about the likely factors, or **variables** (see box), that affect the behavior under observation. Step two involves *formulating tentative explanations*, or a *hypothesis*. During this stage, a researcher makes predictions about the nature of the relationship between variables. Step three involves making *further observations* *and experimenting* (see box). During this stage of the scientific method, observations are made to test the validity of the hypothesis. In step four, *refining and retesting explanations*, researchers reformulate their hypothesis on the basis of the observations made in step three. This might involve exploring the limits of the phenomenon, exploring causes of relationships, or expanding on the relationships discovered. Clearly, the scientific method requires a great deal of time for making careful observations.

Essentially, political psychology represents the merging of two disciplines, psychology and political science, although other disciplines have contributed to the literature and growth of the field, as well. Political psychology can be described as a

---

Variables

A *variable* is what we call something that is thought to influence, or to be influenced by, something else. One seeks to identify them in the first stage of the scientific method. Variables can vary in degree or differentiation. One question of interest in social science is how variance in one variable explains change in something else. When variables are measured, ideally, the researcher wants to have a measurement instrument that is **reliable,** that is, one that will produce the same results when used by another researcher. In addition, the measurement should have **validity,** that is, it should provide an accurate measurement of what it claims to measure.

---

marriage of sorts that fosters a very fruitful dialog. Political psychology involves explaining what people do, by adapting psychological concepts, so that they are useful and relevant to politics, then applying them to the analysis of a political problem or issue. For example, psychologists have been helpful to political scientists who study negative political advertising. Psychologists have done studies whose outcomes provide evidence to suggest that negative political advertisements are often ineffective, because the sponsor of the negative ad is evaluated negatively by same-party voters. Psychologists have brought to political science fresh perspectives on how to make sense of politics, thus expanding our knowledge of the political world. Political scientists bring to the field their knowledge and understanding of politics. For example, psychologists often study the decision-making process employed by groups. Some of the ideas that psychologists have used to guide their theories about how groups make decisions come from real-life group decisions made by political groups (e.g., Bay of Pigs, the decision to enter the Vietnam War). Each must be well-versed in the other field, and together they are able to expand the scope of study in both political science and psychology. As a result, political psychology makes a very important contribution to our understanding of politics and expands the breadth of that understanding.

Merging the two fields is not an easy enterprise. For example, one cannot use many of the experimental techniques of psychology to study politics, yet experiments are vital to psychologists' research and confidence in their findings. Because experiments in psychology are conducted under carefully controlled conditions, they allow psychologists to make inferences about relationships that they suspect exist. Such insights are not possible with other research methodologies, especially those used by political scientists. The patterns of behavior observed in the laboratory, therefore, are not likely to be observed in such pristine quality in the real world, where many extraneous factors cannot be filtered out as influences on behavior. If, for example, a psychologist wants to study group behavior, they can design an experiment in which all other factors (such as competing group loyalties, personality characteristics, gender, or ethnicity) can be made irrelevant to the study. In the real world of politics, these things cannot be extracted from behavior. The simple point is that we cannot expect to see an exact parallel between what the psychologist sees and explains and what we will see and explain in political behavior. Instead, we must take psychological concepts or explanations of behavior and ask ourselves, How are these things likely to be manifest in the real world of politics? This is one of the most difficult aspects of the development of the field of political psychology.

Some simple examples may clarify this problem. If psychologists tell us that personality traits influence behavior, political psychologists must figure out what personality traits are important in politics. Are there certain political personality traits? If so, what are they, and why are they politically important? Political psychologists argue that there are indeed certain political personality traits that are important in influencing political behavior, such as how a person deals with conflict, how complex the person's thought processes are (i.e., how **cognitively complex**), and so on. If psychologists tell us that, under certain conditions, attitudes affect behavior, and we wish to know how this applies to deciding how to vote, then the political question becomes: Which attitudes about politics, under what circumstances, affect how we vote? In the United States, attitudes about candidates, issues, parties, and groups affect how people vote. Those attitudes vary in importance in determining the vote, under differing circumstances. These are examples of the steps that must be taken in applying psychology to the explanation of political behavior. The consequence is that psychology benefits political science, because political scientists use psychological theories to understand political behavior. But political science also benefits psychology, because tests of psychological theories in political settings can help psychologists refine their theories.

Political psychology is a rapidly growing field. Psychology has been used to explain

---

Experiments

The three characteristics that define experimental research are the **manipulation** of an independent variable, **control** over extraneous variables, and random assignment of participants to conditions. An **independent variable** has values set and chosen by the experimenter. If an experimenter wanted to examine the effects of room temperature on mood, then room temperature is the independent variable. The experimenter can randomly assign participants to a room that is 70°F or a room that is 90°F, then observe their mood. Manipulation of the independent variable involves exposing participants to various levels of it and observing its effects on another variable, the **dependent variable**. In an experiment, the dependent variable's values are predicted to change as a function of the independent variable. For example, mood is predicted to change as a function of varying temperatures in a room, with a temperature of 90°F predicted to cause a more negative mood than a room temperature of 70°F. Another characteristic of an experiment is control over **extraneous variables**, which may affect the behavior that a researcher is studying, but which they have no interest in at the moment. If some of the participants just learned that they won the lottery before showing up for the study, then their mood in response to room temperature may be different than if they had not just learned that they won the lottery. The variable "winning the lottery" is an extraneous variable. The manner in which experiments are designed allows a researcher to have a great deal of control over extraneous variables.

---

political behavior for many years, but there has been an explosion in its application to politics since the early 1970s. The field began in the 1920s, with studies of personality and politics and, in particular, with psychoanalytic studies of political leaders. As time and psychology's understanding of personality progressed, political psychologists began looking at personal characteristics, such as motivation and traits, in their analyses of political leaders. Although the psychoanalytic studies tended to use psychobiographies, that is, life stories of a person for data, later studies relied upon new social scientific techniques, such as questionnaires, interviews, experiments, and simulations, for their research. This research is examined in depth in chapters 2 and 5 in this book, as well.

A second wave in the development of political psychology came in the 1940s and 1950s, with increased interest in the systematic study of public opinion and voting behavior in the

United States. Beginning in 1952, researchers at the University of Michigan began collect-
ing survey data on public opinion and voting preferences. In 1960, with the publication of
The American Voter, by Campbell, Converse, Miller, and Stokes, the tradition of using political psychology to study public attitudes toward politics took off. That book presented a
number of centrally important findings about the nature of political attitudes in the United
States. It sparked debate and fueled important, and often differing, models of attitudes and
behavior in the United States. In the years that followed, political psychology has been used
in analyses of political socialization, the role of the media in affecting political attitudes,
racial politics in the United States, and a number of other aspects of American political
behavior. Analyses of public attitudes and political behavior have been done in many other
countries in addition to the United States. Chapters 3, 6, and 7 entertain research in these
areas of political psychology.

The application of political psychology and the development of political psychological
frameworks, for the analysis of behavior in international affairs, was the third wave, and it
came a bit later, beginning in the 1960s, with studies of Soviet–American perceptions of each
other and studies of the conflict in Vietnam (Kelman, 1965; White, 1968). By the 1970s, and
continuing until today, concepts of political psychology have been applied to our understanding of nuclear deterrence, past wars, decision making in crises, nationalism, ethnic conflict,
and a wide variety of additional topics in international politics. This book explores many of
these topics in chapters 5, 7, 8, and 10.

A fourth arena in which political psychology has been used to explain behavior is what Sears
(1993) refers to as "death and horror." This too is a growing body of literature, and it covers the
study of terrorism, ethnic cleansing, genocide, and other patterns of behavior that involve
extraordinary levels of politically motivated violence. We review this literature in chapter 9.

Thus, there are many realms of political behavior amenable to a psychological analysis,
and we explore several of them in this book. There are so many ways of exploring political behavior that the number of concepts can become confusing, in part because different concepts
have emerged in psychology over time, as that field has grown. The growth of any field, be it
political science, psychology, or political psychology, is always haphazard. Concepts often
appear under a new name, but seem strikingly similar to old concepts. Discoveries are made
in one area that were made long before in another area. The lack of cross-fertilization has
meant that scholars looking at one aspect of behavior are often unaware of what those looking
at another aspect of behavior are doing, and therefore they reinvent the wheel over and over
again. One of the tasks of this book is to draw connections between ideas that have emerged
in different realms of the study of political behavior, in order to lessen the confusion that arises
from so many similar ideas, concepts, and arguments with so many different names.

Another outcome of the haphazard development of political psychology is that related but
slightly different concepts have become popular as explanatory tools for different kinds of political behavior. Attitudes, beliefs, schemas, images, and many other concepts appear in the literature, but are rarely discussed in terms of how they overlap and still differ. We undertake
some clarification in this regard, but for the moment let us present our own general picture of
how and why people think and act politically, based on the work that has been generated by
political psychologists over the years. To put it most simply, people are driven to act by internal factors, such as personality, attitudes, and self-identity; they evaluate their environment
and others through cognitive processes that produce images of others; and they decide how to
act when these factors are combined. In politics, people often act as part of a group, and their
behavior as part of a group can be very different than their behavior when they are alone.
Therefore, the political psychology of groups is an essential part of political psychology as a
field. As the book proceeds, each of these factors is developed. In the end, the Political Being

(see Figure 1.1) is described and explained in detail. This is the generic Political Being in their political universe.

At the core of our Political Being is **personality**, which is a central psychological factor influencing political behavior. As we see in chapter 2, personality is unique to the individual, although certain personality traits appear in many people. Many people, for example, have traits in common, such as particular degrees of complexity in their thinking processes and desires for power and achievement, but the combination of those traits differs, and therefore each individual is unique. Consequently, we place personality in the center of the Political Being's brain. It affects other aspects of the thought process and is itself affected by life experiences, but personalities tend to be very stable in terms of amenability to change, and they influence our behavior and behavioral predispositions on an ongoing, constant basis. Moreover, personality affects behavior nonconsciously, in that people rarely sit down and consider the impact of their personalities on their political preferences. It drives behavioral predispositions, without our having to give conscious consideration to the source of those preferences. Personality is, in that sense, a core component of the engine of political thinking and feeling. Much of the discussion of personality in political psychology concerns the personality traits of political leaders and the impact of particular combinations of those traits on their leadership styles. Consequently, much of our discussion of personality in chapter 2 is focused on the leadership dimension, and we have devoted a full chapter (chapter 5) to leadership, with an emphasis on the American president, Bill Clinton.

Next, we have **values** and **identity**, concepts that involve deeply held beliefs about what is right and wrong (values) and a deeply held sense of who a person is (identity). Values often include a strong emotional component. We often feel very strongly about some of our beliefs and goals for ourselves, those we care about, and political principles. For example, a person may have a strongly held value that violence is wrong, which translates into a political predisposition to oppose war, to refuse military service, and to go to prison, if necessary, to defend those values. That person's identity involves personal self-descriptions that are usually tied to, and emerge from, close and enduring personal relationships. For our person with a strong value opposing violence, identity may include, for example, a strong attachment to a religion and religious affiliation. Being religious would be an important part of their identity, and they would strongly value the religious group that is part of their identity. Values, emotions, and identities are also deeply held and fairly permanent aspects of one's psychology, and hence we place them deep in the mind of our Political Being. They are discussed further in chapter 3. Political values, emotions, and identity are also important concepts in our case studies of voting, race and ethnic conflicts, and nationalism, in chapters 6, 7, and 8, respectively.

Next, our Political Being has **attitudes**. As we see in chapter 3, an attitude is defined in different ways by different scholars. Generally, they can be thought of as units of thought composed of some cognitive component (i.e., knowledge) and an emotional response to it (like, dislike, etc.). For example, a person with an attitude on funding for public education may think it is a good thing, know how much their state spends on public education, and feel strongly that this particular level of spending is too low. Many important political attitudes are acquired through socialization, as we see in chapter 6. In the diagram of the Political Being, they are placed toward the top of the mind, because they are accessible to the thinker (who can be asked what they think and feel about an issue and who can articulate an answer) and because they are subject to change through new information, changes in feeling, or persuasion. Attitudes are the focus of attention in political psychology when it comes to voting decisions, political socialization, the impact of the media on how and what people think, and important political notions, such as tolerance, all of which we explore in chapter 6. Studies of voting behavior are central areas in political psychology in general, and chapter 6 provides

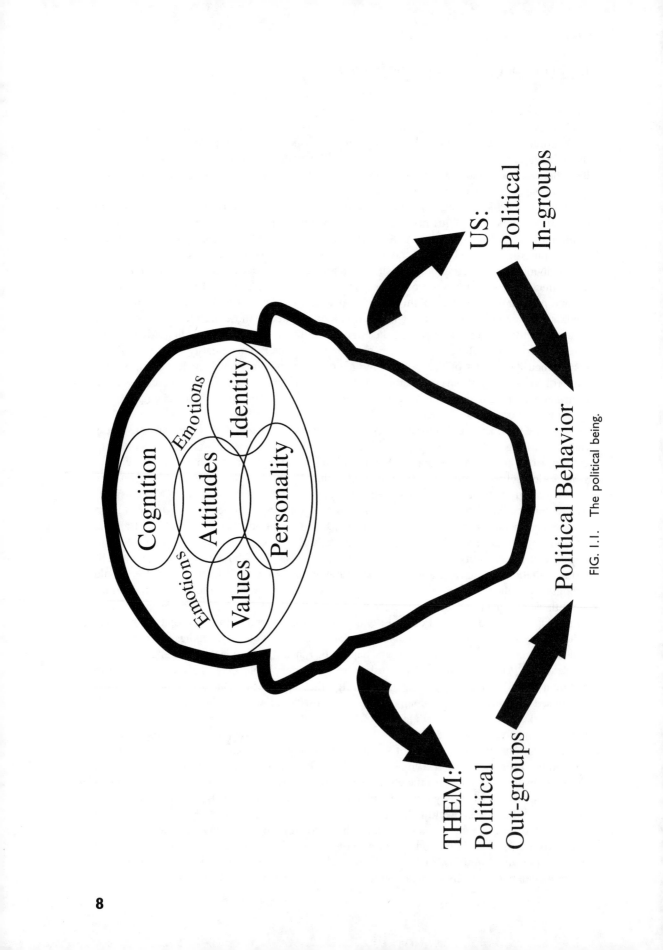

FIG. I.I.   The political being.

an introduction to the topic, with a look at public opinion and voting in the United States and a brief comparison with Great Britain. Voting is, of course, a central component of democratic politics, so it is a logical focus of political psychology.

We have left **emotions** floating in the mind of the Political Being. Politics can be a very emotion-evoking arena of life. Emotions affect all aspects, and are affected by all aspects of the Political Being's mind. Values, identities, and attitudes are emotional or have emotional components, and emotions interact with the next portion of the Political Being's mind: cognition. Emotions permeate politics and the mind of the Political Being: Hence, they are left to freely move about in our picture of the mind of the Political Being. We discuss emotion in every topical chapter in this book.

The final component of the mind of the Political Being is **cognitive processes**, which are the channels through which the mind and the environment first interact. They involve receiving and interpreting information from the outside. They are the mind's computer, in that they facilitate the individual's ability to process information, interpret the environment, and decide how to act toward it. Cognitive processes help us understand an environment that is too complex for any individual to interpret. The cognitive system in our brains helps us organize that environment into understandable and recognizable units and to filter information so that we do not have to consciously assess the utility of every piece of information available to us in the environment. Take this following example. You are students in an institution of higher education. You know that the environment is divided into, among other social groups, professors and students. You know, without thinking, who is a professor and who is a student. You know what you are supposed to do as a student (study, go to lectures and take notes, take tests, write papers), and you know what your professors are supposed to do (give lectures, grade assignments, hold office hours, etc.). If a student walked up to the podium in your classroom and began to lecture, you would think it very odd, disregard the lecture, and not take notes. If the professor, on the other hand, takes over the podium and says exactly the same thing that the student was saying, you would pay attention to it, and you would take notes. These are cognitive processes in operation. They help people understand the environments they live in, without paying close attention. They help us process information. We tend to accept information that is consistent with our preexisting ideas, beliefs, attitudes, and assumptions about the environment in which we live. Cognitive processes and organization are presented in chapter 3.

At this point, we move from the internal components of the mind and look at the Political Being in a broader social and political environment. Political psychology involves not only the individual, but the individual's interaction with their political environment. On one side, we have those important social units, or **groups**, that are politically relevant to the Political Being and to which that Political Being is strongly attached. They constitute *us* in his or her mind, and are assessed in terms of studies of **social identity**. Social identity derives from membership in social groups, such as nationality, gender, age, race, ethnicity, occupation, and other kinds of **group membership**. Groups are depicted in our picture of the Political Being generally in terms of in-groups (those groups people belong to) and out-groups (those they do not belong to). The creation of social categories can produce many important behavioral predispositions, including stereotyping, discrimination, and ethnocentrism. Our social identities, much like our values and attitudes, can strongly motivate behavior. We discuss social identity and groups in chapters 3 and 4, then provide a number of illustrations of their impact on behavior in the chapters that follow.

People belong to many different groups, and we are interested in the role played by attachment to politically relevant groups. Groups themselves have particular dynamics that influence people's behavior, and this is the subject of chapter 4, in which group psychology is introduced in and of itself, and in the context of distinctly political groups. Groups demand loyalty, compliance, and obedience, and those psychological factors can override even strongly held values. Take, for example, perpetrators of genocide in the Holocaust, who explained their behavior in terms of obedience to the norms of the group (e.g., "I did it because I was ordered to do so"). But social identity goes beyond group dynamics. People are influenced by groups, but they are also personally driven to support groups to which they are strongly attached. They make sacrifices that are sometimes extraordinary, for the sake of the group. Illustrations of that behavior, as well as social identity factors, are found in chapter 7 (race and ethnic conflict), chapter 8 (nationalism), and chapter 9, (political extremists). As we see, group dynamics can make people do things that they would never consider doing on their own.

These topics were chosen for in-depth analyses for a number of reasons. Racial discrimination and conflict is a central aspect of American history and current politics, but it also marks the political systems in other countries. Ethnic conflict has many similarities with racial conflict, and the record of the post–Cold War world regarding the prevalence of such conflict and our failure to prevent it from costing hundreds of thousands of deaths, clearly makes it an important issue for a book on political psychology to consider. The same can be said for nationalism, which cost millions of deaths in World War II and which reappeared with ferocity after the Cold War. Political extremists are of concern not just because of the terrorist attack on the World Trade Center and the Pentagon. White racist militias have plagued the American scene for years, and extremists are the people who committed mass killings for political reasons during the Holocaust and other genocides.

The other component of the environment that the Political Being interacts with is *them*, those groups to which that being does not belong, but must interact with in politics. People organize the political environment just as they do the social environment. We look at how people organize the political environment around them. There are a variety of perspectives on this, one of which, image theory, argues that people look at the world around them and organize it in terms of important political actors, such as enemies and allies (and many other categories, as we see in chapter 3). Some of those actors threaten the deeply held values and/or groups with which the Political Being strongly identifies. The enemy is such an actor. Others, such as allies, provide opportunities to achieve desired goals, things that are important to the individual Political Being and to the groups they identify with. In chapter 10, we examine the ultimate conflict with the other—war—and efforts to deter it, which is a matter of importance to everyone in the nuclear era.

All of these psychological elements interact, and all of the patterns of behavior we examine as illustrations are important. Of course, not all of them are functioning all the time. One's attitudes toward political candidates do not affect political preferences every day, but they do during elections. Nationalism is not important in affecting behavior until the nation is either threatened or until an opportunity for its advancement appears. Moreover, at any point in time, one of these factors may be more important than others. Personality can become overwhelmingly important when a president is dealing with a major crisis. Perceptions that another country is an enemy may be important during that crisis, as well. The president's social identity with his ethnic group may not play a role during that crisis, but it may be important when he is pressing for a particular piece of legislation.

Our conceptualization of political psychology sees the political mind as composed of layers or levels. Different layers take on a more or less important role in different kinds of behavior, or at different points in the political action process. Consequently, the following chapters focus on central psychological causes of different types of political behavior. When it comes to small-group behavior and intricate decisions made by the members of that group, we look specifically at the personalities of leaders and at small-group dynamics. When it comes to nationalism-based conflicts, we look at social identity, perceptions or images of other groups, and cognitive processes.

The organization of this book blends concepts and patterns in political psychology and political behavior with detailed illustrations of those concepts and patterns. Chapters 2, 3, and 4 introduce central concepts in political psychology, with examples from psychology and politics for illustration. Then chapters 5 through 10 examine some forms of political behavior, using the concepts introduced in chapters 2 through 4, where appropriate, to explain those behaviors. We encourage readers to try to amplify upon our explanations, as you read the descriptions of the types of political behavior in each chapter. Chapter 5 focuses on political personality traits and leaders. Chapter 6 focuses on the political psychology of the average citizen in the voting booth and in their efforts to learn about and respond to political information. Chapter 7 moves us from the individual level to individuals and groups, in an examination of racial and ethnic politics. Similarly, chapter 8 looks at individual and group political psychology and behavior in the context of nationalism and its impact on domestic politics and foreign policy behavior. Chapter 9 also focuses on individuals and groups, in a look at political extremists—terrorists, those who commit genocide, members of militias, and others. Finally, chapter 10 explores individual and group decision making in international politics, specifically, in international security and efforts to prevent war. Where relevant, as we travel through patterns of political behavior, we conclude chapters with a look at possible approaches to conflict prevention and/or resolution. Each chapter includes a list of key terms and suggestions for further reading.

CONCLUSION

We began this introductory chapter with examples of political behavior that are both disturbing and difficult to explain. Let us conclude the chapter on a more personal note. The psychological causes of political behavior are interesting to study. But for the individuals who live the realities that the following chapters describe, political behavior is not an academic exercise, but a life-shaping and life-altering experience. At the heart of political psychology is the question of whether, by understanding why people behave as they do in politics, we can prevent the worst of human behavior and promote the best. In the pages that follow, we present the work of many political psychologists who believe that this is an achievable goal and a reasonable one to pursue. Indeed, without an understanding of political psychology, it is an impossible goal.

KEY TERMS

Attitudes	**Emotions**	**Social identity**
Cognitive complexity	**Groups**	**Values**
Cognitive processes	**Scientific method**	**Variables**

SUGGESTIONS FOR FURTHER READING

Kressel, N. (Ed.) (1993). *Political psychology: Classic and contemporary readings*. New York: Paragon House.

Monroe, K. R. (Ed.) (2002). *Political psychology*. Mahwah, NJ: Lawrence Erlbaum Associates, Inc.

CHAPTER 2

Personality and Politics

As mentioned in chapter 1, personality is a central concept in psychology. For this reason, personality is placed at the base of the Political Being's brain, representing its roots and, therefore, the most fundamental element. Personality not only affects how people think and behave in the political arena, but it is also affected by the life experiences of individuals. This chapter considers some central questions about personality addressed in political psychology, including such questions as: How does personality affect political behavior? How deep must we go in understanding the development of a person's personality in order to understand their political inclinations (to the unconscious or to more surface, conscious traits and motivations)? What personality characteristics are most politically relevant? Are people completely unique, or do they share personality traits in various combinations, making individuals more or less similar in their political behavior? How should we study personality, because we cannot very well put a political figure on the couch and ask them questions?

The study of personality and politics is the oldest tradition in political psychology (Adorno, Frenkel-Brinswick, Levinson, & Sanford, 1950; Lasswell, 1930, 1948; Leites, 1951). Personality as a concept has been used to evaluate a wide variety of political behaviors, from the psychology of political leaders to psychopathologies of people who have committed politically motivated atrocities (such as Hitler and the Holocaust), to the average citizen and the role personality factors play in attitudes toward race and ethnicity, interest in politics, and willingness to obey authority. However, most studies employing personality-based frameworks focus on the impact of the characteristics of leaders on major decisions and policy-making issues, such as leader–advisor relations. In fact, the studies of political personality and political leadership have developed conjointly in political psychology. As a result, seeking to separate political personality from political leadership research is problematic in any textbook on political psychology.

This chapter discusses some of the broader theoretical arguments about personality and its affect on political behavior. We begin with some of the central questions about the role of personality in political behavior, then turn to the study of personality in psychology and look at some of the major scholars and approaches to personality from the psychological perspective. Next we present an overview of some of the ways in which personality in politics, and particularly personality factors relevant to political leadership, have been studied. The portion of the Political Being emphasized in this chapter is, of course, the personality circle, but you can also see the links between personality and cognition, as well as the impact of personality on interactions with people in the political environment—*us* and *them* in the Political Being diagram.

Despite the central role personality plays in psychology, political science, and political psychology, coming to an acceptable definition of personality is problematic, with research in psychology and political science each tending to focus (and define) the concept quite differently. As Ewen (1998) points out, within the discipline of psychology, "there is no one universally accepted definition of 'personality'" (p. 3), nor is there any one recognized theory of personality. Greenstein (1969) observed that the psychologist's usage of the term *personality* is comprehensive, subsumes all important psychic regularities, and refers to an inferred entity, rather than to a directly observable phenomenon. In other words, *personality* refers to a construct that is introduced to account for the regularities in an individual's behavior as they respond to diverse stimuli (Hermann, Preston, & Young, 1996). Or, as Ewen (1998) notes, *personality*, in the psychological literature, refers to "*important* and *relatively stable* aspects of a person's behavior that account for consistent patterns of behavior," aspects of which "may be observable or unobservable, and conscious or unconsious" (pp. 3–4). DiRenzo (1974) offers a related definition: *Personality* is "one's acquired, relatively enduring, yet dynamic, unique, system of predispositions to psychological and social behavior" (p. 16). At the same time, however, there is tremendous disagreement within the field of psychology, between social psychologists and personality theorists, regarding exactly what should be incorporated into such a comprehensive definition. Personality theorists would include cognition, affect, motivation, and identification, as well as processes of ego-defense, in their conceptions of personality; social psychologists usually seek to limit personality to a residual category that does not include emotion, cognition, or motivation (see Greenstein, 1969; George & George, 1998). There are many different theories of personality in psychology. Schultz (1981), for example, reviewed 20 personality theories organized into 9 categories: psychoanalytic, neopsychoanalytic, interpersonal, trait, developmental, humanistic, cognitive, behavioristic, and limited domain.

In the political psychology literature, in contrast, analysts typically do not worry about arriving at a specific, comprehensive definition of personality. Instead, the focus is upon how particular aspects of personality translate into political behavior. Indeed, the study of personality in political psychology is best characterized as being the study of individual differences. Rather than seek the whole, researchers selectively focus upon any number of individual aspects of a person's makeup (i.e., cognition, motivation, affect, ego, attitudes, etc.) to explain behavior. Obviously, this is a much narrower, more restrictive view of personality than that taken by most psychologists (especially the personality theorists). As a result, it is in our view unproductive to attempt to provide a commonly agreed upon definition of personality for this textbook: There isn't one (Ewen, 1998; Maddi, 1996; Magnavita, 2002). Further, we clearly cannot explore all theories of personality in this chapter. Instead, because our focus is upon political psychology, not psychology, we limit ourselves to those theories most commonly used in political psychology: psychoanalytic, trait, and motivation. Furthermore, we address research that centers upon various kinds of individual differences, to explain leadership, leadership style, and political behavior.

WHEN DO PERSONALITIES MATTER IN POLITICS?

Of course, just because personalities may sometimes matter with relation to policy outcomes, it would be a mistake to argue that they always matter. In fact, during the 1930s and 1940s, Lewin (1935) argued that, to understand behavior, it is necessary to understand both a person's personality and the context in which the behavior is observed, and he emphasized that the interaction between the person and the situation was most important to understanding behavior. Similarly, Mischel (1973) focused attention on the degree to which situational factors govern behavior: He reviewed research on the importance of personality in predicting behavior across a variety of situations and found that people behave far less consistently than had previously been thought. Instead, the situation appears to exert powerful effects on behavior. Indeed, it is generally accepted among scholars who work in the fields of personality or leadership that *context* (or situation) matters more (George, 1980; Greenstein, 1969; Hermann, 1987, 2000; Preston, 2001; Preston & 't Hart, 1999). The situational context provides the stage upon which the person will interact with their environment, providing both opportunities for action and constraints upon it. For example, in his classic book, *Personality and Politics*, Greenstein (1969) observed that, although personality is often unimportant in terms of either political behavior or policy outcomes, the likelihood of personal impact (1) increases to the degree that the environment admits of restructuring, (2) varies with the political actor's location in the environment, and (3) varies with the personal strengths and weaknesses of the actor. In other words, when individuals have the personal power resources, because of their position in the political system (i.e., president, prime minister, general, mayor, etc.), and the situation allows them to exert this power to influence the policy process, what these people are like (i.e., strengths/weaknesses, personality, experience) will have an impact on policy. For Abraham Lincoln, this situation allowed him to educate his cabinet on the importance of the individual leader, when, after a particularly contentious vote, he observed: "Gentlemen, the vote is 11 to 1 and the 1 has it." For Saddam Hussein, it meant that Iraq invaded Kuwait. On the other hand, in contrast to foreign policy, in which there is more freedom of action, American presidents are well-acquainted with their far weaker influence upon domestic policy, in which Congress, the courts, interest groups, and many other actors play substantial roles in determining policy outcomes (see Burke, 1992; Cronin, 1980; Light, 1982; Neustadt, 1990).

THEORIES AND APPROACHES
TO STUDYING PERSONALITY

There are many different approaches or theories regarding personality, only some of which have been used in the study of personalities of political actors. Among the most important are psychoanalytic, trait-based theories, and motive-based theories. As was mentioned earlier, many of the frameworks in political psychology go beyond a single theoretical orientation. Following, we review some personality theories from psychology, then explore their use in political psychology. With each theoretical approach, we discuss some of the research methods typically used to study political actors.

Psychoanalytic Approaches

One of the oldest traditions in personality in psychology are **psychoanalytic** or **psychodynamic theories**. Psychoanalytic theories highlight the role of the **unconscious** in human behavior and the motives and drives that underlie behavior. The father of psychoanalytic theory is Sigmund Freud (1920/1950, 1930/1962, 1932/1951). Freud introduced the idea that the mind is like an iceberg, in that only a small part of the iceberg is visible floating above water, and around 90% is under water and unobservable. Similarly, people are conscious of only a small part of the mind. The majority of the mind's operation is like the portion of the iceberg under water. It is unconscious. Freud viewed the personality as an energy system driven by aggressive and sexual drives. People are motivated to satisfy those drives, a force Freud called the **pleasure principle.** Behavior is a product of these drives and the unconscious efforts by individuals to suppress and channel the desire to act out in search of satisfaction. Living in society, from Freud's perspective, requires people to deny the pleasure principle, and the consequences are pathologies such as anxiety, obsessions, and defense mechanisms.

Freud argued that the structure of personality is based upon three elements. The **id,** which is inherited, includes instincts and responses to bodily functions (e.g., hunger). The id follows the pleasure principle. The **ego** is the part of the personality that moderates between id, and its desire for pleasure, and the realities of the social world. The ego, therefore, follows the **reality principle**, according to which the demands of the id will be blocked or channeled in accordance with reality, but also in accordance with the final element of the personality, the **superego**. This is the moral arm or conscience of the personality (Hall & Lindzey, 1970). Thus, if you interact with an individual whom you do not like at all, the id may inspire you to lash out angrily at that person, but the ego keeps you from doing so, because such behavior is socially inappropriate, and the superego tells you to be kind to all people and forgive them for their obnoxious behavior. When the ego is threatened, people feel **anxiety**, which may be realistic or **neurotic**. Neurotic anxiety is a fear of being punished for doing something the id wants the person to do. Another type of anxiety is moral anxiety, which occurs when there is a conflict between the id and the superego. **Defense mechanisms** are also used to defend the ego. These are unconscious techniques used to distort reality and prevent people from feeling anxiety, and include **repression**, wherein someone involuntarily eliminates an unpleasant memory; **projection**, which involves attributing one's own objectionable impulses to another person, or projecting them onto another; **rationalization**, by which people reinterpret their own objectionable behavior to make it seem less objectionable; and **denial**, wherein people may deny reality (e.g., denying the country is going to war, despite the mobilization of troops), or they may deny an impulse (e.g., proclaiming that you are not angry, when you really are).

Freud's ideas were evident in the theories of many psychologists who succeeded him. Fromm (1941, 1955, 1964), for example, explored the interactions between people and society and argued that change in human society produced freedom from certain restraints, such as serfdom and slavery, but in the process people experienced an increase in alienation and insecurity. To ameliorate this, they could pursue the positive freedom of a humanistic society, in which people treat one another with respect and love, or they could renounce freedom and accept totalitarian and authoritarian political and social systems. Erikson (1950, 1958, 1969) was also a depth psychologist trained as a Freudian, who made many contributions to psychoanalysis. He, too, maintained an interest in politics and political leaders. Erikson is most well known for his work on individual stages of personality development and identity. He maintained that the ego continues to grow after childhood and that society has an impact on personality. Among his important works are studies of Mahatma Gandhi (1969) and Martin Luther (1958).

Psychoanalysts employed a number of techniques that served the roles of data collection—broadly defined—and therapy. Freud and other psychoanalysts believed that much of the unconscious is repressed to avoid painful recollections, and one important component of therapy was to try to bring those repressed ideas and memories to the conscious level. One Freudian approach to therapy is known as free association. This involves having the patient lay on a couch, thinking of things in the past (free association), and saying everything that comes to mind. A second therapeutic technique was dream analysis. Freud believed that dreams are symbolic representations of thoughts—desires, fears, and things that happened. Freud's research was based upon notes about sessions with patients taken after a therapeutic session took place.

Psychobiographies

Clearly, the couch and dream analysis are not options in political psychological research using psychoanalytical theories. Access problems, particularly to political leaders, prevent direct person-to-person psychoanalysis. Therefore, many scholars who adopt a psychoanalytic approach to the analysis of political figures use the psychobiographical method.

Psychobiographies involve an examination of the life history of an individual, but not all psychobiographies are psychoanalytic.[1] Some of these psychobiographies focus upon Freudian analysis or notions of ego-defense (e.g., Glad, 1980; Hargrove, 1988; Link & Glad, 1994; Renshon, 1996); others concentrate upon specific kinds of personality disorders, ranging from narcissism to paranoid personality disorders (e.g., Birt, 1993; Post, 1991, 1993; Volkan, 1980). Usually, psychobiographies take the form of detailed, in-depth case studies of individual leaders, tracing their personal, social, and political development from early childhood through young adulthood. Because it is assumed that leaders' personalities or political styles are shaped by their early childhood socialization experiences, psychobiographies generally seek to identify consistent patterns of behavior, across time, that can be explained using psychoanalysis.[2]

One of the most important examples of high-quality psychobiography is the classic study, *Woodrow Wilson and Colonel House* (1964), in which George and George use a psychoanalytic approach to explain Wilson's highly moralistic, rigid, and uncompromising political style while in the White House. The Georges argue that it was a result of a childhood in a strict Calvinist household, where morality and distinctions between good and evil were emphasized above all else, and where his minister father constantly belittled Woodrow and severely punished him for any perceived transgressions. As a result, Wilson developed a rigid, driven political personality, in which he sought to accomplish great moral deeds to compensate for his own feelings of low self-esteem. Given his difficult relationship with his stern, disciplinarian father, Wilson bridled at authority figures and internalized their criticism as personally directed at him. Not only did he see the world in absolute terms, but Wilson felt that compromise on moral issues was immoral. The Georges argued that these very patterns, developed throughout his childhood and young adult life, followed him into the White House. Indeed, Wilson's efforts to create the League of Nations took on the form of a great moral crusade. His conflict with Senate Majority Leader Henry Cabot Lodge (who ultimately defeated Wilson's efforts to bring the United States into the organization) took the form of a renewed conflict with another strict authoritarian figure—his father. Wilson's political personality and his inability to compromise (not only on what he saw as a moral issue, but also in his conflict with Lodge) were seen by the Georges as the ultimate reason for his political defeat over the League of Nations.

As mentioned, another focus of psychoanalytical studies of personality and politics has been on psychopathology, or psychological disorders. The examination of political leaders' behavior as a possible product of psychopathologies began with Lasswell's *Psychopathology and Politics* (1960), wherein he maintained that the behavior of some people in political roles is affected by their psychopathologies. Lasswell attributed modern understanding of psychopathology to Freud's innovative ideas. Many political figures have also been analyzed based upon the identification of psychopathologies. For example, McCrae and Costa (1985) examined **neuroticism,** a personality disorder they argue is characterized in individuals by anxiety, self-consciousness, vulnerability, hostility, depression, and impulsiveness. In his study of **narcissism**, Volkan (1980) argues that narcissistic people seek leadership roles in a relentless search for power and that they use others in their climb to power. Further, such individuals often seem charismatic, and rise to power in times of crisis, when followers are searching for strong leaders who will improve things. Birt's (1993) analysis of Joseph Stalin found that descriptions of his personality fit the pattern associated with **paranoia**. Paranoid personalities are quite complex. Birt argues that they function along two continua: aggression and narcissism. Aggression can be manifested at one extreme as victim and at the other as the aggressor; narcissism ranges from feelings of inferiority to superiority. Paranoid people swing from one end of each continuum to the other. Birt argues that Stalin's paranoia not only affected the international policies of the Soviet Union, but Stalin's career as well. Stalin, he argues, "is the classical example of a paranoid individual whose paranoia helped him rise to the top of a highly centralized political structure and, once there, turn the bureaucratic institutions of the Soviet Union into extensions of his inner personality disorders" (p. 611). Birt's analysis of one time period in Soviet foreign policy—the blitzkrieg attack by Germany during the Second World War—demonstrates that, before the attack, Stalin was in an aggressor/superior phase and did not believe Hitler would attack. After the attack, Stalin "assumed the position of victim/superior. He deserved better from Hitler. He was slighted. Insecurity set in. To Stalin, he, not the Soviet Union, was under attack" (Birt, 1993, p. 619). As time progressed, he moved into the aggressor/inferior and then the victim/inferior modes, then climbed out of his depression, back to the aggressor/superior mode. Then he was ready for action and the rest of the war was fought with Stalin in that mode.

In general, political psychologists seeking to examine personality disorders in leaders will employ the widely accepted American Psychiatric Association's diagnostic criteria (see Table 2.1) to guide and structure their analysis of leader personality and behavior.

Freud and psychoanalysis in general have received numerous criticisms. Indeed, the criticisms of Freud have been so extensive, Hall and Lindzey (1970) argue, that "no other psychological theory has been subjected to such searching and often bitter criticism than has psychoanalysis. Freud and his theory have been attacked, reviled, ridiculed, and slandered" (p. 68). Among the more legitimate criticisms are those that point to the empirical problems arising from the fact that Freud's research was not controlled, but relied upon his recollections of therapy sessions with patients, which he recorded after the fact. He presented his findings as personal conclusions, without the original data, and those conclusions may have been subject to biases, because he relied on his own recollection of discussions. His method for reaching conclusions was not revealed, and there was "no systematic presentation, either quantitative or qualitative, of his empirical findings" (Hall & Lindzey, 1970, p. 69). A second criticism often made of Freud's theory, and psychoanalysis in general, is that it is not amenable to empirical testing. This is partly because much of Freud's theory about personality is based upon unobservable abstract ideas and partly because there are so many theoretically possible behaviors that are manifestations of psychoanalytic issues a person may have. For example, recall the study of Stalin's paranoia. If diametrically opposite patterns of behavior can result from the same psychoanalytic condition, developing testable, and therefore falsifiable, hypotheses is difficult. As a consequence of these criticisms, as well as the emergence of different perspectives on how important the unconscious is, a number of additional personality theories emerged in psychology, to which we now turn.

Traits, Motives, and Individual Differences

A wealth of personality theories and research looks at individual characteristics (or traits), motivations, and cognitive style variables and how these shape styles of decision making, interpersonal interaction, information processing, and management in office.

Trait Theories

If you were asked to describe your mother, you may say she is smart, funny, loving, tidy, and humble. These are personality traits, which we all use to characterize other people and ourselves. **Traits** are personality characteristics that are stable over time and in different situations (Pervin & John, 1997). Traits produce predispositions to think, feel, or act in particular patterns toward people, events, and situations. Trait theorists also regard traits to be hierarchically

TABLE 2.1
DSM-IV Diagnostic Criteria for Selected Personality Disorders

Personality Disorder	Personality Disorder
	A pervasive pattern of grandiosity (in fantasy or behavior), lack of empathy, and hypersensitivity to the evaluation of others, beginning by early adulthood and present in a variety of contexts, as indicated by at least *five* of the following: 1. Reacts to criticism with feelings of rage, shame, or humiliation (even if not expressed) 2. Is interpersonally exploitative: takes advantage of others to achieve their own ends 3. Has a grandiose sense of self-importance, e. g., exaggerates achievements and talents, expects to be noticed as "special" without appropriate achievement 4. Believes that their problems are unique and can be understood only by other special people
Narcissistic Disorder	5. Is preoccupied with fantasies of unlimited success, power, brilliance, beauty, or ideal love 6. Has a sense of entitlement: unreasonable expectation of especially favorable treatment, e.g., assumes that they do not have to wait in line when others must do so 7. Requires constant attention and admiration, e.g., keeps fishing for compliments 8. Lack of empathy: inability to recognize and experience how others feel, e.g., annoyance and surprise when a friend who is seriously ill cancels a date 9. Is preoccupied with feelings of envy
	A pervasive and unwarranted tendency, beginning by early adulthood and present in a variety of contexts, to interpret the actions of people as deliberately demeaning or threatening, as indicated by at least *four* of the following: 1. Expects, without sufficient basis, to be exploited or harmed by others 2. Questions, without justification, the loyalty or trustworthiness of friends or associates
Paranoid Disorder	3. Reads hidden meaning or threatening meanings into benign remarks or events, e.g., suspects that a neighbor put out trash early to annoy them 4. Bears grudges or is unforgiving of insults or slights 5. Is reluctant to confide in others, because of unwarranted fear that the information will be used against them 6. Is easily slighted and quick to react with anger or to counterattack 7. Questions, without justification, fidelity of spouse or sexual partner

Note: From *Diagnostic and statistical manual of mental disorders* (4th ed., text revision; pp. 690, 714) by American Psychiatric Association, Washington, DC: Author. Copyright by *American Psychiatric Association.* Adopted by permission.

organized. Trait theories in psychology began with the work of Allport (1937, 1961, 1968), who disagreed with Freud's contention that personality dynamics are governed by the unconscious. He also believed that childhood experiences are less important in the adult's personality than Freud maintained. Allport regarded personality traits to be central in determining how people respond to their environments, and he distinguished among cardinal, central, and secondary traits. **Cardinal traits** are critically important and dominate a person's life. An example would be authoritarianism, which is discussed later. Allport believed that cardinal traits are rare and that most people have few or none at all. **Central traits** affect people regularly, but not in every situation, (one example would be honesty). Finally, **secondary traits** are the least important and most irregular in affecting behavior. Allport also emphasized the importance of understanding motivation as a driving force in human behavior. For Allport, motivation was not hidden in the unconscious or derived from childhood experience, but was consciously considered through cognitive processes.

Another trait theorist whose work has influenced political psychology is Eysenck (1975, 1979). He identified three personality trait dimensions: introversion–extroversion, neuroticism, and psychoticism. The **introvert–extrovert trait** refers to how outgoing a person is, the **neuroticism trait** to how emotionally stable a person is, and the **psychoticism trait** refers to how isolated and insensitive to others a person is. Eysenck used questionnaires to gather data on personality traits and employed a statistical technique called **factor analysis** to identify which traits cluster together. Other important early trait theorists include Cattell (1964, 1965); Cattell and Child (1975); and McClelland (1975), both of whom wrote extensively about motivation, a trait factor we consider later.

In recent years, psychologists have sought to develop a taxonomy of personality traits that constitute the basic units of personality. Using several different research techniques, including factor analyses of trait terms commonly used in everyday language, and the analysis of trait questionnaires, psychologists developed five central personality traits. The **Big Five** personality dimensions are neuroticism, extraversion, agreeableness, openness to experience and conscientiousness (Costa & McCrae, 1985). Each trait is arranged on a continuum. For example, those high in neuroticism are characterized as people who worry and are nervous and insecure, whereas those low in neuroticism are calm, secure and unemotional. People who are high in extraversion are sociable, optimistic, fun loving and affectionate, while those low in extraversion are quiet, reserved, and aloof. A person high in openness is curious, creative, and has many interests, while one low in openness is conventional and has narrow interests. People high in agreeableness are trusting, good natured, helpful and soft-hearted, while a person low in agreeableness tends to be cynical, rude, irritable and uncooperative. Finally, a person high in conscientiousness is organized, hardworking and reliable, while a person low in conscientiousness is aimless, unreliable, negligent and hedonistic (Pervin & John, 1997).

Big Five personality research studies are conducted using questionnaires designed to tap how high or low a person is in a particular trait. Studies have looked at a variety of behavioral patterns associated with the Big Five personality traits. Olson and Evans (1999) have examined the relationship between the Big Five personality dimensions or traits and social comparisons. The authors used a new technique (the Rochester Social Comparison Record), wherein experimental subjects keep a diary recording their social comparisons for measuring to whom they compare themselves. The researchers also examined how people feel about those comparisons. They found that people high in neuroticism felt more positive when they compared themselves downward, that is, to others of less stature or status. People high in extroversion compared downward more than people low in extroversion, in part because they had stable positive moods. In addition, Olson and Evans (1999) argue, "along with their greater tendency to experience positive affect, extroverts also might compare downward because of their tendency to be dominant, masterful, and assertive, attributes that are reflected in studies showing them to have a high degree of leadership ability" (p. 1506). This is illustrated later in this chapter and in chapter 5, where we consider leadership in detail. People low in agreeableness tend to see themselves as superior to others, and therefore compared downward

Introversion	**vs.**	**Extroversion**
(Introspective, reserved, seeking solitude)		(Expressiveness and gregariousness)
Sensing	**vs.**	**Intuition**
(Favoring literal, empirical perception)		(Favoring abstract, figurative perception)
Thinking	**vs.**	**Feeling**
(Favoring objective, detached, logical decision making)		(Favoring subjective, value- or emotion-based decision making
Judging	**vs.**	**Perceiving**
(Seeking resolution and order)		(Curious, spontaneous, tolerant of disorder)

FIG. 2.1. MBTI personality types.

Note. From "Presidential character revisited," by M. Lyons, 1997, *Political Psychology, 18,* p. 794.

more than those high in agreeableness. Finally, people high in openness compared themselves to superior groups more than those low in openness and tended not to experience a diminution of positive affect in the process. Also, a body of literature on personality trait affect explores the question of whether traits have particular affects associated with them. Schimmack, Oishi, Diener, and Suh (2000) argue that extroversion includes pleasant affects and neuroticism has unpleasant affects.

The traits used in political psychology are related to traits described in the psychological literature, but they are presented in their political manifestation. Openness to experience, for example, appears as cognitive complexity, interest in politics, integrative complexity, and other traits that are named and described in political form. Traits commonly used in political psychology, and their measurement, are discussed later, in our section on profiling leader characteristics, and in Table 2.3.

Somewhat similar to the Big Five is the application of the Myers-Briggs Type Indicator (MBTI) personality assessment measure to the study of political personality. The MBTI assumes that individual personality reveals itself in the form of specific preferences for certain kinds of environments, tasks, and cognitive patterns (Lyons, 1997). Compared with the Big Five personality traits, the MBTI scales mirror similar factors, with the exception of neuroticism, which is not included in the MBTI system. As shown in Figure 2.1, the MBTI is composed of four scales of preferences, which allow, across the various possible combinations, a total of 16 potential personality types.

For example, applying these measures to former President Bill Clinton's life prior to his arrival in the White House, Lyons (1997) argues that Clinton falls squarely into the extroversion, intuitiveness, feeling, and perceiving categories (an ENFP type) of the MBTI. Given the predictions of the MBTI for the ENFP personality type, Lyons suggests that Clinton would be expected to seek close attachments to other people; be very adept at establishing such attachments; seek out people-to-people work professionally; be optimistic, warmly enthusiastic, high spirited, and charismatic; be brilliantly perceptive about other people, draw followers, and be an excellent politician; appear insincere sometimes, because of a tendency to adapt to other people in the way he presents his objective; be innovative, yet undisciplined, disorganized, and indecisive; hate rules and find it difficult to work within the constraints of institutions; thrive on constant change and begin more projects than can reasonably be completed; find difficulty relaxing and commonly work himself into exhaustion; have his energies divided between competing interests and personal relationships; be ingenious and adaptable in a way that allows him to often improvise success; exhibit a highly empathetic worldview, yet focus on data that confirms his biases, leading to a propensity to make poor choices and make serious mistakes of judgment (Lyons, 1997).

Motive Theories

Some researchers look at the **motives** of individuals. There are many motive theories in psychology and many definitions of the term. In a study done over 40 years ago, for example, Madsen (1961) considered the works of 20 different motive theorists. Interest in motivation has come and gone and come around again in personality theory in psychology. **Motives** are those aspects of personality concerned with goals and goal-directed actions. Motives "energize, direct, and select behavior" (Emmons, 1997, p. 486). The motives that have received the most attention and are regarded as the Big Three in both psychology and political psychology are the **need for power** (i.e., concern for impact and prestige), **need for affiliation intimacy** (i.e., concern for close

> ### What Is Content Analysis?
> Content analysis is a research method used frequently by political psychologists, employing a wide variety of analytical approaches, including those discussed in this chapter and chapter 3. Because, in political psychology, we often lack direct access to policymakers, we look at their statements and infer from those statements some aspects of their political psychological makeup. This is content analysis. To conduct a systematic content analysis, a researcher must (1) decide what materials they will use in the study (e.g., only statements written by the official you are examining, public statements written by others, interviews, etc.) and (2) decide how the material will be analyzed (or coded), i.e., how inferences will be drawn and recorded.

relations with others), and **need for achievement** (i.e., concern with excellence and task accomplishment) (McClelland, 1975; McClelland & Boyatzis, 1982; Winter, 1973, 1987; Winter & Carlson, 1988; Winter, Hermann, Weintraub, & Walker, 1991; Winter & Stewart, 1977). For example, Winter and Stewart (1977) argued that those high in power and low in affiliation make better presidents. Those high in power also require a far greater degree of personal control over the policy process and the actions of subordinates than do low-power personalities. In terms of interpersonal relationships, people high in the need for power exhibit more controlling, domineering behavior toward subordinates than low-power people (McClelland, 1985; Winter, 1973, 1987). Motivation and leadership have received attention in Winter's (1987) study of the appeal of American presidents. He argued that a leader's popular appeal (measured by electoral success) is a function of the fit between his motives and those of society.

In psychology, a method for assessing motives, used by clinical psychologists, is the Thematic Apperception Test (TAT). This method involves giving participants a picture, having them write imaginative stories about it, then doing a content analysis of the stories. The stories reveal underlying personality characteristics. This method has been criticized as unreliable, but, regardless of its reliability, it is not available for the assessment of political leaders, so techniques for measuring motives from a distance have been developed, using **content analysis** of texts, particularly the inaugural speeches of American presidents.[3]

SOME FRAMEWORKS FROM POLITICAL PSYCHOLOGY

In the sections that follow, we introduce readers to political psychological frameworks that employ various combinations of personality psychology just discussed. As mentioned at the outset of this chapter, the use of personality theories by political psychology has been eclectic. The frameworks presented here have drawn liberally from a variety of psychological theories, but they have tried to adapt those theories and concepts to political contexts. For example, personality traits and motivations discussed in psychology may be directly used in political analyses, or they may be presented in a political manifestation. The need for power is directly applicable to politics. Ethnocentrism has been determined to be an important *politically relevant trait*, but is not considered to be a central personality trait in the personality literature.

The Authoritarian Personality

Although research into the authoritarian personality has a long history, interest in exploring authoritarian personality characteristics increased as a result of World War II and the Nazi regime in Germany. The rabid anti-Semitism of that regime, along with its extreme right-wing fascist political principles, led researchers to explore the question of whether this political authoritarianism could be traced to a personality syndrome. The post–World War II study of an authoritarian personalty type began with the work of Adorno et al. *The Authoritarian Personality* (1950) was based on psychoanalytic arguments. Authoritarian personalities were, they argued, the product of authoritarian patterns of childhood upbringing and a resultant weak ego. The parents of authoritarians were insensitive to the difficulties children experience as they try to learn how to control id-derived impulses relating to sexual desires, bodily functions, and aggression. Instead of helping their children develop, these parents were demanding, controlling, and used severe disciplinary techniques. The parents were also described as being determined to raise their children to be highly conventional. As a result, the children did not develop effective ways of controlling their sexual and aggressive impulses, yet feared those impulses. They developed iron-tight defensive techniques that would prevent them from having to confront those impulses. They regard their parents, and subsequent authority in their lives, with a mixture of resentment and dependence. Adorno et al. saw the authoritarian personality as composed of several central personality traits, including conventionalism (rigid adherence to conventional values), submission to authority figures, authoritarian aggression (that is, aggressive impulses toward those who are not conventional), anti-intraception (i.e., rejection of tenderness, imagination, subjectivity), superstition and stereotype (fatalistic belief in mystical determinants of the future and rigid thinking, respectively), high value placed on power and toughness, destructiveness and cynicism, projectivity (i.e., the projection outward of unacceptable impulses), and an excessive concern with the sexual activity of others. Given the era in which the study was done, there was a natural interest in the extent to which authoritarian personalities would be susceptible to fascism of the Nazi Germany variety— antidemocratic and right-wing in political ideology, anti-Semitic, ethnocentric, and hostile toward racial and other minorities.

The Authoritarian Personality study was done using a wide variety of research tools, including questionnaires (with factual questions, opinion–attitude scales, and open-answer questions) and clinical measures (interviews and TAT). The authors developed **scales** to measure several elements of authoritarian political attitudes. Scales combine several items from a questionnaire on the same topic, enabling the researcher to get a broader range of scores for a single person. This increases the reliability of the score. The fascism, or F scale, was developed to test for a person's propensity toward fascism. The other scales were the anti-Semitism scale, the ethnocentrism scale (which included Negro, minority, and patriotism subscales), and the politicoeconomic conservatism scale. Each scale was designed to assess different elements of political authoritarianism. Adorno et al. argued that their empirical evidence demonstrated that this syndrome was closely associated with anti-Semitism, ethnocentrism, and, in turn, with political conservatism. But criticisms quickly emerged on conceptual and methodological grounds. One of the more important criticisms was presented by Shils (1954), who noted that communists, who also held authoritarian political values, scored low in the Adorno et al. measurement scale, the F scale. Therefore, he argued, they apparently tested only for right-wing authoritarianism and not left-wing authoritarianism, and therefore their F scale was not a true measure of authoritarianism. Other criticisms noted that Adorno and his colleagues did not control for education and income, and that the F scale question wording provoked a tendency to agree (acquiesce), thereby producing false positives (Bass, 1955; Gage, Leavitt, & Stone, 1957; Jackson & Messick, 1957). In short, much of the criticism was methodological and revolved around the question of whether the F scale actually tapped true authoritarianism and whether it actually established a relationship between those nine authoritarian personality traits and fascistic political principles.

More recently, additional criticisms have been made about the work of Adorno and his colleagues. For example, Martin (2001) argues that there is a fundamental flaw in the theoretical construct, in that those high in authoritarianism are assumed to have certain syndromes and those low do not. Instead, he argues, the whole issue should be approached as a question, and the difference between low and high should be studied as a continuum. What, for example, are those in the middle like? Second, Martin notes that the Adorno group was willing to distort or dismiss data that showed nonauthoritarian tendencies among the highs and authoritarian tendencies among the lows. This reached its acme in a differential interpretation strategy by which anything good said by a high (but not a low) was evidence of the suppression of its opposite, and anything bad said by a low (but not by a high) was taken as evidence of a healthy acceptance of one's shortcomings (Martin, 2001).

The authoritarian personality debate, and renewed interest in the personality syndrome, was revitalized by the work of Altemeyer (1981, 1988, 1996), whose approach is trait-based rather than psychoanalytic. He uses three of the nine personality traits identified by Adorno et al.: authoritarian submission, authoritarian aggression, and conventionalism. These he regards as central attitudinal clusters (orientations to respond in the same general way toward certain classes of stimuli [1996] in right-wing authoritarianism). Altemeyer did not include the more psychoanalytical traits, because he was not convinced by the original psychoanalytic argument, noting that there was little inter-item consistency among the F scale questions that attempted to trace those traits. Instead, he conceptualized right-wing authoritarianism psychologically, rather than politically (i.e., one ideology vs. another). Psychologically, **right-wing authoritarianism** is submission to perceived authorities, particularly those in the establishment or established system of governance (Altemeyer, 1996). That system could be a repressive right-wing system, as in apartheid South Africa, or a communist system, as in the People's Republic of China, or a democratic system, as in the United States. Hence, right-wing authoritarianism can occur in any political system. Altemeyer has developed a right-wing authoritarianism (RWA) scale, too. The scale includes statements with which the respondent must agree or disagree such as "life imprisonment is justified for certain crimes" and "women should have to promise to obey their husbands when they get married" (1996, p.13).

In Altemeyer's view, right-wing authoritarianism is a product of social learning, a combination of personality predispositions, and life events. Altemeyer argues that those high in right-wing authoritarianism have greater difficulty than low scorers in engaging in critical thinking. They are more likely to agree with a statement of a fact without examining it critically (1996). This is a consequence of having truths dictated to them by those in authority and being prohibited from challenging that authority. Therefore, when a scapegoat is selected upon whom a country's problems are placed, people high in right-wing authoritarianism are more likely to uncritically believe that the scapegoat is responsible. It follows, then, that a second pattern of thinking among those high in right-wing authoritarianism is the acceptance of contradictory ideas and an ability to compartmentalize them, thereby ignoring the contradictions. Any idea that comes from an authority figure is accepted as correct, even if it is in direct contradiction to another idea. Third, Altemeyer argues that those high in right-wing authoritarianism see the world as a very dangerous place. They were taught this by their parents, the resulting fear drives much of their aggression, and this makes them vulnerable to precisely the kind of overstated, emotional, and dangerous assertions a demagogue would make (1996). Fourth, high authoritarians are much more careful in looking for evidence to disprove ideas they are predisposed to reject than to disprove ideas they are predisposed to accept. Finally, Altemeyer argues that high authoritarians are particularly susceptible to the **fundamental attribution error**[1] wherein people attribute the behavior of others to internal dispositions and their own behavior to external forces.

Further research into the authoritarian personality is ongoing. Lambert, Burroughs, and Nguyen (1999) used Altemeyer's RWA scale to examine the relationship between authoritarianism, belief in a just world, and perceptions of risk. They found that high authoritarians perceived risk to be lower if people believed in a just world (i.e., good things come to good people). Low authoritarians did not have the same perception. Chapter 7 discusses some research regarding race-related attitudes and right-wing authoritarianism.

Altemeyer argues that several political attitudes, such as anti-Semitism and hostility toward foreigners, correlate with his three central authoritarian attitude clusters, but others, such as Raden (1999), argue that the clustering of such attitudes is influenced by political and social change; Raden found that anti-Semitism was decreasingly likely to correlate with authoritarian personality characteristics as the twentieth century progressed. Martin (2001) has weighed in on Altemeyer's work, as well, arguing that, although he avoids the methodological problems of the Adorno et al. F scale, he still failed to see authoritarianism as a continuum and does not compare the behavior of lows and highs, but sticks to the examination of the behavior of highs. Furthermore, he does not adequately explain why conventionalism is a manifestation of authoritarianism, and uses evidence of differences in degree (i.e., some lows agreeing with highs and some highs agreeing with lows in some question items) as evidence of a clear-cut, mutually distinct, typological difference.

As mentioned at the beginning of this chapter, studies of personality and leadership in political psychology are rather eclectic, in that they draw not only from psychological personality concepts, but other areas as well. As a result, scholars have built some frameworks that are used to analyze political leaders (but many could be used to examine the average citizen, too). Next, we provide an overview of some of those frameworks, with some examples of their applications to political leaders, but political leaders are discussed in much greater depth in chapter 5.

Leader Analysis Frameworks

There is an extensive literature in political psychology on the leadership or management styles of political leaders, using many different frameworks. Here, we introduce several frameworks used to study political leaders: the presidential character framework developed by Barber, several trait assessment approaches, and the operational code. There also is no common, agreed-upon empirical approach to the study of political leaders in political psychology. Instead, there has developed a broad, methodologically diverse, interdisciplinary literature on the topic, which has been tolerant of hybrid research approaches that borrow individual concepts or variables from a variety of sources. As a result, variables that psychologists would be quick to describe as personality-based (whether Freudian concepts, authoritarian measures, personal traits like need for power, self-confidence, distrust of others, etc.) are routinely combined with clearly non-personality-based variables (such as an individual's first political success, their socialization experiences, their prior policy experience, or operational code belief systems) in the same analysis.

Because the literature addressing the impact of personal variables upon political leader behavior developed over a long process of selective borrowing by political scientists from a broad range of psychological literatures (on personality, cognition, groups, etc.), drawing crisp, clear delineations between personality and political leadership in political psychology is practically impossible. Like the problem often facing surgeons in separating infants born conjoined, these two research traditions in political psychology share too many common elements to easily separate into two distinct bodies. This reality will become more apparent as many of the approaches to the study of personality and politics, as well as political leadership, are viewed in this chapter. There are some personality-based studies that are applied to both leaders and the average person, such as authoritarian personality studies. Next, we provide an overview of several theories and frameworks that focus on individual characteristics and their impact on political behavior.

Trait-Based Studies

Presidential Character

Barber's well-known book, *The Presidential Character* (1972), employs psychobiography to explain the personalities, styles, and character of modern presidents. Avoiding the psychoanalytic focus upon Freudian concepts (id, ego, and superego), Barber's psychobiographies seek patterns in the early lives or political careers of leaders, which create, through a process of socialization, the subsequent patterns of personality, style, and leadership one sees in office. Moreover, Barber argues that personality should not be studied as a set of idiosyncratic traits unique to individual presidents, in which some presidents have a trait others do not. Instead, he argues that personality is a "matter of tendencies" (p. 7), in which traits like aggressiveness, detachment, or compliance are possessed by all presidents, but in differing amounts and combinations. As a result, the components of presidential personality (*character, worldview*, and *style*) are patterned, fitting together in a "dynamic package understandable in psychological terms" (p. 6): *Style* reflects the habitual way a president performs his three political roles (rhetoric, personal relations, and homework); *worldview* consists of the leader's primary, politically relevant beliefs regarding such things as social causality, human nature, and the central moral conflicts of the time (Barber, 1972); and *character* is seen as the way in which a president orients toward life and his own merits (i.e., his sense of self-esteem and the criteria by which he judges himself, such as by achievement or affection) (Barber, 1972). In order to put these pieces together, Barber employs a psychobiographical approach to trace the sociological development, within presidents, of the three patterns comprising personality (character, worldview, and style) from their early lives to their critically important first independent political successes. That first political success sets the pattern that follows, giving the leader a template for successful action and positive feedback, which they emulate and seek to copy throughout their subsequent careers.

Perhaps one of the most famous typologies in political science, Barber's (1972) seeks to capture how *presidential character*, or "the basic stance a man takes toward his Presidential experience" (p. 6), finds itself reflected in two basic dimensions: (1) the energy and effort he puts into the job (*active or passive*); and (2) the personal satisfaction he derives from his presidential duties (*positive or negative*) (Barber). The resulting typology is presented in Table 2.2, along with Barber's examples of American presidents who fit within each of the cells.

Applied to both Bill Clinton and George W. Bush, Barber's (1972) typology leads to a very generalized prediction of behavior and style in office. In Clinton's case, it is clear that he fits into the *active–positive* category of Barber's typology. Indeed, few presidents in American history have been so actively engaged personally in the details of policy making on a day-to-day

TABLE 2.2
Barber's Typology of Presidential Character

		Personal Satisfaction With Presidential Duties	
		Positive	Negative
Energy put into the job	Active	Derives great personal satisfaction and is highly engaged (examples: Jefferson, Roosevelt, Truman, Kennedy, Ford, Carter, Bush, Clinton)	Derives little personal satisfaction yet is highly engaged (examples: Adams, Wilson, Hoover, Johnson, Nixon)
	Passive	Enjoys great personal satisfaction from the job, but puts little energy into it (examples: Madison, Taft, Harding, Reagan, G.W. Bush)	Derives little personal satisfaction and puts little energy into it (examples: Washington, Coolidge, Eisenhower)

basis, or enjoyed their presidential duties and responsibilities, as much as Bill Clinton did in office (Preston, 2001). Barber's predictions for this type of personality are that such individuals want to achieve results and direct much of their energy toward achievement, tend to be self-respecting and happy, are open to new ideas, flexible and able to learn from mistakes, and tend to show great capacity for growth in office. Although one might quibble with some of the predictions that seem to have problems in light of Clinton's White House behaviors regarding interns and the ability to learn from mistakes, the general predictions regarding his emphasis upon results and achievement, his generally happy demeanor, and his widely reported openness to new ideas and policy flexibility, are strongly supported by his record in office.

In contrast, George W. Bush would likely be classified as a *passive–positive*, according to Barber's typology. The early evidence of Bush's style in office supports this designation. He is an individual who tends to be less personally engaged or involved in the formulation and making of policy, preferring instead to delegate these tasks to subordinates, but who, nevertheless, greatly enjoys being president (Dowd, 2001; Kahn, 2000; Milbank, 2001). In terms of predicted behaviors arising from this style type, Barber (1972) describes passive-positives as primarily being after affirmation and support or love from their followers, while showing a tendency for policy drift, especially during times of crisis, in which you would expect to see confusion, delay, and impulsiveness on their parts. There certainly have been numerous examples of confusion, delay, and impulsiveness regarding Bush's policies in the Middle East (especially the Israeli–Palestinian conflict and Iraq), in his reactions toward U.S. participation in many international treaties (ABM and Kyoto being only the most notable), and in his enunciation of an "axis of evil."

Obviously, the typology is exceedingly general in nature, examines only two possible dimensions relating to presidential style, and has an intensely subjective element. Clearly, one could take issue with either the accuracy or usefulness of the Barber model, especially given that it basically places Franklin Roosevelt, Harry Truman, John Kennedy, Gerald Ford, Jimmy Carter, George Bush, Sr., and Clinton all in the active-positive category, and that Ronald Reagan, Warren Harding, and William Taft join George W. Bush as passive-positives. Given such minimal differentiation among such varied presidents, it was apparent to many leadership analysts that a more involved, nuanced approach was required if political psychological techniques were to provide a more nuanced portrait of leaders (Hermann & Preston, 1994, 1998; Preston 2001; Winter et al., 1991).

Looking at other traits, Etheredge (1978), in a study of twentieth century U.S. presidents and foreign policy advisers, noted the importance of traits such as **dominance, interpersonal trust, self-esteem,** and **introversion–extroversion**, in shaping policymaker views and policy preferences. American leaders scoring high on measures of dominance tended to favor using force to settle disputes with the Soviet Union, over the use of arbitration or disarmament. Moreover, leaders scoring high on introversion tended to oppose cooperation, and extroverted ones generally supported cooperation and negotiation with the Soviets. These results built upon earlier studies reported by Etheredge (1978) of over 200 male U.S. foreign service officers, military officers, and domestic affairs specialists, in which those who scored high on traits of dominance and competitiveness were more likely to advocate the use of force and to see the Soviet Union as threatening; those high on interpersonal trust and self-esteem tended to hold a more benign view of the Soviets and to oppose the use of force (Winter, 2003). Other significant work in applying traits to political leaders have been done by Weintraub (1981, 1986, 1989), in his studies of U.S. presidential press conference responses, and by Hermann (1984, 1987, 1988), in her studies of the foreign policy orientations of world leaders.

Leaders' Characteristics: Motives and Traits

A wealth of research also exists surrounding the impact that various individual characteristics of leaders have upon their styles of decision making, interpersonal interactions, information processing, or management behaviors in office (cf. Hermann, 1980a, 1980b, 1983, 1984, 1987; Hermann & Preston, 1994, 1998; Preston, 2001; Preston & 't Hart, 1999; Stogdill & Bass, 1981; Vertzberger, 1990; Winter et al., 1991). In chapter 5, ample illustrations of leader characteristics and decision-making patterns are presented. Several of the most important leader characteristics are next described, along with the measurement techniques discussed.[4] A basic description of some of these characteristics is provided in Table 2.3.

Brief illustrations of three of these individual characteristics (power, complexity, expertise) should provide the reader with a clearer understanding of how these measures tend to be thought of in the literature.

The **need for power** (or dominance) is a personality characteristic that has been extensively studied and linked to specific types of behavior and interactional styles with others (Browning & Jacob, 1964; Hermann, 1980b, 1987; House, 1990; McClelland, 1975; Winter, 1973, 1987; Winter & Stewart, 1977). Specifically, one would expect leaders with progressively higher psychological needs for power to be increasingly dominant and assertive in their leadership styles in office and to assert greater control over subordinates and policy decisions. For example, Fodor and Smith (1982) found that leaders high in need for power were more associated with the suppression of open decision making and discussion within groups than were low-power leaders. Similarly, a number of studies have found high-power leaders requiring a far greater degree of personal control than do low-power leaders, over the policy process and the actions of subordinates (Etheredge, 1978; Hermann, 1980b; Winter, 1973, 1987). In terms of interpersonal relationships, studies have also found that leaders high in the need for power exhibit more controlling, domineering behavior toward subordinates than low-power leaders (Browning & Jacob, 1964; Fodor & Farrow, 1979; McClelland, 1985; Winter & Stewart, 1977).

The **cognitive complexity** of decision makers is another individual characteristic that has long been argued to have a significant impact upon the nature of decision making, style of leadership, assessment of risk, and character of general information processing within decision groups (Driver, 1977; Hermann, 1980b, 1987; Preston, 2001; Stewart, Hermann, & Hermann,

TABLE 2.3
Descriptions of Selected Individual Characteristics

Need for power	Concern with establishing, maintaining, or restoring one's power, i.e., one's impact, control, or influence over others
Locus of control	View of the world in which an individual does or does not perceive some degree of control over situations they are involved in; whether government can influence what happens in or to a nation
Ethnocentrism	View of the world in which one's own nation holds center stage; strong emotional ties to one's own nation; emphasis on national honor and identity
Need for affiliation	Concern with establishing, maintaining, or restoring warm and friendly relationships with other persons or groups
Cognitive complexity	Ability to differentiate the environment: Degree of differentiation person shows in describing or discussing other people, places, policies, ideas, or things
Distrust of others	General feeling of doubt, uneasiness, and misgiving about others; inclination to suspect and doubt others' motives and actions
Self-confidence	Person's sense of self-importance or image of their ability to cope with the environment
Task–interpersonal emphasis	Relative emphasis, in interactions with others, on getting the task done vs. focusing on feelings and needs of others

1989; Tetlock, 1985; Vertzberger, 1990; Wallace & Suedfeld, 1988). For example, Vertzberger (1990), among others, has noted that, as the cognitive complexity of individual decision makers increases, they become more capable of dealing with complex decision environments and information that demand new or subtle distinctions. When making decisions, complex individuals tend to have greater cognitive need for information, are more attentive to incoming information, prefer systematic over heuristic processing, and deal with any overload of information better than their less complex counterparts (Nydegger, 1975; Schroder, Driver, & Streufert, 1967). In terms of interactions with advisers and the acceptance of critical feedback, several studies have shown that complex individuals are far more interested in receiving negative feedback from others—and are more likely to incorporate it into their own decision making—than are those who are less complex (Nydegger, 1975; Ziller, Stone, Jackson, & Terbovic, 1977). Indeed, Vertzberger (1990) and Glad (1983) have both noted that low-complexity individuals tend to show symptoms of dogmatism, view and judge issues in black-and-white terms, ignore information threatening their existing closed belief systems, and have limited ability to adjust their beliefs to new information.

Complexity has also been linked to how attentive or sensitive leaders are to information from (or to nuances from within) their surrounding political or policy environments (Hermann, 1984; Preston, 1997, 2001). In fact, Hermann (1984) notes that the more sensitive the individual is to information from the decision environment, the more receptive the leader is to information regarding the views of colleagues or constituents, the views of outside actors, and the value of alternative viewpoints and discrepant information. In contrast, leaders with a low sensitivity to contextual information will be less receptive to information from the outside environment, will operate from a previously established and strongly held set of beliefs, will selectively perceive and process incoming information in order to support or bolster this prior framework, and will be unreceptive or close-minded toward alternative viewpoints and discrepant information.

In contrast, the **integrative complexity** literature differs slightly from the cognitive complexity literature just discussed, in that it focuses upon both *differentiation* (which is evaluatively distinct dimensions of a problem taken into account by decision makers) and *integration* (which is the connections made by decision makers among differentiated characteristics), whereas the general complexity literature focuses principally upon differentiation alone (Tetlock, 1983). For example, according to Tetlock and Tyler (1996), integrative complexity presupposes a dialectical point–counterpoint style of thinking, in which the speaker recognizes the legitimacy of contradictory points of view, then integrates those evaluatively differentiated cognitions into a higher order synthesis. The concept of cognitive complexity, by contrast, requires merely that one have many distinct ideas or thoughts on a subject, not that those cognitions be in tension with each other or be organized into higher order schemata or knowledge structures. For example, one could be cognitively complex by generating lots of reasons why one is right and one's adversaries are wrong, but still be integratively simple (Totlock & Tyler, 1996).[5]

Finally, the **prior policy experience or expertise** of leaders has a significant impact upon presidential style, the nature of advisory group interactions, and how forcefully leaders assert their own positions on policy issues (cf. Barber, 1972; George, 1980; Hermann, 1986; House, 1990). Past experience provides leaders with a sense of what actions will be effective or ineffective in specific policy situations, as well as which cues from the environment should be attended to and which are irrelevant (Hermann, 1986). It influences how much learning must be accomplished on the job, the inventory of behaviors (standard operating procedures) possessed, and how confident the leader will be in interactions with experts. Leaders with a high degree of prior policy experience are more likely to insist upon personal involvement or control over policy making than are those low in prior policy experience, who will tend to be more dependent upon the views of expert advisers. Indeed, experienced leaders who have expertise in a policy area are far less likely to rely upon the views of advisers or to utilize simplistic stereotypes or analogies to understand policy situations. Such leaders are more interested in gathering detailed information from the policy environment, and they employ a more deliberate decision process than their less experienced counterparts. Similarly, leaders lacking experience or expertise find themselves far more dependent upon expert advisers and more likely to utilize simplistic stereotypes and analogies when making decisions (see Khong, 1992; Levy, 1994; Preston, 2001). Knowing whether a leader is approaching foreign or domestic policy as a relative expert or novice provides insight into predicting how damaging such reliance upon analogy might be to a particular leader's information-management and information-processing styles. This individual characteristic is similar to George's (1980) *sense of efficacy*.

Among the approaches for measuring individual differences and characteristics in leaders, perhaps one of the most widely utilized and empirically rich is the *Leader Evaluation and Assessment at a Distance* (LEAD) profiling technique developed by Hermann (1983, 1999).[6] This method utilizes content analysis of the spontaneous interview responses by political leaders, across differing time periods, audiences, and substantive topic areas, to construct detailed personality profiles of individuals, according to seven different traits: need for power, ethnocentrism, locus of control, complexity, self-confidence, distrust of others, and task/interpersonal emphasis. It has previously been used to construct detailed profiles of more than 140 political leaders in over 40 different countries. Contributing to this large body of empirical research over the past several decades have been studies employing LEAD profiles of modern American presidents, sub-Saharan African leaders, Soviet politburo members, Iranian revolutionary leaders, Sein Fein leader Gerry Adams, and secretaries general of the United Nations (U.N.), among others (Hermann 1984, 1987, 1989; 1999; Hermann et al., 1996; Kaarbo & Hermann 1998; Mastors, 2000; Preston 2001; Preston & 't Hart, 1999; Taysi & Preston, 2001; Winter et al., 1991).

TABLE 2.4

Operational Code Philosophical and Instrumental Beliefs of Leaders

Philosophical Beliefs	Instrumental Beliefs
The fundamental nature of politics and political conflict, and the image of the opponent	The best approach for selecting goals for political action
The general prospects for achieving one's fundamental political values	How such goals and objectives can be pursued most effectively
The extent to which political outcomes are predictable	The best approach to calculation, control, and acceptance of the risks of political action
The extent to which political leaders can influence historical developments and control outcomes	The matter of timing of action
The role of chance	The utility and role of different means for advancing one's interests

Note: From "The causal nexus between cognitive beliefs and decision making behavior" (p.100), by A. L. George, 1979, in L. Falkowski (Ed.), *Psychological models in international politics*, Boulder, CO: Westview.

Operational Code

The last approach presented in this chapter, for studying characteristics of political leaders, is the use of operational codes. Operational codes are constructs representing the overall belief systems of leaders about the world (i.e., how it works, what it is like, what kinds of actions are most likely to be successful, etc.) (George, 1969, 1979; Holsti, 1977; Walker, 1983; Walker, Schafer, & Young, 1998). Why is the discussion of the operational code in a chapter on personality and not in the next chapter, where beliefs are discussed? The explanation is simply that the operational code is unique to the personality of the person under examination and, more important, because the operational code links **motivation** (a personality factor) with beliefs. Scholars who use the framework argue that the beliefs it depicts are motivating forces as well as information-processing filters. As illustrated in Table 2.4 operational code belief systems for leaders are generated by the answers to 10 specific questions regarding their philosophical and instrumental beliefs.

As George (1979) observed, operational code beliefs, unlike attitudes, represent central beliefs, which "are concerned with fundamental, unchanging issues of politics and political action" (p. 99). By understanding the operational codes of leaders, scholars employing this technique argue that a better understanding is gained of their likely decision-making styles and political behavior. Operational codes are constructed, either quantitatively or qualitatively, through an examination of decision makers' speeches, interviews, writings, and other verbal or written materials. This technique has a long history of use in political science and has been used to examine a wide range of political leaders.[7]

For example, in the case of President Vladimir Putin of Russia, an operational code analysis conducted by Stephen Dyson (2001) suggests that, regarding the five basic questions surrounding *philosophical beliefs*, Putin would (1) view political life as harmonious, to the extent that it was governed and regulated by laws, rules, and norms; (2) believe that one can be optimistic about making progress toward one's goals, as long as the rule of law is enforced, but that anarchy and corruption will reign in its absence; (3) believe that the political future is predictable, to the extent that one can rely upon the existence of enforced rules and norms; (4) believe that it is possible to achieve very little direct control over history, but that one's own environment and circumstances can be affected by engaging in an incremental, step-by-step approach; and (5) view chance as something to be avoided as much as possible, through good organization and organizational planning.

In terms of his five basic *instrumental beliefs*, Putin is said to believe that (1) the goals and objectives set for political action should be both achievable and measurable; (2) the best strategy for pursuing goals is to engage in an incremental, backward-mapping approach, planned step-by-step to stay within the norms of expected behavior; (3) political risk can be controlled by keeping a low political profile on his part, while working behind-the-scenes; (4) the best timing of political action is one that preempts major difficulties, but does not preempt so early as to cause difficulties itself; and (5) the prime tools of political interest advancement are incremental backward-mapping and flexibility on the leader's part (Dyson, 2001). Thus, Putin's operational code suggests a leader who is incremental by nature, who judges the acceptability of actions by their chances of success, who sees adherence to norms as essential, and who views those who step outside of such norms as requiring reciprocal or violent treatment (Dyson).

The value of such operational codes in predicting the likely pattern of leader behavior, given the answers to these basic philosophical and instrumental questions, is potentially quite high and of great value to policymakers. For example, in summarizing the findings of the Putin operational code, Dyson (2001) makes a number of potentially important observations regarding the predictability of certain patterns of behavior on the Russian leader's part:

> Putin's central belief in the harmony of political life when governed by rules and norms suggests a reciprocal, *quid pro quo* approach. Putin is unlikely to be impressed by unexpectedly bold or unconventional initiatives. His belief in the necessity of selecting goals which are both achievable and measurable, along with his personal propensity to "backward-map" a "step-by-step" approach towards an objective, suggests that agreements of an incremental design appeal to him. . . . Putin's Operational Code suggests he will, chameleon-like, imitate his environment. One could not expect Putin to act in a norm-bound manner when those with which he is engaged do not. Putin is unlikely to "stick to the rules" in the face of deviation by another. . . . Instead, departure from agreed norms of behavior will in all probability entail a decisive break—an "all bets are off" attitude from Putin . . . . [His] beliefs about political life . . . disposes him to prefer to retain a certain flexibility and freedom to maneuver. A recommendation would therefore be to design agreements and the like with clearly set out rules and schedules, but many "points of exit" for either side. . . . He is unlikely to want to be tied to great statements of intent. Platitudes and vagaries can be expected from him, he will attempt to maintain a low profile until a clear "success" compels him to take political credit. . . . Overall, the policymaker can feel confident that carefully constructed initiatives will not be dismissed out of hand, and that Putin is unlikely to make rash, impulsive, or emotional gestures. . . . However, the policymaker can feel warned that Putin will reciprocate "bad" as well as "good" behavior, and that a break down in cooperation will likely be quite bitter and long-lived. (p. 344)

CONCLUSION

This chapter reviews some of the major theoretical approaches to the study of personality in psychology, but only those that have been used in political psychology. There are many additional psychological theories of personality that are not mentioned in this chapter. In addition, the chapter presents a review of some of the frameworks in political psychology that have been used to analyze personality and leadership in politics. This chapter says little about the average person, because most of the personality-based studies in political psychology are of political leaders. Analyses of the political psychology of the average person are important and are explored in chapter 6. However, the concepts and theories used are those to be found in the next chapter, where we look at cognition and attitudes.

Topics, Theories/Explanations, and Concepts in Chapter 2

Topics	Theories/Explanations and Frameworks	Concepts
Personality	Individual differences	Context
Greenstein's (1969) three factors determining whether personality is important or not	Psychoanalytic approaches	Id, ego, superego
	Disorders	Narcissism, neuroticism
Psychobiographies		
Traits	Big Five personality traits	Neuroticism, extroversion, agreeableness, openness to experience, conscientiousness
Motivations		Power, affiliation, achievement
Authoritarian personality		
Leadership frameworks	Barber's (1974) typology of presidential character	Active/negative, passive/positive
	Operational code	Philosophical/ instrumental beliefs
	Hermann's leader assessment at a distance	
	Leader traits	Need for power, locus of control, ethnocentrism, need for affiliation, conceptual complexity, distrust, self-confidence

KEY TERMS

Achievement motive
Affiliation intimacy
  motive
Agreeableness
Authoritarian
  personality
Big Five
Cognitive complexity
Conscientiousness
Defense mechanisms
Denial
Ego
Ethnocentrism
Extroversion

Fundamental attribution
  error
Id
Locus of control
Motives
Need for achievement
Need for affiliation
  intimacy
Need for power
Neurotic anxiety
Neuroticism
Openness
Operational codes
Power motive

Projection
Psychoanalytic or
  psychodynamic
  theories
Rationalization
Reality principle
Repression
Right-wing
  authoritarianism
Superego
Task–interpersonal
  emphasis
Traits
Unconscious

SUGGESTIONS FOR FURTHER READING

American Psychiatric Association (2000). *Diagnostic and statistical manual of mental disorders* (4th ed., text revision). Washington, DC: Author.

Altemeyer, B. (1996). *The authoritarian specter*. Cambridge: Harvard University Press.

Ewen, R. (1998). *An introduction to theories of personality* (5th ed.). Mahwah, NJ: Lawrence Erlbaum Associates, Inc.

Feldman, O., & Valenty, L. (Eds.) (2001). *Profiling political leaders: Cross-cultural studies of personality and behavior.* Westport, CT: Praeger.

George, A. L., & George, J. L. (1964). *Woodrow Wilson and Colonel House: A personality study*. New York: Dover.

George, A. L., & George, J. L. (1998). *Presidential personality and performance*. Boulder, CO: Westview.

Greenstein, F. I. (1969). *Personality and politics: Problems of evidence, inference, and conceptualization*. Chicago: Markham.

Maddi, S. R. (1996). *Personality theories: A comparative analysis* (6th ed.). Washington, DC: Brooks/Cole.

Magnavita, J. (2002). *Theories of personality: Contemporary approaches to the science of personality.* New York: Wiley.

Post, J. M. (Ed.). (2003). *The psychological assessment of political leaders*. Ann Arbor, MI: University of Michigan Press.

Robins, R. S., & Post, J. (1997). *Political paranoia: The psychopolitics of hatred*. New Haven, CT: Yale University Press.

Smith, C., Atkinson, J., McClelland, D., & Veroff, J. (Eds.). (1992). *Motivation and personality: Handbook of thematic content analysis*. Cambridge, UK: Cambridge University Press.

ENDNOTES

1.   For a critique of psychobiographical method and a discussion of challenges faced by researchers who employ this methodology, see George and George, 1998, and Greenstein, 1969.

2.   Other well-known studies of political leaders that rely upon psychobiography, with some elements of psychoanalytic analysis, include those exploring the personalities of former U.S. Secretary of Defense James Forrestal (Rogow, 1963); Vladimir Lenin, Leon Trotsky, and Mahatma Gandhi (Wolfenstein, 1971); John F. Kennedy (Mongar, 1974); former U.S. Secretary of State Henry Kissinger (Isaak, 1975); Richard Nixon (Brodie, 1981); Jimmy Carter (Glad, 1980; Hargrove, 1988); Ronald Reagan (Glad, 1989); Iraqi President Saddam Hussein (Post, 1991, 1993); Josef Stalin (Birt, 1993); and Bill Clinton (Renshon, 1996). Some of these psychobiographies focus on Freudian notions of ego-defense (e.g., Glad, 1980; Hargrove, 1988; Link and Glad, 1994; Renshon, 1996); others concentrate upon specific kinds of personality disorders in these leaders, ranging from narcissism to paranoid personality disorders (e.g., Volkan, 1980; Post, 1991, 1993; Birt, 1993).

3.   Examples of leader studies using Winter's motive scoring technique (which looks at power, achievement, and affiliation) include Richard Nixon (Winter & Carlson, 1988), U.S. presidents (Winter, 1987); African political leaders (Winter, 1980), and Mikhail Gorbachev (Winter et al., 1991). For a more detailed discussion of motives and various coding techniques surrounding them, see Smith, Atkinson, McClelland, and Veroff's (1992) volume, *Motivation and Personality: Handbook of Thematic Content Analysis*, published by Cambridge University Press.

4.   Among the political psychology or psychological studies that have focused on the traits themselves, or how they relate to leaders, have been ones examining personal needs for power (Etheredge, 1978; Hermann, 1984, 1987; House, 1990; McClelland, 1975; Winter, 1973, 1987), personal needs for affiliation (Browning & Jacob, 1964; McClelland & Boyatzis, 1982; Winter, 1987; Winter & Stewart, 1977), conceptual complexity (Driver, 1977; Hermann, 1984, 1987; Suedfeld & Rank, 1976; Suedfeld & Tetlock, 1977; Tetlock, 1985), locus of control (Davis & Phares, 1967; Hermann, 1984, 1987; Rotter, 1966), achievement or task/interpersonal emphasis (Bales, 1951; Bass, 1981; Byars, 1972, 1973; Hermann, 1987; Nutt, 1990; Rowe & Mason, 1987; Winter & Stewart, 1977), ethnocentrism (Glad, 1983; Levine & Campbell, 1972), and self-confidence (Hermann, 1987; House, 1990; Winter et al., 1991). For a more detailed discussion of these traits, see Hermann (1999) and Smith et al. (1992).

5.   Included in this literature are studies of Winston Churchill (Tetlock & Tyler, 1996), revolutionary leaders (Suedfeld & Rank, 1976), the British House of Commons (Tetlock, 1984), and the Middle East (Suedfeld & Tetlock, 1977), the Soviet politburo (Wallace & Suedfeld, 1988), and Mikhail Gorbachev (Wallace, Suedfeld, & Thachuk, 1996).

6.   This technique was originally known as the *Personality Assessment-at-a-Distance* approach. Hermann changed the name of the technique in 2001.

7.   See, for example, operational code studies of the Soviet politburo and the Bolsheviks (Leites, 1951, 1953), John Foster Dulles (Holsti, 1970; Stuart & Starr, 1981), John F. Kennedy (Stuart & Starr, 1981), Henry Kissinger (Walker, 1977; Stuart & Starr, 1981), Woodrow Wilson (Walker, 1995), U.S. presidents and secretaries of state (Walker & Falkowski, 1984), and Lyndon B. Johnson and his advisors (Walker & Schafer, 2000).

Cognition, Social Identity, Emotions, and Attitudes in Political Psychology

This chapter explores how individuals make sense of others and themselves in the context of political issues, choices, and conflict. How do people understand the political world? How do they interpret information and make decisions? How organized are their thoughts? How do emotions affect thoughts and actions in politics? This chapter reflects the thinking and feeling portions of the Political Being's mind: cognition, emotion, social identity, and attitudes and beliefs. We examine a number of ideas about how people process political information, the psychological techniques and mechanisms used to understand others and the environment in which they live, the importance of the groups to which people belong, and how people regard those groups they do not belong to. In addition, we explore the importance of emotion in politics, as well as in political attitudes. A number of concepts are introduced, including cognition, cognitive categories and schemas, social identity, images, affect and emotion, and attitudes. These concepts are tied to different kinds of political behavior in this chapter and are detailed in the chapters that follow. Once again, the depiction of the Political Being in this chapter highlights the concepts that are covered here, and does so in a way that layers them. Attitudes and cognitive processes are at the top of consciousness: These are things we are well aware of, and they are important in information processing and everyday decision making. Values and social identities are deeper. We have to think harder to figure out how they affect our behavior. Emotions saturate the mind and influence the entire process of deciding how to act politically. In addition, more detail is provided on the *us* and *them* portions of the Political Being's environment.

We proceed with building blocks. First, we examine the thinking part of the Political Being. We begin with the topic of information processing and the limits people have in their abilities to process information. In doing so, we introduce two theoretical areas that provide insights into the patterns and causes of patterns in human information processing: attribution theory and consistency theories. Next, we turn to the question of how people make sense of the world they live in, through a process called cognitive categorization. In examining cognitive categorization, we discuss how people organize and simplify the complex social and political world in which they live, and we introduce the related notion of a stereotype. Next, we proceed to social identity theory, which provides us with information concerning how people see the groups that they belong to and those that they do not belong to—in-groups and out-groups. After that, we introduce a model of categories of other political actors—the political equivalent of out-groups—called image theory.

From here, we turn to the emotional part of the Political Being and look at emotions in politics. This is a relatively new area of political psychological research, but it is very important, because of the power of emotions in politically motivated violence and other patterns of behavior. After discussing emotions, we discuss attitudes, which combine emotion and thinking about politics. Our goal for this chapter is to introduce a wide range of central political psychological concepts regarding thinking and feeling about politics and the behavioral

37

predispositions that result. These concepts are used throughout the rest of the book, as we look at different kinds of political behavior.

Let us begin with some puzzles. First, people need to understand the world around them, and particularly the people in that world. Perceivers need to explain and predict the behavior of others. In order to do this, they need to process incoming information from their environments and to evaluate it. People like to think that they are good at processing information. We assume that we recognize and evaluate important information and that we store it in memory quite accurately. This is incorrect. Consider the following example:

In the criminal justice system, eyewitness testimony is commonly accepted as notoriously inaccurate and as having a strong impact on juries. As Loftus (1979) explains:

> Before a witness can recall a complex incident, the incident must be accurately perceived at the outset; it must be stored in memory. Before it can be stored, it must be within a witness's perceptual range, which means that it must be loud enough and close enough so that the ordinary senses pick it up. If visual details are to be perceived, the situation must be reasonably well illuminated. Before some information can be recalled, a witness must have paid attention to it. But even though an event is bright enough, loud enough, and close enough, and even though attention is being paid, we can still find significant errors in a witness's recollection of the event, and it is common for two witnesses to the same event to recall it very differently. (p. 22)

Second, people tend to see what they expect to see. They fit incoming information into the ideas or beliefs they already hold to be true, and they typically do not recognize that they do this. Discrepant information is often not noticed or rejected as incorrect. Consider some examples from the battlefields of World War II:

> Common also are cases of outright refusal to believe reports that contradict a firm belief. . . . When Hermann Göring was informed that an Allied fighter has been shot down over Aachen, thus proving that the Allies had produced a long-range fighter that could protect bombers over Germany, he told the pilot who had commanded the German planes in the engagement: "I'm an experienced fighter pilot myself. I know what is possible. But I know what isn't too. . . . I officially assert that American fighter planes did not reach Aachen. . . . I herewith give you an official order that they weren't there." Similarly, when the secretary of the navy was told of the Japanese attack on Pearl Harbor, he said, "My God, this can't be true. This [message] must mean the Philippines." It is not without significance that the common reaction is not that the report *is* incorrect, but that it *must be* incorrect. (Jervis, 1976, pp. 144–145)

These examples illustrate several important topics that we begin with in this chapter. The eyewitness testimony example shows important instances in which people do not process or remember information very well. People are imperfect information processors, and of course this will affect their processing, evaluation, and retention of political information, just like any other kind of information. Second, people do not process information on a tabula rasa. They have certain psychological mechanisms that facilitate the processing of information.

In psychology, the concept of **cognition** is central to understanding how people process information and understand the world around them. **Cognition** is "a collective term for the psychological processes involved in the acquisition, organization, and the use of knowledge" (Bullock & Stallybrass, 1977, p. 109). The knowledge is organized in our minds in a **cognitive system**. For example, our knowledge of birds is organized as follows: birds have wings, feathers, and beaks, they use the wings to fly, they eat insects or seeds and are eaten by people. The terms *beliefs* or *attitudes* are often used to describe these components of the cognitive system. **Beliefs** are associations people create between an object and its attributes (Eagly & Chaiken, 1998). We believe that birds have wings and that Democrats are liberal. **Cognitive processes** is a term that refers to what happens in the mind while people move from observation of a stimulus to a response to that stimulus. Cognitive processes include everything from perception, memory, attention, and problem solving to information processing, language, thinking, and imagery. Let us turn first to cognitive processes involved with the acquisition of information from the environment and its evaluation.

INFORMATION PROCESSING

People are bombarded with vast amounts of information all the time. They cannot attend to all of it, and the mind has developed techniques for deciding what information is important and relevant and what information can be ignored. Several theories in psychology address patterns of information processing and provide explanations for different propensities in attending to and interpreting information. One theoretical school in psychology that has conducted numerous studies of how people judge and evaluate others is **attribution theory**. One of the earliest attribution theorists was Heider (1958), along with Jones and Davis (1965), Kelley (1967), and Weiner (1986). Attribution theorists also have a number of insights into information processing. They argue that people process information as though they are "naive scientists," that is, they search for cause in the behavior of others, just as scientists search for the cause of a disease. However, people often do not properly employ the scientific method, and they tend to make a number of errors in this quest for the cause of others' behavior. Attribution theorists argue that individuals use **heuristics**, which are mental shortcuts, in processing information about others. Among the most important heuristics is the **availability heuristic**, wherein people predict the likelihood of something, based on the ease with which they can think of instances or examples of it (Tversky & Kahneman, 1982), for example, estimating the distribution of As in a political science class, based on how many people you can think of who got As in the class last year. The **representativeness heuristic** is another common example. This is a probability judgment. A person may, for example, evaluate the characteristics of another person and estimate the likelihood that that person belongs to a particular occupation (Fiske & Taylor, 1991). For example, medical professionals are commonly seen with stethoscopes. If you see someone with a stethoscope, you will assume that it is probable that that person is a medical professional.

In interpreting and evaluating information regarding the cause of behavior of other people, one of the most important aspects of perceptions of causality is whether it is attributed to internal states (personality) or to external forces (circumstance). People are more likely to attribute others' behavior to their general dispositions (personality traits or attitudes) than to the situation they are in. This is known as the **fundamental attribution error** (Ross, 1977). A study by Jones and Harris (1967) provides a clear illustration of the fundamental attribution error. Participants in that study were asked to read essays about a controversial topic—Cuba under the rule of Fidel Castro. Participants were told that the essay writer had either freely chosen to take a pro-Castro or anti-Castro position, or they were told that the essay writer had been assigned a particular essay position. Even when the essay writer was assigned the position, participants overestimated the role of internal dispositions (the writer's true position on Castro) and underestimated the role of the situation (lack of choice about which position to take), when asked to explain the position taken in the essay.

Another set of theories that contributes to our understanding of information processing comes under the general rubric of consistency theories. One of the earliest consistency theories was Heider's (1946, 1958) **balance theory**, which presented research indicating that people try to keep the components of the cognitive system in **balance**. He described **balance** as "a harmonious state, one in which the entities comprising the situation and *the feelings about them* fit together without stress" (Heider, 1958, p. 180; italics added). In other words, people want to see their environment, the people in it, and their feelings about it as a coherent, consistent picture. For example, if you consider yourself a responsible and serious student, you would not neglect your studies and go out partying with your friends the night before an exam. If you did, the cognitive system representing your knowledge about yourself would be out of balance, and you would try to change it. Partying, rather than studying the night before an exam, is not consistent with your self-perception that you are a serious student. A friend of one of the authors presents another example. She is a lifelong liberal Democrat from an eastern city, who advised a politician on his state's education policy. That politician was a Republican. She liked him, found him charming, and was proud that his policies improved education in his state. She would like to vote for him, and is appalled at herself. How can she, a lifelong liberal Democrat, consider voting for a conservative Republican? That behavior would not be balanced, because it is inconsistent with her political beliefs. To achieve balance, she would either have to vote Democratic, change her ideology and join the Republican party, or consider this single Republican vote an anomaly.

A related type of consistency pattern is described in **dissonance theory**, which deals with the inconsistencies between people's attitudes and behaviors (Festinger, 1957). *Dissonance* refers to an aversive state that results when our behavior is inconsistent with our attitudes. Dissonance creates psychological tension, which people feel motivated to avoid through selective attention to information. Once dissonance is experienced, people are motivated to relieve it. For example, suppose you ate a big piece of chocolate cake while you were on a diet. There are at least three ways that people can reduce dissonance: People can change their behavior (in this case, that is not possible, because you already ate the cake); people can engage in cognitive strategies, such as trivialization (e.g., "It's not really that bad if I ate a big piece of chocolate cake") or distortions of information (e.g., "Chocolate cake has lots of nutritional value"); or people can change their attitude (e.g., "I really don't need to be dieting anyway"). Typically, people reduce dissonance by changing their attitude.

People can live with inconsistency and imbalance, but they would prefer not to. When inconsistency is extreme, it can be psychologically painful, for example, as when your significant other and best friend cannot abide one another. Individuals can avoid inconsistency through information processing, and they can reestablish consistency in their cognitive system by changing whatever is easiest to change. If our friend's attachment to the Democratic party is weaker than her liking for the Republican politician, she will change parties. If not, she will either vote Democratic or consider the situation an anomaly (incidentally, she voted for the Democrat, which is an illustration of the power of political socialization, which we discuss in chapter 6).

Vertzberger notes that the drive for consistency occurs on three levels: within attitudes between affect and cognition (thinking and feeling the same way); across attitudes; and throughout what he calls the "cognitive entirety" (1990, p. 137), that is, attitudes, beliefs, and values. The drive for consistency affects information processing in a number of ways. First, it produces selective perception, which includes "*selective exposure* (seeking consistent information not already present), *selective attention* (looking at consistent information once it is there), and *selective interpretation* (translating ambiguous information to be consistent)" (Fiske & Taylor, 1991, p. 469). Inconsistent information can be ignored, or it can be distorted so that it appears consistent with attitudes or cognitive categories. Inconsistent behaviors can be compartmentalized so that people refuse to recognize their own actions as serious. The process of balancing and avoiding inconsistency can also lead to **bolstering**, which involves selective exposure to information, as people search for information supporting their decision and avoid information that would be critical of it. Bolstering also occurs when people denigrate the alternative not chosen and amplify the attractive aspects of the decision they did make. Bolstering occurred in the Kennedy administration, before the Bay of Pigs invasion, by convincing themselves that American involvement would remain secret and by avoiding arguments to the contrary. This incident is discussed (in chapter 4) in the context of groupthink, a group decision-making error involving faulty information processing. President Johnson's decision in 1965 to use air power in Vietnam gave evidence of bolstering, as well, in his belief that the air campaign would not have to last long and that the war would end quickly (George, 1980).

The drive for consistency in information processing has a number of important political consequences. Accepting only information that conforms with expectations can lead people to miss important information, for example, about a candidate's stand on a political issue, if that position is inconsistent with their party or other issue positions. Interpreting information so that it conforms to expectations, rather than to some other possibility, can lead to spiraling conflicts between countries or political groups. Distorting information in a search for consistency can produce a failure to recognize the need for value trade-offs in politics. The **avoidance of value trade-offs** occurs when people mistakenly believe that a policy that "contributes to one value . . . also contributes to several other values, even though there is no reason why the world should be constructed in such a neat and helpful manner" (Jervis, 1976, p. 128). An example comes from the Vietnam War:

> Officials who favored bombing North Vietnam felt that this would: (1) decrease American casualties, (2) drastically increase the cost of the war to the North; (3) increase the chance of the North's entering negotiations, without increasing the danger of Soviet or Chinese intervention. Those who opposed bombing disagreed on all points. (Jervis, 1976, p. 134)

These patterns are tendencies, not absolutes. They occur often, but not always. People may be aware of, but ignore, inconsistent information, if it is unimportant to them. They may be forced by situational conditions to attend and respond to inconsistent information.

CATEGORIZATION

So far, we have noted that people organize and simplify their environment; they process information about that environment, based on the way they understand it; and they search for causes in the behavior of others. People keep the knowledge that is most useful about an environment, then use it to filter subsequent information. We expect the environment to be consistent and that what we know about it will be repeated. We accept as true information that conforms to our preexisting knowledge and reject as untrue, or irrelevant, information that does not conform. Consequently, the cognitive system helps us filter incoming information. If, for example, your cognitive system of politicians includes the belief that all politicians are dishonest, if you have evidence both confirming and disconfirming that politician Smith has taken a bribe, then you will believe the confirming evidence. But cognitive systems are more than a set of bits of knowledge. They are organized in order to enable people to move through their worlds without thinking too much and yet manage their environments effectively. Cognitive systems help people understand their world. Knowledge about the environment that people live in is organized, simplified, and used to make sense of complex social and physical realities. If we did not organize and simplify the environment, then we would not be able to process all the information available to us and could never make decisions. The world is too complex for our brains to handle. As Allport wrote in 1954:

> The human mind must think with the aid of categories. . . . Once formed, categories are the basis for normal prejudgment. We cannot possibly avoid this process. Orderly living depends upon it. . . . What this means is that our experience in life tends to form itself into clusters . . . and while we may call on the right cluster at the wrong time, or the wrong cluster at the right time, still the process in question dominates our entire mental life. A million events befall us everyday. We cannot handle so many events. If we think of them at all, we type them. . . . Bertrand Russell . . . has summed up the matter in a phrase, "a mind perpetually open will be a mind perpetually vacant." (pp. 19–20)

People form and use cognitive categories that aid them in their need to process information efficiently. There is no set recipe by which categories are formed. Categories, the attributes or characteristics associated with them, and the beliefs about them, are formed through experience. Rosch (1978) argues that there are two principles involved in category formation. First, categories must provide the perceiver with a large amount of information with as little mental effort as possible. People need categories that enable them to discern and understand the world around them, but that also allow them to reduce small and irrelevant differences among people and objects. Second, people need categories that are suited to their own social and physical realities. If you live in a high crime, heavily populated urban area, you will need different social categories to understand and deal with people than if you live in a rural area with almost no crime and few people.

One way of looking at this is to think of the way that people organize and simplify their environment as creating a mental model of the environment that emphasizes only the most important points. People form categories of the most important elements of the environment. For example, in the natural world, we think of categories such as dogs, cats, horses, and birds. As we said before, the category of birds is filled with important information about what a bird is and how it behaves. The same is true of the categories of dog, cat, and so on. Of course, some birds are not good fits with the common characteristics associated with birds. Penguins do not fly, but they swim and have scrawny wings that they use like flippers. They do not fit the bird category very well in our minds. The same is true of the human world. We categorize people into groups, such as racial groups (Caucasian, Black, Oriental), ethnic groups (Latino or Hispanic, Italian-American), nationality groups (American, German, Chinese), and religious groups (Christian, Muslim, Jewish). This is to say, we organize the social world in terms of social categories. We all make assumptions about other people, ourselves, and the situations we are in. Sometimes we are very wrong, but often our expectations are functional. The first step in perceiving another person is to classify the person or situation as fitting a familiar category. Once you recognize someone as filling a particular role (e.g., a police officer or a professor) on the basis of particular attributes (uniform, gun, billy club; glasses, briefcase, lecture notes), then you can apply your knowledge about the role to guide the subsequent interaction with that person.

Once a person or situation is classified into a category, people apply organized generic knowledge, in the form of a category or **schema**, to process information about the person or situation and to make decisions about it or them. The terms *cognitive category* and *schema* are often used interchangeably. Psychologists define *schema* as "a cognitive structure that represents knowledge about a concept or type of stimulus, including its attributes and the relations among those attributes" (Fiske & Taylor, 1991, p. 8).

Stereotypes are a particular type of social cognitive category. The psychological roots of stereotypes, the reasons for their occurrence, and the impact they have on the behavior of those using them and those viewed through them, have been widely studied in psychology and political science (see Fiske, 1998, for a review). *Stereotypes* are beliefs about the attributes of people in particular groups or social categories, and should be a very familiar concept. Everyone has stereotypes or at least knows about stereotypes of others. Consider, for example, the well-known stereotype of Jewish people, called the anti-Semitic stereotype, which is based on an assumption that a particular group is an overachieving minority, superior in wealth and talent. It is also assumed that they are able to construct complex conspiracies that will increase their material wealth and influence. Finally, they are seen as standoffish, cliquish, and consider themselves to be superior to everyone else (Hunter, 1991). Other people who have been seen through the same stereotype are the Indians and Pakistanis in East Africa, the overseas Chinese in Southeast Asia, the Armenians in the Middle East, and the Ibos in Nigeria. Other stereotypes familiar to most readers denigrate people who are considered inferior. Most Americans are familiar with American racism, which is a result of holding negative stereotypes of African Americans. Stereotypes are not limited to personality trait descriptions (e.g., "Germans are conscientious and hardworking"), but can include any personal attribute—physical, affective, visual, or behavioral—that can be seen as characteristic of that group (e.g., "Germans are fair, tall, and rigid"). Stereotyping, as in all social categorization, is a mental short-cut that enables people to "know" quite a bit about a person or group of persons, whether that knowledge is accurate or not. It occurs quickly and without conscious thought (Fiske, 1998). We discuss social stereotypes in more detail in chapters 7, 8, and 9.

Discrimination is not an inevitable consequence of stereotyping. Recent research (e.g., Devine & Elliot, 1995) suggests that, even though people possess knowledge of stereotypes, they are not necessarily prejudiced. Only those high in prejudice tend to accept stereotypes about a group of people. A person can have knowledge of stereotypes and not discriminate. For the moment, let us leave it that stereotypes are social categories, and that, when people are evaluated through a stereotype, they often suffer from discrimination. They are assumed to have the characteristics of a stereotype, whether they do or not. Those who hold the stereotype and behave toward that group in a discriminatory fashion are said to be prejudiced.

Once information about a person is noticed, it is classified nominally in terms of what it is about or which category or attitude it is relevant for. If you notice a person who is tall, blond, blue-eyed, and speaks with an accent, you may classify that person in the category "German." The availability heuristic is important in this stage, because information is more likely to be classified in categories that are readily accessible. Hence, you may be more likely to use the German social category if you are in a town with a high percentage of German immigrants. Once this judgment has been made, the information is evaluated in terms of its fit in to the category. If, for example, you walk into a classroom and the professor looks like he is 15 years old, is wearing shorts, a ripped t-shirt, and no shoes, that information about him is not typical of what you expect to see when interacting with a professor. It affects how you regard this particular person in his role as professor. He may be a professor, but maybe he is not very qualified, because he looks young and dresses like a teenager. Moreover, when this kind of social judgment is made, it is also influenced by **assimilation** and **contrast** effects. The prototypical example of a social category serves as an anchor or central reference point for incoming information. Information is compared to that anchor and, when it is different from expectations, the contrast effect makes it seem moreso. For example, most people would expect a priest to be honest. Learning that a priest has done something objectively moderately dishonest will be interpreted as extremely dishonest, in the context of having been done by someone from whom complete honesty is expected. The assimilation effect produces the opposite perception. Information similar to that which is expected can be perceived as even more similar than it objectively is (Eiser & Stroebe, 1972; Herr, 1986; Manis, Nelson, & Shedler, 1988). The category in which a person, group, or country is placed has yet another effect on information and information processing. Missing information can be supplied by the category or image itself. If you do not know if a person has a particular characteristic, because you do not have the information, then you can guess, based on the social category in which the person is placed (Taylor & Crocker, 1981).

We also categorize the political world. Some scholars argue that we organize the international environment in terms of types of states, such as the enemy or the ally. These cognitive categories are called **images**, and images function very much like stereotypes. **Image theory** is a political psychological approach that draws connections between policymakers' image of other countries and their resulting behavior (Blanton, 1996; Cottam, 1986, 1994; Cottam, 1977; Herrmann, 1985a, 1985b, 1988, 1991; Herrmann Voss; Schooler, & Ciarrochi, 1997; Holsti, 1962; Schafer, 1997; Shimko 1991). Images contain information about a country's capabilities, culture, intentions, kinds of decision-making groups (lots of people involved in decision making or only a few), and perceptions of threat or opportunity. Capabilities include economic characteristics, military strength, and domestic political stability and effective policy making and implementation. Cultural attributes consist of judgments of cultural sophistication. When assessing a country, decision makers judge whether its capabilities and culture are equal, inferior, or superior to their own country. Another appraisal is whether the country or group has threatening or defensive (good) intentions or presents an opportunity to achieve an important goal. Lessons of history that policymakers associate with a particular type of state are also included in each image. In other words, leaders use historical incidents to explain a conflict and to make predictions about the outcome of a conflict. Policymakers also draw upon a variety of policy options, which are measures that they see as appropriate in dealing with a country. Some policy options include military threat, economic sanctions or incentives, and diplomatic protests. The model also proposes that certain tactics are relevant to each image. For example, when decision makers hold the so-called colonial or client image of another country, they consider that country and its people to be inferior in terms of culture and capabilities. They also assume that the people are incompetent and childlike and are ruled by a small elite, who are generally not a threat and who are often corrupt. This image produces behavioral tendencies that are coercive and noncompromising (you do not negotiate with children, you tell them what to do).When an enemy image is held, that country is seen as equal in capability and culture, and threatening in intentions. The enemy is ruled by a small elite, but one that can cleverly strategize policies that will attempt to hurt the perceiver's country. The tactics used in responding to such a state are global in focus, competitive, and noncompromising, because you cannot trust such a country to keep its word.

The ally is perceived as equal in terms of its capability and culture, but also as very similar to your own group in values. The intentions of an ally are believed to be good. Barbarians are superior in capability and inferior in culture. They are also aggressive in intentions, which makes them very frightening. An imperialist country is perceived to be superior in culture and capability, but its intentions can be either harmful or benevolent. Either way, imperialists are a dominating people, and resisting them would be very difficult. The rogue is inferior in capability and culture, but is also very harmful in their intentions. This is the "bad seed," the irresponsible child, who, it is believed, can and should be punished until they reform their ways. Last, there is the image of the degenerate. A degenerate may be powerful and culturally

TABLE 3.1
Images

	Capability	Culture	Intentions	Decision Makers	Threat or Opportunity
Enemy	Equal	Equal	Harmful	Small elite	Threat
Barbarian	Superior	Inferior	Harmful	Small elite	Threat
Imperialist	Superior	Superior	Harmful	A few groups	Threat
Colonial	Inferior	Inferior	Benign	Small elite	Opportunity
Degenerate	Superior or equal	Weak-willed	Harmful	Confused, differentiated	Opportunity
Rogue	Inferior	Inferior	Harmful	Small elite	Threat
Ally	Equal	Equal	Good	Many groups	Threat

advanced, but also weak-willed, undisciplined, and lacking the will to follow through on expressed goals and plans of action.

The ways that policymakers make distinctions among these types of images are a matter of their perceptions of the country's capabilities, culture, threat, response alternatives, and event scripts. The images are summarized in Table 3.1.

Although this particular example demonstrates images of other countries used by policymakers in foreign affairs, images are used to organize and guide responses to people's action in any political domain. In fact, Jackson (2001) has gathered impressive data concerning the images used by police officers of the communities in their districts and the patterns of response to crime associated with those images. We return to the discussion of images later, after introducing some additional psychological concepts. Chapters 7, 8, and 9 also contain many examples of how images affect political behavior.

SOCIAL IDENTITY

We classify others into groups, and we classify ourselves into groups, as well. Groups we belong to are called **in-groups**, and those we do not belong to are **out-groups**. Conflict among political groups is, of course, a central issue in political psychology. Group conflict and behavior are examined in detail in chapter 4. Here, we want to consider groups as social categories and as part of the general cognitive organization of the social and political world.

Much of the work on the social psychology of intergroup relations has focused on intergroup conflict and discrimination. The seminal research using this approach can be found in Tajfel's (1970) work on intergroup conflict, in which the author speculated that something about group membership alone might stimulate conflict with other relevant groups. He postulated that individuals are likely to act in a discriminatory manner whenever they are in a situation in which intergroup categorization is made salient and relevant.

In other words, whenever individuals find themselves in a situation in which there exists clear evidence of a *us* and a *them*, they are likely to discriminate against the out-group (*them*) and in favor of the in-group (*us*). To test this idea, Tajfel (1970) designed a series of experiments based on the minimal group paradigm: in which individuals are arbitrarily assigned to one of two groups. In one typical experiment, assignment to a group was based on whether individuals tended to overestimate or underestimate a series of dots presented on a screen. Individuals participating in the experiment were then assigned to either the overestimator or underestimator group, presumably on the basis of their estimating tendencies. In reality, this assignment was purely arbitrary; the tendency to over- or underestimate was in no way related to accuracy. This arbitrary assignment procedure proved to be important and necessary, for several reasons. First, it ensured that there was no personal reason for one group to discriminate against the other group. An individual presumably had nothing to gain personally by discriminating against the other group. Second, the procedure ensured that there was no existing hostility between the groups. Prior to categorization, individuals never thought of themselves as being a member of a group that tends to underestimate, or that other individuals are members of a group that overestimate, for example. Further, there was no chance for the groups to interact with one another, thus eliminating any possibility that group members would come to like the in-group or dislike the out-group. Third, such a procedure ensured that individuals had no conflicts of interest. There was nothing inherently valuable about being a member of a group that under- or overestimates.

Following this categorization procedure, individuals were asked to assign rewards and penalties, by allocating small amounts of money to two anonymous group members (see Brewer, 1979; Insko & Schopler, 1987; Turner, 1978, for a review of allocation matrices). To eliminate self-interest as a possible influence, individuals were told that they should not allocate any money to themselves. The results of this experiment showed that, even in this minimal group, the allocation decisions, concerning both an in-group and out-group member, led to in-group favoritism and out-group discrimination. Individuals gave more money to members of their own group than to members of the other group. Thus, even though these individuals were assigned to a group on the basis of unimportant and seemingly meaningless criteria, they still acted in a discriminatory or competitive manner. Providing an explanation for this effect is what led to Tajfel and Turner's (1979, 1986) social identity theory.

According to Tajfel (1978), *social identity* is "that part of an individual's self-concept which derives from his [her] knowledge of his [her] membership in a social group (groups) together with the value and emotional significance attached to that membership" (p. 63). Tajfel and Turner (1979) summarized this theory with three theoretical principles. First, group members strive to achieve or maintain a sense of positive social identity. Second, group members base this social identity on favorable comparisons that can be made between in-group and relevant out-group members. The social categories or groups of which individuals are members provide individuals with a social identity, by enabling them to compare their in-group with relevant out-groups. These comparisons are said to contribute to individuals' self-esteem, because they allow individuals to define the members of their group as being better than other groups. In other words, in an attempt to gain a positive sense of self, individuals compare their group with other groups, to create a favorable distinction between the groups. Third, group members will attempt to leave their group or join a more positively distinct group, when their social identity is not satisfactory to them.

Tajfel and Turner (1979) imply that intergroup discrimination is a result of a motivation to evaluate one's own group more positively than a relevant out-group. By comparing one's in-group to a relevant out-group, individuals attempt to differentiate their group from other groups, so that their social identity will be enhanced. In addition to the necessary precondition of social categorization into in-group and out-group, Tajfel and Turner (1979) maintained that there are at least three additional variables that should influence intergroup differentiation. First, members of a group must have internalized their group membership as an aspect of their self-concept. In other words, they must clearly perceive themselves as a member of the in-group and be likely to describe themselves as a group member, if asked a question such as, Who are you? Second, the social situation must allow for intergroup comparisons. Group members must be able to make evaluative group comparisons, in order to perceive their in-group as positively distinct from the out-group. Third, the out-group must be perceived as a relevant comparison group. Members of an in-group do not compare their group to any available out-group. Instead, factors such as similarity, proximity, and situational salience determine whether an out-group is considered a valid and reliable comparison group (see Campbell, 1958).

Tajfel (1978) and Tajfel and Turner (1979) also discuss three ways in which individuals might react to threatened or actual negative social identity. *Social mobility* is the enhancement of positive social identity by advancement to a group of higher status. If an individual's social identity is threatened or is perceived as being negative, the individual will attempt to dissociate themselves from the in-group by joining a group that is higher in status. A second reaction to threatened or negative social identity is *social creativity*, which includes three strategies: (1) comparing the in-group to the out-group on a different dimension; (2) reevaluating the comparison dimension, so that previously negative dimensions are perceived as positive; and (3) comparing one's in-group to a different or lower status out-group. Finally, *social competition* is another reaction to a threatened or negative social identity. In-group members might directly compete with the out-group to attain positive distinctiveness or positive social identity, or at least with the intention of attaining a positive social identity.

In a review of research that has examined strategies of identity enhancement, van Knippenberg and Ellemers (1990) concluded that the permeability of group boundaries appears to play a key role in determining which strategy is used to enhance social identity. For example, when it is relatively easy for a group member to move to a higher status group, then that member is more likely to move to the new group than when it is more difficult to change group memberships.

Much of the research on social identity has tested the original in-group bias effect, that is, whether individuals tend to favor their own group over a relevant out-group, and has shown this to be true (see Brewer, 1979). The arbitrary assignment of individuals to groups has been repeatedly demonstrated to result in preferential reward allocations to in-group members (e.g., Billig & Tajfel, 1973; Tajfel & Billig, 1974), heightened in-group attractiveness (e.g., Rabbie & Wilkins, 1971), perceptions of in-group similarity and homogeneity (e.g., Allen & Wilder, 1979; Linville & Jones, 1980), and assignment of positive traits to in-group members (e.g., Howard & Rothbart, 1980). Thus, when individuals are categorized into two distinct groups, there is a tendency for individuals to favor their own group over another relevant group, presumably to enhance their social identity. However, some research has sought to identify ways in which in-groups and out-groups may cooperate with one another or extinguish the tendency to compete.

There are instances in which people accept a group's inferior situation, if they believe that their position is just and legitimate. These kinds of patterns were evident historically in the submission to and eventual rejection of colonial domination. People in territories that were conquered by such colonial powers as Britain, France, Germany, and others, often accepted that domination. They perceived the colonial powers through the imperialist image and thus saw them as superior in culture and capability. Resisting that domination would have brought severe punishment, and they often accepted domination as just and legitimate. But, over time, independence movements grew, and political activists in the colonies argued that their subservience to the colonial power was unfair, unjust, and illegitimate. Once that change in perception occurred, they began to compare their situations with that of the colonial power and decided that the colonial country was rich and they were poor, and that difference was unacceptable, particularly because the colonial power took the resources of the colonies and used them to enrich itself. The result was a willingness by the subjugated colonized people to risk everything, even their lives, for independence. They did so when they believed independence was a real possibility. In other words, they compared themselves to the other group (the colonial power), found the comparison to be unacceptably negative, sought and found an alternative, and engaged in social competition (rebellion) to achieve it.

AFFECT AND EMOTION

Our discussion so far has centered around cognition and politics. But the discussion of social identity leads easily to another important element in political psychology: emotion. People have emotional responses to political issues, actors, and events, and also to political principles and ideals that they value. When social categories and stereotypes are discussed, there is a tendency for the emphasis to be placed on cognitive processes and properties, such as beliefs, assumptions, and knowledge about different kinds of people, groups, or countries. But clearly cognitive phenomena, such as stereotypes, information processing, and making political decisions, such as for whom to vote, involve affect and emotion, too. Analysts tend to focus on cognition versus affect, depending upon what they are studying and the relative importance of each in affecting how people think. Affect and emotions are difficult to study, because of considerable disagreement about what they are and how to measure them, and, in political science, it is often argued that rational decision making must be unemotional. Nevertheless, it is crucial that political psychology make advances in understanding the impact of affect and emotions on behavior. Not only is emotion, in the form of prejudice, more closely associated with behavior than the cognitive component (Fiske, 1998), but we cannot understand mass violence, including genocide, without understanding the role of emotions. Moreover, emotion can play a positive role in decision making. One study found, for example, that suppressing emotions impairs memory (Richards & Gross, 1999). Thus, not only is emotion important, but trying to be unemotional can actually impede important elements in decision making.

Affect and emotion have been defined differently by various scholars. Fiske and Taylor (1991) define **affect** as "a generic term for a whole range of preferences, evaluations, moods and emotions" (p. 410). Affect can be positive or negative, that is, evaluations or preferences that are either pleasant or unpleasant. Ottati and Wyer (1995), on the other hand, have a more narrow definition and consider affect to be a physiological state that is experienced as either pleasant or unpleasant, positive or negative. Fiske and Taylor (1991) regard **emotion** as a "complex assortment of affects, beyond merely good feelings or bad to include delight, serenity, anger, sadness, fear and more" (p. 411), but Ottati and Wyer (1995) define emotions as affective states that are more precisely labeled, such as anger, hatred, fear, love, and respect. How affect and cognition are interrelated is an issue of debate. As we already noted, cognition is "a collective term for both the psychological processes involved in the acquisition, organization, and the use of knowledge" (Bullock & Stallybrass, 1977, p. 109). Some have argued that affect precedes cognition. In other words, a person makes a cognitive appraisal, then affect is evoked. The alternative picture is that people feel first, and this then evokes cognition (Marcus, Newman, & MacKuen, 2000; Zajonc, 1980a). Stephan and Stephan (1993) present a network model of affect and cognition, in which they maintain that cognition and affect are a set of interconnected parallel systems. In other words, people have a cognitive system (a system of thoughts, ideas, knowledge) and an affective system (a system of feelings and various emotions). They are separate systems in the mind, linked by various cognitive and affective nodes. The links can vary in strength.

Is it important to have a better understanding of the relationship between affect and cognition? We suggest that it is. As we see in chapter 6, the relationship between affect and cognition in influencing political tolerance in American is an important area of research. Another important area of inquiry is the role of cognition and emotion in politically motivated violence, and we examine many cases of such violence, in chapters 7, 8, and 9. When does emotion take over in the process of committing acts of violence? Are some conflicts dominated by cognitive factors and others dominated by affect? An interesting study by a clinical psychologist, Beck (1999), compares domestic violence with group-to-group violence and to international violence. He emphasizes the cognitive side of violent actions, in the sense that he explores what people are thinking before they attack someone—their spouse or children—and he notes that it is difficult to get people to recognize what they are thinking before they lash out in violence: They really do not think they are thinking anything in particular, but, when really pressed, they recognize self-demeaning thoughts and hurt feeling that precede the violence. On the flip side, there is the question of what happens to the thought process when emotions are essentially turned off, if they are, when people commit atrocities over a long period of time. We see cases of this in chapter 9, when we look at people who commit torture and genocide.

Affect and emotions clearly influence information processing, decision making, and some predispositions for behavior. Isen (1993), in a review of studies of positive affect, notes that positive affect and emotions promote improvements in problem solving, negotiating, and decision making. Positive affect seems to expand peoples' abilities to see interrelationships and connections among cognitive items. On the other hand, when compared to neutral affect, positive and negative affect, but particularly positive affect, reduce peoples' ability to perceive variability in other groups (Park & Banaji, 2000; Stroessner & Mackie, 1993). Predispositions for behavior resulting from particular emotions have also been studied. Anger, for example, has been found to be associated with moving against, or lashing out at, the perceived source of the anger (Izard, 1977). Contempt, on the other hand, is described by Izard (1977) as cold and distant, leading to depersonalization and dehumanization of others: "It is because of these characteristics that contempt can motivate murder and mass destruction of people" (p. 340).

Emotions and the behaviors they influence are intricately related to goals at stake in a situation. Political goals naturally vary over time, given particular political contexts and values. Even so, people generally assume that out-groups hinder in-group goals, and therefore the out-group is automatically associated with negative emotions. Out-groups, by definition, are assumed to be different and thus have different goals.

Emotions also vary in intensity, which can increase in response to certain psychological properties, as well as to the nature and impact of events. One of those event characteristics is simply how real the event seems to the person experiencing the emotion (Ortony, Clore, & Collins, 1988). Second, the closer the emotion-producing situation is in time, that is, its proximity, the greater the intensity of the emotion. Third, unexpected events or actions increase intensity. Fourth, physical arousal and the flow of adrenaline increase the emotional intensity. Fifth, in terms of psychological properties, leaving aside individual differences, the salience of social identity groups will increase emotion intensity. The stronger the sense of belonging to a group, the more important belonging is to members' self-esteem, the more salient will be group membership, and the more intense will be emotions generated by that membership. Emotional reactions to events affecting the group may not be observed often, even when one identifies strongly with that group. As long as things are normal, there may be little emotion. However, intense relationships produce the potential for strong emotions, when that relationship, and normal forms of behavior in the context of that relationship, are interrupted (Berscheid, 1987). Thus, one can expect politically motivated emotions to be intense when important political identity groups face threats or unusual opportunities. The intensity of the emotion may come as a great surprise to outside observers, if it has not been witnessed before.

The intensity of affect and emotion is also determined by perceptions of the other group. Out-groups are reacted to more negatively and with greater intensity than are in-groups. Also, extreme stereotyping corresponds with more extreme affect. Groups perceived to be threatening (e.g., out-groups) are seen as more homogeneous and extreme as threat percep-tions increase (Corneille, Yzerbyt, Rogier, & Buidin, 2001). Conversely, more complex cognitive processes are associated with more moderate reactions (Linville, 1982). Thus, be-cause a group member perceives their group more complexly than the out-group, evalua-tions of the in-group are typically less extreme than evaluations of an out-group. However, research (Marques, Abrams, Paez, & Hogg, 2001) shows that, when an in-group member engages in positive behavior or is described in positive terms, they are evaluated more fa-vorably than an out-group member who engages in the same behavior or is described in the same positive terms. But, when an in-group member engages in negative behavior or is de-scribed in unfavorable terms, they are evaluated more unfavorably than an out-group mem-ber who engages in similar behavior or is described in unfavorable terms. This has been termed the *black sheep effect* (Marques & Leyens 1988). Group members might derogate a "bad" in-group member, so that they can distance themselves from that member thus restor-ing their sense of positive social identity. The purpose of that study was to test the hypoth-esis that strength of group identification is related to strength of derogation of an errant in-group member.

Generally, we would expect positive emotions to be associated with in-groups and negative emotions with out-groups. This is an important principle to keep in mind when looking at emotion and political behavior. Social psychologists have examined the emotions associated with social groups that are lower or higher in power and status, under varying circumstances, which help with another important pattern regarding emotion and politics (Smith, 1993; Duckitt, 1994). Those studies can be complex, because emotions can be bundled together. Prejudice, the affective partner of a cognitive stereotype, is a good example of this. "Hot prej-udices" are composed of these emotions: disgust, resentment, hostility, and anger. Let us turn to a number of politically relevant emotions first, then consider how they may cluster with different political groups.

The list of negative emotions is long, and one in particular, anger, is an emotion often found in political behavior. Anger is a negative emotion, wherein blame for undesirable behavior, and resulting undesirable events, is directed at another person or group. It occurs when goals are thwarted and attention is focused on the source of the obstacle to the goal (Stein, Trabasso, & Liwag, 1993). Anger produces a desire to regain control, remove the obstruction, and, if nec-essary, attack the source of injury (Frijda, 1986; Izard, 1977; Lazarus, 1991). Whether a per-son acts on their anger depends on the situation, norms and values, and the characteristics of the offending party. Anger can also be triggered by particular schema. When a person has experienced intense emotion, such as anger, in a previous situation, the schema of that situation can trigger anger when a similar situation is identified. If, for example, a person witnessed an act of cruelty and was angered by it, the same emotion can be triggered by similar situations, or even by thinking about acts of cruelty in general.

Other emotions are closely related to anger and are also politically important, including frustration, resentment, contempt, and disgust. Disgust involves being repulsed by the ac-tions or characteristics of others. It can be quite severe and lead people to fear that the very social order is being contaminated. The behavior that disgust can produce includes the pos-sibility of wanting to destroy the offending group. On the other hand, because the level of in-terest and degree of distress when one is disgusted is lower than when one is angry, disgust does not produce as much aggression as anger. Contempt, on the other hand, involves feeling superior to another group and can lead to domination and dehumanization of others (Frijda, 1986). Dehumanization, in turn, leads to extremely violent behavior, even genocide (Izard, 1977; Kressel, 1996). The less human another person or group appears, the easier it is to kill them en masse.

Guilt, shame, sympathy, pity, envy, and jealousy can also affect political behavior. Guilt occurs when people do something they consider morally unacceptable and people want to atone or make amends to those they have hurt (Lazarus, 1991; Swim & Miller, 1999). Shame, on the other hand, occurs when a person does something that violates how they see themselves. When feeling shame, people tend to avoid others who have observed whatever they did to produce the shame.

Fear and anxiety, two other emotions important in politics, both occur when danger is perceived, but they differ, in that fear is associated with a clear and certain threat, and anxiety is associated with uncertainty about the threat. Typically, when people experience fear, they want to avoid or escape the threat. When they experience anxiety, however, they do not really know what to do or how to respond, and they tend to worry about what to do and how to do it (Lazarus, 1991).

There are positive emotions that are also important in politics, such as pride in the achievements of one's group or country or happiness, when an opportunity to achieve an important goal occurs. As mentioned earlier, positive emotions tend to make people more flexible and more creative in problem solving. They are able to see more nuances and have more complex evaluations of other people, when feeling positive emotions. Clearly, these emotions, such as pride in your country, or joy and happiness when the country does well in things like economic development and growth, or in international athletic competitions, are associated with politics.

As alluded to earlier, there are a few psychological studies of emotions that are associated with groups of varying degrees of power, in different contexts. Duckitt (1994), for example, looked at emotion and behavior patterns associated with groups considered malicious superior, oppressive, inferior, threatening, and powerful. He found punitiveness, intropunitive abasement, extrapunitive hostility, hostility, derogation, and superficial tolerance associated with each, respectively. Smith (1993) also examined perceptions of different groups (strong or weak, compared to the perceiver's group and the emotions associated with it), in a study of emotions and stereotyping. Smith found that minorities with low power felt fear regarding high-power or majority groups; members of high-status groups felt disgust in regard to low-status groups; contempt was felt by any group toward any out-group; anger was felt by members of high-power or majority groups when low-power or minorities made demands or threats; and jealousy emerged among low-status groups toward high-status groups.

Mackie, Devos, and Smith (2000) also examined an important issue regarding the experience of negative emotions resulting from interactions with an out-group. They argue that either fight (e.g., anger) or flight (e.g., fear) emotions are possible, depending upon appraisals of the out-group by, and in relation to, the in-group. Marcus et al. (2000) examined emotion in the American electoral context, in an interesting study that drew upon current studies in neurosciences, among other fields: They argued that there are "two systems associated with the brain's limbic region, the disposition and the surveillance systems" (p. 9). From the dispositional system come the emotions of satisfaction and enthusiasm or frustration and depression. The surveillance system determines feelings of relaxation and calm or anxiety and unease, depending upon political conditions. Both cause people to be more or less attentive to the political arena and their evaluation of candidates and participation in politics. In a look at emotions and images of other states, Cottam and Cottam (2001) argued that certain emotions are closely associated with particular images. Some of these images can be translated to domestic contexts, as well. Following is a review of the images and emotions associated with them. These patterns are beginning to receive empirical verification from experimental studies (Alexander, Brewer, & Herrmann, 1999). The images and strategic patterns discussed next are summarized in Figure 3.1.

Image of Other Political Actor		Threat/Opportunity		Strategic Preference
Enemy image	⟶	Threat high	⟶	Containment
Barbarian image	⟶	Threat high	⟶	Search for allies, augment power
Imperial image	⟶	Threat high	⟶	Submit/revolt when possible
Rogue image	⟶	Threat moderate/low	⟶	Crush
Degenerate image	⟶	Opportunity high/ moderate	⟶	Challenge, take risks
Colonial image	⟶	Opportunity high	⟶	Control, direct, exploit
Ally image	⟶	Threat/opportunity (Will help in either context)	⟶	Negotiate agreements Common strategy

FIG. 3.1.   Images and strategic preferences.

The Diabolical Enemy

The image of an enemy is associated with intensely perceived threat and very intense affect and emotions. The enemy is perceived as relatively equal in capability and culture. In its most extreme form, the diabolical enemy is seen as irrevocably aggressive in motivation, mono-lithic in decisional structure, and highly rational in decision making (to the point of being able to generate and orchestrate multiple complex conspiracies). Citizens who do not share this im-age, or who merely have a more complex view of the enemy, are often accused of being, at best, dupes of the enemy and possibly even traitors. This is unfortunate, particularly because the ability to view the threatener in more complex terms makes it possible to identify a broader range of policy options, some of which might stave off a crisis or at least allow for a more complex strategic response.

Some of the emotions associated with the enemy would include anger, frustration, envy, jeal-ousy, fear, distrust, and possibly grudging respect. An enemy's successes are considered unfair, and when bad things happen and goals are not met, the enemy is blamed. People tend to be both antagonistic and reactant in responding to an enemy. People compete with the enemy and try to prevent the enemy from gaining anything. The approach to conflict makes sense in light of the cognitive properties of the image. The enemy is as powerful and capable as one's own country, so there is an even chance of losing, if the approach to the conflict is entirely zero sum. Thus the enemy image makes a strong, aggressive defense the logical choice. If such a defense should eliminate the threatener altogether, so much the better. However, a strategy of **containment** may be the only recognized alternative in most political contexts, simply because the odds of defeat-ing an enemy are 50–50, at best. Containing your enemy, preventing them from becoming more powerful or achieving its desired goals, may be all you can do.

The consequences of stereotypical enemy image can be tragic, when the motivations of the country considered to be an enemy are really misunderstood, that is, when the people and leaders are essentially acting toward that country based upon a stereotype of an enemy. It can produce a self-fulfilling prophecy. The people and leaders of enemy countries will see them-selves as having been aggressed against and will develop an enemy image (or mirror image), because each sees the other as an enemy and will adopt the same tough strategy. The result could be an unnecessary and disastrous **security dilemma** that would be extremely difficult to overcome. **Security dilemmas** are situations in which the efforts made by one state to defend itself are simultaneously seen as threatening to its opponents, even if those actions were not intended to be threatening. They easily lead to **spiral conflicts** in which each side matches and one-ups the actions taken by the other side. This can produce arms races and other types of aggression that result from misunderstanding each others' motives. The enemy stereotype is virtually nonfalsifiable. It can explain any response, including appeasement, on the part of the enemy. In chapters 7 and 8, a number of cases are presented in which this image is evident. Spiral conflicts and the security dilemma are discussed in more depth in chapter 10.

The Barbarian

The barbarian image appears when an intense threat is perceived as emanating from a political entity viewed as superior in terms of capability, but as inferior culturally. Historical examples of this image can be found in the ancient Greek depiction of the Germanic tribes to the north. The image of the barbarian is of an aggressive people who are monolithic in decisional structure, cunning, and willing to resort to unspeakable brutality including genocide, and who are determined to take full advantage of their superiority. Emotions commonly associated with this image are disgust more than contempt (because the barbarian is considered greater in capability, even though culturally inferior), anger, and fear. The latter is a product of the superior capability of the barbarian. People who do not share this image will be accused of cowardice and treason.

Because of both cognitive and emotional properties, this image does not lead to an aggressive defense posture. Fear produced by capability asymmetries will make people prefer to avoid direct conflict. A more reasonable primary course of action for dealing with a barbarian is a search for allies who can be persuaded of the probability that a failure to deal with this threat will affect, seriously and adversely, their own national interests. In social identity theoretical terms, perceivers would probably like to engage in direct competition with this hated and disgusting opponent, in the most violent form of eliminating the threat altogether, but they cannot, because they are too weak. Instead, they must build coalitions to overcome their weakness and improve their ability to at least contain the barbarian.

There are some examples of this image in recent international and domestic political conflicts. International cases include Israeli perceptions of the Arab world. Although the Arab states are not superior in military capability to Israel, their large populations and resource advantages lead to an Israeli expectation that they have the potential for becoming superior. Despite perceived cultural inferiority, the probabilities are seen as high that superiority in conventional arms is not only attainable but unavoidable. A second example occurred in the disintegration of Yugoslavia (explored in detail in chapter 8), in which the Croatians believed themselves to be culturally superior to the Serbs, but much weaker in capability (Cottam & Cottam, 2001). In both cases, allies were sought: Israel looked to the United States and Europe, and the Croatians looked to Slovenia and other European states for support in their efforts to achieve independence from Yugoslavia.

The Imperial Image

This image occurs when the people of a polity perceive threat from another polity viewed as superior in terms of both capability and culture. That is a situation that was fairly commonplace during the height of colonialism in the nineteenth century. The imperial stereotype now is viewed primarily in a neocolonial variation, reflecting the disappearance of formal colonialism. The imperial power is perceived to be motivated by the desire to exploit the resources of the colonized people. The decisional structure of the imperial power is viewed as less monolithic than in the enemy and barbarian images, because an anti-imperialism element is frequently perceived to be present in the imperial power. People assume that decisions are made in a subtle and discrete manner in the imperial power, in the form of an elaborate web of institutions and individuals. People also believe that, even though their own country has its own institutions and leader, the imperial power is pulling the strings, often at a very detailed level. The imperial power is viewed as having the capacity to orchestrate developments of extraordinary complexity and to do so with great subtlety. The style is often described as operating through a "hidden hand," which is what gives the imperial power superiority in capability. People who collaborate with the imperial power are viewed by those resisting it as profiting hugely from the relationship and are judged as having betrayed their nation. But the reality is that, historically, many people in colonial and neocolonial countries did collaborate with the imperial powers. From a social identity standpoint, this makes sense, if comparisons were not made by collaborators between themselves and the imperial power, but between themselves and other groups in the colony dominated by the imperial power. They may have seen imperial control as just and legitimate, and thereby accepted their own inferior status, if they saw their own circumstances improved, compared to other groups, because of the imperial power's presence. Therefore, the image is sometimes associated with strong perceptions of injustice and illegitimacy, but not by everyone.

The complex of emotions associated with this image is affected by perceptions of whether or not the relationship is a just or legitimate one. When the colonial–imperial relationship is seen as legitimate or just, emotions associated with the image include fear of the imperial power. The behavioral tendencies that result involve self-protection and avoiding conflict with the fear-inducing agent (Duckitt, 1994). In addition, when the relationship is considered just and legitimate, respect is likely by the subordinate people for the imperial group, as is benevolent paternalistic affection by the imperial group for the subordinate group (Duckitt, 1994). The behavioral preferences would be simply to maintain the relationship as it is currently conducted, with the imperial group making major decisions and allowing symbolic concessions to the colonial subject group.

Emotions and action preferences are different on both sides, when the relationship and interaction is considered unjust by the weaker, subordinate group. The extremity of mutual stereotyping increases in such situations, and the people in the subordinate position start to make demands for greater equality. They may feel jealousy, anger, and shame that they are in the inferior position (Smith, 1993). These perceptions and emotions can push people toward antagonistic and hostile actions toward the superior group, including rebellion, even though they are well aware of the potential consequences. However, actions as risky as outright rebellion tend to occur only when social mobility and creativity options are not available and when real alternatives are perceived to exist. For example, after World War II, the European colonial powers were so weak that the prospect of actually achieving independence looked good enough to leaders of independence movements to push hard for the end of colonialism. This image is also important in a case study presented in chapter 8 of U.S.–Mexico relations in the war on drugs.

The Rogue Image

The rogue image is relatively new. During the Cold War, leaders of the West held an image of a dependent of the enemy, in which a country was viewed as inferior in capability and culture, but controlled and supported by the enemy. That image disappeared with the end of the Cold War and the demise of the Soviet Union. Nevertheless, former allies of the Soviet Union, along with some other countries (such as North Korea, Cuba, Iraq, Libya, Serbia, and Iran), were seen as both inferior and threatening. American policymakers often refer to rogue states. For example, Anthony Lake (1994), when national security adviser, wrote:

> Our policy must face the reality of recalcitrant and outlaw states that not only choose to remain outside the family [of nations] but also assault its basic values. There are few "backlash" states: Cuba, North Korea, Iran, Iraq and Libya. For now they lack the resources of a superpower, which would enable them to seriously threaten the democratic order being created around them. Nevertheless, their behavior is often aggressive and defiant. . . . These backlash states have some common characteristics. Ruled by cliques that control power through coercion . . . these nations exhibit a chronic inability to engage constructively with the outside world, and they do not function effectively in alliances. . . . Finally, they share a siege mentality. Accordingly, they are embarked on ambitious and costly military programs. (pp. 45–46)

Look at the words Lake used. There are references to a family (bad children), the weakness of these states, the incompatibility of their values with those of the rest of the family of nations, their aggressive behavior, decisions are made by a small elite, and they cannot be dealt with rationally and constructively. Responses to this type of state are driven by a sense of superiority. They are bad children who must be taught a lesson, and that lesson is taught with force. One does not negotiate with bad children, one punishes them. There are many examples. American reaction to Saddam Hussein's resistance to weapons inspection was to attack with the full force of America's military might. President Bush repeatedly stated that there would be no negotiations with Saddam Hussein and that he had to do what he was told to do or be punished. When Slobodan Milošević resisted points in the Rambouillet accords that would have given North Atlantic Treaty Organization (NATO) forces the right to wander unimpeded throughout Yugoslavia, negotiations ceased and Yugoslavia was bombed. When Manuel Noriega thumbed his nose at U.S. efforts to promote free elections, Panama was bombed. Often, one individual is assumed to be responsible for the behavior of the rogue state (e.g., eliminate Noriega, Saddam, or Milošević, and the problem will be solved overnight).

The Degenerate Image

The degenerate image is one associated with the perception of an opportunity to achieve a goal at the expense of a country that is seen as relatively equal or even greater in capability and culture. Even though a country seen as a degenerate may be more powerful than the perceiver's country, it is also seen as uncertain and confused in motivation and is characterized by a highly differentiated leadership that lacks a clear sense of direction and that is incapable of constructing an effective strategy. They are believed to be unable to muster the will and determination to make effective use of their power instruments or to mobilize effective public support. Fellow citizens who do not share this image are seen as wimps. As in the case of the enemy stereotype, disconfirming evidence is likely to be interpreted as confirming and the image is extremely difficult to falsify.

The emotions associated with the image are disgust, contempt, scorn, and anger all of which, may ultimately turn to hatred. This combination leads to a desire to eliminate the offensive group and can lead to a dangerous underestimation of an adversary's abilities (Izard, 1977). Contempt and disgust combine with anger and scorn, and this can lead to dehumanization and to genocidal violence. Because the motivations of a country seen as a degenerate are assumed to be harmful, the drive to eliminate the problem is likely to be strong.

Leaders of Germany and Japan before World War II made statements about, and committed acts toward Great Britain, the United States, and France, that indicated their degenerate image of those countries. A more recent example of this stereotypical view was Saddam Hussein of Iraq, in his confrontation with the United States and its allies in 1990. Saddam Hussein apparently believed to the end that the United States and its allies would not have the will to engage him on the issue of the invasion of Kuwait. More typical was the operating worldview of Hitler, Mussolini, and the Japanese military. They at least did possess formidable war capabilities, and all saw a reality that made plausible the achievement of their aggressive ends.

The Colonial Image

A second stereotypical image associated with perception of opportunity is the colonial image, which is the flip side of the imperial image. It occurs when an opportunity is identified to gain control over another polity or group perceived as significantly inferior in capability and culture. The people are perceived as childlike and inferior, and the political elite are typically perceived to fall into one of two groups: One group is seen as behaving moderately and responsibly, as is indicated by its willingness to collaborate with the imperial power; the other group, in contrast, is seen as behaving in an agitating and irresponsible manner, opposing the imperial purpose, sometimes to the point of allying with and serving the interests of enemies of the imperial power. The moderate, responsible section is motivated to support what is perceived as the civilizing mission of the imperial power. The agitating group is seen as monolithic in decisional structure and cunningly destructive, as it tries to mobilize the most alert elements in a mostly apolitical and passive populace. The imperial power capability advantage rests on the perceived immaturity of the colonial population, as manifest in an inability effectively to recruit, organize, and lead a military force and to make effective use of advanced weaponry. Those citizens of the imperial power who do not share this essentially contemptuous view will be regarded as having "gone native" and lost perspective.

Members of the imperial power polity tend to regard the colonial populace with disgust and contempt, but also with pity. Behaviors associated with the image and its emotional baggage include wanting to avoid contamination from contact with the inferior, or moving forcefully against them to punish bad behavior. This was the Cold War pattern in U.S. foreign policy. Countries in this image, who moved in political directions that U.S. policymakers did not approve of, were punished, sometimes through the overthrow of their governments. Examples include the overthrow of the governments in Iran (1953), Guatemala (1954), and Chile (1973). The fear was that they would become infected with socialism and that it would spread to other countries, and they were simply not going to be allowed to do this. In less dangerous contexts, such as disagreements regarding economic matters, there is little a colonial country can do to seriously threaten the imperial power, and policy preferences are for nonviolent repression in the form of economic sanctions, isolation, refusal to give trade preferences, and so on. The actions and demands of the colonial country are still considered illegitimate and inconsistent with the goals of the perceiver, and responsibility for the conflict is attributed to the colonial country.

We describe this image in terms of international politics, but the dynamic repeats itself in any domestic political context in which one group considers itself vastly superior to, and therefore rightfully in control of, another group. White resistance to the civil rights movement in the United States in the 1960s South is an example. African American political leaders were also divided into "moderate" and the "irresponsible" classifications. This image is also evident in the case study of U.S.–Mexico interaction in chapter 8.

ATTITUDES

The discussion of images and their emotional components tells us something about the inter-action of cognition and emotion. There has also been a great deal of research on the cognitive and emotional elements in the individual attitudes that make up a cognitive system. The concept is defined and thought of in different ways by different psychologists. A standard definition of **attitudes** is that they are an enduring system of positive or negative **beliefs** (the cognitive component), **affective** feelings and emotions, and action tendencies regarding **attitude objects**, that is, the entity being evaluated. Stone and Schaffner (1988), for example, regard attitudes as "an organized set of beliefs, persisting over time, which is useful in explaining the individual response to tendencies" (p. 63). Eagly and Chaiken (1998) define attitudes as "a psychological tendency that is expressed by evaluating a particular entity with some degree of favor or disfavor" (p. 269). Duckitt (1994) reviews two different ways in which attitudes have been conceptualized in psychology. In one, they are seen to be com-posed of cognitive, affective, and behavioral components. However, there were many criti-cisms of this conceptualization of attitudes, because there was little in the way of specifics as to how these three components interacted and whether they were always consistent with each other. We saw earlier, in our discussion of balance and consistency, that affect and cognition are not always consistent, and most people know from personal experience that attitudes and behavior are often inconsistent.

One of the most important controversies in attitude research has concerned the behavioral component in the original conceptualization of attitudes. Originally, it was simply assumed that a person's attitudes determine his behavior. A person who favors a certain politician is likely to vote for him. A person who smokes marijuana is likely to support bills legalizing marijuana. A person who is racially prejudiced is unlikely to send their child to a school where African Americans and Hispanic Americans, or whoever the person does not like, are in the majority. In 1934, however, a major study was done, which found interesting results and which challenged the notion that there is a direct connection between attitudes and behavior. This study was conducted by La Pierre, who was a Caucasian professor. He toured the United States with a Chinese couple during a period when there was a great deal of prejudice against Asian people in this country. They stopped at 66 hotels and 184 restaurants. Only once were they turned away by a hotel and never by a restaurant. Later, a letter was sent to the same ho-tels and restaurants, asking whether they would accept Chinese customers. Ninety-two per-cent of those who responded (128) said that they would not. The study showed that people do not always behave in accordance with their attitudes. Later studies raised similar concerns (Deutscher, 1973; Katz & Stotland, 1959; Kuntner, Wilkins, & Yarrow, 1952; Minard, 1952) This, of course, led to the question of when and under what circumstances attitudes and behavior are likely to coincide.

Attitudes that are strong, clear, and consistent over time, and that are directly and specifically relevant to the behavior under examination, are more likely to be associated with attitude–behavior consistency (Fazio & Williams, 1986; Fishbein & Ajzen, 1980; Krosnick, 1989). Inconsistencies can come from weak or ambivalent affect. In addition, the affective and cognitive components of an attitude may be in some conflict, which also reduces the changes of attitude–behavior consistency. For example, some men and women may think intellectually gender-based discrimination is wrong, but they are emotionally upset when men and women do not conform to gender-related roles. Also, if one is going to study the relationship between attitudes and behaviors, one needs to look at behaviors that are directly related to attitudes, to get an accurate picture of the relationship. For example, several studies tried to examine the relationship between religious attitudes and religious behavior, by asking subjects whether they believe in God or consider themselves religious, then noting whether they attended church. Usually, there was only a weak relationship between the two. The problem is that going to church is not directly related to belief in God or even to being religious. Many people who believe in God do not go to church. Other people go to church for social reasons, more than because they believe in God. In addition, it may be important to look at a series of a person's actions over time, to get an accurate picture of the relationship between attitudes and behavior (Epstein, 1979; Fiske & Taylor, 1991). This eliminates interference from situational conditions that interfere in the attitude–behavior relationship.

This brings us to situational pressures, which can also affect the relationship between attitudes and behavior. Whenever a person engages in overt behavior, they can be influenced both by their attitudes and by the situation they are in. When situational pressures are very strong, attitudes are not likely to be as strong a determinant of behavior as when situational pressures are relatively weak. Situational pressure can include social norms (a person may be a bigot, but know that others will think poorly of him if he acts that way) or contextual effects, which heighten the salience of or perspective on, a certain attitude (Bentler & Speckart, 1981; Fishbein & Ajzen, 1975; La Pierre, 1934). Individual differences are also important in explaining inconsistencies between what people think and how they behave. Some people are high self-monitors, meaning that they are very attentive to social norms and the impression they make in social situations. They are less likely to act consistently on the basis of their attitudes and instead act as they think the situation demands (Perloff, 1993; Snyder, 1987).

Given these issues, other perspectives on attitudes have been offered. Fishbein and Ajzen (1980) offer a unidimensional approach to attitudes, wherein they regard attitudes solely as affect. They separate the cognitive and behavioral components and argue that these should be observed and measured separately. As Duckitt (1994) explains, this approach

> does not expect a strong relationship between an attitude to an object and specific behaviors to that object. To predict a specific act, both the attitude to that act and act-specific social norms need to be considered as well. On the other hand, a generalized attitude toward an object should predict the overall tendency to behave in a generally favorable or unfavorable way toward that object, as aggregating over a variety of different situations and acts should largely average out normative and situational influences. (p. 13)

Judd and Krosnik (1989) take a similar approach and define an attitude as "an evaluation of an attitude object that is stored in memory" (p. 100). Others have limited attitudes to affect and beliefs alone (Levin & Levin, 1982).

No agreement exists on a universally accepted understanding of what an attitude is and how its component parts relate to each other, but the attitude concept has been widely used in studies of voting behavior, persuasion, and media effects on political behavior, as seen in chapter 6. Unlike the image and stereotype concepts, the attitude concept can more easily separate cognition and affect, and for that reason it can be very useful in studying voting behavior, particularly in a country such as the United States, where people have political attitudes that often are based upon little, and often inaccurate, cognition. An attitude can be driven mostly by affect, but as our discussion of images and stereotypes shows, there is considerable knowledge, although often inaccurate, embodied in them. Alternatively, an attitude may be primarily cognitive in content, that is, based solely on beliefs without affect (Eagly & Chaiken, 1998).

Attitude studies are concerned with many issues, one of which is, as mentioned, the relationship between cognition and affect, particularly when they are not consistent (i.e., what you think about an object and how you feel about it are different). Marcus et al. (2000) examine the role affect plays in the behavior of American citizens in elections and regarding important issues. They argue that emotions help people monitor and take surveillance of politics. Their study includes survey results demonstrating the importance of enthusiasm and anxiety in electoral preferences for the presidency in the 1980s. For example, enthusiasm for Reagan and lack of anxiety about the country's circumstances, they argue, contributed strongly to Reagan's reelection in 1984. They also explain the lack of everyday interest in politics in America by noting that the average citizen uses emotions to act as an alarm: when the citizen starts to feel anxiety, they then turn to the news and find out more about what is going on. The emotional system is a watchdog that operates nonconsciously. We discuss this research in more detail in chapter 6.

Another broad issue concerns the consistency among, and structure of, attitudes, for example, whether Republicans are consistently conservative and Democrats are consistently liberal on all political issues, and how those attitudes are linked together. Attitudes can be bipolar, wherein people recognize and understand both sides of an issue, or they can be unipolar, in which case people see only their preferred position. Eagly and Chiaken (1998) cite a number of studies that suggest that attitudes on controversial issues are likely to be bipolar (e.g., Pratkanis, 1989; Sherif, Sherif, & Nebergall, 1965). In addition, there is a large body of literature on the complexity of beliefs, which we introduce in chapter 2 and explore in detail in chapter 5, where political leaders are discussed. Many studies concerning how political attitudes are formed, and how they change, are examined in chapter 6.

CONCLUSION

This chapter has introduced readers to many different concepts in cognitive and social psychology, and it has briefly introduced their application to political psychology. We began with basic patterns in information processing, then turned to an overview of the cognitive system. To this, we added the importance of the groups to which people belong (in-groups) and their reactions to groups to which they do not belong (out-groups). We presented a model of out-groups (image theory), which depicts out-groups in international politics, but which can be used in domestic political arenas as well. In subsequent chapters, where we examine race, ethnicity, nationalism, and political extremists, we explore some of the groups in politics to which people have powerful attachments, as well as patterns of behavior toward out-groups. We looked at emotion in politics, and readers may find that, although emotions have not been systematically examined in the patterns of political behavior we discuss in succeeding chapters, they are deeply important. Indeed, readers may find themselves having powerful emotional reactions to some of the cases presented in the chapters that follow. Finally, we presented the concept of attitudes, to which we return when we look at public opinion and voting in chapter 6. Thus far, in chapters 2 and 3, we have explored the content of the Political Being's mind. In the next chapter, we turn to the Political Being and the outside world, with a look at groups and group behavior.

Topics, Theories/Explanations, and Concepts in Chapter 3

Topics	Theories	Concepts
Information processing	Attribution theory	Heuristics: availability, representativeness, fundamental attribution error
	Balance theory dissonance theory	Need for consistency: selective exposure, attention, interpretation bolstering, avoidance of value trade-offs
Cognition and cognitive systems	Categorization Social Identity	Cognitive categories, schemas, stereotypes, in-groups and out-groups
	Image theory	Enemy, barbarian, imperial, rogue, degenerate, colonial
Emotions		
Attitudes		

KEY TERMS

Affect
Ally image
Assimilation effect
Attitudes
Attribution theory
Availability heuristic
Avoidance of value
   trade-offs
Balance
Barbarian image
Beliefs
Bolstering

Cognition
Cognitive
   processes
Colonial image
Contrast effect
Degenerate image
Dissonance
Emotion
Enemy image
Fundamental attribution
   error
Heuristic

Image
Imperialist image
In-group
Out-group
Representativeness
   heuristic
Rogue image
Schema
Security
   dilemmas
Social identity
Stereotypes

SUGGESTIONS FOR FURTHER READING

Alexander, M. G., Brewer, M. B., and Herrmann, R. K. (1999). Images and affect: A functional analysis of out-group stereotypes. *Journal of Personality and Social Psychology, 77,* 78–93.

Cottam, M. (1994). *Images and intervention.* Pittsburgh, PA: University of Pittsburgh Press.

Cottam, M., & Cottam R. (2001). *Nationalism and politics: The political behavior of nation states.* Boulder, CO: Lynne Rienner.

Eagly, A. H., & Chaiken S. (1998). Attitude structure and function. In D. T. Gilbert, S. T. Fiske, & G. Lindzey (Eds.), *The handbook of social psychology* (4th ed.) New York: McGraw-Hill.

Fiske, S., & Taylor, S. E. (1991). *Social cognition.* New York: McGraw-Hill.

Frijda, N. (1986). *The emotions.* Cambridge, UK: Cambridge University Press.

Mackie, D., & Hamilton, D. (Eds.). (1993). *Affect, cognition and stereotyping: Interactive processes in group perception.* New York: Academic.

Marcus, G., Neuman, W. R., & MacKeun, M. (2000). *Affective intelligence and political judgment.* Chicago: University of Chicago Press.

Tajfel, H. (1982). *Human groups and social categories.* Cambridge, UK: Cambridge University Press.

CHAPTER 4

The Political Psychology of Groups

This chapter looks at the Political Being in their environment, that is, in the presence of, and as a member of, groups. Groups have a prominent role in politics. Small groups are often given the responsibility of making important political decisions, creating political policies, and generally conducting political business. Larger groups, such as the Senate, also hold a special place in politics and are responsible for larger-scale decisions and tasks such as passing legislation. Finally, large groups, such as states and countries, carry with them their own dynamics, especially regarding how they view each other and how they get along. Because so much political behavior is performed by groups, it behooves us to learn more about the basic processes that govern groups. Although groups are comprised of individuals, understanding group behavior cannot be attained from an understanding of individual behavior. Obviously, understanding groups involves an understanding of the individuals who comprise a group, but there are dynamics of groups that cannot be observed from examining individuals alone. Many observers (e.g., Durkheim, 1938/1966; LeBon, 1895/1960) note that individuals often behave quite differently when they are together than when they are alone. Consequently, although the workings of the Political Being's mind are still operative, we are interested in the impact of the sociopolitical environment on behavior in this chapter.

The study of groups in social psychology has a short history, with some of the first studies being conducted just before World War II (e.g., Lewin, Lippitt, & White, 1939; Newcomb, 1943; Sherif, 1936; Whyte, 1943). Nonetheless, a vast amount of information is available about group behavior, and most of it can be applied to the study of groups in political settings. In this chapter, we review a variety of information about groups. The first half of the chapter focuses on the structural characteristics of groups, such as composition, formation, and development. The second half of the chapter focuses on the unique behaviors that take place in groups or because of groups, including influence, performance, decision making, and intergroup conflict.

THE NATURE OF GROUPS

Definition of a Group

Imagine all of the different types of collectives that exist in political settings. People work together to solve problems, set political policies and agendas, serve constituents, make legal decisions, run political campaigns, and make decisions about world problems. Do all of these collectives constitute groups? Groups researchers have been unable to answer that question. There is little consensus in the field about what characteristics of a collective make a group. Although most social psychologists would agree that a **group** is a collection of people who are perceived to belong together and are dependent on one another, there are other ways to conceptualize groups. For example, Moreland (1987) discusses "groupiness" or social integration as a quality that every collection of individuals possesses to some degree. As the level of social integration increases, people start to think and act more like a group than a collection of individuals. Other social psychologists (Dasgupta, Banji, & Abelson, 1999; Lickel et al., 2000) maintain the importance of the perception, named **entiativity**, which refers to the extent to which a collection of people is perceived as a coherent entity. Some groups, such as people in line at a bank, are perceived as being low in entiativity. Other groups, such as members of a family or members of a professional sport team, are perceived as being high in entiativity.

Group Composition

Groups come in all shapes and sizes, and political groups are no exception. Groups can differ in size, composition, and type. Concerning group size, research suggests that naturally occurring groups are typically small, containing just two or three persons (Desportes & Lemaine, 1988). People may prefer smaller groups because they are confused by large groups (James, 1951) or because they cannot easily control what happens to them in larger groups (Lawler, 1992). Research has examined some interesting effects of group size. For example, as the size of the group increases, group members participate less (Patterson & Schaeffer, 1977), display less commitment to the group (Widmeyer, Brawley, & Carron, 1990), and show higher levels of tardiness, absenteeism, and turnover (Durand, 1985; Spink & Carron, 1992). Other group dynamics are also affected by group size. In larger groups, there tends to be more conflict (O'Dell, 1968), less cooperation (Brewer & Kramer, 1986), and less conformity to group norms (Olson & Caddell, 1994). Finally, group performance can also be affected by the size of a group. In large groups, coordination is more difficult (Diehl & Stroebe, 1987; Latane, Williams, & Harkins, 1979), leading to decrements in performance and it is easier to social loaf and free ride, which can have harmful effects on the performance of a group (Karau & Williams, 1993). In the chapters that follow, we examine large groups, such as ethnic, national, and racial groups, and small groups involved in political decision making and small groups involved in political violence.

Groups can also differ in terms of their composition. The characteristics of individual group members, such as sex, race, ethnicity, and physical attractiveness, can be very important to the functioning of the group. Recently, however, attention has focused on the diversity within a group (Levine & Moreland, 1998). Research examining the effects of diversity on communication suggests that diversity can be harmful. As the degree of diversity increases, group members tend to communicate with each other less and in more formal ways (Zenger & Lawrence, 1989). When group members communicate less often, interpersonal conflicts become more likely (Maznevski,1994). Diversity, however, can be beneficial to group performance (McLeod & Lobel, 1992). Diversity allows a group to be more flexible, foster innovation, and improve the quantity and quality of relationships outside of the group.

Groups can also be distinguished by their type. In a recent study (Lickel et al., 2000), participants were asked to categorize a large number of groups. Their sorting resulted in four categories of groups: First, some groups, such as families and romantic relationships, were categorized as *intimacy groups*; second, *task-oriented groups* consisted of groups such as committees and work groups; third, groups such as women and Americans were categorized as *social categories*; and, finally, *weak social relationships or associations* included such groups as those who enjoy a certain type of music or those who live in the same neighborhood. Political groups certainly fall into the task-oriented type, whether they are government working groups, juries, political interest groups such as Green Peace or Human Rights Watch, or committees and subcommittees in Congress. Political groups can also be social categories, such as ethnic groups, racial groups, or women, all with particular political issues of concern.

Group Structure

Another important characteristic of a group is its structure. Every group has a structure, and it tends to develop quickly and change slowly in most groups (Levine & Moreland, 1998). Apparently, group members need to know what the structure of a group is and are reluctant to alter it once it is set. For example, understanding the structure of a group, and how aspects of a group's structure can influence conflict and performance, is important. Aspects of group structure include status, roles, norms, and cohesion.

Status in a group refers to how power is distributed among its members. Indicators of high status include nonverbal behavior, such as standing more erect, maintaining eye contact, and being more physically intrusive (Leffler, Gillespie, & Conaty, 1982), as well as verbal behavior, such as speaking more, interrupting more, and being more likely to be spoken to (Skovertz, 1988). The manner in which people acquire or are assigned status can be explained by two theories: Expectation states theory (Berger, Rosenholtz, & Zelditch, 1980) suggests that the expectations of a person, based on their personal characteristics, contribute to group members' sense of the sorts of accomplishments a person can achieve; ethological theories (Mazur, 1985) maintain that a group member acquires status when other group members assess the person's strength by evaluating their demeanor and appearance. However status is acquired, it is generally slow to change. Because high status is associated with rewards, those high in status are reluctant to give it up. And, because those high in status are usually evaluated more favorably than those low in status, other group members are reluctant to remove status (Messe, Kerr, & Sattler, 1992).

The various roles that group members hold constitute another important component of group structure. **Roles** are expectations about how a person ought to behave. Little is known about how roles in groups develop (Levine & Moreland, 1998), except that task roles emerge before socioemotional ones. Regardless of how roles develop, it is clear that well-played roles can be beneficial to a group (Barley & Bechky, 1994; Bastien & Hostager, 1988). Much of the research on roles in groups focuses on the conflicts they create. Some role conflicts occur as a result of *role assignment*, which refers to the decisions that are made about who plays what role. Other conflicts center on *role ambiguity* (uncertainty about how to behave in a role) or *role strain* (lacking knowledge or ability to fulfill the role).

The norms of a group can be an important aspect of group structure. **Norms** refer to expectations about how all group members should behave. Like roles, the formation of norms in a group can be difficult to identify. Some argue that a group's initial behavior can be transformed into norms (Feldman, 1984). Others argue that norms can arise from the expectations for behavior that people bring with them when they join a group (Bettenhausen & Murnighan, 1991). Regardless of how norms are formed, there is strong pressure to maintain them. Group members can impose strong sanctions on members who violate the standards of behavior, and for good reason. Research suggests that adherence to norms improves the performance of a group (Seashore, 1954). For example, in groups that have norms of productivity or success, group members become more motivated to engage in behaviors or tasks that ensure the success of the group. On the other hand, adherence to norms can sometimes impede the performance of a group. If a norm of laziness develops, for example, then group members might work less hard to achieve their goals.

Cohesion refers to the factors that cause a group member to remain in the group (Festinger, 1950). The importance of cohesion to a group's well-being cannot be underestimated. It exerts powerful effects on a group's longevity. As such, understanding how cohesion in a group develops is important. There are several factors that affect the development of group cohesion. First, the more time group members spend together, the more cohesive they become (Griffith & Greenlees, 1993). Second, the more group members like each other, the more cohesive is the group (Lott & Lott, 1965). Third, groups that are more rewarding to their members are more cohesive (Ruder & Gill, 1982). Fourth, external threats to a group can increase the group's cohesiveness (Dion, 1979). Fifth, groups are more cohesive when leaders encourage feelings of warmth among group members. Most studies on the effects of cohesion on well-being and performance find a positive relationship. For example, members of cohesive groups are more likely to participate in group activities and to remain in the group (Brawley, Carron, & Widmeyer, 1988), and, in a meta-analysis on the effects of cohesion on performance, Mullen and Copper (1994) found that cohesive groups tend to perform better.

There are many studies of political decision-making groups, particularly American presidents and their close advisors, that show differences among those groups in status, roles, norms, and cohesion. These studies are reviewed extensively in chapter 5. Here, let us simply take a couple of examples. President John F. Kennedy preferred an advisory group that was collegial. Although he was at the top in terms of status, the various advisors in his group were seen as colleagues. The group was formed at the outset of the administration, and each member had his own domain of expertise, which provided him with a particular role. In terms of norms, conflicting viewpoints were encouraged, and all sides were taken into account in searching for solutions to problems. President Nixon was very different. His advisory group structure was hierarchical, with him on top. Again, each advisor had a role to play, but conflict and brainstorming were not encouraged. The emphasis in problem solving was on technical rather than political considerations. In the Clinton administration, role assignments were ambiguous. As you can see in chapter 5, this led to many delays and much turmoil in policy making in the Clinton administration.

Group Formation

If you think about all of the groups you are a member of, do you know how or why each of those groups formed? What were the circumstances surrounding the formation of each of your groups? Some of the answers may be easier than others: For example, the animal shelter you volunteer at formed because there was a need to care for stray dogs and cats, and the group of people you spend time with formed because the members liked one another. But how did the church you attend get started? Why did the intramural softball team form that you play on every Tuesday night? Groups researchers have yet to develop a comprehensive theory to explain how and why groups form, but there are two perspectives that offer promise. The *functional perspective* suggests that groups form because they serve a useful function or fulfill a need for their individual members (Mackie & Goethals, 1987). For example, your animal shelter formed to fulfill the need created by so many homeless dogs and cats. The *interpersonal attraction perspective* suggests that groups form because its members like one another and seek to spend time together. Thus, the group of friends you spend time with formed because you all liked one another and wanted to spend time together.

Functional Perspective

According to the functional perspective, groups satisfy many needs, including survival, psychological, informational, interpersonal, and collective. Groups can be functional, in that they can fulfill many of our *survival* needs, including feeding, defense, nurturance, and reproduction

(Bertram, 1978; Harvey & Greene, 1981; Scott, 1981). Many of these needs were stronger during earlier periods in history, but we still rely on groups to fulfill many of these functions today. For example, we rely heavily on our military forces to defend our country. We depend on farmers to provide some of our food. And, to the extent that we have a need to defend our country, for example, we might decide to join one of our country's armed forces.

Groups can also satisfy a host of psychological needs, some of which we introduced in chapter 2. For example, joining a group can satisfy the **need for affiliation.** Those with a high need for affiliation join groups more often, communicate with others frequently, and seek social approval (McClelland, 1985). Groups can also satisfy the **need for power**. People with a high need for power want to control others (Winter, 1973). This need can often be accomplished by joining a group. Finally, Schutz's **Fundamental Interpersonal**

> ## Political Action Groups and the Internet
> The Internet seems to affect everything, even group formation patterns. Take, for example, a political action group called Moveon. Moveon was organized by two Silicon Valley entrepreneurs, Joan Blades and Wes Boyd, in 1998, when they reached a level of frustration with the effort to impeach President Clinton. Then, after 9/11, Eli Pariser started an online petition for peace. They joined forces and have an international association of over 2 million online activists and formed the MoveOn.org political action committee. This is an example of a cybergroup formed to achieve functional goals of affecting politics through interest group activity. Will the opportunity to form and join cybergroups affect group psychology? Will it affect group influence in politics? (To learn about Moveon, naturally, you should visit their Web site, www.moveon.org.)

Relations Orientation (FIRO) can explain how joining a group can fulfill psychological needs (Schutz, 1958). According to this perspective, joining a group can satisfy three basic needs: *inclusion* (the desire to be part of a group), *control* (the need to organize an aspect of the group), and *affection* (the desire to establish positive relations with others). For individuals with these needs, joining a group offers them a way to fulfill these needs.

Another category of needs that can often be served well by groups is informational needs. Festinger (1950, 1954) argued that people join groups to provide standards with which to compare their own beliefs, opinions, and attitudes. People often have a need to determine if their own viewpoints are correct or accurate. One way to make such determinations is to seek similar people with when to compare our views. This perspective suggests that people join groups to better understand social reality.

Groups can also meet people's interpersonal needs. Many groups can provide social support, giving emotional sustenance, advice, and valuable feedback. Social support can be a valuable function of groups. Groups can protect us from the harmful effects of stress (Barrera, 1986). The social support of groups can also protect us from being lonely. Research indicates that people who were members of many groups reported less loneliness (Rubenstein & Shaver, 1980). College students who eat dinner with others and spend time with their friends also report being less lonely (Russell, Peplau, & Cutrona, 1980).

Finally, groups can fulfill important collective needs. Sometimes, groups can be more productive and efficient than individuals working alone. Groups often form because individuals believe that pooling the efforts of multiple people will lead to better outcomes than if individuals simply work alone. Some of the collective goals sought by groups include engaging in the performing arts, enriching the leisure time of its members, changing the opinions of persons outside the group, and making routine individual tasks more tolerable (Zander, 1985).

Interpersonal Attraction Perspective

Sometimes, groups form because individuals discover that they like each other and want to spend more time together. There are many factors that influence our liking of another. First, we tend to be attracted to those who are most similar to us in attitudes, beliefs, socioeconomic status, physical appearance, and so on (Newcomb, 1960, 1961). This suggests that we prefer to form or join groups with people who are most similar to us. Second, we tend to form relationships with those who are physically closer to us (Festinger, Schachter, & Back, 1950). Thus, we tend to make friends with those who live next door, those we sit next to in class, and those with whom we work closely. We are likely, then, to form or join groups with people who are physically close. Third, we like people who like us (Newcomb, 1979). We are thus more likely to form or join groups with people who are fond of us. Fourth, we are attracted to people who are physically attractive. With the exception of those who are extremely attractive, physically attractive people are more accepted than those less physically attractive.

In summary, people join groups for a variety of reasons. One reason that people join and form groups is to satisfy a number of important needs, including survival, psychological, informational, interpersonal, and collective needs. We are more likely to join groups that can effectively satisfy our needs. Another reason that people join groups is to spend more time with people they like. Such situations, especially when reciprocal, can be very rewarding.

Group Development

Think again about the groups you belong to. Have they remained the same over time, or have they changed somehow? Most likely, groups that you are a member of have changed somewhat over time, but how? *Group development* refers to the stages of growth and change that occur in a group, from its formation to its dissolution (Forsyth, 1990). Of course, there is disagreement among groups researchers about the number and type of stages, but most models include the following basic stages: forming, storming, norming, performing, and adjourning (Tuckman, 1965; Tuckman & Jensen, 1977).

The first stage refers to the point during which the collection of individuals is **forming**. This stage is also referred to as the orientation stage, because prospective members are orienting themselves to the group. During this stage, individuals are getting to know one another. The stage is often characterized as one with a fair amount of tension—prospective group members are on guard, reluctant to share much information or to discuss their personal views. Also, as you can imagine, group norms have not yet formed, making this a difficult period of development. In fact, the tension can be so high that those who believe they lack the skills necessary to effectively handle such a situation try to avoid group membership (Cook, 1977; Leary, 1983). Over time, tensions lessen and group members begin to exchange more information. Also, feelings of interdependence—one of the defining features of a group—increase during this stage. In chapter 9, we look at a number of groups of political extremists, such as the Nazi SS: There, careful attention is given to this stage to ensure that only people with particular characteristics are included.

The second stage of group development, **storming**, is characterized as one of conflict. Many types of conflict exist. Some conflicts occur when a person's position or action is misinterpreted (Deutsch, 1973). Other conflicts arise when a group member's behavior is deemed to be distracting, such as when a group member consistently arrives 15 minutes late for meetings. Other types of conflicts can escalate, such as when minor disagreements turn into major points of contention. Although conflicts, especially those that escalate, can disrupt the group, they can serve as important catalysts for group development. Conflicts can serve to promote group unity, interdependence and stability, and cohesion (Bennis & Shepard, 1956; Coser, 1956; Deutsch, 1969).

Norming, the third stage of group development, is a phase in which conflict is replaced with cohesion and feelings of unity. When groups become more cohesive, they have a heightened sense of unity. The relationships among members become stronger, as do individual members' sense of belonging. The degree of group members' identification is heightened during this period. Another characteristic of groups in this stage of development is stability. There is a low turnover of members, a low absentee rate, and a high rate of involvement. During this stage of development, group members also report a high degree of satisfaction with the group. They enjoy the group more, note increases in self-esteem and security, and have lower levels of anxiety. Finally, the internal dynamics of the group begin to intensify. There is greater acceptance of the group's goals by group members, a low tolerance for disagreement, and increased pressures to conform.

The fourth stage of group development is characterized by **performing**. Performance usually only occurs when groups mature and have successfully gone through the previous stages of development (Forsyth, 1990). In a study of neighborhood action groups (Zurcher, 1969), only 1 of 12 groups reached the performing stage. All others were stuck in the conflict or cohesion stages.

A group's decision to dissolve (**adjourning**) can either be planned or spontaneous. A planned dissolution occurs when the group accomplishes its intended goals or

Urban Street Gangs as Groups

Urban street gangs in the United States, and elsewhere, provide illustrations of the power of group demands for loyalty, conformity, and obedience. In the book *Monster: The autobiography of an L.A. gang member* (1993), Sanyika Shakur, a.k.a. Monster Kody, describes those group dynamics:

1. Belonging to the group enhances self-esteem, and cohesive groups demand strong loyalty: "Actually, I wasn't fully aware of the gang's strong gravitational pull. I knew, for instance, that the total lawlessness was alluring, and that the sense of importance, self-worth, and raw power was exciting, stimulating, and intoxicating beyond any other high on this planet. But still I could not explain what had happened to pull me in so far that *nothing* outside of my set mattered" (p. 70).

2. Loyalty and solidarity are described in passages such as this: "I went to trial [for murder] three months later. The gang turnout was surprising. Along with my family, at least fifteen of my homeboys came. All were in full gear (gear as in gang clothes, colors and hats—actually uniforms)" (p. 23).

3. Norms: Among the norms of his gang are: "You are your brother's keeper"; trouble (fighting, drinking, drugs, and sex); toughness; smartness (respect for streetwise savvy); fatalism (they did not believe they would grow old); autonomy (reject family and other agents, like the schools and teachers and police, so that they can associate with the gang); respect and honor for others according to their status; protect the gang turf; retaliate against all perceived offenses; and, when war is declared, all members are expected to fight.

exhausts its time and resources. Examples of groups with planned dissolutions include a jury who has reached a verdict, a softball team playing its last game of the season, or a class that dissolves because the semester has come to an end. Spontaneous dissolutions occur when unanticipated problems arise that prevent the group from continuing. Examples of groups with unplanned dissolutions include those that have repeatedly failed or those that fail to satisfy their members' needs.

INFLUENCE IN GROUPS

Groups can exert a great deal of influence over their members. When people are in groups, there is a strong tendency to adhere to the groups' norms. When group members act in accord with group norms, they are conforming. **Conformity** refers to the tendency to change one's beliefs or behaviors so that they are consistent with the standards set by the group. Americans tend to be ambivalent about the notion of conformity. On the one hand, to conform is to be "spineless" and "wishy-washy"; because Americans tend to value individualism, being labeled a conformist can be a negative label. On the other hand, conformity is valued because it leads to harmony and peace. Imagine a world in which no one conformed. In this section, we examine some of the early studies on norm formation and conformity. We also explore the reasons that people conform, as well as when people conform.

One of the earliest studies of conformity was conducted by Sherif (1936), who was interested in how group norms form. To understand norm formation, he made use of the *autokinetic effect*, which refers to a perceptual illusion that occurs when a single point of light in a darkened room appears to be moving. In Sherif's experiments, he asked participants to stare at the point of light and estimate how far it moved. In reality, the light does not move at all, so there is no correct answer on this task. In his first experiment, Sherif asked individual participants to estimate, over a series of trials, how far the light moved. The pattern of responses was nearly identical for all participants: initially, their estimates were quite variable, but over time, they settled on a single estimate, such as 3 inches, for example. In the next experiment, Sherif asked pairs of participants to estimate, over a series of trials, how far the light moved. Again, the pattern of responses for each pair was nearly the same—variability in their initial estimates, then convergence on how far the light moved. These experiments were important in showing how norms form. Eventually, individual or pairs of participants formed a standard for how far the light moved. In Sherif's third experiment, he sought to determine if people could be persuaded to conform to the judgment of another person. Participants in this experiment made judgments in groups of two. In reality, only one of the persons was a real participant; the other was a confederate of the researcher. The confederate was asked to make estimates either lower or higher than the real participant. Over time, the participant began to make estimates that were close to the estimates of the confederate, suggesting that participants were conforming to the standards set by the confederate. These experiments were important in demonstrating that, in ambiguous situations, where there is no correct answer, people tend to conform to a norm.

Another researcher, Asch (1955), wondered if participants would be as likely to conform when the situation was not so ambiguous, that is, when there was a correct answer on a judgment task. To answer this query, Asch asked five participants to take part in a perceptual judgment task. The participants were shown a series of three lines, varying in length. Their task was to determine which of the three lines matched a target line. The task was designed to be unambiguous: there was clearly a correct answer. Each participant, in turn, was asked to indicate, aloud, his answer to the experimenter. In reality, the first four participants were confederates of the experimenter. The person sitting in the fifth position was the real participant. On half of the trials, the four confederates were instructed to give the (clearly) wrong answer. The question was, would the fifth (real) participant also give the wrong answer. The results showed that 75% of the participants went along with the group and gave the wrong answer at least once. Apparently, the pressure to conform was so strong that, even on this unambiguous task with a clearly correct answer, participants were willing to give an answer that they knew was wrong.

Both of these experiments are important in showing that people conform. But why do they? Research suggests that people conform for two reasons: to be liked and to be correct (Cialdini &

Trost, 1998). In Sherif's (1936) study, people conformed because they wanted to be correct. One way to be correct is to gather as much information as possible before acting or making a decision. For example, one of the authors was recently in London and had to take a train to the airport. Not knowing where or how to buy a train ticket or where to board the train, she spent time observing what other people were doing. In doing so, she gathered enough information so that she was able to successfully purchase a train ticket and board the correct train. Whenever we use other people's actions or opinions to define reality, we conform because of informational social influence.

Conformity on the basis of informational social influence occurs whenever we are uncertain about the correct or appropriate action. In the Sherif (1936) studies, for example, the task was novel and ambiguous. Under these circumstances, the best course of action is to gather information from other participants, to arrive at the best answer. If we have a great deal of confidence in our knowledge or ability to make the right decision, then there is little reason to rely on others for information. Research suggests that, when our motivation to be correct is high, we tend to conform more when we are uncertain about the correct answer than when we are certain (Baron, Vandello, & Brunsman, 1996).

In Asch's study (1955), people conformed because they wanted to be liked. Conforming to be correct is referred to as *informational social influence*. Conforming to be liked and accepted is referred to as **normative social influence**. Sometimes, as in the Asch line study, people give a clearly wrong answer in order to be liked and accepted by the group. In these situations, the group has a powerful, if unspoken, influence over group members' behavior. In an interesting twist on normative social influence, two social psychologists have investigated "jeer pressure," or the tendency to conform in order to avoid rejection from peers (Janes & Olson, 2000). When we observe another person being rejected by the group, there is a tendency to conform even more strongly to the standards set by the group, presumably to avoid similar rejection from group members.

Situational Conformity

If you think about your own behavior, there probably have been times when you conformed or felt the pressure to conform more than others. Some aspects of a situation lead to more pressure to conform than do others. These factors include the size of the group, group unanimity, commitment to the group, and individuation and deindividuation.

Intuitively, one would predict that the pressure to conform is greater as the **size** of the group increases. Early research (Asch, 1956) suggested that, as group size increased, so did conformity, but only to a point. Once the size of the group reached about three members, conformity seemed to level off. But more recent research (Bond & Smith, 1996) suggests that conformity increases up to a group size of eight members. So, it seems that the larger the group, the greater is our tendency to conform. **Group unanimity** is also important. Imagine being in the Asch line study—in which all of the group members give the (clearly) wrong answer. Now, it is your turn to give your answer. What do you do? Asch's results suggest that you would give the wrong answer at least once. But now imagine that just one other member of the group gives the correct answer, one that disagrees with the other group members. Now, what answer would you give? Research (Asch, 1955; Morris & Miller, 1975) suggests that conformity drops if there is even just one dissenter in the group.

Groups whose members are highly **committed** to the group are more likely to conform to the group than members with less commitment (Forsyth, 1990). Obviously, group members who are highly committed to the group want to be liked and accepted by other group members. One way to ensure being liked and accepted is to go along with the group.

One individual difference variable that predicts the tendency to conform or not is **individuation**. Individuation refers to the desire to be distinguishable from others on some aspect (Maslach, Stapp, & Santee, 1985; Whitney, Sagrestano, & Maslach, 1994). Some people have a greater desire than others to differentiate themselves. Those high in the desire for individuation are less likely to conform than those low in individuation. Conversely, **deindividuation** can increase conformity. When this occurs, people attribute their behavior to being part of the group's behavior, and there is a diffusion of responsibility. People feel less responsible for their actions when those actions take place in a group context than they would if they committed those acts alone.

Power

Implicit in our discussion of influence in groups is power. *Power* is the capacity to influence other people (French & Raven, 1959). In groups, power can be advantageous. Powerful group members can resolve group conflicts more efficiently than those with less power (Levine & Moreland, 1998), and powerful members are better-liked and are deferred to more than less powerful group members (Shaw, 1981). Of course, the possession of power can also serve as a disadvantage: Those with power are granted the responsibility to be effective leaders (Hollander, 1985), exercising

The Tulsa Race Riot, May 31–June 1, 1921

Mobs and riots are one of the most frightening and destructive instances of group behavior, resulting, in part, from situational conformity factors. One example of mob behavior with racist motivations occurred in Tulsa, Oklahoma, in 1921. At that time, Tulsa was home to the most prosperous African American community in the United States, called Greenwood. About 10,000 people lived in this 34-block neighborhood. It was separated from the White community by railroad tracks. Tensions between the Black and White communities increased in May, 1921, when a Black man was accused of assaulting a White woman. Fighting ensued, and on May 31 a White mob pushed the Blacks across the railroad track and proceeded to burn down Greenwood. It soon became evident that the Whites would settle for nothing less than the complete destruction of the Black community and every vestige of Black prosperity. They spread gasoline inside homes and businesses and set them on fire. Blacks fled, some were shot down while they ran, and some burned to death in the buildings. The Whites arrested any Blacks they caught but didn't kill. Before they burned, they looted and stole Blacks' personal property. It still is not known if the mob acted spontaneously, or if it was organized by the KKK or the police or any other entity. For the full story, read Tim Madigan's book, *The Burning* (2001).

power can be stressful (Fodor, 1985), and exercising power can lead to faulty perceptions of oneself and others (Kipnis, 1984). In this section, we examine the bases of power, as well as the reactions of group members to the exercise of power.

One of the most influential typologies of power is French and Raven's (1959; Raven, 1965) critical **bases of power**. The typology assumes that a group member's ability to exert power over another group member or the entire group can be derived from one or more of the following kinds of power: reward, coercive, legitimate, referent, and expert. **Reward power** is defined as the ability to control the distribution of positive and negative reinforcers. In groups, many rewards are to be had: praise for good performance, money for work completed, and trophies for winning championships. Group members who can control the distribution of those rewards are granted the most power. For example, teachers can exert power over students to study hard, because they control the distribution of good grades. Of course, the group member who controls the distribution of rewards is only powerful if the rewards are valued by the group member, the group member depends on the power holder for the reward, and the power holder's promises are sincere (Forsyth, 1990). When a power holder is the only one in the group who can distribute rewards, their position as a power holder becomes more secure.

Coercive power refers to the capacity to punish those who do not comply with requests or demands. For example, if one country threatens another with attacks or boycotts, then the country is using coercive power. Teachers can use coercive power to get students to work harder, by assigning extra work. Research suggests that, given the choice of using reward or coercive power, most will choose reward (Molm, 1987, 1988). Those with **legitimate power** have a right, by virtue of their position, to require compliance. For example, when a military officer orders troops into battle, that officer is exerting legitimate power. With legitimate power, the power holder has the right to exercise power, and the target has a duty to obey the power holder. An interesting characteristic of legitimate power is that the power holder is typically chosen to occupy the position of power, granting them the support of the majority.

When we identify with someone because they are similar to us or because we want to be like them, the person then possesses **referent power**. When someone tries to imitate a teacher or family member, because they want to be like them, this is an example of referent power. Of course, advertisers might make use of referent power, when, for example, they encourage young people to purchase cigarettes, so they will look like the attractive models in the advertisements.

Special knowledge, skill, or ability that one possesses can serve as a basis for **expert power**. Physicians, for example, are often afforded a great deal of power, because of the knowledge and ability they possess. Of course, expert power can only be exerted if the target of power is aware of the power holder's special knowledge or talent (Foschi, Warriner, & Hart, 1985).

Reactions to Use of Power

One of the goals of power exertion is to affect change. When one country threatens to attack another country, if that country does not comply with certain demands, there is an expectation that the target country will change. Of course, other changes may occur in the target country as a result of the use of power tactics, including compliance, attraction, conflict, rebellion, motivation, and self-blame (Forsyth, 1990). **Compliance** occurs when a powerful member of the group asks a less powerful member of the group to do something, and the member does what is asked. This response is consistent with the *complementarity hypothesis* (Carson, 1969; Gifford & O'Connor, 1987; Kiesler, 1983): When one person acts in a powerful manner, the other person becomes submissive. Such a response also ensures that the power holder will retain their power. Of course, the complying group member need not change their attitudes or behaviors permanently. In fact, although a group member agrees to the demands or requests of the power holder, this does not necessarily correspond to a permanent change in behavior or attitude (Kelman, 1958, 1961). Only when the target of power internalizes the power holder's views does a permanent change in behavior or belief occur. Note that compliance is different than conformity, although both types of social influence can result in a change in behavior. Compliance involves behavior motivated by a particular request; conformity involves behavior motivated by a need to be liked or a need to be correct.

Attraction is also affected by having power. A potential consequence of having power is not being liked by targets of power. In general, we tend not to like those who use power in direct and irrational ways (Forsyth, 1990). This is not to suggest that we dislike all powerful people. Research indicates that the targets of power tend to like those who influence them via discussion, persuasion, or expertise, more than those who influence them via manipulation, evasion, or threat (Falbo, 1977). Regarding the bases of power discussed earlier, research shows that managers who use referent power are liked the most, and those who use coercive power are liked the least (Shaw & Condelli, 1986).

Another consequence of the use of power in a group is **conflict** and tension (Forsyth, 1990). Some types of power use engender more conflict than others. For example, group members often respond to coercive power with anger and hostility (Johnson & Ewens, 1971), except in situations when the group is successful (Michener & Lawler, 1975), they have a trusted leader (Friedland, 1976), or the use of coercive power is normative for the group (Michener & Burt, 1975). One problem with responses that involve anger and conflict is that the functioning of the group might be compromised (Forsyth, 1990). One group member's anger can be fueled by another group member's anger, which can result in an escalation of anger and hostility.

Research suggests that, if a group member abuses their power, a typical response is **rebellion** on the part of other group members (Lawler & Thompson, 1978). Abuses of power can also lead to *reactance*, a feeling that one's freedom has been limited or taken away (Brehm, 1976). When group members believe that their freedom (of choice, for example) has been removed, they respond by becoming defiant and refusing to go along with the leader (Worchel & Brehm, 1971).

Motivation can also be influenced when power is exercised in a group. Often, group members are motivated intrinsically, that is, they enjoy being productive and doing good work, because they are personally satisfied by it. But, if a leader uses reward or coercive power, which often involves the use of extrinsic rewards (e.g., money, promises), it can lead group members to become less motivated to work hard and do a good job.

In some circumstances, a leader might be so abusive that they cause group members to suffer tremendously. If group members believe that the world is just, then they are likely to think that they got what they deserve (Lerner & Miller, 1978). That is, they might come to believe that they deserve to suffer and will engage in **self-blame**. A belief such as this allows suffering group members to make sense of their plight.

Group leaders can exercise their power in a number of ways. They have at their disposal several bases of power, some of which are more conducive to certain situations than others. If group leaders have a choice about which bases of power to use, it behooves them to carefully consider the consequences of the use of that base of power. As we have seen, the use of power can engender many reactions, some of which can be good for the functioning and well-being of the group, but others of which can be detrimental to the group.

Minority Influence

A final topic of interest for the study of social influence in groups is minority influence. Sometimes, in groups, there are lone dissenters or a small faction of the group that refuses to go along with the group. Of interest to social psychologists is how successful minorities are in exerting influence on the group. Research suggests that minorities successfully influence majorities under specific circumstances (Kaarbo, 1998; Kaarbo & Beasley, 1998; Moscovici, 1985). First, for minorities to be successful in exerting influence on majorities, they must be consistent in their opposition (Wood, Lundgter, Ouellete, Busceme, & Blackstorie, 1994). Members of a consistent minority are perceived as being more honest and competent (Bassili & Provencal, 1988). If they are inconsistent or appear divided in any way, then their influence is greatly diminished. Second, minorities are more successful if they are able to refute the majority's arguments successfully (Clark, 1990). Third, minorities are more successful if the issue is not of great personal relevance to members of the majority (Trost, Maass, & Kendrick, 1992). Finally, minorities are likely to be successful when they are similar to the majority groups in most respects, except for the disagreement at hand (Volpato, Maass, Mucchi-Faina, & Vitti, 1990). For example, if a member of the Republican party was trying to convince other Republicans to change their views on homeland security, that member would be more successful than if the would-be persuader was a Democrat. In this case, the Republican dissenter is more similar (in terms of party membership) to the majority than is the Democrat.

Successful minorities may be able to change the position of the majority, which, in the political realm, may amount to a policy change. Short of affecting policy as a whole, they may be able to have an indirect effect through pressuring the majority to move in a particular direction, or affecting the information received by the majority. Finally, studies show that minorities can improve the quality of a group's decision making (Nemeth, 1986). Given the inter-agency nature of many government decisionmaking units, which makes the presence of minorities a frequent occurrence, understanding the role of minorities can help us understand both change in policy and shifts in policy. Kaarbo and Gruenfeld (1998) point to a number of examples: Change in Japan's foreign aid policy, from one that emphasized Japan's self-interest to one that reflected humanitarian interest, was the result of a small minority in the foreign ministry, was pitted against the large and powerful ministries of finance and international trade. Soviet policy toward Czechoslovakia, in 1968, was changed by the prointerventionist minority, who, through manipulation of information and the decisionmaking process, moved themselves from the minority to the majority.

GROUP PERFORMANCE

One of the primary functions of a group is to perform a task, and one of the unique characteristics of a group is that its tasks are typically performed in the presence of others. For some groups, tasks are performed in the presence of other people, such as in a factory. For other groups, tasks require that group members depend on one another to successfully complete the task, such as in an assembly line. In this section, we examine research suggesting that sometimes the presence of other people enhances performance (social facilitation) and that, at other times, it hinders performance (inhibition).

Groups are often assumed to accomplish more than individuals and to perform better than individuals. Yet, research suggests that groups do not always perform better than individuals. We examine the various productivity losses in groups, including coordination and motivation losses. Finally, we explore some of the techniques used to help groups function more effectively.

Social Facilitation and Inhibition

Have you ever noticed that, when you run a 5K race, for example, your time is always better than when you time yourself during training? Why is it that the speech you gave in your communications class was better than when you practiced it at home by yourself? In some situations, we appear to perform better in the presence of other people than when alone, which is an effect known as *social facilitation*. One of the first experiments ever conducted in social psychology was designed to examine the effects of the presence of others on an individual's performance. Norman Triplett (1898) tested the hypothesis that people perform better in the presence of others than when alone. In his study, he had children play a game alone or with one other person. His results confirmed his hypothesis: When paired with another person, individual performance is better than when performing alone. This and subsequent research suggests that, if given a choice between working alone or in the presence of other people, we would be better off performing a task in the presence of others.

Now imagine another situation. You are playing on a basketball team. Your coach spends hours helping you learn to shoot a left-handed layup, which is not an easy shot for a right-handed person. When by yourself, you can shoot 20 left-handed layups easily. But what happens when you are playing a game in front of a cheering audience? Evidence suggests that you would miss the layup. This effect, known as *social inhibition*, occurs when the presence of others inhibits performance. According to research in this area, we would be better off working alone than in the presence of others.

These two effects—facilitation and inhibition—seem contradictory. One suggests that working in groups can enhance performance, but the other suggests that it can inhibit it. Zajonc (1965) reconciled these two seemingly contradictory findings, by suggesting that the presence of others enhances performance on well-learned or simple tasks, but inhibits performance on difficult or novel tasks. The presence of other people enhances the tendency to display the *dominant* (well-learned) response and inhibits the tendency to suppress the *nondominant* response. Because running is a fairly simple task, the presence of others during a race should enhance performance. But shooting a left-handed layup when you are right-handed is a difficult task, so the presence of a cheering crowd or other teammates should hurt performance, because our tendency is to shoot the ball with our right hand. A comprehensive review of research in this area basically confirms Zajonc's perspective (Bond & Titus, 1983). The presence of others improves the quantity of performance on simple tasks and decreases the quality and quantity of performance on difficult tasks.

Zajonc's (1965) perspective explains when facilitation and inhibition occur, but why do these effects occur? What is it about the social situation that causes improvement in performance on simple tasks, but decreases performance on difficult tasks? Researchers in the area have developed three explanations: arousal, evaluation apprehension, and distraction. Zajonc (1965, 1980b) argued that the mere presence of others increases the **arousal** level of the performer. When individuals are in a heightened state of arousal, the tendency to display a dominant response is increased. If the dominant response (shooting the ball with your right hand) is the correct one, then social facilitation occurs. If the dominant response is not the correct one, then social inhibition occurs. Cottrell (1972) agrees that the presence of others causes arousal, but he argues that the source of arousal is **evaluation apprehension**, or the anxiety created by the fear that one is being evaluated. In a study to test this idea (Cottrell, Wack, Sekerak, & Rittle, 1968), participants were asked to work on a task alone, in the presence of others who were also working on the task, or in the presence of others who were blindfolded (and thus could not see what participants were doing). The results showed that social facilitation occurred only when the others present could see the participant perform the task. When the possibility of evaluation was removed (in the blindfolded participants' condition), social facilitation did not occur. Finally, according to the **distraction** explanation, the presence of others is potentially distracting. When one is distracted, paying attention to the task at hand can be difficult. Such distractions create conflict as to whether to pay attention to the audience or to the task. When one is distracted, more effort is required to focus attention on the task, thereby improving performance on simple or well-learned tasks. When tasks are difficult, even the increase in effort is not enough to improve performance and usually leads to impaired performance (Baron, 1989; Groff, Baron, & Moore, 1983).

Productivity Losses

As mentioned previously, there is a belief that groups will be more productive than individuals. More than likely, you have been in a group that seems not to have lived up to its fullest potential. Clearly, groups are not always as productive as they should be. According to Steiner (1972), there are two reasons for process losses in groups. One reason is that the responses of individual group members are not combined in a way that enhances group productivity. Decrements in performance caused by poor coordination are known as *coordination losses*. In an operating room, for example, coordination losses occur if the surgeon is not handed the correct surgical instruments. Another reason for productivity losses is known as *motivation losses*. These occur when individual group members fail to exert their maximum effort on a task. The operating room team will not perform at its maximum level if one of the team members does not complete their assignment effectively. Although both coordination and motivation losses in groups are interesting, most attention has been paid to motivation losses. One such motivation loss that has received a great deal of attention is social loafing.

Social loafing refers to the tendency of group members to work less hard when in a group than when working alone. One of the earliest studies of social loafing was conducted by Ringelman (1913), who found that people exerted less effort, when pulling a rope or pushing a cart, if they worked in a group than if they worked alone. In another interesting study (Latane et al., 1979), groups of six participants were asked to wear a blindfold, sit in a semicircle, and listen (via headphones) to the noise of people shouting. Participants were asked to shout as loud as they could, while listening to the noise through their headphones. On some trials, participants believed that they were shouting alone or with one other person. On other trials, they believed that everyone was shouting. When participants thought they were shouting with one other person, they shouted 82% as intensely as when they thought they were alone. When they thought everyone was shouting, they shouted 75% as intensely.

Because social loafing can lead to severe performance decrements in groups, efforts have been made to reduce or eliminate it. First, social loafing can be reduced if each group member's contributions are clearly identifiable (Hardy & Latane, 1986; Kerr & Bruun, 1981). When the possibility of being evaluated is evident, group members appear to give maximum effort (Harkins, 1987). Second, if group members find the work to be interesting and involving, then they are less likely to loaf (Brickner, Harkins, & Ostrom, 1986; Harkins & Petty, 1982; Zaccaro, 1984). Third, if group members take personal responsibility for the group's outcome, then they are less likely to loaf (Kerr & Bruun, 1983). Group members need to believe that their individual efforts will have an impact on the group's outcome.

Improving Productivity

In addition to efforts to reduce social loafing in groups, researchers have developed techniques to help groups function more effectively and avoid production losses of any kind. One such technique is *team development*, which includes a variety of techniques, such as sensitivity training, problem identification, and role analysis (Dyer, 1987). Techniques such as these are designed to improve both the task and interpersonal skills of group members. A similar technique involves the use of *quality circles* (Marks, Mirvis, Hackett, & Grady, 1986). If group members engage in regular meetings to discuss problems with productivity and ways to solve the problems, then productivity losses can often be reduced. Another technique involves the use of *autonomous work groups* (Pearson, 1992). This technique involves the use of self-managed work teams who can control how tasks are performed.

Many of these techniques require that groups change how they function. There are also techniques that focus on individual group members. For example, in *participative goal setting*, individual group members are responsible for setting the group's productivity goals (Pearson, 1987; Pritchard, Jones, Roth, Stuebing, & Ekeberg, 1988). Another technique, *task design*, involves changing the attributes of the task to make it more attractive to group members (Hackman & Lawler, 1971). Both of these techniques involve changing group members' perceptions of the task, rather than the task itself.

GROUP DECISION MAKING

The discussion of group productivity attests to the fact that groups are frequently called upon to perform a variety of activities. An important activity that groups, especially political ones, are often asked to do is to make decisions. Political groups are often responsible for making decisions with large-scale consequences, such as whether to send troops to a region in conflict or to escalate an existing conflict. As in productivity tasks, groups are often assumed to make better decisions than individuals. Groups can pool all of the best resources that individual group members can offer. In this section, we examine the group decision-making process, including how decisions are made, the stages of group decision making, and how individual resources are pooled; then we examine research on the effectiveness of individual versus group decisions. We also look at research suggesting that groups often make bad decisions, and, finally, we explore some tactics to improve the decisions made by groups.

The Decision-Making Process

Imagine that a group of people, such as a jury, have been assembled to make an important decision. A jury spends time listening to testimony and the presentation of evidence. When all of the evidence has been presented, the jury meets to discuss their verdict. At the end of their deliberations, which can last from a couple of minutes to weeks and months, they reach a final, typically unanimous, decision. From the perspective of an observer, the jury appears to leave the courtroom and magically return with a verdict. But what happened between the time the jury left the courtroom to deliberate and when they returned with a verdict? How did this group of people reach a decision about what should happen to the defendant? The group decision-making process has been studied extensively, and several models exist that can help us understand how groups arrive at a decision.

Three-Stage Model of Group Decision Making

According to Bales and Strodtbeck (1951), groups proceed through three stages, before eventually arriving at a decision. In the *orientation* stage, group members spend time defining the problem and planning their strategy for solving the problem. Research (Hackman & Morris, 1975) suggests that most groups spend little time in this phase, assuming that planning is a waste of their time, but that groups who spend a fair amount of time in the orientation phase are more successful than groups that do not (Hackman, Brousseau, & Weiss, 1976; Hirokawa, 1980). In the *discussion* stage, group members spend their time gathering information, identifying and evaluating alternatives. The amount of time groups spend in this stage is also related to the quality of the group's decisions (Harper & Askling, 1980; Laughlin, 1988). However, groups do not often make full use of this stage (Janis & Mann, 1977; Stasser & Titus, 1987). In addition, the use of information by groups at this stage is problematic, in that new information brought forth by one member of the group, but unknown to other members, is not fully considered in discussion. In fact, groups tend to "omit unshared information from discussions while focusing on information that all members already know" (Wittenbaum & Stasser, 1996, p. 5). In the *decision-making* stage, groups choose a solution. How groups combine the individual preferences to reach a group decision can be explained by understanding the group's social-decision scheme.

Social-Decision Schemes

Social-decision schemes refer to the process by which groups combine the preferences of all the members of the group to arrive at a single group decision (Stasser, Kerr, & Davis,

1989). If groups use the *majority-wins rule*, then they combine individual preferences by opting for whatever position is supported by the greatest number of group members. For example, if 10 of 12 jury members believe they should deliver a "guilty" verdict, then the group's final decision will be "Guilty." In the *truth-wins rule*, group members tend to be persuaded by the truth of a particular position. This rule tends to be adopted when group members are discussing facts rather than opinions. Another decision scheme that groups use is the *first-shift rule*, by which groups tend to adopt the decision that is consistent with the first shift in group members' opinions.

Describing social-decision schemes from a research perspective may leave you with a sense that the process occurs without pressures or emotions, but pressures, such as conformity pressures, occur during this process, and they can be extreme. A book describing jury deliberations in a murder case, written by the foreman of the jury, describes the pressure put upon the only person reluctant to vote "Not guilty":

> Without pausing, I took the cards out of my pocket and passed them around. . . . There was silence as the cards started to come back, each folded in half. I counted them. Nine. We waited, and two more came in. Eleven. We waited. Still eleven.
>
> At this point there was no confusion about who still held a card. Adelle [the holdout] sat at the corner of the table to my left. . . . She was looking fixedly away, up, behind her, out the window.
>
> No one spoke. . . . One sensed everyone in the room concentrating on the black card in rapt meditation. Adelle breathed audibly, wrote something rapidly on the card, closed it on itself, and pushed it into the middle of the table.
>
> I placed it, consciously and more or less conspicuously, at the bottom of the pile. I wanted the full dismay of the room to land on her if she had voted for a conviction. Then I began to open the cards and read them: not guilty, not guilty. . . . And the last one: Not guilty. (Burnett, 2001, p. 166)

Groups and Political Decision-Making Units

Political decisions are made in response to a perceived problem, and they tend to occur sequentially, that is, frequently a set of decisions is made, one after another, without pausing to evaluate the effect of each decision along the way. Decisions are also made by different actors, agencies, and coalitions. The type of group making authoritative decisions can have an impact on the policies that result. Hermann (2001) has proposed a model of foreign policy decision making by groups, which can also be used in domestic political contexts. She argues that there are three types of decision-making groups, or units. The **predominant leader** group has "a single individual who has the ability to stifle all opposition and dissent as well as the power to make a decision alone, if necessary" (p. 56). The **single group** is a decision unit that includes "a set of individuals, all of whom are members of a single body, who collectively select a course of action in consultation with each other" (p. 57). This can be an ad hoc group set up to respond to a crisis, such as the Office of Homeland Security established by President Bush after the attack of September 11, 2001, or a standing bureaucracy (which Homeland Security eventually became) or interagency committee. Finally, a **coalition of autonomous actors** is a decision unit that is composed of multiple groups that can act independently. U.S. trade policy, for example, is affected by a wide variety of domestic and international interest groups, multilateral organizations, government bureaucracies, and so forth. Each can act independently, and each has some impact at different times on decisions and policies.

Hermann maintains that each kind of decision-making unit has different decision processes and different behavioral patterns. The first two kinds of decision units can be analyzed with political psychological concepts. In the *predominant leader unit*, the most important factors affecting how the group behaves and makes decisions are the personality characteristics of the leader, which are discussed in chapter 2. The *single group pattern* is determined by group psychology, particularly the techniques used by the group to handle disagreements and conflict in the group. There are three alternatives: groupthink (discussed in more detail later), wherein groups attempt to minimize disagreement by promoting conformity; bureaucratic politics, wherein group members acknowledge that disagreements will occur and attempt "to resolve the conflict through debate and compromise" (Hermann, 2001, p. 65); and finally, the implementation of a social-decision scheme, discussed earlier.

Individual vs. Group Decision Making

Evidence indicates that groups are not necessarily better decision makers than individuals (Hill, 1982). According to Hastie (1986), whether groups make better decisions than individuals often depends on the characteristics of the task. On numerical estimation tasks, for example, group judgments tend to be a little better than the average individual judgment, but on problem-solving tasks, such as logic problems, group solutions tend to be much better than average individual judgments, but worse than the best individual judgment. One of the keys to determining the superiority of group or individual judgments, according to Hastie (1986), is whether the task involves a demonstrably correct solution: When there is, groups tend to perform better than individuals. Some recent research indicates that groups make better decisions than individuals when they have been working together for a long time and the task is important to the group members (Michaelsen, Watson, & Black, 1989; Watson, Michaelsen, & Sharp, 1991).

Individual solutions have also been compared to group solutions in *brainstorming* tasks, which require participants to generate as many different suggestions as they can. Intuition suggests that groups would perform better than individuals on brainstorming tasks (more people should produce more ideas), but research suggests that individuals often produce more and better ideas when working alone than when working in brainstorming groups (Mullen, Johnson, & Salas, 1991; Taylor, Berry, & Block, 1958). Several explanations have been offered for the failure of groups to perform as well as individuals on brainstorming tasks. First, when one group member is speaking, another is prevented from speaking at the same time, which often causes other group members to forget what they were going to say (Brown & Paulus, 1996). This situation might lead to a loss of ideas. Second, group members may have evaluation anxiety and fear that their ideas will be ridiculed by other group members (Camacho & Paulus, 1995). As a consequence, they might be reluctant to share new ideas.

Consistent with the idea that groups often perform worse than do individuals on problem-solving or brainstorming tasks is the notion that groups often make worse decisions than individuals. In fact, many group decisions in political history (e.g., Bay of Pigs, Vietnam War) suggest that groups often make bad decisions with serious consequences. Researchers have identified several faulty decision-making processes, to describe some of the bad decisions that groups make, including groupthink, new group syndrome, bureaucratic politics, group polarization, and the escalation of commitment.

Groupthink

Groupthink refers to an irrational style of thinking that causes group members to make poor decisions (Janis, 1972). Janis maintained that many major political decisions, such as the Bay of

Pigs invasion, US failure to defend against the attack on Pearl Harbor, the Vietnam War, and Watergate, provide evidence for groupthink. According to Janis, (1982), there are a number of observable features of these groups that provide evidence for the existence of groupthink. First, in all of these decision-making groups, group members felt a strong pressure to *conform* to the group. There were strong sanctions for disagreeing with other group members or criticizing their opinions. Second, *self-censorship* was present in most of the groups. Although many group members may have disagreed with the decisions that were being made, they felt pressured to not express these disagreements openly. Third, *mindguards* in the group prevented group members from learning of new information that might disrupt the flow of the group's proceedings. Fourth, there was an *apparent unanimity* of opinion. All of the group members seemed to agree with one another. Fifth, *illusions of invulnerability* allowed group members to feel confident in their decisions. Most group members believed that their judgments could not be wrong. Sixth, *illusions of morality* prevented group members from ever questioning the morality of their decisions. They believed that because they were a member of an elite decision-making group, all of their decisions were moral and justified. Seventh, group members had a *biased perception of the other group*. In the Bay of Pigs decision, a decision by the Kennedy administration to sponsor a group seeking to overthrow Fidel Castro in Cuba in 1961, members of the President's advisory committee believed Castro to be a weak and evil leader. Derogatory comments about Castro were frequently voiced during meetings. Finally, many of the decisions made by these groups represented *defective decision-making strategies*. Decisions made in groupthink situations are often described as "fiascos," "blunders," and "debacles."

In addition to specifying the characteristics of the group and the group decision-making process that indicates evidence for groupthink, Janis (1972) also specified the causes of groupthink. One cause is *cohesiveness*. When groups are very cohesive, as was the case in the Bay of Pigs advisory committee, disagreements are typically held to a minimum, creating the perfect conditions for faulty decision making. Another cause of groupthink is *isolation*. When groups, such as the president's advisory committee, are discussing top-secret issues, they do so in isolation, which prevents outsiders from entering the group to review the group's deliberations. Another cause of groupthink is the presence of a *directive leader*, who has control over the discussion and can prevent any disagreements from being voiced. Finally, *stress* can also create symptoms of groupthink.

In the only booklength study of the groupthink phenomenon, 't Hart (1990/1994) expanded upon Janis's concept by noting that, in addition to groupthink being a product of high in-group cohesion under stress, it may also emerge as the result of **anticipatory compliance** by group members seeking to reach decisions that they believe will meet the views or desires of powerful leaders or peers. Further, 't Hart (1990/1994) notes that the situational conditions in which groupthink becomes most likely include situations of threat and stress (the context emphasized originally by Janis) and situations perceived by group members as major opportunities requiring rapid and major commitment to a pet project or policy to achieve major success (Fuller & Aldag, 1997).

Groupthink has received mixed support (Levine & Moreland, 1998). Some studies support parts of the groupthink model. For example, one study (Tetlock, Peterson, McGuire, Chang, & Feld, 1992) analyzed records of 12 different political decisions and found that it was possible to distinguish between groups whose decisions were indicative of groupthink and those that reflected good decision making. But the research was not especially successful in locating evidence for all of the factors thought to cause groupthink. Other work (Aldag & Fuller, 1993; Fuller & Aldag, 1997) suggests that research has failed to provide convincing support for the existence of groupthink and that the model itself has become an unnecessary constraint upon researchers seeking to adequately examine the true dynamics of group decision making under the conditions explored by Janis. Indeed, Fuller and Aldag suggest, along with many current scholars of political group dynamics (see 't Hart, Stern & Sundelius, 1997), that, rather than proceed with further studies utilizing the outdated groupthink model, scholars should unpack the various component parts from the model and embrace a wider range of new research and literature on group function and dynamics, which better reflects the behavior of actual political decision groups.

New Group Syndrome

Another analysis of conformity problems in group decision making is called *new group syndrome*, which is part of a recent collection of articles seeking to move beyond groupthink ('t Hart et al., 1997). Stern (1997; see also Stern & Sundelius, 1994) uses social psychological findings regarding the life cycle of groups in a reexamination of the Bay of Pigs disaster, one of Janis's groupthink cases. Group cohesion, norms, status hierarchy, and strength of group identity, all change as the group ages. With good performance, cohesion increases. With time, the status hierarchies and role responsibilities become clear and routine. Norms and accepted decision rules are internalized. When groups are new, Stern (1997) argues, members bring with them extragroup baggage, in the form of values, beliefs, and past experiences, which affect the decision making in the new group. In addition, leaders are particularly important in the early stages of a group's life, and that is particularly the case when the leader is the president of the United States. At this stage, leaders can establish roles, norms, and group decision-making processes that lead to effective and critical policy option deliberation, rather than to group conformity. Some leaders do this early on, but others do not, and this leads to new group syndrome. When a leader does not establish norms and decision-making patterns, "there is a serious risk that group interaction will spontaneously evolve in a fashion leading to excessive degrees of conformity or conflict (an abrupt shift into the storming stage)" (Stern, 1997, p. 163). In this early forming stage, the group members are uncertain about how they should behave, are anxious to do a good job, and, therefore, are very vulnerable to conformity pressures, if group leaders do not encourage the opposite by establishing roles, norms, and decision-making procedures. This is new group syndrome. As an explanation of excessive group conformity, it differs from groupthink, in that it is not dependent upon situation pressures such as extreme stress. The phenomenon can occur in any group, in any context.

The Bay of Pigs fiasco shows evidence of new group syndrome. Kennedy had been in office for only 4 months, the plan itself came from the previous administration, Kennedy was under pressure to do something about Castro, and the advisory group he used in making the decision was informal and interagency in nature. Kennedy had campaigned against the Republicans, in part, on the platform that they had been lackadaisical in confronting communism, and he swept away the previous administration's policy-making system. Stern (1997) describes the group culture in the decision-making group as follows:

> A number of analysts have suggested that a norm of "boldness" associated with the "New Frontier" mentality permeated the proceedings. Another important norm appears to have been "rally to the President" when his "project" came under the criticism of outsiders. . . . Another apparent norm that proved dysfunctional was "deference to experts." Finally, an emergent norm of deference to the leader is noticeable, a norm of which the president himself appears to have been unaware. . . . Kennedy, having little previous management experience, reportedly had a relatively simplistic view of small group and organizational management. He placed a premium on talent, believing that this quality was the key to achieving policy and political success. In other words, he

believed that it was enough to assemble a number of talented people, throw them in a room together, and wait for good things to happen. (pp. 174, 177)

What he got instead was failure. The Cuban exiles, sponsored by the United States to invade Cuba and overthrow Castro, landed in a swamp, the Bay of Pigs, and were quickly captured by the Cuban military. The popular uprising against Castro, which they counted on in their plan to overthrow Castro, never happened.

Bureaucratic Politics

Another set of group-related decision-making problems that plague political decisions comes under the rubric of bureaucratic politics. Although political systems differ widely, many political decisions are affected by the interactions of groups based in governmental bureaucracies. Those groups have differing perspectives and interests; they see issues and problems differently, and they compete for policy dominance and resources. At the same time, these groups have to interact in a variety of policy contexts and need to work together. Consequently, their interactions are often characterized as "pulling and hauling," that is, bargaining, coalition formation, compromise, competition, and the selective use and sharing of information to enhance the position of the group or faction in question. The result is policy decision making based upon organizational and group interests, rather than on an objective assessment of the policy issue. The often quoted phrase, "Where you stand depends on where you sit," reflects this pattern.

Early studies of bureaucratic politics focused primarily on the standard operating procedures and conflicts among bureaucratic groups, both of which can negatively affect decision making. The seminal study by Allison (1971), on the Cuban missile crisis of 1962, illustrated the impact of bureaucratic struggles in one of the most dangerous episodes of American foreign policy, which nearly led to nuclear war. Rather than keeping a focus on the national interest, the bureaucracies fought continuously for control of the policy. In August 1962, there were increasing concerns in the Central Intelligence Agency (CIA) that the Soviet Union was placing, or would place, offensive nuclear missiles in Cuba. During the next month, these concerns spread, and the question of whether to send U-2 spy planes to take pictures of Cuba, in search of missile sights, was discussed. This was considered to be a risky enterprise, because of the diplomatic fallout should a U-2 be shot down. Bickering between the Air Force and CIA, over which agency would get to fly the U-2s over Cuba, caused a 10-day delay in spotting the missiles. Those 10 days were crucial for the installation and arming of the missiles and made the conflict that followed, between the United States and USSR, much more dangerous.

More recent studies of bureaucratic politics have focused more precisely on the group nature of decision making in bureaucracies (Preston & 't Hart, 1999; Stern & Sundelius, 1997; Vertzberger, 1990). This has enabled analyses of the whole range of decision-making patterns that can emerge from group interaction in bureaucracies, a range that spans from consensus seeking, the most extreme form of which is groupthink, to extreme intergroup conflict verging on bureaucratic warfare. Consensus and cohesion occurs within groups, particularly when pressured by intense intergroup conflict. Hence, bureaucracies can be the locale of a long continuum of group-produced behaviors (see Figure 4.1).

For example, Preston and 't Hart (1999) have argued that the actual degree to which bureaucratic politics pervades the policy-making process is variable, and that it is important to see bureaucratic politics as a continuum in which such dynamics will have varying degrees of impact (both positive and negative) upon the quality of the decision-making process. They employ three criteria developed by George (1980), for evaluating the quality of decision making on that continuum. The three criteria are *reality testing* (Does information get to the central decision

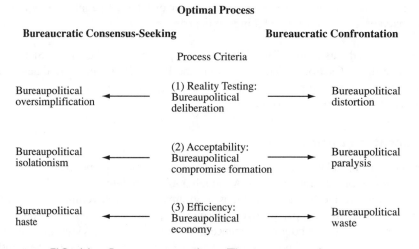

FIG. 4.1.   Bureaucratic politics: The normative dimensions.

makers, and are multiple options considered?), *acceptability* (Are relevant players involved in the decision-making group and are they listened to?), and *efficiency* (What are the costs of the decision-making process?). Preston and 't Hart (1999) argue that, at the consensus end of the spectrum, one sees the decision-making pathologies of bureaupolitical *oversimplification*, when reality testing is poor; *isolationism*, when acceptability is poor; and *hasty decision making*, when efficiency is poor. On the extreme conflict end of the scale, one sees bureaupolitical *distortion*, when reality testing is poor; *paralysis*, when acceptability is poor; and *waste*, when efficiency is poor.

Manipulation

Manipulation occurs when a group member, often a leader, rigs decision making, and may get a group to "accept a commitment which would have been rejected out of hand had the full implications and full extent of the project been revealed from the start" (Stern & Sundelius, 1997, p. 131). Manipulators use at least three strategies: They affect the group's structure, so that their allies dominate decision making; they manipulate the procedures the group follows, by setting the agenda and framing issues in a particular way; and they manipulate their personal relationships with group members, both formally and informally, to put themselves in a favorable position to influence the decision's outcome (Hoyt & Garrison, 1997).

Group Polarization

Groups researchers have long been interested in whether groups make riskier decisions than individuals. Janis's (1972) groupthink model suggests that groups take risky courses of action that cannot be justified. Research on the *risky shift* phenomenon suggests that the decisions made by groups are often riskier than those made by individuals (Stoner, 1961; Wallach, Kogan, & Bem, 1962). But there also exists evidence suggesting that groups sometimes make more cautious decisions than individuals (Wallach et al. 1962), and some evidence suggests that groups make **both** more risky and more cautious decisions (Doise, 1969).

Groups make both very risky and very cautious decisions, compared to individuals. When in a group, there is a tendency to make **extreme** decisions. Whether the decision is extremely risky or extremely cautious depends on what position dominated at the outset of the discussion. **Group polarization** refers to the tendency for individuals' opinions to become more extreme after discussion than before discussion (Myers & Lamm, 1976). For example, if group member A's pre-group-discussion opinion tended to be moderately cautious, then their post-group-discussion opinion would probably be extremely cautious. Likewise, if group member B's pre-group-discussion opinion was moderately risky, it will become even more risky after group discussion. Although there is a tendency to assume that extreme decisions, in either direction, are bad decisions, such is not the case. Extremely risky or cautious decisions can have positive or negative outcomes.

A number of explanations have been offered to account for polarization effects. One explanation is based on the *persuasive arguments perspective*, which assumes people are likely to be exposed to persuasive arguments that favor their initial position (Burnstein & Vinokur, 1977). Although group discussions are likely to contain some arguments for and against an individual's initial position, there is a tendency to sample information that is consistent with our own point of view. Such biased information sampling is likely to shift a group member's opinion further in the direction of their initial position. Additionally, a group member is likely to share their initial position with the rest of the group. The mere expression and restatement of ideas may increase the shift toward a more extreme view (Brauer, Judd, & Gliner, 1995). Those members committed to a more risk-prone decision may be more committed, more vocal, and hence more influential in persuading others. However, as Vertzberger notes (1997), when more cautious members are more committed, they can sway the group toward that pole.

Another explanation for group polarization is based on *social comparison* processes. According to this perspective, group members often compare themselves to others, in order to gain approval for their views. Comparisons with other group members might lead to the realization that others have similar opinions and still others have more extreme opinions. Motivated by a need to be viewed positively by other group members, individuals may shift their opinions to a more extreme position (Brown, 1974; Myers, 1978). Social comparison processes can be so strong that polarization can be produced by merely knowing of others' positions, in the absence of exposure to supporting arguments (Isenberg, 1986).

A third explanation for group polarization is based on *social identity* processes (Hogg, Turner, & Davidson, 1990; Mackie, 1986). According to this perspective, group discussion causes individual group members to focus on the group, which can often lead to pressures toward conformity. Rather than perceiving the average opinion of the group, individual group members often perceive the group's opinion to be more extreme. Pressures to conform lead individuals to adopt a position that is more extreme than their initial position.

Escalation of Commitment

In making political decisions, people sometimes decide on a course of action that proves detrimental to the achievement of their goals. Both individuals and groups can become overly committed to these failing endeavors. Situations such as these have been referred to as escalation situations (Staw & Ross, 1989), or situations in which some course of action has led to losses, but in which there is a possibility of achieving better outcomes by investing further time, money, or effort (Brockner, 1992; Staw & Ross, 1987, 1989). Thus, there is still a glimmer of hope that, by investing additional resources, the project will become successful. Three characteristics define escalation situations (Staw & Ross, 1987). First, escalation situations involve some loss or cost. Second, there must be a lapse in time from the initial decision: Escalation situations do not refer to one-shot decisions; instead, they refer to a series of decisions made over time. Third, withdrawal from the situation is not obvious or easy. Countless examples of these escalation situations exist at both the individual and group levels (Ross & Staw, 1986). Individual-level examples include a person deciding whether to invest more money in a broken car or in a declining stock.

Decision making during the war in Vietnam illustrates the impact of commitment. In his memoir, former Secretary of Defense Robert McNamara reviews the debates within the policy advisory circles of the Johnson administration. The administration, under the influence of the *domino theory* prominent during the Cold War, believed that, if South Vietnam were overtaken by the communist government of North Vietnam, regimes all over Asia would become communist as well, like dominoes falling. Yet the government of the South was corrupt and illegitimate, and the determination of the North, as well as of the Viet Cong (the guerrillas operating in the South) was clear. Important voices in the military warned that the administration's hopes in 1964—that the insurgency problem could be solved by bombing the North, thereby eliminating the need for U.S. ground troops—would not work. Bombing North Vietnam into oblivion would still not stop the Viet Cong's efforts to overthrow the government of South Vietnam. They also knew, from an intelligence report, that the chances of a stable South Vietnamese government emerging—one with popular support and that could pursue the war on its own terms—was very unlikely. As McNamara (1995) recalls:

> These two assessments should have led us to rethink our basic objective and the likelihood of ever achieving it. We did not do so, in large part because no one was willing to discuss getting out. . . . We . . . wished to do nothing that might lead to a break in the "commitment dike" as long as there appeared to be some alternative. . . . It is clear that disengagement was the course we should have chosen.
>
> We did not.
>
> Instead we continued to be preoccupied by the question of which military course to follow. (pp. 154, 164).

They decided to pursue a course that led to a quagmire from which they could not and would not extract themselves, a situation causing thousands of American and Vietnamese casualties, which would have been avoided by an earlier withdrawal of American military forces.

Project, psychological, social, and organizational factors could all affect escalation behavior. Project factors are the most obvious determinants of commitment to a failing course of action. The manner in which a failing project is structured seems to influence whether an individual or group withdraws from it or persists. One such factor is whether a setback is the result of permanent or temporary causes (Leatherwood & Conlon, 1987). Commitment is more likely to escalate when the setback results from a temporary cause. In the Vietnam case, the focus upon military options led the decision-making group to think that a change in military strategy would work and that their inability to win the war was a temporary result of incorrect military strategy, rather than the result of permanent irremediable political realities. Similarly, when future costs required for the project's success are expected to be small, commitment is more likely to escalate (Brockner, Rubin & Lang, 1981). Escalation of commitment can also depend on how often previous commitments have succeeded (Goltz, 1992; Hantula, 1992; McCain, 1986). When previous investments have been successful, people are more likely to escalate their commitment to a project, even when the project is currently failing. Commitment to a failing project is also more likely to escalate if the size of the initial investment is relatively large (Teger, 1980). Finally, escalation of commitment is stronger when the size of the payoff from continued investment is likely to be high (Rubin & Brockner, 1975).

There are also several psychological factors that can influence persistence in an escalation situation. Information-processing errors, for example, can be very important. Individuals often misinterpret or seek data in a manner that supports their beliefs (Frey, 1986), thus strengthening their commitment to a failing course of action (Bazerman, Beekun, & Schoorman, 1982; Caldwell & O'Reilly, 1982; Conlon & Parks, 1987). A related factor is the type of goal individuals set before initiating the project. If people do not set explicit goals about the maximum size of their investment (Kernan & Lord, 1989) or the extent of their commitment (Brockner, Shaw, & Rubin, 1979), then they are likely to escalate their commitment to a failing project. The pattern was also evident in Vietnam. The escalation of force was gradual and incremental, with no set limit on size or time at which point there would be an evaluation of the effort to determine if it had failed, and no upper limit was identified on how many U.S. troops would be committed.

Self-justification is another psychological factor that has been shown to influence commitment. Individuals often commit further resources to a losing course of action to justify previous behavior, such as advocating the project in the first place (Bazerman et al., 1982; Bazerman, Giuliano, & Appelman, 1984; Staw, 1976; Staw & Fox, 1977). Recent research suggests that conscientiousness can also impact whether individuals escalate their commitment. When individuals felt a sense of duty, they escalated less than did individuals who were motivated by an achievement obligation (Moon, 2001). Finally, groups whose members identify strongly with their group are more likely to escalate their commitment to a failing project than groups whose members identify weakly with a project (Dietz-Uhler, 1996).

Another set of factors that can influence the escalation of commitment is social in nature. One such factor is the need for external justification. Individuals or groups may persist in order to save face or avoid losing credibility with others (Brockner et al., 1981; Fox & Staw, 1979). Another factor that might influence persistence is external binding, which occurs when individuals or groups become strongly linked with their actions related to a project. For example, a project may become so associated with the primary decision maker (e.g., Reaganomics) that withdrawal is difficult or impossible (Staw & Ross, 1989). Research on the "hero effect" has found that, under some conditions, people who remain committed to a failing project are evaluated more favorably than people who withdraw (Staw & Ross, 1989).

Finally, structural or organizational factors can also influence commitment to a failing project. One such determinant of persistence is institutional inertia. Because change in an organization (especially a large organization) is often difficult, it may seem easier to persist in a losing course of action than to somehow mobilize the organization for change (Staw & Ross, 1989). Another organizational determinant of persistence is the operation of political forces. There may be strong political support for the continuation of a project, even though it is not economically feasible. Groups that are interdependent or politically aligned with a project may also demand support for it (Staw & Ross, 1989). Finally, cultural norms can also affect the likelihood of escalating commitment (Geiger, Robertson, & Irwin, 1998; Greer & Stephens, 2001).

Escalation of commitment to a failing project is a robust phenomenon. Escalations of commitment have been demonstrated in many laboratory and real-life situations, and many factors have been shown to account for the phenomenon in such situations: What is so intriguing is that the decisions appear to be so irrational. From a rational point of view, it often seems that the best choice in these situations is to withdraw and avoid greater losses. However, several researchers (Barton, Duchon, & Dunegan, 1989; Beeler, 1998; Beeler & Hunton, 1997; Bowen, 1987; Northcraft & Neale, 1986; Northcraft & Wolf, 1984) have noted that decisions to continue investment in a failing project are not necessarily irrational, at least from the perspective of the decision maker(s). For example, Northcraft & Wolf (1984), and Whyte

(1986) have argued, from an information-processing perspective, that the manner in which decisions are framed determines whether individuals escalate their commitment to a failing project. If a decision is framed as a certain loss, then people tend to abandon the project. However, if a decision is framed as an attempt to recoup an investment, then people tend to escalate their commitment to the project. In escalation situations, decisions are often framed as an attempt to recoup an investment. Thus, to an outside observer, these decisions seem to be irrational, but, to the decision maker(s), they can seem quite rational, because of the way in which they have been framed.

Improving Group Decisions

Because the decisions made by groups have often been disappointing, efforts have been made to develop techniques to improve groups' decisions. One technique that has been suggested is to appoint a group member to serve as a devil's advocate (Hirt & Markman, 1995). The role of the devil's advocate is to disagree with and criticize whatever plan is being considered by the group. This technique can be effective, because it encourages group members to think more carefully about the decisions they are contemplating. A related approach involves the use of authentic dissent, in which one or more members of the group actively disagree with the group's initial plans, without being assigned to this role (Nemeth, Connell, Rogers, & Brown, 2001). This technique can be effective, because it encourages the group to consider alternatives and often moves the group away from their initial preferences.

A technique that makes a great deal of sense in political decision making is **multiple advocacy** (George, 1980; George & Stern, 2002). In this process, manipulation is avoided by having the deliberation procedures managed by a neutral person, a custodian manager, while the advocates of different positions are allowed to fully develop their proposals and advocate the advantages. Mutual criticism by the advocates of various proposals should, in theory, flesh out the strengths and weaknesses of the different policy options. This is done for the benefit of the final decision maker, or chief executive (the president, prime minister, etc.), who listens, evaluates the options, and makes an informed decision. Many American presidents have tried to use this approach for improving decision making in their administrations. In fact, the National Security Council (NSC), and particularly the national security advisor, has evolved into the role of the custodian manager, since its foundation in 1947. As George (1980) describes it, the NSC has taken on a number of tasks in its role as custodian manager:

1. Balancing actor resources within the policymaking system
2. Strengthening weaker advocates
3. Bringing in new advisers to argue for unpopular options
4. Setting up new channels of information so that the president and other advisors are not dependent upon a single channel
5. Arranging for independent evaluation of decisional premises and options, when necessary
6. Monitoring the workings of the policy-making process to identify possibly dangerous malfunctions and institute appropriate corrective action (pp. 195–196)

Nevertheless, establishing and consistently using a multiple advocacy system to improve group decision making is difficult, and many presidents fail to keep it alive. First, the custodian manager has to ensure that a wide range of views and proposals is heard and that the appropriate people are involved in the group deliberations. This is difficult to achieve, particularly given the fact that this role is typically held by someone from the administration and therefore a person with their own political perspective and career, subject to pressure from many different agencies and individuals ('t Hart, 1997). For similar reasons, it is difficult for the chief executive to use the system. Choosing the best option is often impossible, because of domestic or international political pressures and obstacles. Finally, some presidents, such as Ronald Reagan, do not want to hear the debate and discussion of multiple options.

CONFLICT IN GROUPS

When people are working together to achieve a goal, there will inevitably be some conflict, which occurs when group members believe their goals are not compatible (Pruitt & Rubin, 1986). Group members can conflict with another in many ways. For example, if group members have to compete for scarce resources, conflict can arise. Group members can also experience conflict when one group member tries to exert influence or gain prestige in the group (Levine & Moreland, 1998). In this section, we examine the various types of conflict that can ...... particularly in situations in which group members are motivated to both com-......te. A discussion of the causes of conflict in groups follows, then we briefly ......ation of coalitions in groups. Finally, we examine strategies designed to re-......roups.

......flict: Social Dilemmas

......arch on conflict in groups examines mixed-motive situations—ones in which ......compete is mixed with the motivation to cooperate. Perhaps the most famous ......me is the **prisoner's dilemma game** (Luce & Raiffa, 1957; see Figure 4.2). Research of this type is used to determine how tendencies to cooperate and compete can lead to various outcomes for groups. In this game, participants cannot communicate with one

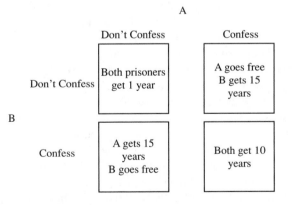

FIG. 4.2.   The prisoner's dilemma. In this classic game, two prisoners, A and B, accused of a crime, have the options of confessing or not confessing. If they maintain their alliance and neither confesses, both get short sentences. If each of them confesses, they each get a heavy sentence. But if one confesses and the other does not, the prisoner who confessed is rewarded with freedom, while the one who did not confess gets a severely heavy sentence. The dilemma for each prisoner is that, if he trusts the other not to confess, his best option is to rat out his partner in crime.

another, yet the outcome of the game for each person is contingent on what the other person decides. The game is set up so that, (1) if both players cooperate, they receive a moderately favorable outcome; (2) if one cooperates and the other competes, the cooperator receives an unfavorable outcome and the competitor receives a favorable outcome; and (3) if both players compete, they receive a moderately unfavorable outcome. In this situation, the dilemma is whether to compete or cooperate. The situation is rigged, so that both players benefit equally if they cooperate, but there is a tendency to not trust the other player, so many people compete (Pruitt & Kimmell, 1977). More recently, research on mixed-motive interactions has used an N-person social dilemma that is, a social dilemma with more than two people (Levine & Moreland, 1998). In these dilemmas, several outcomes are possible. First, a player always benefits more from a noncooperative than cooperative choice. Second, a noncooperative choice is harmful to others in the group. Third, the amount of harm to others, as a result of a noncooperative choice, is larger than the profit received as a result of any choice.

There are several types of social dilemmas (Messick & Brewer, 1983). In a **collective trap**, behaviors that reward an individual group member can be harmful to the rest of the group, especially if engaged in by enough group members. For example, during a water shortage, individuals who use too much water harm everyone else by prolonging the shortage. The best strategy for the collective is if each individual takes a little. In **collective fences**, the entire group is harmed if behaviors that are costly to individuals are avoided by enough people. For example, if each person does not donate money to medical research, then everyone will be worse off. The best strategy is for everyone to give a little. In either situation, people are tempted to "free ride" or enjoy the group's resources without penalty. Research using collective traps and collective fences can tell us much about human tendencies to be selfish or prosocial, as well as how a person's value orientation (e.g., cooperative or competitive) can influence their behavior in social dilemmas.

Causes of Conflict

Conflicts, such as social dilemmas, typically arise when group members have competing goals or see their goals as being incompatible. There are many factors that can contribute to the origination of conflict, as well as to its escalation. In the previous chapter, the concept of **attributions** was introduced. They play a role in group conflict, as well as in individual perceptions. *Attributions* refer to the explanations generated for the causes of our own and others' behavior. Imagine playing a prisoner's dilemma game, in which you realize that the best strategy is for you to cooperate, but your partner seems to always make the competitive choice. Why? There are many reasons why your partner makes the competitive choice: Perhaps they do not understand the game; perhaps they were told by the experimenter to make consistently competitive choices; or maybe they are just an evil person. Attributing the cause of another's behavior to dispositional, rather than situational, factors is the **fundamental attribution error** (Ross, 1977). If, during conflict, we blame another group member, conflict is likely to escalate, rather than to be resolved (Forsyth, 1990). Thus, if you blame your partner's personality for the competitive choices they make, then you are likely to also make competitive choices. People also have a tendency to perceive their own views as correct and objective, but to perceive others' views to be biased (Keltner & Robinson, 1997; Robinson, Keltner, Ward, & Ross, 1995). A consequence of this bias in perception is that we are likely to exaggerate the difference in perspective between ourselves and another group member, which is likely to serve as fuel for conflict.

Second, when in potential conflict situations, communicating effectively can be difficult. Sometimes, group members criticize one another harshly. If you have ever been on the receiving end of harsh criticism, then you realize that it can be unpleasant and uncomfortable. Such discomfort can often instigate revenge, which only serves to escalate the conflict (Cropanzano, 1993). If group members do not communicate reasonably and effectively, then conflict will likely occur and may even be escalated. One particularly destructive variant of faulty communication is *nay-saying*, a pattern in which group discussions are crippled and paralyzed by negativism and bickering over everything, down to the smallest details of a decision (Stern & Sundelius, 1997). Whenever conflict becomes stronger, so do anxiety and tension (Blascovich, Nash, & Ginsburg, 1978; Van Egeren, 1979). According to the arousal/aggression hypothesis (Berkowitz, 1989), group members become frustrated when they are unable to attain their goals. Frustration can lead to aggression, which is often displayed by lashing out at other group members. If group members are aggressive, then conflict will occur and probably escalate.

Finally, in the review of the research on escalation of commitment, we learned how group members can easily become committed to a course of action, even if it is a failing one. Group members can also become committed to their viewpoints, especially when they are under attack (Staw & Ross, 1987), for several reasons. First, we tend to seek information to confirm, rather than to refute, our beliefs (Petty & Cacioppo, 1986). Such action tends to make us even more committed to our beliefs. Second, in a public situation, there is often a desire to appear strong and having conviction in our beliefs. Third, once an individual commits to a belief, they rationalize their choice by overestimating its favorableness and increasing their dedication to it (Batson, 1975). Fourth, attacks from other group members can create reactance (Brehm, 1976), which occurs whenever we sense a loss of freedom. The consequence is that we become even more committed to our belief or position.

Coalitions

Sometimes, conflicts exist between more than two group members. Sometimes, group members persuade other group members to join forces by forming a **coalition**, a small collection of group members who cooperate in order to achieve a mutually desired goal. Coalitions have a number of characteristics in common (Forsyth, 1990). First, they all typically involve group members who disagree on fundamental issues, but who decide to set aside those differences and focus on the problem at hand. Second, they form for the purpose of achieving certain goals. Third, coalitions tend to be temporary, and there is often little commitment on the part of the participants, except to the current goal. Fourth, coalitions typically form in mixed-motive situations: Group members who formerly competed with one another must cooperate to achieve the current goal. Fifth, coalitions are adversaries. The goal is to make sure, in the end, that they are better off and that another coalition is worse off.

There are a number of theories that have been put forth to explain when and why certain coalitions are likely to form. According to **minimum-resource theory** (Gamson, 1961, 1964), group members form coalitions on the basis of equal input–equal output. That is, the most likely grouping of people is one that involves the fewest number of people with the fewest number of resources, yet that is most likely to win. The theory makes two assumptions: First, people in groups are primarily motivated by the need to maximize power and payoffs and believe that forming coalitions will satisfy this goal; second, members of coalitions believe that the distribution of power and rewards should be divided equally among the members of the coalition.

Another theory that explains when and why coalitions form is **minimum-power theory** (Shapley, 1953). According to this theory, coalition members expect payoffs that are directly proportional to their ability to turn a losing coalition into a winning one. This type of power is referred to as pivotal power (Miller, 1980). In this theory, power, not resources, is the most important determinant of coalition formation. The pivotal power of any group member is determined by the number of times that member could turn a winning coalition into a losing one by withdrawing from the coalition. Thus, coalitions form on the basis of the highest chances of winning with the lowest amount of pivotal power.

According to **bargaining theory** (Komorita & Nagao, 1983), coalitions form on the basis of considering expected payoffs, which are based on norms of equity and equality, and group members will appeal to whichever norm provides them with the largest payoff. This theory assumes that group members prefer to form coalitions with those who will not withdraw. It also assumes that the amount of payoff may change over time, to compensate for extra rewards given to coalition members who are being tempted to join another coalition.

In addition to these theories of coalition formation, research has identified other factors that influence the formation of coalitions, including the number and size of existing coalitions (Komorita & Miller, 1986; Kravitz, 1987), expectations of each group member in forming coalitions (Miller & Komorita, 1986), and the availability of other influence strategies that do not require the formation of coalitions (Komorita, Hamilton, & Kravitz, 1984).

Conflict Resolution

Conflicts in groups can be difficult, but they are not impossible to resolve. Groups have at their disposal a number of tactics to help them resolve disputes and disagreements. Forsyth (1990) suggests a number of techniques that groups can use to settle conflicts. Groups can engage in **imposition**, in which one coalition or subgroup is forced to accept another subgroup's position. Another tactic is **withdrawal**, in which one collective leaves the group. Parties can also do nothing or as little as possible about the conflict, which is a tactic referred to as **inaction**. Disagreeing parties can **yield**, so that one side withdraws their demands. Parties can also **compromise**, meaning that acceptable alternatives are located somewhere between two conflicting parties' positions. Finally, groups can **problem solve**: They can try to identify the source of the conflict, then agree to a solution.

Of course, groups are not always able to resolve conflicts on their own. Sometimes, a **third-party intervention** is necessary. Third parties can help to reduce conflict in a group by serving various functions (Forsyth, 1990). First, they allow both groups to express themselves, by providing a safe and peaceful environment. Second, they can help disputing parties communicate more clearly and effectively. Third, they can allow disputing parties to save face by putting the burden for compromise on the negotiator, rather than on the compromising party. Fourth, they may have the ability to generate ideas and solutions that neither party considered. Fifth, they are given the power to set the location, time, and composition of meetings between the disputing parties. Research suggests that third-party interventions are most effective when the conflict is very intense (Hiltrop & Rubin, 1982); otherwise, the third party may simply make minor conflicts more severe.

CONCLUSION

This chapter reviewed some of the central findings from psychological research on groups and their behavior. We have also reviewed some of the key patterns of group behavior in politics, and we have discussed how and why groups form, how they make decisions, and what problems arise in group decision making. We examined intra- and intergroup conflict dynamics, as well as some techniques for conflict resolution. Several of the chapters that follow provide additional information and illustrations of group behavior. Chapter 5 provides examples of small-group dynamics in leadership management styles. Chapters 7 and 8 provide examples of group behavior in cases of race, ethnic, and nationalist group conflicts. Chapter 9 looks at the behavior of extremist groups, such as terrorist organizations, perpetrators of genocide, and others. Chapter 9 provides several illustrations of obedience to, and compliance with, groups demands.

Topics, Theories/Explanations, and Concepts Covered in Chapter 4

Topics	Theories/Explanations	Concepts
Definition of groups		Entiativity
Central characteristics: size, composition, type		
Group structure: status, roles, norms, cohesion	Expectation states theory Ethological theories	
Group formation	Functional perspective Interpersonal attraction perspective	
Group development		Stages: forming, storming, norming, performing, adjourning
Influence in groups		Conformity
Conformity	Informational social influence Normative social influence	
Situational conformity	Group size Group unanimity Commitment to the group Individuation	
Minority influence		
Power: reward, coercive, legitimate, referent, expert		
Reaction to power: compliance, attraction, conflict, rebellion, motivation, self-blame	Complementarity hypothesis	
Group performance		
Social facilitation and inhibition	Arousal Evaluation apprehension Distraction	
Productivity losses	Social loafing	
Group decision making	Three-stage model	
Groups and political decision-making units		Predominant leader Single group Coalitions

Topics, Theories/Explanations, and Concepts Covered in Chapter 4
(continued)

Topics	Theories/Explanations	Concepts
Group decision making	Groupthink New group syndrome Bureaucratic politics Manipulation Group polarization Escalation of commitment	
Improving group decisions		
Conflict in groups		Social dilemmas Collective traps Collective fences
Causes of conflict	Faulty attributions Faulty communications Biased perceptions Personality Commitment Arousal and aggression	
Coalitions	Minimum-resource theory Minimum-power theory Bargaining theory	
Conflict resolution		

KEY TERMS

Autokinetic effect
Bargaining theory
Coercive power
Cohesion
Collective fences
Collective trap
Conformity
Deindividuation
Entiativity
Escalation of commitment
Expected payoffs
Forming

Fundamental
   interpersonal relations
   orientation (FIRO)
Group
Group development
Group polarization
Groupthink
Minimum-power theory
Minimum-resource
   theory
Norming
Norms

Performing
Prisoner's dilemma
Referent power
Reward power
Roles
Social-decision schemes
Social loafing
Status
Storming
Three-stage model of
   group decision making
Third-party intervention

SUGGESTIONS FOR FURTHER READING

Forsyth, D. R. (1990). *Group dynamics*. Pacific Grove, CA: Brooks/Cole.
George, A., & Stern, E. (2002). Harnessing conflict in foreign policy making: From devil's advocate to multiple advocacy. *Presidential Studies Quarterly, 32,* 484–508.

Janis, I. L. (1982). *Groupthink: Psychological studies of policy decisions and fiascoes* (2nd ed.). Boston: Houghton Mifflin.

LeBon, G. (1960). *The crowd: A study of the popular mind.* New York: Viking. (Original work published in 1895).

Levine, J. M., & Moreland, R. L. (1998). Small groups. In D. T. Gilbert, S. T. Fiske & G. Lindzeq. (Eds.) *The handbook of social psychology* (4th ed., pp. 415–469). New York: McGraw-Hill.

Moscovici, S., & Doise, S. (1994). *Conflict and consensus: A general theory of collective decisions.* London: Sage.

Prentice, D., & Miller, D. (Eds.). (1999). *Cultural divides: Understanding and overcoming group conflict.* New York: Sage.

Preston, T., & 't Hart, P. (1999). Understanding and evaluating bureaucratic politics: The nexus between political leaders and advisory systems. *Political Psychology, 20,* 49–98.

't Hart, P. (1994). *Groupthink in government: A study of small groups and policy failure.* Baltimore: Johns Hopkins University Press. (Original work published 1990).

't. Hart, P., Stern, E. K., & Sundelius, B. (1997). *Beyond groupthink: Political group dynamics and foreign policy-making.* Ann Arbor: University of Michigan Press.

CHAPTER 5

The Study of Political Leaders

The preceding chapters have developed a number of important concepts, theories, and analytical frameworks in political psychology. We can now turn to an examination of important topics in political psychology, and we begin with a look at leaders. In this chapter, aspects of personality, cognition, and small-group behavior, all considered in depth in the previous chapters, are brought together to explore political leaders' management and leadership styles. We begin with a consideration of types of leaders, then explore a number of analytical frameworks. The case of President Bill Clinton is used to illustrate the concepts in leader analysis. The Political Being considered in this chapter is, of course, a leader. The elements of the Political Being of interest in this chapter are personality, cognition, emotion, and also the interaction with *us*, that is, political in-groups in the form of advisors.

We can begin with an illustration of the importance of the personality of political leaders. In recalling the Cuban Missile Crisis, Robert Kennedy remarked: "The fourteen people involved were very significant—bright, able, dedicated people, all of whom had the greatest affection for the U.S. . . . If six of them had been President of the U.S., I think that the world might have been blown up" (Steel, 1969, p. 22). Robert Kennedy's chilling observation about the men within President John F. Kennedy's decision-making group (Executive Committee of the National Security Council or Ex Comm), during the Cuban Missile Crisis of 1962, dramatically illustrates the importance of personality and other individual leader characteristics in politics. What a leader is like, in terms of personality, background, beliefs, and style of leadership, can have a tremendous impact upon the policy-making process and its outcomes. In the case of Cuba, Kennedy's pragmatism, sensitivity to the needs of his adversaries, his openness to advice and feedback from his staff, and his own extensive, personal foreign policy expertise, led to a willingness on his part to debate the pros and cons of the airstrike option (which he initially favored) and to consider arguments in favor of the less confrontational blockade option to remove the Soviet missiles. Within the decision group itself, Kennedy's collegiality enabled advisers to express their unvarnished opinions during Ex Comm sessions, and his desire for outside advice led to the inclusion within the group of several notable foreign policy experts from outside of his administration. More important, his willingness to consider the possible consequences of his policy actions and his sensitivity to the need for his opponent (Khrushchev) to have a face-saving way out of the crisis enabled Kennedy to successfully avoid war (Allison, 1971; Allison & Zelikon, 1999; Preston, 2001).

Would a different president have brought the same personal qualities or style of leadership to the situation? For Robert Kennedy, the answer was clearly, No. Among the Ex Comm advisers, there were many who lacked Kennedy's pragmatism, favoring instead an aggressive, immediate response to resolve the crisis. Others lacked his empathy toward Khrushchev and his awareness of his opponent's domestic political position. Some clearly had less need for information when making decisions, less desire to search out alternative viewpoints on policy matters, and far lower tolerances for dissent or disagreement over policy than had Kennedy.

Had any of these individuals been president instead of JFK, the outcome of the Cuban Missile Crisis might have been very different indeed.

In his classic book *Leadership* (1978), Burns describes *two basic types of leadership*: the **transactional** and **transformating**. According to Burns (1992), "Leadership over human beings is exercised when persons with certain motives and purposes mobilize, in competition or conflict with others, institutional, political, psychological, and other resources so as to arouse, engage, and satisfy the motives of followers" (p. 24). This definition is significant, because it distinguishes between relationships based upon naked power and those based upon leadership. For Burns, true leadership involves a relationship between the leader and followers, in which the leader taps the motives of followers, in order to realize mutually held goals. This can take the form of either *transactional* leadership, in which the leader approaches followers with an eye toward exchanging one valued thing for another (e.g., jobs for votes, subsidies for campaign contributions, etc.), or *transformational* leadership, in which leaders engage their followers in such a way that they raise each other to higher levels of motivation and morality. As Burns (1992) describes it:

> Transforming leadership ultimately becomes *moral* in that it raises the level of human conduct and ethical aspiration of both leader and led, and thus it has a transforming effect on both. Perhaps the best modern example is Gandhi, who aroused and elevated the hopes and demands of millions of Indians and whose

Are Leaders Born or Made?

A substantial debate in leadership studies has revolved around the issue of whether leaders are born or are made. The "**great man**" **theory of leadership** suggests that people who become leaders are special, that they have personal qualities or characteristics that set them apart from nonleaders. According to this line of thinking, Abraham Lincoln and Winston Churchill were special and would have become great leaders, even in the absence of the crises during which they emerged (the American Civil War and World War II, respectively). On the other hand, the **situational (or zeitgeist) theory of leadership** holds that it is the context that is special, not the person, and that the situation itself determines the type of leaders and leadership that will occur. For example, in the absence of the outbreak of the World War II and Chamberlain's political humiliation by Adolf Hitler at Munich, Winston Churchill would have remained in the shadows and never risen to the rank of British prime minister. It was the particular nature of the times and the dire crisis facing Britain (i.e., the hardships of the blitz, Britain's isolation and lack of allies, and the danger of imminent invasion by Germany) that created the stage for the charismatic, strong, uncompromising Churchill to lead. Further, just as the war had created the proper situational context for Churchill's leadership, the end of the war resulted in a dramatically altered context and his defeat in the first postwar national elections in 1945. Thus, it was the convergence of a unique situation with an individual whose personal qualities matched up well with the requirements of the situation that led to the emergence of Churchill's leadership.

life and personality were enhanced in the process. Transcending leadership is dynamic leadership in the sense that the leaders throw themselves into a relationship with followers who will feel "elevated" by it and often become more active themselves, thereby creating new cadres of leaders. (p. 26)

On the other hand, the use of naked power is not leadership, but instead is based purely upon a coercive, one-sided relationship with followers, built upon a leader's own power position or resources (Burns, 1992). No exchange of valued commodities takes place and the followers' motives are irrelevant to the leader. Instead, the leader employing naked power enters into neither a transactional or transformational relationship with followers, but merely forces them to comply with the leader's own desires.

Later scholars, such as Kellerman (1984), have expanded upon Burn's explicitly moral, normative definition of transformational leadership, by including the notion that such leaders can also tap into their follower's needs for authority or for the "security of a firm and coercive program" (p. 81). Thus, the transformation brought about by the leader can be either elevating (as Burns argues) or debasing. In particular, charismatic leaders often embody, for followers, by virtue of their unusual personal qualities, the promise or hope of salvation (or deliverance from distress) and, as a result, take on a transformational role: This relationship, in which the leader evokes so strong an emotional response that his misdeeds and mistakes are ignored or trivialized, can lead to elevation or disaster. If the charismatic leader is transforming, they will, according to Burns (1978), capitalize on the strength of their followers' devotion and engagement, to improve humanity. But another kind of charismatic leader, such as Hitler or Jim Jones, will lead his still-willing followers to destruction. Yet, whether we who are outside the group judge the charismatic leader to be benign or malignant, the main point here is that they apparently emerge in response to some deeply felt group need or wish. Building upon and paralleling Burns's focus upon leadership and followership are a number of studies in political science, especially in the field of presidential studies, dealing explicitly with the leadership (or management) styles of presidents and how these impact their interactions with advisers (followers). Although the primary focus of most of that work still rests squarely upon the personal qualities and characteristics of the leaders themselves, usually taking the form of discussions of types of presidential style, implicit in all of these discussions is the importance of the leader–follower relationships. This is illustrated in chapter 2, where we discussed the presidential character studies by Barber (1972).[1] Indeed, reflecting upon the centrality of this leader–follower relationship, Greenstein (1988) observed, "Leadership in the modern presidency is not carried out by the president alone, but rather by presidents with their associates. It depends therefore on both the president's strengths and weaknesses and on the quality of the aides' support"(p. 352). Yet, across this broad literature, Hermann and Preston (1994) have argued that there are five main types of leadership variables that appear to be routinely identified as having an impact upon the style of leaders and their subsequent structuring and use of advisory systems: (1) involvement in the policy-making process; (2) willingness to tolerate conflict; (3) motivation or reason for leading; (4) preferred strategies for managing information; and (5) preferred strategies for resolving conflict.

The focus on types of leadership style, personality, or character in the political science literature can be traced back to Lasswell, who first argued, in his classic *Psychopathology and Politics* (1930), that classifying leaders as particular types is possible, because, although leaders are different in fine details, important similarities can be seen across leaders, which allow us to argue that two or more leaders are of the same type. For example, after Barber's (1972) active–passive/positive–negative typology of presidential character, perhaps the best known typology of presidential management style is Johnson's (1974) classification scheme. Johnson argued that there was a consistent pattern of three White House management styles found among modern-day presidents: the **formalistic, competitive, and collegial styles** (see Table 5.1 and Figure 5.1).

These management styles essentially establish group **norms**, which is an important part of group behavior presented in chapter 4. The formalistic style (Harry S. Truman, Dwight Eisenhower, Richard Nixon, Ronald Reagan) is designed to reduce the effects of human error, through a well-designed management system that is hierarchical, nonconfrontational, focused on issues rather than personalities, and oriented toward generating options and making the best decision. The focus of this style is on preserving the president's time for the big decisions. In contrast, the collegial and competitive styles emphasize less hierarchical organization. The collegial style (John F. Kennedy, Jimmy Carter, Bill Clinton) focuses on working as a team,

TABLE 5.1

General Characteristics of Johnson's Typology of Formalistic, Competitive, and Collegial
Management Styles

Management Style	Advisory System Characteristics
Formalistic (examples: Truman, Eisenhower, Nixon, and Reagan administrations)	Emphasis upon strict hierarchical, orderly decision structures Formalized staff system funnels information to top, where leader weights options on their merit Emphasis upon technical instead of political considerations (underplays politics) Analytical and dispassionate advisors selected Stress on finding best solution to problems, instead of working out compromises among conflicting views Discourages staff conflict; emphasis upon order and analysis
Competitive (example: Franklin Roosevelt administration)	Relatively unstructured information network, with leader placed in arbiter position among competing advisers with overlapping areas of authority Leader thrives on conflict and uses it to stay informed and to exploit existing political environment Seeks aggressive advisers with divergent opinions Encourages staff conflict as means of generating creative ideas and opposing viewpoints Emphasizes bargaining over analysis, with tendency to settle upon short-term solutions
Collegial (examples: Kennedy, Carter, and Bush administrations)	Emphasizes teamwork, shared responsibility, and problem solving within group Advisors seen as colleagues who work as cooperative group to fuse strongest elements of divergent views Leader has strong interpersonal skills and will work collegially with advisors, rather than dominate group by pushing one position Discourages staff conflict, encourages conflicting viewpoints, takes into account all sides of issues, to forge solutions substantively and that are politically acceptable

sharing responsibility, and consensus-building, with an interest in generating options, openness to information, and reaching a doable, as well as best, decision. Leaders organizing their
advisers around the collegial style want to be involved in policy making and are uncomfortable when they are not in the middle of things. On the other hand, the competitive style
(Franklin Roosevelt) centers around confrontation, with the leader setting up an organization
with overlapping areas of authority, to maximize the availability of information and differing
perspectives. The emphasis in competitive systems is upon debate and advocacy, with the
leader playing the role of final arbiter.

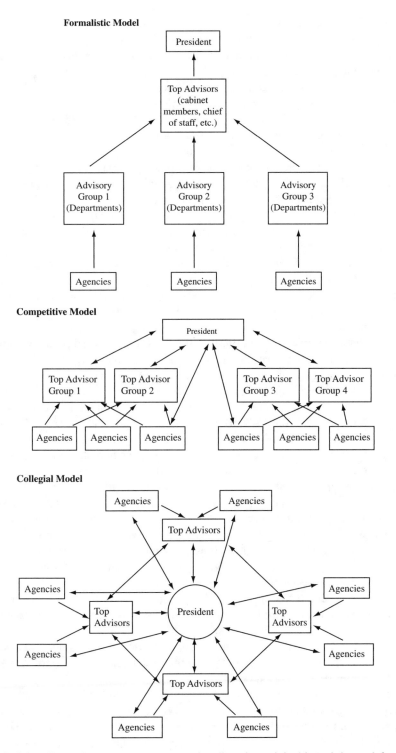

FIG. 5.1. Formalistic, competitive and collegial models. *Note:* Adapted from *Presidential decision-making in foreign policy* (pp. 152–156), by A. L. George, 1980. Boulder, CO: Westview. Copyright by Westview.

George (1980) built on Johnson's work, abstracting out three stylistic variables that seemed to shape what presidential advisers do. The first, **cognitive style**, refers to the way presidents gather and process information from their environment. Do presidents come with a well-formulated vision or agenda that helps to shape how they perceive, interpret, and act on information, or are they interested in sounding out the situation and political context before defining a problem and seeking options? The way this question is answered suggests the types of advisers presidents will have around them and the kinds of information presidents will want in making a decision. In the first instance, presidents seek advisers and information that are supportive of their predispositions; in the second instance, they are interested in experts or representatives of various constituencies who will provide them with insights into the political context and problem at any point in time. At issue in this second instance is what fits with the context, that is, what is doable at this particular moment.

The second stylistic variable centers around **sense of efficacy** or competence. Sense of efficacy for George (1980) relates to how agendas are formed. The problems presidents feel most comfortable tackling and the areas they are most interested in are likely to dominate their agendas. If, like George H.W. Bush, a president feels more at ease with foreign than domestic policy, his presidency will probably favor foreign over domestic policy. If, like Ronald Reagan, he has an arena of problems that are of particular importance, such as building the military strength of the United States vis-à-vis the Soviet Union, these issues may dominate much of the time of his administration.

The third stylistic variable George (1980) calls **orientation toward political conflict**. How open are presidents to face-to-face disagreements and confrontations among their advisers? The more open presidents are to such debate and crossfire, the easier it is to forge an advisory system exhibiting the characteristics of Johnson's competitive model; the more uncomfortable such a milieu makes them, the more likely presidents are to want an advisory system that either emphasizes teamwork (all of us work together) or formal rules (here are the gatekeepers who manage what gets to the president). George (1980) argues that this orientation tends to shape presidents' dealings with the cabinets and the executive bureaucracy, as well as with the White House staff. It colors the way presidents want the advisory system to run. Moreover, it helps to define the type of control presidents will want over the policy-making process and how much loyalty will be demanded from those around them. If conflict is to be minimized, presidents will have to expend resources to keep it under control; one way to achieve such control is to choose advisers who are loyal and who have served them for some time. If conflict can be tolerated and, perhaps, even used, presidents may see high turnover among staff, as egos are bruised or tempers flare. But advisers are more likely to be policy advocates and know what they want a president to do. Examples of presidents with low tolerances for political conflict include Richard Nixon and Lyndon Johnson. Indeed, Johnson's intolerance of dissent from advisers, and his desire for loyalty among advisers on policy lines adopted by the administration, were defining characteristics of his Vietnam policy style (Preston, 2001; Preston & 't Hart, 1999). On the other hand, Franklin Roosevelt's skillful use of a competitive management style provides the prototypical example of the leader high in tolerance of political conflict (George, 1980; Johnson, 1974).

Other scholars particularly interested in the presidency (Campbell, 1986; Crabb & Mulcahy, 1988; Smith, 1988) have added to what Johnson and George have described. These writers have been interested in leadership style variables that are relational in form; that is, they focus on what a president does vis-à-vis advisers and the bureaucracy. One such variable is the degree to which presidents do business personally or through institutionalized routines. Is the president a hands-on person like Lyndon Johnson, who wanted to talk to commanders in Vietnam or the ambassador in the Dominican Republic about what was really going on, or is the president more likely to want what comes up through the bureaucracy to be culled and organized, before it gets to the president for reflection? Anyone can become an adviser to the first type of president: The gatekeepers at the end become the advisers for the second type of president.

Another relational variable concerns how proactive versus reactive presidents' policy making is. Are presidents interested in shaping policy and enlisting the aid of others in selling the policy, or are presidents more responsive to what comes from others, rather than searching out activities? Proactive presidents are more likely to want a loyal staff with similar predispositions, who are sold on the president's program and who are ready to enlist support for it. Consider the staff that supported Reagan in seeking the release of American hostages in Lebanon by selling arms to Iran. Reactive presidents become more dependent on how others define and represent problems and the pressure others place on them to act. The issues that more reactive presidents focus on are a function of those on their staff.

A third relational variable centers around distrust of the bureaucracy. How much does a president trust the executive branch bureaucracy to carry out decisions and programs? Those presidents, such as Nixon, with an inherent distrust of what the bureaucracy will do to their policies, often centralize authority so that it rests with those they can trust, or they bypass the bureaucracy altogether by bringing policy making into the White House and under their control. With more trust of the bureaucracy comes more interest in recommendations from those further down in the hierarchy and more interest in interagency commissions and task forces. Scholars writing about political leadership in general (Hermann, 1987; Kotter & Lawrence, 1974) have stressed several further leadership styles that can influence how advisers are chosen. The first focuses on the leader's preferred strategies for resolving conflict. Which of the following strategies does the leader generally use to resolve conflict among advisers: leader preferences, unanimity/consensus, or majority rule? Each strategy suggests a difference in the advisory system. If the strategy focuses on ensuring that the leader's preferences prevail, the leader is going to play a more forceful role in the proceedings than if the strategy involves building a consensus or engaging a coalition to make a majority. Consensus building demands more of a facilitative role from the leader; engaging in coalition formation suggests an emphasis on negotiation and bargaining, with trade-offs and side payments. Moreover, the advisers the leader selects may differ with these strategies. If leaders generally want their preferences to prevail, they will probably seek out advisers who have a similar philosophy, are loyal, and are predisposed to please them. If consensus is the name of the game, leaders will seek out advisers who are, like themselves, interested in facilitating the process of bringing different views together and who are more conciliative than confrontational. Advisers to leaders whose preferred strategy is coalition building probably need skills in ascertaining where constituents stand and persuading others to join with them.

The last leadership style variable centers around the general operating goal of the leader— What is driving the leader to accept a leadership position? Why is a person interested in running for president? The type of goal indicates who the leader or president is likely to seek for advisers. Leaders interested in a particular cause seek advocates around them; those interested in support seek a cohesive group around them; those interested in power and influence seek implementors around them; those who want to accomplish some task or change some policy seek experts around them. Advisers are sought who complement the leaders' needs and who facilitate the leaders doing what they perceive needs to be done.

Thinking more broadly regarding the leader–follower relationship, Hermann et al. (1996) propose a typology of foreign policy leadership style types for world leaders, based upon three dimensions: (1) responsiveness to (or awareness of) constraints; (2) openness to information; and (3) motivational focus (i.e., task/problem accomplishment vs. interpersonal/relationship

TABLE 5.2

Leadership Style as Function of Responsiveness to Constraints, Openness to Information, and Motivation

Responsiveness to Constraints	Openness to Information	Problem Focus Motivation	Relationship Focus Motivation
Challenges constraints	Closed to information	*Expansionistic* (Focus of attention is on expanding leader's, government's, and state's span of control)	*Evangelistic* (Focus of attention is on persuading others to join in one's mission and in mobilizing others around one's message)
Challenges constraints	Open to information	*Actively independent* (Focus of attention is on maintaining one's own and the government's maneuverability and independence, in a world that is perceived to continually try to limit both)	*Directive* (Focus of attention is on maintaining one's own and the government's status and acceptance by others, by engaging in actions on the world stage that enhance the state's reputation)
Respects constraints	Closed to information	*Incremental* (Focus of attention is on improving state's economy and/or security in incremental steps, while avoiding the obstacles that will inevitably arise along the way)	*Influential* (Focus of attention is on building cooperative relationships with other governments and states, in order to play a leadership role; by working with others, one can gain more than is possible on one's own)
Respects constraints	Open to information	*Opportunistic* (Focus of attention is on assessing what is possible in the current situation and context, given what one wants to achieve and considering what important constituencies will allow	*Collegial* (Focus of attention is on reconciling differences and building consensus—on gaining prestige and status through empowering others and sharing accountability)

emphasis). As Table 5.2 illustrates, the dimensions result in eight specific foreign policy styles: expansionistic, evangelistic, actively independent, directive, incremental, influential, opportunistic, and collegial.

Finally, another recent typology of leadership style proposed in the political psychology literature focuses upon two main dimensions: the leader's need for control and involvement in the policy process; and the leader's need for information and general sensitivity to context (Preston, 2001). Measuring the individual characteristics of past American presidents using Hermann's LEAD technique, discussed in chapter 2, Preston suggests that a leader's need for power and their prior experience/policy expertise in a given policy domain will shape how much control or involvement a president will insist upon having in the policy-making process.

TABLE 5.3

Presidential Need for Control and Involvement in Policy Process

	Prior Policy Experience or Expertise in Policy Area (General Interest Level of Desire for Involvement in Policy)	
	High	*Low*
	Director	*Magistrate*
Need for Power High	Decision making centralized in inner circle Preference for direct control and involvement throughout policy process Advocate own policy views, frame issues, and set specific policy guidelines Leader relies upon own policy judgments more than on those of expert advisers	Decision making centralized in inner circle Preference for direct control over decisions, but limited need for involvement throughout policy process Sets general policy guidelines, but delegates policy formulation and implementation Leader relies more upon views of expert advisers than upon own
	Administrator	*Delegator*
Need for Power Low	Decision making less centralized and more collegial; leader requires less direct control over policy process and subordinates Enhanced roles of subordinates Actively advocates own views, frames issues, and sets specific policy guidelines Leader relies more upon own judgments than on those of expert advisers	Decision making less centralized, and more collegial; leader requires little/no direct control/involvement in policy process Enhanced roles of subordinates Delegates policy formulation and implementation to subordinates Tendency to rely upon (and adopt) views of expert advisers in final policy decision

Note: From *The president & his inner circle* (pp. 16–17), by T. Preston, 2000. Copyright by Columbia University Press. Reprinted with permission.

Indeed, as the psychological literature on the need for power suggests, individuals differ greatly in their desire for control over their environments, with some insisting upon a more active role than others (see Table 5.3).

In terms of the second dimension (cognitive complexity), Preston (2001) uses cognitive complexity and prior experience/policy expertise in the policy domain as indicators of a president's *general sensitivity to context* (i.e., their general cognitive need for information, their attentiveness and sensitivity to the characteristics of the surrounding policy environment, and the views of others). As the literature on complexity and experience illustrates, individuals differ greatly in terms of their general awareness of, or sensitivity toward, their surrounding environments. Indeed, individuals vary radically even in their general cognitive need for information when making decisions: Some prefer broad information search before reaching conclusions; others prefer to rely more upon their own existing views and other simplifying heuristics. In Table 5.4, the leaders' cognitive complexity interacts with their prior substantive policy experience or expertise, to produce an overall style regarding the need for information and sensitivity to external context.

TABLE 5.4

Sensitivity to Context (For example, to the policy environment, institutional constraints, the views of subordinates.)

	Navigator	Observer
Cognitive complexity high	High general need for information and interest in foreign policy Active collector of information from policy environment Greater sensitivity to constraints and enhanced search for information and advice from outside actors	High general need for information, but limited personal interest in foreign policy Interested in information on policy specifics, but heavily dependent on expert advice Reduced sensitivity to constraints on policy and less awareness of (search for) information and advice from outside actors
	Sentinel	Maverick
Cognitive complexity low	High personal interest in foreign policy but low need for information Greater sensitivity to constraints and advice from outside actors Seeks to guide policy along path consistent with own personal principles, views, or past experience Avoids broad search for policy information beyond that deemed relevant, given past experience or existing personal views	Low need for information and limited personal interest in foreign policy Avoids broad collection of general information; decisions driven by own idiosyncratic policy views and principles Reduced sensitivity to constraints on policy and less awareness of (search for) information and advice from outs

Note: From *The president & his inner circle* (pp. 22–23), by T. Preston, 2001. New York: Columbia University Press, Copyright by Columbia University Press. Reprinted with permission.

Developed through empirical testing of its hypothesized relationships between leader characteristics and their foreign policy decision making and uses of advisory systems against the archival record in the presidential libraries, Preston's (2001) model produces a nuanced, composite style typology that is sensitive to differences in leaders across these two dimensions and across differing policy domains (see Table 5.5). In other words, this allows presidents to vary from one another in more than just the one simple dimension of their need for control and involvement in the policy process (as in the typologies of Barber [discussed in chapter 2] and Johnson), but also in terms of their general sensitivity to policy information and context. In addition to providing greater variation in style types, the resulting typology provides greater analytical capability to study the impact of leadership styles across different policy domains, by incorporating a more contingent notion of leadership style into the analysis of presidents. For example, a serious weakness of previous typologies has been their firm roots in either foreign policy or domestic policy, with presidential styles generally appearing to be incompatible between the two domains. Although personality traits (e.g., need for power and complexity) are stable in form, over time, within individuals, and should have the same impact upon presidential behavior, regardless of policy domain (foreign or domestic), this is not the case for non personality-based characteristics, such as prior policy experience or expertise (see Hermann, 1980a; McCrae,

TABLE 5.5
Composite Leadership Style Types

	Foreign Policy	*Domestic Policy*
Truman	Magistrate–maverick	Director–sentinel
Eisenhower	Director–navigator	Magistrate–observer
Kennedy	Director–navigator	Magistrate–observer
Johnson	Magistrate–maverick	Director–sentinel
Reagan	Director–maverick	Sentinel–maverick
Bush	Administrator–navigator	Delegator–observer
Clinton	Delegator–observer	Administrator–navigator
G.W. Bush	Delegator–maverick	Delegator–maverick

Note: From *The president and his inner circle* (p. 28), by T. Preston, 2001, New York: Columbia University Press. Copyright by Columbia University Press. Reprinted by permission.

1993; Winter, 1973). In the typology presented here, leadership styles for presidents vary across the foreign and domestic policy domains, based upon the leaders' degree of prior policy experience in the particular area. Table 5.5 compares the composite leadership style designations for a number of modern U.S. presidents, across both foreign and domestic policy.

ILLUSTRATION OF APPLICATION OF POLITICAL PSYCHOLOGY APPROACHES TO LEADERS

In the final section of this chapter, an illustration is provided of how a number of the political psychological approaches discussed so far can be applied to a political leader—Bill Clinton. Obviously, examples of all of the techniques discussed would be impractical, given the space constraints in a textbook. Although some illustrations are provided in chapter 2, a lengthy examination of Bill Clinton's characteristics, using two additional approaches, demonstrates the utility of leadership analysis for understanding the behavior of this president.

The Example of Bill Clinton

Political psychology approaches to the study of political leaders can range from those that make fairly general, simple predictions of overall styles of behavior, to those providing much more involved, detailed analyses. An example of the former would be Barber's (1972) typology focusing on the two dimensions of active–passive (i.e., how much energy do presidents put into the job) and positive–negative (i.e., the personal satisfaction they derive from presidential duties), which we discussed in chapter 2 with reference to Presidents Clinton and Bush. Examples of more complex approaches would include more involved leader profiles using the LEAD approach of Hermann (1999), discussed in chapter 2, or the style typology developed by Preston (2001).

Again using the example of Clinton, Hermann's (1999a) LEAD technique, employing content analysis of leader interviews to produce profile scores along seven characteristics (i.e., need for power, locus of control, ethnocentrism, task–interpersonal focus, complexity, self-confidence, and distrust of others), suggests quite different style consequences for the two presidents. For example, in terms of Hermann et al.'s (1996) typology focusing upon whether leaders *challenge or respect constraints* and whether they are *open or closed to information*, Bill Clinton (based upon his measured, moderate profile scores on need for power and locus of control) is seen as generally accepting of (or respectful of) constraints, but, under certain circumstances, can challenge what appear to be inappropriate or unfounded limitations on his role (Hermann, 1999b). As Hermann (1999b) notes, leaders with moderate scores, such as Clinton's, will work within the parameters they perceive to structure their political environment, and, because of the limitations within which they perceive they have to work, building consensus and achieving compromise are important skills for a politician to have and to exercise. Clinton's high scores on complexity and self-confidence suggest that he is open to information, is more highly attuned to feedback from the political environment, and is much more active in monitoring his surroundings and gathering advice when making decisions. At the same time, however, such intensive monitoring of the environment for feedback and information, before taking actions, can lead outside observers to see their behavior as erratic and opportunistic (Hermann, 1999b). In terms of the degree to which he is *motivated by the problem or the relationship*, Clinton's moderate score on task–interpersonal emphasis suggests that he has the ability to direct his attention to the problem when that is appropriate to the situation at hand, or to building relationships when that seems more relevant, essentially shifting between these, as called for by the context (Hermann, 1999b). As Hermann explains regarding Clinton's style:

> Clinton's pattern of scores on the seven traits help us determine the kind of leadership style he will exhibit. By ascertaining that he is likely to (1) generally respect constraints in his political environment, (2) be open to, and search out, information in the situation, (3) be motivated by both solving the problem and keeping morale high, and (4) view politics as the art of the possible and mutually beneficial, we know from extensive research that Clinton will exhibit a collegial leadership style. His focus of attention is on reconciling differences and building consensus, on retaining power and authority through building relationships and taking advantage of opportunities to work with others toward specific ends. Clinton's leadership style predisposes him toward the team-building approach to politics. Like the captain of a football or basketball team, the leader is dependent on others to work with him to make things happen. Such leaders see themselves at the center of the information-gathering process. With regard to the advisory process, working as a team means that advisers are empowered to participate in all aspects of policymaking but also to share in the accountability for what occurs. Members of the team are expected to be sensitive to and supportive of the beliefs and values of the leader. (pp. 4–5)

Another approach that can be applied to Clinton and Bush is Preston's (2001) typology of leadership style, which also makes use of the LEAD technique to obtain scores for a president's need for power and complexity, but adds a measure for prior policy experience or expertise. In the foreign policy arena, Clinton, who scores low in need for power and prior policy experience, but high in complexity, is classified as a *delegator–observer*. As a result, the typology would predict that, although interested in policy matters, Clinton would require less direct personal control over the policy process, would actively delegate policy formulation and implementation tasks to subordinates, and would rely heavily upon the expertise or policy judgments of his senior specialist advisers, when making decisions. On the other hand, his high complexity suggests that he has a high need for information when making decisions. This would lead him to seek out multiple policy perspectives from advisers, engage in extensive search in the policy environment for information and feedback, and exhibit a more tentative, less decisive decision style that avoids rigid, black-and-white reasoning, while focusing upon the shades of gray in issues. Clinton would be expected to demonstrate a pragmatic approach to policy issues and would not rigidly adhere to a given ideological or political position, if feedback from the policy environment suggested a different context. Advisers would be drawn not only from those who share his views, but also from those who express varied and competing viewpoints.

In contrast, George W. Bush, who scores low in power, complexity, and prior policy experience, would fit the *delegator–maverick* style (the same style as Ronald Reagan). Even more than Clinton, Bush would be expected to not require active personal involvement in policy-making tasks, to heavily delegate policy formulation and implementation tasks to subordinates, and to be almost entirely dependant upon the expertise or policy judgments of his senior specialist advisers when making decisions. Unlike Clinton, however, Bush's low complexity and lack of policy expertise results in an information-processing style that does not require much information or advice when making decisions. Instead, one would expect a very rapid, decisive decision-making style driven by black-and-white reasoning, rigid adherence to existing ideological beliefs, extensive use of simple stereotypes and analogies, and the use of advisers who share his general idiosyncratic views of the world. Bush would not be expected to monitor his political environment for diverse information or feedback on policy or political issues, but would instead proceed from the basis of his own ideological or political belief system.

Moving beyond this discussion, which merely lays out how some of the many different types of political psychological approaches might explain or predict a political leader's behavior, we now take one specific example from Preston's (2001) typology, and discuss in a more detailed fashion the empirical evidence supporting its predictions, to illustrate the application of such approaches to the study of the personality and style of leaders. At the same time, let us emphasize that there are many available elaborations of the approaches discussed in this chapter in published research on political leaders, which are worth examining in more depth than is allowed in any textbook chapter. For example, the psychoanalytic approach has previously been applied to Bill Clinton by Renshon (1996), the operational code by Schafer and Crichlow (2000), and the MBTI (covering introversion vs. extroversion, sensing vs. intuition, thinking vs. feeling, and judging vs. perceiving scales) by Lyons (1997; discussed in chapter 2). All provide useful takes on the different dimensions of personality or individual characteristics that make up Bill Clinton. Together, they provide scholars and students alike with a more nuanced, well-rounded portrait of a complex individual. None of the approaches alone provides all of the answers. Rather, the scholarship on personality and leadership, across the political psychology literature, provides us with multiple methods and approaches to the study of individuals across many differing dimensions. Such approaches can be applied to political leaders across cultural and national boundaries, as well as to nonleaders and individual citizens (see Hermann, 1984, 1987; Kaarbo & Hermann, 1998; Taysi & Preston, 2001; Winter et al., 1991). The research question you ask should drive your selection of approach and what dimensions of personality, style, or leadership that you focus upon. The purpose of this chapter is to lay out some of the options on this lengthy menu.

Bill Clinton as Delegator–Observer: A Case Study

Based upon his LEAD profile scores, Bill Clinton would be expected to exhibit the delegator's preferences for control and involvement in the policy process and the observer's needs for information and sensitivity to the contextual environment in his foreign policy decision making.[2] Table 5.6 provides a summary of the composite delegator–observer leadership style predicted for Clinton in foreign affairs. In the following section, the predictions of the typology

TABLE 5.6
Expectations for Composite Delegator–Observer Leadership Style

Composite Style (Delegator–Observer)	Expectations: Leader Style and Use of Advisers
Dimensions of leader control and involvement in policy process	Delegative presidential style in which leader requires limited direct personal control over the policy process
	Preference for informal, less hierarchical advisory structures designed to enhance participation by subordinates
	Leader actively delegates policy formulation and implementation tasks to subordinates and adopts (relies upon) the expertise and policy judgments of specialist advisers, when making decisions
	Inner circle decision rule: Advisory group outputs and leader policy preferences reflect the dominant views expressed by either expert advisers or the majority of group members
	High cognitive need for information and multiple policy perspectives; extensive search for feedback or advice from advisers in surrounding policy environment; use of both formal and informal advice networks
Dimension of leader need for information and general sensitivity to context	Because of policy inexperience, leader exhibits less sensitivity to the external policy environment, less awareness of constraints on policy, and limited search for advice from relevant outside actors
	Less decisive decision style; avoidance of rigid black-and-white reasoning; emphasis in decision making upon data gathered from environment, rather than preconceived views or stereotypes; tolerant of, and willing to consider, discrepant information or advice
	High self-monitoring and "inductive novice" style of information processing

Note: From *The president and his inner circle* (p. 221), by T. Preston, New York: Columbia University Press. Copyright by Columbia University Press. Reprinted with permission.

are compared to the secondary literature on Clinton, his former advisers' recollections, and his leadership style and decision making on Korea during the crisis of 1994.

Limited Foreign Policy Expertise and Involvement in Policy Making

Although, in domestic politics, Clinton is routinely described by colleagues as one of the best politicians they have ever seen (Morris, 1997; Reich, 1997; Stephanopoulos, 1999), Clinton entered the White House with an extremely limited foreign affairs background. With the exception of his work on Senator William Fulbright's staff and his Rhodes Scholar experience in England during his early 20s, Clinton had no other significant foreign policy experience (Allen & Portis, 1992; Maraniss 1995). Devoting himself to his true policy interests, Clinton developed tremendous expertise in domestic policy and the art of political campaigning (Maraniss, 1995). Indeed, Clinton has been described as a student of government, in the truest sense of the phrase, having spent virtually his entire adult life in politics and elective office (Watson, 1993). However, this pursuit was strictly domestic in flavor, with foreign affairs never capturing the future president's interests, as did domestic issues. A virtuoso in domestic politics, Clinton was noticeably out of his element when dealing with foreign affairs:

> Clinton on domestic policy is a sort of controlled volcano, ad-libbing furiously, tearing off ideas. Clinton on foreign policy is far less confident. When he speaks to congressional leaders on the telephone he writes his own script; when he calls foreign leaders he sets up a speakerphone so aides can listen in and, if necessary, quietly pass him notes. The president rarely departs from the prepared text of foreign policy speeches, which often makes them sound wooden. (Elliot & Cohn, 1994, p. 28)

Generally, White House aides have noted that Clinton saw foreign policy as a distraction from his domestic agenda and sought to delegate its formulation to others, whenever possible. As a result, Secretary of State Warren Christopher and NSC Adviser Anthony Lake's role in the new administration was to "not let foreign policy get in the President's way as he focused on domestic policy" (Drew, 1994, p. 28). In this respect, Clinton bears a striking resemblance to Truman, Johnson, and George W. Bush, who also had limited foreign policy backgrounds, relied heavily upon expert advisers, and delegated significant policy-making tasks to subordinates.

Preference for Informal, Less Hierarchical Advisory Structures

A hallmark of the Clinton White House, in both foreign and domestic policy, was the president's informal, nonhierarchical advisory structure and collegial style of leadership (Campbell, 1996; Drew, 1994; Jones, 1996; Watson, 1993). In fact, this loose, free-ranging management style mimicked that used by Clinton during his years as governor of Arkansas (Maraniss, 1995). Unfortunately, although this open advisory system allowed an immense range of feedback to reach the White House, the nearly complete lack of coordination and structure often resulted in information overload and a painfully slow decision process (Reich, 1997; Stephanopoulos, 1999). To maximize his information gathering, Clinton frequently used ad hoc problem-solving groups, such as special task forces, policy councils, and loosely defined clusters of friends and advisors, to make policy and maximize his information gathering (Watson, 1993). Given our discussion of problems faced during the **forming** and **storming** stages of group development, we can anticipate that, with frequently formed new groups, these groups would be prone to tension and argument. As former Secretary of Labor Robert Reich (1997) observed, Clinton "doesn't give a fig for formal lines of authority. He'll seek advice from anyone he wants to hear it from, for as long as he thinks he's getting what he needs" (p. 217). Indeed, no president since Lyndon Johnson has come close to matching Clinton's voracious information needs when making decisions. However, Johnson was principally interested in obtaining political information that would support the accomplishment of his goals and no more, but Clinton, a true policy wonk, cast his net as widely as possible in what some staff have criticized as a "love affair with details" (Campbell, 1996, p. 75). Former White House Chief of Staff Leon Panetta comments that Clinton was like "a lion looking for every last morsel of information" from his advisory system (Woodward, 1996, p. 417).

The resulting informal White House organization served to encourage a high degree of staff access to the president and active participation by them in the policy-making process:

> Clinton's inclusiveness was initially a joy to his staff. The unhierarchical structure and the collegial style of the Clinton White House seemed, at first, wonderful. Clinton himself contributed to the informality, often wandering the halls and dropping in on aides or on the Vice President. Aides felt fairly free to drop in on. . . . A large number of people were in on meetings with him. Clinton encouraged it. (Drew, 1994, p. 28)

However, as Colin Powell (1995) observed, discussions in these meetings tended to meander like "graduate student bull sessions" or "think tank seminars" (p. 576), with low-level staffers often sounding off with the authority of cabinet officers and openly arguing with their superiors during meetings. Noting that Clinton had an "academic streak" and seemed to enjoy these marathon debates, Powell (1995) nevertheless believed that the president "was not well-served by the wandering deliberations he permitted" (p. 577). In Powell's view, the norms established in these groups hurt their performance (see chapter 4 for a review of norms and performance). Similarly, former Treasury Secretary Lloyd Bentsen criticized Clinton for not delegating properly and failing to separate important from nonimportant decisions, thereby complicating the decision process (Woodward, 1996). Adding to the confusion, Clinton failed to establish clear structures of delegation within his advisory system, resulting in both a free-for-all among his advisers, who were unclear who had responsibility for what, and an overall lack of coordination among policy groups (Drew, 1994; Greenstein, 1995; Woodward, 1996). As one staff member observed, "It's a floating crap game about who runs what around here. The last person who has an idea can often get it done, whether it's part of the strategy or not" (Drew, 1994, p. 241). Indeed, Stephanopoulos (1999) observed: "What happens in the White House is a reflection of the way he thinks. He doesn't want hierarchy. He doesn't want a strong Chief of Staff. He doesn't want a single economic adviser. He wants all kinds of advisers swirling around him constantly" (p. 99).

However, although the president frequently chaired and actively participated in domestic policy staff meetings, he rarely attended formal meetings of the NSC during his first term and seldom participated in policy discussions (Drew, 1994; Campbell, 1996). Recognizing the problem, Lake noted that Clinton did not engage himself sufficiently in "larger contemplative discussions" of foreign affairs and needed to have more "sit-back-and-think-about-this kind of meetings" to improve his handling of foreign policy (Campbell, 1996, p. 76). But this never came to pass, and Clinton continued to pay only sporadic attention to the NSC during his first term (Campbell, 1996).

As Jones (1996) notes, Clinton's informal, freewheeling style did not invite a chief of staff system of organization, and, through much of the first term, the overall functioning of the advisory system lacked much coordination or coherent structure. Indeed, prior to Mack McClarty's replacement by Leon Panetta as White House chief of staff, as many as 10 different advisers had direct access to Clinton, in addition to outside consultants like James Carville and Mandy Grunwald, who served as unofficial advisers to the president (Clift & Cohn, 1993). The chain of command inside the White House was so loose that some senior aides were "roamers" with no clear responsibilities, and staff meetings were so unstructured that they often became just talking sessions that never led anywhere (we saw in chapter 4 that ambiguous group roles tend to promote conflict in groups). Meetings in the Oval Office were often so large that officials joked that the room "needed bleachers to hold everyone" (Mitchell, 1995, p. A16). Panetta had been warned by Stephanopoulos (1999) that, to be effective, he had to insist on being given "the power not to be overridden" (pp. 284–285), because Clinton had never given McClarty any real authority or mandate, which had led to his ineffectiveness. Panetta responded by immediately banning the free-floating advisers, limiting Oval Office access (including that of Stephanopoulos) to people he approved or who Clinton expressly requested, and restricted staff meetings to senior aides only (Harris, 1997; Mitchell, 1995). Clinton and Panetta described their relationship as "a balancing act between Panetta's desire for order and Clinton's desire to deliberate and discuss every decision with a wide group of people" (Harris, 1997, p. 11).

However, unwilling to be limited to the flow of advice within the White House, Clinton utilized a broad informal network of advisers, to reach beyond those within his formal inner circle. Often referred to as Friends of Bill (FOBs), this network was comprised of an extensive collection of outside supporters, including former politicians, prominent journalists, lobbyists, and campaign advisers, who Clinton gathered over the years and frequently called for independent advice (Clift & Cohn, 1993; Gerth, 1996; Maraniss, 1995; Morris, 1997). For example, recalling the informal relationships Lyndon Johnson had with outside advisers Abe Fortas and Clark Clifford, Clinton constantly met with his own close friend and informal adviser Vernon Jordan, to discuss a wide range of sensitive issues in foreign and domestic policy (Gerth, 1996). Further, Clinton met privately with many of his inner circle advisers, especially Gore, to informally discuss or debate issues of importance to the president (Sciolino & Purdum, 1995; Woodward, 1996).

Further illustrating Clinton's desire for broad feedback and debate were his efforts to emulate Franklin Roosevelt's competitive decision style of sitting back, letting his advisers argue different positions, and assigning them crosscutting policy responsibilities. Those who have worked within Clinton's inner circle note that the president's approach was geared toward having competing advisers counteracting each other's arguments or influence within the administration, preventing dominance of any one position and providing a more balanced debate of the issues (Drew, 1994; Morris, 1997; Reich, 1997; Renshon, 1996; Stephanopoulos, 1999). For example, Stephanopoulos (1999) recalls that Clinton's typical pattern was to allow all of his advisers to have their say, then ask pointed questions and play them off against one another. However, given Clinton's loose style of management and lack of formal structures of control, copying FDR's competitive model poses significant problems. Indeed, although noting that "no single adviser could ever fully own Clinton," because "he was too smart and too stubborn for that," Stephanopoulos (1999, p. 335) observed that the president lacked the firm directiveness that had allowed FDR to avoid the near-total anarchy the competition between staff sometimes created in the White House (Reich, 1997). Often, advisers were left guessing as to what Clinton expected of them or wanted to hear. For example, during one series of stormy interactions with Dick Morris over domestic policy, as both advisers competed for the president's ear, a frustrated Stephanopoulos belatedly recognized that "Clinton *is* pulling an FDR. He want's Dick's energy and ideas, but he wants us to check him too. He wants us to get along, but he doesn't want me to give up" (Stephanopoulos, 1999, p. 338). Clearly, the norms Clinton promoted among his advisory groups did not always result in high-quality group performance.

Active Delegation and Reliance Upon Expert Advisers

As would be expected of a leader with limited experience, Clinton tended to rely heavily upon subordinates with the expertise he lacked, when making decisions. Indeed, in a style reminiscent of Truman's reliance upon Marshall and Acheson, Clinton consistently delegated the general formulation and implementation of foreign policy to his two secretaries of state, Warren Christopher and Madeline Albright, as well as to subordinates such as Al Gore and NSC Advisers Tony Lake and Sandy Berger (Berman & Goldman, 1996; Drew, 1994; Greenstein, 1995; Sciolino &

Purdum, 1995). For example, Gore took a leading diplomatic role in the administration, by establishing a series of commissions with foreign leaders to manage the bilateral relationships between the United States and those countries. The most famous of these, the Gore–Chernomyrdin
Commission, served as the ultimate back channel to the Russian government during Clinton's
first term and played a guiding role in U.S.–Russian relations (Sciolino & Purdum, 1995). Gore's
policy advice was valued to such an extent that the president did not make any decision of significance without him (Sciolino & Purdum, 1995). Similarly, during the crisis with Iraq, in the
fall of 1998 through early 1999, Albright was widely credited with being the architect of U.S.
foreign policy (Gordon & Sciolino, 1998). Given Clinton's limited interest in foreign affairs and
his desire to focus upon domestic issues, the clear pattern that consistently emerged within foreign policy making—whether in Bosnia, Iraq, Russia, or Kosovo—was that of delegation to his
expert subordinates, by the president, of foreign policy formulation and implementation (Bert,
1997; Gordon & Sciolino, 1998; Hermann & Preston, 1998; Sigal, 1998).

High Need for Information and Sensitivity to Political Environment

Perhaps Clinton's greatest individual strength was the innate complexity of his mind—his
ability to see multiple perspectives and the shades of gray on issues, his probing curiosity, his
unrelenting search for ever more information or advice on problems, and his amazing sensitivity to the political environment and the needs of his constituents. As the Republican, former
governor of New Jersey, Thomas Kean, once noted, Clinton "has a first-class intellect as well
as a sensitivity to the needs of others. You'll often find politicians with one or the other, but not
both. It's quite a combination" (Rockman, 1996, p. 345). In the information-processing literature, such qualities are usually regarded as those characteristic of a high-quality process,
leading to a greater likelihood of well-considered, competent decision making (Schroder,
Driver, & Streufert, 1967; Vertzberger, 1990). At the same time, however, such complexity can
also be a profound liability, not only in terms of the dangers of information overload and
reduced speed of decision making, but also in the political perception it creates. Just as his
high-complexity predecessors (Eisenhower, Kennedy, Carter, Bush) were criticized for indecisiveness, tentative decision making, and waffling on the issues, Clinton's complexity of
mind has led to similar characterizations of his own presidency (Berman & Goldman, 1996;
Campbell, 1996; Drew, 1994; Woodward, 1996). As Rockman (1996) observed:

> Clinton is the rare combination of a complex policy thinker and a sophisticated thinker
> about politics—perhaps too complex and too sophisticated for his own good. Clinton's
> policy complexity often resists being boiled down to a succinct and memorable position
> or slogan. The public has had a hard time figuring out what he is about. By seeing so
> many angles to problems and by seeing that varying solutions have both costs and ben-
> efits of different sorts, Clinton often suffers from that which afflicted his equally brainy,
> if less sophisticated, predecessor Jimmy Carter, namely, paralysis by analysis. (p. 347)

Being open-minded and sensitive to policy facts, as well as to their interplay with the
political environment, resulted in an almost endless process of Clinton making up his mind—
resulting in indecision, uncertainty, and delay (Rockman, 1996). Agreeing with this diagnosis,
Betsey Wright, Clinton's White House secretary and former Arkansas chief of staff, noted that
Clinton "has this restless intellectual curiosity," which "complicates" matters, because of his
constant search for ever greater amounts of information and advice. Recognizing the positive
aspects of this Clinton quality, Wright nevertheless observes the political problems it creates:

"There's an openness I don't think he gets credit for; he gets denigrated for it" (Purdum, 1996, p. 1). Indeed, as Robert Reich notes, efforts to narrow the president's policy focus or search for information is almost doomed to failure:

> [Clinton] doesn't operate this way. His mind is too restless, and there's too much in it to begin with. He is constitutionally incapable of sticking to a single sound bite, or even to a single theme, let alone one broad unifying idea. He likes to gab about the whole range of policies, themes, and ideas, long into the night. (Reich, 1997, pp. 103–104)

Clinton's highly inquisitive style and constant search for additional information often made decisions difficult to obtain from the president. Finding it difficult to get the president to sign off on a recommendation, Panetta recalls, "I would say, 'I think this is what we have to do' . . . and he would say, 'Yeah, but I want to reach out here, I want to reach out there.' He is an individual who by his very nature wants to get as much information as possible" (Harris, 1997, p. 11).

Colleagues have often remarked that Clinton tended to focus on multiple tasks at once, even during briefings, asking "what else" to staff when he had catalogued information and was ready to move on, and ending conversations with one of his favorite phrases: "Keep your ear to the ground" (Maraniss, 1995, p. 383; Reich, 1997). Further, Clinton was well-known for constantly working phones for inside information, for advice from his FOB network, or from members of his own inner circle (Maraniss, 1995; Reich, 1997; Stephanopoulos, 1999). As Drew (1994) remarked, Clinton is "a man of large appetites. . . . His keen intellect and ability to absorb a lot of material caused him to immerse himself in a great many issues— which wasn't altogether to his benefit" (p. 94):

> What Clinton does instinctively is carry around in his head a lot of feedback from people, whether or not it's consistent. He sends out the sonar, tests out ideas, gives a speech and watches and listens for responses. He'll talk to people, asking, "What do you think?" This is a process of constant sonar, and he'll carry in his head different views from different people until they evolve into policy, or he'll try to set forth a problem and leave it to other people to come up with proposals and solutions. What this means is he's sitting in the middle of a cacophony of voices and ideas. It also means that those who have the most time with him have the most influence, so there's a great deal of stampeding around him to have the most time with him. (Drew, 1994, p. 99)

Seeking to collect diverse, even conflicting, perspectives on policy issues, Clinton populated his advisory system with advisers who would not necessarily agree with one another. For example, in his cabinet appointments, one sees both strong left-of-center leanings (Donna Shalala, Henry Cisneros, Robert Reich) and strong moderate leanings (Lloyd Bentsen, Janet Reno, William Cohen) among his appointees, thereby ensuring that Clinton would get conflicting views from his advisers (Renshon, 1996). It has also been noted that Clinton was uncomfortable with unanimity of opinion from his advisers and liked to hear contradictory things from his staff (Woodward, 1994). Clinton often would push debate to "the point of chaos," reflecting the "intellectual, ruminative side of his personality" (Woodward, pp. 210–211). As one White House aide remarked, Clinton's constant search for multiple policy perspectives often led to

> these extended debates where they essentially talked to death the inevitable. Clinton was always trying to pick out a new course, move the debate or the policy slightly. The dynamic had a pattern. Clinton, unaccepting of the conventional wisdom, especially

about Congress, would test the edges of what was possible, stretching the boundaries of the Washington and congressional playing field. (Woodward: p. 298)

Stan Greenberg, another Clinton adviser, noted that the president "might make some decisions from memos and options, but on major things he wants to sit down for two or three hours and talk to people about it. You need to create structure that enables him to do that" (quoted in Drew, 1994, pp. 239–240). Recognizing this element, Stephanopoulos (1999) noted that the decision-making process within the early Clinton White House had to adapt, to better compensate for the president's information needs:

We have to work on our internal decision-making structure. We have to come up with a system that lets Clinton be Clinton—even more, *help* Clinton be Clinton. He needs the time to talk, to bring people together. What we have to do to help him is shorten the frame between his discussions . . . and his decision. If he wants to talk to a lot of people, make sure the work has been done, and then he does the deciding. All the backup work has to be done more quickly, more precisely, so that he can get on with the decisions. (p. 56)

Although Clinton has sometimes been criticized for basing policy decisions upon polls (Berman & Goldman, 1996) or governing with an eye to the next election (Jones, 1996), this represents just another facet of his thirst for yet more information and feedback from the political environment. As Morris (1997) recalled, regarding the president's use of polls for foreign policy making:

Bill Clinton did care what America thought. He cared not just so he would get reelected but because he . . . knew that without popular support no policy would work. He was not, in this respect, a prisoner of polls. He rarely consulted them to decide what foreign policy should be. He used polling instead to discover what arguments would be most persuasive in getting popular support for a decision. (p. 247)

Another example of Clinton's use of his interpersonal skills to gather information and feedback during conversations is his longtime friend John Issacson's observation that the president's conversational style has always been characterized by two basic moves:

(1) the Sponge move and (2) the Radar move: "The Sponge move was to soak information and give it back. The Radar move was Clintonesque. He was not so much a talker as a bouncer. He would try out different versions of what he thought and bounce them off you while looking at your eyes. That was his radar system. When the radar hit the eyes, he knew it." (Maraniss, 1995, p. 144)

Less Decisive Decision Style

As expected for a high-complexity leader, Clinton's decision style placed tremendous importance upon deliberate process in which immense amounts of information are gathered and analyzed prior to making decisions (Campbell, 1996; Hermann & Preston, 1998). As a result, very few decisions were made. Indeed, some associates have noted that Clinton had "a decision-making method that is a postponement process" (Drew, 1994, p. 232). Of course, for high-complexity leaders who see the shades of gray on all policy matters and recognize that most problems can be seen from any number of perspectives, final decisions requiring closing off options or deciding not to gather all the available information or advice possible on a problem is difficult (Preston, 1996; Renshon, 1996). As a result of their high need for information and sensitivity to context, it is almost inevitable that such leaders will have less decisive, deliberative decision processes.

Although Clinton's high need for information often led him to actively participate in meetings with his staff on even minor topics (especially in domestic matters), his participation generally slowed things down. In fact, Reich, observing that the Clinton White House was not a place where "decisions are precisely made," remarks that it was often necessary to "coax the decision-making process along," in order to make progress (Reich, 1997, p. 232). Advisers have noted that one of the reasons for Clinton's indecisiveness was that he "never stops thinking" and that it was "Clinton's way" to have "a lot of last-minute decisions and changes" (Drew, 1994, p. 67). Participants at these meetings note:

> His decision-making style is not to make a decision the way others do—toting up the costs and benefits. He makes a decision when he absolutely has to. Sometimes when he must make a decision that he's not ready to make, the decision doesn't get made. . . . You couldn't really tell when he was making a decision and when he wasn't. (Drew, 1994, p. 67)

At the same time, however, those who have observed Clinton from both within his inner circle and outside of it have noted that he was not rigidly ideological or partisan, but was willing to consider alternative viewpoints, in his quest for addressing policy problems and achieving policy goals (Campbell, 1996; Hermann & Preston, 1998; Rockman, 1996). This is also consistent with the expectations for an open-minded, high-complexity leader.

In *High Self-Monitoring, Attention to Interpersonal Relations, and Avoidance of Conflict*, Betsey Wright has commented that "the foremost thing about this man [Clinton] is that he loves people, he genuinely adores people, and wants that love back. . . . In fact he goes crazy if he can't have it" (Purdum, 1996, p. 14). In fact, Clinton's need for affirmation and interaction with people has consistently been seen as one of the strongest elements of his personality, and a large factor in his desire to please everyone (Drew, 1994; Reich, 1997; Stephanopoulos, 1999). As Maraniss (1998) noted, "Clinton's ability to empathize with others, his desire to become a peacemaker and bring diverse groups together, always struck me as the better part of his character" (p. 18).

However, this stereotypical image of Clinton's personality as being one dominated by the need to be liked by others may actually confuse his affiliative needs with his validation needs. As Renshon (1996) observed:

> At least two theoretical and factual difficulties stand in the way of this argument. First, there is Clinton's very high level of self-confidence. Ordinarily, the need to be liked would not be associated with such personal confidence. Second, the idea of a 'need to be liked' does not fully come to grips with Clinton's well-documented tendency toward public and private displays of anger . . . [and] fails to address . . . his tendency to demonize, build up, and then lash out against those who oppose his policies. . . . Presidents, like others, can be known by and benefit from having certain kinds of enemies. However, for a man who is said to have such a strong need to be liked, the list of enemies is rather long and his characterizations of them often harsh. . . . The central emotional issue for Clinton is a strong need to be validated. . . . [which] is reflected in a person's efforts to be acknowledged for the specific ambitions, skills, and accomplishments by which he defines himself. It is important that these specific aspects of oneself be met with appreciation and acknowledgment from important others. (pp. 99–100)

These observations by Renshon are consistent with the behaviors one would expect, given Clinton's LEAD scores, which show a low need for affiliation and a high need for task achievement, but significantly, one of the highest scores for self-confidence recorded in a 94-world-leader data set. But whatever their origins, clearly most observers see Clinton as highly attentive to interpersonal relations (for either personal or political reasons), a high self-monitor who constantly probes the environment (through polls, FOBs, etc.) for feedback regarding his performance and for signals regarding what policies are popular, and as someone who generally avoids serious conflicts with others, when possible (Drew, 1994; Maraniss, 1995; Reich, 1997; Stephanopoulos, 1999; Woodward, 1996).

Reflecting this chameleon-like quality of the high self-monitor, Stephanopoulos notes that watching Clinton was like looking into a kaleidoscope: "What you see is where you stand and where you're looking at him. He will put one facet toward you, but that is only one facet" (Woodward, 1994, p. 211). The true empath, Clinton projects attentiveness, sympathy, warmth—whatever the audience requires—which is one reason why supplicants advocating a certain policy position before the president often came away believing (erroneously) that Clinton had agreed with them or adopted their positions. Although tremendously useful for a politician, this characteristic also has a double edge, when these supplicants, having heard what they wanted to hear, later view Clinton's lack of policy movement as evidence of waffling or a policy flip-flop (Reich, 1997; Stephanopoulos, 1999).

For Clinton, friends are links in an ever-expanding network of contacts, useful for both future political support and as a source of advice (Maraniss, 1995). Possessing a skill reminiscent of Lyndon Johnson, Clinton had a "novelistic sensibility about people" (Maraniss, 1995, p. 240) and remembered for future use important things about their lives, the names of their family members, their home towns, their interests. Clinton friends have remarked that he "had a way of making you feel you were the most important friend in his life and what happened to you was the most important thing that ever happened" (Maraniss, 1995, p. 220), or, as Reich described it, Clinton's "you-are-the-only-person-in-the-world-who-matters gaze" (Reich, 1997, p. 133). Further, Clinton was "a master of sustained eye contact, hunting reactions in the eyes of an audience of one or a thousand" (Woodward, 1994, p. 5). As Stephanopoulos (1999) notes:

> When he was "on" before a live audience, Clinton was like a jazz genius, jamming with his pals. He poured his whole body into the speech, swaying to the rhythms of his words, losing himself in a wonky melody, soaring from the text with riffs synthesized from a lifetime of hard study and sympathetic listening. If he sensed a pocket of resistance in the crowd, he leaned its way, determined to move them with raw will if sweet reason didn't work. (pp. 202–203)

Part of the reason behind this Clinton emphasis upon interpersonal relations undoubtedly centers around his extraordinarily high self-confidence, internal locus of control, and complexity. As Reich (1997) noted:

> [Clinton] is an eternal optimist, convinced that there's always a deal lying out there *somewhere*. That's what makes him a supersalesman: He is absolutely certain that every single person he meets—Newt Gingrich, Yasir Arafat, whoever—*wants* to find common ground. It's simply a matter of discovering where it is. (p. 238)

Clinton viewed himself as a fighter who does his best when under the gun. Demonstrating his internal locus of control, colleagues note that Clinton rarely conceded that a problem was insoluble (Drew, 1994). Instead, his motivation to successfully address the problem rose to the challenge, driven by his steadfast belief that he was personally capable of resolving the issue through his own efforts (Drew, 1994; Maraniss, 1995; Renshon, 1996). For example, Stephanopoulos (1999) recalls that "Clinton's favorite remedy for personal and political malaise was to hit the road. . . . If his staff couldn't get the message out, he'd do it himself (i.e., crisscross the country on fund-raisers, rallies, talk-radio shows, etc.)" (p. 317). Indeed, the president's remarkable interpersonal skills translated into a tremendous political asset, allowing Clinton confidence that he could reach out and bring audiences to his side.

Finally, as would be expected, given Clinton's emphasis upon interpersonal relationships, he generally sought to avoid direct conflict with others. Clinton would often use surrogates to present alternative ideas during Oval Office meetings or to make arguments that the president himself felt uncomfortable making (Reich, 1997; Stephanopoulos, 1999). Further, he had a well-known distaste for dispensing bad news, preferring to use surrogates for those tasks as well, such as firing individuals, reassigning them, and so on (Drew, 1994; Maraniss, 1995; Morris, 1997; Purdum, 1996; Stephanopoulos, 1999). At the same time, Clinton was also renowned for having a tremendous temper, which was frequently unleashed at aides, including Stephanopoulos, who named the variants of these tempers: the slow boil, the show outburst, the last gasp outburst, and the silent scream (which was essentially a version of the LBJ silent treatment). But these were usually momentary outbursts and, as Stephanopoulos (1999) also notes, "Clinton has political grace; he doesn't stand on ceremony and goes out of his way to share political credit" with his staff (p. 313). For the most part, Clinton sought happy, non-confrontational associations with those around him and, like Bush, was noted for performing more than "the political average of thoughtful gestures—making a considerate phone call, doing something special for someone who had been slighted" (Maraniss, 1995: 47; Drew, 1994).

The Nuclear Crisis With North Korea (1993–1994)

One of the first foreign policy crises faced by Clinton involved a problem inherited from the Bush administration, namely, North Korea's possible pursuit of a nuclear weapons program. For a number of years, suspicion had been growing about Pyongyang's nuclear ambitions, suspicions heightened by the construction of a plutonium reprocessing plant at Yongbyon, which would allow weapons-grade material to be separated from spent fuel from North Korea's three nuclear reactors. Between 1989 and 1991, the International Atomic Energy Agency (IAEA) reported that Pyongyang had reprocessed spent fuel at least three times, leading the U.S. intelligence community to suspect that material had been diverted to weapons production (Mazaar, 1995; Sigal, 1998). Policy making on Korea was delegated, within the Clinton administration, to the president's foreign policy team (NSC Adviser Lake, Secretary of State Christopher, Defense Secretary Les Aspin) and their staffs. As expected for a delegator–observer, Clinton, whose interests lay in domestic policy, took little direct interest in the shaping of U.S. policy and was not personally involved in the crisis until well over a year later.

Throughout 1993, Lake sought to "frame consensus positions" and accommodate "differences of view" (Sigal, 1998, p. 53) between departments, as tremendous outside political pressure began building in support of a military response. As Sigal (1998) observed, the issue quickly "devolved to the lower ranks" (p. 54), with Assistant Secretary of State for Politico-Military Affairs Robert Gallucci finally taking charge of policy in late Spring of 1993. However, as an assistant secretary, Gallucci lacked bureaucratic clout or standing within the State Department to put together a deal, had no one-on-one meetings with Christopher, and had to clear all of his initiatives with lower level superiors, such as Undersecretary of State for

Politico-Military Affairs Lynn Davis and Undersecretary for Political Affairs Peter Tarnoff, neither of whom supported diplomatic initiatives with Pyongyang. Although high-level talks did resume, staffers observed that North Korea policy "was a series of ad hoc improvisations without any organizing concept" (Sigal, 1998, p. 55). Further, significant disputes soon erupted between State and Defense over control of North Korean policy, with Defense officials pushing for a military response, instead of the diplomatic approach favored by State. Because interagency agreement could not be obtained for anything else, U.S. diplomatic efforts by Gallucci avoided dealing with any substantive issues and focused solely upon promising continued high-level talks to Pyongyang as an inducement to avoid reprocessing (Sigal, 1998).

This pattern of U.S.–North Korean negotiations continued through the fall, with little progress being made. Policymakers in Washington remained at odds over the direction of policy, and the NSC was unable to provide coherent direction. As Assistant Secretary of Defense Ashton Carter observed: "It was such a dysfunctional NSC system at that time that nothing could get done. There was almost an aversion to clarity because it binds one's hands. It used to drive me nuts. Everything was still up for grabs" (Sigal, 1998, pp. 80–81). By November 7, 1993, when Clinton publicly stated that "North Korea cannot be allowed to develop a nuclear bomb," a draft National Intelligence Estimate (NIE), circulating within the government, had put the odds at better than even that Pyongyang already had one or two bombs (quoted in Engleberg & Gordon, 1993; Sigal, 1998).

At the November 15 NSC principals meeting, State, Defense, and the Joint Chiefs of Staff continued to debate the proper direction of U.S. policy. The State Department's proposal, which set preconditions for a new round of bilateral talks and which proposed a package deal —covering a range of nuclear, economic, and political issues of interest to both sides, but focusing first upon the nuclear issue—was eventually accepted (Sigal, 1998). However, once the November NIE was released, CIA Director James Woolsey publicly announced that his agency believed there was little chance of restoring inspections to Pyongyang's nuclear facilities and warned that the North could soon resume reprocessing, which built pressure for military action. At the December 6 NSC principal's meeting, after considerable debate between Lake and Aspin, Clinton agreed to continue diplomacy, but then took until April 4, 1994, to actually establish a formal advisory structure to help set the priorities for these talks. The Senior Policy Steering Group on Korea, chaired by Gallucci, who was given the rank of ambassador-at-large and freed from his normal duties at State, was authorized to report directly to the NSC and, for the first time, established a full-time group within the administration to carry out nuclear diplomacy with North Korea (Sigal, 1998). Thus, for well over a year, Clinton was mostly uninvolved in the policy debate, delegated policy formulation to low-level staff (where it was subjected to intense bureaucratic infighting), and failed to establish formal structures to coordinate policy.

By June 1994, the crisis had worsened considerably, with North Korea beginning to reprocess spent fuel, the United States attempting without success to gain support for economic sanctions from Pyongyang's neighbors (China, Japan, and South Korea), and domestic political pressure building for a military response (Mazaar, 1995; Sigal, 1998). Then, the American ambassador to South Korea, James Laney, helped trigger the chain of events leading to former President Carter's trip to Pyongyang and the eventual resolution of the crisis. Laney, concerned about the administration's policy approach of pursuing sanctions and sending military reinforcements to South Korea, contacted Carter to urge his involvement. After phoning Clinton on June 1, to express his concern over U.S. policy, Gallucci was dispatched to brief the former president, who decided that North Korean leader Kim Il Sung needed to be communicated with directly, to avert disaster. After Carter sent Clinton a letter stating that he intended to go to North Korea, Clinton decided to take the political gamble and approved

Carter's trip. Carter was briefed by administration officials and was told by Lake that he would have no official authority to speak for the United States or to negotiate a change in existing U.S. policy toward the North. Instead, his role was only to offer Sung a way out of the crisis (Sigal, 1998).

As Carter negotiated, Clinton convened the NSC on June 16, to discuss the crisis and to authorize U.S. military reinforcements for Seoul, prior to the imposition of sanctions against the North. The CIA warned the president that the planned reinforcements (an initial 23,000 troops of an estimated 400,000 troops required if war broke out) might trigger a North Korean mobilization and raise the risk of preemptive war. In contrast, recalling Somalia, Joint Chiefs Chairman John Shalikashvili and Defense Secretary William Perry warned of the risks of not sending the reinforcements—an argument which led Clinton to approve the deployment. But events soon took a dramatic turn, as Carter interrupted this meeting with a phone call, not only announcing that Kim Il Sung had agreed to freeze his nuclear weapons program under IAEA monitoring and to resume high-level talks on a comprehensive settlement of the nuclear issue, but also that he (Carter) planned to immediately announce the agreement live on CNN. Speaking to CNN, Carter, repudiated the U.S. policy of pursuing sanctions, effectively killing the sanctions movement in the United Nations Security Council (Sigal, 1998). As one top official later noted, "It blindsided us" (Sigal, 1998, p. 157).

Although Clinton officials were furious at being upstaged in public by Carter, Gore suggested making "lemonade out of this lemon," by taking the Carter–Kim deal and interpreting it to Washington's advantage—essentially borrowing a page from Kennedy's handling of the Cuban Missile Crisis, when he responded to the second, not the first, Khrushchev letter (Sigal, 1998). Drafting a response, Clinton's senior advisers proposed raising the bar, before resuming talks—requiring that the North not restart the Yongbyon reactor—and quickly consulted with the South Korean and Japanese foreign ministers. However, Carter, who disagreed with the continued U.S. pursuit of sanctions, used an open CNN microphone, during a subsequent meeting with Kim, to say, "I would like to inform you that they have stopped the sanctions activity in the United Nations" (Watson, 1994, p. 39). As one diplomat later noted, Carter's "larger purpose was to prevent the one thing from happening that the North had warned would be the point of no return" (Sigal, 1998, pp. 161–162). Although reluctant to give up its sanctions strategy and concerned about appearing to appease North Korea, Clinton was not inflexible and proved willing to take advantage of the opportunity created by Carter to settle the crisis. As Clinton later told his NSC staffers, the agreement would "give the North Koreans an exit. . . . If an ex-president came to them, that was something they could respond to. It would allow them a graceful climb-down" (Sigal, 1998, p. 160). Further, although Clinton's willingness to seize the opportunity to avoid a confrontation represented an abrupt shift of policy, "it also showed his political courage in the face of fierce opposition" (Sigal, 1998, p. 162). On June 22, the deal was announced, including North Korea's promise to allow IAEA inspections of its reactors and to cease all reprocessing/reloading activities until after a third round of peace talks—negotiations which eventually led to the Agreed Framework of October 1994, ending the crisis (Berman & Goldman, 1996; Mazaar, 1995; Sigal, 1998).

Consistent with expectations, Clinton's foreign policy style during the Korean case followed the delegator–observer pattern, that is, limited presidential involvement, extensive delegation of policy formulation and implementation to subordinates, heavy reliance upon expert advisers when making decisions, limited sensitivity to the external environment, but substantial emphasis upon the domestic environment in his information gathering. Further, as predicted by the framework presented in Preston and 't Hart (1999), which is discussed in chapter 4, Clinton's personal characteristics led to extensive bureaucratic in-fighting among lower level staff and departments to whom policy formulation had been delegated, resulting in both overanalysis of policy problems and inefficient decision making. At the same time, Clinton's constant search for information, flexibility, and willingness to consider alternative policy approaches (such as a Carter mission) was clearly displayed in this case and played a significant role in the eventual peaceful resolution of the conflict.

CONCLUSION

Obviously, this chapter serves as only a starting point for students interested in political psychological approaches to personality or leadership. However, this overview of a number of the more widely known psychological approaches used in research on political questions, as well as the case study application example just described, should give the reader a sense of how these approaches tend to be employed. These leader personality and style variables, discussed in this chapter, also have significant impact upon the group processes, bureaucratic politics, and political behavior discussed in chapter 4.

KEY TERMS

Cognitive style
Collegial management
  style
Competitive management
  style

Formalistic management
  style
Orientation toward
  political conflict
Sense of efficacy

Transactional leadership
Transformational
  leadership

Topics, Theories/Explanations/Frameworks, and Cases in Chapter 5

Topics	Theories/Frameworks	Cases
Burn's transactional and transformational types of leadership		
Leader management style	Johnson's (1974) formalistic, competitive, and collegial management styles	
	George's (1980) cognitive style, sense of efficacy, tolerance of political conflict	
	Hermann et al.'s (1996) three leadership style dimensions: responsiveness to constraints, openness to information, and motivational focus	
	Preston's (2001) typology and three style dimensions: *leader need for control, prior policy experience/expertise, and sensitivity to context*	Clinton

SUGGESTIONS FOR FURTHER READING

George, A. L. (1980). *Presidential decisionmaking in foreign policy: The effective use of information and advice.* Boulder, CO: Westview.

George, A. L., & George, J. L. (1998). *Presidential personality and performance.* Boulder, CO: Westview.

Greenstein, F. I. (1988). *Leadership in the modern presidency.* Cambridge, MA: Harvard University Press.

Preston, T. (2001). *The president and his inner circle: Leadership style and the advisory process in foreign policy making.* New York: Columbia University Press.

Preston, T., & 't Hart, P. (1999). Understanding and evaluating bureaucratic politics: The nexus between political leaders and advisory systems. *Political Psychology, 20,* 49–98.

Preston, T., & Hermann, M. G. (1998). Presidential leadership style and the foreign policy advisory process. In E. Wittkopf & J. McCormich (Eds.), *The domestic sources of American foreign policy: Insights and evidence* (4th ed.). Lanham, MD: Rowman & Littlefield.

ENDNOTES

1.   See also Burke and Greenstein, 1991; Campbell, 1986; Crabb and Mulcahy, 1986; George, 1980; George and George, 1998; Greenstein, 1982, 2000; Haney, 1997; Hargrove, 1988; Johnson, 1974; Jones, 1988; Pika, 1988; Porter, 1980; Preston, 1997, 2001.

2.   Clinton scored low on measures of prior foreign policy experience, as well as on LEAD measures of power (.16), affiliation (.10), ethnocentrism (.15), and distrust of others (.07). He scored high on cognitive complexity (.50), locus of control (.59), and self-confidence (.94). These scores place Clinton over three standard deviations lower in needs for power and ethnocentrism than the averages in the 94-world-leader data set. Clinton was also one standard deviation lower in distrust of others, but over one standard deviation higher than average in both his locus of control and self-confidence. Clinton profile courtesy of Margaret Hermann. For more information, see www.socialscienceautomation.com

CHAPTER 6

Voting, Role of the Media, and Tolerance

How do Americans think and feel about politics? The political thoughts and feelings of the American public have been the subject of intense and prolific research since the 1950s. Questions such as, How sophisticated is the public about politics and democratic ideals? How much attention do Americans pay to political information? How do people process and use information (particularly during electoral campaigns)? and How do Americans make decisions when deciding for whom to vote? have been important in political psychology. In addition, political psychologists have been interested in the impact of the media on American political thinking.

Another important question raised by political psychologists about American political beliefs concerns the issue of how tolerant Americans are of views contrary to their own. Needless to say, in a democracy this is an extremely important matter, because democratic ideals hinge upon the notion that even very unpopular views may be expressed without fear of reprisal or repression. This chapter looks at some of the findings and controversies in political psychology regarding the political attitudes of ordinary American citizens. The Political Being in this chapter is an average citizen. We focus primarily upon the attitudes and cognition component of their mind and the *us* part of the political environment: We are looking at the Political Being in the context of politics at home in the United States (and Britain).

We begin with some concepts, then turn to the classic study by the Michigan school of thought on the nature of American political attitudes and sophistication. We then consider some critics of the Michigan school's perspective. From that topic, we turn to studies of how people process information during campaigns and how their feelings affect for whom they decide to vote. We then discuss the media in American politics, political socialization in the United States, and political tolerance in America, all of which are important topics in studies of public opinion. After that we compare American political attitudes with those in Great Britain. To begin, let us review some of the central concepts analysts use to study public opinion.

BELIEFS, VALUES, IDEOLOGY, ATTITUDES, AND SCHEMAS

In chapter 3, the term **beliefs** was defined as associations people create between an object and its attributes (Eagly & Chaiken, 1998). Another useful definition of beliefs is "cognitive components that make up our understanding of the way things are" (Glynn, Herbst, O'Keefe, Shapiro, 1999, p. 104). When beliefs are clustered together, we call it a **belief system**. Most Americans, for example, have a belief system about democracy that includes such beliefs as "Free speech is a necessity," "The people have a right to decide who holds political power," and "All citizens should have the right to vote."

Values are closely related, but have an ideal component. Beliefs reflect what we think is true; values reflect what we wish to see come about, even if it is not currently true. Rokeach (1973)

125

argued that there are two types of values, *terminal values*, which are goals, and *instrumental values*, which endorse the means to achieve those goals. For example, Americans want a safe society and want the police to maintain law and order. This is a terminal value—a concern for the well-being of the people. At the same time, Americans value civil liberties, defined in the constitution, and endorse only those behaviors by the police that enforce public safety and order through means that do not violate civil liberties. This is an example of instrumental values.

Values and beliefs are closely related, and when we refer to political values and belief systems, we call it an **ideology**, which is "a particularly elaborate, close-woven, and far-ranging structure" of attitudes and beliefs (Campbell et al., 1964, p. 111). American political values and ideology are rooted in Lockean liberalism, that is, the philosophical ideas of John Locke, and, although attitudes about many issues have changed over time, these values remain much the same, even after more than 200 years (McClosky & Zaller, 1984).

A central concept in the study of political psychology used in this chapter is **attitudes**, which we present in chapter 3 as an enduring system of positive or negative beliefs, affective feelings and emotions, and subsequent action tendencies regarding an attitude object, that is, the entity being evaluated. Some of the controversies regarding this type of definition are discussed in chapter 3, as well. In terms of research on the political psychology of Americans and their subsequent political behavior, some central questions regarding attitudes have been: (1) Are attitudes consistent with one another? In other words, do people have consistently liberal or consistently conservative attitudes? (2) Are political attitudes consistently related to political behavior? For example, do people who consider themselves to be Republicans, and who hold Republican views on political issues, also vote for Republican party candidates? (3) How do people use attitudes to process political information? (4) How do people acquire their political attitudes? (5) How sophisticated are political attitudes in a given population? Are they cognitively complex? (6) If people do have inconsistent attitudes, how do they balance the inconsistencies?

The attitude concept has a long tradition in the study of public opinion, but, more recently, the schema concept was introduced. As we saw in chapter 3, a **schema** is defined as a "cognitive structure that represents knowledge about a concept or type of stimulus, including its attributes and the relations among those attributes" (Fiske & Taylor, 1991, p. 8).[1]

POLITICAL SOPHISTICATION IN AMERICA

Beginning in the late 1940s, researchers armed with surveys set out to investigate the nature of American political attitudes. They were interested in the question of how sophisticated Americans were and in the internal consistency of their attitudes. The deeper question underlying this research concerned the quality of democracy in America. Presumably, a functioning democracy requires citizens to make informed decisions when they vote. This requires some degree of political sophistication, that is, knowledge about the political system they live in and the issues that are important. However, despite the importance attributed to political sophistication, there is considerable disagreement as to whether it should be considered knowledge about politics, or, more broadly, knowledge, attention, interest, and involvement in politics (McGraw, 2000).

The Michigan School

The groundbreaking study of American political sophistication, *The American Voter* (Campbell et al., 1960, 1964), was discouraging for those who believe democracy must be founded on a citizenry interested in, and informed and thoughtful about, democratic principles and political issues of the day. Because *The American Voter* was based upon survey results from the Survey Research Center at the University of Michigan, its model of the American voter became known as the Michigan school, or Michigan model. Specifically, the researchers were interested in finding out whether people had consistently liberal or conservative values; whether those values were related to their party identification and loyalty and to their policy preferences; and how they determined for whom to vote.

The authors began with the assumption that Americans should have an integrated mental map of the political system:

> "The individual voter sees the several elements of national politics as more than a collection of discrete, unrelated objects. After all, they are parts of one political system and are connected in the real world by a variety of relations that are visible in some degree to the electorate. A *candidate* is the nominee of his *party*; party and candidate are oriented to the same *issues* or *groups*, and so forth. Moreover, we may assume that the individual strives to give order and coherence to his image of these objects." (Campbell et al., 1964, p. 27)

In other words, these are the cognitive categories utilized by Americans to simplify and organize American politics.

Campbell et al. then anticipated that American attitudes about candidates, issues, party, and group interests would be structured, that is, would be functionally related to each other and to an ideology. Ideally, people should know what liberal and conservative values are, what positions on important political issues are liberal and conservative positions, which party represents liberal and which party represents conservative principles, and which candidates stand for which issues. For example, a person who opposes big government (a conservative ideological attitude) should also feel an attachment to the Republican party (the conservative party in the United States), vote for candidates espousing similar views, and belong to groups that benefit from minimal government. In addition, that person should favor other conservative positions on other issues, such as taxes, labor rights, federal versus state power, and so on. This type of person could justifiably be called an ideologue. A liberal ideologue would be equally consistent, with liberal attitudes regarding party (Democratic party), issues, and candidate preferences. An ideologue was considered a political sophisticate in the sense that such a person would presumably be politically aware, could understand and process political information consistently, and would make political choices suitable for their personal, group, and value-based interests.

What the authors of *The American Voter* (1964) reported, however, was that very few Americans fit the profile of an ideologue, that is, of a person who understood the differences between liberal and conservative principles and who could locate each party and the issues along liberal and conservative dimensions. They conducted surveys in which they asked people what they liked and disliked about the parties and candidates and coded the surveys in terms of the nature of the response. If the respondent expressed likes and dislikes in terms of ideological principles, that person was considered an ideologue. They classified people into one of several possible **levels of conceptualization**, on the basis of the primary attitudes used to express likes and dislikes about the parties and candidates. The levels of conceptualization are arranged in terms of degrees of sophistication. In fact, they found that only about 2.5% of their respondents fell into the ideologue level of conceptualization. The second level of conceptualization of respondents was called the "near-ideologues." These people claimed to know the differences between liberal and conservative principles, but were less confident about, and less able to articulate, those principles. About 9.5% of the sample fell into the near-ideologue level of conceptualization.

The next level of conceptualization, the "group benefits" level, was populated by people who saw political issues in terms of concrete benefits for their group, compared to those for other groups in society. At this level, "there is little comprehension of 'long-range plans for social betterment,' or of basic philosophies rooted in postures toward change or abstract conceptions of social and economic structure or causation" (Campbell et al., 1964, p. 135). Forty-two percent of the respondents fell into this category. Level four was populated by "nature of the times" folks, who had no conception of ideology, no recognition of group interests, and who, when they did think of politics, thought simply in terms of whether times were good or bad for themselves and their families. Good times meant that the party of the president was good; bad times meant that the party of the president should be punished. The category also included people who identified a single isolated issue with a party (e.g., Social Security benefits and the Democratic party). Twenty-four percent of the respondents fell into this category.

The final level was "absence of issue content"—the boobie prize level. These people, 22.5%, knew nothing about political issues and approached politics solely in terms of party membership (absent any understanding of the party's position on issues) or candidate appeals (looks, religion, or sincerity, rather than issue positions), when they had anything resembling a political opinion. Few of the people at this level of conceptualization bothered to vote.

What this study demonstrated was that Americans are not political philosophers and that a deep understanding of politics and democracy was not the foundation of their decisions on how to vote. Subsequent studies using similar survey tools (but with important changes in question wording, which positively affected respondents' ability to express knowledge of politics) found an improvement in knowledge after the 1950s. In particular, *The Changing American Voter* (1976), by Nie, Verba, and Petrocik, covered elections from 1952 through 1976, and found that, as politics became more exciting in the 1960s, levels of conceptualization improved in terms of the numbers in the highest levels (they identified 31% ideologues), as did levels of issue consistency (i.e., people tended to take consistently liberal or conservative positions on a number of issues). However, a significant number of people remained fairly ignorant about politics. Later works, such as *The Unchanging American Voter* (1989), by Smith, although critical of important components of *The American Voter* (particularly the levels of conceptualization idea, which Smith argues is not a valid measurement of how people actually think about politics), provide further data supporting the argument that American political attitudes do not revolve around sophisticated political ideologies and ideological thinking. The political attitudes of Americans do not have a cognitive component sophisticated enough to understand abstractions such as liberalism and conservatism. Table 6.1 shows trends in levels of conceptualization over time. From this table, the reader can easily see that there was an upsurge in ideologues during the "hot politics" years of the 1960s and early 1970s. But, by and large, the American public remains nonideological.

Just how little Americans know about politics is revealed in the findings of survey researchers. For example, for many years, pollsters have asked people, after a national election, which party won the most seats in the House of Representatives and which party has the most members in the House. In 1980, only 14% knew both (Smith, 1989). In 1986, 24% of Americans were either unable to recognize Vice President George Bush's name, or could not identify his office, even though he had been in the office of vice president for 6 years (Zaller, 1992). In a 1966 national election study, only 1.9% of the public could name even half of the members of the Supreme Court, and not one of the 1,500 people surveyed could name all nine members of the Supreme Court (Zaller, 1992). In March 2000, after months of intense and often bitter competition, both Al Gore and George W. Bush had secured enough delegates to get the nomination for the presidential candidacy from the Democratic and Republic parties, respectively. But only 66% of Americans could correctly name both candidates, and 20% could

TABLE 6.1
Levels of Conceptualization Over Time

Levels of Conceptualization	1956	1960	1964	1968	1972	1976	1980	1984	1988
Ideologues	12%	19%	27%	26%	22%	21%	21%	19%	18%
Group benefit	42	31	27	24	27	26	31	26	36
Nature of the times	24	26	20	29	34	30	30	35	25
No issue content	22	23	26	21	17	24	19	19	21
N	1,740	1,741	1,431	1,319	1,372	2,870	1,612	2,257	2,040

Note: From Controversies in voting behavior (3rd ed., p. 89), by R. Niemi and W. Weisberg (Eds.), 1993, Washington, DC: Congressional Quarterly.

name neither (Gallup Poll, 2000). A Gallup poll taken in July 2001 found that only 11% of Americans claimed to follow the national missile defense issue closely, despite heavy news coverage of that controversial proposal by the Bush administration. Fifty-eight percent thought that the United States already had a missile defense system, and only 28% knew that the United States did not have a missile defense system. On a more humorous note, a 1998 study by the National Constitution Center found that only 41% of American teenagers can name the three branches of government, but 59% know the names of the Three Stooges. And although only 2% know the name of the chief justice of the Supreme Court, we can all be comforted by the fact that 95% know the name of the actor who played the Fresh Prince of Bel Air on television (Will Smith) (Spokesman Review, "Teens Sharper," 1998).

The political attitudes that many Americans do have are not **constrained** or consistent, nor are they **stable**, that is, the same over time (Converse, 1964). In terms of constraint, this means that people do not have consistently liberal or conservative attitudes: They may be conservative on one issue and liberal on another. Without an underlying ideological guideline, such lack of constraint is not surprising, but the implication in terms of American political sophistication is controversial. In terms of stability, Converse (1964) noted that responses to attitude questions, for some people, remained very stable, but for others the responses changed in an apparently random pattern. He called this the **black and white model** of attitude change. We shall return to the issue of how Americans organize and process political information later but let us turn now to the question of which attitudes affect how Americans vote, and how they have changed.

The authors of The American Voter, and others included in the Michigan school, presented a model of political attitudes, and their relationship to each other, that depicted the causes of the vote. The model is called the **funnel of causality** (see Figure 6.1), and it distinguishes between **long-term** factors or attitudes that affect how Americans vote (which are attachment to a party, or **party identification,** and **group interests**) and **short-term** factors (currently important **issues** and **candidates'** personal characteristics). Party identification is an attitude by which a person considers themselves to be a Democrat or a Republican. Party identification is acquired through socialization and other life experiences and, the authors argued, tends to remain fairly stable, that is, it does not change over one's lifetime. Partisanship does vary in intensity, and the Michigan school scholars argued that those who were more strongly attached to a political party were more likely to be interested in and involved in politics. They were more likely to know more about politics and to vote. In the United States, the strength of attachment to the political parties diminished over the generations, since the height of party loyalty and attachment in the Great Depression, at which

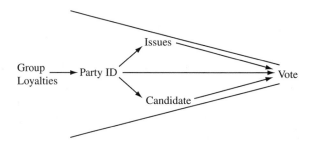

FIG. 6.1.   The funnel of causality.

time the Democratic party became the majority. Bartels (2000), however, presents data indicating that attachment to the parties reached its low point in 1996 and has since increased,
but only for those who actually vote. Another change since the Depression is that, as new
generations have entered the electorate, the Democratic party's majority status has changed.
The Depression generation was strongly attracted to the Democratic party, because of its
perception that Franklin Roosevelt and his New Deal policies, designed to end the Depression, were beneficial to the workers, the young, and immigrants who recently acquired citizenship. As that generation passes on and new generations come of voting age without the
same strong pull, the Democratic and Republican parties have become about equal in voter
identification, and over one third of voters (about 35% in the 1990s) consider themselves to
be Independent today, as well (although two thirds of the self-identified Independents lean
toward one of the two parties). According to the U.S. Census Bureau (1998), in 1994, the
distribution of party identifiers was as follows:

Strong Democrat	15%
Weak Democrat	19%
Independent Democrat	13%
Independent	10%
Independent Republican	12%
Weak Republican	15%
Strong Republican	16%

Party identification has a strong effect on how people vote, particularly on those who
identify intensely with their party. When you consider how little Americans actually know
about politics, the importance of party identification seems obvious. If people know little
about the current issues, those who identify always have their party attachment to guide
them in the voting booth. Party identification also affects how people view short-term
forces, such as issues and candidates. It is used to screen information and colors the voter's
interpretation of issues and candidates. But people do not always vote for candidates of their
own party, nor do they always agree with their party's stance on particular issues. When people defect and vote for the other party's candidates, it is the result of short-term forces. For
example, a moderate conservative who is a member of the Republican party, but who favors
reproductive choice, might decide not to vote for George W. Bush, because he is opposed to
abortion rights. Or, recall our friend from chapter 3, who is a lifelong Democrat and a strong
party loyalist, who briefly considered voting for George W. Bush, but ended up voting for Al
Gore. Education policy was one of several important short-term forces for her (the others
favoring Gore), and partisanship kept its strong pull.

The Michigan school developed a formula for analyzing the impact of partisanship, issues, and candidate characteristics in each election. Because partisanship is a long-term factor affecting the vote, they reasoned that an election in which people voted according to their party identification, and in which Independents split evenly between the two parties, could be considered a baseline, or an ideal typical election. They labeled such an election a **normal vote** (Converse, 1966). They could then look at different elections and determine the relative importance of partisanship, issues, and candidate characteristics. In the 1950s, 1960s, and 1970s, when the Democratic party was the majority party, a normal vote was 54% Democratic and 46% Republican (the distribution of party identification changed in the last part of the twentieth century, so that Republican and Democratic identifiers are each roughly 33% and independents are the other 33%). Thus, the 1952 and 1956 elections deviated from the normal vote, because Dwight Eisenhower, the Republican candidate for the presidency, won. His election was mostly the result of candidate appeal short-term forces (he was immensely popular)—pro-Republican foreign policy attitudes and a negative popular reaction to Democratic skills in managing government.

The arguments that partisanship lasts a lifetime, even when one defects repeatedly and votes for the other party, and that it outweighs short-term factors when people decide how to vote, have come under attack. Rational choice analysts, who are not political psychologists, argue that people vote on issues in terms of self-interest calculations and that partisanship itself is a collage of short- and long-term forces (e.g., Brody & Rothenberg, 1988; Fiorina, 1981; Franklin, 1992; Franklin & Jackson, 1983; Markus & Converse, 1979; Page & Jones, 1979). Political psychologists, on the other hand, have studied candidate evaluations from a cognitive information-processing perspective, findings to which we turn a bit later. The Michigan model's emphasis on partisanship was defended in 1996, with the publication of *The New American Voter,* by Miller and Shanks.

The Maximalists

The Michigan model is not the final word on the sophistication of the American voter. Lane (1962, also; Lane & Sears, 1964) and others had a more optimistic evaluation of the quality and quantity of political knowledge Americans had and sought. Some argue that, even if Americans do not have consistently liberal or conservative political attitudes, they may organize their attitudes, anyway, but in a way different than that expected by the Michigan school. Perhaps the biggest political psychological challenge to the Michigan model is the Maximalist school. These scholars maintain that the Michigan model is a minimalist picture of the American political worldview. They argue that, looked at differently, Americans are much more politically sophisticated than the Michigan model maintains.

Sniderman, Brody, and Tetlock (1991) trace the challenge to the minimalist picture of the American political thinker to the alternative picture painted in *The Changing American Voter* (Nie et al., 1976) and to an article by Stimson (1975). The former we have already mentioned—they provided data indicating that, when politics gets more exciting, the public becomes more informed and sophisticated. Stimson, and later Neuman (1986), argued that the problem with the Michigan model is that it attempts to treat the public as one group, but, in reality, there is great variation across the public. Neuman (1986) maintains that there are three publics: (1) the political sophisticates (about 5%), who know a great deal about politics and who are very active; (2) the majority (about 75% of the public), who have advanced education and, in effect, have cognitive abilities, but who are not often strongly motivated to use them in the realm of politics; and (3) those who are truly apolitical (about 20% of the population), who will never be interested or involved and who lack the cognitive capabilities to be so, even if they wanted to.

The Maximalists challenged the Michigan model's basic premises about how people think about politics (the cognitive component), and they added the importance of affect into the process of thinking about politics (Sniderman et al., 1991). Their argument maintains that the Michigan school's assumption that people organize their political thoughts in a linear (liberal to conservative) manner diverts attention from how people actually think about politics. In their own words:

> Belief systems, we reasoned, acquired structure through reasoning about choices. To see the structure they possessed, it was necessary to identify how people managed choices—that is, the considerations that they took into account and the relative weights they placed on them. The standard approach in effect asked: To what extent is one idea element connected to another *on the assumption the connections are approximately the same for everyone.*
>
> From our perspective, idea elements could, and likely were, connected in a variety of ways depending upon both the characteristics of the problem that a person was trying to work through and the characteristics of the person trying to work it through. Political choices pose problems, and the object of political psychology accordingly is to give an account, not simply of how people recollect their preferred solution to a problem, but of how they figured it out in the first place. (Sniderman et al., 1991, p. 3–4)

The authors pose a question: The minimalist model assumes that liberals and conservatives should have consistent positions on two issues, for example, government spending and pornography, but how does one get from one of those issues to the other (Sniderman et al., 1991)? Because they are not obviously related, one can connect them using only a higher order construct, that is, liberal or conservative ideology. Using ideology as a guideline, a person is expected to take either liberal or conservative positions on both issues, in order to be considered politically sophisticated by the minimalists. But why should we assume that this is the reasoning path people follow, and why grant this path the honor of being the hallmark of political sophistication? Why assume that such a deductive inference (i.e., using the higher order construct to connect the issues) is more likely to occur than a paired association (in this case, there is none, so why should one expect a related position on both issues)? According to Sniderman et al. (1991), the minimalist school

> asks us to suppose that the positions we take on issues, so far as we arrive at them through reasoning, are the product of logical entailment. This is an excessively cerebral account of political thinking, minimizing the role of affect, or feelings in political reasoning. (p. 7)

They maintain that, although not expert in political philosophies of liberalism and conservatism, people can process political information and decide where they stand on political issues, which we consider later.

Sniderman and Tetlock (1986) argue that the minimalist view of belief system structure assumes that it is, and should be, organized in a straight line along a liberal–conservative continuum. They offer a different perspective, and argue that beliefs can also be seen as organized in a weblike structure, with pockets of beliefs consistently related to other pockets. They note studies of Americans during the Cold War that demonstrated that people have internally coherent outlooks on topics, such as the rights of communists to speak freely, write, and work in mass media, universities, and even in defense plants. A person who granted communists one of those rights tended to grant them the others, too. Moreover, this pocket of beliefs would often be linked to other pockets. People who granted civil rights to one group of people did so not only because of their beliefs about civil liberties, but also because of their feelings toward other groups, beliefs about tolerance, and so forth. Sniderman and Tetlock (1986) argued that there can be many such pockets or only a few, depending on how cognitively complex the individual in question is. Cognitive complexity, in turn, depended on how adept the person is at abstract reasoning. From this perspective, they determined that at least one third of the mass public is cognitively complex and that another third is well-organized, at least in terms of the basic American values regarding democracy and capitalism.

Having reviewed some of the debate on the level of political sophistication in America, at least in terms of how much people know about politics, we can turn to the question of whether it matters. Do people take issue positions and vote in accordance with their interests, despite variations in levels of information and knowledge? Delli Carpini and Keeter (1996) argue that they do not, noting that those who were poorly informed did not connect their votes to their views on issues. Bartels (1996) agrees that there is an important difference in the voting patterns of informed and uninformed voters and that many uninformed voters would vote differently if they had full information. On the other hand, Lau and Redlawsk (1997) conducted experiments on voting and information. They defined "correct" voting as voting in accordance with the voters' own values. Subjects in the experiments were given limited information before voting and full information after voting, with the chance to change their vote. Only 30% chose to change their votes when given additional information.

Knowledge Structures

A related approach to reconceptualizing attitude complexity looks at **knowledge structures**. In a recent review of this literature, McGraw (2000) divided it into three categories: The first focuses on how people mentally organize information about political actors, a second body of research explores how those knowledge structures (e.g., stereotypes of the political parties) affect learning and decisions about political candidates, and a third body of literature examines how attitudes about issues are represented in the mind. Lavine (2002) divides the literature somewhat differently. He argues that one body of literature maintains that attitudes are affected by people's **memory**—what they recall about a candidate when they decide for whom to vote and what they think about issues. Another body of literature is one that examines **online** information processing, wherein people keep a running tally of information as they form attitudes on political issues.

The architecture of knowledge (or online) structures is a subject of debate. As mentioned earlier, Sniderman et al. (1991) believe that the architecture varies in complexity from individual to individual, but that it exists in weblike pockets of attitudes related to one another. Similarly, Judd and Krosnik (1989), along with McGraw and Steenbergen (1995), argue that people have **associative networks**, that is, knowledge structures embedded in long-term memory, which consist of nodes linked to one another, forming a network of associations. When nodes are linked together, thinking about one draws thoughts about the other(s). This is illustrated with a network of knowledge regarding a candidate, which becomes more complex as more is learned about the candidate. An associative network of a candidate would look like Figure 6.2.

As Judd and Krosnik (1989) explain, the linked nodes may be within a single category of political objects, or between different categories altogether:

> Thus, for instance, the policy of affirmative action may be linked to the policy of school integration. At the same time, the policy of affirmative action is also likely to be linked to more abstract value nodes, such as freedom or equality, as well as to object nodes representing political reference groups (e.g., Blacks) and candidates. (p. 109)

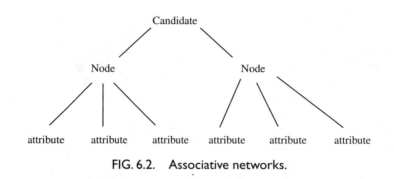

FIG. 6.2.   Associative networks.

Linked nodes imply that there is a positive or negative relationship between them (e.g., affirmative action is positively associated with equality and negatively associated with freedom). Nodes, and subsequently their links, also vary in strength, which affects the probability that the activation of one node will activate another, as well as the likelihood that the associated evaluations will be consistent (Judd & Krosnick, 1989). The stronger a node, the more likely it is to be linked to other relevant nodes in a consistent manner. The more nodes and the more links among them, the more consistent and complex a person's attitudes toward politics. One interesting aspect of this model is that is it entirely conceivable that a person may be quite sophisticated about politics in one domain, such as domestic politics, but not at all in another domain, such as foreign affairs. Indeed, in chapter 5, we saw that this even occurs among people very sophisticated about politics, such as President Clinton. In addition, when people are more complex in their thinking, they look for and process more information, when an attitude is important to them (Berent & Krosnick, 1995).

There is, however, considerable debate about whether Americans have such precomputed opinions about issues (Lavine, 2002). Part of the reason for this debate about the political sophistication of Americans is that this research relies very heavily upon surveys. As Zaller (1992), explains, surveys are likely to pick up what is on the top of the respondent's head:

> Most people really aren't sure what their opinions are on most political matters, including even such completely personal matters as their level of interest in politics. They're not sure because there are few occasions, outside of a standard interview situation, in which they are called upon to formulate and express political opinions. So, when confronted by rapid-fire questions in a public opinion survey, they make up attitude reports as best they can as they go along. But because they are hurrying, they are heavily influenced by whatever ideas happen to be at the top of their minds. (p. 76)

Zaller takes this point beyond surveys, however. He also maintains that people really are ambivalent on many political issues much of the time. Putting the public in the context of politics, in the midst of debate about an issue, enables one to see the complexity of the multiple attitudes involved. A person may, for example, support a woman's right to reproductive choice generally, but may be very ambivalent about late-term partial birth abortions. When politicians discuss complex issues, they frequently do so in terms of summary judgments, a conclusion that overrides underlying ambivalence. Survey questions ask respondents to do the same thing, and therefore, they pick up seeming instability in responses, because ambivalent attitudes can swing in different directions when a summary judgment is required.

In Zaller's (1992) view, people do not have true attitudes, such as those expected by the Michigan school,

> but a series of partially independent and often inconsistent ones. Which of a person's attitudes is expressed at different times depends on which has been made most immediately salient by change and the details of questionnaire construction, especially the ordering and framing of questions. (p. 93)

The debate has turned to the question of how people actually do process political information in America, and to that discussion we now turn.

INFORMATION PROCESSING AND VOTING

A central question addressed by the knowledge structure inquiries concerns how those structures are used to process information and make political choices, such as how to evaluate a candidate and for whom to vote. Those who know a lot about politics, and who are interested in it, will process information differently than those who know little and are not interested in politics (Lodge & Hamill, 1986; Sniderman, Glaser, & Griffin, 1990). But even people who have a great deal of interest in, and knowledge about, politics will take information shortcuts. They rely upon **attitudes, schemas,** and **heuristics** to help process information and make decisions. Pratkanis (1989) reminds us that a schema (or category) consists

> of both *content* (information in the schema and its organization) and *procedure* (the usage of this information in knowing). The dual role of a schema . . . is similar to that of the heuristic as cue (an evaluation stored in memory) and strategy (the use of this cue in problem solving). A schema differs from a heuristic in its complexity. A heuristic is one simple rule, whereas a schema is an organization of many rules and pieces of data within a domain. (p. 89)

Associative network models argue that nodes and links with greater strength are more easily summoned for thinking and information processing than are those with weak links (Judd & Krosnick, 1989; McGraw & Steenbergen, 1995). Associative network studies drew upon schema research to develop ideas about information processing. The accessibility of political schemas will influence how people think and what they are alert to. Those that are more frequently and most recently used will be readily available for use again (Popkin, 1994; Ottati & Wyer, 1993). Schemas are used to filter information, providing people with a means for deciding which information is correct, irrelevant, or incorrect. Schemas or category-based knowledge, that is, preexisting beliefs already present in a person's political mind, is also used as a source for substitute information, when current information about a political issue or candidate is missing.

How do people process political information? The steps through which people presumably proceed, upon receiving information, are as follows: Information is received, and the appropriate node or schema is primed; the information is matched to the knowledge structure and appropriate nodes; the information is assessed and stored in memory; finally, that evaluation is retrieved from memory, when the individual is called upon to make a decision about a political action (how to vote, what to think about a policy, etc.) (Anderson, 1983; Brewer, 1988; Fiske & Pavelchak, 1986; Graber, 1984; Lodge & Stroh, 1995; Ottati & Wyer, 1990). In the process, feelings about candidates also emerge and are stored in memory (Rahn, Aldrich,

Borgida, & Sullivan, 1990). Rather than placing feeling along a continuum from very negative to very positive, Lavine (2002) argues that people have stores or stockpiles of negative and positive feelings toward candidates, issues, and groups.

Of course, attention to information can be very selective (Iyengar, 1990; Ottati & Wyer, 1990). Some people are members of issue publics and are interested in particular issues. For example, the so-called soccer moms were intensely interested in education, child care, and health insurance issues, during the 1992 and 1996 elections. People can easily be more interested in one issue than another, and hence attentive to information about the issues they are interested in, but not to information about the issues they are not interested in. Delli Carpini and Keeter (1993, 1996) found that political elites have a remarkably large amount of information about politics and the political system. They pay very close attention to politics. For these people—political elites and issue publics—schemas related to political issues will be quite accessible. The more accessible a schema or node is, the more information related to it will be noticed by the perceiver. Accessibility varies, depending on how important an attitude is to the perceiver (Berent & Krosnick, 1995; Holtz & Miller, 1985; Huckfeldt, Levine, Morgan, & Sprague, 1999; Krosnick, 1988, 1989). Also, Lau (1995) maintains that people use those schemas or nodes that are primed, that is, are most readily accessible. In addition, as is discussed in more detail later, issue nodes can be made more accessible when the media focuses on a particular issue in depth (Iyengar, 1990).

Not only are people selective in their attention to information, but studies have questioned how well people actually remember information as campaigns progress. Lodge and Stroh (1995; see also Lodge, 1995; Lodge, McGraw, & Stroh, 1989) argue that, as information is acquired, it is used to enhance, or update, beliefs about a candidate or party, and the specific details of the information are forgotten. Likes and dislikes are influenced by the information, and are remembered, but a person may well be hard-pressed to explain what the liking or disliking is based upon. This **impression-based model** of information processing, memory, and evaluation of political candidates, stands in contrast to more traditional models, which maintain that people store in memory the evidence supporting their evaluations (see Dreben, Fiske, & Hastie, 1979; Hastie & Park, 1986; McGraw, Lodge, & Stroh, 1990; Srull & Ottati, 1995; Srull & Wyer, 1989). In another study looking at voters' use of information, Lodge, Steenbergen, and Brau (1995) also addressed the question of how much information voters remember from the campaign, when they go to vote. They argue that voters do forget lots of information, but that does not mean the information did not have an impact on their knowledge level when it was received. Voters keep a running tally or an online tally, from which information is used in forming an impression of the candidates. The specifics of the information may be forgotten, but the overall impression remains and is important in determining the vote.

A number of different heuristics, knowledge structures, and schema are important in processing political information (Lau, 1986; Ottati & Wyer, 1990; Rahn et al., 1990). There are many different heuristics serving as shortcuts in political information processing and judgments. Fiorina (1981) presents evidence of a retrospective voting heuristic, wherein voters make decisions about current candidates for office, based upon those candidates' performance in the past. The representativeness heuristic, presented in chapter 3, also plays an important role in political judgments. Recall that the representativeness heuristic is a rule of thumb for deciding what kind of person someone is, based on how closely that person fits a stereotype.

In deciding for whom to vote, according to Popkin (1994), "the most critical use of this heuristic involves projecting from a personal assessment of a candidate to an assessment of what kind of leader he[sic] was in previous offices or to what kind of president he[sic] will be in the future" (p. 74). People decide how well a candidate will perform in office based upon the goodness of fit between the candidate and the perceiver's stereotype of a good president or mayor or whatever office the person is running for. Popkin goes on to argue that this results in the generation of narratives about people, wherein specific traits serve as the foundation of a fuller picture of the individual under observation. This, in turn, results in **Gresham's law of political information,** which says that

> personal information can drive more relevant political information out of consideration. Thus there can be a perverse relationship between the amount of information voters are given about a candidate and the amount of information they actually use: a small amount of personal information can dominate a large amount of historical information about a past record. (Popkin, 1994, p. 79)

Another informational shortcut is the **drunkard's search,** named after the drunkard who lost his keys in the street and looks for them under the lamppost, because the light is better there, not because that is where he lost the keys. This is analogous to the use of information in political decisions, when people reduce complicated issues and choices among candidates to simple comparisons, because that is easier. This occurs in comparisons of candidates for office, when people use one-dimensional searches, focusing on obvious single issues or candidate characteristics, rather than searching for the complexities of both candidates and issues (Popkin, 1993; Jervis, 1995).

Heuristics are one form of mental shortcuts, and schemas are another. Among the most important schemas for Americans are partisanship, issues, and candidate schemas. The role of each type of schema is difficult to separate, because they interact with one another. Ottati and Wyer (1990) illustrate this with the following possibilities:

> A voter may infer that a candidate endorses a given set of issue positions (e.g., favors bombing Libya or favors military intervention in Nicaragua) because he or she believes the candidate has certain personal traits (e.g., assertive) that combine to form the candidate's "image." Conversely, a voter may infer the candidate's personal traits from his or her stands on various issues. Analogously, a voter's perception of a candidate's personal characteristics or issue orientation may elicit emotional responses to the candidate. On the other hand, a voter's assessment of his or her own reactions to the candidate may lead the voter to infer that the candidate has certain personal characteristics or holds issue positions that are evaluatively consistent with these reactions. (p. 205)

The earliest studies of voting behavior demonstrated the importance of partisanship as a schema. *The American Voter* (Campbell et al., 1964) described *partisanship* as an attitude used early on in information acquisition and that a candidate's party is the first consideration, with issue positions and a candidate's personal characteristics second. Party also affects people's impressions of candidates, so, from this perspective, it is the most important schema (Markus & Converse, 1979). For example, the schema or category "Democrat" has multiple pieces of information embodied in it. If a person is a Democrat, has the appropriate schema, and knows that candidate Smith is a Democrat, but has not bothered to get any information about where candidate Smith stands on issues, the association with the Democratic party will lead to assumptions that Smith agrees with the perceiver on important issues. A study by Lodge and Hamill (1986) shows some of the effects of partisan schema on information processing. When presented with statements by a fictitious congressional leader, people with party schemas were more able to correctly categorize statements as being Republican or Democrat than were people without party schemas. Those with schemas were better able to recall statements that were consistent with the party than those that were inconsistent.

Schematics also "systematically distort the congressman's stance on the issue by imposing more schematic order on his policy positions than was actually present in the campaign message" (Lodge & Hamill, 1986, p. 518) indicating a bias in political information processing.

Candidate schemas or knowledge structures have been studied extensively and are believed to be closely associated with how a particular candidate appeals to voters on particular issues (Funk, 1999; Graber, 1984; Jacobs & Shapiro, 1994; Kaid & Chanslor, 1995; Kinder, 1986; Markus, 1982; Miller & Shanks, 1996; Rahn et al., 1990). Miller, Wattenberg, and Malanchuk (1986) examined whether there exists a presidential schema, or a prototype of the president. In other words, do individuals have a preexisting schema about the president that they use to evaluate a candidate? In their examination of elections from 1952 to 1985, those authors found that individuals do in fact hold a presidential schema, central to which is the notion of competence (past political experience, ability as statesman, comprehension of political issues, and intelligence), which they regard as a performance-related criterion. Other dimensions, such as integrity (i.e., trustworthiness, honesty, sincerity, just another politician) and reliability (i.e., dependable, strong, hardworking, decisive, aggressive), became more relevant after 1964. Miller et al. (1986) note that these expectations about the performance of presidents "appear to reflect in part the actions of past presidents and in part the agenda set by the media or by current candidates" (p. 535).

The importance of candidate schemas in information processing is further emphasized by Rahn et al. (1990), who maintain that, although different people rely differentially on schemas of parties, issues, candidates, or groups, almost all of the massive amount of information available to voters during an election can be used in evaluating candidates. Hence, candidate appraisals are particularly important. Moreover, they maintain that, in election after election, five characteristics of candidates are important in determining how much voters like or dislike a candidate: competence, integrity, reliability, charisma, and personal characteristics (Rahn et al., 1990). Funk (1999) found that candidates and campaigns vary in the underlying trait dimensions that emerge as important in evaluations of candidates. The substantive content of traits makes a difference. In her study, Funk found that the leadership characteristic significantly affected overall evaluations of George Bush and Michael Dukakis in 1988. In 1992, Bush was evaluated in terms of leadership and empathy characteristics. Ronald Reagan, in 1984, was evaluated in terms of empathy and integrity; Walter Mondale, his opponent, was evaluated in terms of leadership during that election. In 1992 and 1996, Bill Clinton was evaluated in terms of all three characteristics: leadership, empathy, and integrity.

Schemas and attitudes about issues compose a third important element in the American view of politics. An **issue** is a dispute about public policy. Popkin (1994) argues that issues are effective in waging a campaign for office only when voters see connections "(1) between the issue and the office; (2) between the issue and the candidate; and (3) between the issue and the benefits they care about" (p. 100). People are more likely to attend to issues about which information is easily acquired, that is, issues that are immediate in their lives and that are easy to understand. This presents a formidable task for candidates for office. If candidates wish to campaign on issues, they must make the potential voters aware of where they stand on issues, that their position will benefit the voter, and that once in office they will actually have the power to affect the promised change.

Consequently, how issues are **framed** by candidates for office makes a big difference in whether or not, and how, the public will consider the issues (Gamson, 1992; Nelson & Oxley, 1999; Popkin, 1994; Zaller, 1992). Issue frames are "alternative definitions, constructions, or depictions of a policy problem" (Nelson & Oxley, 1999, p. 1041). How issues are framed influences the way voters look at the issues, and it also affects how accessible the issue attitude is in the perceivers' minds. Studies have shown framing to be important in presidential politics, as well as in race-related politics in the United States, which is a topic covered in chapter 7 (Kinder & Sanders, 1996; Mendelberg, 2001; Popkin, 1994). The studies done at Columbia University in 1948, for example, showed that the campaign changed the relative importance of international issues versus domestic issues, in voters' minds. Thinking about the positions of the candidates on domestic issues, instead of on international issues, affected voter preference in that election, because they framed the candidates differently. Popkin (1994) summarizes the findings regarding presidential politics and framing, as follows:

> There is enough differentiation in people's images of presidents for formulation effects to matter; changing people's ideas about problems facing the president changes the way people think about presidents; and changing the ways people think about presidents affects their assessments of presidents as well as their votes. (p. 84)

Candidates who engage in *frame alignment* (pointing out how their position on issues is consistent with voters' position) are likely to gain more support than candidates who do not.

EMOTION AND VOTING

In chapter 3, the importance of emotion in political behavior is discussed, and the work of Marcus et al. (2000) was introduced. In 1993, Marcus and MacKuen published a study that pointed to the importance of anxiety and enthusiasm in political learning and involvement. They argued that people do not simply respond to candidates positively or negatively (i.e., valence), but with specific emotions. Traditional notions of the effect of emotions on voting maintained that positive or negative feelings toward candidates directly influence how people vote. Marcus and MacKuen (1993), however, offered a more precise picture of how emotions affect political behavior during election time. Two emotions are central in responses to political events and candidates: fear (or anxiety) and enthusiasm. Enthusiasm affects the decision of for whom to vote; anxiety increases the search for information about candidates. When people do not experience anxiety, they tend to rely upon habit in determining how they will vote (e.g., party identification). Thus, anxiety has an important role in information processing, and it stimulates learning.

This argument is presented as a theory of affective intelligence in *Affective Intelligence and Political Judgment* (Marcus et al., 2000). Those authors examined interviews with people during the 1980, 1984, 1988, 1992, and 1996 presidential election campaigns, looking for trends in emotional responses to the candidates and voting decisions. They made assessments of voters' preferences, using the "standing choice" factors for these elections, that is, partisanship, issues, and the candidates' personal qualities. Then they added in an analysis of voters' enthusiasm and anxiety. For example, in the 1980 election, President Jimmy Carter began the campaign with public support and sympathy in the midst of the Iran hostage crisis and the Soviet invasion of Afghanistan. By October, however, the hostage rescue scheme had failed, the economy was in the doldrums, and public enthusiasm for Carter had waned. In addition, public anxiety regarding the competence of the administration grew, albeit modestly. Enthusiasm for Ronald Reagan, Carter's 1980 opponent, was modest, but the study shows an increase in anxiety regarding Reagan, after the Democrats launched a scare campaign in an effort to persuade voters that Reagan would be dangerous in foreign policy. In the 1984 campaign, enthusiasm for Reagan, by then a popular president, was high, and anxiety was not. The challenger, Walter Mondale, evoked neither enthusiasm nor anxiety. In 1988, when Vice President George Bush ran against Massachusetts Governor Michael Dukakis, the public's anxiety about

Dukakis was increased by the famous Willie Horton ads (discussed in more detail in chapter 7), which portrayed Dukakis as weak on crime. Overall, in their analyses of all five races from 1980 to 1996, Marcus et al. (2000) found that anxious voters were much less likely to rely upon partisanship in making a voting decision and much more likely to look for and attend to information about the candidates's personal qualities and issue positions. A caveat is that this anxiety must involve the voter's own candidate, the one they would ordinarily vote for, based upon partisanship. To be anxious about the other candidate is normal—one is always anxious about the candidate from the other party, nothing unusual about that, but doubts about the person one would ordinarily vote for produces anxiety.

MEDIA FRAMING AND PUBLIC OPINION

Does the media shape public opinion, and, if so, how? Many analysts agree with Cohen (1963), who wrote, "The press may not be successful much of the time in telling people what to think, but it is stunningly successful in telling its readers what to think about" (p. 13). People are limited in how much time and attention they can or wish to devote to politics. They rely upon the media to tell them which issues need attention and in what form. This is referred to as **agenda setting**. Studies have examined the amount of reporting issues received and find strong correlations between quantity of coverage and the importance attributed to issues by the public (McCombs & Shaw, 1972). Other studies have looked at the order in which issues are covered by the press and are regarded as important by the public, and have found that the press reporting comes first, followed by public perceptions of an issue's importance (Glynn et al., 1999).

Explanations of this pattern are based on the psychological concept of **priming.** Because political issues are many in number and extraordinarily complex, people need help in deciding which issues are important and which aspects of those issues need to be attended to. The news media provide that guidance by priming, that is, pointing out to the public which elements of which issues are important (Glynn et al., 1999; Iyengar & Kinder, 1987). For example, when primed by the media on an issue such as rising gas prices, individuals will judge President Bush on how well they think he has kept rising prices at bay. How does this work? As Miller and Krosnick (1996) explain, when making day-to-day decisions, people tend to **satisfice**, that is, they make a decision that is adequate rather than optimally based upon full consideration of all relevant information. They also do this when making political judgements. Using the example of how people rate presidential performance, those authors elaborate:

> To decide how well the president is doing his job, a person could evaluate how well he has been handling all issues on which he has been working. This would be a very tough task, however, because presidents typically address a great many issues in very short periods of time. In his first year in office, for example, President Clinton worked on a number of issues, including reform of the U.S. health care system, staffing of the U.S. military, abortion laws, reducing the deficit, appointments to his Cabinet, U.S. involvement in Somalia, the North American Free Trade Agreement, Supreme Court appointments, and more. A careful evaluator could have graded his handling of each of these issues and then averaged those grades together into an overall assessment. Most Americans, however, probably had neither the information nor the motivation to do such labor-intensive thinking. Instead, they probably satisficed his handling of just a few issues. (p. 260)

Again, the media plays an important role in the priming process, because they determine which issues come to the forefront. Therefore, to use another of the authors' examples, if the media pays attention to the economy, and people think about this issue, then the economy will probably become a consideration when evaluating presidential performance. What is the specific impact of any media story? In other words, does one story about an issue prime another issue? Those authors believe that, in related issues, this may occur. In their view, if policies are viewed as related, coverage of one will prime the other. For example, affirmative action and school busing (the former priming the latter) are viewed as related, because both could be seen as related to improving the lives of minorities. However, news coverage of affirmative action probably would not prime inflation.

The existence of priming has been supported by several experimental studies (see Iyengar, 1991; Iyengar & Kinder, 1987; Iyengar, Peters, & Kinder, 1982; Iyengar, Peters, Kinder, & Krosnick, 1984). In subsequent literature, the application of priming to the political realm in a nonlaboratory setting has also been explored on a variety of issues, such as presidential performance, race, and supremacist groups (see, for example, Krosnick & Kinder, 1990; Miller & Krosnick, 1996, 2000; Nelson, Clawson, & Oxley, 1997; Nelson & Kinder, 1996; Nelson & Oxley, 1999). Krosnick and Kinder (1990), for example, found that the decline in the popularity of President Reagan was a result of two elements: (1) the media's newfound fascination with covert aid to the Contras and (2) the public's opposition to intervention in Central America. In their look at priming and presidential evaluations through several case studies (President Bush and the Gulf War and the 1992 election, Ronald Reagan and Iran–Contra), Miller and Krosnick (1996) argue that what the media decides to cover does impact the standards by which people evaluate the president. Moreover, media coverage can affect the cognitive complexity of the public's evaluation of issues. Milburn and McGrail (1992) found that the effect of vivid images in news coverage was a reduction of recall of information among viewers, as well as a reduction in cognitive complexity in their discussions of the issues involved.

Another important aspect regarding issue framing, and what the media focuses on, concerns the presentation of an issue, or what is often referred to as "spin." How an issue is reported on can make a difference. Most political issues have multiple elements, but the media may focus on only one or two. Those elements then receive attention, and the resulting debate regarding moral and/or policy implications revolves around those elements, rather than others. Entman (1993) illustrated this with an example from the Cold War. During that time, civil wars in other societies were discussed in the American media in terms of the implications for alliances with either the United States or the Soviet Union, rather than in terms of the domestic issues in those societies that led up to civil war. Nelson et al., (1997) present another example in a study of local television news outlets and a rally by the Ku Klux Klan in Ohio. Among their findings, media framing influenced the opinions of individuals toward the KKK. Specifically, if the media presented the story as having implications for free speech, individuals had more tolerance for the KKK. However, they had less tolerance for the KKK, if the media framed the rally as one that may bring about a clash between two angry groups.

In a related argument, Patterson (1993) notes that journalists operate with different schemas than those used by voters, which in turn produces a particular pattern in framing issues and candidates during campaigns, in particular, he argues, journalists' dominant schema "is structured around the notion that politics is a strategic game" (p. 57), rather than competing ideas about issues, appropriate policies, and matters of principle. The public, on the other hand, functions with a schema that views politics as an arena in which policies are discussed and in which leaders are selected who will attempt to implement particular policies. These game and governance schemas interact, and voters and journalists have cognizance of each other's perspective, but Patterson (1993) argues that, because of the press game schema, the focus of the news buries and distorts the substance of the information conveyed to the public during a campaign.

Having noted the importance of the media in priming people to attend to particular issues, some caveats must necessarily be added. First, the impact of the media is, not surprisingly, strongest on those who have little independent interest in politics, who are weakly attached to a party, and who are less educated (Iyengar & Kinder, 1987). In addition, personal involvement with an issue affects its salience, and, therefore, people for whom an issue is personally salient will attend to that issue, regardless of the amount of media coverage. Iyengar and Kinder (1987), for example, found in their experiments that subjects who were unemployed attended to media stories about employment more than those who were employed during a period of low unemployment, but that even people who were employed attended to unemployment stories during periods of higher unemployment. They concluded that employment was of concern only to the unemployed during periods of low unemployment, but that everyone felt a stronger personal stake in employment issues during periods of higher unemployment.

If the media influences what people think about, does it also influence how they think, that is, their attitudes toward an issue or a political candidate? This question has been answered differently over generations of analysis. Early studies of the effects of the media, in campaigns in the 1940s and 1950s (Lazarsfeld, Berelson, & Gaudet, 1944; Berelson, Lazarsfeld, & McPhee, 1954), found that partisanship was so solid for so many people that the media's effect on their attitudes was much less than anticipated. Instead, people attended to information in the media that supported their preexisting preferences. Moreover, people who did not have candidate preferences early in the campaign tended to be influenced more by family and friends than by the media. Later studies, reflecting societal changes, such as the advent of television, the general weakening of partisanship, and the diminished importance of extended families and communities as important influences on political attitudes, argue that media has a stronger impact on the content and complexity of public attitudes (Milburn, 1991). People are influenced by opinions expressed by reporters, of which there are more now than in the past, by experts, and by popular presidents. Glynn et al. (1999) summarize the current perspective on media influence as follows:

> Most theories of media influence today generate from a view of audiences being largely active players in choosing what they hear, watch, or read, and responding accordingly. However, we cannot reject the notion that at times people are quite passive or reactive in attending to media—or in everyday conversations for that matter, simply letting words or images wash over them, leaving themselves more open to influence or manipulation. This juxtaposition of more active versus more passive possibilities for audience involvement with media has led many researchers to look at media effects on public opinion as a more *interactive* or *transactional* process. The nature of the relationship between audiences and media likely changes and shifts across different personal traits, moods, contexts, and situations. (p. 407)

In a democracy such as the United States, one of the most important times in which the media may influence public opinion is during campaigns. Candidates use the media as part of their campaign strategy to deliver their campaign message, and the media also report on the candidates, issues, and campaign as an independent observer. In addition, the media cover candidate debates. The media have been widely criticized for providing only lightweight coverage of issues during elections, focusing instead on poll standings of candidates, character issues, and campaign gaffes, rather than on core issues regarding policy positions and past performance in office (Ansolabehere, Behr, & Iyengar, 1993; Mayer, 1996; Sabato, 1991). There is also the question of media bias. Does the media favor one candidate over another? A commonly held argument, particularly among conservatives, is that the media is biased in a liberal direction, but, in a recent study of the 1992 election, Beck, Dalton, Greene, and Huckfeldt (2002) found no clear pattern of bias. In fact, they argue that, "where there was partisan favoritism in news reports and editorials, it was demonstrably small in most cases. A majority of those exposed to television received messages that were close to evenly balanced; similarly, biases in newspaper coverage were often slight" (p. 62). They also found that people who were highly partisan perceived a bias against their preferred candidate, even when none existed.

POLITICAL SOCIALIZATION

How do people acquire their political attitudes in America? Research on political socialization began in the 1950s and looked at the ways in which "people acquire relatively enduring orientations toward politics in general and toward their own particular political systems" (Merelman, 1986, p. 279). The research reached its peak in the 1970s and suffered a decline, then a renewed interest in the 1990s (for earlier reviews, see Merelman, 1986; Niemi, 1973; Sears, 1975). Why did the field suffer a decline? As Niemi and Hepburn (1995) put it, "The field atrophied because it was based on exaggerated premises and because of misinterpreted and misunderstood research findings (and lack of findings)" (p. 7). Thus, there have been several efforts to revitalize the field and offer new directions for research (see Merelman, 1986; Niemi & Hepburn 1995; Sigel, 1995). Let us begin with a brief look at the development of this body of literature, as seen through the eyes of the scholars themselves, and then discuss ways in which they suggest bringing it back to life.

The earliest socialization studies focused on children. Studies were conducted on their views of political authority figures (see, for example, Easton & Dennis, 1973) and on their acquisition of political attitudes. The first authority figures recognized by children, as they became aware of politics, were the president and the policeman (Easton & Dennis, 1973). As children mature, their cognitive abilities increase, and they can advance from thinking of government in personal concrete terms (e.g., George Washington and the flag) to more abstract notions, such as institutions and lawmaking. Moreover, these studies found that children like government. Easton and Dennis (1973) suggested that children proceed through stages in political socialization: politicization (learning there is authority beyond family and school); personalization (becoming aware of authorities, through individuals such as police and the president); idealization (the belief that political authority is trustworthy and benevolent); and institutionalization (association with depersonalized objects, such as government) (Niemi, 1973). Concerning the acquisition of political attitudes, family was considered to be the most important agent of transmission (Jennings & Niemi, 1974; Maccoby, Matthews, & Morton, 1954), followed by schools (Hess & Torney, 1969), then peers, media, and events (Jennings & Niemi, 1974). Jennings and Niemi (1974), for example, found that parents transmit partisanship to their children, although the attachment tends to be weaker in the children.

The aforementioned studies shed considerable light on how children are socialized, but whether or not they continued to have those same attitudes into adulthood was also an important question. The early socialization studies examined children precisely because they thought that socialization was completed by age 18 years or so, and that the attitudes were retained through the life cycle. But, as Niemi and Hepburn (1995) explain:

These studies were fascinating and often had amusing twists. The problem, however, was in trying to determine their long-term significance. Here, socialization research fell victim to two assumptions that are, at best, highly questionable. First, it was assumed that what was learned prior to adulthood remained unchanged later in life. This "primacy" principle was most explicit in political science with respect to partisanship. . . . Party identification was very nearly immutable both between generations and across lifetimes. Yet even as socialization work was getting up a full head of steam, the first cracks in this assumption were appearing, as the number of independents underwent a significant increase in the late 1960s. (p. 8)

The primacy principle, advanced by the claims in *The American Voter* (Campbell et al., 1964), was subsequently challenged by many studies indicating that partisanship is not necessarily constant. Other elements, such as political trust, also changed over time. Niemi and Hepburn's (1995) conclusion is that attitudes and behavior do change over time and that what is learned early on may not be relevant later in life. Instead of the focus being on children, it should turn to individuals between the ages of 14 and 25 years. Why? "First, there is little dispute that youth is a time of extraordinary psychological and social change. Second, these are the years during which our society traditionally attempts to educate youth for citizen participation" (Niemi & Hepburn, 1995, p. 9). Those authors also offer several ways to "reestablish socialization as a viable and vibrant field of study" (pp. 13–14). First, eliminate what, for many purposes, is the artificial distinction between those aged under 18 and those 18 and over. Second, undertake a major new socialization study devoted specifically to the study of intergenerational and youthful change and development. Third, conduct more major youth studies and be more involved in new studies at the design stage. Fourth, pay more attention to high school and college courses and their probable effects on young people. Fifth, think more theoretically and write about all aspects of socialization. Sixth, conduct more comparative socialization work, especially if it is to contribute to our understanding of the significance of learning in early childhood.

In another assessment, Sigel (1995) points out that there are four problems with socialization research: lack of conceptual clarity, poor choice of subjects, insufficient attention to historical and cultural factors, and inappropriate methodology. As Sigel explains the first problem:

What really do we understand by the term *political socialization*? As currently used in the literature, the term is applied to many different phenomena. Scholars not only disagree among themselves in their definitions of it, but at times operate with a variety of definitions or conceptualizations even in their own work, applying one definition at one time and another—not necessarily a compatible one—at another, and often doing so in the same research enterprise. (p. 17)

Reviewing the literature, Sigel found numerous definitions of political socialization, including learning (political knowledge and comprehension), the developmental sequence through which knowledge and comprehension are acquired, continuity over time of knowledge and attitudes, acquisition and internalization of society's norms and behaviors, and synonyms for civic or political education.

The second problem is the focus of the studies on young children. Like Niemi and Hepburn, Sigel (1995) asks whether these views carry over into later years. In addition, "virtually no literature exists that has actually studied and observed the manner by which 'agents' [those who do imprinting] do or do not make influence attempts" (p. 18). Finally, she questions the idea that young people are passive and gullible to outside influences. The author suggests taking a life-span approach to understanding why orientations are maintained, modified, or abandoned. In addition, more attention should be paid to the historical and cultural context in which the observations of attitudes are made. Finally, political scientists need to pay more attention to methodology. The reliance upon close-ended survey questionnaires has been criticized as inappropriate for studying the process of attitude change along the life span. Sigel (1995) suggests other methods, such as field observations, collection of life histories, simulations, or direct observations.

Socialization studies are certainly interesting and important. They can help us understand the foundations of support for a political system. There is, as mentioned, a renewed interest in studying political socialization. In September 1999, for example, a collection of articles on political socialization appeared in *Political Psychology*. The studies are cross-national, including studies in Germany, the Netherlands, Sweden, the United States, and the Arab–Israeli conflict. As Special Editor Richard Niemi points out, although these authors concentrate on different aspects of socialization research, they demonstrate the resurgence of the subject, and a new approach that is cognizant of the problems with previous research.

In addition to those studies, there is another, broader, approach to the study of political socialization, which is particularly evident in the works of Milburn and his colleagues (Milburn & Conrad, 1996; Milburn, Conrad, Sala, & Carberry, 1995). Drawing upon earlier works by Lasswell (1960) and Merelman (1969), these scholars argue that much of the traditional political socialization literature has focused too narrowly upon the transmission of political attitudes from parents to children. Instead, Milburn et al. take an approach to political socialization that employs cognitive and emotional elements in the development of political ideas, or lack thereof. A central thesis is that "childhood experiences can affect the way we view the world and the political perceptions and understanding we develop" (Milburn & Conrad, 1996, p. 3), but that that understanding includes not only what we think and feel, but what we refuse to think about, that is, the political realities that people cannot face, because they are too painful and threatening. They also argue that anger from childhood treatment by parents contributes to long-term political attitudes. That anger is displaced onto political issues, and people with particularly punitive upbringings tend to be attracted to conservative ideologies.

POLITICAL TOLERANCE

If asked, most Americans are likely to maintain that the United States is a country with a great deal of tolerance for minority viewpoints on political issues. After all, the Constitution provides assurances that majority rule will not result in the repression of the rights of minorities. Since 1937, researchers have asked how much tolerance Americans have for politically deviant groups. At that time, the questions mainly revolved around tolerance for civil liberties for communists and their rights to free speech, to hold public office, to have public meetings, and so forth. The early studies found that most Americans favored restrictions on communists' rights in these areas. A major study conducted by Stouffer in 1955 found high levels of intolerance. For example, only 59% thought that a person who favors government ownership of all the railroads and big industries (an indicator of socialist ideas) should be allowed to speak in their community. Only 37% would allow a person to speak against religion. Only 27% would allow an admitted communist to speak. Community leaders were more tolerant than the average citizen, however: 84% would allow a socialist to speak, 64% an atheist, and 51% an admitted communist. Higher levels of education also correlated with greater tolerance. Stouffer argued that education teaches people not to stereotype or to rigidly categorize people into groups, and to have respect for differing points of view.

Studies show an increase in tolerance between 1954 and 1973, when another major study (Nunn, Crockett, & Williams, 1978) in an effort to replicate Stouffer's study, was conducted. Now 52% would permit an admitted communist to speak publicly, and 65% would let an atheist speak. However, Sullivan, Piereson and Marcus (1979, 1982) suggest that, although tolerance toward communists, atheists, and socialists increased, it may only have been a product of diminished perceptions of threat from these groups. People may have become less worried about these groups, and thus had less motivation to deny them their freedoms, but that does not necessarily mean that tolerance in a general sense had increased. Sullivan et al. argue that tolerance should only be said to exist when one is willing to tolerate those groups one dislikes. It is irrelevant in responses to groups one likes.

Sullivan et al. (1982) are essentially making the argument that tolerance, or lack thereof, is a political position driven primarily by emotion, rather than by cognition. One can only test levels of tolerance by looking at attitudes toward groups a person dislikes. Therefore, a person on the left end of the political spectrum who expresses a willingness to grant civil liberties to a communist is probably not expressing tolerance, because that person does not dislike communists in the first place. Ask that same person how they feel about granting civil liberties to a Nazi, then you will see how tolerant they really are. Sullivan et al. (1982) are fairly pessimistic about levels of tolerance in the United States, because it has been studied mostly in the context of attitudes toward leftist political groups, which, as noted above, are less threatening now, and therefore are less likely to evoke negative emotions. Therefore, increased willingness to grant those groups their civil liberties is meaningless as a reflection of growth in tolerance. Empirical studies supported this argument: Sullivan et al. (1982) let their respondents decide which groups they disliked, rather than presenting them with a group the researchers assumed they disliked—a technique they called a "content-controlled" measurement of tolerance. When looked at that way, they found that levels of tolerance had not increased since the 1950s. Another implication of this approach to the study of tolerance is that American ideals regarding basic civil liberties are much less important in producing tolerance than are emotional responses to groups people dislike.

Sniderman et al. (1991) disagree. They examined tolerance toward a different variety of groups, including

> people who are against all churches and religion; people who believe that blacks are genetically inferior; people who admit they are communists; people who advocate doing away with elections and letting the military run the country; and people who admit they are homosexual. (p. 123)

This assortment of groups was guaranteed to evoke dislike for at least one group by the various respondents. They found consistent responses toward the groups, meaning that, if people were tolerant toward one group, they were tolerant toward the others. Therefore, the implication is that, if people hold tolerance as a value, their attitudes toward all groups reflect that attitude, even if they personally dislike the group in question. Given that at least one group would be disliked by every respondent, the researchers maintained that people are responding on the basis of their principles regarding tolerance, rather than on the basis of which group they dislike or like.

The difference between these two assessments of tolerance is a reflection of different emphases: affect versus cognition. The relative role of thinking and feeling, when it comes to political tolerance in the United States, is an interesting and important topic. A study by Kuklinski, Riggle, Ottati, Schwartz, & Wyer (1991), for example, found that, although people initially endorse tolerance, that is, they respond in support of the value, the more they think about the group in question, the more intolerant they become, because the negative affect toward the group takes precedence over principle. The role of affect and cognition will continue to be debated and studied as time goes on. In the meantime, one clear trend is that the increase in tolerance, evident from the 1950s to the 1970s, has slowed down, although public opinion polls in some areas, such as civil liberties for homosexuals, continue to show increases in tolerance. In 1977, for example, 56% of respondents to a Gallup poll supported equal rights, in terms of job opportunities for homosexuals, whereas, in 1999, 83% supported equal rights (www.gallup.com/poll/indicators/indhomosexual.asp).

VOTING BEHAVIOR IN BRITAIN

Needless to say, the United States is not the only country whose public's political behavior has been studied. However, the approaches used to study voting behavior in other countries are generally American in origin, with a heavy reliance on survey data. Like the United States, party identification in Britain has been studied extensively. During the 1950s and 1960s, people tended to align strongly with either the Conservative or Labour parties. Two widely accepted factors determined a person's party identification: parents' affiliation and class. People tended to identify with their parents' party; working-class folks belonged to the Labour party, and middle- and upper-class people overwhelmingly identified with the Conservative party. The association between class and partisanship in Britain was very strong. The central difference between Britain and the United States, in terms of party alignment, was the greater importance of class in partisan alignment in Britain than in the United States. Other factors, such as age, sex, religion, and region, had some influence in British party alignments, but much less so than did class and family (Butler & Stokes, 1974; Denver, 1994). As in the United States, British voters were affected by shortterm factors, which may have caused them to defect and vote for the other party. Indeed, during the 1950s and 1960s, the Conservative party would never have won an election were it not for short-term factors that led the majority Labour party identifiers to defect and vote Tory.

Beginning in 1970, Britain began to experience both partisan and class dealignment, which means that fewer people identify with the traditionally dominant Labour and Conservative parties, and those who do identify with a party do so with less strength of attachment. By 1997, less than 20% of the electorate in Britain identified strongly with either the Labour or Conservative parties, down from 38% in 1964 (Jones & Kavanagh, 1998). In part, partisan dealignment was a result of the pull from other parties, including the Liberal party and the nationalist parties in Scotland and Wales: the Scottish Nationalist party and Plaid Cymru, respectively. Other factors leading to dealignment were increases in levels of education, enabling more independent judgments by voters, rather than reliance upon the parties for issue positions; a decline in support for the more social welfare, pro-union principles of the Labour party; changes in campaigns, allowing for more

What Is Social Class?

Although an important concept in social science, the term *social class* does not have a universally accepted definition. We generally think about class in terms of occupation, income, and lifestyle. Often, classes are divided into upper, middle, and working class. For purposes of measuring public opinion, classes are categorized as (A) high-level professional, managerial and administrative; (B) middle management, professional or administrative; (C1) supervisor, clerical, nonmanual; (C2) skilled manual labor; (D) semi- or unskilled manual; (E) occasionally employed or reliant upon government benefits (Denver, 1998). These are then grouped together as manual workers (C2, D, E) and nonmanual workers (A, B, C1). This is known as the Alford Index. In recent years, there has been considerable debate as to whether or not a manual worker–nonmanual worker basis for distinguishing class is useful for postindustrial societies in which heavy industry is no longer dominant in the economy.

direct and challenging reporting on candidates and issues; and general dissatisfaction with the performance of the two dominant parties when in office (Denver, 1994). Class dealignment also took place after 1970, meaning that people were less and less likely to vote for the party associated with their class. As Britain moved from a predominantly blue-collar to white-collar society and economy, class interests became more diverse. For example, the working class of pre–World War II days had divided into different subclasses, with vestiges of the old working class—those who work in factories, live in council houses (i.e., government funded housing), and so on—and a newer, more affluent working class with more skills, who work in light manufacturing and who own their own homes. As Norris (1997) puts it, "The nature of class inequalities has become more complex in postindustrial society" (p. 90). Other social identities, including region, ethnicity, and religion, have increased in importance and influence on the vote in Britain, as class identity has fragmented (Bartle, 1998; Norris, 1997).

During the alignment era, British voters, like Americans, tended to be fairly ignorant of political issues. Butler and Stokes (1974) found that, when British voters did express attitudes on issues, the attitudes changed frequently, indicating that they were not true attitudes, but randomly changing opinions. In a series of four interviews with the same respondents, only 43% were consistent in their positions on nationalization of industries, which was an important issue in Britain at the time. In addition, respondents' attitudes were not consistently related to other attitudes. For example, in principle, a person who is pro-private enterprise should oppose a growth in trade union power, but this was not often the case in Britain in the era of alignment. Most people used partisanship to make a voting decision, rather than attitudes toward issues.

After dealignment, however, British voters began to engage in issue voting. Studies of voting in Britain use the same standards of analysis as studies of American voting. A voting decision is considered to be based on an issue (issue voting), if the voter is aware of the issue, has a position on the issue, understands where the parties stand and how they differ from each other on the issue, and finally, votes for the party perceived to be closest to their own position on the issue (Butler & Stokes, 1974). A number of studies maintain that the majority of British voters have been casting issue votes in the dealignment era (summarized in Denver, 1994). Issues such as taxes and government spending, unemployment, privatization of publicly owned industries, the European Union, racial conflict, and the status of Scotland and Northern Ireland, among others, have influenced the vote in Britain in recent years.

The transformation of the Labour party in Britain, and its spectacular success in the 1997 election, is plausibly a reflection of the changes in the British voter. Since 1974, the Labour party had been regularly beaten by the Conservative party. In 1979, Margaret Thatcher became prime minister and stayed in office for 12 years. She was succeeded by another Conservative, John Major, and, even in the context of a struggling economy, Labour lost in 1992. This sparked a reform effort and the emergence of new leadership. According to the Labour party director of communications, David Hill, the party had come to be regarded as "too old fashioned, too tied to the past, too linked to minorities rather than majorities, and too associated with old images of the trades unions" (quoted in Seyd, 1998, p. 51). The public had become mistrustful of Labour's stance on taxation, support for income redistribution, support for trade unions, and other traditional positions. Tony Blair, a relatively young man of 41, became the party's new leader in 1994 and set about devising some fundamental reforms of the party, referring to it as the New Labour party. Among those reforms was a revision of clause 4 in the party's charter, which changed the party's emphasis from supporting trade unions, first and foremost, to making trade unions only one among many important sectors, along with a thriving private sector, which the party promised to work for. This move was strongly supported by the party's members, and it is a reflection of change in class, society, and the economy in

Britain. The Labour party was set to target the middle class and to address increases in issue voting. The Conservative party, on the other hand, had made a series of blunders since 1992, including economic failures, which destroyed its reputation for financial competence, and association with a number of scandals (Denver, 1998; King, 1998).

CONCLUSION

This chapter examined public opinion and voting behavior in the United States and Britain. We began the chapter with a review of some of the concepts first presented in chapter 3, such as attitudes, beliefs, and schemas, in addition to new concepts such as values and ideology, all of which are commonly used in the analysis of public opinion and voting behavior. The analysis of American voting behavior was more thorough, looking at the Michigan school versus the Maximalist views of attitudes and political sophistication in the United States, ideology, information processing and voting behavior, emotions and voting, the impact of the media, and the issues of political socialization and political tolerance. In the case of Great Britain, the British were noted to be traditionally much more reliant upon class as a basis for partisanship than are Americans. We also looked at issue trends in British elections and the reemergence of the Labour party under the auspices of New Labour.

One of the central issues underlying the study of voting behavior is the question of how those who participate in politics—the average voters—affect the quality of a democracy. Ideally, a democracy should run on the basis of decisions made by informed and thoughtful citizens. We believe that a careful study of the political psychology of voting behavior, particularly the role of ideology, information-processing patterns, and the influence of the media, will give students a better basis for coming to their own conclusions about the quality of democracy in America and elsewhere.

Topics, Theories/Explanations, and Cases Covered in Chapter 6

Topics	Theories/Concepts	Cases
Public opinion	Beliefs, belief systems	Political sophistication in America
	Values	
	Attitudes	
	Schema	
	Ideology	
Voting in America	Michigan school	Normal vote
	Levels of conceptualization	Long-term and short-term forces
	Funnel of causality	
	Maximalists	Knowledge structures
Information processing and voting	Cognitive patterns	Elections
	Role of emotion	
Media effects	Priming	Campaigns
	Framing	
Political socialization	Primacy principle	New studies
Political tolerance		
Voting in Great Britain	Class	

KEY TERMS

Agenda setting
Associative networks
Belief system
Black and white model
Drunkard's search
Funnel of causality
Gresham's law of political
   information

Ideologue
Ideology
Impression-based model
   of information
   processing
Issue
Issue frames
Knowledge structures

Levels of
   conceptualization
Maximalists
Michigan model
Normal vote
Party identification
Priming
Values

SUGGESTIONS FOR FURTHER READING

Ansolabehere, S., Behr, R., & Iyengar, S. (1993). *The media game*. New York: Macmillan.

Campbell, A., Converse, P., Miller, W., & Stokes, D. (1964). *The American voter*. New York: Wiley.

Denver, D. (1994). *Elections and voting behaviour in Britain*. London: Harvester Wheatsheaf.

Glynn, C., Herbst, S., O'Keefe, G., & Shapiro, R. (1999). *Public opinion*. Boulder, CO: Westview.

Iyengar, S. (1991). *Is anyone responsible? How television frames political issues*. Chicago: University of Chicago Press.

Inyengar, S., & McGuire, W. (Eds.). (1995). *Explorations in political psychology*. Durham, NC: Duke University Press.

Marcus, G., Neuman, W. R., & MacKeun, M. (2000). *Affective intelligence and political judgment*. Chicago: University of Chicago Press.

Miller, W., & Shanks, M. 1996. *The new American voter*. Cambridge, MA: Harvard University Press.

Patterson, T. (1993). *Out of control*. New York: Knopf.

Popkin, S. (1994). *The reasoning voter: Communication and persuasion in presidential campaigns*. Chicago: University of Chicago Press.

Smith, E. (1989). *The unchanging American voter*. Berkeley: University of California Press.

ENDNOTE

1.   There has been some debate as to whether schemas and attitudes are the same thing. Kuklinski, Luskin, and Bolland (1991) maintain that they are the same concept; Conòver and Feldman (1991) maintain that they are not. They argue:

> The central meaning of the attitude concept—the meaning common to all competing definitions—is fundamentally *affective* in nature. At its core, an attitude is a "person's evaluation of an object of thought" (Pratkanis & Greenwald, 1989, p. 247). The central meaning of the schema concept stands in sharp contrast. Though it, too, has been defined in a variety of ways, at its core a schema is fundamentally a *cognitive* structure. . . . Traditionally, attitudes have been linked to consistency theories while schemata are tied to information-processing theories. (p. 1366)

Others claim that attitude theories have always looked at attitudes as information-processing filters, hence they are cognitive in nature and the same as schemas (e.g., Eagly & Chaiken, 1998).

Each argument has some validity, but, in our view, the debate is making a mountain out of a molehill. Neither concept needs to replace the other, and the different concepts have been used mostly to examine different questions. Early research on public opinion found that American political attitudes are sorely lacking in cognitive content (i.e., Americans know little about politics), and hence the concept of attitude did emphasize affect (as in art, people may not know much about politics, but they know what they like and dislike). Later researchers were curious about how people process political information. Newly developed theories about information processing, emphasizing cognitive properties, were used to explore information processing, using the concepts of schema and heuristics.

The Political Psychology
of Race and Ethnicity

Racism and ethnocentrism are sources of intransigent political conflict worldwide. Racial prejudice and discrimination have been considered the "great American dilemma" (Myrdal, 1944) for decades. Racism was responsible for one of the most repressive regimes in modern history—the apartheid government of South Africa. Ethnic hatred has been held responsible for countless violent incidents globally, some involving genocide. Looking at these conflicts from a political psychological perspective can provide insights that other approaches cannot provide. First, explaining racial and ethnic conflicts as a consequence of competition for resources and power fails to explain why people would engage in these conflicts, when they result in the destruction of wealth and resources, indeed, of the very countries where power is distributed. Second, if there were no underlying psychological processes influencing ethnic and racial conflict, they could be settled once and for all, but, from the political psychological perspective, we can understand the intransigence of group conflict as the result of the continual human drive to form in-groups and out-groups and to compare their groups with others. Political psychology also enables us to understand how racial and ethnic groups can live together harmoniously for years, then erupt in horrific internecine violence. Identities can be manipulated by leaders, and emotions can rise to extremes of hatred and fear, when people are convinced by leaders and by rumors that their group is threatened by others. Political psychology also turns our attention to the ways in which issues can be framed to produce particular anxieties in the minds of citizens. Stereotypes can be subtly or openly manipulated to produce stereotype-driven behaviors and attitudes.

This chapter looks at the underlying causes of political conflicts produced by racism and ethnocentrism. We begin with some concepts and definitions—some introduced in earlier chapters, others new—that enable us to have a common understanding of the perceptions and behaviors involved in race and ethnicity. This chapter explores most of the Political Being's personality attitudes, cognition, emotions, and identities, in relation to *us* (in-groups) and *them* (out-groups). We look at race and politics in the United States, Brazil, and South Africa. The cases of ethnic conflict we examine include Nigeria, Bosnia, and Guatemala. The chapter concludes with an examination of conflict prevention and resolution in race and ethnic conflicts.

Race and ethnicity are social constructs, not scientific distinctions, and they are often confounded, as the history of racism in the United States shows. George Fredrickson (1999) notes:

> Throughout its history, the United States has been inhabited by a variety of interacting racial or ethnic groups. In addition to the obvious "color line" structuring relationships between dominant Whites and lower-status Blacks, Indians, and Asians, there have at times been important social distinctions among those of White or European ancestry. Today we think of the differences between white Anglo-Saxon Protestants and Irish, Italian, Polish, and Jewish Americans as purely cultural or religious, but in earlier times

these groups were sometimes thought of as "races" or "subraces"—people possessing innate or inborn characteristics and capabilities that affected their fitness for American citizenship.

It can therefore be misleading to make a sharp distinction between race and ethnicity when considering intergroup relations. . . . Ethnicity is "racialized" whenever distinctive group characteristics, however defined or explained, are used as the basis for a status hierarchy of groups who are thought to differ in ancestry or descent. (p. 23)

Having set forth this caution, we look at race and ethnicity separately, only as a reflection of their social construction in real situations. In other words, when societies consider race to be race rather than ethnicity, so do we, in order to reflect the language used in those societies and the studies published about them.

This chapter is concerned with race and ethnicity because group differentiations, in terms of race and ethnicity, are so frequently associated with political inequalities and violence. These patterns of political activity stem from stereotyping of, and prejudice toward, groups of different race or ethnicity. What is **prejudice**? It is a commonly used term, but there are many differences in definition. Reviewing various interpretations of prejudice, Sniderman, Piazza, and Harvey (1998) note four components of prejudice that are generally agreed upon in the literature: a response to group members, based upon their membership in the group; a negative evaluative orientation toward a group and consequently an aversion to group members; an attribution of negative characteristics toward a group and its members that is incorrect; and, finally, consistency in the negative orientation toward the group and its members.

Prejudice is closely associated with a concept we introduced in chapter 3: a **stereotype**, which we defined as "a set of beliefs about the personal attributes of a group of people" (Duckitt, 1994, p. 8). Stereotypes and prejudices that produce discriminatory behavior are filled with negative evaluations of the group and its members. Rothbart and Johns (1993) note that stereotypes have descriptive and evaluative components. The problem, they argue, "is that the evaluative component, which is a judgment that the observer makes about the group, is not perceived as a judgment *about* the group, but as an attribute *of* the group itself" (p. 40). This is called the **phenomenal absolutism error**. For example, a group that does not spend a great deal of money can be thought of as thrifty or as stingy. Either characterization is an evaluation of a behavior, but that evaluation comes to be considered a characteristic of the group, not an evaluation or one of several possible evaluations, of the behavior noticed. In a negative stereotype, a group whose members do not spend much money may be considered inherently stingy people. The use of prejudices and preexisting beliefs in evaluation of others also occurs in ambiguous situations, which is a phenomenon known as the **ultimate attribution error** (Pettigrew, 1979).

EXPLAINING RACISM AND ETHNOCENTRISM

Why do people stereotype others and engage in discriminatory behavior? One of the oldest explanations for prejudice and discrimination is **realistic conflict theory** (Bobo, 1983). According to this explanation, discrimination is a result of competition over scarce resources, such as jobs, housing, and good schools. Whenever such commodities are in short supply, the demand for them increases. Additionally, research suggests that, as competition becomes more severe, those involved tend to view the other in increasingly negative terms (White, 1977). For example, members of groups tend to solidify the boundaries that exist between them, derogate the other group, and believe that their own group is superior. One of the earliest investigations of realistic conflict theory was conducted by Sherif, Harvey, White, Hood, and Sherif (1961). That study involved dividing a group of 11-year-old boys, who were attending a summer camp, into two groups. For 1 week, the boys in each group lived together, ate together, played together, and generally engaged in enjoyable activities. Then, the boys in both groups were told that they would be engaging in a number of competitions, the winners of which would receive valuable prizes (e.g., trophies). Over the next 2 weeks, as the boys competed with another, tensions escalated. They taunted each other, attacked one another's cabins, overturned beds, and destroyed some of the others' personal belongings. In only 2 short weeks, the boys, who were friends before study, came to behave in hostile ways toward one another, as a result of the competition.

In an attempt to restore the boys' friendships, Sherif and his colleagues (1961) created a series of *superordinate goals*—ones that both groups desired and that required the cooperation of both groups to achieve. When their water supply was severely reduced (as a consequence of being sabotaged by the researchers), for example, both groups of boys had to work together to restore it. Similarly, when the boys wanted to rent a movie, but could not afford it on their own, they pooled their money. The introduction of these superordinate goals worked to reduce the tensions created as a result of the competitions. Additionally, many of the boys, who were in different groups, were able to restore their friendships. This investigation is important in revealing how competition over scarce resources can quickly escalate into full-scale conflict.

A second explanation for prejudice and discrimination is **social learning theory**. According to this view, children learn negative attitudes and discriminatory behavior from their parents, teachers, family, friends, and others, when they are rewarded for such behavior. Rewards can be in the form of praise, agreement, love, and so on. Children have a strong need to be accepted and loved by those who are important to them. One way to be accepted and loved is to adopt the same attitudes that valued others have toward certain groups. *Social norms* (rules governing appropriate and acceptable behavior) are also a powerful mechanism for learning prejudice. Most people choose to conform to their own group's norms. The development and expression of prejudice can stem from conformity to group norms. For example, a child might assume that if a member of their group does not like another group, then the child will also not like the other group. Recent research (Towles-Schwen & Fazio, 2001) suggests that individuals' attitudes toward particular racial groups is determined by the attitudes of their parents, as well as by their childhood experiences with members of minority groups. Those with less prejudiced parents and more positive experiences with minority group members have more favorable racial attitudes. The media also plays a strong role in shaping our attitudes toward members of racial groups. When minority group members are portrayed (on television, in movies, in commercials) in stereotypical ways, media consumers tend to adopt stereotypical (prejudiced) attitudes.

Another explanation for the development of prejudice is **social identity theory**, first presented in chapter 3. Social identity studies have found that prejudice and stereotyping among groups occurs even in the absence of conflicting goals. Competition can occur even when the stakes are only psychological, and among groups that are arbitrarily formed by experimenters with no real interaction or conflicting goals (the **minimal group paradigm**) (Tajfel, 1982; see Brewer & Brown, 1998, for a thorough review). In chapter 3, we note that social categorization and social identity are partially responsible for the initial process of group differentiation into in-groups and out-groups. With this process comes the accompanying perception of the superiority of in-groups. In addition, psychologists have found that people remember negative behaviors of out-groups far better than positive behaviors and positive behaviors of the in-groups far better than negative behaviors (Rothbart & John, 1993; Fiske, 1998), but this kind of bias in favor of the in-group is not in and of itself stereotyping and prejudice. As Allport (1954) noted many years ago, "Not every overblown generalization is a prejudice" (p. 9). Such generalizations become prejudices when they are resistant to disconfirming information, that is, when information indicating that they are wrong is ignored, disbelieved, or rejected out of hand.

A core argument in social identity theory is that social categorization produces a basic motivation for intergroup social competition. Once social categories are formed, people strive for positive social identity, which, in turn, creates intergroup competition. This causes perceptual biases and discriminatory behavioral patterns, as people strive to view their in-group in a positive light, compared to out-groups. This explanation helps us understand general ethnocentrism: It directs our attention to the role of social cues that make salient intergroup distinctions and to the importance of status differentials, that is, the need to see one's own group as superior to others. But does it explain why prejudice toward some groups is so deep, but almost nonexistent for others? Not really. To do this, we must add in factors relating to the social context, the perceived legitimacy of intergroup relations, and individual personality characteristics.

Motivation and **personality traits** have also been examined in efforts to explain the causes of racism and ethnocentrism. One additional explanation for racial and ethnic prejudice that should be considered is related to studies of personality, discussed in chapter 2. As mentioned in that chapter, there has been a revival in the study of the authoritarian personality. Studies by Altemeyer (1981, 1988, 1996) and others argue that three central characteristics of the authoritarian personality covary across cultures and are directly related to ethnocentrism and prejudice. Those characteristics are authoritarian submission (to authority), aggression (against nonconformist groups), and conventionalism (blind acceptance of social norms). Altemeyer (1996) argues that these characteristics are strongly linked to right-wing authoritarianism in particular, and his studies have found them to be highly correlated with ethnocentrism. People who earn high scores in measures of authoritarianism tend to be more prejudiced toward low-status out-groups than are people whose authoritarianism scores are low (Altemeyer, 1996; Meloen, 1994). Those high-scoring individuals stereotype out-groups as inferior to their own groups. In general, despite ongoing debates about theory and method, evidence indicates that individual differences account for degrees of racism, prejudice, and ethnocentrism. Those people who score high in authoritarianism are more prejudiced against out-groups (particularly those who are visible and low-status), more likely to be ethnocentric, less cognitively complex, and more likely to rely on stereotypes in ambiguous contexts (Perreault & Bourhis, 1999). Other personality traits have also been associated with ethnocentrism. Perreault and Bourhis (1999), for example, found that ethnocentrism and personal need for structure predicted both in-group identification and discriminatory behavior.

Another explanation that examines personality characteristics, but that is also group-related, is the **social dominance theory** (Pratto, Sidanius, Stallworth, & Malle, 1994; Sidanius, 1993; Sidanius & Pratto, 1993, 1999; Sidanius, Singh, Hetts, & Federico, 2000). Social dominance theory presented a social dominance orientation measure that differentiates those who prefer social group relations to be equal or hierarchical, and the extent to which people want their in-group to dominate out-groups. Social dominance orientation personality dimensions concern the degree to which a person favors an unequal, hierarchical, dominance-oriented relationship among groups (the actual scale is in the side box). Clearly, those high in social dominance orientation would strongly agree with questions 1–8 and disagree with 9–16. The scale has produced results similar to the right-wing authoritarian measurements by Altemeyer (1998), although those high in social dominance are unlike authoritarians, in that religion is not particularly important to them, and they "do not claim to be benevolent" (p. 61), but right-wing authoritarians do so (Whitley, 1999).

Sidanius (1993) argues that, despite its strengths, social identity theory cannot explain experimental findings that demonstrate out-group favoritism, and it cannot predict how and along what dimensions, discrimination against out-groups will occur. He argues that the social identity theory model expects out-group discrimination, yet studies have found evidence of low-status groups admiring high-status out-groups.[1] How can one explain this? Social dominance theory seeks to explain these behaviors as a product of social status and a human predisposition to form social groups that are arranged in a social hierarchy. There are three broad hierarchies in societies: gender (males dominate females); age (adults rule); and a third category, which varies from society to society, but that consistently includes socially constructed groups identified as differentiated in terms of race, ethnicity, class, clan, or nationality. The studies are primarily concerned with "the specific mechanisms by which social hierarchies are established and maintained and the consequences these mechanisms have for the nature and distribution of social attitudes and the functioning of social institutions within social systems" (Sidanius, 1993, p. 198). Those mechanisms are ideologies and political values that ascribe legitimacy to the social hierarchy. The people who support and promote such ideologies (e.g., the Protestant work ethnic and liberalism/conservatism) are, of course, those who are at the top of the group hierarchy. They are able to use their dominance to perpetuate ideas and institutions that maintain their dominance. People accept inferiority because they are socialized to do so, and those at the top of the hierarchy accept their superiority for the same reasons. To ensure that these systems of hierarchy survive, governments use coercion, when necessary, to defeat challengers.

> **Social Dominance Scale**
>
> The social dominance orientation scale is based upon responses to the following questions. On a seven-point scale, respondents are asked to strongly disagree to strongly agree.
>
> 1. Some groups of people are just more worthy than others.
> 2. In getting what your group wants, it is sometimes necessary to use force against other groups.
> 3. Superior groups should dominate inferior groups.
> 4. To get ahead in life, it is sometimes necessary to step on other groups.
> 5. If certain groups of people stayed in their place, we would have fewer problems.
> 6. It is probably a good thing that certain groups are at the top and other groups are at the bottom.
> 7. Inferior groups should stay in their place.
> 8. Sometimes other groups must be kept in their place.
> 9. It would be good if all groups could be equal.
> 10. Group equality should be our ideal.
> 11. All groups should be given an equal chance in life.
> 12. We should do what we can to equalize conditions for different groups.
> 13. Increased social equality.
> 14. We would have fewer problems if we treated different groups more equally.
> 15. We should strive to make incomes more equal.
> 16. No one group should dominate in society.
>
> (Sidanius et al., 2000, pp. 234–235)

In essence, the theory attempts to look at individual, group, and social-structural variables to explain racism. People in dominant groups are socialized, as individuals, to have a social dominance orientation. They belong to groups that are on the top of the hierarchy, the social and political system benefits them the most, and they use social and political structures to maintain the hierarchical relationships among groups (Sears, Hetts, Sidanius, & Bobo, 2000; see also Rabinowitz, 1999). The theory also has been applied to groups in the United States and other countries (e.g., Levin & Sidanius, 1999).

The why question—why racism and ethnocentrism occur—must be followed by the who question—What explains who the particular targets are? This is particularly perplexing when one considers the artificiality of race. As we noted earlier, people tend to think of race as denoting biological differences among people, but in fact it is largely socially constructed. Why is it that race is so important as an identifying marker for discrimination and prejudice in the United States, particularly when it comes to African-Americans as perceived by Euro-Americans? Why were Jews the scapegoats in Nazi Germany, the Armenians in Turkey, the Tutsis in Rwanda, and the Maya in Guatemala and other parts of Central America? What determines who gets picked on in a society? In addition, perceptions of those who are targets for harsh treatment vary. Some, like the Maya in Guatemala or African-Americans in the United States, are perceived to be inferior and have been victims of chronic and systematic discrimination. Others, like the Armenians, Jews, and Tutsis, are identified as the culprits to blame for bad things happening to society and as having far more than their fair share of power or wealth.

The social dominance perspective has provided one explanation about which groups receive the worst treatment: There are three potential hierarchies, and society maintains the status differentials through legitimizing myths, institutions, and force, if necessary. Likewise, realistic conflict theory cites competition for resources as a motivating factor producing prejudice. But does that hostility necessarily evolve into the view of the other group as inferior? For example, did the Nazis and Hutus perceive the Jews and Tutsis, respectively, as inferior, or was that perception preceded by a perception that they were in a superior position in society? If so, how and why does that perception occur?

Social identity theory provides some insights here. It maintains that **scapegoating** is a result of social causality assessments—finding an out-group to blame for bad things that happen to the in-group (Hogg & Abrams, 1988; Kecmanovic, 1996; Staub, 1989). It is sensible that out-groups identified as responsible for some problem the in-group is facing will have negative characteristics attributed to it. Whether the scapegoat begins in a superior position or not, they are ultimately described as inferior. Some analysts draw more from psychoanalytic concepts and argue that **projection**, that is, ascribing one's own unacceptable and repressed impulses or attributes to out-groups, explains why they are regarded as inferior. In particular, repressed anger is displaced onto the scapegoat, and that group is not only regarded with contempt, but reacted to with powerful emotions of anger, fear, and resentment (Milburn & Conrad, 1996). Experimental studies, such as those of Rogers and Prentice-Dunn (1981), demonstrate the importance of anger, for example, in studies that found that White subjects, when not angered, react with more hostility toward Whites than toward Blacks, but when White subjects were angered in the experiment, they reacted with more hostility toward Blacks than toward Whites.

RACE IN THE UNITED STATES, BRAZIL, AND SOUTH AFRICA

Let us now turn to three examples of race and politics—the cases of the United States, Brazil, and South Africa. Each case shows the manner in which race is socially constructed and the different patterns of behavior that emerge in situations of stereotyping and prejudice.

The United States

American attitudes on race and race-related issues go right to the heart of democratic principles. Those attitudes have changed greatly since the 1950s, and in a positive direction, in terms of the democratic principles of equality.[2] Nevertheless, the socioeconomic reality of Black and White American living standards indicate continuity in the wide disparity of wealth and power. Changing attitudes have not produced socioeconomic equality between Blacks and Whites in the United States. For example, in 1968, 8.4% of White families with children lived in poverty, and 34.6% of Black families with children lived in poverty. In 1998, the figures were 6.1 and 30.5, respectively, an improvement, but still a great disparity in percent of families living in poverty, when White and Black families are compared (Joint Center for Political and Economic Studies, 2001). More African-Americans attend college today than in the 1940s, and more graduate from high school. However, the increase of Black college attendance in the 1970s has since been reversed, as has the rate of Black graduation from college (Farley, 1996). More Blacks are employed in white-collar jobs today, up from 5% in 1940 to 32% in 1990 (Sears et al. 2000), but Blacks still make less money than Whites, even with equal levels of education. Black women with high school diplomas earn $926 for every $1,000 earned by a White female high school graduate. Black men with a high school education earn $723 for every $1,000 earned by a White male high school graduate. The figures for Black and White male college graduates are $767 for every $1,000, respectively (Shipler, 1997).

Racial attitudes have also changed dramatically in the United States, but not enough to eradicate racism. For the most part, White Americans no longer regard African-Americans as biologically inferior to Whites, as they did during slavery and the Jim Crow era that followed. As late as 1942, survey data indicated that more that half of Whites believed Blacks to be less intelligent than Whites and opposed integration of schools and public transportation (Schuman, Steeh, Bobo, & Krysan, 1997). By the end of the century, those attitudes had changed dramatically, with over 90% of Whites favoring school integration and willing to vote for a Black political candidate, and only around 10% believing that Blacks are inherently unequal to Whites (Schuman et al., 1997). Studies have found that racist attitudes in the United States have diminished as education levels increased over the years. Those with more formal education are less likely to express racist attitudes. But their support for policies designed to address inequality between the races is another issue entirely, as we see later (Jackman, 1978; Carmines & Merriman, 1993; Schuman et al., 1997).

Nevertheless, vestiges of the past remain. Peffley and Hurwitz (1998), for example, found that a plurality of Whites have a positive perception of Blacks, but a surprisingly high proportion still see Blacks as lazy (31%), not willing to succeed (22%), aggressive (50%), and undisciplined (60%). At the heart of all of this is affect—negative feelings toward Blacks by Whites.

Needless to say, the topic of race relations in America today is enormously complex. It can be understood best by breaking it down into component parts and central questions. First, what is the relationship between attitudes toward race and positions on central political issues? This is a confoundingly difficult question to answer.

In the past, how one stood on equal housing, busing, affirmative action, voting rights, equal access to public facilities, and so on, was determined by how one felt about African-Americans. Sniderman and Piazza (1993) argue that, today, a distinction must be made among policies directed at equal treatment (e.g., in housing, schools, etc.); policy areas that are explicitly racially conscious, such as affirmative action; and social welfare-related policies. They argue that only equal treatment and race-conscious policies are uniquely related to racial attitudes. Social welfare policies involve programs for the poor, regardless of race or ethnicity. A person's positions on the social welfare issues reflect attitudes toward the role of government, its size, influence on the lives of citizens, and role as agent of social change, rather than simply on race.

More generally, Schuman et al. (1997) examined trends in White racial attitudes regarding principles of equal treatment, implementation of equal treatment, social distance, beliefs about inequality, and affirmative action. Looking at survey results for several decades (when possible), they found a number of interesting patterns. There was an increase in White acceptance of the principles of equal treatment, but less change when Whites were asked about policies that would implement those principles. For example, White support increased for implementation of open access to public accommodation and housing, but a gap remained between those supporting the principle and those supporting policy to implement the principle, and the percent supporting federal government efforts to integrate schools actually declined over time (Schuman et al., 1997). The social distance patterns were also mixed. Over the years, Whites expressed an increased willingness to send their children to schools with Black children in attendance, to the point that nearly 100% accepted integrated schools by the 1990s. But when they were asked about truly integrated schools, schools in which their children may be a minority (i.e., 51% black children), the picture changed. By 1996, 49% of White parents said they would not send their children to a school that was over 50% Black (Schuman et al., 1997). Acceptance of integrated neighborhoods showed a similar pattern, with 13% of Whites indicating that they would only live in an all-White neighborhood in 1994, compared to 28% in 1976, but with little change in those wanting to live in a mostly White neighborhood (Schuman et al., 1997). In terms of beliefs about the causes of inequality, the percentage of Whites who believe that African-American socioeconomic disadvantages are the product of slavery and discrimination has declined since the mid-1960s. Whites today prefer explanations that divide the blame between Blacks themselves and historical social discrimination against Blacks (Schuman et al., 1997). Finally, regarding affirmative action programs that explicitly attempt to compensate Blacks for past discrimination in housing, jobs, and access to education, White support has remained at or below one third (Schuman et al., 1997). Sniderman and Piazza (1993) sum up the results of the various surveys with the following evaluation:

> With the exception only of citizens who are uncommonly well educated and uncommonly liberal, what is striking is the sheer pervasiveness throughout contemporary American society of negative characterizations of Blacks—particularly the stereotype that most Blacks on welfare could get a job. Perceptions of Blacks as inferior were supposed to represent an archaic stock of beliefs that were in the process of dying out, and some indeed do appear to be fading out. But it completely misreads contemporary American culture to suppose that all negative characterizations of Blacks are dwindling away. On the contrary, images of Blacks as failing to make a genuine effort to work hard and to deal responsibly with their obligations is a standard belief throughout most of American society. (pp. 50–51)

Nevertheless, there is a deep disagreement among political psychologists in their answers to questions of how prevalent and how deep racial prejudice is in the United States today. One camp is led by Sniderman, Piazza, Tetlock, Kluegel, and others. They propose a model, which they have not named, but which we call the **politics-is-complicated model** (also known as the **principled objection** model), wherein it is argued that White Americans vary in the degree to which they blame the inequalities between the races on structural factors (such as the historical legacy of slavery and current system-wide discrimination), as opposed to individual factors (individual acts of prejudice and discrimination, rather than system-wide factors). The other camp, led by Kinder and Sears, maintains that what we have in America today is **symbolic racism** disguised as traditional American individualist values. Let us look at each argument in some detail.

Data do not provide clear-cut evidence about the degree of racism among White Americans. For example, Sniderman and Piazza (1993) report 81% of surveyed Whites agreeing that Blacks on welfare could find jobs; 43% agreed that Blacks need to try harder, 36% agreed that Blacks have a chip on their shoulder, but only 6% agreed that Blacks are born with less ability.

Are people who agree with a negative description of another group of people necessarily prejudiced toward that group? The politics-is-complicated camp's answer is no: "Apart only from the characterization of Blacks as inherently inferior to Whites, [the negative characterizations] cannot be entirely reduced to bigotry, for these characterizations capture real features of everyday experience" (Sniderman & Piazza, 1993, p. 43). Moreover, they note that Blacks have even harsher characterizations of Blacks than Whites do. Fifty-nine percent of Blacks agree that Blacks are aggressive, compared to 52% of Whites; 39% of Blacks agree that Blacks are lazy, compared to 34% of Whites; and 40% of Blacks agree that Blacks are irresponsible, compared to 21% of Whites (p. 45).

There are racists in American today, but scholars in this school of thought maintain that true racists are people who express prejudicial attitudes toward Blacks and that they also systematically express anti-Semitic attitudes toward Jews and hostility toward other minorities. They accept stereotypes of Blacks as lazy, violent, and innately inferior to Whites, and of Jews as shady in business practices, arrogant, and concerned only with the well-being of other Jews, for example (Peffley & Hurwitz, 1998; Sniderman & Piazza, 1993). This indicates that such people are broadly ethnocentric, hold a number of social stereotypes, and are generally socially intolerant. Advocates of the politics-is-complicated model argue that values related to authoritarianism, such as obedience to authority and hostility toward those different from one's own group, are more strongly correlated with negative attitudes toward Blacks than with values of individualism (i.e., the symbolic racism model) (Peffley & Hurwitz, 1998; Sniderman & Piazza, 1993).

An additional problem is a lack of consistency between support for equality between the races and lack of support for policies to achieve that equality. The politics-is-complicated model maintains that the inconsistency is not racism, but is attributable to changes in American politics and in attitudes about policies related to race, but also to other political attitudes. Attitudes toward race, they argue, do not always dominate political choice. For example, if two people (one liberal and one conservative) both express support for equality, but only the liberal supports spending by the federal government to help Blacks, is the conservative then inconsistent and a closet racist? From the politics-is-complicated perspective, the answer is no, because a conservative would believe that federal spending per se should be opposed. The conservative would maintain that they support racial equality, but that less government is more important and/or that government support for Blacks actually produces dependence on government, rather than giving a leg up. This point is extended to explain one of the paradoxes found among those with higher levels of education. The more educated White people are, the more likely they are to respond to political issues associated with race in terms of affect (liking or disliking Blacks) and cognition (understanding the broader political context and linking issues to ideological principles). The resulting cognitive complexity allows people to consider a variety of differentiated considerations in making a policy choice. Hence, more educated people are more likely to consider issues other than, or in addition to, race, when deciding on their issue positions. Therefore, the conservative described earlier will consider race, but several other principles and policy characteristics, along with race, will also affect their decision, thus diminishing race-related principles in the overall decision-making process (Sniderman et al., 1991).

The politics-is-complicated framework maintains that, in America today, there are "multiple agendas in racial politics, distinguishing the equal treatment agenda from the social welfare and the race conscious agendas" (Sniderman, Crosby, & Howell, 2000, p. 257). Some of those agendas, while having race-related implications, are not dominated by race-based attitudes, when policy choices are expressed. The politics of race has changed since the 1950s and 1960s, when they centered around legally sanctioned racial inequality, that is, Jim Crow laws, which created and enforced racial segregation and discrimination in schools, public facilities, housing, employment, and voting rights. Today's issues are more complex and include government enforcement of school integration through busing, affirmative action, assistance to Blacks to improve their economic situation, and government guarantees of equal opportunity.

Sniderman and Piazza (1993) maintained that there are three issue agendas in the United States today: the social welfare agenda, the equal treatment agenda, and the race-conscious agenda. The social welfare agenda is broadly defined to include governmental assistance to the disadvantaged, regardless of their race. However, because Blacks generally are at lower socioeconomic levels than Whites, race can become an issue in approving or rejecting social welfare policies. Sniderman and Piazza (1993) argue that "Whites tend to base their position on social welfare assistance for Blacks to a significant degree on judgments about effort and fairness" (p. 118). Whites are more likely to approve of social welfare policies, if they believe Blacks have been the victims of prejudice and discrimination, regardless of the White person's level of education. Whites are more likely to oppose these policies, if they believe that Blacks do not try hard enough, again, regardless of levels of education.

Ideology influences judgments of social welfare policies, as well, particularly among the more educated, who, as noted, are more cognitively complex. Conservatives are more likely than liberals to believe Blacks do not try hard enough and less likely than liberals to believe that Blacks have been treated unfairly in America. Ideology plays a role for the more educated, but not for the less educated, in determining their support for social welfare policies. The implication here is that, for the less educated, prejudice toward Blacks leads to the view that they have not been treated poorly and do not try hard enough, but for the more educated, ideology, rather than prejudice toward Blacks, produces opposition to welfare policies. Sniderman and Piazza (1993) explicitly note that the "more prejudiced a person is, the more likely he or she is to perceive Blacks to be failing to make a genuine effort to deal with their problems on their own" (p. 120), and that this attitude is a result of a general negative view of Blacks as lazy and irresponsible. They maintain that, in statistical analysis, there is little correlation between prejudices (which they continue to assess not only by anti-Black attitudes, but also by anti-Semitic attitudes) and ideology. This means that conservatism and prejudice can be statistically pulled apart and are not found to hang together. Hence, they maintain that ideology (liberalism and conservatism) plays a separate and distinct role in determining attitudes toward social welfare policies. Specifically, it is Whites' acceptance of the importance of individuals succeeding through hard work, rather than through help from the government, that produces their unwillingness to approve of social welfare-related policies, not a general dislike of Blacks. This also affects White responses to the next issue agenda—equality (Sniderman & Hagen, 1985).

Looking at the equal treatment agenda, Sniderman and Piazza (1993) examine attitudes about antidiscrimination laws. Here, they find that support or opposition for laws, such as fair housing, are only slightly related to the reasons Whites favor or oppose social welfare support by the federal government for Blacks. In the issue area of fair housing, prejudiced opposition stems from social distance factors: Prejudiced Whites do not want to live close to Black people. Again, Sniderman and Piazza (1993) found that prejudice is low among those with higher levels of education. For those with higher education, opposition to fair housing laws stems from the belief that government power should not be used to enforce equality.

Finally, in their examination of the race-conscious agenda, Sniderman and Piazza (1993) examine attitudes toward affirmative action. There is generally strong White opposition to affirmative action, although the authors found about 40% willing to support set-asides (in which a certain portion of federal contracts are reserved for minorities). White opposition to affirmative action is profound, regardless of whether or not they like or dislike Blacks. In a study by Sniderman and Carmines (1997) 9 of 10 prejudiced Whites opposed affirmative action, and 8 of 10 Whites who were neutral in their attitudes toward Blacks objected. In short, this is the politics-is-complicated model. Different issue agendas related to attitudes toward race are also related to attitudes toward other principles in American politics. They are more complicated than race alone, and must be examined in terms of that complexity.

This school of thought is strongly opposed by the advocates of the symbolic or new racism model, led by Sears and Kinder (1971; Kinder & Sears, 1981) and a number of others who have taken the argument in different directions (e.g., Bobo & Smith, 1994; Gaertner & Dovidio, 1986; Kinder & Sanders, 1996; Mendelberg, 2001; Pettigrew & Meertens, 1995). Symbolic racism arguments maintain that a new form of racism has replaced that of the old pre–civil rights era racism and that, rather than being rooted in self-interest or group competition, the new racism has its foundation in conservative political values and the Protestant ethic's moral values. There is substantial White resentment of Blacks today, a resentment embodied in and fueled by the campaigns and policies of Nixon and Reagan, along with other politicians (Kinder & Sanders, 1996). Kinder and Sanders (1996) ask the important question of whether racial resentment is associated with racial stereotyping, and, looking at the results of surveys, they found that racial resentment and stereotyping are closely related. However, the data indicate that modern White prejudice toward Blacks is not based on the old notions of biological inferiority, but on a belief that Blacks fail to try hard enough.

Symbolic racism advocates maintain that the lack of consistency between support for equality between the races and support for policies to achieve that equality is evidence of underlying ongoing racism in White America. (see Figure 7.1) Negative views of Blacks are still socialized into White Americans, who are conditioned to respond negatively to particular symbols regarding race-related issues, such as school busing (Sears, 1993). In terms of content, this new racism embodies the beliefs that "discrimination no longer poses a major barrier to the advancement of Blacks, that Blacks should try harder to make it on their own, that they are demanding too much, and that they are too often given special treatment by government and other elites" (Sears, et al., 2000, p. 17). More specifically, symbolic racism is composed of a conviction that Blacks are no longer treated unfairly; that they do not have traditional American values, such as the work ethic and obedience to authority; that, despite this, they

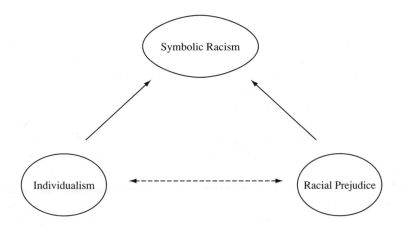

FIG. 7.1. Model of constituent elements defining the new racism. *Note.* From "The politics of race" (p. 241), by P. Sniderman, G. Crosby, and W. Howell, (2000), in D. O. Sears, J. Sidanius, and L. Bobo (Eds.), *Racialized politics,* Chicago: University of Chicago Press. Copyright by The University of Chicago Press. Adapted by permission.

continue to demand special treatment from the government; and that they get that special treatment undeservedly (Sears, Henry, & Kosterman, 2000). Sears et al. (2000) maintain that these attitudes and beliefs account more powerfully for the attitudes on policy issues just discussed than does ideology.

The dispute between the two models centers mostly around the relationship between conservative values, particularly those ranking individualism very high, and racism. The role of individualism is particularly important, because it emphasizes the importance of an individual "pulling themselves up by their boot straps" and not being reliant on government help to get ahead. Those who fail to do this are looked upon with disdain. Because many White Americans believe that Black Americans do not work hard enough, they regard Blacks with disdain: This is a new form of racism, based upon American values. Those values giving primacy to individualism are held most strongly by conservatives, whereas liberals tend to value equality (of opportunity, under the law, etc.) more highly. Hence, the relationship between conservative values and the new racism. Thus, the symbolic racism school maintains that hostile feelings toward Blacks blend with conservative values to produce a new form of racism. The politics-is-complicated model claims that conservative values are independent of prejudice (as discussed previously).

Also of importance to the symbolic racism school is the use of race-related issues in electoral campaigns. In the previous chapter, we discussed the role played by **framing** and **priming** during campaigns in American politics. Those factors play a particularly important role in race-related issues during elections. The two dominant parties in the United States are deeply divided by the social cleavage of race. During the civil rights era, the Democratic party moved left and the Republican party moved right, in positions on issues related to government intervention on behalf of racial equality for African-Americans. The Democratic party became the party to which most African-Americans hold allegiance, and many southern Whites left the Democratic party (Kinder & Sanders, 1996; Mendelberg, 2001). Strategically, therefore, Democratic candidates will want to mobilize Black votes, without alienating White voters in the process. Democratic candidates are frequently accused of merely ignoring Black interests, assuming that Blacks have little choice other than to vote Democratic. Republican candidates will generally want to mobilize White voters who hold conservative views on race-related matters, without alienating more moderate Whites. Added to the strategic problems is the advent of the norm of racial egalitarianism. The overwhelming majority of White Americans do not openly endorse racist ideas or practices: They embrace the norm of racial equality. However, as we have seen, racial resentment remains a real part of race relations in the United States.

These trends in White attitudes and emotions produce a strategic dilemma, particularly for Republicans running for office. Democrats need only keep quiet on race to keep their coalition of Black and White voters together. Republicans, however, must appeal to racial conservatives while not alienating moderate Whites, and they must do that without violating the social norm of racial equality. In other words, they cannot get caught "playing the race card" openly. Consequently, according to symbolic racism studies, they do it implicitly, through the use of code words, whereby an implicit reference to race is made, and, by being implicit, it can be denied. References to issues like law and order, urban crime, local control of schools, voting blocs, and protection of property rights, are all code words or phrases used to implicitly prime resentments against African-Americans among those who believe that Blacks do not try hard enough and are lazy, violent, and take power away from Whites. This pattern was noted in Richard Nixon's campaign strategy in 1968, as well as in the Reagan campaigns in the 1980s (Kinder & Sanders, 1996; Mendelberg, 2001). Perhaps the most infamous and hotly debate example of the use of implicit campaign advertisements is the Willie Horton campaign during the 1988 George H.W. Bush campaign (see box).

This area of research is important for the symbolic racism argument, because it digs through the layers of denial that these scholars believe cover latent racism in America (see also Milburn & Conrad, 1996). The denial is not difficult to understand, because it is a way of avoiding painful conflicts between competing ideas and emotions. The psychological processes are familiar ones, as Mendelberg (2001) notes:

The conflict between negative racial predisposition and the norm of racial equality can generate ambivalence; in turn, ambivalence creates a greater susceptibility to messages. A racial appeal thus has the capacity to affect public opinion about matters related to race. It is most likely to do so by making negative racial predispositions—stereotypes, fears, and resentments—more accessible. Once primed by a message, these predispositions are given greater weight when white Americans make political decisions that carry racial associations. . . . Racial priming can take place without the awareness of the individual, safeguarding the person's commitment to egalitarian conduct. (p. 112)

> ### Willie Horton and the Race Card
> In the 1988 presidential race, Vice President George H. W. Bush squared off against Massachusetts Governor Michael Dukakis. In an effort to demonstrate that Bush was tougher on crime than Dukakis, a pro-Bush campaign organization, in collaboration with the Bush team, developed an ad showing the mug shot of Willie Horton, an African-American convicted of murder in Massachusetts, who was allowed weekend furloughs from jail. During one of the furloughs, Horton ran away, ending up in Maryland, where he brutally beat a man and repeatedly raped a woman. Dukakis refused to revoke the furlough policy. The Bush team argued this was evidence that Dukakis was soft on crime. However, many argued that the Willie Horton ad was an implicit effort to use the race card. Horton was shown on television with a big afro, scruffy beard, and scary scowl. He looked like a criminal, and he was Black. Jesse Jackson accused the Bush campaign of making a racial appeal to White voters. Despite their denials, Bush officials knew that Horton was Black, and his race influenced their decision to use the Horton case in the campaign (Mendelberg, 2001).

The disagreement between the politics-is-complicated and symbolic racism camps about race in America cannot be settled here. Much of it rests on disagreements regarding the meaning and appropriate measurement of individualism. The book *Racialized Politics: The Debate About Racism in America*, edited by Sears, Sidanius, and Bobo (2000), contains recent and informative discussions of both debates. Nevertheless, we can say that there is a real conceptual disagreement here that may be unresolvable. The politics-is-complicated school clearly believes that people think in an additive way, that is, people hold a number of distinct ideas (about policy, government's role, and Blacks); they nonconsciously weigh those cognitive properties when making decisions; and, based upon the priority they give them separately, they produce a policy position on race-related issues. They regard the cognitive process as complex and linear, moving from cognition to recognition of information regarding political realities and policy options among which the people must chose, to a choice. The symbolic racism camp takes more of a gestalt view of how people think, with ideas, values, information, and choice occurring in an ebb and flow, with complexity lying in their interaction and, most important, the idea that the mental system is a unique system that is different from the sum of its parts. The symbolic racism camp believes that the interaction of portions of the race-related mind should not be separated, because that gives an inaccurate and artificial picture of the nature of modern racism.

Having reviewed some of the central scholarly arguments about race in America, let us return to a more anecdotal conclusion. Clearly, blatant racism remains in America. Clearly, there has been change in that over time, but it is very difficult for Black and White Americans to interact comfortably. We are, as Shipler (1997) puts it, a country of strangers. Let us illustrate this point with a few passages from Shipler's look at Black and White interaction, or lack thereof. Blacks and Whites each assume the other wants no interaction, and so none takes place. Shipler interviewed White college students, asking if they would talk to blacks in the self-selected "Black section" of the college cafeteria:

> "It wouldn't be something you would do," explained a young White woman. . . . "You aren't invited." Do you have to be invited to sit down with somebody in the lunchroom? "Well, no, but when you sit down with somebody at a table, you don't just sit down with people that you don't know. And if they don't invite you, you're not going to walk over."
>
> "It's like an attitude, I don't know," one woman said. "It's like they try to scare you. I don't know."
>
> Can you be precise? What do they do to scare you?
>
> "I don't know, I feel like they're looking at me like I think that I'm better than them, even though I don't. But they just perceive that we all think that, so they try and, like, have this rule by fear, like the only way maybe to defend themselves is to scare you, I guess."
>
> So it's the look? body language? "Yeah, they would look at you 'Why are you coming to sit with us?' Or sometimes they think that you're trying to be, like, diversified . . . so then they have the attitude 'Oh, you're just coming over here because you want to meet us because we're Black."
>
> Did that ever actually happen to you? "No." She giggled. (Shipler, 1997, pp. 27–28)

Here, a White woman feels uncomfortable about interacting with Black people, because she is concerned, based upon no actual evidence, that she would be snubbed for her willingness to do so. Her statement reflects fear of African-Americans, fear of even trying to interact with them on an individual level, and some sense of an assumption that African-Americans are responsible for their own segregation.

In a discussion of the cultural divide between Black and White Americans, Shipler notes that African-Americans are not free to behave in accordance with African-American culture, when in the White world. They have to adapt; Whites do not. They have to learn to walk in two worlds; Whites do not. For example:

> Every morning, Consuella Lewis consciously transformed herself as she drove to her job as director of the Office of Black Studies at Claremont-McKenna College. About a block away from the . . . campus . . . she reached down to her radio, lowered the volume, and changed the music from throbbing rap to soothing classical. . . . She had no apologies, even for the change of radio stations. "You're riding around, you may see someone, it's a small community, so you do the switching thing," she explained. (p. 71)

Or:

> The differences come in explicit and subtle forms. Daphne LeCesne, an African-American psychologist . . . used culture to explain issues of time, status, and organization that affect how she thought Black children learned. Her comparisons were heavily

value laden. "African-American learners," she insisted, "respond to a warm, interactive style, sensitivity to relational issues, and interact with you—accept interaction from you—on the basis of your personal attributes. The reason is, in a slave culture . . . you acquire strength and power by being verbally adroit. . . . Whereas there's tons of research that suggests that a European style is more dependent upon positional authority: your status, your role, the job you've been given . . . It's more European to be very time-conscious and role-conscious.

"Suburban birthday parties are a wonderful example," she said . . . ."A great suburban birthday party for White folks—I discovered with the first party I went to—starts promptly at two, just like it says on the invitation. And if you run late, people will call you and say, 'You comin'?' 'Of course we're coming,' 'Well, we're waiting.' 'You're waiting? You're holding up the party and waiting? OK, we'll be there.' You go, it starts promptly, there are no parents in sight. Everyone drops off their kids, they leave. When you stay, they look at you like 'You have an anxiety problem or something? You know you can go shop.' 'Well, I don't leave my kids and go shop.' 'Well, OK, fine.' 'You need any help?' They look affronted: 'You think I'm not organized here?' And at four, these people come back, and they take their kids. And of course, since you came late and your kids aren't used to this, they're like, 'Can we stay and play?'

"A great African-American party . . . doesn't start on time. If you come on time you expect to cook, OK? And you're needed to help cook because this is an extended family event. You better have food enough for the adults, and you better have adult quality food. It's terrible—you got hot dogs here. Where's the chicken? Don't expect it to start on time, and don't expect it to end abruptly." (pp. 80–81)

At the end of this chapter, we discuss the importance of forging a common third identity in resolving conflicts among ethnic groups. Americans think this is a done deal in the United States; our ethnic heritage is a source of pride, but in the end we are all Americans. But a recent study by Barlow, Taylor, and Lambert (2000) shows that African-Americans (women in this study) perceived themselves to be Americans, but doubted that White Americans see them as American. This is a reflection of the lack of interaction, the extent to which there is still a large social distance between Whites and Blacks in the United States, and a sad illustration of the ongoing legacy of slavery.

Race in Brazil

The United States is not the only country in the Western Hemisphere with a history of slavery. Indeed, Brazil had the largest slave population in the hemisphere. Despite myths to the contrary (e.g., Freyre, 1956; Tannenbaum, 1947), slavery in Brazil was brutal. Slave death rates were so high that reproduction rates were low, the average mining slave lived only 7–12 years, and 80% of slave children did not live long enough to reach adulthood (Marx, 1998; Mattoso, 1986). Slaves died from disease and harsh working conditions, and, because of the terrible conditions in which they lived, there were numerous slave revolts. Finally, in 1888, slavery was abolished, but the Black former slaves were left in dreadful conditions, "lacking any means to advance themselves or to compete, isolated in rural areas or in the newly emerging urban slums, or favelas." (Marx, 1998, p. 161)

Despite the legacy of slavery, Brazil prides itself on having a nonracist society. This is also a myth, one that has been increasingly decried by Brazil's Afro-Brazilian community. The myth arises from the fact that, after abolition of slavery, Brazil sought to avoid the kind of race-based conflicts that occurred in the United States. This was done through a conscious policy of miscegenation, encouraging the intermarriage of Black and White people in order to water down African heritage (in sharp contrast to the prohibition on such race mixing in the United States after slavery). There was certainly racial prejudice in Brazil. After slavery, for example, Whites were encouraged to immigrate from European countries, and Africans were prohibited, but formal discrimination was prohibited by law. In addition, Brazilians appreciated and embraced many African cultural remnants in art, music, and dance, in particular. This, along with official encouragement of people to label themselves White, reduced Black racial group identity, and reduced the incentives of Blacks to mobilize politically. Inequality was socially, rather than politically, enforced. The average White income is twice that of Blacks; Afro-Brazilians have a higher unemployment rate than Whites, and, when employed, they are in lower skilled and lower pay jobs; Afro-Brazilians have shorter life expectancies than Whites; and race is correlated with poorer physical health, as well (Hanchard, 1993; Marx, 1998).

Beginning in the late 1970s, in part as the result of the beginning of a gradual return to civilian government following 20 years of military rule, Brazil began to experience a newly mobilized Afro-Brazilian movement, particularly the *Movimento Negro Unificado*. Yet, many Afro-Brazilians, including Black politicians, are still reluctant to challenge the myth of Brazil's racial democracy. The great irony in Brazil is that, without systematic and institutional racial discrimination, group identity and mobilization have been limited, despite the fact that race matters in Brazil, and Afro-Brazilians have a great deal to complain about in terms of de facto inequality in Brazilian society.

South Africa

In 1948, the system of apartheid, which divided people according to racial categories, was instituted in South Africa. According to Eades (1999), "Apartheid was a radical and extreme extension of a system of segregation originating with colonial conquest and gradually evolving into complex sometimes uncoordinated institutions in the late nineteenth and early twentieth centuries" (p. 4). Within the system of apartheid were four racial categories: the Whites, the Coloreds, the Indians, and the Africans. Beginning with the Whites, each category was considered inferior to the one preceding it; In other words, Whites were considered superior to Coloreds, Indians, and Africans; Coloreds were superior to Indians and Africans; and so forth.

The Whites were made up of British English-speaking settlers and Dutch Afrikaner settlers. Even though they were considered part of the same "White" category, Afrikaners and English speakers were not a unified, homogenous group. There were considerable clashes between these two distinct ethnic groups, exhibited most notably during the Boer War (1899–1902), as both tried to assert their power in South Africa (Marx, 1998). But, as Eades (1999) explains,

> as Afrikaners came to dominate state power in South Africa, their sense of identity and destiny increasingly became more racial than cultural. A study carried out among Afrikaners in 1977 illustrated this shift. Before 1948 most of the Afrikaners' focus was on distinguishing themselves from the English-speakers. After 1948, however, the focus changed to race as apartheid based itself on racial distinction and had to be made legitimate. (p. 35)

The Coloreds were a broad racial category that included slaves from Madagascar, Indonesia, and tropical Africa, as well as indigenous Khoisan people. They were Christians and Muslims, farm laborers and artisans, and had many cultural differences (Eades, 1999). The mostly Hindu Indians were descendants of workers who were brought to work on sugar plantations between 1860 and 1911. Another wave of Indian immigrants, who were mostly Muslim, came as British subjects, beginning in the 1870s. Finally, the Africans were the largest category, making up 70% of the population of South Africa. This category encompassed many different tribes and clans and was not by any means a homogenous group.

In addition to classifying individuals, other legislation was passed that prohibited the mixing of races by marriage or sexual contact between them. The Bantu Authorities Act also established "homelands," which were essentially independent states that each African was assigned to. Thus, Africans became citizens of a homeland and not South Africa. Therefore, they had no national political rights. In essence, the apartheid system determined the political, social, and economic status of an individual, because being in a certain group afforded one a certain status. In this system, Whites benefited the most. Thus, Afrikaners, in particular, had a vested interest in maintaining such a system. They did this through brutal repression of the non-White population.

The dismantling of the apartheid system began in February 1990, when President F. W. deKlerk announced sweeping changes in the country. The constitution was rewritten, and elections were held, bringing Nelson Mandela, an African, to the presidency. Why, after all those years, did this system of institutionalized racism finally end? There was significant pressure internationally and on the South African government to end apartheid. In addition, domestic pressure became more intense. Possibly, deKlerk and many other Afrikaners realized that they could not maintain such a system, given that the Black majority, in particular, would no longer accept their inferior status in society.

The end of apartheid is also understandable in the context of the political psychological theories set forth at the beginning of this chapter. White powerholders did not give up without a struggle. Perceptual change among Whites was gradual, and is attributable in part to a freer media, which showed the opposition as reasonable and organized, thereby pushing the "skeptical master race to the necessity of negotiations as equals" (Adam & Moodley, 1993, p. 230). Increased defacto integration in universities and churches also influenced a change in White values. But it was perhaps the strategy of the African National Congress (ANC), the umbrella opposition organization, of inclusive national identity, that was crucial. By informing the South African Whites that they would be included as equals, not punished, in the post-apartheid South Africa, the ANC reduced the threat to the white identity group. Whites came to understand that things would change, but that they would not face retribution. After apartheid ended, South Africa engaged in extensive efforts to heal the wounds. The truth and reconciliation process in South Africa is discussed in detail in chapter 9.

The South African case is interesting, because it demonstrates patterns anticipated by both realistic conflict theory and social identity theory, and by patterns of group formation discussed in chapter 4. With regard to realistic conflict theory, the non-White groups competed with each other for resources (access to jobs, rights, etc.), until a superordinate goal— eliminating apartheid—united them. In terms of social identity, the South African case shows the malleability of race and ethnicity. The architects of apartheid clearly categorized people in terms of skin color. By doing so, they unwittingly created a form of social categorization that would unite non-Whites. African ethnic groups ("tribes") had many conflicts among themselves and were divided from the Coloreds. However, apartheid gave them a common cause and enabled them to bridge their differences, thus changing ethnicity as a central political dividing point to race as a central factor in uniting these groups to oppose the apartheid regime (Marx, 1998).

Duckitt (1994) has examined the political psychology of racism in South Africa and argues that getting to its roots is complicated, when the system as a whole institutionalizes racism. It offers the opportunity to explore the role of conformity pressures in producing prejudice, as well as arguments that authoritarian personality characteristics are associated with prejudice toward out-groups. After reviewing a number of studies, Duckitt (1994) relates that studies of authoritarianism, using Altemeyer's right-wing authoritarianism scale, did find that authoritarianism is important in producing prejudice in South Africa. In addition, during the apartheid era in South Africa, there were differences in degrees of racism, with English-speaking Whites being less racist than Afrikaans-speaking Whites. As in the United States, education made a difference, with prejudice falling as years of education increased. However, conformity pressures did not emerge as an important factor in prejudice in South Africa. Instead, racially prejudiced attitudes are learned early through socialization.

Finally, South Africa also offers a laboratory for the study of perceptions by the previously oppressed of their former oppressors, once the power tables have been turned. Duckitt and Mphuthing (1998) examined this question. Studies from the apartheid era show that Black Africans resented the power and privilege of Afrikaners more than that of English-speaking Whites. The supremacy of the Afrikaners was seen as illegitimate. Black Africans perceived themselves to be disadvantaged, compared to Afrikaners, and were outraged about it. The Duckitt and Mphuthing study examined African attitudes toward Afrikaners, before and after the first democratic election in South Africa, in May 1994. The two studies were done just 4 months apart. Before the election, Black Africans held the view just described of Afrikaners. Four months later, after the election, which was won by Nelson Mandela and which ended the Afrikaner lock on political power, Africans saw themselves as less disadvantaged relative to Afrikaners. Duckitt and Mphuthing note that, in a 4-month period, the socioeconomic disadvantages of the African communities did not change significantly. What did change was the power they held and their sense that the political system was legitimate and just. Under those circumstances, "inequality in post-transition South Africa could be viewed as less unfair and less inequitable than it was before the election" (1998, p. 827).

ETHNIC CONFLICT

What does it mean to be Italian-American, or Swiss German, or Yoruba, or Azeri? These labels, used to delineate groups of people from each other all over the world, are actually ethnic identities. Ethnic groups have cultural, religious, and linguistic commonalities, as well as a shared view that the group has a common origin or a unique heritage or birthright (Smith, 1981; Young, 1976). As Rothschild (1981) explains, ethnic groups are "collective groups whose membership is largely defined by real or putative ancestral inherited ties, and who perceive these ties as systematically affecting their place and fate in the political and socioeconomic structures of their state and society" (p. 9). Ethnic groups are considered exclusive rather than inclusive: Outsiders cannot join an ethnic group with which they do not share a common heritage. For example, a person from Zimbabwe could move to India, work, vote in national elections, and speak Hindi, becoming part of the Indian nation, but could not ever be accepted as an ethnic Indian, because that person does not possess a common ancestral heritage with other ethnic Indians.

Ethnicity has become a particular focus of attention in political psychology, because of the explosion of ethnic conflicts in various states within the past decade. However, interest in **ethnocentrism** can be traced back to William Graham Sumner's introduction of the term in 1906. He described it as "the view of things in which one's own group is the center of everything . . . and looks with contempt on outsiders" (p. 12). Although ethnic conflict has always existed, with the end of the Cold War the focus and attention of the international community has shifted from conflict between the superpowers to ethnic conflicts within countries. In countries where internal conflict has erupted, the state is no longer able to function as an authority over the groups. The conflicts are perplexing and surprising in many cases, because members of one ethnic group are now willing to kill members of another group who were formerly seen as neighbors, coworkers, people they went to school with, and perhaps even friends. It is evident that ethnicity has an enormous impact upon group relations within countries and unfortunately has resulted in atrocities being committed by one group against another. Rwanda, Bosnia, Chechnya, Congo, Liberia, Sierra Leone, Kosovo, and East Timor are only a few of the countries or regions that have experienced severe ethnic conflict and violence, many of which are ongoing. And, even if there is said to be the achievement of peace, frequently, no real political solution has been found. As a result, conflict can resume at any time.

Multiethnic or Multisectarian States

Before looking at cases of ethnic conflict, it is important to describe some of the political characteristics of the countries most likely to experience ethnic conflict. In multiethnic or multisectarian states, there are at least two ethnic groups, neither of which is capable of assimilating or absorbing the other or of seceding and maintaining independence. This is an important definitional point. Multinational countries, which are discussed in the next chapter, do have national identity groups capable of existing as independent countries. But, by definition, multiethnic and multisectarian states are composed of ethnic groups that cannot realistically establish independent countries. People in multiethnic or multisectarian countries give primary loyalty to their ethnic or sectarian group, rather than to the broader community living in the country (see Figure 7.2). The ethnic groups frequently realize that they do not have the resources to form their own state, but they may strive for the maximum autonomy possible and/or a large share of political and economic power in the state they share with other ethnic groups. Often, members of the groups in multiethnic states maintain separate, geographically concentrated communities, but there are many instances in which ethnic group members are dispersed across the country. As is seen in the Bosnia case, ethnic groups sometimes have ethnic kin living close by in an independent country. In Bosnia, Bosnian Serbs and Croatians wanted to join Serbia and Croatia, respectively. To do that, however, required "ethnic cleansing" of one another and of the Muslims living in Bosnia. This case is discussed in detail later. The disintegration of Yugoslavia, of which Bosnia was a part, is discussed more fully in chapter 8, because, with the exception of its republic of Bosnia-Herzegovina, Yugoslavia was a multinational state.

Many of the multiethnic states found today are former colonies. As a result of colonialism, the ethnic groups found themselves part of a state structure created by and imposed upon them by the colonial power. These are artificial states in the sense that they were literally drawn on

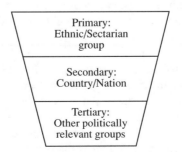

FIG. 7.2.   Political identity and loyalty in multiethnic and multisectarian states.

a map by an external power. In many cases, dominant ethnic groups within these colonial states took on the role as a local elite, by serving the interests of the colonial power. And frequently, after independence, they attempted to gain complete control of the state, resulting in ethnicity-based political competition for resources and power. Their political behaviors are a reflection of their concern with matters such as the security, autonomy, and welfare of their ethnic group, rather than those of the country as a whole.

In order to accommodate different ethnic groups' concerns, several structural options are employed by many multiethnic states, including consociationalism and federalism. These devices permit some degree of autonomy, by offering some local political control, but they also allow for national governmental control to exist. Both consociationalism and federalism are particularly appealing to those states that have geographically concentrated communities.

Consociationalism, or power sharing, as it is also referred to, has several features. Political parties, representing the ethnic groups, first form a coalition government, and each group is represented in this coalition government through proportional representation. Rules are then implemented that are used to govern the public sector. Each group is also afforded a degree of autonomy over matters deemed important to them. Finally, there are constitutional vetoes put in place for minority groups. Switzerland, with its strong German, French, and Italian ethnic groups, each with their own cantons, or governing regions, is a classic example of consociationalism.

In federal structures, there is a separation between a central government and provincial governments, each having different spheres of influence. This type of government has a governing constitution and bicameral legislature. In constitutional matters, both levels of government must give their approval. As a general rule, in the legislatures, smaller parties are over-represented.

Even if either of these structures are put in place, there is no guarantee that they will completely solve the conflict between groups within multiethnic states. In former colonies in particular, groups that have engaged in conflict do not have short memories of the acts perpetrated against them. For this reason, it is very difficult to foster a sense of community between the groups. An examination of some cases of ethnic conflict will demonstrate how quickly they can become inflamed, how violent they can be, and how difficult they are to stop. Many multiethnic states employ federalist institutional structures. Russia is one, and Nigeria, a case described shortly, is another.

Explanations of Conflict

The same psychological explanations of racial conflicts can be used to explain ethnic conflict. There is some basis for realistic conflict and competition among these ethnic groups for power, influence, and autonomy in a political system. In good times, cooperation in pursuit of common goals is possible. In bad times, competition for resources and power can be fierce. But these conflicts are not simply contingent upon good or bad times. The roots are psychological and so deep that conflicts easily erupt when an opportunity or threat is perceived by one ethnic group vis-á-vis another and when at least one group is mobilized, often by political leaders, to challenge the perceived threat or opportunity. From social identity theory, we know that groups engage in social comparison. When the outcome of that comparison is negative, groups are motivated to change their status. An insecure social comparison results in a conclusion that an out-group has an unfair advantage and that the relationship among the groups is conceived of as unfair, among other perceived inequities. One strategy for changing a group's status is social competition, which takes place when a subordinate group engages in direct competition with the dominant group. The group in the dominant position will feel threatened by the challenge to its status by a subordinate group. When this occurs, competition can lead to conflict.

Many of the ethnic conflicts that have occurred in the post–Cold War era have been shockingly brutal. The discussions of group behavior in chapters 3 and 4 provide some insights into how violence can become so severe. These are situations in which intense threat to the group is perceived, which, in turn, increases cohesion; dehumanization of other groups; deindividuation, so people see the group as responsible for events, not their own actions as individuals; and strong pressures for conformity and unanimity in the face of threat. Strong emotions associated with out-groups, discussed in chapter 3, erupt and add to the violence. The emotions emanating from ethnic out-group stereotypes are often extremely powerful. They can change from simmering bitterness and resentment to rage and hatred toward other ethnic groups, when underlying conflicts increase in intensity. At the same time, people experience increased love and attachment to their own ethnic group. In addition, in ethnic conflicts, one is unlikely to find the reticence evident in American racial politics, in which political elites resort to implicit code word references to race in race-related issues. In ethnic conflicts, such as those discussed in the next section, political leaders actively manipulate the stereotypes and emotions, in order to mobilize their ethnic brethren against other ethnic groups. They use stereotypes and emotions to arouse intense feelings of hatred and anger toward other ethnic groups. As Kaufman (2001) notes, "If emotional appeals to ethnic themes are simultaneously appeals to ideas that lead one to blame another group, those appeals are apt simultaneously to arouse the feelings of anger and aggression most likely to motivate people to want to fight" (p. 9). Leaders play an important role in defining a threat or an opportunity, in sharpening perceptions of ethnic identity, and in furthering conflict by obstructing diplomatic solutions. In the process, committing acts of violence against others, for the sake of the in-group, becomes more likely, even if the victims once were friends.

Case Illustrations of Ethnic Conflict

Ethnic Clashes in Nigeria

Nigeria is a multiethnic state that was a product of colonialism. Nigeria was colonized by the British. Three main ethnic groups make up two-thirds of the population: the Hausa/Fulani (who are Muslim), the Yoruba (who are Christian and Muslims), and the Ibo (who are Christian). Within these three groups, there are many subdivisions, so that, as a whole, Nigeria has more than 248 distinct ethnic groups (Diamond, 1988). The Hausa/Fulani are found in the north, the Yoruba in the west, and the Ibo in the east. However, each region does contain other ethnic groups.

Social stereotypes, group conflict, and social comparison processes are important factors in understanding ethnic conflict in Nigeria. Under British colonialism, Nigeria was partitioned into three regions, each dominated by an ethnic group. The Hausa were chosen by the British to be their administrative representatives. Although the Hausa were permitted to keep their traditional class hierarchy, social structure, and educational system based upon the Koran, the British imposed their own education system and made the common language English in the areas dominated by Yoruba and Ibo. This set forth the basis for ethnic competition after independence: An outside power, the British colonizers, had already established the basis for Hausa superiority, in terms of political power; The other groups' self-comparison with the Hausa would be negative, at least from the standpoint of political power.

Nigeria achieved its independence from Britain in 1960, and the colonial regional structuring based on ethnicity was initially left in place in a federated political system. Ethnic competition preceded independence and quickly became a central factor in Nigerian politics after independence. The Ibos, in the southeast, were tired of the domination by the north. In the early colonial era, the British had considered the Ibo to be the most backward and inferior of Nigeria's ethnic groups. But during the 1930s, the social and economic position of the Ibo had improved. The perception by the British of the Ibo as backward had shifted to view them as "dynamic, aggressive, upwardly mobile" (Young, 1983, p. 206).

During the 1950s, the Ibo became strongly nationalistic, desiring a role in the existing national institutions. The Ibos also tended to be very entrepreneurial and moved into Hausa and Yoruba regions. Their economic success, as well as their desire for greater participation and political power, was perceived as threatening to other groups. Increasingly, the Ibo were seen, through an anti-Semitic type of stereotype, as insular, elitist, devious, and power- and wealth-acquisitive. Thus, stereotyping and social identity patterns appear in this case. The Ibos were downtrodden and sought to alter their social, economic, and political roles in Nigeria. This was threatening to the other groups, who had a strong stereotype of Ibos as bad in a variety of ways, and they were not about to let change occur.

In January 1966, Ibo military officers led a successful coup, overthrowing the government. They, in turn, were ousted later that same year by northerners, bringing Lieutenant Colonel Yakubu Gowon to power. Ethnic clashes followed, and many Ibos were killed, particularly in the north. Continued persecution prompted the Ibos to declare independence in the region of the country where they were the numerical majority, which they called Biafra. The federal government refused to let them secede, and, in 1967, a civil war broke out between the Ibos, seeking to establish an independent Biafra, and the federal government of Nigeria. The war, which lasted for 3 years, ended in a loss for the Ibos and claimed the lives of over 1 million people, mostly Ibos. After the war, the federal government developed a very important approach to the defeated Ibo: reincorporation into the country, opportunities in education, and reconstruction. This type of policy is crucial to the future of any multiethnic state that contains a defeated breakaway group. And it worked in Nigeria. Despite the 1 million Biafran deaths, the war is not a topic of discussion and continued resentment in Iboland today.

After the war, ethnic divisiveness continued to plague Nigerian politics. General Gowon was overthrown in a coup in 1975 (Ihonvbere, 1994). General Olusegun Obasanjo, a Yoruba, took power and adopted measures to pave the way for democratic reform and a return to civilian rule. Those reforms included the creation of a new constitution, with provisions that would accommodate ethnic diversity. A new federal state structure was introduced, with 19 states. In order to win the presidency, a candidate would have to receive at least one third of the popular vote and at least one fourth of the vote in two thirds of the 19 states (Shively, 1999).

Since the end of the first 13 years of military rule in 1979, Nigeria has only had a few years of intermittent civilian rule, and ethnic conflict and competition have been instrumental in inhibiting the establishment of stable democracy. For example, elections were finally held in 1979, as promised by Obansanjo, bringing the northerner, Shehu Shagari, to power. However, he was overthrown in 1983, amid accusations of corruption, a failing economy, and his inability to deal with ethnic divisions (Shively, 1993). In 1993, Chief Moshood Abiola, a Yoruba, won the election. However, General Ibrahim Babangida, a northerner who had been in power since 1985, nullified the results. Babangida finally stepped down, naming Ernest Shonekan, a civilian, as interim leader for a few months, until the defense minister, General Sani Abacha, took control. In June 1994, Abacha arrested Abiola and charged him with treason. When Abacha suddenly died in June 1998, an interim leader, General Abdulsalami Abubakar, succeeded him. After years of promises, elections were finally held, and Olusegun Obansanjo took office once again on May 29, 1999. However, Obansanjo took office amid election irregularities such as inflated turnout, the stuffing of ballot boxes, intimidation and bribery of election officials and voters, and alteration of results (Human Rights Watch, 2000). Obasanjo won reelection in 2003, again amid accusations of irregularities in the electoral process. In each case of regime change, the ethnicity of the old and new power holders is centrally important to the people of Nigeria. Each group continually compares itself with the others, and the propensity to identify some basis for a negative social comparison is strong. The power and economic pie in Nigeria is small. Nigeria is a poor country despite its oil, and each group fears the others will get more than their fair share.

The Nigerian case shows how ethnicity and national identification can become mutually exclusive. In Nigeria, control of the state was associated with ethnicity, so extensively that each of the three dominant ethnic groups was susceptible to ethnicity-based political parties and issues. They were constantly fearful that the essence of being Nigerian would be captured by one of the other ethnic groups, and their own group would lose out on power and security. In fact, the Biafran war served as a catalyst for a struggling Nigerian identity to gain momentum. According to Oyovbaire (1984):

> The quantum or quality of national consciousness generated by [federal efforts during the war] is impossible to assess, but there is no doubt that a new public consciousness of the role of the centre previously unknown in the politics, economics and management of the federation had been generated by the civil war. . . . If before the Biafran occupation, Nigeria was just a name—lacking meaning, attachment and symbolism to the literate and nonliterate, the urban unemployed and rural dwellers—after that experience Nigeria became a fact of existence, the federal government being regarded as protector and benefactor. (pp. 132–133)

Nevertheless, ethnicity continues to be a dominant factor in Nigerian politics, and it continues to cause frequent outbreaks of violence, resulting in hundreds of deaths, on a regular basis. To satisfy ethnic demands, the country has been divided repeatedly into more and more states, currently standing at 36. In the process, the three largest and dominant ethnic groups have been distributed among several states. Thus, Nigerian identity remains secondary to ethnic identities and is unlikely to be enhanced by the ongoing corruption, political instability, poverty, and repression of ethnic discontent, such as the execution in 1995 of nine ethnic Ogoni leaders who protested government policies in Ogoniland. This leaves the glaring question of how Nigeria as a state survives, and the answer must be that no group sees an alternative.

Ethnic Cleansing in Bosnia

Yugoslavia was a multinational and multiethnic country. For many years, the people from different ethnic groups lived together harmoniously. After World War II, Yugoslavia's government was headed by a very charismatic leader, Josip Broz Tito, who encouraged a common Yugoslav political identity. In 1980, Tito died, and during the next decade the unity and brotherhood encouraged by Tito gradually unraveled. The final disintegration of Yugoslavia began on June 25, 1991, with the declaration of independence of Croatia and Slovenia. The Yugoslav republic of Bosnia-Herzegovina declared itself an independent country on April 5, 1992, and was subsequently recognized as such by the international community. This left a rump Yugoslavia composed of what was left—Serbia and Montenegro.

The powerful pull of in-groups, as well as the impact of negative threatening images of others, are useful in explaining the conflict that erupted in Bosnia. Bosnia has three main ethnic groups: the Serbs (who are Eastern Orthodox), the Muslims, and the Croatians (who are Roman Catholic). The Serbs and Croatians in Bosnia were part of larger ethnic groups in the

Croatian and Serbian republics of Yugoslavia. As Thomas (1996) explains, during the days of Yugoslavian unity

> in Bosnia-Herzegovina, whether Muslim, Orthodox Christian or Roman Catholic Serbs, Croats and Muslims were all comfortable being labeled "Bosnian" even if they believed themselves to be Bosnian Serb, Croat or Muslim. This was because Bosnia was a smaller and narrower representation of the larger concept of multi-ethnic Yugoslavia, a country voluntarily created in 1918 for the South Slav peoples. . . . Bosnia-Herzegovina, like Yugoslavia, denoted territorial space and not ethnic identity. (p. 30)

The 1991 census demonstrated the importance of ethnic identity, however: 44% self-identified as Muslim, 31.5% Serb, 17% Croat, and only 5.5% Yugoslav. As a republic in Yugoslavia before it disintegrated, Bosnia-Herzegovina could and did provide these groups with opportunities for social mobilization and social creativity. The Yugoslav state prevented one group from being dominant and provided opportunities for all ethnic groups. In fact, the state created the concept of Bosnian Muslims as a distinct ethnic identity in the 1960s, which was more preferable to the Muslims than their previous identities as Croat or Serb Muslims (Thomas, 1996). Intergroup competition was held in check by the Yugoslav government while efforts were made to forge a common identity.

As Yugoslavia fell apart, the three ethnic communities in Bosnia faced a real dilemma. Should they remain part of Yugoslavia or attempt independence? None of the three had the power to dominate an independent Bosnia. The ethnic populations were territorially dispersed, and there was significant intermarriage among the groups. Therefore, the groups could not simply be divided up geographically, providing each its own state in a multiethnic country. Nor, given the distribution of ethnic populations and the complexity of their intermixture, could Bosnia simply be divided up, with its Croatian and Serbian ethnics annexed to their re-spective national states, Croatia and Serbia. The dilemma, by 1991, therefore, became whether to stay with Yugoslavia, which now consisted primarily of Serbs, or attempt independence. Staying in Yugoslavia was threatening to the Muslim and Croat populations. Bosnian Serbs, on the other hand, had every reason to want to remain in what was left of Yugoslavia, where Serbs would be the dominant group. It was in this context that a referendum was held to de-cide upon independence. The Serbs boycotted the referendum, and the Muslims and Croats voted for independence from Yugoslavia.

Bosnian leaders quickly developed a power-sharing arrangement among the parties repre-senting all three ethnic groups in an autonomous Bosnia. That arrangement was doomed to failure, however. The Croatian and Serb communities in Bosnia each saw an opportunity to join their ethnic brethren in Croatia and Serbia. The strong pull of group identity made this op-tion very attractive for the Bosnian Croats and Bosnian Serbs. This destroyed any basis for power sharing. The Bosnian Serbs declared themselves part of the Serb nation. The Bosnian Croats insisted that they would not remain in Bosnia, if Bosnia remained in Yugoslavia (Woodward, 1995). Eventually, Bosnian Croats marked for themselves a Croat state in west-ern Bosnia-Herzegovina. The Muslim community, recognizing its inability to maintain sover-eign independence for long in this setting, was faced with the options of emigration or ac-cepting minority status in Croatia or Serbia.

Threat perceptions in all three communities were very high. Croatians traditionally saw Serbs as barbarians, that is, through the barbarian image (see chapter 3); Serbs were horrified at the prospect of being separated from the Serb population that had dominated the old Yugoslavia, at least in size and presence in the military. Moreover, the Serbs recalled the slaughter of Serbs by Croatians during World War II. The Muslims feared both Croatians and

Serbs, with good reason. They too had received brutal treatment from the Croatians during World War II, and the Serbs maintained an historical animosity toward the Muslims that went back hundreds of years.

The war that ensued was a brutal one. All three ethnic communities had been mobilized and galvanized by leaders (Serbian President Slobodan Milošević, Croatian President Franjo Tudjman, and Bosnian Muslim leader Alija Izetbegovic) in the years preceding Bosnia's war, while Yugoslavia, as a whole, disintegrated (Kaufman, 2001). Local Bosnian Serb, Croatian, and Muslim leaders also contributed to the slandering and dehumanization of the other ethnic groups. The means selected by all three groups for solving the question of the future of Bosnia-Herzegovina was ethnic cleansing. If living with the other groups is too threatening, they thought, they would just get rid of them. In the spring of 1992, Serb-dominated Yugoslav forces, together with Bosnian Serbs, began a campaign to ethnically cleanse the other groups from the country. In addition to forcing Muslims and Croats to flee the country, the list of atrocities committed by the Serbs against the other groups included mass killings, rape, and the creation of concentration camps. The other groups also committed atrocities, but not on the same scale as the Serbs.

In November 1995, the United States brokered talks, which resulted in the Dayton Peace Accord. Bosnian Serbs did not negotiate for themselves, but were represented by Slobodan Milošević. Under the agreement, a Bosnian Serb Republic and Muslim–Croat federation were established. A federal government, with a presidency that rotates among the groups, was also created. NATO peacekeeping troops were also brought in to ensure a peaceful transition.

In Their Own Words: Radovan Karadzic on the Situation of the Bosnian Serbs

Below are some excerpts from a speech given by Radovan Karadzic to the Parliament of Bosnian Serbia, (Republika Srpska) in 1996. Karadzic was the President of Republika Srpska at the time. He is now under indictment for war crimes. Try to identify the phrases that would galvanize hostility toward other ethnic groups as well as increase Serb solidarity.

"Five years have passed since the first multi party elections in the former Bosnia-Herzegovina, four years and three months since the founding of the Republic and four years since the beginning of the war.

There are few nations in the world who were exposed to such trials and suffering in such a short period as our people have been. Centuries and decades which our enemies had spent working on the denationalization of the Serbs west from the Drina and on their separation from the mother Serbia.

Regardless of whether those guilty for this war will be tried, we shall always hold them responsible and will never forget what they did to us. . . . Three weeks after the recognition of our state we were forced to defend it with arms. Our armed struggle and the defense of the state and the people are among the brightest examples of knightly self-sacrifice. . . . We fought against huge powers. Against a more numerous and better equipped enemy . . . The people was on our side, and the God was on our side. . . . Our goal was, and remains, the united state of all Serbs. . . . We saved our people from a genocide and secured a significant proportion of its historic territories. Some precious territories we didn't include in our state, and we will never accept that that loss is definitive." (Karadzic, 1996, pp. 1–2)

However, this war, which claimed the lives of an estimated 200,000 people (Power, 2002), may not be over. Hatred in this conflict erupted quickly, in part because of the efforts of leaders to provoke it. It cannot be expected to disappear overnight, particularly after so many have died. The box text on page 178 illustrates the extent to which hatred associated with extreme stereotypes spreads like an infectious disease in conflicts such as these.

Ethnic cleansing in Bosnia is a classic example of the group patterns leading to violence, which were discussed earlier. Without the Yugoslav state to manage ethnic group competition, concerns began to arise about the domination by one ethnic group. Wrongs done by each group to the others in the past were recalled, threat perceptions increased, stereotyping increased, the salience of group attachments increased, and eventually war erupted. Once the fighting started, it was increasingly possible to dehumanize the others, to divest oneself of personal responsibility for violence, and ethnic cleaning, ethnic rape, and thousands of deaths occurred.

The Maya of Guatemala

The last case of ethnic conflict we consider also involves various aspects of social identity theory and group competition. In this case, the indigenous Maya of Guatemala were a downtrodden people who were kept in an inferior socioeconomic situation and who lacked political power. The dominant group, the ladino (non-indigenous) population in general, and the military in particular, looked at them with contempt. During the worst years of the conflict there, they were dehumanized by the military, who slaughtered thousands of Maya.

In Guatemala, 60% of the 12.5 million citizens are Maya; the rest are ladinos. The two differ in language and custom, but not in appearance, because most ladinos have Mayan ancestry. Ladinos speak Spanish, wear western clothing, and engage in capitalist enterprise. The Maya of Guatemala, however, are composed of 23 subgroups and languages, some of which are mutually unintelligible. Many Maya do not speak Spanish, and many are bilingual (Warren,

---

Ethnic Hatreds

Journalist Anthony Loyd's (1999) report from the battlegrounds of Bosnia provides a first-hand illustration of ethnic stereotyping and hatred:

"I had left Citluk at dawn and after walking a few miles had been picked up by a heavily built middle-aged Bosnian Croat woman. . . . Naively I had imagined having to listen to tales of grandchildren or cats for the next leg of my journey. Instead she had launched into a tirade against Islam that gathered momentum with each dragging mile. There were thousands of Arab mujahidin swarming through the hills, she told me. They had radicalized the minds of the Bosnian Muslims who were now waging a jihad, a holy war, upon the beleaguered Croat people who for so long had been persecuted by the filth of the Ottoman Empire. Bosnia was now Europe's frontier against the fundamentalist legions of Allah, the Croatian people the brave hajduk vanguard in the battle for Christianity. As for the Serbs, not one of them would find salvation. . . . Spittle began to fly like sparks from the edge of her mouth." Describing his next lift Loyd wrote: "Within five minutes I was hearing the same story: mujahidin, fudamentalism, the Ottoman empire, jihad, Turks, Christ. . . . It was the key to so much of what was happening in Bosnia. If I, a relatively impartial foreigner, . . . could be frightened by local scaremongering and propaganda, imagine what it was doing to the minds of isolated rural communities with no access to outside news, no experience of media impartiality. . . . You could pop common sense from the minds of villagers in Bosnia like a pea from a pod. Make them afraid by resurrecting real or imagined threats, catalyse it with a bit of bloodletting, and you were only two steps from massacre and mayhem." (pp. 70–71)

1993). They often wear traditional colorful clothing and maintain a traditional communal lifestyle.

Since the Spanish conquest of the Maya in the 16th century, the central direction of change has been toward the assimilation of the Maya into Spanish culture. One was ladino or one was Maya. The two identities were not complementary. Being ladino meant one was Guatemalan, whereas being Maya meant one was not. The indigenous Maya were stereotyped as racially and culturally inferior. Their socioeconomic characteristics and political powerlessness reflected this perception of them by the ladino society.

Over the centuries since conquest by Spain, the Maya remained at the bottom of the social and economic ladder in Guatemala. The first stage of the mobilization of the Maya to change this situation began in 1944, with the establishment of a reform-minded government, and ended with the 1954 overthrow of that government and the brutal repression that followed. But, by the late 1970s, the indigenous people were politically and socially mobilized again. This is an illustration of the efforts people make, when they perceive a realistic opportunity, to change their group's status. At that point, they were participating in political party activities, running for office, and had established a Mayan-led labor organization, the Committee of Peasant Unity. This took place in the context of broader social and political discontent in Guatemala, which included sectors of the ladino population. The period also witnessed the emergence of left-wing guerrilla groups intent on overthrowing the government. The guerrilla military offensive reached its height in 1980–1981, with 6–8,000 armed fighters and 250,000–500,000 active collaborators and supporters, and operated in most parts of the country (Schirmer, 1998).

This movement was seen as threatening to the dominance of the ladinos in general and of the wealthy landowner ladinos in particular. The military government's response was a scorched-earth assault on all opposition, including the Mayan communities in rural areas, which were suspected of supporting the guerrillas. The violence was horrific, and the intention was to eliminate as many guerrillas and their supporters as possible and to terrorize the Mayan communities into submission. The tactics used were very brutal. Witness accounts, such as the following, were common:

A North American priest described how this process took place in an isolated northern province where he worked during the early years of the violence:

"Between 1975 and 1997, 47 project leaders were assassinated or disappeared. One returned. He suffered torture and witnessed the murder of some 30 members of his community . . . . In March, 1981, 15 members of our co-op were dragged from their homes and murdered by the military. In December 1981, assassins in army uniforms and with government trucks entered a remote village and assassinated several co-op leaders. Five others were found later, crucified with sharp sticks to the ground and tortured to death."

Another respondent . . . a Peace Corps volunteer, described the following situation in the Indian town where she worked:

"I was working in one town which was trying to organize a bread-baking and shirt-making co-op to raise funds for community projects such as a pharmacy. Several of the members were murdered in an attack by uniformed government soldiers. I did not witness this, but I saw the effects on the project and the source was truthful beyond any doubt. I later read an account in a U.S. publication that said that these "terrorists" (bread makers) had been roasted alive in the schoolyard in front of their friends and families." (Davies, 1992, 22–23)

Moreover, the military was unabashed about their conduct. They admitted to the tactics they used and felt quite justified in using them. The press secretary for General Ríos Montt, who took control of the dictatorship after a coup in 1983, stated:

The guerrillas won over many Indian collaborators. Therefore, the Indians were subversives. And how do you fight subversion? Clearly you had to kill Indians because they were collaborating with subversion. And then it would be said that you were killing innocent people. But they weren't innocent; they had sold out to subversion. (quoted in Carmack, 1992, p. 57)

Villages were routinely attacked, many suspected subversives were killed, women were gang raped, victims were tortured, and the soldiers even engaged in ritual cannibalism, in order to terrorize the civilians (Stoll, 1992).

For the Maya, the consequences of this "dirty-war" were disastrous, approaching a "demographic, social and cultural 'holocaust'" (Davies, 1992, p. 21). More than 150,000 people were killed, depending on when one starts the count; 150,000 went into exile in Mexico; and half a million people became internal refugees. Guatemala ended up with more than 40,000 disappearances. Eighty-three percent of the victims of the scorched-earth policy were Maya. Ninety-three percent of human rights violations were attributed to the military or paramilitaries. If the Maya fled the army's assaults by going into the mountainous highlands or Mexico, they faced hunger and misery. When they tried to return, they were imprisoned in "poles of development" (*pollos de desarrollo*)—internment camps for Mayan returnees where they were to be indoctrinated in anti-communism, and where their way of life was to be systematically destroyed. The campaign was not simply directed at the Maya, but was an ideologically based internal security campaign, which combined with ongoing ethnocentrism to devastate the indigenous population.

The military turned the reins of government back to civilians in 1985, but this was only a cosmetic democracy. The military was free to continue to run its counterinsurgency program, and the Mayan people continued to suffer. Although the guerrillas had a resurgence in the late 1980s, they by then recognized that the war could not be won by either side. They suggested peace talks, but it was not until December 1996 that the final peace agreement was reached. The UN brokered the talks and the subsequent reforms of the political system.

Now that the war is over, the Mayan communities have again mobilized, this time to ensure their participation in the establishment of a new Guatemala. Of central importance is that their mobilization appears to be toward achieving a new definition of the national community and what it means to be Guatemalan. During the early 1990s, many ladinos began to accept and prize aspects of Maya culture, the teaching of Mayan languages in schools, and the participation of Maya political organizations in the political system (LaBaron, 1993). That in and of itself did not mean that the ladino community was interested in the creation of a new common third identity incorporating elements of Maya culture. But, by 1996, there were signs that this too may be changing: The Accord on the Identity and Rights of Indigenous Peoples, and constitutional changes agreed to by the government, will, if put into effect, turn Guatemala into a multiethnic, multicultural, and multilinguistic society. It appears, then, that Guatemala has a chance to reconcile competing indigenous versus ladino identities, so that they may still be different, but both will be Guatemalan. We return to this process, in our discussion of conflict resolution.

RESOLVING RACIAL AND ETHNIC CONFLICTS

A crucial first step in conflict resolution in the aftermath of extreme violence is for people to feel safe. Once the fighting has stopped, people still have highly charged emotions about other groups, and they will quite reasonably fear that their own safety is still in jeopardy. This makes peacebuilding, that is, reconstructing a new peaceful society, very difficult. Leaders are crucial who have skills enabling them to build coalitions and calm fears. Neutral third-party mediators are also often sought, whose role is to mediate negotiations, offer resources, and inspect the actions of the various groups involved in the conflict, to ensure they are abiding by their agreements. However, as Kaufman (2001) notes, this approach rarely works in ethnic conflicts. Instead, for third parties, "the most effective tool of reassurance is peacekeeping, the nonviolent use of third-party armed forces to maintain peace among belligerents. In general, peacekeeping only works with the consent and cooperation of the key parties to the conflict" (p. 41).

Over the long term, whether discussing racial or ethnic separation and conflict, integration and the elimination of inequalities and their causes have long been considered essential to conflict resolution and avoidance. Integration without discrimination is really the only practical solution in many cases, because separation is not an option. In the following sections, we discuss two types of integration strategies: shared sovereignty and utilitarian. A central feature of these conflicts is fear—the development of a security dilemma wherein different identity groups (racial or ethnic) fear that they will lose out in competition for power and justice, fear the destruction of their group as an identity group, or even fear for their very existence. People mobilize to defend themselves against perceived threat from other groups.

Ultimately, the best long-term solution to these conflicts is the development of an overarching common identity among the groups: "Yes, I am White and you are Black, but we are both Americans first and can live together harmoniously" or "I am Ibo and you are Hausa, but we are both Nigerians first and can live together harmoniously." An ideal integration strategy to achieve this end would be a plan for developing a population-wide, first-intensity identity with the territorial community, for example, with America or Nigeria or Guatemala. Indeed, this is the goal in the peace process in Guatemala, to establish a common and multifaceted Guatemalan identity that incorporates both ladino and Mayan culture, rather than ladino alone. But, in some cases, the development of an overarching identity, which receives all groups' primary and most intense loyalty, is neither desirable nor possible. Often, distrust is too high or people do not want to be assimilated into a dominant culture and lose their cultural uniqueness.[3] Nevertheless, integration strategies can be developed to resolve conflict in those cases, as well. To be successful, an integration strategy requires eliminating racial or ethnic prejudice and the accompanying structural (legal, social) factors that maintain it.[4]

Successful integration strategies require a number of political and psychological components. Psychologically, integration strategies would have to provide different identity groups in a polity with options for social mobility and social creativity, so they need not rely on competition and conflict to satisfy identity needs, and can move toward the development of a common third identity while not threatening the existence of the primary identity. Integration strategies need to establish an environment in which groups feel secure that their identities are not threatened. The greater the disparity in cultural, religious, and racial characteristics, the more complicated the problem. A multifaceted formula is needed here, in which different group characteristics are looked at positively when comparisons are made. When social comparisons are different, but equally positive, conflict can be avoided (Van den Heuvel & Maeertens, 1989). For example, in the United States, the "black is beautiful" campaign during the civil rights movement, and other more current efforts to promote multiculturalism, all attempt to recognize cultural and racial differences and to celebrate those differences as equally valuable and equally American.

A second psychological element involves a need to address stereotypes and social distance among groups. Possibly most important in this process is addressing perceptions of group inferiority or superiority. Breaking such stereotypes and images is central to a workable integration strategy. The objective should be the replacement of a highly simplified and negative view of the other group with a far more complex and nonjudgmental view. This requires acceptance of, and respect for, group differences and changed expectations about other group members' behavior (Hewstone, 1989; Van den Heuvel & Martins, 1989). An early idea about how to do this was the **contact hypothesis**, which proposed increasing intergroup contact, and exposing people to the complexity of group members and thereby providing information that breaks down stereotypes. But the contact hypothesis works only in an environment or institutional context that is supportive, where contact can be ongoing, and in which groups are equal in status (Allport, 1954; Brewer & Brown, 1998; Fiske, 1998). A number of studies note that increased contact may merely lead people to assume that the member of another group who appears to be different from the stereotypical member is simply atypical of the group, meaning that the stereotype of the group will stand, but a particular individual will be seen as different, not like the others (Brewer & Miller, 1984; Hewstone & Brown, 1986; Mackie & Hamilton, 1993).

The political or policy aspect of integration strategies would have to meet these psychological requirements. Policies would have to address the particular needs, demands, and alternatives regarding conflicting groups' capability, power, and rewards accrued within the political system. Mechanisms used for this part of an integration strategy include supplying multiple channels for acquiring power, so that no group dominates limited channels; promoting intragroup, rather than intergroup, conflict; policies that promote intergroup cooperation; policies that encourage cross-group alignments based on interests, rather than on group identity; and policies that reduce various kinds of disparities between groups, thereby reducing dissatisfaction (Horowitz, 1985). Politically, the strategy has to be tuned to the distribution of power among groups. Ethnic and racial identity groups often vary greatly, in terms of perceived power and influence in their political systems. Those who see themselves as strong enough to possibly achieve independence would only be satisfied with institutional and social conditions offering broad autonomy just short of independence. At the other end of the scale are groups far too weak to achieve independence, and, for these groups, integration, in the form of assurances of equality with other groups, rather than autonomy, would be satisfactory.

Shared sovereignty and utilitarian strategies are good examples of the importance of blending political structures, institutions, and distribution of power with psychological patterns. The strategies recognize that identities are not negotiable, but that interests are (Burton, 1990; Gurr, 1994; Rothman & Olson, 2001).

Shared Sovereignty Strategies

The first type of integration strategy considered here is one in which an ethnic or racial group is given some degree of self-rule. It accommodates a group's desire to maintain its integrity as an identity group and the primacy of that identity for group members. People must be confident that the integrity, indeed the very continuity, of their primary identity groups will be secure, for these conflicts to be resolvable. Shared sovereignty strategies usually provide for some degree of regional political autonomy, or statewide confederation or federation, that is, some form of shared homeland (Rabie, 1994). Autonomy, confederation, and federation all involve the devolution of power. Which of these arrangements works best depends greatly on the specific characteristics of group interaction and settlement patterns (i.e., whether ethnic and national groups are clearly divided territorially or are dispersed and intermixed). In the cases we reviewed in this chapter, shared sovereignty strategies, incorporating some form of autonomy or self-rule designed to reduce threat perceptions, have been attempted in Nigeria, Bosnia, and Guatemala.

Autonomy may be preferred by an ethnic group that understands that it does not have the capability necessary to achieve independence. In this type of situation, the option of autonomy can set into motion a gradually intensifying identification with the broader national community. Unfortunately, as the Nigerian case shows, these efforts often fail. As Horowitz (1985) notes,

> Most such agreements are concluded against a background of secessionist warfare or terrorist violence. Where central authority is secure . . . the appropriate decisions can be made and implemented by the center. But, where the very question is how far the authority of the center will run, devolution is a matter of bilateral agreement, and an enduring agreement is an elusive thing. (p. 623)

These forms of integration strategy address the important political issues of providing groups increased capability and decision-making power in their region or state and with competitive power in the broader country government.

These institutional arrangements can accommodate identity needs of groups, particularly when a group's identity is threatened. But reducing stereotypes and promoting equality in group comparisons is very difficult to realize. Often, policymakers rely upon the contact hypothesis, wherein, as mentioned, it is assumed that, if people get to know members of groups that they discriminate against, the interaction will disprove those stereotypical ideas, and tolerance and acceptance will result. But, in fact, contact is limited in countries where shared sovereignty strategies are employed, because groups tend to be geographically concentrated. Moreover, failure to identify group variability increases with intense emotions (Mackie et al., 2000; Park & Banaji, 2000; Stroessner & Mackie, 1993), and shared sovereignty integrative strategies often come into play after serious and violent clashes between ethnic or racial groups have occurred. Thus, intense emotion is likely to prevail in these situations, making the breakdown of preexisting stereotyped images extremely difficult.

Integration strategies should explicitly address intergroup perceptions. Some steps can be taken, through policies that prevent systematic discrimination against ethnic or racial groups, even in autonomous regions in which they are minorities, or that ensure that national institutions, such as the military, are not dominated by one particular ethnic or racial group. Such control can easily cause resentment, because it often involves the reduction in power of dominant ethnic or racial groups. However, over time, learning nonstereotyped responses to others is crucial to a change in image. People change perceptions of others by acting differently, not just thinking differently (Pettigrew & Martin, 1989). In other words, people can be trained not to stereotype (Kawakami, Dovidio, Moll, Hermson, & Russin, 2000). In fact, it may be that change in American racial attitudes is a good example of just this. From a policy standpoint, this requires the explicit promotion of tasks that require intergroup cooperation to achieve goals and interdependence at equal status levels. Equal status in group member interaction is important for disconfirming stereotypes (Allport, 1954; Bizman & Amir, 1984; Van Oudenhoven, 1989).

Emotions are involved in changing stereotypes, too. Perceptions that the elite of another group is inferior tend to generate anger among those considered inferior, as well as anger and guilt among those considered superior (Duckitt, 1994; Swim & Miller, 1999). This, as was mentioned, can be counterproductive, because strong emotions tend to inhibit the identification of group variance and, thus, the breaking down of stereotypes. On the other hand, emotions can also be used to reduce stereotyping. **Perspective-taking**, for example, involves empathizing with others, experiencing their perspective and the emotions it generates in them. Galinsky and Moskowitz (2000) argue that perspective-taking "appears to diminish not just the expression of stereotypes but their accessibility. The constructive process of taking and realizing another person's perspective furthers the egalitarian principles themselves" (p. 722). Other studies have found that people do both adopt and change stereotypes, when given information about how other in-group members think about the out-group (Sechrist & Stangor, 2000; Stangor, Sechrist, & Jost, 2001).

Utilitarian Integration Strategies

The institutional options of independence or autonomy are not available when the groups are geographically intermingled across a country or minorities are low in power and capabilities. Social distance factors are very important in these cases, as are the nature of existing stereotypes or images. The contact hypothesis probably will be relied upon by policymakers to naturally reduce group stereotyping images, because contact is more likely to occur in countries where ethnic and racial groups intermingle and can be more easily promoted by government agencies as a solution to group stereotyping. Of the cases reviewed here, this type of strategy would be prominent in conflict resolution in the United States, Brazil, and South Africa.

An essential feature of a utilitarian integration strategy is to satisfy the populations' needs, and this requires removing any obstacles to equality of access to important political positions in the country. This most immediately involves unimpeded access to state educational institutions and the elimination of any state-sponsored social discrimination, but the speed with which integration develops varies with the social distances between groups. The greater the distances, the harder and slower integration will be. Memories of historical relationships, such as slavery, and the depth of institutional discrimination also affect the speed of integration.

One of the greatest difficulties in this type of integration strategy is changing traditional perceptions of groups that have been regarded as inferior. The task is complicated when the self-imagery within the subordinate minority is also negative. This kind of imagery is the imperial–colonial pattern referred to Chapter 3. As mentioned there, conquered people can, through years of repression, come to accept, as just, the conditions and position in which they live. In countries with histories of this kind of repression, in which one or more of the identity communities is perceived as, and perceives itself as, underachieving, there is likely to be a strongly persisting inclination toward the colonial and imperial images. Our earlier discussion of racism in America (in this chapter) illustrated this, as well. Breaking these stereotypes requires making opportunities for those in the minority community and persuading them that they can and should try to take advantage of those opportunities.

A key aspect of the utilitarian strategy, in this case, is attracting qualified individuals in the minority community or communities into positions that exceed their expectations, and the majority's. Affirmative action programs are designed to do this. This should help break stereotypes of inferiority, eventually, as people from minority groups come to be increasingly associated with high achievement. A study by Sinclair and Kunda (1999), for example, shows that American subjects high in prejudice did not activate their racial prejudice, when motivated to have high regard for a Black person. In their experiments, when subjects were induced to have high regard for a Black doctor, they invoked the doctor stereotype, not the racist anti-Black stereotype.

The American affirmative action program illustrates both the promise and problems associated with this component of the strategy. Inevitably, those perceiving the minority groups through the contemptuous colonial image will make the case that the program is ideologically driven and that the individuals who benefit from affirmative action lack the requisite qualifications. The program, they argue, is damaging both in the placement of inherently unqualified individuals into positions in which they will not perform adequately and in causing serious hardship among those who are qualified in achieving communities. Plus, Brown, Charnasangavej, Keough, Newman, and Rentfrow (2000) offer experimental evidence that affirmative action programs may be self-defeating, if they become "reminders of peoples' stigmatized status," which can "have dramatic, detrimental effects on their performance. A phenomenon referred to as 'stereotype threat'" (p. 737). Thus, the stereotype of inferiority can become a self-fulfilling prophesy: People who are considered inferior are given fewer opportunities and are inferior in education, income, social standing, and so on, and they know they are. Meanwhile, the highly achieving group minority will see integration as an unattractive prospect.

Clearly, dominant groups that are numerical minorities can be pushed from power, but not all dominant groups are numerical minorities, as in the case of White Americans, and it would be hoped that violence can be avoided. What is also clear is that, for utilitarian strategies to occur and for violence to be avoided, dominant groups, whether numerical majorities or minorities, must choose to accept equality with subordinate groups. As both the United States and South African cases show, perceptual change must accompany internal and external pressures for structural change. Stereotypes are shaken when expectations are consistently disconfirmed. The utilitarian strategy applied to subordinate groups should, if successful, do this. As subordinate groups achieve more, the dominant group's expectations, rooted in the colonial image, would not be realized, and the image would be challenged. The impact should be a decline in opposition to further expanding access to opportunities and, gradually, a diminution of the colonial image of the disadvantaged groups. Image disconfirmation in this direction also can occur through the direct efforts of the subject of the colonial image to alter it by disconfirming it. This occurs through group mobilization and organization, demonstrating power and control unexpected of those perceived through the colonial image.

Let us conclude this chapter on a practical note, with a look at one component of conflict resolution in divided societies that illustrates the importance of using political institutions to tackle the underlying political psychology of ethnic or racial conflict. It has recently become more and more apparent that one of the central elements in conflict resolution and reconciliation, in divided societies that have experienced intense violence, is the training of a new, impartial, and professional police force. Political science is only now learning this lesson, but, from a political psychology standpoint, it is not surprising. One of the most important elements in the governance process in a country is the criminal justice system, particularly the police. They can ameliorate competition and perceptions of inequality, or they can exacerbate those perceptions. They are the representatives of government with whom people interact on a daily basis, and, as such, they are the central source of perceptions of justice, or lack thereof, in the political system. They have to be seen as impartial and unbiased in the treatment of citizens, regardless of ethnicity. They are crucial in conflict resolution, because, although military peacekeepers may disarm combatants, police provide the order necessary for people to feel secure. Without this, political reconstruction cannot occur.

In multiethnic countries, too often the police force itself becomes a tool of one ethnic group. Often, the police in a deeply divided multiethnic country are characterized by bias in law enforcement, they are politicized and identified with a repressive regime, the dominant ethnic group monopolizes top positions, they are not held accountable by authorities for abuses of power, and they have extraordinary power to control the subordinate population (Call & Barnett, 2000; Mani, 2000). When this pattern occurs, it erodes state legitimacy, increases resentment against the state by unrepresented ethnic groups, and increases the possibility of ethnic conflict and the need of the state to employ coercion to quell that conflict.

The importance of impartial policing in conflict resolution has been recognized in the cases of ethnic conflict discussed earlier. Let us return to the Guatemalan case for illustration. Guatemala's Mayan population suffered violence on the scale of mass killing, if not genocide, although cultural genocide was certainly intended. There were death squads operative and a campaign of state terror. Mass murder took place indiscriminantly in Mayan villages, committed by the military and its police. Nevertheless, despite many difficulties, Guatemala is today undergoing political reforms that are attempting to dismantle the counterinsurgency state.

During the war, the military and police committed numerous and appalling human rights violations. One of the most important aspects of reform is the separation of the police and military institutions. Before the peace accords, the police in Guatemala were part of the military. This is the case in most Latin American countries. Now the police are a separate institution and have authority in internal security matters. The military's domain is left to external security. The enabling legislation and the regulations for the new National Civilian Police were designed primarily by the Spanish police, who also took the lead in training and advising the new Guatemalan police force. The reform of the police was actually part of the peace accords themselves, and the government—particularly then President Alvaro Arzu—was committed. The accord provided the broad outlines for the police, including the provisions that it would be under the authority of the ministry of the interior, rather than under the military; that there would be established a separate academy for police training; and that the police force would take into account the multiethnic nature of the society and would form specialized agencies in that regard. This was to be done in the context of a reformed and impartial justice system.

Progress has been slow. On the negative side, the policing portion of the peace accords was very general and lacked important details. There were no provisions made regarding the inclusion of police officers from the old order; no provisions for vetting officers, to eliminate those involved in human rights abuses during the dirty war years (imagine having your local police officer be the same person who tortured you during the civil war); and no details about the content of training, organization, or disciplinary measures, including no education level requirements, which is an issue in countries with high levels of illiteracy.

The law that went into effect, implementing the government's agreement with the rebels, had no requirement that the new police include members of the different Mayan groups in Guatemala. Only about one fifth of the new recruits are indigenous. And former military personnel, who are prohibited from joining the police, have managed to get in. Guatemala has had a tremendous increase in crime, and the government has permitted joint military–police patrol to combat it, which is a dangerous practice. Finally

> the Constitutional reforms that would have consolidated the separation of police and military functions . . . was defeated in May 1999 in a nation-wide referendum . . . [so] the . . . military continues to have the Constitutional authority to be involved in internal security, and the future division of roles remains unclear. (Byrne, Stanley, and Garst, 2000, p. 5)

On the positive side, the government is clearly committed to this reform. By October 1999, the new police were 17,339 strong, and 36.5% were new recruits. The force is more service-oriented and has been positively received by the public. Complaints about human rights violations and corruption have diminished. Those are signs of a healing society and reasons for optimism that Guatemala may recover from its violent past.

CONCLUSION

In this chapter, a number of theories are used to look at different aspects of race and ethnic conflicts. Although race in the United States has received the lion's share of study in political psychology, we did look at some crossnational examples in Brazil and South Africa. The theories used to examine different takes on race relations included realistic conflict theory, social identity theory, social learning theory, and social dominance theory. In our discussion of race, we entertained difficult arguments found in the literature about how much racism remains in the United States. One camp argues that attitudes toward politics have changed, in that race-related issues are not judged by many Whites in terms of racial attitudes, but in terms of other attitudes. Hence, for example, White Americans who favor racial integration may oppose school busing, not because they are closet racists, but because they do not want their children going to schools miles away from home. On the other side of the debate is the symbolic racism school, which maintains that racism is alive and well in America, but that people know it is considered inappropriate to be openly racist, so they hide their racist views behind traditional values such as the Protestant ethic and individualism. They say they disapprove of policies designed to help Black Americans, not because the beneficiaries are Black, but because no one, White or Black, should get a government handout. Although not explicitly argued, there is a strong relationship between symbolic racism arguments and the arguments made in social learning theory, that people learn racial attitudes from their families and societies and are rewarded for them.

Realistic conflict theory and social identity theory are also useful in understanding conflict, as are some of the patterns discussed in chapter 4, on groups. Ethnic conflicts are often bubbling under the surface of multiethnic societies. We examined cases that have involved considerable amounts of mass violence and killing. Governments of many multiethnic states, particularly those that are poor and where resources are the object of tough competition, are constantly forced to fight against upsurges of ethnic conflict. At the end of the chapter, we considered some strategies to promote integration and reduce the chances of violence.

Topics, Theories/Explanations, and Cases Covered in Chapter 7

Topics	Theories	Cases
Race	Realistic conflict theory	United States
	Social learning theory	Brazil
	Social identity theory	South Africa
	Social dominance theory	
	Politics-is-complicated model	
	Symbolic racism model	
Ethnic conflict	Realistic conflict theory	Nigeria
	Social identity theory	Bosnia
	Group conflict (chapter 4)	Guatemala
Conflict resolution	Integration strategies	Policing in Guatemala
	Shared sovereignty	
	Utilitarian	

KEY TERMS

Contact hypothesis

Ethnocentrism

Minimal group paradigm

Perspective-taking

Phenomenal absolutism
error

Politics-is-complicated
model

Prejudice

Projection

Realistic conflict theory

Scapegoat

Shared sovereignty
strategies

Social dominance
theory

Social learning
theory

Symbolic racism

Ultimate attribution
error

Utilitarian integration
strategy

SUGGESTIONS FOR FURTHER READING

Duckitt, J. (1994). *The social psychology of prejudice.* New York: Praeger.

Fiske, S. (1998). Stereotyping, prejudice, and discrimination. In D. T. Gilbert, S. T. Fiske, and G. Lindzey (Eds.), *The handbook of social psychology,* Vol. 2 (4th ed. pp. 357–411). New York: McGraw-Hill.

Horowitz, D. (1985). *Ethnic groups in conflict.* Berkeley: University of California Press.

Ihonvbere, J. O. (1994). *Nigeria: The politics of adjustment and democracy.* New Brunswick NJ: Transaction Books.

Kinder, D., & Sanders, L. (1996). *Divided by color: Racial politics and democratic ideals.* Chicago: University of Chicago Press.

Loyd, A. (1999). *My war gone by, I miss it so.* New York: Penguin.

Marx, A. (1998). *Making race and nation: A comparison of the United States, South Africa, and Brazil.* Cambridge, UK: Cambridge University Press.

McGarry, J., & O'Leary, B. (Eds.) (1993). *The politics of ethnic conflict.* New York: Routledge.

Sears, D., Sidanius, J., & Bobo, L (Eds.) (2000). *Racialized politics: The debate about racism in America.* Chicago: University of Chicago Press.

Shipler, D. (1997). *A country of strangers: Blacks and Whites in America.* New York: Knopf.

Sniderman, P., & Carmines, E. (1997). *Reaching beyond race.* Cambridge, MA: Harvard University Press.

ENDNOTES

1.   Social identity theory is simplified in this critique, in that it maintains that comparisons that result in out-group derogation are only made with relevant groups, not all groups. A university student, for example, would simply not compare his group's socioeconomic status with that of his professors' group, because that is not a relevant comparison group. On the other hand, if a student found students in a neighboring university to be generally more wealthy than his own group of students, that would be a relevant comparison group, and it may be stereotyped as "a bunch of lazy rich kids who go to school to please their wealthy parents and who don't study." Moreover, social identity theory does maintain that people do not select social competition, that is behaviors that seek to alter the social status relationship of their group with those who have greater advantages, unless they identify a clear alternative future.

2.   There are many important methodological issues associated with getting and measuring an accurate picture of racial attitudes. Question wording, the nature of survey research

from which most of the data is drawn, race of the interviewer, and the use of telephone or person-to-person interviews, are all important in affecting the data. See Schuman et al., 1997, chapter 3, for a review of those issues in layman's terms.

3.   When a multiethnic state has one or more ethnic communities desirous of independence, and which have the capability to achieve independence, conflict can best be avoided when those communities are territorially homogeneous, by granting them the right of national self-determination. As long as such communities perceive a real option for independence, they are unlikely to respond to efforts to attract a primary attachment to the territorial community.

4.   We explore only integration strategies that are relatively noncoercive here. There are many examples of forced integration, wherein a regime simply crushes and eliminates the cultural uniqueness of an identity group. This happened throughout the Western Hemisphere with colonial power destruction of indigenous communities, for example. For a discussion of other cases and patterns, see Byman (2000).

CHAPTER 8

The Political Psychology of Nationalism

For the past 200 years or so, nationalism has been an important driving force in political behavior. Nationalism is not universal, not everyone is a nationalist, and it is not always present, but it lies dormant until a threat or opportunity to the nation is perceived by the populace. Nationalism emerged first in Europe with the development of the modern state, following the French Revolution. Nationalism has been considered one of the most dangerous sources of political behavior in the twentieth century. German nationalism is blamed for World War II, and it certainly played a major role in causing that conflict. The nationalisms of various communities in Yugoslavia tore that country apart in the 1990s. Conflict between the United States and its Latin American neighbors often rests upon nationalistic indignation by one at the behavior of the other. The causes of nationalism and the impact of nationalism on political behavior are the topics of this chapter. They are illustrated with many examples from different regions of the world. Various conflict resolution strategies, which can be used to ameliorate these conflicts, are then addressed.

We begin with a general discussion of nationalism, its definition, the patterns of nationalistic behavior, the psychological roots of nationalism, and a description of different kinds of states with varying arrays of nationalists and nationalism. This is followed by a discussion of the political psychological causes of nationalist passions and behavior. From there, we present case illustrations of patterns of behavior. We begin with a look at nationalists' responses to perceived threats to national values and the case of Western European responses to immigrants. Next, we look at nationalism and the strong desire nationalists have for unity and independence for their people. This is illustrated in the cases of Northern Ireland, Yugoslavia's breakup, the Albanian revolt in Kosovo, the conflict in Cyprus, German unification, the revolt in Chechnya, and the Kurds' drive for independence from Turkey. Then we turn to the impact of nationalism on foreign policy behavior, and we look at World War II, the war on drugs in U.S.–Mexico relations, and Russian and Chinese nationalism in post–Cold War foreign policy. We conclude with a look at some conflict resolution techniques in nationalistic conflicts.

AN OVERVIEW OF NATIONALISM

Definition and Patterns of Behavior

Before beginning any discussion of nationalistic behavior, a definition of the concept is necessary. In this chapter, Emerson's (1960) definition of **nationalism** is used:

> The nation is a community of people who feel they belong together in the double sense that they share deeply significant elements of a common heritage and that they have a

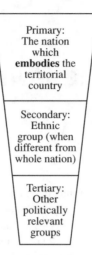

FIG. 8.1.   Political identities and loyalty in nation-states.

common destiny for the future. . . . The nation is today the largest community which, when the chips are down, effectively commands . . . loyalty, overriding the claims both of the lesser communities within it and those which cut across it or potentially enfold it within a still greater society. . . . In this sense the nation can be called a terminal community with the implication that it is for present purposes the effective end of the road for man as a social animal. (pp. 95–96)

As Emerson explains, nationalists give their primary loyalty to their perceived nation, which can be considered a political identity in-group—a concept introduced in chapter 3 (see Figure 8.1). For example, people can call themselves Irish and see themselves as part of that nation of people. A **nation-state** exists when the average citizen of a country is a nationalist. Those who see themselves as part of the Mexican nation would consider the territorial boundaries of Mexico the nation-state. Alternatively, those in Ireland who see themselves as part of the Irish nation would consider the territorial state of Ireland the nation-state. Countries in which people are generally not nationalistic are countries in which primary political loyalty is directed elsewhere, such as to an ethnic group, as we saw in chapter 7, rather than to the community living within the territorial boundaries of the state.

Being strongly attached to their nation, nationalists are committed to the unity, independence, dignity, and well-being of the national community and the nation-state. Even when they dislike their government, they love the nation itself. The concept of nationalism is similar to that of social identity, which is discussed in detail in chapter 3. Recall that *social identity* refers to the positive sense of self-esteem that people derive from their memberships in social groups and categories (Tajfel & Turner, 1986). People are motivated to feel good about their groups. Nationalists are group members who are motivated to have a strong, positive attachment to their nation.

Several patterns of behavior occur in nation-states, and by nationalists, which are not so evident in states where people are not nationalistic, that is, nonnation-states. First, nationalists tend to be more sensitive than nonnationalists to threats to the nation-state, and the image through which they view the threatener is extreme. Research (see Dietz-Uhler, 1999) suggests that people who identify strongly with a group react strongly when their sense of positive social identity is threatened. Similarly, nationalists, particularly nationalistic leaders, are very sensitive to opportunities to advance their country's influence and are more likely than nonnationalists to seriously consider the option to expand state influence at the expense of others.

Third, there will be a greater tendency among the public of nation-states to be deeply concerned with the objective of gathering together communities existing outside the borders of the state, whom they regard as a part of their national community. Generally, nationalists desire a territorial state for their people, and they want all of the community to live in that state. This is referred to as **irridentism**—the desire to join together all parts of a national community within a single territorial state. Those members of the nation who live outside the territory of the country are called a **diaspora**. Irridentism was an important factor in Bismarck's wars for German national unification in the late nineteenth century and, at the beginning of World War II, in the German conquest of Poland and Czechoslovakia where millions of ethnic Germans lived.

Fourth, nationalists are more concerned with their country's prestige and dignity than are nonnationalists, and nationalists are more willing to take action to rectify perceived affronts. Fifth, there is more likelihood that the public of a nation-state will be susceptible to grandeur interests and will therefore want to see national prestige and status enhanced and recognized globally. Sixth, leaders of nation-states, compared to nonnation-states, are better able to make effective appeals to the citizens to make great sacrifices to enhance the power of the state. Seventh, the public is more willing to serve in the military and to have a more intense commitment to the defense of that state. Finally, the citizens of a nation-state are more likely to grant leaders considerable freedom to take risks in defending the country's interests. However, leaders who fail will be punished by nationalistic people. They will not grant those leaders the freedom to accept defeats or the loss of face.

Given these patterns of behavior, we can begin to generalize about governance in nation-states. All governments have certain tools available to them to keep their populations stable and supportive. They can and must satisfy the utilitarian needs of the population through a functioning economy and political system. They also have at their disposal coercive instruments such as the police and the military, which can be used to keep order, prevent instability, and, if necessary, force the society to comply with the government's decisions. Many governments combine these tools and have a public accustomed to compliance and political stability. The habit of the public is to obey the laws of the government and accept governmental authority.

However, the governments and leaders of nation-states have an added instrument that helps them govern and, when necessary, mobilize the population to make great sacrifices for the country: They can use nationalistic symbols to arouse passionate feelings of devotion to the nation—symbols such as the flag; historic events, such as success in a great battle; or the idea of the motherland or fatherland. Because nationalists deeply value the independence, unity, dignity, and well-being of their national community, they respond readily to the use of symbols to mobilize them to achieve national goals. Experimental research in social psychology has examined the effectiveness of group symbols in arousing and making salient one's group (or national) identity. For example, Wilder and Shapiro (1984) found that the mere presence of an out-group symbol was sufficient to make salient one's in-group identity. Specifically, participants were exposed to a pennant of either their own university (in-group condition) or a rival university (out-group condition). Participants were asked to review a list of words, then were later given a word recognition test. The words in the recognition test included words related to either the in-group or the out-group. The results showed that participants were more likely to falsely recognize in-group-related words when an out-group symbol was present. More important, the presence of an out-group was sufficient to increase group members' adherence to their own group's norms. Thus, nationalistic symbols can be powerful motivators of pro-nation behavior.

Nationalism in Nonnation States

On the other hand, there are some countries that are **multinational states**, in which several groups of people, who think of themselves as separate nations and who actually have the capacity to establish viable independent states, live together in a single country. They do not see the populations of the country as their primary identity group. Instead, their primary identity group is the nationality they belong to (see Figure 8.2). Examples include the Russians and Ukrainians who lived in the Soviet Union. Their primary identity was with the Russian or Ukrainian national community, not the Soviet Union. In these cases, no nation completely controls its own destiny, and no nation has its own independent state. The dynamics of nationalism are likely to be directed toward striving for independence. Thus, multinational states have chronic disintegrative forces that they must try to prevent from exploding. Northern Ireland is a case in point, as we see later. Finally, a third type of state—which is not a nation-state, strictly speaking, but whose leaders often behave like nationalists—is called a **core community nonnation-state**. These are countries with a dominant ethnic or sectarian community who believe that they are the primary nation embodied in the country and who identify with that nation in the strongest terms. In addition, that community tends to be politically dominant and controls the political system. However, also present within the territorial state are other communities, which give primary loyalty to their ethnic groups. These secondary groups desire autonomy or independent statehood, but they do not have sufficient resources to sustain it. A good example of a core community nonnation-state is Russia. Russians are clearly the dominant group, and Russians tend to be quite nationalistic. Yet, there are many other ethnic groups living in Russia, who speak Russian and are part of the country's political system, but who have a different ethnic identity.

In many of these cases, the core community advocates the integration and assimilation of the other groups, encouraging the minorities to speak the dominant group's language, abandon their customs, identify with the country as a whole, and perhaps intermarry (indeed, this is discussed as a pattern of conflict prevention and resolution in chapter 7). Under these circumstances, minority groups can use social mobility as an option and assimilate into the

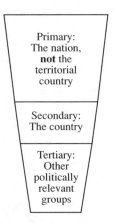

FIG. 8.2.   Political identities and loyalty in multinational states.

core community. Social mobility is one of the strategies suggested by Tajfel and Turner (1979) to cope with a threatened or negative social identity. When a group member's (especially a low-status group member) social identity is at risk, one option is to leave the group and join a group that is positively valued. Of course, this option is only available when group membership is achieved, rather than ascribed. However, the option of assimilation or social mobility is not always welcome, if assimilation requires the complete abandonment of group identity, and, if the existence of the group is threatened, political conflict may occur. Resistance to assimilation may also come from members of the core community who view these other groups as undesirable. Under some circumstances, such as the events leading up to the Albanian revolt in Kosovo and the Chechnyan revolt in Russia, those small communities may identify a chance to break free and go for independence, despite the prospect of tremendous loss of life.

CAUSES OF NATIONALISTIC BEHAVIOR

We have already mentioned the importance of social identity theory as an explanation for the power of nationalism. To review, social identity theory notes that people need to belong to groups, and they see their groups (in-groups) as better than other groups (out-groups). Nations are groups and, for nationalists, are a deeply important in-group. Central to in-group–out-group relations is the concept of social categorization. Members of a group see themselves as similar, sharing common attributes, and this group identification inspires group behavior. Members of a group also tend to accentuate their positive attributes when they compare their in-groups to relevant out-groups, which they do regularly. When engaging in social comparison, the self-esteem of group members is enhanced when that comparison is positive for the in-group. Sometimes, conflict is a result of engaging in social comparison.

As noted in chapter 3, the social comparison process is a complicated one. When the comparison is unsatisfactory, people can switch to a new group; they can engage in social creativity strategies, which change the comparison process itself, so that people can find a positive basis for comparison to replace a negative one; or they can engage in competition. The important thing to remember about nationalists is that the first option is out: They are committed to their nation as a group. The second and third options are acceptable, but the potential to engage in the third option (competition with other countries or nationalities within a single country) is high, when they perceive a threat to the nation or an opportunity to achieve some important goal. Nationalists reach this point quicker and with greater intensity than nonnationalists. Members of a nation or nation-state—an in-group—will perceive themselves as better than their social comparison groups. They are highly cohesive and very willing to sacrifice for the nation. They are also more likely to be sensitive to things such as insults, frustrations, and aggressive behavior by out-groups (Cottam & Cottam, 2001; Searle-White, 2001). As Cottam and Cottam (2001) further explain, "The nation as an identity group is highly salient for nationalist citizens, indicating that the intensity of emotional responses to threats or opportunities for the national will be strong and volatile" (p. 95).

Nationalism involves very strong positive emotions associated with the nation and also a propensity for heightened negative emotions associated with the out-group. If the nation is considered an in-group, which it is for nationalists, we can expect a range of positive emotions to be associated with the nation, such as pride in the achievements of one's group or country or happiness when an opportunity to achieve an important goal occurs. As mentioned in chapter 3, positive emotions tend to make people more flexible and more creative in problem solving. They are able to see more nuances and have more complex evaluations of other people when feeling positive emotions. Clearly, these emotions, such as pride in your country and joy and happiness when the country does well in things like economic development and growth or in international athletic competitions, are associated with politics. There is a potential downside to this, however—and this is commonly observed in the behavior of nationalists: an inability to look critically at one's own country's behavior. If pride is strong, then recognition of one's own inadequacies is less likely than is the assumption that, when things go wrong, someone else is responsible. Our policies cannot be to blame. This refusal to look at the country's own role in national difficulties also encourages a search for **scapegoats** upon whom to blame the poor circumstances. This, in turn, can produce behaviors ranging from violation of civil and human rights to genocide. More generally, Kecmanovic (1996) and Searle-White (2001) argue that, in terms of affective properties, nationalistic behavior resembles crowd behavior, in that there is low tolerance for differing views; oversimplification; diminished personal responsibility; a reluctance to consider alternate views; a readiness to act out; a sense of being endowed with unrivaled power, which makes people less critically minded; intensified emotional reactions; and feelings of persecution.

In addition, group factors, such as group loyalty and obedience (discussed in chapter 4 and, in the context of political extremists, in chapter 9), come into play, in terms of conformity to the in-group's position toward the out-group. There are tremendous internal and social pressures on people to conform, when nationalism is aroused. One either faces ostracism and condemnation by friends, neighbors, the community, and even family, or one participates in the flag waving or becomes a passive bystander. This was, and is, certainly evident in the United States after 9/11.

Exactly how nationalists will respond to other countries depends upon the *image* (see chapter 3) of other countries or nationalities within a single multinational country. They will confront an enemy with different tactics than a barbarian or an imperialist, for example. The emotions attached to the image will be supercharged among nationalists, because they are so intensely attached to the nation. To refresh the reader's memory, Table 8.1 outlines the images and their attributes.

Let us turn to some case studies. Given the previous description of patterns of nationalistic behavior and the use of social identity theory to explain the underlying psychological causes of nationalism, we use *nationalism* as the political psychological concept in explaining the cases, rather than repeat the elements of social identity theory over and over

TABLE 8.1
Images

Image	Capability	Culture	Intentions	Decision Makers	Threat or Opportunity
Enemy	Equal	Equal	Harmful	Small elite	Threat
Barbarian	Superior	Inferior	Harmful	Small elite	Threat
Imperialist	Superior	Superior	Harmful	A few groups	Threat
Colonial	Inferior	Inferior	Benign	Small elite	Opportunity
Degenerate	Superior or equal	Weak-willed	Harmful	Confused differentiated	Opportunity
Rogue	Inferior	Inferior	Harmful	Small elite	Threat
Ally	Equal	Equal	Good	Many groups	Threat

again. We also point out the operative images that accompany nationalism and that affect the exact nature of behaviors in the cases that follow.

CASE ILLUSTRATIONS OF NATIONALISM

Nationalism and Perceived Threats to National Values: Western Europe and Immigrants

We mentioned above that, as a group, nationalists see themselves as distinct and better than others. They are strongly devoted to the identity of the group as it stands, and view any perceived contamination of the group, through the imposition of alien values, as extremely threatening. During the 1990s and into the new century, much attention has been devoted to the growth in hostility toward non-European immigrants in Western European countries. This is an illustration of what happens when nationalists perceive a threat to their group identity. The hostility has been particularly intense toward immigrants from third world countries whose cultures (as well as racial makeup) are distinctly different from European cultures.

This pattern is manifested in the acceptance of falsehood about the impact of immigrants on European societies and in fear of cultural contamination and change. Many Europeans, for example, believe incorrect myths, such as the idea that immigrants take jobs from citizens. In fact, countries such as Germany, Italy, and Denmark need immigrant laborers, because their own birthrates are falling (Fijalkowski, 1996). Immigrants are also believed to be responsible for increased levels of crime, and surveys show that Europeans fear that immigrants will change their European culture. Many Europeans explicitly reject multicultural practices that allow immigrants to keep aspects of their culture. Hence, they do not believe that immigrants can enrich the culture of their nation, and they reject instruction of immigrants in native languages. Surveys demonstrate this pattern. For example, in 1992, two thirds of Italians surveyed explicitly rejected the possibility that their culture could benefit from the influence of immigrants, and two thirds of Danes objected to educating immigrants in their native languages. In 1990, 45% of Austrians agreed that foreigners were a threat to Austrian identity and way of life (Fijalkowski, 1996).

Indeed, by 1999, hostility toward immigrants was so strong in Austria that the anti-immigrant Freedom Party, led by Joerg Haider, had enough political power to be part of the governing coalition in Austria. Although the controversial Haider stepped down as party leader, the party held the vice chancellor's office and the ministries of justice and defense. Moreover, in coalition with the right-wing People's party, the governing coalition held 104 of the 183 seats in Parliament. Other European countries, as well as the United States, reacted strongly and negatively to these events. Although most Europeans condemn violence committed against foreigners, this is an example of the rise of antiforeigner nationalism in Europe, resulting from perceived threats to the nation as a group and the values associated with that group.

Nationalism and the Desire for Unity and Independence

Following are a number of case studies illustrating the importance that nationalists attach to independence and unity. Given a perceived opportunity, a perceived realistic chance of achieving independence and unity, or a sense that the deprivation of independence and unity is unacceptably unjust, nationalists will make great sacrifices to achieve those goals. The cases covered are Northern Ireland, the breakup of Yugoslavia, the Albanian revolt in Kosovo, the conflict in Cyprus, the revolt in Chechnya, the Kurds' drive for independence from Turkey, and German unification.

Northern Ireland

Historical background.   Northern Ireland is a region within the United Kingdom, which, since its creation in 1920, has been immersed in nationalism and national identity-based conflict. The Northern Ireland conflict is over national identity, involving several groups, notably British Protestant Unionists and British Protestant Loyalists (the majority) and Irish Catholic Nationalists and Irish Catholic Republicans (the minority).

Until 1972, Northern Ireland enjoyed devolved status, meaning that the regional parliament enjoyed a great deal of autonomy, except in fiscal and foreign affairs. The regional Parliament was dominated by the Unionist majority, and allegations soon surfaced of discrimination in areas such as elections, housing, and employment. As a result of the perceived discrimination against Irish Catholic Nationalist, the Northern Ireland Civil Rights Association (NICRA) formed in 1967. The association intended to protest discrimination using nonviolent means such as marches, meetings and sit-ins. NICRA held its first march on August 24, 1968, but the Orange Order, a Protestant organization formed during the late 1700s, had also planned a march for the same day. To avoid clashes, the Royal Ulster Constabulary (RUC) police force attempted to reroute the Catholic marchers. When some Catholics resisted, the march was broken up by the police and the B Specials—a unit established in 1920 to augment the Ulster police (disbanded in 1969)—resulting in rioting by Catholic Nationalists. The treatment of the marchers by the police sparked allegations of brutality. By 1969, the violence between Protestant Unionists and Catholic Nationalists escalated, which prompted the British government to send 6,000 troops to quell the disturbances. The British Army assumed responsibility for restoring public order and directing internal security, and the RUC was reserved the authority to investigate criminal activity.

At first, the Nationalist population welcomed the troops, but soon resented their presence, because the army was viewed as biased in favor of the Protestants. On July 3, 1970, the army raided a Catholic area of Belfast in search of illegal arms. When the army encountered resistance from the Republican paramilitary group known as the Irish Republican Army (IRA), they imposed a curfew. After subsequent clashes between members of the IRA, other Nationalist Catholic civilians, and the army, internment was introduced on August 9, 1971. Internment is a practice of detaining people without formal arrest and is often associated with brutal treatment or torture, including forcing people to stand for long hours with their hands against a wall, putting a hood over their heads for sensory deprivation, continuous noise, deprivation of food and sleep, beatings, and terror, produced by making prisoners believe they will be tossed out of helicopters alive (Conroy, 2000). Of the 342 men interned that same day, only two were Protestants.

Perhaps the most significant incident that enraged the Nationalist community occurred in Derry in January 1972. The army had decided to block the exit from the Catholic area, to contain the marchers, some of whom rioted in response. The army then fired upon the marchers, killing 13 people. That day became known as Bloody Sunday. The army claimed that they were provoked, although the allegation was never substantiated.

After the Bloody Sunday incident, the British government proposed assuming total responsibility for the maintenance of order in the North. The RUC was then permanently reserved the authority to investigate criminal activity. When the Unionist government rejected the proposal, the British government dissolved the Northern Irish parliament and imposed direct rule on the region. The 6 counties were then represented in the British Parliament at Westminster by 12 members elected within the North. Thus, legislation involving Northern Ireland was to be debated in London. However, there were fundamental disagreements over the British solution.

The political psychology of the conflict.

There are many ways to characterize the Northern Ireland conflict, but social identity factors, and images held of one another, are crucial. In terms of social identity, one way is to delineate and define the groups in the conflict by religion, notably as Catholics and Protestants. However, this characterization simplifies the conflict as one over religious preference. In doing so, it does not indicate that Catholics and Protestants are part of two distinct national groups—British and Irish—with differing **national identities** and aspirations. Distinct groups within these national groups have their own political parties and paramilitary groups. The Protestant factions identify with Great Britain and consider themselves to be British. The Catholic factions identify with Ireland and consider themselves to be Irish. The terms *Unionist* and *Loyalist* are used to describe British national groups who are pitted against their Irish counterparts, known as Nationalists and Republicans. Unionists and Loyalists also have differing perceptions of the appropriate tactics to use in the conflict (specifically, differences about the utility of force and paramilitaries vs. working in the political system), but they are both British in national identity. Nationalists and Republicans also have different tactical preferences regarding how the conflict is to be fought and won, but they are both Irish in national identity. Yet, the underlying conflict over national identity has not changed since the inception of the state, even though, over the years, political parties and paramilitary groups under Unionist/Loyalist and Nationalist/Republican auspices have emerged, renamed or reconstituted.

Unionists and Loyalists believe that they are British and that Northern Ireland is rightfully part of the United Kingdom and should remain that way. They perceive their Nationalist and Republican counterparts as threatening. Any discussion of the **images** that they hold of Nationalists and Republicans must also include their perceptions of the Irish government, because the Republic is perceived as a looming **enemy** with threatening intentions. This enemy has designs on Northern Ireland, and Nationalists and Republicans are merely the dependent arms (**colonial image**) of the enemy. Together, they make up a pannationalist front, whose intent is to break apart the United Kingdom.

Unionists and Loyalists both proclaim their "Britishness," but they are not a united front, because they are divided over the acceptable use of tactics to ensure their union with Britain. Unionists work through the political process; Loyalists, although represented by political parties, also have corresponding paramilitary groups, such as the Ulster Volunteer Force, who believe in the use of force to achieve their goal. Thus, their **images of each other** further complicate the group relationships in Northern Ireland. Loyalists, for example, are seen by Unionists as their dependent children (**colonial**

The Right to March: Demonstrations of Nationalism

Marching season in Northern Ireland begins in the early summer. Marching parades are a way for both British Protestant Unionists, who see themselves as British subjects, and Irish Catholic Nationalists, who see themselves as Irish subjects, to commemorate their heritage. Thousands of marches take place throughout the summer (the majority of which are Unionist), but at times the marches result in violent clashes between the police and the marchers, as well as between the two communities. In July 2000, several areas of the region were again paralyzed by 10 days of rioting, the catalyst of which was the decision by the police, fearing a confrontation between the two communities, to refuse to allow the Unionists to march through a Nationalist section of Portadown, located outside of Belfast.

image), who need guidance from the Unionists. Loyalists, however, see the Unionists as weak **allies**, because, in their view, Loyalists parties and paramilitary groups had to form to represent the working-class Protestants, a group of Unionists overlooked and never represented.

Nationalists and Republicans believe they are Irish and that Great Britain should relinquish its illegal rule over the region. Their goal is to see both parts of Ireland reunited. Nationalists and Republicans see the British government as an **imperialist** power that is holding the North hostage. The British were responsible for partitioning Ireland and creating an artificial majority of Unionists and Loyalists, who are essentially the colonial elite. Like their British counterparts, Nationalists are divided over the acceptable use of tactics. Nationalists, like the Unionists, work through the political process; Republicans, like the Loyalists, have both political parties and corresponding paramilitary groups, most notably, on the Republican side, the Provisional Irish Republican Army. However, Nationalists and Republicans essentially see each other as **allies** who represent the same communities, are the same people culturally, and share the same problems of discrimination.

Direct rule was viewed as a temporary solution to the problems of this nationalist conflict. But, despite many efforts by the Irish and British governments, including the most recent creation of a devolved powersharing assembly, and despite the fact that paramilitary groups on both sides are holding cease-fires, the groups have not found a long-term solution. The fundamental problem still remains: National groups with differing identities want to be part of two different countries, and each holds threatening images of the other. The groups are unable to put aside their long-held and deep-rooted hatred and threatening images of each other and to join forces for the greater good of governing the region.

Yugoslavia

Historical background. One of the most often mentioned cases, in which nationalists of different nationalities took great risks and committed great acts of violence in pursuit of national independence, is found in what used to be Yugoslavia. There were six nationalities in Yugoslavia before it fell apart: Serbians, Croatians, Macedonians, Slovenians, Montenegrans, and Bosnian Muslims, who were recognized as a national identity group in the 1970s. Except for Slovenians and Bosnian Muslims, each of these peoples had once existed as a medieval state. Some of the nationalities had also been conquered by, and incorporated into, great empires: first the Ottoman Empire, and then the Austro-Hungarian Empire. The people of each nation identified with a defined territory, and they differed in language, alphabet, culture, and, most important, religion. Yet the majority were ethnically South Slav.

After centuries of conquest by different empires, Yugoslavia was formed as a single South Slav state in 1918. The government was a compromise among the strongest nations, particularly Serbia and Croatia, and reflected their national symbols, religions, and the Cyrillic and Latin alphabets used in Serbia and Croatia, respectively. Their union was motivated primarily by political and security concerns (Crnobrnja, 1994).

Yugoslavia was decimated during the Second World War, and horrible atrocities were committed during that time by the nationalities against one another. Germany invaded Yugoslavia and found allies in the Croatian fascists, whose military forces, the Ustashe, slaughtered Serbs by the thousands. Serbian royalists formed a military force, the Chetniks, who fought against the German Nazi forces, as well as against the Ustashe and the partisans. The partisan forces, led by Josip Broz Tito, were the only military force whose members considered themselves Yugoslavs and who fought for the federation (Crnobrnja, 1994). Tito was also the head of the Yugoslavian Communist Party. The war cost an estimated 1 million lives in Yugoslavia, half of them Serbs.

After the war, Tito's partisan forces quickly took control of the country, and Tito became the head of state. He developed a program for governing Yugoslavia that directly addressed the nationalities problem. His strategy included a brotherhood and unity campaign that promoted a common Yugoslav identity among all nationalities in the country, but not at the complete expense of the national identities. The brotherhood and unity campaign attempted to transform national identities, such as Serbian or Croatian, into ethnic identities, leaving Yugoslav identity as the national identity of all. He hoped to make Yugoslavia the nation to which all gave primary loyalty and with which people identified most strongly. Instead of being a multinational country, he intended to have Yugoslavia become a multiethnic federation. Yugoslavia was divided into six republics, or federal units, which were nationally based in terms of territory (with the exception of Serbs, many of whom lived outside of the Serb Republic): Serbia, Croatia, Bosnia-Herzegovina, Slovenia, Macedonia, and Montenegro. In addition, there were two autonomous provinces in Serbia: Kosovo and Vojvodina. For a communist country, the Yugoslavian state was unusually decentralized. Tito carefully avoided using the largest nation, Serbia, as a foundation for a common Yugoslav identity. In fact, Serbian power, which was in part a result of the fact that the Serb population was the largest of the nationalities in Yugoslavia, was purposefully reduced by Tito. The 1974 constitution is an example of this reduction of power. In that constitution, Tito gave Kosovo and Vojvodina more power and autonomy (their own assembly, representation in the Serbian assembly, and a turn in the rotating presidency), Serbian power was reduced, and the other republics were reassured that Serbia would not be able to control the federal government.

In addition, the Communist party and ideology were used to counteract periodic upsurges of nationalist sentiment, as well as too-liberal reform movements. Tito believed that the communist ideology would bring the country together as Yugoslavia and ultimately reduce nationalism to a cultural artifact, rather than remain a political element in Yugoslavia (Schöpflin, 1993). Nationalism was a crime, and those found guilty were punished with long prison terms. The nationalists in Croatia, in particular, were severely punished in the 1970s.

Tito himself became a unifying symbol. He was charismatic and very popular among the citizens of Yugoslavia. While he was alive, the international behavior of Yugoslavia appeared to be quite nationalistic. This was enhanced by the existence of an external threat to Yugoslav independence. Shortly after World War II, Yugoslavia was pressured by the Soviet Union to follow the Soviet model, which they strongly resisted. In later years, Tito became one of the founders of the nonaligned movement, which was an organization of countries that rejected being pulled into either the U.S. or Soviet camp in the Cold War. Yugoslavs enjoyed the grandeur acquired by having this leadership role in an international movement. Yugoslavia also achieved considerable economic success.

Ironically, the successes of Tito's strategy produced forces that ultimately caused the country to fall apart. With economic success came further economic liberalization in the 1960s, which, in turn, made the republics more autonomous and weakened the central state. Constitutional changes, in 1974, gave each republic and the two provinces a central bank, police, and educational and judicial systems. By the time Tito died in 1980, the economy was on a downward spiral, and no political leader had emerged who could fill Tito's role as national unifier. His importance in keeping Yugoslavia whole was evident in the failure of the federal presidency after Tito died. He did not promote a successor, but instead developed the peculiar idea of a rotating federal presidency, which would rotate among the republics annually. This made it virtually impossible for any single political figure to emerge as a national leader, and it fueled the rise of nationalism among the separate nationalities in Yugoslavia. The presidency was used as a bargaining tool by the different republics. In 1986, for example, Slovenia gave its turn in the presidency to Bosnia in exchange for concessions on economic reforms (Woodward, 1995).

The political psychology of the conflict. The Serbs were the most numerous of the peoples and were dominant in the military officer corps (Silber & Little, 1996). After Tito's death, Serbia's role and position in the federation became increasingly galling to **Serbian nationalists**. They believed that they were unfairly deprived of their just desserts. First, unlike the other nationalities, Serbs were not unified in a single republic. Second, they believed that Serbs should control Kosovo and Vojvodina, but particularly Kosovo, which was a central symbol of Serbian nationalism and the cradle of Serbian civilization. The symbolic importance of Kosovo made irrelevant the fact that only 10% of its residents were ethnic Serbs and the rest Albanian. Meanwhile, as Serbian nationalism surged, Slobodan Milošević maneuvered his way to the top of the Communist party in Serbia, by defeating party rivals less inclined toward radical nationalism (Silber & Little, 1996). He then managed to gain de facto control of the votes of Kosovo, Vojvodina, and Montenegro in the federal government. The upsurge of Serbian nationalism follows the patterns we described earlier, when nationalists believe they have the capability for autonomous statehood, and who, when comparing themselves to other out-groups, come to believe that they have been mistreated and deprived of natural rights. The case also demonstrates the important role **leaders** play in manipulating nationalism to mobilize people to fight against other na-

Leader Manipulation of Nationalism

In the post-Tito era, Serbian nationalism was inflamed by a memorandum produced by the Serbian Academy of Sciences and Arts in 1986. It focused on Kosovo, where the situation was described as the "physical, political, legal and cultural genocide of the Serbian people" (quoted in Doder and Branson, 1999, p. 37). The document was crafted by Dobrica Cosic, an important author and a leader of intellectual nationalists in Serbia. Slobodan Milošević early on recognized the potential opportunity for his own political ambitions embedded in the arousal of nationalism by the intellectual nationalist camp. In 1987, Milošević, by then leader of the Communist party, was sent by the president of the Serb Republic to Kosovo to address concerns of the Serb minority there about mistreatment by the Albanian majority. In response to protestors' assertion that they were being beaten by Albanians, Milošević stated: "No one will ever dare beat you again . . . You must stay here. Your land is here. . . . You are not going to leave them, are you, because life is hard and because you are subject to injustice and humiliation? It was never in the spirit of the Serb . . . people to succumb before obstacles, to quit when one has to fight, to be demoralized in the face of hardship" (quoted in Doder & Branson, 1999, pp. 43–44). With this statement, and others that followed, Milošević manipulated Serb nationalist symbols, mobilized Serb nationalists, and won the mantle of the defender of Serb nationalism.

tional groups in defense of their own nation (see box). As Kaufman (2001) notes, "Yugoslav politics makes sense only in the context of the nationalist myths and symbols that the peoples of Yugoslavia found so moving. The power of Milošević had everything to do with his ability to appropriate and manipulate [those symbols]" (p. 199).

Meanwhile, nationalist passions were on the rise in the other republics, particularly Slovenia and Croatia. The Slovenes considered themselves to be culturally superior to their fellow Yugoslavs, particularly the Serbs (they were Roman Catholic; the Serbs were Eastern Orthodox). The Slovenes saw themselves as more like Western Europeans, and their economy was more advanced than those of the other nationalities in Yugoslavia. This also enhanced their self-image. The **Slovene nationalists** wanted greater autonomy from the rest of the republics and more decentralization in the country. Although Serb nationalists wanted more centralization, not decentralization, they tended not to have severe conflicts with the Slovenes in this regard, because they were far apart geographically, and there were very few Serbs living in the

Slovene republic. Eventually, Slovenia pushed for greater and greater autonomy, rejected the legitimacy of federal control, and appeared to be heading toward secession, which the Serbs would not agree to. Conflict between the two republics was then inflamed in 1988, when the Slovenian government supported a strike by ethnic Albanian miners in Kosovo and condemned Serbian efforts to revoke Kosovo's status as an autonomous province and simply make it part of the Serb republic. Slovenian Communist party leader Milan Kucan "portrayed Serbia as the enemy of Slovene democracy, as witnessed by its repression of Albanian rights" in Kosovo (Woodward, 1995, p. 98; Remington, 1996). Serb nationalists were infuriated that the Slovenes would side with the Albanians in Kosovo, who, they believed, prevented Serbians from having their own national territory.

The growth of Serbian power in Yugoslavia, as well as the upsurge in Serb nationalism, contributed to the rise of nationalism in Croatia. Croatians, like the Slovenians, viewed themselves as culturally superior to the Serbs (Silber & Little, 1996); The Serbs were peasants, the Croatians were sophisticated; Serbs were Orthodox, Croatians were Roman Catholic. Because the Serbs were also powerful, having a strong presence in the military, the Croatian leadership quickly developed a **barbarian image** of Serbia. In chapter 3, this image is described as one of people who are perceived to be superior to the perceiver in capability, inferior in culture, and aggressive in intentions. This image could only have been reinforced by statements such as that by Milošević regarding the breakup of Yugoslavia: "If we have to, we'll fight. I hope they won't be so crazy as to fight against us. Because if we don't know how to work and do business, at least we know how to fight" (quoted in Silber & Little, 1996, p. 129).

Croatia had pockets of Serbs in Krajina who revolted from the newly forming Croatian state. Given the legacy of World War II, they naturally would not want to live in an independent Croatia nor would the Serbs of Serbia want them to. The rebellion spread to other Serbian-dominant communities in Croatia, in the first half of 1991. The Yugoslav army was dominated by Serbs, but was still the army of the federation, and intervened when the Croatian police tried to crush the Krajina Serb revolt. Although the Yugoslav army did not support the rebels, both Slovenia and Croatia interpreted the intervention as an ominous sign that the Yugoslav army was a tool of the Serbs. This was the final straw in their decisions to secede from Yugoslavia. Milošević's official position was that both Croatia and Slovenia had the right to secede from Yugoslavia, but that Serbs living in either one, meaning Croatia, had the right to live in Serbia. Therefore, borders would have to be redrawn, and portions of Croatia where Serbs lived would have to stay in Yugoslavia, but this was unacceptable to **Croatian nationalists**.

The impact of the Croatian barbarian image of Serbia, on both the mobilization of Croatian nationalism and its movement toward secession, can be seen in late 1990 and early 1991. We noted in chapter 3 that, when this image is present, people will look for alliances, rather than take on the barbarian directly. Croatia, under President Franjo Tudjman, initially advocated a confederation with the rest of Yugoslavia, rather than complete independence, indicating that they did not want a direct confrontation with Serbia or the Yugoslav army. Croatia did look for allies—which is what one would expect when the barbarian image is operative, and found one in Slovenia. As Slovenia moved toward a bid for independence, Croatia was faced with two options: isolation in the federation, along with a rebellious Serb population in the eastern regions; or declaring independence, as Slovenia had done, and searching for international support as an independent sovereign state. Slovenia had a referendum on independence in December 1990, and Croatia did so in May 1991. Both declared independence on June 25, 1991. Violence escalated in the regions of Croatia where Serbs were in rebellion.

The difference in Serbia's response to Slovenian and Croatian independence is evident in the differences in the wars that followed. The Yugoslav army tried to prevent Slovenia from leaving the federation in a 2-week-long conflict with few dead, which ended with a cease-fire agreement, and Slovenia seceded from the Yugoslav federation. This heralded the end of Yugoslavia as a multinational federation, and it became merely another name for Serbia. The Yugoslav army was no longer the military force of the federation, but was Serbia's army, which would be used in a much more destructive war to prevent Croatia from seceding. The difference in these wars is attributable to a number of perceptual factors. Slovenians and Serbians did not have the history of ethnic genocide, and Croatians and Serbs did. The Serbian nationalists believed that their own national kindred must be protected from a repeat of the slaughter of World War II and that they should be incorporated into the territory the nation deserved and had been denied for so long. This was not an issue with Slovenia.

Kosovo and Albanian Independence

Historical background. Kosovo was a province within the Serb Republic of Yugoslavia. Of the 2 million people who inhabit Kosovo, 90% are Albanian and 10% are Serbian. In 1974, when Yugoslavia changed its constitution, the province was granted autonomous status within the Serb Republic of Yugoslavia, angering many Serb nationalists. During the next 15 years, the Albanian majority engaged in ethnic discrimination against the minority Serb population. Kosovo's autonomy was taken away in 1989, by Yugoslav President Slobodan Milošević. In doing this, Milošević abrogated provisions in the constitution, that allowed for such things as the Albanian language to be used in schools, as well as for the observance of Islamic holy days. Milošević also sent troops and police to the region. In the view of Milošević and other Serb nationalists, Kosovo is an integral part of Serbian history and a cradle of their civilization. Serbs trace this history to 1389, when they fought and lost the province to Ottoman rule under the Turks.

The Albanians did not want to abide by their loss of autonomy and in effect created a shadow government in 1992, led by Ibrahim Rugova. By 1996, the Kosovo Liberation Army (KLA) had formed in order to gain independence for the region. They began with attacks on the Serb forces. Over the next few years, clashes between the Serbian forces and the KLA increased. Albanians were divided in loyalties, with some supporting the KLA and others, such as Rugova, who was not an advocate of armed resistance to the Serbs, and who preferred a negotiated settlement to the conflict. While the fighting escalated, the Serbs were strongly resistant to outside interference. In a referendum held in April 1998, 95% of Serb voters rejected foreign mediation of the conflict (Judah, 2000). Sanctions were imposed on Serbia in late April, and, in May, Milošević and Rugova agreed to talk. However, Rugova had no influence over the KLA and lacked the authority to end the fighting.

In September 1998, the UN Security Council voted in favor of a resolution, that called for a cease-fire in Kosovo, because they were concerned about the fighting and the number of refugees fleeing the fighting. The council also warned the Yugoslav government that it would take additional action if they did not comply. In addition to the cease-fire, the UN demanded the withdrawal of Serbian troops from the region, peace talks, a return of the refugees, full access by aid agencies, and cooperation with the International War Crimes Tribunal at The Hague. In October, Richard Holbrooke, the U.S. nominee for ambassador to the UN, met with Milošević. After a series of talks, an agreement was settled on. In that agreement, Serb forces were to be withdrawn, a force of 2000 troops from the Organization for Security and Cooperation in Europe (OSCE) would verify compliance with the agreement tasks on the ground, and NATO would be permitted to perform air verifications. Finally, elections were to be held in 9 months' time.

By mid-October, Milošević was not complying with the guidelines negotiated with Holbrooke. For example, Milošević did move the largest army battalion out of Kosovo, but only just over the Kosovo border. NATO warned again that, if Milošević did not comply, air strikes would ensue. On October 25, the UN Security Council passed another resolution, implicit in which was that military action would take place, again, if Milošević did not abide by the negotiated agreement. Russia and China, however, opposed any unilateral action against Serbia.

By January 1999, it was apparent that, despite negotiations, the fighting had not ceased. Among the incidents were the capture of eight Serbian soldiers by the KLA and the murder of 45 Albanians in the village of Racak. In addition, OSCE observers, who were unarmed, were encountering resistance from the Serb forces. Serbia, represented by Minister of Foreign Affairs Milan Milutinovic, once again began to participate in negotiations in Rambouillet, France, on February 6. In that meeting, it was reported that Milutinovic had agreed to autonomy for Kosovo, as well as a cease-fire. However, also proposed in the so-called Rambouillet Agreement was not only that NATO forces be placed in the region, but also that they "shall enjoy . . . unrestricted passage and unimpeded access throughout the FRY [Federal Republic of Yugoslavia] including airspace and territorial waters" (p. 47).

This proposal was unacceptable to the Serbian government, which is not surprising, considering that Serbs are very nationalistic and that this was a direct threat to the unity and independence of Serbia. As we have seen, unity and independence are core nationalistic values. Essentially, what was proposed was an occupation force in all of Serbia. At this point, Holbrooke reemerged, but was not successful in trying to convince the Serbs to accept this aspect of the accord. NATO responded by beginning a bombing campaign on March 24, 1999, which lasted 78 days. On June 12, UN forces (Unmik) and NATO forces (K-for) entered the region, at which point Kosovo was considered an international protectorate.

The political psychology of the conflict.   The strength of **Serbian nationalism** enables us to understand why they were so determined to keep Kosovo part of Serbia. This is an outcome of their attachment to the symbols of the country and the people and the desire for unity. Kosovo Albanians, on the other hand, saw an **opportunity for independence** and for their own unity and took advantage of that opportunity. They knew the history of international (UN and NATO) involvement in Bosnia as Yugoslavia broke up (see chapter 7), and they had reason to believe that, if the international community intervened to support the Bosnian Muslims' effort to split from Yugoslavia and Serb domination—which it did—then the international community would help them, too.

The question remains, why Slobodan Milošević would take on the greatest military powers on earth. Here, images play an important role in helping us understand his behavior. Evidence indicates that Milošević had a **degenerate image** of NATO countries, and he simply did not believe that they would carry out their threats to attack Serbia. His previous experiences in negotiating with Holbrooke; the fact that threats had been made before and not carried out; his belief that, even if NATO did attack, Serbs were strong enough to resist; his knowledge of disagreements on the use of force within NATO; and many other factors all supported a degenerate image of NATO countries (Cottam, Mahdasian, & Sarac, 2000). With that image, he could have concluded that risking resistance to NATO demands was worth the gamble to achieve goals driven by nationalism.

A related question is, Why would the Albanians rise up and fight for independence from Serbia? **Social identity theory** and its implications for nationalism provide a plausible answer to that question, as well. The theory tells us that people will try to change their group's status and position—in this case a change toward independence—when they identify a realistic cognitive alternative. In the case of the Albanians, there can be no doubt that they too watched as the UN and NATO came to the aid of the Muslims in Bosnia, and they figured that the same could realistically happen for them. Hence, the chances of actually achieving independence would have seemed better in the late 1990s than at any time in history.

Although the bombing succeeded in forcing Milošević to withdraw Serb forces from the region, and restored the autonomy of the region, it did not mend the hatred between the still-segregated Serbs and Albanians. The desire for independence by Albanians, and the Serbian view that Kosovo is part of Serbia, remain unchanged. Furthermore, it was not until the October 2000 elections that Milošević was ousted from power, succeeded by Vojislav Kostunica. At first, it did not seem that Milošević would accept the outcome of the election, but widespread protests helped convince him to step down. Milošević remained a face in Serbian politics. Another blow, however, was dealt to his party when Kostunica's alliance, the Democratic Opposition of Serbia, won two thirds of the seats in the December 24 parliamentary elections. Milošević, now considered an international war criminal, is being tried by the International Court of Justice.

What is clear about the situation in Kosovo is that its future remains uncertain. The desire for independence, the emergence of another Albanian guerilla group with ties to former KLA guerillas, who are fighting to attach part of the Presevo Valley in Serbia to Kosovo, and the Serbian insistence that Kosovo remain part of Serbia, indicates that the conflict has not ended.

Cyprus

Historical background.   Like Northern Ireland, the Cypriot conflict involves two countries, Greece and Turkey, whose people believe that they are rightful owners of Cyprus. However, unlike Northern Ireland, ethnic Greek and Turkish Cypriots coexist on the island as part of two separate nation-states: the Turkish Republic of Northern Cyprus and the Republic of Cyprus. Cyprus was a colony of the British by 1925. In 1955, the Greek majority (about 80%) decided that they did not want to be under British rule and started a campaign known as *Enosis*, which means union. Greek Cypriots wanted to be unified with Greece. In 1959, the British reluctantly granted unification, and the following year the Republic of Cyprus was established. The Greeks, Turks, and British settled on a Greek president and a Turkish vice president, as well as on proportional power-sharing within the legislature. The British also were given two sovereign military bases. The three powers also left themselves as guarantors, meaning that, if there was any constitutional disruption, they would have the right to intervene.

It was not long before communal violence between the two national groups had broken out. In 1964, the UN sent in peacekeeping troops to deal with the island, because of the violence. By this point, the Turks and the Greeks had established their own enclaves. The situation was further exacerbated by the toppling of the Greek Cypriot president by what Turks argued was a pro-*Enosis* Greek government. As a result, in 1974, the Turkish government invaded the island, arguing they had the right under the Treaty of Guarantee. The Turks established a partition line, known as the Attila Line, resulting in the creation of two countries on the island.

The political psychology of the conflict.   The Cyprus conflict is problematic, because it involves two warring national groups—the Greek and Turkish Cypriots—but is further compounded by the involvement of their respective mother countries, Greece and Turkey. Greece and Turkey are highly nationalistic countries and have a long and historical animosity for each other. They are essentially enemies whose perception of each other is highly threatening. The island of Cyprus represents a battleground for these enemies, much like many developing countries were for the United States and the Soviet Union during the Cold War. The Greek and Turkish governments desire to protect and ultimately bolster the power of their own people. And, because of their long-standing historical animosity, both Turkey and Greece have a strategic interest in the island, ultimately not wanting the other to control the island.

The national groups on the island, the Greek and Turkish Cypriots, are simply Greek and Turk **diasporas**. They do not see themselves as Cypriots with common heritages and goals. In essence, then, there is no conception of a common Cypriot nation (Fisher, 2001). Their view of each other is highly threatening, each perceiving the other to be an arm of the Greek or Turkish government. This is especially problematic for nation building, which would require that they overcome their perceptions of each other and begin to see themselves as one nation whose aim it is to build a country beneficial to both groups.

Chechnya

Historical background.   The nationalist uprising in Chechnya has been an ongoing problem for the Russian government. Chechnya is one of six republics in Russia. Chechens are an indigenous group, descendants of herdsmen and farmers, who speak their own distinct language (Kline, 1998). Chechens have a long history of nationalist resistance to Russian rule. As Payin and Popov (1996) explain, about the early nineteenth century:

> Russian imperialism in the Caucasus lasted several centuries and met its most deter-mined and well-organized resistance on [in] the territory of Chechnya and the bordering regions of Dagestan. There, for a quarter of a century, Shamil's Islamic proto-state fought the Russian army until 1864. The Republic of the North Caucasus, that included Chechnya, declared independence soon after the Bolshevik revolution in May 1918 . . . and fought a brutal war against the Tsarist army, commanded by General Denikin. . . . After Denikin's defeat, the Red Army entered Chechnya in early 1920, and a new rebel-lion erupted, this time against the Bolsheviks. This revolt was not suppressed until fall 1921. . . . Over the ensuing three years, Chechnya, Ingushetia, and a number of other autonomous *oblasts* of the Northern Caucuses became independent. A brief period of relative tranquility was cut short by the mass political repression of the collectivization campaign during the late 1920s and early 1930s. This sparked a new wave of anti-Soviet uprisings in Chechnya that continued for the next ten years, gradually taking on the character of guerilla warfare. (p. 2)

In 1944, Soviet leader Joseph Stalin banished the Chechens to Kazakhstan, after he accused them of collaborating with the Germans. Chechens were permitted to return to their homeland by Nikita Khrushchev, in 1957.

The most recent conflict with Russia began in October 1991, when Chechen General Dzhokhar Dadaev declared independence for Chechnya. As in the case of Kosovo's Albani-ans, it is very likely that the Chechen rebels saw the disintegration of the Soviet Union, and the subsequent independence of neighboring countries, as an indication that a realistic opportu-nity existed for them to make a successful break from Russia. As we noted in the case of Kosovo, this is something social identity theory would lead us to expect. Similarly, national-ism explains the Russian response: *Nyet*! Russia had already experienced numerous humilia-tions, such as loss of territory, severe economic problems, and loss of international status as a superpower. There was no way a nationalistic people would tolerate the further humiliation of losing Chechnya. Consequently, the Russians, who claimed that the republic was rightfully part of the Russian Federation, did not recognize an independent Chechnya. In 1994, Russia sent 40,000 troops to the republic. Even though the Russians were able to occupy the urban centers, they were unable to defeat the guerrillas in the south. The guerrillas were able to retake Grozny, the capital (Grozny was later renamed Djohar by Chechens). Although the Russians anticipated a quick victory, this was not to be. In July 1996, after more than 80,000 people had died, 40,000 homes were destroyed, and an estimated 300,000–400,000 people were displaced, the war-torn Russian army were forced to withdraw their forces (Kline, 1998). Within the peace agreement signed, in August 1996, by Russian General Alexander Lebed and Chechen Chief of Staff Aslan Maskhadov (who was elected president of Chechnya in January 1997), there was a provision that independence would be addressed in 5 years, in 2001.

In August 1999, the Chechens invaded neighboring Dagestan, in order to help Islamic forces there gain independence. Russia once again invaded Chechnya with 100,000 troops, and, since then, they have been accused of human rights abuses, from torture, summary executions, kidnappings and disappearances, to looting and extortion (Peterson, 2000a). Russian President Vladimir Putin initially saw the solution as direct rule from the Kremlin, which is obviously a different outcome of national liberation than envisioned by the rebels (Weir, 2000). Russia continued to claim that victory over the rebels was imminent. In March 2003, a referendum was called for by the Russian government, which would provide Chechnya with a new constitution and limited autonomy, although it was clearly to remain a part of Russia. In the meantime, the region remains devastated by war and in dire need of a rebuilding of its infrastructure.

The political psychology of the conflict.   The position taken by the Russian government, and its actions, shed light on the **image** it holds of the Chechens. The nationalistic Chechens represent a threat to the Russians, but they are also perceived by them to be inferior in terms of capability and culture, which explains the Russian view that this **rogue** group needs to be taught a lesson and must be defeated by force. The Russians are also highly nationalistic, and granting the demands of the Chechens would compromise the territorial integrity of a greater Russia. On the other hand, the Chechens clearly believe that the Russians are **imperialists** with far superior capability. However, the relationship between them is seen by the Chechens as unjust, explaining why they have repeatedly challenged Russian rule, despite the country's perceived superior capability. Negotiating an end to the conflict would certainly require the perceptions of one group to change: Either the Russians would have to accept that the Chechens are a unique national/ethnic group, relinquishing control over the region, or the Chechens would have to see themselves as part of a greater Russia, thus not perceiving themselves as distinct within the country.

Turkey and the Kurdish Revolt

Historical background.   Since 1984, 30,000 people have died as a result of the conflict between the Kurds and the Turkish government. The Kurds, a minority group of 12 million people concentrated in southeastern Turkey, are predominantly Sunni Muslims, who speak two distinct dialects: Kurmanji and Zara. This minority has expressed demands ranging from complete independence to autonomy. The Turkish government, however, believes the Kurds should assimilate into Turkish society and has banned the Kurdish language, television, and the arts.

The conflict between the Kurds and the Turks did not begin with the Kurdish offensive of 1984, nor is it a problem situated solely in Turkey. The Kurds are a nation of around 25 million people without a state. Their traditional homeland is in the area where Turkey, Iraq, and Iran share borders. The majority of the Kurds live in those three countries, with smaller Kurd populations in Syria and Azerbaijan. They have revolted against the governments of Iran and Iraq in recent years, and their aspirations for nation statehood have been repressed, often brutally. The conflict in Turkey can be traced to the creation of the post–Ottoman Empire Turkish state in 1923. At the end of the First World War, the Ottoman Empire was defeated, and the Treaty of Lausanne (1923) divided the multinational holdings of the empire. The Republic of Turkey was established, but the Kurds were left without a homeland. There were three major revolts against the Turkish government between 1925 and 1939, in the southeastern part of the country, where the Kurds resided, and the Turkish government responded with brutal repression, attempting to assimilate the minority group. Martial law remained in effect until 1946.

The Kurdistan Workers Party (PKK) formed in 1978. Defining their struggle as one of anticolonialism, the group demanded independence. With the military coup of 1980, and a campaign of repression against the Kurds by that regime, many members of the PKK fled to Iran, Iraq, and Syria. In Syria, members of the PKK were supplied with money, weapons, and training. In 1987, the Syrians agreed to no longer support the PKK and claimed that their bases had been closed. However, in reality, the PKK simply moved their bases to an area in Lebanon controlled by Syria and continued their campaign (Graham-Brown & Sackur, 1995).

Beginning in 1984, the campaign was responded to with a declaration of a state of emergency in 10 of Turkey's southeastern provinces. The following year, Prime Minister Turgut Ozal created a system of village guards, whereby local citizens were recruited to help the armed forces fight the PKK (Graham-Brown & Sackur, 1995). In recent years, with the weakening of the movement, the leader of the PKK, Abdullah Ocalan, has claimed that he is willing to discuss a political settlement, possibly including autonomy rather than independence (O'Toole, 2000). Ocalan was arrested in Kenya in February 1999 and was given a death sentence. After his arrest, he called for a cease-fire with the Turks. Most of the guerillas have retreated to Northern Iraq and Iran. The PKK claims that they are no longer at war with the Turks (BBC News, "Turkish Troops," 2000). However, in the spring of 2000, Turkish troops crossed into Northern Iraq in an offensive against them signaling that the Turkish government did not believe the conflict was over. The Turkish government was still threatened by Kurdish nationalist sentiments and were still driven by the perception that this rogue group was not to be negotiated with, but defeated.

The political psychology of the conflict.   This conflict can also be explained in terms of conflicts about the meaning of national identity, as well as images. The Kurds had a nationalist awakening fairly late in the game, after their nation had already been divided among other countries (Gunter, 1990). During the time when nationalism was sweeping through Turkey and Iran, the Kurds were still divided into parochial communities, that is, communities where the strongest identities were with the clan or tribe, rather than with the Kurdish nation. Indeed, those identities remain very strong in the Kurdish population, and there are significant animosities among the Kurds. As Gunter (1990) notes, in "all of the Kurdish revolts of the twentieth century . . . —whether in Turkey, Iraq, or Iran—significant numbers of Kurds have supported the government because of their tribal antipathies for those rebelling" (p. 6). Kurds also have linguistic divisions. The language has two major dialects (Kurdi and Kurmanji), as well as subdialects, and some are mutually incomprehensible. As national identity grew, however, they came to see the Turks as oppressive **imperialists**. Kurds in other countries saw their governing regimes in the same manner. By the late 1900s, they had reached the conclusion that a favorable international environment would improve their chances of attaining an independent Kurdistan. We return to this point later.

Turkish nationalists, on the other hand, do not want the Kurds to have either independence or autonomy within Turkey. They have attempted to force assimilation of the Kurds, through repressing their language and culture. But this is not just the determination of one group to suppress another. When modern Turkey emerged from the ashes of the Ottoman Empire, whose heart was in Istanbul, it was not precisely clear who was a Turk. Islam provided a common link between the Turks and Kurds, but the new Turkey was to be a secular state. In the process of repressing the revolts between 1925 and 1939, Turks increasingly denied the existence of an ethnic or national group of Kurds. Instead, they began to refer to them as "mountain Turks" and attempted to force them to assimilate into Turkish society. Speaking the Kurdish language was illegal until 1991. As recently as 1999, after the capture of Ocalan and 15 years of war against the PKK, one member of Parliament refused to acknowledge that there is a "Kurdish" problem in Turkey. He was quoted as saying, "We call it the southeast problem. We don't separate any ethnicity in Turkey in our hearts and minds" (Freeman A., 1999).

With Turkey pushing to be considered as a member of the European Union, they are coming under increasing pressure by the members to grant rights to the Kurdish minority. Turkey argues that granting rights, such as allowing education in the Kurdish language and lifting the ban on broadcast-

---

The Power of National Identity

Bruni (2003) wrote the following story about a 15-year-old Kurdish boy, Bayram, which illustrates the extent to which Turkey is determined to force the assimilation of the Kurds:

"On a school day last November, his teachers in this remote, poor, densely Kurdish area of southeastern Turkey asked him to lead his classmates in the customary Turkish pledge of allegiance, which includes the line 'Happy is one who calls himself a Turk.' Bayram ... balked ... [The teachers] insisted that he press ahead. So he did, and what they heard him say was this: 'Happy is one who calls himself a Kurd.' The teachers not only sent him home from school for the day, but also summoned the police. Bayram now stands accused of 'inciting hatred and enmity on the basis of religion, race, language or regional differences.' ... Bayram's case provides a glimpse into the extreme vigilance of Turkish government officials against any possible flicker of Kurdish separatism, a watchfulness that continues to shape the country's response to the war in Iraq." (p. A3) Bayram faced up to 5 years in prison if convicted.

---

ing, could foster separatism (Bruni, 2003). However, the most significant opportunity for the Kurds of Turkey may come from the Kurds in Iraq. With the Gulf War of the first President Bush, they rebelled against the Iraqi Republican Guard, and the United States decided to protect them from retaliation by creating a safety zone in northern Iraq. This in essence established a rump Kurdish state. Then came the second Gulf War, the product of decisions made by the second President Bush, which presented a spectacular opportunity for the Iraqi Kurds to establish a larger and fully independent state. They moved quickly against the Iraqi military. At this writing, the Kurdish military forces have taken over Mosul and Kirkuk and the rich oil wells there. The whole prospect of instability (i.e., war) in Iraq is deeply worrying to the Turkish government, because they understand full well the impact, for the Kurdish community in Turkey, of an independent Kurdistan in portions of what used to be Iraq, particularly portions with oil wealth. It would present them with a clear-cut opportunity to try to revolt and to unite with the Iraqi Kurds. The United States has insisted that the Kurds in Iraq will be asked to pull back, but the future remains very unclear. The next case demonstrates full well the power of nationalism when the opportunity for unity of a national identity group appears.

German Unification

Our last example of the power of the desire that nationalists have to live together in a unified, independent country is a more positive one—German unification in 1990. Germans are commonly considered to be very nationalistic, and German nationalism is considered a primary cause of World War II (see later). German political behavior is historically replete with examples of popular sacrifice for the sake of the country and the German people. This is a pattern of behavior that derives from strong attachment to the nation as an in-group.

After World War II, however, Germany was divided into the Federal Republic of Germany (commonly referred to as West Germany), and the German Democratic Republic (commonly referred to as East Germany). The East became a Soviet ally, and the West became an American and Western European ally. During the Cold War, the option of unification did not exist, despite Soviet statements to the contrary. This led to uncertainty as to the composition of the German national community. Was it the territorial community of both Germanies, or were there two German national communities: the West and East? If the latter, then both West and East Germany could be considered distinctive nation-states. If not, then the desire for national unification would still exist, even if only in a dormant state, because of the constraints imposed on the possibility of unification by the Cold War. The answer to the question of how many German nations there were was dramatically apparent as the Soviet Union relinquished its control in East Europe. The German people moved quickly to take up the new option of reunification.

One of the most interesting aspects of German unification is that it was so attractive to Germans who had in the preceding years demonstrated less and less interest in reunification. West Germany had become prosperous and was closely identified with the NATO alliance. In 1969, the West German government began a process of neutralizing conflict with Eastern Europe, which in effect signaled acceptance of the status quo (Grosser, 1992; Mahncke, 1992). Public opinion polls conducted in West Germany also demonstrated the diminution of hope for unification and the low expectation that it would ever materialize. A 1986 survey found that one third of the West Germans polled believed that East Germany was a foreign land. This was particularly the case among those aged 14–29: 51% of this age group regarded the East as foreign (Plock, 1993). Only 9% of respondents believed Germany would be united in their lifetimes, but Germans still approved of the idea of reunification, as shown in a 1987 poll, in which 70–80% of respondents were advocates of reunification (Plock, 1993). When the opportunity finally came, it took only 1 year from the disintegration of the East German government, in October 1989, to formal unification, on October 3, 1990, even though the German government had to convince the United States, Britain, France, and the Soviet Union that a newly unified Germany would not be aggressive and would commit to undertaking the enormous financial commitment and sacrifice that unification would require.

Nationalism and Foreign Policy[1]

Nationalism also has an impact on foreign policy behavior. The heightened propensity to identify threats and opportunities, the importance of national grandeur, and the tendency to be quicker and more extreme in using stereotypical images of others, all influence foreign policy predispositions among nationalists. In addition, nationalists are more easily mobilized by their governments, through the manipulation of symbols important to them, to make sacrifices for foreign policies designed to respond to threats or take advantage of opportunities. Here, we examine a few cases of nationalism and foreign policy.

World War II

World War II is considered possibly the most horrendous illustration of the impact of nationalism on the foreign policy behavior of nation-states. But, if we look at the policies of two of the major nation-states in the conflict—Germany and the United States—we can see that, although nationalism drove Germans to embark on a policy of expansion that ultimately cost 50 million lives, it also enabled the United States to mobilize the American population in order to prevent Hitler from achieving his goals.

Germany in the 1920s was in terrible condition. The country had been defeated in World War I, and the settlement ending the war, the Versailles Treaty, imposed onerous war reparations and peace conditions upon the country. There was severe inflation in the early 1920s, which wiped out much of the savings of the middle class. The government of the post-war state, known as the Weimar Republic, could not meet the basic needs of the public. Moreover, the Weimar Republic had been imposed by the victors of World War I and was politically alien to Germans, who had never previously lived under democratic rule. The institution of the monarchy had been overturned when Germany was defeated in World War I, and there was an uncertain attachment to the new republican institutions. In short, Germany was not politically stable. The Weimar government could not guarantee that Germans would obey its decisions or support it out of principle or habit, and it did not have the ability to provide conditions of economic prosperity for the people. Because of its lack of legitimacy, the government could not mobilize the nationalistic German people by manipulating nationalistic symbols, thereby encouraging them to make sacrifices necessary to rebuild and get through the hard times. Any serious effort to manipulate German national symbols would most likely have led the public to insist on the rectification of German national humiliation and to a questioning of the nationalist legitimacy of the Weimar Republic, which submitted to this humiliation. The Weimar Republic was a consequence of military defeat, that is, it was a symbol of national humiliation (Cassels, 1975; James, 1989).

Under the circumstances, it is not surprising that a right-wing nationalist leader such as Adolf Hitler would appear on the scene to challenge the Weimar Republic, and that they would be attractive to the German people. They were able to manipulate those symbols, and they were determined to restructure the German government and remove the governing elite of the Weimar Republic, who they saw as being unwilling to defend the grandeur of the German nation.

Hitler's ability to manipulate national symbols was a major factor in his rise to power in Germany. His defiant nationalism both silenced his opposition and increased his support base (James, 1989). Nevertheless, when he actually came to power, he not only lacked majority support, but also was viewed by large sections of the public with a mixture of fear and loathing (Steinert, 1977). Thus, he developed a system of coercive control that would ensure his authority, by intimidating his opposition through violence. It started with street violence during electoral campaigns, even before he came to power, and continued with the development of institutionalized coercion and terror, after he came to power. Opponents of the regime were threatened simultaneously with brutal coercion and with appearing unpatriotic by opposing a government that wrapped itself in the flag, by declaring itself the savior of the German nation.

By using nationalistic symbols, condemning the humiliations and territorial losses Germany had experienced after World War I, and instituting a strong coercive control system, Hitler was able to mobilize the German people to make the sacrifices necessary to construct a military machine so strong that the Nazi leadership could embark on a plan that not only recovered land lost after World War I, but that also included a goal of vast expansion. He saw an opportunity to achieve nationalist goals, the rectification of the punishment of Versailles, the expansion of Germany into much-needed territory (*lebensraum*), and the reunification of Germans living in Poland, Czechoslovakia, and Hungary with the broader German nation. German nationalists supported these goals, and the threat of coercive retribution prevented opponents from objecting to those policies. As World War II progressed, the same tactics produced an acceptance of a terrible loss of life and devastating destruction, even as it became clearer and clearer that the goal could not be achieved. The German people became resigned to war (Steinert, 1977). Meanwhile, Germany's opponents were demonized and Jews were identified as the scapegoats upon whom the blame for Germany's problems was placed.

We often think of the United States's involvement in World War II as simply the fight of good against evil and a normal response to the attack by the Japanese, Hitler's ally, on Pearl Harbor. But American behavior is also attributable to American nationalism. By the 1920s, the United States was a country whose populace was nationalistic. This explains in part why the country made it through the Great Depression without serious instability. The economic crisis of the depression years was a shock to the stability of the system, but the government did not have to respond to instability with coercion. Instead, President Franklin Roosevelt was able to call upon American nationalism to generate a willingness to accept the sacrifices necessary to deal with the economic crisis.

Roosevelt recognized the dangers to the United States emanating from the crisis developing in Europe in the 1930s, but the American public did not yet see events in the same way that Roosevelt did (Dallek, 1983). Instead, the public was concerned with the threat to the nation caused by the economic crisis. Many Americans were isolationists during these years and believed that the national interest lay in avoiding another involvement in European squabbles. Roosevelt was clearly aware of the public's preference and acquiesced to it, despite his concerns, as early as 1935, about the possibility of German aggression in Europe (Dallek, 1979).

The Japanese attack on Pearl Harbor on December 7, 1941, erased American isolationism. After the attack, Roosevelt found it easy to mobilize the country. He announced a program to use America's industrial base, resources, and people, to create an overwhelmingly powerful military force. He asked for and received enormous material sacrifices, personal sacrifices, and a willingness to risk lives to deal with this threat to the security of the nation. His request was received with approval and even enthusiasm, and with little dissent. Americans did not have to be forced to fight for the nation, and were willing to die for it.

This case illustrates one of the most important features of nationalistic behavior: the willingness of a national community to make enormous sacrifices in order to construct the instruments—military, diplomatic, intelligence, and economic—necessary for dealing with an external threat. This ability to generate a willingness to make sacrifices is the most important impact of nationalism on a country's foreign policy. Nationalism makes a state more powerful, because people are willing to make great sacrifices for it. But these cases also show that nationalists can be mobilized by the identification of opportunities to achieve a desired goal, as in Germany, as well as by threats to the nation, as in the United States.

The War on Drugs

U.S. domestic and international counternarcotics policy, known as the "war on drugs," and the responses of other countries to that policy, is another arena that bears the marks of nationalism. Both the United States and Mexico are nation-states, and Mexican and American nationalism has influenced the war on drugs (Cottam & Cottam, 2001; Cottam & Marenin, 1999). Typical of nationalists, American policymakers have difficulty believing that Americans are responsible for their own drug use. Instead, U.S. policymakers view the drug war predominantly in supply-side terms. In other words, drugs are a problem because they are produced in other countries and sold to Americans, and, although demand for drugs is also seen as a problem, the central solution to drug abuse has been identified as cutting off the supply. To deal with the supply of drugs coming into the country, U.S. policymakers have adopted an interdiction campaign on U.S. borders, at ports of entry, on the high seas, and on major foreign transshipment routes and production sites. Other methods include crop eradication in source countries, as well as money for training and supplies for source countries.

Relations between Mexico and the United States became publicized in the early 1970s, with Operation Intercept. The idea behind Operation Intercept, initiated by the United States, was in effect to close the borders by slowly searching border traffic for illicit drugs, snarling traffic, and dissuading millions of American and Mexicans from trying to cross the borders on regular business and tourist activities. The Mexicans did comply with U.S. demands that it improve its drug interdiction efforts, resulting in increased U.S. aid to the Mexico, the establishment of Mexico's Northern Boarder Response Force, and increased collaboration between the Mexican military and police with U.S. military counternarcotics officials and civilian law enforcement agencies (Dunn, 1996). However, because the United States unilaterally launched Operation Intercept, it placed a great strain on U.S.–Mexican relations. The United States has since then adopted a more bilateral approach, through Operation Cooperation, but that operation was still a result of U.S. demands for improvement in drug interdiction.

U.S. policy toward Mexico, concerning drug interdiction, has continually strained relations between the two countries, evoking nationalist resentment in Mexico. International narcotics matters offer plenty of opportunities for threat to nationalist sensitivities, because cooperation requires, at a minimum, an overlap of law enforcement activities. Mexicans are very cautious about that interaction. From their perspective, if you give the United States an inch, they may take a mile. If concessions of Mexican sovereignty are made on this issue, the United States will soon be making similar demands in other areas such as immigration. Mexicans are highly suspicious about the intentions of the United States and have indicated a strong resistance to any effort to give American law enforcement officials free reign on Mexican soil. The United States has added credence to this perspective by demanding a certain amount of freedom to operate as law enforcement agents on Mexican soil. In the late 1980s, for example, in response to the murder of a DEA agent in Mexico, U.S. agents participated in the kidnapping of a Mexican national, who was then taken to the United States to stand trial for his role in the murder. The U.S. Supreme Court upheld this action, which infuriated Mexican nationalists. Mexico argued that the United States could not send agents to Mexico and kidnap Mexican nationals to stand trial for a crime committed in Mexico.

Another U.S. policy that inflames nationalist sentiments is the certification process, whereby U.S. monetary funds (as well as international funds, because of U.S. pressure) are withheld if a country is not seen as cooperating with the United States in narcotics control. Every year, the executive branch must certify other countries before the U.S. Congress. Any country that is not evaluated positively as cooperating with the United States in its drug war policy is denied assistance from this country in matters unrelated to drugs. In addition, the United States will recommend against the granting of funds from international aid sources. This is deeply insulting to nationalistic Mexicans, who refuse to recognize certification, arguing that it is a violation of international law and a certain illustration of American ignorance and imperialism. Who is the United States to grade other countries, they ask? Moreover, Mexican nationalism is inflamed when the United States argues that Mexico should control the flow of drugs into the United States. It is a supply problem, but, when Mexican authorities complain that illegal firearms flood into Mexican criminals' hands from the United States, American officials say it is Mexico's demand that is at fault. They maintain that this too is an illustration of American imperialism and hypocrisy.

Nationalists in both countries seek others to blame for what is clearly a transnational problem, requiring international cooperation. But nationalists have a difficult time recognizing their own countries' weaknesses, such as a heavy appetite for drugs in the United States and corruption and trafficking in Mexico. More-over, nationalists in both countries loath having any other country interfere in their domestic politics. Hence, Mexicans do not want the United States to tell them how to conduct policing in Mexico, and Americans do not want Mexicans telling them this country has a major public health problem that Americans need to address.

Post–Cold War Nationalism in Russia and China

The end of the Cold War and the disinte-gration of the Soviet Union produced new implications for nationalists in Russia and China. The end of the Cold War brought opportunities for the reemergence of na-tionalism in Russia. The Soviet Union had been ideologically opposed to the manifes-

> **The AIDS Controversy: A Case Study in South African Nationalism**
>
> In April 2000, South African President Thabo Mbeki made public a letter to U.S. President Bill Clinton, in which he declared that South Africa must find its own solution to HIV-AIDS, which is estimated to have in-fected at least 4 million South Africans. The rate of infection in all of Africa indicates a seriously growing epidemic. According to Mbeki, "a simple superimposition of West-ern experience on African reality would be absurd and illogical." Mbeki sparked further controversy when he questioned whether or not HIV caused AIDS and seriously inquired whether or not current cocktail treatments for AIDS were even effective in the treatment of HIV and AIDS. ("Mbeki's letter" 2000)

tation of nationalism. Now, Russian nationalists were free to express loyalty to the Russian nation. However, the disintegration of the Soviet Union brought a decline in prestige and power in international politics for Russia. Russia's economic problems and political turmoil placed the country in a position of weakness and in need of aid and mercy from its former Cold War opponents. This constitutes a humiliation for proud nationalists and also brought insecurity, because, as the Soviet empire and the associated Warsaw Pact disappeared, the al-liance of the Western Cold War powers, NATO, expanded. That expansion began with the "partnership for peace," which would gradually prepare a number of applicants for member-ship. The first three full-fledged post–Cold War members were Hungary, the Czech Republic, and Poland, which were admitted in 1999. These countries were formerly part of the Eastern-bloc Cold War alliance, the Warsaw Pact, of which the former Soviet Union was the head. The plans to expand NATO into what Russia claims to be its sphere of influence is perceived to be threatening to them, especially when the offer of NATO membership is extended to bor-der countries that Russia has strained relations with, and when the situation in Russia is dire, with the war in Chechnya, a failing economic situation, weakened armed forces, and a host of other problems.

After the fall of the Soviet Union, the new Russian leaders made it clear that they regarded Russia as a great power worthy of a central role in international politics. President Boris Yeltsin remarked, in 1992, that "Russia is rightfully a great power by virtue of its history, its place in the world and its material and spiritual potential" (quoted in Webber, 1996, p. 120). But nationalism in Russia has a number of faces, in part as a readjustment to the shocks of economic depression in the 1990s, and in part as a result of the question of what role an independent Russia would play in world politics. One of those faces is called the New Right Eurasianism. Advocates argue that Russia's orientation should be toward the East, not the West, and, reflecting this, in 1998, Prime Minister Primakov suggested the formation of a strategic triangle among Russia, China, and India. To some extent, this is a result of increas-ing anti-Americanism, wherein the United States is identified by nationalistic Russians as the scapegoat for Russia's economic failures and decline in international power and prestige (Shiraev & Zubok, 2000).

Russian nationalism has contributed to disagreements with the United States on a number of important issue areas. First, there is the expansion of NATO, which is perceived as threatening to Russia. In a September 1999 survey, for example, 66% of Russian respondents believed that the expansion of NATO was a threat to Russia (Shiraev & Zubok, 2000). Second, there was disagreement about U.S. and NATO policy toward Serbia, in the conflicts in Bosnia and in Kosovo. Russians and Serbs are traditional allies, and, in both Bosnia and Kosovo, the Russians believed that they were not given due consideration and attention in handling the crises. They disagreed with the policy of vilifying the Serbs, and they believed that Americans were acting in an imperialistic manner in directing the international community's policy. The United States was warned that it could not play the role of international policeman (Broder, 1999). These policy positions make clear the importance of national prestige for Russians, a value that we noted is common among nationalists. Finally, there is the issue of nuclear weapons. Distrust of the United States led to a long delay in the Russian Duma's ratification of the Strategic Arms Reduction Agreement of 1992 (START II), and the renewed American interest in a national missile defense system (NMD, discussed in chapter 10) further exacerbated Russian concerns about American intentions and their own security and independence. The fear is that, if the United States develops and deploys a national missile defense system, this country will then be able to launch an offensive attack on Russia without fear of retaliation. Again, heightened sensitivity to threats is common among nationalist peoples such as the Russians.

China is another country with a nationalistic populace. Despite its enormous population, its linguistic and ethnic diversity, and the late arrival of an institutionalized state and accompanying national identity, nationalism is an important factor in Chinese foreign policy. There has been an upsurge in nationalism in China in recent years (Bernstein & Munro, 1997; Scalapino, 1999; Zhao, 2000). As in the case of Russia, there are different domestic manifestations of nationalism in China. Zhao (2000), for example, argues that there are three distinct interpretations of Chinese nationalism: nativism, which rejects all things foreign, antitraditionalism, which calls for adaptation to the international environment, in search of China's greatness; and pragmatism, which sits in between. All three are sensitive to threats to China's interests and territorial integrity. Like Russians, Chinese nationalists believe that their country has suffered humiliation at the hands of imperialism, historically, and many identify the United States as the modern-day imperialist bent on dictating to them and inhibiting them from their natural leadership role in international politics. There is a belief that the United States is attempting to contain China and is trying to assert unipolar dominance in Asia. Hence, Chinese foreign policy has included a strategy of multipolarism, that is, the development of diverse partnerships, including one with Russia, to counter American hegemony (Scalapino, 1999). Chinese nationalists are also concerned about threats to their country's security, as a result of U.S. actions, such as the bombing of the Chinese Embassy in Belgrade, Yugoslavia, in the course of the Kosovo war, and the accident that occurred when an American reconnaissance plane was buzzed by a Chinese fighter plane, resulting in the death of the Chinese pilot and emergency landing of the U.S. plane on Chinese territory. The Chinese are concerned, as are the Russians, about the American consideration of a NMD system.

Territorial integrity is among the most important foreign policy issues related to Chinese nationalism. Chinese leaders have insisted upon the return of territory taken from China as a result of nineteenth century imperialism (Hong Kong, Macao, and the South China Sea islands) and a reunion with Taiwan, which was first taken from China by Japanese conquest in 1905 and later split from the mainland by the losing side in China's revolution. Chinese leaders have insisted that Taiwan may not declare independence and that reunification is inevitable. It may, in their view, be done through peaceful negotiations or, if necessary, by force. Because Taiwan has become increasingly democratic, however, there is a growing popular movement against reunification. China implicitly warned Taiwan not to move toward an independence-minded president, by engaging in military exercises using live ordinance, before the presidential election of 1996. Similar threats were made before the next presidential election in 2000, in an effort to prevent the ascent of a new president willing to declare independence for Taiwan. The issue remains one of the most dangerous in Asia, particularly in light of the election in Taiwan, in March 2000, of Chen Shui-bian of the Democratic Progressive party, a pro-independence party. A crucial actor in this conflict is still the United States, which has encouraged Taiwan to negotiate with China, but whose response to military action by China against Taiwan is uncertain.

A second important international issue for Chinese nationalists is human rights. China has been criticized by the United States and others for its lack of political freedoms and repression of political dissidents. These criticisms have been fairly constant since the Tiananmen Square massacre of 1989, when several thousand dissident pro-democracy demonstrators, mostly students, were killed by Chinese military forces, after staging a peaceful sit-in for several days. To the Chinese, criticism is interference in domestic affairs, and an affront to national dignity and prestige, which are central nationalist values.

Most of all, Chinese and Russian nationalists wish to be treated as equals to the great powers in the post–Cold War world, the most important of which is the United States. Nationalistic values of prestige, dignity, security, and unity are all seen to be at stake in the issue areas that are of concern to these countries. Russians want to be consulted in international decision making. Chinese nationalists want full membership in the international community, too, including the World Trade Organization and other central international institutions. They both resent any American action that thwarts their desire for equality.

CONFLICT PREVENTION AND RESOLUTION STRATEGIES

Nationalism is likely to be a source of domestic and international conflict for decades to come. As long as states are common political units, identification with the community residing in their territories will continue, and, when that identity is primary and intense, nationalism will continue. We conclude this chapter with a look at a few conflict resolution issues related to nationalism. These conflicts are difficult to resolve, but they can be dealt with. Ayers (2000) provides a glimpse of the conflict resolution track record. Of 77 intrastate nationalist conflicts from 1945 to 1996, he found 27 on-going as of 1996, 22 ending in defeat, 22 ending in agreements, 4 cease fires, and 2 that simply petered out.

Noted at the outset of this chapter was that nationalists are very sensitive to threats and opportunities in foreign policy. They tend to use extreme stereotypes of others, when perceptions of threat or opportunity are great. More precisely, nationalists are sensitive to threat and opportunity to the values of unity, independence, grandeur, and well-being of the national community. As we saw earlier, Germany's instigation of World War II demonstrates the power of the perception of opportunity to enhance those values, whereas the American response demonstrated perception of threat to those values. Today, as our discussion of China and Russia demonstrates, there is the danger of two nuclear powers perceiving a threat to those values. There is also a danger of the United States, another nuclear nation-state, perceiving an opportunity to enhance those values. Either perception can lead to aggressive behavior.

There are diplomatic techniques that are useful in avoiding nationalistic conflicts. Permitting nationalistic people to save face by employing quiet diplomacy, rather than scolding them publicly, is one obvious example. But, more generally, conflict resolution and prevention depends very much upon having the correct assessment of nationalism. If policymakers understand in advance that the people of another country are very nationalistic, they can anticipate that those people will be very sensitive to threats and opportunities and that they will engage in extreme stereotyping of others when they perceive threats or opportunities to their nation. If they act aggressively because they perceive a threat to the nation, then the **security dilemma**, discussed in chapters 3 and 10, will be operative, and measures to ameliorate misidentified threat perceptions must be put into effect. Unfortunately, the power of operative images makes this difficult, particularly if the image in question is heavily laden with threat perceptions from the very outset, before the conflict escalated. In those cases (enemy, barbarian, rogue, and imperialist), the problem of nonfalsifiability is difficult to overcome. Recalling chapter 3, this is a problem that emerges because the images are so firmly held that virtually any action or nonaction, which could and should disconfirm the image, can be explained away as a product of the nasty nature of the opponent. Nevertheless, consistently and clearly acting in a way that disconfirms the operative image, and thereby lessening the perception of threat, is crucial to conflict prevention and resolution.

On the other hand, if the nationalist country in question has leaders pursuing an opportunity, the situation is completely different and demands a policy of **deterrence and containment** (also discussed in chapter 10). **Deterrence** is the threat by one political actor to take actions in response to another actor's potential actions, which would make the costs (or losses) incurred far outweigh any possible benefits (or gains) obtained by the aggressor. In these situations, the appropriate strategy for preventing or stopping aggressive actions has to go straight to the heart of the identified opportunity, and the other state must be made to understand clearly that what the leaders perceive as an opportunity would instead be an unacceptably costly mistake. This is what Chamberlain failed to do with Hitler before World War II. By appeasing Hitler's demands, he provided evidence to Hitler that the rest of Europe conceded to his ambitions, that they did not have the will to stop him, and that therefore the opportunity he identified was real and worth a gamble to achieve.

Once nationalists do go to war, getting them to pull back is more difficult than it is with nonnationalists. The importance attached to the nation, the sacrifices nationalists are willing to make, and the costs failure is likely to impose on the leadership, makes determination to fight on very strong. Consequently, providing an exiting strategy for a losing nationalistic people is very important, because it can prevent the perception of total humiliation and the instability which that can bring.

Other types of nationalism-related conflicts discussed here are those resulting from nationalities searching for independence, as the examples presented earlier illustrate. In chapter 7, we discuss conflicts in which separation is not possible and a number of conflict prevention and resolution strategies. Here, we restrict ourselves to a discussion of measures suggested by the Carnegie Commission on Preventing Deadly Conflict and the issue of what the international community can or should do when faced with the demands of a national group for secession from a multinational country. In 1997, the Carnegie Commission produced a report that was a result of careful study of numerous post–Cold War conflicts (see also Jentleson, 2000; Lund, 1996). The report maintains that there are four essential measures for preventing deadly conflict: early warning and response; preventive diplomacy; economic measures, including both sanctions and inducements; and, when necessary, the use of force (1997). Although we report on these findings in this chapter on nationalism, they are equally applicable in the next chapter, where ethnic and racial conflicts are discussed.

Early warning and response requires attention to important signs that violence is imminent, including human rights abuses, brutal political oppression, the acquisition of arms, and the use of the media to inflame the public. According to the report:

> During the early stages of a crisis, policymakers should not only be attentive to how circumstances could worsen, but they should also be alert for opportunities to make constructive use of local issues and processes that could help avoid violence. And they should exercise great care as to whom they support and how that support is offered. (Carnegie Commission,1997, p. xxi)

Preventive diplomacy goes beyond traditional diplomacy, in that it uses more urgent unilateral and multilateral techniques to "pressure, cajole, arbitrate, mediate, or lend 'good offices' to encourage dialogue and facilitate a nonviolent resolution of the crisis" (Carnegie Commission,1997, p. xxii). The report recommends that governments maintain diplomatic relations with leaders and groups in conflict-prone situations, rather than suspending relations to show disapproval of their actions. Moderates should be supported and the UN should immediately become involved and should stay abreast of unfolding events, through its own agencies and through other nongovernmental organizations. The economic measures, sanctions, and inducements should be employed to provide punishment for violence and rewards for constructive actions. Finally, if force becomes necessary, it should only be used as a last resort and should not be the only instrument used. Diplomacy and economic measures should be included as part of an integrated strategy. The use of force involves peacekeeping in the aftermath of violence.

Although this sounds sensible, it often does not happen. This approach requires, first and foremost, an attentive and interested international community able to recognize danger signals (George & Hall, 2000; Lund, 1996). This requires the ability to overcome preexisting images of the participants in a conflict and also requires a fundamental understanding of the causes of nationalist and ethnic conflicts, both to enable identification and recognition of early warning signs and to prevent spillover effects, wherein the action taken in response to one crisis unintentionally affects another crisis.

The extensive history of the disintegration of Yugoslavia illustrates all of these points (Cottam & Cottam, 2001; Lund, 2000; Woodward, 1995, 2000). First, as Slovenia and Croatia made it increasingly clear that they intended to secede, the international community was divided and confused. The Bush administration deemed this a European problem, in 1991, and declined involvement. German recognition of Croatian independence inspired Serbian fears, based in the World War II slaughter of Serbs by Croatians. What would happen to the Serbs left in Croatia? Could a Serbian nationalist not insist that their Serbian cousins in Croatia had the right to live in Serbia? The international community, not understanding the importance of Serbian nationalism and the legacy of World War II, neglected essential causes of these conflicts, and in fact exacerbated them by recognizing Croatian independence, then was dismayed when Serbia (i.e., Yugoslavia) went to war to either prevent Croatia's secession or to redraw the borders, so that Serbs in Croatia remained in Yugoslavia.

The next crisis in Yugoslavia's demise came in Bosnia (discussed in chapter 7), which never had a chance as an independent state, because of competing national loyalties (the Serbs and Croatians there wanted to live in Serbia or Croatia). Again, the international community did not recognize the inevitability of war in Bosnia and did not take concerted action until hundreds of thousands of people had died. Then, by the time the combatants were finally convinced to attend the peace talks in Dayton, Ohio, the Bosnian Serbs had been so demonized that they were not permitted to negotiate for themselves. Instead, Slobodan Milošević negotiated for them (another example of a stereotype—a Serb is a Serb, they are a homogeneous group, their interests are all the same), which was a guarantee that the Dayton agreements would be next to impossible to fulfill. This amounted to the imposition of a peace agreement upon the Bosnian Serbs. They had no say in their own future, and by that time Milošević was ready to make great concessions on their behalf (such as giving up Sarajevo), without their agreement. Once the international community did become involved in Bosnia, they demonstrated to the restive Albanian population in Kosovo that, if a minority does choose to break away from Serbia, and if the Serbs are brutal enough, the international community will come to its aid. This is the wrong message to a population waiting for the opportunity. By then, the image of Milošević was the extreme rogue image, and the approach used to convince him to do the international community's bidding was typical of strategies used with a rogue: Tell him what to do and punish him if he does not do it. Hence, the unacceptable Rambouillet accord, which was most certainly going to be unacceptable to any nationalist (Cottam et al., 2000).

Clearly, the ideas of the Carnegie report are good. However, implementing those ideas requires that policymakers understand the causes of nationalistic and ethnic conflicts, if they are to prevent them from exploding into violence. Indeed, they need a course on political psychology. They also need the political will to use their country's resources to do things like provide economic incentives—and this is very difficult politically. An international response that is seen as neutral needs to be a truly international response, whether it is regional or global, through the UN. This means that countries need to agree on standards, procedures, costs, and risks, before a conflict occurs; that they have the resources available for rapid response to crises; and that they share in the burdens. Local conditions also must be appropriate for conflict resolution accords to be acceptable to the populace. The conflicting groups need enough trust in one another, so that they cannot only negotiate, but can accept an agreement without fear of being betrayed. The peace agreement has to be sensible in terms of the social, geographic, and political conditions needed for successful implementation, and the agreement has to be seen as locally produced, not imposed from outside. Finally, identity-based conflicts such as these have added elements of difficulty are discussed at the conclusion of chapter 7. Conflict resolution in nationalist, ethnic, and racial conflicts is very difficult to achieve, but not impossible (Jentleson, 2000).

CONCLUSION

This chapter has examined the role of nationalism as a political psychological factor affecting a variety of political conflicts. We looked at nationalistic desires for unity and independence in a number of civil conflicts, from Europe (Northern Ireland, Yugoslavia, Kosovo) to Russia, to the Middle East (Turkey and the Kurds, Cyprus). We also examined the power of nationalism to promote the peace and unity required for substantial sacrifices, in the case of German unification. Fear of contamination of national unity and values was discussed in the case of Western European concerns about immigrants from the third world. Finally, the impact of nationalism on foreign policy was discussed.

Nationalism has been popularly condemned as bad and a force for great violence. And it has indeed been the cause of millions of deaths and tremendous suffering. However, it can also produce great sacrifice for others. When one looks at it from the standpoint of political psychology, one can see that it is normal in-group behavior. It therefore is going to be a factor in politics as long as nations exist, and understanding that it is neither good nor bad, that it simply is a reality that produces particular patterns of behavior, is much more constructive than merely condemning it. By understanding the political psychology of groups and social identity, one can understand nationalism. In turn, understanding the images nationalists have of out-groups helps in predicting the tactics they will use against them. This should be the basis for preventing nationalism from causing violence, and using it for good.

Topics, Theories/Explanations, and Cases in Chapter 8

Topics	Theories	Cases
Nationalism defined		
Nationalistic behavior described		
Nationalism explained	Social identity theory Image theory	
Nationalism and the drive for unity and independence		Northern Ireland Yugoslavia Kosovo Cyprus Chechnya Turkey German unification
Nationalism and foreign policy		World War II Drug war Russian foreign policy Chinese foreign policy
Conflict prevention and resolution		

KEY TERMS

Ally image
Barbarian image
Colonial image
Core community
   nonnation states
Degenerate image

Deterrence
Enemy image
Imperialist image
Irridentism
Multinational states
Nation state

Nationalism
Rogue image
Scapegoat
Security dilemma
Social identity theory

SUGGESTIONS FOR FURTHER READING

Carnegie Commission on Preventing Deadly Conflict. (1997). *Preventing deadly conflict: Final report.* New York: Carnegie Corporation of New York.

Cottam, M., & Cottam R. (2001). *Nationalism and politics: The political behavior of nation states.* Boulder, CO: Lynne Rienner.

Farnen, R. (Ed.). (1994). *Nationalism, ethnicity, and identity.* New Brunswick, NJ: Transaction, Books.

Fijalkawski, J. (1996). Aggressive nationalism and immigration in Germany. In R. Caplan & J. Feffer (Eds.), *Europe's new nationalism: States and minorities in conflict.* Oxford, UK: Oxford University Press.

Keckmanovic, D. (1996). *The mass psychology of ethnonationalism*. New York: Plenum.
Searle-White, J. (2001). *The psychology of nationalism*. New York: Palgrave.
Silber, L., & Little, A. (1996). *Yugoslavia: Death of a nation*. New York: Penguin.

ENDNOTE

   1.   Many of the cases that follow are developed in greater detail in Cottam & Cottam, 2001.

CHAPTER 9

The Political Psychology of Political Extremists

Immediately after the April 19, 1995, Oklahoma City bombing, Americans asked themselves, Who could commit such a violent act? Were Arab terrorists to blame? Or had some other group committed this act? When Timothy McVeigh and Terry Nichols were apprehended, many Americans had their first glimpse of men who would go to extremes because of their political ideas. Words like militias and patriots became part of our vocabularies. And more and more we wanted to understand these men. Were McVeigh and Nichols monsters or sociopaths, were they simply insane, or were they normal? How could a normal person commit such a horrific act?

Extremist groups have many different views and perspectives, as well as agendas. There are many extremist groups, in the United States alone. They are as diverse as White supremacist organizations such as the Aryan Nations, Ku Klux Klan, the National Alliance, and Spokane Skins; sovereign citizens who do not believe in the legitimacy of the federal government; and militias such as the Michigan Militia, whose members train so that they can defend the United States from the new world order. There are also tax protestors, antienvironmental and antiabortion extremists, terrorists, and gangs. Some extremist groups are associated with political parties, and some are just political parties.

Extremist groups are not only found in the United States, but also in other parts of the world. Other countries have their share of terrorist organizations (such as the Provisional Irish Republican Army in Northern Ireland), government sanctioned and unsanctioned paramilitaries/death squads (such as the United Self-Defense Forces of Colombia), and many racist groups, such as the National Front political party in France. As in the case of the United States, some of these groups are associated with political parties, others are not, and some are political parties. In addition, many have transnational contacts with one another (Kaplan & Weinberg, 1998). Often, extremists are also portrayed as members of the radical right, but it is important to note that although many extremist groups are found on the right of the ideological spectrum, plenty of groups are also found on the left of that spectrum. The actions of political extremists can range from bombing a building known to be empty to targeting an entire group of people for mass extermination, that is, genocide.

In this chapter, we present case studies of extremist groups. We examine racist groups in the United States, terrorist groups, terror committed by governments against their own people, paramilitaries/death squads, and the perpetrators of genocide. One of the central themes of this chapter is that political psychological studies of such people demonstrate that, under the right circumstances, the most ordinary people can be the perpetrators of extremist actions, or they can be passive bystanders who watch while such acts are carried out and do nothing to stop them. What is an extremist and what makes a person an extremist? An **extremist** is a person who is

excessive and inappropriately enthusiastic and/or inappropriately concerned with significant life purposes, implying a focused and highly personalized interpretation of the world. Politically, it is behavior that is strongly controlled by ideology, where the influence of ideology is such that it excludes or attenuates other social, political or personal forces that might be expected to control and influence behavior. (Taylor, 1991, p. 33)

Extremists, then, are concerned only with the logic of their own behavior and their ideological construction of the world. Extremists tend to disregard the lives of others. They also tend to disregard alternatives. As George and Wilcox (1996) write:

> In our study of extremism we have become very aware that all human beings have biases and tend to see events from certain perspectives. We recognize the "Rashomon" principle, whereby individuals tend to interpret, and even distort events in order to preserve their own integrity and sense of self-esteem. (p. 8)

In striving for consistency, then, regardless of what is true, "extremists believe what they prefer to be true" (George & Wilcox, 1996, p. 9). It follows that extremists are very resistant to change.

THE POLITICAL PSYCHOLOGY
OF POLITICAL EXTREMISTS

Political psychologists have some thoughts on why people are extremists. There are several explanations, ranging from personality attributes to the need for group conformity. Let us examine these insights more closely.

One thing that is clear is that political extremists, or fanatics, are not all suffering from mental illness. Take the case of Timothy McVeigh, who admitted orchestrating the Oklahoma City bombing, and who considered the deaths of 19 children "collateral damage" (a term used by the U.S. military to describe civilian death during times of war). After 25 hr of psychiatric evaluation, a psychiatrist "concluded that his patient was deeply depressed and singularly focused, but not insane" (Romano, 2001, p. 3). As the execution of McVeigh approached, the weekly magazine *Newsweek* published a special edition on evil, and the journalist (Begley, 2001) writing the story was quickly disabused of any notion that people who commit serial killings, mass genocide, or terrorist acts, like those committed by McVeigh or Ted Kazinski, the Unabomber, are irrational or insane. According to the psychiatrists and psychologists interviewed for the magazine article, we all have the capacity to commit evil acts.

> "The capacity for evil is a human universal," says psychiatrist Robert I. Simon. . . . "There is a continuum of evil, of course, ranging from 'trivial evils' like cutting someone off in traffic, to greater evils like acts of prejudice, to massive evils like those perpetrated by serial killers. But within us all are the roots of evil." (Begleg, 2001, p. 32)

People who commit extremist actions are typically lacking in empathy for others and tend to dehumanize their victims (witness McVeigh's proclamation that the children were collateral damage). However

> "you can have people who have a well-developed capacity for empathy, relating, who are very close to their friends, but who have been raised in an ideology that teaches them that people of another religion, color, or ethnic group are bad," says psychologist Bruce

Perry.... "They will act in a way that is essentially evil based upon cognition rather than emotion." But the heart and the head interact. People who grew up amid violence and cruelty are more susceptible to ideologies that dehumanize the other in favor of the self. (Begley, p. 33)

Having said this, there is disagreement in political psychology as to whether there are particular personality traits commonly found among political extremists. Studies of terrorists, for example, simply do not agree on this matter. Scholars such as de Cataldo Neuberger and Valentini (1996), Pearlstein (1991), and Post (1990) have attempted to identify common terrorist personality disorders. Others (Braungart & Braungart, 1992; Crenshaw, 2000; Rabbie, 1991; Ross, 1994; Silke, 1998) argue that there is no terrorist personality. According to Crenshaw (2000):

Most analysts of terrorism do not think that personality factors account for terrorist behavior, nor do they see significant gender differences. One of the basic research findings of the field is that terrorism is primarily a group activity. It is typically not the result of psychopathology or a single personality type. Shared ideological commitment and group solidarity are much more important determinants of terrorist behavior than individual characteristics. (p. 409)

Similarly, studies of torturers in Greece and Latin America do not find any particular personality syndrome that differentiates them from people who do not torture. For example, Mika Haritos-Fatouros (1988) did not find evidence of sadism or extreme authoritarianism in Greek torturers before they entered the armed forces. Rosenberg's (1992) studies of torturers in Argentina, although journalistic rather than scientific, described normal, career-minded officers who were in charge of the Argentine torture unit. Claudia Reyes-Quilodran (2001) argues that there appear to be two types of torturers: those motivated by ideology, training, and loyalty to the military; and those who are simple criminals—but she also found no particular personality type.

Although there does not appear to be a particular personality associated with political extremists such as terrorists, personality is not unimportant. One personality characteristic that is arguably important in explaining the actions of extremists is their response to authority. As we explained in chapters 2 and 7, in his work on the authoritarian personality, Altemeyer (1996) discussed the attributes of submission to authority, aggression against nonconformist groups, and conventionalism, which are strongly linked to right-wing authoritarianism, but other studies have demonstrated that it is not only people who are high in authoritarianism who can respond very strongly to instructions from authority. People with more education tend to at least say that they would resist authority. The **locus of control** personality trait influences susceptibility to authority. **Internals,** that is, people who believe they have considerable control over their fate, are more likely to resist authority than **externals,** people who believe the external environment determines strongly what happens to them (Blass, 1991; Kressel, 1996). Also, people who do not care much about the impression they make on others (low self-monitors) are less susceptible to authority's demands (Kressel, 1996). The series of experiments by Milgram (1974) are among the most often cited studies that demonstrate the power of authority.

In the Milgram (1974) experiments, subjects were told that they were going to participate in an experiment on learning. They were instructed, by an experimenter in a laboratory setting, to deliver shocks to a "learner" when he made a mistake (the learner was in fact a confederate in the experiment). With each mistake, the subjects were told to increase the electrical voltage.

When the learner started to moan, claiming a bad heart, the subjects were told to keep delivering the shocks, with instructions such as "The experiment requires you to go on," and "You have no other choice." More than 62% of the subjects delivered the highest level of voltage, ignoring the printed warnings of danger and the screams and protestations of the learner. Most of the subjects who persisted in delivering the shocks did so with great reluctance and asked for permission to discontinue the shocks, or called the experimenter's attention to their learner's suffering, demonstrating that the subjects did not hate the learners, nor did they even dislike them.

Examining the results of his study, Milgram (1974) argued that the subjects were not sadistic, because the context of the action had to be considered, that is, there is an important person–situation interaction effect. The experimenter appeared to have the legitimate authority to know what could be done, that is, how much electrical voltage the subject could endure. The subjects became integrated into a situation that carried its own momentum. The problem for individuals is how to become disengaged from a situation that has moved in an apparently terrible direction. In subsequent experiments, Milgram (1974) found that obedience diminishes rapidly if one person in a group refuses to obey. In addition, distance from the experimenter reduced compliance. If the experimenter sat next to the subject, compliance was high. The farther away he was physically, the more likely people were to refuse to continue administering the shocks. Personality plays a role, as well: Elms and Milgram (1966) found that people higher in authoritarianism were more likely to be obedient to authority.

Examining extremists, from a group perspective, also yields some interesting insights into their behavior. As Baumeister (1997) notes, extremist acts of violence are

> nearly always fostered by groups, as opposed to individuals. When someone kills for the sake of promoting a higher good, he may find support and encouragement if he is acting as part of a group of people who share that belief. If he acts as a lone individual, the same act is likely to brand him as a dangerous nut. (p. 190)

Let us return once again to social identity theory. In earlier chapters, we discussed the importance of belonging to groups and seeing those groups positively in comparison to others. When this is not possible, people look for some out-group to blame. Under normal conditions, conflicts among groups can occur over scarce resources, territory, values, ideology, status, security, power, and many other things (Fisher, 1990). In conditions of severe socioeconomic and political despair and depression, the environment is often conducive to the identification of one group as a **scapegoat**, a group that is blamed for all of society's illnesses. During hard times, the groups that people are particularly attracted to are those that "provide an ideological blueprint for a better world and an enemy who must be destroyed to fulfill the ideology" (Staub, 1989, p. 17). This is called **social causality** (Hogg & Abrams, 1988). Typically, a negative stereotype of that group is promulgated on a society-wide scale. Next, **social justification** occurs, wherein that group's poor treatment is justified. The most extreme form of this is **dehumanization** of the scapegoat, wherein those people are regularly described as less than human, and therefore deserving of treatment one would not administer to a human being. In Germany during the Hitler era, Jews were regularly vilified and called rats. In Rwanda, before that genocide, the Tutsis were called insects and cockroaches by the Hutu extremists. Under these conditions, hating the enemy becomes a noble and righteous cause in the minds of group members.

The identification of an out-group upon whom to place blame is important for groups and their members, in order to provide an explanation for their own circumstances, but, as noted in chapter 4, the group also offers individual members important psychological benefits.

Although there are certainly many reasons a person may join a group, such as ideology and a sense of social support, among others, once they become members, uniform views tend to reinforce the conformity of individuals. In addition, members face so-called psychological traps and the group experiences the escalation of commitment pattern discussed in chapter 4 (Taylor, 1991). People find themselves in circumstances that require a great amount of time and effort toward the accomplishment of the group's goals. It follows that the more investment a person makes in a goal, the harder it becomes to abandon the group, regardless of actual accomplishment of that goal. Commitment to a group, then—especially one that requires the use of violent behavior—is psychologically very demanding. The more acts of violence one commits, the more psychologically entrapped a person becomes.

At this point, we can pull together some of the patterns we have reviewed in individual and group behavior with the obedience-to-authority patterns present in the Milgram experiment. People are obedient not only to individual authority figures, but to groups and their authority structure, as well. Why? In chapter 4, we discussed several reasons for conformity in groups, including informational social influence, wherein people conform to group norms because they wish to be correct, and conforming enables people to gather information. Normative social influence was also mentioned, in which people conform in order to be liked.

Situational factors, such as group size and unanimity, affect conforming, as well. Commitment to the group is also an important situational factor. Consider what will happen if you are not loyal and obedient to a group. If you do not conform to group norms and goals, the most likely outcome is that everyone in the group will dislike you. In fact, you may even be expelled from the group, which can be very threatening, particularly when the group is cohesive, when members are isolated from other groups, and when the group is an important component of a personal identity.

Yet, there is a caveat, because how you conduct your deviance from a group makes a significant difference. For example, heretics who do not disavow their membership, but who deviate from the group, fare better than renegades who denounce their membership in a group, because a renegade is questioning the core values of a group, as opposed to questioning group tactics. Examples of this pattern can be found in Ezekiel's (1996) study of American neo-Nazis and Klansmen. Those groups tend to be highly fluid, with members moving in and out, but about one third of the members are hard-core loyalists. Those who leave the group without denouncing White racism can return. But those who denounce the racist ideas are branded "race traitors" and are despised.

An individual can be obedient to a group, even when the group acts in a way that is contrary to an individual's values. However, whether an individual is obedient depends on the social context in which the authority is being used, the character of the authority holders, and the nature of the demands that they make. Individuals are more likely to obey when the action is authorized by authority; when the action is routinized, making it mechanical and possible to do with little thought; and when the victim is dehumanized. Obedience is also more likely when the individual wants to comply, not because they necessarily agree with the activity, but because of the positive impression gained from compliance (Kelman & Hamilton, 1989; Sabini & Silver, 1993; Staub, 1989). Often, the most fanatical members become group leaders, and they act strongly to prevent dissension within the group.

Groups and their members interact in a symbiotic fashion, and being obedient to group norms and the demands of its authority are not simply the product of fear or rejection. Groups often indoctrinate members through initiation rites, training, and providing a feeling of being part of a family. These are the forming and norming stages of group development discussed in chapter 4. The process can be dramatic. Group members who have had to undergo severe initiations, or who have had to endure harsh pain and suffering to become a member, tend to be more committed to the group than group members who do not have to suffer to join the group (Aronson & Mills, 1959; Wicklund, Cooper, & Linder, 1967). Indoctrination and initiation rites can be brutal, giving the member who survives and becomes a member of the group a strong sense of belonging, having passed the test of strength and will. Indoctrination presents the member with a worldview. Torturers in Northern Ireland and Guatemala, for example, were often given horrifically brutal training and indoctrination in anticommunist ideology, the idea being that they were saving the country by torturing deviants (Conroy, 2000; Reyes-Quilodran, 2001). People do not want to let the group down. Staub (1989, 1999, 2000) and Kelman (1990), among others, argue that the factor of human needs must also be introduced to fully understand this type of phenomenon. Generally, the point is that people are not just cogs in these groups' machinery. The perception of hard times is deeply threatening to the extremists, and this activates basic survival needs. They join groups they think will satisfy those fundamental survival needs. The groups are more than social. Obedience and compliance with group norms, which demand extremism and violence, are done out of more than fear of rejection or punishment: They are done willingly. The group makes it easier, true enough. The group makes it possible for people to distance themselves from the violence, by distributing and diffusing responsibility for it. The group provides the moral authority for the actions the individual takes. Groups with this type of cohesion and dedication to a cause are more likely to experience groupthink (discussed in chapter 4), particularly if their leaders are charismatic and/or narcissistic and unwilling to hear disagreement or critical information.

Finally, research on how perpetrators of acts that are condemnatory perceive their own actions provides important insights on why people do things that cause great suffering and harm. Baumeister's (1997) research found that perpetrators see their actions as much less wrong than the victims do. They minimize the harm done and often explain their actions as justified by the evil nature of the victim. This is an example of patterns of perception described by attribution theory. We see this later, in the cases of racist antigovernment militias, and among torturers, terrorists, and those who commit acts of genocide.

The following illustrations of extremist groups enable us to flesh out some of these political psychological patterns.

EXTREMIST GROUPS

There are certainly many ways to classify extremist groups. In looking at these groups, we have found that there are not only too many groups to mention, but that there is considerable overlap in their views. For example, many militia and Klan groups believe in Christian Identity, just like those in the White supremacist group, Aryan Nations. We have done our best to simplify this classification. Therefore, rather than discuss the groups individually, presenting all of their views, we want to provide a more general discussion of each category, so that we have a macroview of those groups. We have also provided some discussion boxes that talk about certain groups more specifically.

Extremist Groups in the United States: Patriots, Ku Klux Klan, Skinheads, Neo-Nazis, and Others

The cluster of right-wing extremist groups in the United States and Europe includes a wide variety of groups loosely organized through a circuit of leaders and lieutenants (Ezekiel, 1996). The Southern Poverty Law Center is an organization that carefully tracks hate groups in the United States. It listed 602 active hate groups, as of 2000, and classified them into the Klan,

Neo-Nazi, Racist Skinhead, Christian Identity, Neo-Confederate, and Black Separatist groups. Estimates of membership size in these groups varies greatly. Abanes (1996) argues that there are possibly 5 to 12 million members, but the Southern Poverty Law Center and Center for Democratic Renewal maintain that hard-core membership is about 23,000–25,000, with another 150,000 sympathizers and possibly half a million interested enough to read movement literature (Ezekiel, 1996). The number of militias has dropped dramatically since the Oklahoma City bombing, from 858 in 1996 to only 194 in 2000 (*Idaho Spokesman Review*, 2001), because McVeigh's association with the militia movement discredited it. Given the breadth of the militia movements, there is not one single view or philosophy that can be used to describe all of the groups involved. However, there are a few elements that provide a basis for understanding their wide-ranging views. The members of these groups have four common beliefs (Abanes, 1996): (1) an obsessive suspicion of the government; (2) belief in antigovernment conspiracy theories; (3) a deep-seated hatred of government officials; and (4) a feeling that the U.S. Constitution, for all intents and purposes, has been discarded by Washington bureaucrats. Abanes also adds that most patriots believe that the government is illegitimate.

These groups hate government officials for what they see as excessive governmental regulation and restrictions, which intrude on

---

The Turner Diaries and the Order

The Turner Diaries is a fictional book written in 1978 by William Pierce, which is widely read by White supremacist groups. The book is supposed to be the diary of Earl Turner, a member of a White patriot group called The Order, which is part of a larger group called The Organization. In his "diary," Turner chronicles the actions of his group during a war (which occurs between 1991 and 1993) between the government and the Whites, after the government outlawed firearms. Turner describes an escalation of the war in which Jews, Blacks, and other people of color are killed by beatings, hangings, guns, and knives.

The book inspired a man named Robert Matthews to recruit some members of the Aryan Nations, a neo-Nazi group based in northern Idaho at the time, to form The Order, in 1983. "In the beginning the goals were loosely defined, but everyone agreed the new organization would fight for a territorial imperative that defined the northwestern United States as 'the last bastion of white predominance,' and called for its secession" (Ridgeway, 1995, p. 109). At first, the members used legitimate means to raise money, but they soon engaged in criminal activity, including armed robberies and counterfeiting. In June 1984, they murdered Jewish talk show host Alan Berg. Because of extensive law enforcement efforts, members of the group were eventually apprehended. Two members were given 150-year sentences for the murder of Berg (George & Wilcox, 1996).

---

their lives and violate their rights. For example, ranchers and loggers resent environmental regulation that they believe seriously and negatively impacts their way of life. The right-wing militias, Patriots, and Christian Identity groups live their lives according to their interpretation of the Constitution and Bill of Rights. One of the most important elements in their interpretation of the Constitution lies in the 14th amendment. In the patriot movement's view, no one may change the constitution. Before the 14th amendment, everyone was a natural citizen of the state or republic in which they were born. The 14th amendment grants citizenship to former slaves and others who become citizens of the federal government and receive benefits from it. This, in the view of the patriots, is an inferior and secondary form of citizenship, entered into by Americans who have been duped by the federal government and who unknowingly place themselves under the authority of that government by entering into illegal contracts with it (e.g., birth certificates, drivers licenses, and social security numbers). These documents make one a federal citizen and revoke the superior state citizenship. This particular interpretation of the 14th amendment is the reason why many patriots refuse to pay federal taxes. Another example of patriot thinking is found on the American Patriot Network (2002) homepage, where they ask, "How dead are the Bill of Rights?" They proceed to describe the ways in which the Bill of Rights has been unlawfully changed by the federal government via court cases or laws passed. For example, the 2nd amendment is said to be 90% dead. The culprit they point to is the Crime Bill of 1994, which banned 19 types of semiautomatic rifles.

An integral part of their group identity is the belief that the federal government is not only untrustworthy, but conspiratorial. As George and Wilcox (1996) explain:

> The range of conspiracy theories may be almost encyclopedic, but they all have one thing in common: some kind of diabolical plot by the dark forces to do in the champions of righteousness and freedom. The details vary considerably, but they usually involve secrecy and deception, complicated scenarios by which the people are fooled, sometimes even by those claiming to oppose the plotters. All this ends with the control or enslavement of the masses by a self-appointed elite. (p. 266)

More specifically, these theories range from a plot by the UN to establish a one-world government, to government coverups of UFOs. Many militia group members prepare themselves for armed conflict by stockpiling weapons, ammunition, and food, among other things, which they will need to survive. They believe that this is necessary because of the inevitable consolidation of the new world order. There are some small variations in the explanation of the true meaning of the new world order and who is behind it; however, it can be generalized as a wide conspiracy of different individuals, including international bankers, socialists, liberals, politicians, members of the military, and elites whose aim is to form a UN-centered, one-world government. Militia members are readying themselves to defend American sovereignty. The following song, which was written by Carl Klang and published in the patriot newspaper, *The Idaho Observer,* in February 1998, encapsulates these beliefs and demonstrates the extent of such theories.

EVIL, FILTHY, ROTTEN CONSPIRACY

Now have you seen them flying saucers
Or some of them black helicopters
Flyin' down low and over my back yard recently?
Seen them foreign troops in ninja suits
Leavin' imprints of their combat boots
In the meadow down near the neighbor next to me?
Heard they're buildin' concentration camps
From the rate hike off our postage stamps
To protect and defend their great democracy
Though my vote in the last election
Didn't quite match the same projection
Made by those beautiful talking heads on my TV
When I called them to complain—and asked them to explain
They just said that it proves you're not in the groove
Of the new majority
Well just between you and me—can't you just feel the conspiracy?
Can't you sense the hypocrisy as they call it democracy

Well it's a threat to your sanity, not to mention your liberty
And it's all an evil filthy rotten conspiracy . . .

So as they redirect our mail
And all our incoming phone calls
To the Central Intelligence Agency
We'll just hope and pray someday they'll see
That you and me are not the enemy
Nor do we believe in cult theology
And as their police try to bust us
We'll keep tryin' to find some justice
Though its hidden behind a wall of masonry
We'll keep working out our Salvation
With the feelin' and fear and tremblin'
Hopin' and praying someday that truth might set us all free
And just 'cause the media won't respond—don't mean there's nothin' going on
And brother what'll ya do if there's somethin' to
All the words inside this song? (p. 1)

An element of many of these groups is **Christian Identity,** an unusual reading of the Bible. Central to Christian Identity is that the notion that the true descendants of the Israelites are White Europeans. They also believe that White people descended from Adam and Eve, but non-Whites, whom they deem "mud people," came from another form of creation. Christian Identity believers also argue that Jews are descendants of Satan (as a result of Eve mating with the serpent). The religious doctrine justifies, in their minds, their derogation of African-Americans and their deep anti-Semitism (Bushart, Craig, & Barnes, 1998).

Not all right-wing extremist group members follow Christian Identity. However, racists and anti-Semites have found common ground with the Christian Identity movement, because both believe that the end of the world will occur after a battle between good and evil. The difference lies in the former believing that a race war will occur after the destruction of the Jews (government is a pawn of the Jews), with Whites emerging victorious; the latter "view Washington politicians as evil conspirators laying the foundation for the soon-to-be revealed Antichrist, whose reign of terror will end only when Jesus Christ returns to earth in glory" (Abanes, 1996, p. 3). How is it that they share such beliefs? According to Abanes (1996):

a preoccupation with the end-times is shared by Christians and White supremacists because many White supremacists emerged from mainstream Christian denominations. Unfortunately, these non-Christian defectors from the faith have borrowed heavily from their Christian roots, picking up those doctrines that are most appealing—especially beliefs associated with end-times—and blending them with racial prejudice. (p. 3)

Studies of these groups have found some of the same dynamics among individuals and groups that we described as generally pertaining to extremist groups. The members have a sense of injustice, of being deprived of their rightful status in society, of being left behind. They are concerned about, and threatened by, social change, including influxes of immigrants, perceived special privileges given to minorities and women, changes in gender roles, race-mixing and other trends (Ezekiel, 1996; Green, Abelson, & Garnett, 1999; Langer, 1990). There is little systematic analysis available of the leaders and members. One study, by Ezekiel (1996), argues that the groups draw from lower income sectors of White society, although the

Christian Patriots also draw from the middle class. One leader of the Michigan patriot movement, Robert Miles, put it bluntly: "We work with losers" (quoted in Ezekiel, 1996, p. 30). In fact, the decline in the militia movement is attributed in part to Timothy McVeigh, but also to the improvement in the economy during the last part of the 1990s, the improved availability of jobs, and the end of the Clinton administration, despite the irony of that administration's oversight of economic growth and prosperity. According to one former Michigan militia member, "The militia grew because of fear, and without fear, the militia will recede. People [i.e., militia members] have the feeling George Bush is America's savior. They have cable TV, and the beer's cold" ("McVeigh helped speed," 2001)

Membership tends to fluctuate, but committed leaders recruit constantly. Leaders such as Tom Metzger of the White Aryan Resistance are well-versed in the importance of using music and the Internet to recruit members. There are White supremacist recording labels, such as Resistance Records, and numerous racist bands with names like Angry Aryans (latest CD being *Racially Motivated Violence*), Blue Eyed Devils, and Beserkr (*Crush the Weak*). The leaders are men, and most of the members are, as well. Women are expected to perform traditional roles in the group (Ezekiel,

> **Morris Dees Takes On White Supremacists**
>
> Morris Dees, a lawyer with the Southern Poverty Law Center, brought some high-level suits against the United Klans of America in 1991 and Aryan Nations in 2000. The case against the Klan involved a 1981 murder of a Black teenager. Dees won the suit against the United Klans and several of its members. The headquarters of the Klan was sold and the proceeds given to the mother of the victim. The Klan was formed in 1866 by a group of Confederate soldiers, in order to amuse themselves. At first, the organization simply engaged in practical jokes, but soon evolved into a group that would intimidate, harass, whip, and murder Blacks (Ridgeway, 1995). Several Klan groups still exist, but the organization has been seriously weakened not only by the efforts of Dees, but also by the Federal Bureau of Investigation.
>
> In the case of the Aryan Nations, Victoria Keenan and her son Jason were driving by the compound of the Aryan Nations in North Idaho when their car backfired. The guards in the compound pursued them for 2 miles, and shot at them. After their car went into a ditch, they were then assaulted by the guards. Dees won $330,000 in compensatory damages and $6 million in punitive damages, for the woman and her son, against Saphire Inc., the corporate body of the Aryan Nations.

1996). The organizations glorify violence and reinforce group members' loyalty through rituals associated with religion and mythology, as well as by uniforms, banners, hierarchy, and symbols such as the swastika.

The International Connection

Is there an international movement of groups such as the militias, patriots, neo-Nazis, and skinheads? In their book, Kaplan and Weinberg (1998) tackle this question, providing an account of what they call the Euro-American right, which consists not only of extremist groups, but also of political parties. The authors examine the relationship between groups in the United States and Europe. They argue that there are several conditions evident in both Europe and the United States that have aided in the mobilization of this transatlantic movement. According to Kaplan and Weinberg (1998), "Movements are sustained interactions between aggrieved social actors and allies, and opponents and public authorities" (p. 77). These factors include the rise in the number of immigrants seeking a better life in advanced industrial countries, the weakening of the family, a changing economic situation, and less confidence in democratic institutions. The authors also suggest that the recent emergence of radical-right groups represents a counterrevolution against new social movements, such as environmentalism, women's movements, and so on.

The Euro-American right share a common subculture: "It consists of a shared set of myths, symbols, beliefs, and forms of artistic expression that set it apart on a transnational basis from other subcultures" (Kaplan and Weinburg, 1998, p. 18). They also have a common identity, which, for the most part, is White racial solidarity. However, cultural affinity, common historical experience, and shared destiny can also form the basis of this identity. Connections have been made across Europe and the Atlantic with like-minded groups (Lee, 1997). In fact, much of the influence is from east to west. These connections may be personal, a result of "movement entrepreneurs," who want to spread the word in person or distribute materials abroad. Contact could also be through a "cybercommunity." Kaplan and Weinberg (1998) conclude that the existence of such a movement is not an immediate threat to Western democracy. In other words, they are not a "single minded conspiratorial organization" (p. 77). Nevertheless, these connections do take place, and the conditions exist to keep the connections alive.

Terrorists

"Each year, terrorist groups commit hundreds of acts of violence." This is the sentence with which the authors started the section on terrorism 6 months before the attack on the World Trade Center in New York City on September 11, 2001. Before that attack, volumes of research and case studies on terrorist groups had already been produced. But so much of the thinking and behavior of terrorists and of terrorist organizations are still not understood, in part because they are very difficult to interview. In fact, there is still little agreement as to how to define terrorism. Crenshaw (2000), a leading scholar on terrorism, captures the essence of this debate:

> The problem of defining terrorism has hindered analysis since the inception of studies of terrorism in the early 1970s. One set of problems is due to the fact that the concept of terrorism is deeply contested. The use of the term is often polemical and rhetorical. It can be a pejorative label, meant to condemn an opponent's cause as illegitimate rather than describe behavior. Moreover, even if the term is used objectively as an analytical tool, it is still difficult to arrive at a satisfactory definition that distinguishes terrorism from other violent phenomena. In principle, terrorism is deliberate and systematic violence performed by small numbers of people, whereas communal violence is spontaneous, sporadic, and requires mass participation. The purpose of terrorism is to intimidate a watching popular audience by harming only a few, whereas genocide is the elimination of entire communities. Terrorism is meant to hurt, not to destroy. Terrorism is preeminently political and symbolic, whereas guerilla warfare is a military activity. Repressive "terror" from above is the action of those in power, whereas terrorism is a clandestine resistance to authority. Yet in practice, events cannot always be precisely categorized. (p. 406)

Crenshaw goes on to argue that the wide-ranging tactics used by terrorists further complicate the problem . For example, some use methods such as kidnapping and hostage taking, others bomb, some use assassination, some may use all of these, and some mix and match. Terrorism can also be state-sponsored, when independent non-state terrorist organizations are supported by states. They are also organized differently, ranging from hierarchical and centralized to anarchical and decentralized. Finally, classification of terrorist groups is complicated, because terrorist groups have many different goals and motivations.

We cannot settle the definitional debate here. Suffice to say that, for the purposes of this book, we have taken elements from existing definitions and include groups that are composed of small numbers of people who use, or threaten to use, systematic violence in order to accomplish a political goal. Acts of terrorism are symbolic, that is, the targets of terrorists are symbols of the state or of social norms and structure.

Terrorists do come from all socioeconomic classes, but the initial leadership tends to be held by middle- and upper middle-class people; the masses tend to be drawn from those with lower or working-class backgrounds. How do people become terrorists? One method is through public appeal. For example, Colonel Mu'ammar Qadhafi placed ads in newspapers all over the Muslim world. Many young men in Saudi Arabia are subject to a pervasive recruitment environment through the use of fatwas (religious edicts), fliers, and several media venues, asking them to fight jihad as part of their religious duty, in far away places such as Afghanistan, Chechnya, and Kashmir. Another recruitment tool is through personal contact. This is particularly true in the case of terrorist organizations, whose reliance on secrecy is key to their ability to survive, especially against state security organizations. Those who join terrorist groups usually do so gradually, through a series of steps that remove people from their old lives and lead them to new ones. When an individual joins an existing terrorist organization, there is usually a period of disassociation, when previous social and emotional ties are loosened. For some people, this process is started after some dramatic change in life, such as divorce, drug and alcohol abuse, or educational failure. Thus, understanding the personal motivations of those who join terrorist groups may be key to gaining insight into why people join them in the first place and why they are driven to commit acts of violence against others. An estimate of the number of terrorist incidents can be found in Figure 9.1.

Terrorist groups have the same dynamics that we described for other extremist groups. They attract people who have a very strong need to belong, who are often alienated from society, and whose attachment to the group is like that to a family. Post (1986b) argues that "underlying the need to belong is an incomplete or fragmented psychosocial identity, so that the only way the member feels reasonably complete is in relationship to the group; belonging to the group becomes an important component of the member's self concept" (p. 215). Yet, membership rates fluctuate. As we saw with the White supremacist groups, there appears to be a difference between those completely committed to a terrorist group, who derive all identity from the group, and those who were ambivalent about joining the group in the first place and who maintain the ability to think critically about the group (Post, 1986b). The latter often drop out. The enforcement of group norms is rigid, and members are isolated from other groups and associates. Taylor and Quale (1994) illustrate this in interviews with IRA activists, who describe how those who betray the organization are killed. The organizations also teach members how to become accustomed to violence, and they provide the diffusion of responsibility necessary to carry out acts of violence. Group norms are also solidified through the adoption of a common identity, ideology, and worldview. Nationalist terrorist groups, such as the

1-5-10-15-20-25-30-35-40-45-50-55-60-65-70-75

2000–2001	——— (15)
1990–1999	———————————————————————————————— (73)
1980–1989	—————————————— (32)
1970–1979	——— (11)
1960–1969	— (4)

FIG. 9.1. Terrorist incidents. This is the U.S. Department of State estimate of terrorist incidents over time, up to September 11, 2001. *Note:* From http://usinfo.state.gov

Kurdish PKK, Kosovo Albanian KLA, the Liberation Tigers in Sri Lanka, and the Basque separatist organization *Euskadi ta Askatasuna* (or ETA), attempt to consolidate national group identity and direct it in opposition to identity with the existing state (Byman, 1998).

The question of whether there is a particular terrorist personality was discussed earlier, with most scholars arguing that there may be some common characteristics, but no such thing as a terrorist personality syndrome. There remains disagreement as to whether or not terrorists have certain personality defects, however. A number of scholars argue that terrorists have had childhood experiences, such as humiliation and other negative experiences, producing lack of self-esteem, an inability to cope with stress, and propensity for aggression (Kaplan, 1981; Post, 1984, 1986b, 1987; see also, the arguments about childhood experiences in Milburn & Conrad, 1996). As mentioned, Post (1986b) argues that these people often are looking for something to belong to. He also maintains that there are two different personality types among terrorists: the anarchic-ideologue and the nationalist secessionist. The former comes from a dysfunctional family and rebels against their parents. They take certain political conditions, such as poverty and injustice, as analogous to parental authority and rebel against those situational conditions through terrorist actions. The nationalist-secessionist, on the other hand, was a loyal child and is obedient to authority, but rebels against social and political conditions they associate with the sufferings of their families.

In contrast to the personality-based models of terrorists are those grounded in a social learning theory (see chapter 4). From this perspective, "terrorism does not result from *dysfunctional* or defective personality traits; rather it is largely a result of societal influences and unique learning experiences that form the foundation of *functional* character traits or behavioral tendencies" (Ruby, 2002, p. 18). This is the view of Crenshaw, as noted earlier. From this perspective, terrorists are no more dysfunctional than a regular soldier in a regular army, but they differ, because the terrorist has no traditional army to join. Upon joining a terrorist organization, the members are subject to the cohesive group pressures discussed previously and in chapter 4. They are taught to conform to group standards, to minimize contact with outsiders, and to adopt group norms concerning actions to be taken against the perceived enemy. Often, as in the case of Northern Ireland, they are socialized to hold particular ideas and ideals: a sense that their group is threatened by another, a desire for autonomy, and ideology that is passed from generation to generation. They are also endowed with a notion of who the enemy is, and they carry a strong enemy stereotype or image (Mastors, 1998). Conspiracy thinking is also common in terrorist groups, and it is used to vilify and dehumanize the opposition. Terrorists often believe that they are forced to be violent and that the circumstances and nature of the opposition leave them with no choice (Taylor & Quayle, 1994). Finally, they are rewarded for successful acts of violence and are therefore more likely to act in that manner in the future (Ruby, 2002).

Since September 11, 2001, and in light of the violence in the West Bank in 2001 and 2002, the brand of terrorist known as **suicide bombers** has received considerable attention. What makes someone willing to commit suicide in order to ensure maximum effectiveness in a terrorist attack? The men who flew the planes into the World Trade Center and the Pentagon and the individuals who strap explosives to their bodies and blow up themselves and others in buses, restaurants, and other establishments populated by innocent civilians, are both frightening and mysterious. Who does it, and why?

Suicidal terrorist acts are not new and not unique to Middle Eastern terrorist organizations. Indeed, from 1983 to 2000, the Liberation Tigers of Tamil Eslam (the Black Tigers), in Sri Lanka, committed more suicide attacks than any other organization. Organizations that use terrorism vary in the extent to which suicide attacks are institutionalized in the organization's strategy. Some use this form of attack regularly; other organizations use it only occasionally and as a temporary tactic. According to Sprinzak (2000), neither Hamas nor Hezbollah have permanent suicide units, but recruit bombers on an ad hoc basis.

What motivates the bombers? First, not all suicide bombers are acting in pursuit of religious martyrdom. The Black Tigers, for example, are an ideological nationalist group, not a religious organization. The bombers are people willing to give their lives for a cause. They are not forced to give up their lives, but are recruited because they appear to have a predisposition to be willing to do so. According to Sprinzak (2000):

> recruiters will often exploit religious beliefs when indoctrinating would-be bombers, using their subjects' faith in a reward in paradise to strengthen and solidify preexisting sacrificial motives. But other powerful motives reinforce tendencies toward martyrdom including patriotism, hatred of the enemy, and a profound sense of victimization. (p. 69)

Suicide Bombers

149 suicide bombers, from 1993 to April 2002, were profiled by Dickey (2002) as follows:

Organization:

Al Aqsa (a branch of the PLO): 19.8%
Popular Front for the Liberation of Palestine: 4.9%
Hamas: 47%
Islamic Jihad: 28.3%

Age:

17–23: 67.1%
24–30: 30.9%
31–48: 2%

Education:

Primary school: 26.8%
Some or full high school: 37.6%
Some college: 35.6% (p. 30)

In the spring of 2002, suicide attacks by Palestinians in Israel increased dramatically and came to include young women bombers, as well as men.

Of particular interest, since September 11, 2001, is the terrorist organization responsible for the attacks in the United States. **Al Qaeda** represents a terrorist group with significant cross-cultural appeal. Al Qaeda recruits from many national groups that are spread across the world, from the Philippines to the United States. Although many are drawn from the Middle East (countries such as Libya, Egypt, Saudi Arabia, etc.), some of its members are Europeans whose parents immigrated from the Middle East and North Africa. Others were born and raised in the United States (i.e., Jose Padilla, an Islamic convert of Puerto Rican descent), and in European countries, notably France, and were first converted to Islam before joining al Qaeda. Before joining al Qaeda, many were also soldiers in holy wars fought in Afghanistan against the Northern Alliance, in Chechnya, and in Bosnia. Their participation in jihad represents a rite of passage for many, although it is certainly not a precondition for joining the organization. However, as is discussed next, participation in jihad in Afghanistan, against the Soviets, was the starting point for the founding members of the organization.

Al Qaeda has its roots in the war in Afghanistan in the 1980s. In 1979, the Soviet Union invaded Afghanistan in an effort to prevent the downfall of a pro-Soviet socialist government there. This was met with resistance by guerrilla forces of **mujahedin**, or holy warriors, fighting to get the infidel atheist Soviet Union out of Muslim Afghanistan. They came from all over the world. Many service organizations, based in Peshawar, Pakistan, provided training, spiritual guidance, and support for the mujahedin. One of the most prominent of these was Maktab al-Khidamat, headed by a Palestinian, Abdallah Azzam.

Osama bin Laden was among the many young men who went to fight the Soviets. He was the son of a wealthy Saudi family of Yemeni origin. The family fortunes came from their construction business, and Osama bin Laden's personal wealth came from the family fortune, as well as from his own ability to grow his money. Bin Laden was born in 1957 and was educated at King Abdul Aziz University in Jeddah. There he came under the influence of Azzam, who, it is thought, is responsible for bin Laden's interest in conducting a holy war against nonbelievers. Bin Laden is a follower of Wahabism, a puritanical fundamentalist version of Islam. After the Soviets invaded Afghanistan, bin Laden went first to Pakistan, where he used his wealth to provide services for refugees from the fighting in Afghanistan. In the mid-1980s, he went to Afghanistan and eventually became a warrior. After the Soviets were defeated, bin Laden and other mujahedin went home, many to join fundamentalist movements in their home countries. Al Qaeda evolved from the organizations developed during the fighting in Afghanistan.

Bin Laden and other veterans of the Afghan war were committed to the establishment of Islamic governments in their own and other countries. After the war, bin Laden returned to Saudi Arabia and worked for the family business, but he also retained his commitment to his religious goals. He and other veterans of the Afghan conflict founded al Qaeda, "the base," as an organization that would facilitate the establishment of fundamentalist governments. Bin Laden believed that his own government was not following the tenants of Islam, and the Saudi Arabian and Egyptian governments were his first target. Then, in August 1990, Iraq invaded Kuwait, and an international force led by the United States initiated a military campaign in the Persian Gulf. The Saudi government not only supported the war, but allowed U.S. troops to establish a presence in Saudi Arabia, where they stayed even after the war. This infuriated bin Laden and other members of al Qaeda. Saudi Arabia is home to two of the holiest places in the Muslim world, Mecca and Medina, and, in bin Laden's view, the royal family that governed Saudi Arabia had permitted an infidel imperialist power to occupy its lands. According to bin Laden,

> For over seven years the United States has been occupying the lands of Islam in the holiest of places, the Arabian Peninsula, plundering its riches, distancing its rulers, humiliating its people, terrorizing its neighbors, and turning its bases in the Peninsula into a spearhead through which to fight the neighboring Muslim peoples. . . . We . . . call on Muslim ulema, leaders, youths, and soldiers to launch the raid on Satan's U.S. troops and the devil's supporters allying with them, and to displace those who are behind them so that they may learn a lesson. The ruling to kill the Americans and their allies—civilians and military—is an individual duty for every Muslim who can do it in any country in which it is possible to do it, in order to liberate the al-Aqsa Mosque and the holy mosque [Mecca] from their grip, and in order for their armies to move out of all the lands of Islam, defeated and unable to threaten any Muslim. (December 23, 1998, quoted in Frontline, 1998)

Now al Qaeda and bin Laden had a new goal—driving the United States out of the Middle East. From this point on, the United States became al Qaeda's principal target. Bin Laden's opposition to the Saudi government eventually got him in trouble in Saudi Arabia, and he went to Sudan in 1992. His Saudi citizenship was revoked in 1994. In Sudan, he invested in legitimate businesses, set up terrorist training camps, and used his wealth to finance al Qaeda operations, as well as those of other terrorist organizations, including a bomb in a hotel in Yemen, whose target was American service personnel, and the World Trade Center bombing in 1993. In 1996, under pressure from the United States, Sudanese leaders made it clear bin Laden should leave, and he moved to Afghanistan. In August, 1996, he issued his first declaration of jihad, or holy war, against the United States.

In Afghanistan, bin Laden and al Qaeda established training camps for terrorists. Al Qaeda conducted its own attacks, but it also supported and contracted out attacks by other terrorist organizations, such as the Algerian group, the Salafist Group for Call and Combat. There have been extensive contacts and interactions with Egyptian Islamic Jihad or al Jihad, an Egyptian group committed to overthrowing the Egyptian government and establishing an Islamic state. Indeed, its leader, an Egyptian doctor named Ayman al Zawahiri, is a longtime mentor and advisor to bin Laden. In fact, in 2001, Islamic Jihad and al Qaeda formally merged to form al Qaeda al Jihad. Zawahiri is considered the number-two man in the organization. Among the terrorist actions al Qaeda is responsible for are the August 1998 bombings of two U.S. embassies in Kenya and Tanzania, which killed 224 people and injured over 4,500. The terrorist group is thought to have extensive financial networks and is very skilled at using the Internet for communications.

The political psychological roots of organizations like al Qaeda, and of people like bin Laden, are complex, but if you turn back to the discussion of extremist groups in America, the patterns are very similar. These are people who have watched their governments fail in wars (1967, 1973), fail to provide the masses with basic needs, and fail to provide what they see as opportunities for representation. In many cases, these people have experienced a sense of personal failure. Their level of frustration and cynicism is high. Joining extremist groups satisfies survival needs and provides them with a clear vision of what is wrong and what must be done to fix it. They associate in exclusive, tight-knit groups, undergo rigorous training, are severely punished if they defect, and often obtain admiration from others for their dedication to the cause. Their enemy is clearly identified, which helps cement group cohesion, and it is depersonalized and dehumanized as the imperialist demon, the infidel, and the evil exploiter of their people. Many al Qaeda members have not come face to face with the enemy (i.e., never having traveled to the United States or Europe and experienced Western culture firsthand), but many of the 9/11 hijackers had traveled to Europe to be educated and were exposed to Western culture. Several also spent time in the United States. However, in these cases, they were not positively impacted by this exposure. In fact, their interaction may have served to further cement their already defined anti-Western notions. For example, the suspected leader of the al Qaeda attack, Mohammad Atta, was an Egyptian who had legal residence in Germany and attended Hamburg University, as did many of the others in that Hamburg-based terrorist cell. Those who were born and raised in Europe often had experienced personal failure and/or felt unwelcome and discriminated against. These people may look to organizations such as al Qaeda to fill the void and provide them with a sense of group identity. The one terrorist who did not make the flight, because he was in jail on visa violations, Zacarias Moussaoui, was a French citizen of Moroccan decent, who was educated in Western schools. As briefly mentioned earlier, there are also several notable examples of European citizens who converted to Islam after a life-changing event, ultimately joining al Qaeda.

State Terror and Cultures of Fear

Another form of terror consists of systematic efforts by a government to terrorize the population of the country through torture, political murder, genocide, and other atrocities (Rummel, 1994, Sluka, 2000a). The goal is to terrorize the population into political submission and obedience, while opponents of the government are being violently repressed or killed. This occurs frequently and across the globe. Amnesty International reported, in 1996, that, out of 150 countries examined, 55% used torture and that 41% had politically motivated murders of opponents of the governing regimes (Sluka, 2000a). In Latin America during the 1970s and 1980s, this occurred in Brazil, Chile, Argentina, and Uruguay, among other countries. They came to be known as "dirty wars" and a new term was coined for victims of repression: *desaparecidos*, or the disappeared. Although the exact number of deaths is not known, and probably never will be known, approximately 30,000 people were killed or disappeared in Argentina, and between 9,000 and 30,000 people suffered similar fates in Chile. Torture was a common instrument used to extract information from "subversives," who included anyone expressing opposition to the government or associated with those expressing opposition to the government (relatives, friends, neighbors, students, etc.). Anyone was a potential target.

The populations of these countries were terrorized into submission through the gradual establishment of a **culture of terror**. As Sluka (2000a) describes:

> A culture of terror . . . is an institutionalized system of permanent intimidation of the masses or subordinated communities by the elite, characterized by the use of torture and disappearances and other forms of extrajudicial death squad killings as standard practice. A culture of terror establishes "collective fear" as a brutal means of social control. In these systems there is a constant threat of repression, torture, and death for anyone who is actively critical of the political status quo. (pp. 22–23)

Typically, in these situations, people have little access to substantiated information. Rumors abound, but there is little concrete

---

State-Sponsored Terrorism

State-sponsored terrorism occurs when a state supports a terrorist organization either directly or indirectly. In its report on state-sponsored terrorism, the U.S. government has identified Cuba, Iran, Iraq, Libya, North Korea, Sudan, and Syria as governments who support or engage in terrorism. Libya, led by Colonel Muammar Qadhafi, is an example of a country that not only engages in terrorist activity, but also backs terrorist organizations. Libyan agents were accused of the 1988 bombing of Pan Am Flight 103, which exploded over Lockerbie, Scotland. UN sanctions were imposed on Libya until 1999, when Qadhafi surrendered two men. They were tried in a Scottish court, and, in January 2001, one was found guilty and the other acquitted. In the past, Qadhafi has also been accused of supplying many terrorist groups with weapons and training, including the Provisional Irish Republican Army and various Palestinian groups.

Like Libya, the North Korean government has also been accused of engaging in and backing terrorist activity. For example, in 1983, a bomb exploded, killing 17 South Korean officials who were visiting Burma (Myanmar). Two North Korean officers were caught and confessed. In another incident, in 1987, Korean Airlines flight 858 was the target. All 115 people aboard were killed in that midair bombing. North Korea is also providing a safe haven for members of the Japanese Communist League–Red Army Faction, who hijacked a Japanese Airlines flight to North Korea in 1970.

---

information about what is happening, to whom, and how. Lack of concrete information increases fear of the unknown, and it allows the average person to ignore what is going on or to not even try to find out, because, if one knows, one may be the next victim. Knowledge is dangerous in these situations, so people hunker down, attend to their own personal situations, and try not to make waves. This facilitates the state's control of the population, by making the political killings possible and the population, passively acceptant. In these cases, the entire population becomes a massive bystander.

The Dirty War in Argentina

In 1976, the Argentine military overthrew President Isabela Perón, after a period of economic and political turmoil. During the preceding years, in the late 1960s and early 1970s, the military had begun a campaign against a leftist guerrilla organization, the Montoneros, who engaged in various acts of political violence, such as blowing up banks and kidnapping wealthy people. In response, right-wing death squads were formed, which then proceeded to kill even more people than the Montoneros killed. By the time the military took power in 1976, it had already suppressed the Montoneros. It then turned to any other apparent dissidents. Those not executed immediately were taken to various locations for the extraction of information. Among the most notorious was the Navy Mechanics School, where people were tortured and killed. But not all prisoners were killed: Some were turned into informants, and some survived by performing important functions for the unit, similar to the concentration camps in Nazi Germany. Others, after being tortured, were drugged, stripped naked, placed in airplanes, and thrown, alive, into the Atlantic Ocean. These were some of the many who simply disappeared. In response, Argentine society became silent. The major exception were the mothers of some of the disappeared. These brave women assembled every Thursday at the Plaza de Mayo, wearing white scarves bearing the names of their missing children. Known as the Madres de la Plaza de Mayo, they still assemble every Thursday, still seeking to know what became of their children.

The behavior of the torturers was reflective of the patterns discussed earlier. They were a tight unit composed of carefully selected men committed to the idea that they were saving Argentina from its own worst enemies: political activists. The torturers were isolated, living in the Navy Mechanics School building and permitted to see their families only three times per month (Rosenberg, 1992). They were well rewarded with money and other perks, such as the personal belongings of those they disappeared. They dehumanized their victims and joked about them, referring to two French nuns who were tossed into the ocean as "the flying nuns," for example. The torturers used euphemisms for their actions. When prisoners were thrown out of planes into the ocean they were "transferred" or "sent up." Torturers referred to the administration of electric shocks as "giving the machine" (Rosenberg, 1992, 90). Many of the torturers believe to this day that they were only doing their duty and that the victims were to blame for their treatment. In the words of one torturer:

> At first, I'll be honest, it was hard to accustom ourselves to put up with torture. We're like everyone else. The person who likes war is crazy. We all would have preferred to fight in uniforms, a gentlemen's fight where you all go out to have dinner afterward. The last thing we wanted to do was interrogate.
>
> In the first phase of the war everyone who was captured was executed. . . . We knew if we put them into the courts they would ask for all the guarantees of the system they were attacking. They'd have been freed. . . . Let's say that ten thousand guerrillas disappeared. If we hadn't done it, how many more people would have died at the hands of the guerrillas? How many more young people would have joined them? It's a barbarity, but that's what war is. (quoted in Rosenberg, 1992, pp. 129–130)

This particular torturer simply saw this as another justifiable battle, not something to be ashamed of.

In addition, the silence of Argentine society, as in so many other cases, encouraged the implementors of state repression to continue with it. They did, indeed, have support for their actions. The individual just quoted also stated:

> We had the backing of the church. . . . Not that priests would say 'go ahead and torture,' but that the church said there were two groups here and we were the ones who

were right. I really feel that any armed forces with a decent level of culture and human feeling would do the same as we did. (quoted in Rosenberg, 1992, p. 130)

This form of terror was extremely effective in silencing Argentine society. Indeed, when the military left power, it did so because it lost a war with Great Britain over the Falklands/ Malvinas Islands, not because of popular protest of the brutality of the regime.

Paramilitaries/Death Squads

Violence can also be committed by organized groups, called paramilitaries or death squads, on behalf of a state, whether sanctioned by that state or not. Usually, the state will either turn a blind eye to the actions of these groups or drag its feet when it comes to apprehending them. Paramilitaries and death squads are difficult to define distinctly. Sluka (2000a) defines **death squads** as "progovernment groups who engage in extrajudicial killings of people they define as enemies of the state" (p. 141). Cubides (2001) defines **paramilitaries** as "organizations that resort to the physical elimination of presumed auxiliaries of rebel groups and of individuals seen as subversive of the moral order. . . . They mostly operate through death squads" (p. 129). Clearly, they are part of the same organization. They often act as a close-knit clandestine organization, which many know about, but whose members try to hide their association with the group, although the leader of the largest paramilitary in Colombia is well known and the paramilitary has a Web site. They kidnap, torture, and kill victims identified as belonging to political groups they believe are undermining them and their country. Thus, the element of intensely perceived threat to the group operates in these cases, as in the others discussed in this chapter.

Death squads and paramilitaries are effective, insofar as they not only destroy the opposition, but terrorize into silence those who object to their activities. Death squads and paramilitaries have appeared in many countries experiencing severe political instability, and they are not confined to the third world. The Protestant–Loyalist paramilitaries in Northern Ireland— the Ulster Defense Association and Ulster Volunteer Force and the loyalist death squads, the Ulster Freedom Fighters, Red Hand Commandos, Protestant Action Force, and others—have killed around 700 Catholic civilians (Sluka, 2000b). There were many paramilitaries and death squads operating in Latin America during the era of repressive military regimes in the 1960s and 1970s, as well as during the civil wars in Central America during the 1970s and 1980s. In El Salvador, for example, a civil war was being fought between the government and leftist rebels called the Farabundo Martí Liberation Front, who wanted to gain control of the government. The ARENA party was the most militant of the right-wing parties in El Salvador and was known to be associated with death squads. Many people from political parties, labor organizations, peasant organizations, universities, and the clergy died at the hands of these squads, if they were even thought to have been colluding with the enemy.

The Colombian government has been battling the leftist Revolutionary Armed Forces of Colombia (FARC) and the National Liberation Army (ELN) for over 30 years. Although the army is deeply engaged in this war, some Colombians have taken it upon themselves to defend their country from the FARC and the ELN. On December 22, 2000, the paramilitary group called United Self-Defense Forces of Colombia (AUC) declared war on these groups and their supporters (Wilson, 2001a). The AUC has become infamous for its brutal acts of violence used in their counterinsurgency campaign. For example, in April 2001, in the village of Naya, at least 40 civilians were killed with machine guns, machetes, and chain saws (Wilson, 2001b). Allegations of army collusion have led to questions of whether or not they really want to put an end to such activity. Sixty-two members of the AUC were finally apprehended in April, and

Colombian President Andres Pastrana argued that, despite international and domestic criticism, this signaled that the government is not tolerating their activities.

THE PERPETRATORS OF GENOCIDE

The final act of political extremists that we look at here is genocide. In some cases, such as Rwanda, genocide is planned by an organized group of political extremists. But in other cases, such as the Holocaust in Europe during World War II, it is the product not only of a group (the SS), but also of a large, complex bureaucratic system. In addition, having the discussion in this chapter should not mislead readers into thinking that genocide is only the product of extremist groups. In theory, the conditions that produce genocide can occur anywhere, and genocide can be committed by ordinary people.

What is genocide? The UN defines **genocide** as "acts committed with the intent to destroy in part or in whole a national, ethnic, racial, or religious group as such," which Staub (2000, p. 8) objects to on several grounds. First, it does not include political groups as specific possible targets of genocide. Second, it groups killing the group "in whole" or "in part" as constituting genocide, whereas Staub argues that killing "in part" is mass killing. Mass killing may kill many people, as does genocide, but genocide as an act is designed to eliminate the group from the face of the earth.

Genocide is a result of an intense feeling of frustration and threat, produced by a combination of many of the psychological patterns discussed in chapters 3 and 4—social identity factors, stereotyping, and group loyalties—usually operating in the context of difficult social economic and political circumstances. As Staub (1989) explains:

> Powerful self-protective motives then arise: the motive to defend the physical self (one's life and safety) and the motive to defend the psychological self (one's self-concept, values, and ways of life). There is a need to both protect self-esteem and to protect values and traditions. There is also a need to elevate a diminished self. (p. 15)[1]

If an enemy is not readily identified as the cause of the condition, one is created: a scapegoat. Although some argue that certain cultures are more disposed to this than others (e.g., Staub, 1989), the potential for violence of this magnitude exists in most cultures. The more cohesive a group is, the most likely the potential, particularly when it is accompanied by a sense of superiority. This is especially evident when nationalism is strong in a country. Strong respect for authority and strong inclination for obedience, which everyone has to some degree, are other predisposing characteristics for mass killing and genocide. Those characteristics make it more likely that personal responsibility will be relinquished and that leaders will be followed without question. In addition, people are susceptible to the "foot in the door" technique, wherein they will respond positively to a small request, then become much more likely to respond positively to subsequent requests. Freedman and Fraser (1966) argue that, in the process of complying to first one, then another, request, people change their attitudes about what they are doing, and they may also change their attitudes about themselves (from, for example, "I'm not the kind of person who hits others" to "I am the kind of person who hits others, and hitting is not a bad thing to do").

In the twentieth century, there were a number of horrific cases of genocidal violence. Genocide occurred in Turkey, where approximately 1.5 million Armenians lost their lives from 1915 to 1917, and in Cambodia, where 2 million died from 1975 to 1979. The greatest loss of life in a genocide took place in the Holocaust during World War II, but the genocide in

Rwanda, which took the lives of over 1 million, occurred in the space of 3 months, from April through June of 1994, a kill ratio five times greater per day than during the Holocaust. The Holocaust and the Rwanda genocide offer evidence of all of the political psychological patterns we discussed earlier.

The Holocaust

As we have seen in the previous chapter, Germans were strongly nationalistic, and hence devoted to the nation as a group. Germany had suffered terribly from the demands of the Treaty of Versailles and the Great Depression of the 1930s. The Weimar Republic was seen as a government imposed by the victors of World War I, and there was considerable political instability on top of the social and economic problems. In 1933, Adolf Hitler achieved his goal of being appointed chancellor of the German Reichstag, or parliament, and was able to capture the mantle of German nationalism. His regime, the Third Reich, once established, instituted a repressive political system that made dissent increasingly dangerous. The SS (*Schutzstaffeln*, i.e., security echelon), which began in 1922 as Hitler's personal security force, later became the organization responsible for most of the genocide. When Hitler came to power, he established control over the entire police system in Germany, and used it to repress dissent. The concentration camps were set up in 1933, but initially they were used to detain political enemies from leftist political parties, the clergy, liberals, and "undesirables," such as homosexuals (Dicks, 1972).

Thus, the German nation held the in-group quality previously discussed, the political and economic situation contained the ingredients that motivate the search for a scapegoat in order to bolster positive group esteem, and Jews were an easy target for vilification and dehumanization by the Nazis. Political repression made resistance difficult and passive acquiescence easy. For those who complied, resistance was far more difficult than under the conditions of the Milgram (1974) experiment, and we saw how many complied under those weak conditions. Finally, the Holocaust did not occur overnight. It was a gradual process beginning in 1933, with relatively mild (compared with what was to come) forms of discrimination against Jews in things like employment and civil rights. Later, they were prohibited from owning businesses and were forced to wear a yellow six-pointed star to identify them as Jews. The deportation of Jews to concentration camps began in 1938, but mass extermination in the concentration camps did not come until the order was given by Hitler in 1941, by which time the maltreatment of, and discrimination against, Jews had become normal. These characteristics of German politics and political psychology help us understand both the willingness to identify with the nation, to vilify a scapegoat, and, for those who did not agree with the government, to become passive bystanders.

Still, there are other important ingredients in this case that help us understand how Germany went from a condition of intolerance, repression, and scapegoating to the establishment of a giant death machine that sought ultimately to annihilate the Jewish population of Europe. A look at the characteristics of the Nazi leadership, as well as the followers who carried out the genocide, is also important. Many Nazi leaders claimed that they did what they did because they were following orders, behaving like good citizens and soldiers. But this is far too simple an explanation of their deeds. They did not just follow orders, but willingly carried out and developed enormous acts of cruelty designed not only to kill, but to make victims suffer terribly before they died. Studies have been done of leaders in the SS and report both significant elements of authoritarian personality in many, and fanatical loyalty to the SS, which then led to a refusal to disobey orders or to admit to qualms about carrying out genocide (Dicks, 1972; Steiner, 1972; Staub, 1989).

SS training techniques were similar to those that we have described in other extremist groups—harsh discipline, ideological indoctrination, glorification of the group, and fanaticism. In addition, belonging to the SS provided career opportunities, which was reportedly important for many. The people who participated in the killings of Jews did so under the auspices of authorities who they viewed as legitimate. By obeying these legitimate governmental authorities, perpetrators' judgment was subordinated to them. That being so, they were able to participate in the murdering of Jews, despite, in some cases, personal misgivings and feelings of guilt. Dicks (1972), a psychiatrist who interviewed SS officers imprisoned for their crimes against humanity, has an interesting assessment of these men. He notes their ordinariness, but also the fact that they

> at some point crossed the line between their previous "law abiding" lives and their subsequent killer careers. And—their SS roles ended or interrupted—these same "fiends incarnate" in various ways disappeared quietly into civilian life, in some instances resumed orderly and normal careers, and are in prison "the easiest convicts to handle." (p. 234)

Dicks (1972) and Lifton (1986) both believe that the SS were able to oversee and participate in the extermination of millions of people because they could split or compartmentalize those actions from the rest of their lives. Hence, they could be loving fathers at home and murderers at work. They varied in personality, of course, some coming to the extermination of Jews reluctantly, others with enthusiasm. One generalization that can be made is that they were, not insane, but were, for personal reasons, susceptible to the SS indoctrination, and thereafter group dynamics and the nature of fanaticism took over.

In addition to the group dynamics, the Nazi political system had some important elements that facilitated the size of the genocide. Much of this was done in concentration camps, but the political police and *Einstazgruppen* (special mission groups) in the SS units followed the German army as it swept eastward through eastern Europe and executed thousands of undesirables—Jews, Gypsies, communists, homosexuals, and others: Typically, they were rounded up, a big ditch was dug, and they were shot and thrown into the ditch, dead or alive. The task was extremely difficult, even for the most dedicated Nazis. Personal contact with those who were to be executed proved to be a major problem. The *Einstzgruppen* men were actually told they did not have to participate in the executions, because the officers understood that compelling them to do so could backfire and break the units (Browning, 1992). They were also given plenty of alcohol and were required to work only for short periods of time.

Depersonalization was also important in facilitating the genocide. The camps were organized in such a way that personal identification with the victims did not need to occur. Gas chambers were constructed to kill on a massive scale and to eliminate personal responsibility for the killing. Some Jews were spared, so that they, not the SS, could remove gold from the mouths of victims, collect their clothing, and so on. Then there was the massive bureaucracy that divided the entire process, provided bureaucratic rules guiding the process, and permitted people who participated in the process of exterminating the Jews to deny personal responsibility, (Sabini & Silver, 1993). The engineer who drove the cattle cars filled with people destined for the gas chambers could avoid responsibility, because he just drove the train, he did not kill anyone. Different ministries handled different portions of the destruction of the Jewish population, one taking their property, another firing them from their jobs, another rounding them up, and another sending them off to die.

This situation parallels the Milgram (1974) obedience experiments described earlier. In those experiments, the learner (the person who was supposedly receiving electrical shocks) was out of view of the teacher (the person administering the shock). In some ways, this situation allowed the learners to be depersonalized, making it easier for the participant to administer such high levels of shock. This situation also parallels the Milgram experiment because the teacher did not feel responsibility for shocking the learner. This **diffusion of responsibility** occurs when there is more than one person present in the situation to take all or some of the responsibility for the outcomes. In the Milgram experiment, many of the participants asked the experimenter if he was going to take responsibility for whatever happened to the learner. When the experimenter responded that he would, this gave the participants a green light to continue shocking the learner.

Rwanda

For roughly 3 months in the spring of 1994, the international community witnessed, and did nothing to stop, the genocide of Tutsis and moderate Hutus by more extremist Hutus in Rwanda. In public view, Tutsis were systematically rounded up and shot, stabbed, beaten, or hacked to death with machetes. The *New York Times* reported, on April 10, 1994, just 4 days after the violence started, "that 'tens of thousands' were dead, 8000 in Kigali [the capital city] alone, and that corpses were in the houses, in the streets, everywhere" (quoted in Powers, 2002, p. 256). How could this have happened?

Rwanda, like many African countries, was colonized by Europeans—first Germany, then Belgium. Before colonialism, the Hutus and Tutsis lived in relative harmony. They spoke the same language, practiced the same religion, and were economically interdependent. Tutsis were herders and Hutus usually were farmers. As Peterson (2000b) notes, the "caste system was largely apolitical: Tutsi came to mean 'rich,' someone with many long-horned cows; Hutu, or 'servant' came to mean someone with fewer than ten cows" (p. 258). Under certain circumstances, a Hutu could become a Tutsi. Eventually, the Tutsi, along with a few Hutu, became the economic and political elite.

When the Belgians arrived in Rwanda after World War I, they sought to impose their own colonial administration. Even though Hutus were the majority, the Belgians chose to put Tutsis in positions of power. The Belgians chose the Tutsis because they had aquiline features and thus looked more similar to the Belgians than did than Hutus; therefore, the Belgians reasoned, the Tutsis must be the superior group (Human Rights Watch, 1999). The Belgians created a system of colonial administration in which the Tutsis were favored in jobs and education. Ethnic identity cards were issued. Tutsis became the administrative elite for Belgian colonial rule. Because they were able to benefit from the colonial system, Hutus considered Tutsis an elitist class, and an arm of the colonial state. Ethnicity was thereby politicized by colonialism and would return to haunt Rwanda many times. Rwanda gained its independence from Belgium in 1959, when the Hutu overthrew the colonizers. During this drive for independence, many Tutsis were driven into exile.

By the late 1980s, the Tutsis in exile desired a permanent home and wanted to return to Rwanda. However, in 1986, the Hutu government, led by General Juvenal Habyarimana, argued that Rwanda was overpopulated and could not accommodate the refugees. By July 1990, the government seemed to be making progress toward their accommodation. Habyarimana not only needed to facilitate the return of the Tutsi refugees, but also to establish a democratic government that replaced a one-party state dominated by him (Human Rights Watch, 1999). On October 1, 1990, hoping to overthrow Habyarimana, the RPF left Uganda and attacked a small detachment of the Rwandan military. From there, they made their way to Kigali, the capital. In response, Habyarimana falsely claimed that the RPF had actually attacked the capital, hoping to mobilize Hutus against the RPF and to gain the support of the international community. The government cracked down and 13,000 people were arrested and detained

(Human Rights Watch, 1999). Habyarimana's strategy was to divide those Hutus who supported him from those Tutsis and Hutus who collaborated with the enemy. This resulted in the deaths of many Tutsis and moderate Hutus.

By 1991, support for Habyarimana was waning, as opposition parties demanding change began to emerge. Habyarimana and his supporters created a militia known as the *Interahamwe,* whose members were allowed to attack Tutsis without any repercussions. Civilian defense groups were also created. But the RPF continued to make advances and forced the Habyarimana government to enter into negotiations. The RPF and the government finally signed a cease-fire in Arusha, Tanzania, in July 1992, and a series of agreements, which became known as the Arusha Accords, were finally signed in August 1993. This was a power-sharing agreement wherein military commanders would be 50–50 Tutsi–Hutu, and troops would be 40% Tutsi and 60% Hutu. This clearly did not reflect the distribution of Tutsi and Hutu population in Rwanda, which was 14% and 85%, respectively. In an attempt to monitor the implementation of the accords, on October 5, 1993, under the name the UN Assistance Mission in Rwanda, the UN finally allocated 2,548 peacekeeping troops. Despite the accords, the killing of Tutsis continued, but Hutu extremists were planning much worse to come.

On April 6, 1994, Habyarimana was returning from Tanzania, when his plane was hit by two surface-to-air missiles. Even though the identity of those responsible is not certain, after the news of his death broke, the Hutus mobilized. A well-organized and systematic campaign to rid Rwanda of Tutsis, and of Hutus who were suspected of not supporting the government-backed campaign to eradicate the Tutsis, was begun by the armed forces, including the police and the paramilitaries—the *Interahamwe* and the *Impuzamugambi*. This campaign lasted roughly 3 months, and it is estimated that over 1 million people were killed. By April 21, after the murder and mutilation of 10 Belgian peacekeepers, the UN withdrew the rest of its forces from the country. The slaughter of Tutsis continued unabated for 3 months. When it ended, as one Hutu told a journalist "It's not out of kindness . . . but because there are so few Tutsis left alive" (Peterson, 2000b, p. 288).

In July 1994, the RPF defeated the Hutu government. Paul Kagame, the leader of the RPF, installed Pasteur Bizimungu as president. A Hutu, Bizimungu was chosen to reflect the diversity of the new administration, although it is widely believed that Kagame was running the government from behind the scenes (Simpson, 2000b). In March 2000, Bizimungu resigned, and Kagame was chosen by Parliament to officially become the president of Rwanda.

For the first time since independence, the Tutsis were the governing ethnic group. Yet, the conflict does not seem to be over, because the *Interahamwe* militia has regrouped and is now waging a war against the government, from the Congo. This has prompted Rwandan and Ugandan troops, together with the Congolese rebel group, the Congolese Rally for Democracy, to wage a war against the Congolese President Laurent Kabila's (Kabila was assassinated on January 17, 2000, and his son Joseph became president) government troops and the Rwandan and Burundian militia fighters (Talbot, 2000). Because ethnicity is the primary basis for group loyalty, and served as a basis to the conflict, the question remains, How long will Tutsis be able to remain in power?

The Rwanda genocide shares many of the characteristics of the Holocaust, but there are also some important differences. Social and economic conditions in Rwanda before the massacre were difficult, as was the case in Germany when Hitler came to power. Rwanda was overpopulated and one of the poorest countries in Africa. All but 5% of its land was under cultivation, the average woman had nine children, and hunger was rampant (Peterson, 2000b). The majority Hutus had suffered significant strategic losses to the Tutsi rebel forces and faced the prospect of having to share power with them. Germany too had experienced the defeat of World War I, which was a factor in setting the stage for that genocide. In addition, as in

Germany, there was a legacy of Hutu–Tutsi stereotyping, which had been worsened through the influence of the colonial powers. By the time this holocaust took place, Tutsis were dehumanized by the Hutus, who called the Tutsis *inyenzi*, cockroaches. The Hutu extremists were organized into a political party, the *Mouvement Révolutionnaire National pour le Développement* (National Revolutionary Movement for Development [MRND]), which, in turn, had the paramilitary organization, the *Interahamwe*. The *Impuzamugambi* were associated with the hardline Hutu organization, the *Coalition pour la Défense de la République* (Coalition for the Defense of the Republic). The party and its leaders promoted an ideology of "Hutu power," complete with a document of anti-Tutsi principles, such as "every Hutu should know that every Tutsi is dishonest in business. His only aim is the supremacy of this ethnic group. . . . All strategic positions . . . should be entrusted to Hutus. . . . The Hutu should stop having mercy on the Tutsi" (quoted in Power, 2002, p. 339). Any Hutu who did not agree was considered a traitor. Again, this resembles Germany with the Nazi party and Nazi ideology.

As in Germany, this genocide was planned in advance by the Hutu political and military leaders. The Rwandan army began to train the *Interahamwe* in 1990, which resembled the Nazi SS, by offering members strong psychological and material rewards. Prominent Hutu leaders began publicly to call for the elimination of the Tutsis, as early as 1992. For example, Leoin Mugesera, a member of the MRND, stated in 1992, "The fatal mistake we made in 1959 was to let [the Tutsi] get out. . . . They belong in Ethiopia and we are going to find them a shortcut to get there by throwing them into the Nyabarongo River. I must insist on this point. We have to act. Wipe them all out!" (quoted in Power, 2002, pp. 339–340) And finally, as in the case of the German commanders of the Holocaust, who claimed to be only following orders, the perpetrators of this violence have demonstrated little remorse.

But there are differences in these genocides. Rwanda's was not as technical, depersonalized, and hidden as Germany's was. There was no complex bureaucracy that carried out the genocide in bits and pieces. Here, every Hutu was either involved in the killing or hiding to avoid having to participate in the killings. Although this permitted diffusion of responsibility, as was the case in Germany, the average citizen took a hand in the direct killing in Rwanda, that is, publicly hacking Tutsis with machetes and clubs, stabbing them, or, if merciful, shooting them. As a *Frontline* (1995) report states:

> The main agents of the genocide were the ordinary peasants themselves. . . . Even in the cases where people did not move spontaneously but were forced to take part in the killings, they were helped along into violence by the mental and emotional lubricant of ideology. We can see it for example in the testimony of this seventy-four-year-old "killer" captured by the RPF: "I regret what I did. . . . I am ashamed, but what would you have done if you had been in my place? Either you took part in the massacre or else you were massacred yourself. So I took weapons and *I defended the members of my tribe against the Tutsi.*" (p. 4)

BYSTANDERS AND ALTRUISTS

In New York City, one night in 1963, a woman named Kitty Genovese was stabbed to death. Her assailant beat and stabbed her for close to an hour, while dozens of people heard her screams and saw her being attacked, but did nothing. This tragic story is often used to illustrate the bystander phenomenon—when people do nothing to help others. Why does this happen? There is a tendency to blame the bystanders as being apathetic or uncaring. But researchers Latane and Darley (1970) argued that situational factors can explain the lack of help given to Kitty Genovese. When people are bystanders in an emergency situation, they sometimes experience *pluralistic ignorance*. They do not know how to respond, so they look to others to see how to respond (much like informational social influence, described in chapter 4). The problem is, everyone is looking at everyone else to figure out how to respond. Unfortunately, the result is that bystanders become paralyzed and do not respond at all. A second situational determinant, which can often explain the lack of help given to those in emergency situations, is **diffusion of responsibility**. If you were the only person available to help, then you would have 100% of the responsibility to give help. But if just one other person is present, then your sense of responsibility drops to 50%. The more people who are present in a situation, the more diffused is responsibility. This is partly the result of group characteristics. When people are part of a group, there is a diffusion of responsibility, and people feel less compelled to intervene and help. Many analysts believe that the **bystander phenomenon** is a crucial component in genocide.

Bystanders know, at least implicitly, that something wrong is happening, but they do nothing about it. Bystanders can be a person, a group, an organization, or a country. Indeed, the entire international community knew about the genocide unfolding in Europe, and in Rwanda 50 years later, and did nothing. They engaged in **denial**. Stanley Cohen (2001) argues that denial "includes *cognition* (not acknowledging the facts); *emotion* (not feeling, not being disturbed); *morality* (not recognizing wrongness or responsibility); and *action* (not taking steps in response to knowledge)" (p. 9). Milburn and Conrad (1996) argue that, at the individual and social levels, denial is a product of an unwillingness to face a reality that is horrifically painful. This, they argue, stems from childhood denial of punitive parental treatment. Denial is also often a subtle social pressure. Everyone knows and no one admits what is happening. Those who do are condemned or ostracized by the group. To admit that something bad is happening is often threatening to the group's self-image, so avoiding or ignoring information is necessary to maintain the positive self-image, and to be complicit in the general denial. Hence, many Germans could ignore the evidence that Jews and others were being exterminated in death camps, because Germans are good people, and good people do not do such things. For individuals, not to be bystanders in the face of political violence is often difficult. They are often threatened with severe punishment, if not death; they do not know what to do or how to act; and they know that as individuals they have little power to do anything. Yet, some individuals do act, hiding a Jew or a Tutsi, managing to save lives, one at a time.

Denial comes in many forms. People deny that they inflicted pain ("It was an accident"), that an injury occurred ("No one was really hurt"), that the victim is a victim ("He deserved it"), or that they had no knowledge about atrocities. Denial also comes in degrees, from knowing about but refusing to believe information, to knowing but maintaining only a vague awareness of the facts, to knowing, being aware, and choosing to do nothing (Cohen, 2001). For example, arguments abound to this day as to how much ordinary Germans knew about the Holocaust, and those arguments will inevitably continue, because many Germans did not then, and cannot now, recognize the extent to which they knew, but did not attend to information about the extermination of Jews and others. As Laqueur (1980) wrote, "It is, in fact, quite likely that while many Germans thought that the Jews were no longer alive, they did not necessarily believe that they were dead" (p. 201).

The likelihood that people will engage in denial, and will refuse to help victims of violence, is augmented when there are many people involved (as in a crowd surrounding an accident victim), when the situation is ambiguous, and when people are fearful of the reaction of others. People are also influenced by the belief in a just world. They believe that the world is benevolent, and that bad things only happen to bad people. Therefore, if someone is hauled off by the SS, they must have done something wrong. This belief comforts people by letting them think that the world is stable, certain, and predictable (Cohen, 2001; Staub, 1989;). These patterns can be seen in Germany and in Argentina, where bystanders abounded. In both cases, the information was, for many, very ambiguous. In both cases, there was no free press that provided concrete and undeniable information that atrocities were occurring. To speak out against regime policies was dangerous and deadly and was certainly discouraged by others, who did not want to rock the boat. And, as in so many cases of genocide and state terror, there was pride in a civilization that led people to believe that nothing so horrible could happen here.

In cases of state terror and genocide, there are always some people who help others and who speak out. The Madres de la Plaza de Mayo are an example. In Europe during the Holocaust, 90% of the Jewish population in Latvia, Lithuania, Poland, and Hungary died. But 90% survived in Denmark, and, in Belgium, where there was resistance to German dictates for rounding up Jews, 53% survived (Staub, 1989). Studies of **rescuers** or **altruists**, as these brave people are called, have found that one central characteristic is an ability to empathize with others, to imagine themselves suffering in the same way (Beck, 1999; Cohen, 2001). **Empathy** is defined as "an 'other centered' emotion which is produced by observing another individual in need and taking that individual's perspective" (Batson, 1991; Rumble, 2003, p. 8). Rumble (2003) cites numerous studies of empathy and notes that the evidence indicates that people will be empathetic when they see another person in need and when they can adopt that person's perspective. In addition, rescuers tend to have an ability to identify with humanity at large, rather than only with their families, local community, or country. Oliner and Oliner (1988) found, in a study of 406 people who attempted to rescue Jews during the Holocaust, that they also had a strong sense of personal responsibility. Finally, Cohen (2001) notes that "these people reacted instinctively: they did not look for accounts or neutralizations for why *not* to help" (p. 263).

CONFLICT AND RECONCILIATION IN THE CONTEXT OF POLITICAL EXTREMISM

In this section, we consider the aftermath of conflict, particularly the question of how people can live together again after catastrophic levels of violence, whether in the form of terrorism by a small group or genocide by a political system. Punishment for crimes against humanity has always been a part of this process. The trials of the Nazi leadership in Nuremberg, the identification of Bosnian Serbs guilty of mass murder, the trials of Rwanda's killers, and the execution of Timothy McVeigh, all illustrate the importance attached to punishment by the international community and by victims of the violence. Punishment also is supposed to act as a deterrent to others who would commit such acts. But, at some point, punishment stops, and conflict resolution and reconciliation require returning to the source of the conflict to begin with.

Many studies of conflicts, such as those discussed in this chapter, draw upon social identity and human needs theories to explain the conflicts and to propose methods of prevention, resolution, and reconciliation. From this perspective, conflict arises in societies because basic human needs are not being met, whether those needs are physical and objective, or psychological and subjective. If one's primary identity groups are threatened, then a basic need for safety, through higher needs such as self-esteem, are not being met. As Staub (2000) argues:

> Economic problems, political conflict and disorganization, and intense and rapid social change (separately or in combination) not only have material effects, but also profoundly frustrate basic human needs. . . . To satisfy needs for identity and connection, people often turn to a group. They elevate the group . . . by psychologically or

physically diminishing other groups. They scapegoat another group for life problems, which protects their identity, strengthens connection within the group, and provides a psychologically useful (even if false) understanding of events. (pp. 369–370)

Every group we considered in this chapter reflects these dynamics. In previous chapters, we examined strategies for reducing perceptions of inequality and threat. We also discussed, in chapter 8, the importance of early detection of possible genocidal situations and the importance of eliminating the bystander effect. But, recognizing that terrorists, militia members, and other extremist groups are not always going to be stopped before they commit violent actions, what can be done to promote reconciliation afterward?

Reconciliation is necessary to prevent violence from becoming cyclical, with one group seeking violent revenge against another. In addition to punishment, reconciliation requires recognition of the humanity of one another, forgiveness, and the reestablishment of trust. Victims must have an audience that acknowledges their trauma. Perpetrators must explain their actions, which often results in a description of the perceptions of their reality and their sense of mistreatment, and must express contrition. There is then an outlet for understanding for the victims, however unpalatable that understanding may be. In the process, victims recognize that what happened to them is not a result of their own inhumanity (Staub, 2000).

A number of methods have been used, in the aftermath of conflict, to promote resolution and reconciliation. No approach is perfect and, as Minow (1998) notes, "At best they can only seek a path between too much memory and too much forgetting" (p. 4). Some, in fact many, societies choose not to confront the past, to try to forget the horrors they have experienced and to move on. But, for others, this is too much forgetting, and they employ approaches ranging from trials and purges, wherein at least some of the perpetrators are put on trial for crimes against humanity, and others are removed from positions of authority. This is what happened in Nuremberg after World War II, when Nazi leaders were tried. It was not until nearly 50 years later that another round of international trials for crimes against humanity was established. In 1993 and 1994, the UN established war crimes tribunals for Yugoslavia and Rwanda, respectively. The Yugoslavia trials are currently under way in the International Court at the Hague. Many of the 76 people indicted have been accused of human rights abuses during the war in Bosnia. The most famous person on trial there is Slobodan Milošević himself. Those accused of committing acts of genocide in Rwanda are on trial in Arusha, Tanzania, at the International Crimes Tribunal for Rwanda. Sixty-two people have been indicted for the Rwanda genocide. Students interested in following these trials can log onto their Web sites, at http://www.un.org/icty for Yugoslavia and http://www.ictr.org for Rwanda. The UN recently decided to establish a permanent International Court (which the United States does not support).

War crimes trials have a number of criticisms. The Nuremberg Trials, conducted by an International Military Tribunal, have been criticized for being little more than vengeance by the victors of World War II. The laws, procedures, and judges were all selected by the allies, and the victorious allies, who had committed some horrifying acts of violence against civilians, including the fire bombing of Dresden and the atomic bombing of Hiroshima and Nagasaki, were not held accountable for their actions. The crimes defendants were accused of were retroactive, that is, they were not clearly crimes at the time of their commission. The Nuremberg trials were also criticized for going too far and not going far enough. There were 85,882 cases prosecuted, but only 7,000 convictions. Some argued that these individuals should not be held accountable for actions conducted by a state government; others noted that putting only 185 people on trial could hardly be considered enough.

War crimes trials being held today are less susceptible to criticisms that the laws and procedures are arbitrary, because, in the years since the establishment of the UN there have been international agreements as to what constitutes genocide and violations of human rights. The UN built upon the Nuremberg trials and used them as precedents for the codification of international laws. The Hague and Geneva Conventions are also important legal statements. These developments help address the retroactivity issue. Now, certain actions have been deemed crimes, in accordance with international laws agreed to by an international organization and its members. Procedures for trials are also established by the International Court. Nevertheless, the complaint remains that participants in violence are not treated equally. For example, many Serbs maintain that Croatians and Muslims who committed atrocities against Serbs during the Yugoslavian wars are not pursued as vigorously as Serbs are. In addition, the ongoing war crimes trials only seek to indict and try the commanders who gave orders, not those who actually committed the violence, reasoning that the latter were only following orders and would have been shot had they disobeyed. This gives little satisfaction to victims' families, however.

In addition to international trials, individual governments have held trials to bring to justice people who participate in atrocities and state terror. Trials have been held in Argentina, Chile, and Brazil, and in several Eastern European countries after the fall of the communist regimes there. However, it is not always easy to carry out effective trials. In both Chile and Argentina, for example, the return to democracy was done under the watchful gaze of the military. Governments seeking to punish those who commit politically motivated crimes must be in control of the situation, and, in both of these cases, the military could conceivably act again to overthrow the civilian governments. Therefore, in Argentina, after the return to civilian rule in 1982, the newly elected president, Raul Alfonsín, ordered nine top level military officers to be tried, five of whom were convicted. Middle and junior ranking officers were not tried. But his successor, President Carlos Menem, fearful of the military and wanting to close the past, pardoned the officers and forbade future trials, but efforts to bring these officers to accountability did not stop. In 1997, for example, an Argentine lawyer, representing 13 families of victims who were disappeared, used the courts to try to bypass that prohibition, by maintaining that the pardons of officers was illegal, because the kidnapping of the victims is continuing, because they were never found. In March 2001, an Argentine judge struck down the amnesty laws that protected middle-level and junior officers from prosecution. In addition, Spain and France are both trying to use legal means to punish Argentine perpetrators of violence against their citizens, such as the "flying nuns," who were captured and disappeared by the military regime.

To carry out trials, governments and societies must have the power and will to punish those responsible. However, the trials will never be sufficient to punish everyone in every case, particularly in situations like Rwanda, where so many people were involved in the slaughter of Tutsis. Moreover, trials do not produce reconciliation or forgiveness. To achieve these, people must admit their wrongdoing, and often one finds in trials that that is exactly what people will not admit. A different technique for recovering from violence is the **truth and reconciliation commission**, which is designed to reveal the truths of political violence, to let the revelation of truth allow the victims or their survivors to grieve, and to achieve some measure of reconciliation and forgiveness. Truth commissions gather evidence, determine accountability, and often recommend policies for the treatment of victims and perpetrators. As Rigby (2001) notes:

> Whereas trials and purges are aimed at punishing the perpetrators of crimes against their fellow citizens, the prime concern of the truth commission approach is with the victims. The aim is to identify them, to acknowledge them and the wrongs done to them, and to arrive at appropriate compensation. (p. 6)

Truth and reconciliation commissions were established in a number of countries following periods of massive violations of human rights. Argentina, Chile, El Salvador, and South Africa have all used truth and reconciliation commissions. Truth commissions are often used in situations in which the government replacing the power holders who committed the acts of violence is not powerful or stable enough to challenge all of those agents. This was the case in Argentina, as noted, wherein the new civilian government could not prosecute all of the military officers responsible for the repression. The military made it clear that this would not be tolerated. Argentina's truth commission was established in 1983 and was called the National Commission on Disappeared People. Its primary mission was to discover what happened to those who disappeared and where their remains could be found. It ultimately produced a 50,000-page report called *Nunca Mass* (Never Again), as well as a documentary. However, as Rigby (2001) argues:

> To many of the relatives and friends of the victims, who were what can be termed secondary victims of the military junta, the report was a whitewash. They knew who the victims were: what they wanted was the names of those who had tortured, raped, and killed them. (pp. 69–70)

Another reason for the use of truth and reconciliation commissions is that often the number of people involved in one way or another with the commission of violence is so great that the prosecutorial approach would only serve to make impossible reconciliation and the reconstruction of a working political and social system. Guilt and blame are also often difficult to discern. How does one condemn a person who breaks under torture, turns into an informant and who, then, in that role, causes someone else to be tortured? Truth and reconciliation commissions are also useful in trading amnesty for information about what happened to whom. In many cases, families of victims have no idea what happened to their loved ones, and, when perpetrators of violence are granted amnesty, they are more likely to provide vital information about the fates of victims. They may also provide details on the conduct of violence, including who had what kind of decision-making authority. Finally, truth and reconciliation commissions do serve the fundamental need of the victims and their families to have an audience willing to listen to their accounts and acknowledge publicly the wrongs done to them.

The South African Truth and Reconciliation Commission (TRC), which lasted from 1996 to 1998, is perhaps the most famous example. During apartheid, tremendous violations of human rights took place, as Whites attempted to suppress the desires of Black South Africans for equality. As shown in chapter 7, after years of struggle, the White power structure finally dismantled the apartheid state, through a negotiated process, and free elections were held. The last apartheid-era White president, F. W. de Klerk, made it clear during the negotiations that a peaceful transition from apartheid to democracy would not be possible if trials were in the offing to punish members of the apartheid establishment. Nelson Mandela, who was the leader of the ANC resistance movement, and who had been held prisoner by the regime for 27 years, was elected to hold the office of president of the new democratic government. The new government approved a law called the Promotion of National Unity and Reconciliation Act, in 1995, thus establishing the TRC. The TRC was headed by another hero of the antiapartheid resistance, Archbishop Desmond Tutu. The TRC aspired for transparency in its deliberations and attempted therefore to be very public and open in procedures, gathering of testimony, and decision making. The TRC gathered testimony from thousands of victims, and included testimony from those abused by the resistance, as well as by the regime. It was also empowered to grant amnesty to perpetrators of violence who applied for amnesty and confessed about what they did. In this way, information was obtained about victims and the chain of command, and often perpetrators apologized to victims. Not all victims testified publicly, but those who were willing to do so had their testimonies broadcast on radio and television and are available on the TRC's Web site (http://www.doj.gov.za/trc/). For victims, the experience can be very therapeutic (Minow, 1998).

A centrally important element in the South African TRC was the amnesty condition. Unlike Argentina, there was no blanket amnesty. Instead, perpetrators had to apply for amnesty and admit to their actions. Amnesty was not granted until the admission of guilt was evaluated, to determine that the actions were politically motivated, rather than personal or criminal. They had a limited time in which to do this, and those who refused were susceptible to criminal prosecution. In the end, over 8,000 people asked for amnesty.

In South Africa, the human rights abuses were mostly done by the members of the government's security forces. There were also many bystanders—White people who benefitted from the apartheid system, but who had not committed human rights abuses themselves. In order to enable these people to admit guilt and shame for indirect complicity, "and to extend the domain of truth telling beyond the confines of the Commission hearings, a Reconciliation Register was opened, with books kept at various locations where people could go and sign them as a personal symbol of regret for their past culpability and commitment to a new beginning" (Rigby, 2001, p. 130).

Do truth commissions accomplish their goals? In some respects, they do. Victims get an opportunity to express their outrage, and it is heard. Families find out what happened to their lost loved ones, and a country learns about the systems of abuse, that is, who ordered what, when, and why. But many victims and their relatives object to amnesty for perpetrators and resent the fact that those individuals are free to go on with life. Then there is the question of what the truth is. It is not always clear-cut, nor is it immune to wide variations in perceptions. In fact, the South Africa TRC's final report discussed four truths: factual, personal, social, and healing. Factual is just that, objective, measurable truth; personal is the victims' stories; social is the discussion of conflicting interpretations of what happened; and healing is reconciliation and compensation (Cohen, 2001; Tepperman, 2002).

There is also a question as to what reconciliation really is and whether truth commissions can achieve it. Reconciliation is usually thought to occur when there is a willingness to forgive, to tolerate one another, and to live together in harmony in the future. Yet, in South Africa, public opinion polls taken after the TRC finished found that "two thirds of South Africans felt the commission's revelations had only made them angrier and contributed to a worsening of race relations" (Tepperman, 2002, p. 134). It is also necessary to question who considers whom to be a victim. Normally, we think of those who suffered the abuse as victims, and the perpetrators need to accept responsibility and make amends. But it is quite likely that, although some perpetrators apologize, other perpetrators see themselves as victims, persecuted by truth commissions, persecuted for only doing their jobs, or persecuted for having tried to save the country. As Minow (1998) puts it "Perhaps acknowledgment of wrongs is most helpful to the victimized and the entire society when it comes from perpetrators, yet no sincere acknowledgment can be ordered or forced" (p. 76). Is reconciliation possible without it?

CONCLUSION

In this chapter, we have covered the political psychology of political extremists and some of the brutal forms of political violence that they commit. We hope to have convinced the reader that these actions are undertaken, not by lunatics, but by ordinary people in extraordinary situations. Once again, understanding the underlying psychological factors helps us understand the behavior of those who commit these acts of violence and of those who stand by and let it happen. Reconciliation after atrocities of this magnitude will clearly be difficult, but, we hope, not impossible.

Topics, Theories/Explanations, and Cases in Chapter 9

Topics	Theories/Concepts	Cases
Political extremists	Personality studies Obedience Social identity theory Group loyalty	U.S. groups: Militias, racists, skinheads, etc. Terrorists
Terrorists		al-Qaeda
State terror	Culture of terror	Argentina
Paramilitaries/death squads		Colombia
Genocide	Social identity Stereotyping Group loyalty Obedience	The Holocaust Rwanda
Denial and bystanders		The Holocaust Argentina
Reconciliation		War crimes trials Truth and reconciliation commissions

KEY TERMS

Altruists

Bystander phenomenon

Christian Identity

Culture of terror

Dehumanization

Death squads

Denial

Diffusion of responsibility

Empathy

Externals

Extremist

Genocide

Internals

Mujahedin

Paramilitaries

Social causality

Social justification

Suicide bomber

Terrorism

Truth and reconciliation
    commission

SUGGESTIONS FOR FURTHER READING

Cohen, S. (2001). *States of denial: Knowing about atrocities and suffering*. Oxford, UK: Blackwell.

Conroy, J. (2000). *Unspeakable acts, ordinary people*. New York: Knopf.

Ezekiel, R. (1996). *The racist mind: Portraits of American neo-Nazis*. New York: Penguin.

Kressel, N. (1996). *Mass hate: The global rise of genocide and terror*. New York: Plenum.

Minow, M. (1998). *Between vengeance and forgiveness: Facing history after genocide and mass violence*. Boston: Beacon Press.

Peterson, S. (2000). *Me against my brother: At war in Somalia, Sudan, and Rwanda.* New York: Routledge.

Rigby, A. (2001). *Justice and reconciliation after the violence.* Boulder: Lynne Rienner Press

Rosenberg, T. (1991). *Children of Cain: Violence and the violent in Latin America.* New York: Penguin Books.

Staub, E. (1989). *The roots of evil: The origins of genocide and other group violence.* Cambridge: Cambridge University Press.

ENDNOTE

1.   A significant body of literature (Milburn & Conrad, 1996; Miller, 1983) explains the propensity of individuals who are products of harsh childhood upbringing to be attracted to these groups.

CHAPTER 10

The Political Psychology of International Security and Conflict

Throughout history, people have seemingly been embroiled almost constantly in violence, conflict, and war. And, for an equally long period of time, writers from numerous disciplines have sought to understand the causes of such strife (Brown, 1987; Nieburg, 1969). Although a discussion of this subject could reasonably be seen to require a review of the voluminous research into violence and aggression that has been conducted in psychology and sociology, that is really beyond the limited scope of this chapter. In fact, much of this literature is already discussed in our other chapters dealing with ethnic nationalism, violence, and genocide. Instead, this chapter seeks to use international security and conflict as an example, in order to illustrate how political psychological approaches have been applied by political scientists to better understand such problems as the causes of war, the security dilemma, and deterrence. In doing so, it is hoped that students will better appreciate how psychological concepts can be usefully applied to real-world political problems. The portions of the Political Being focused upon in this chapter are cognition, emotion, and perceptions of *them*.

WHY VIOLENCE AND WAR?

There have been many competing explanations for violence and war proposed over time, by scholars across numerous disciplines (Brown, 1987). Some, for example, looked to biology, to suggest that humankind was genetically predisposed to be innately violent (Freud, 1932/1951, 1920/1950, 1930/1962; Lorenz, 1966; Scott, 1969; Shaw & Wong, 1989; Wilson, 1978) Others have suggested that human aggression was more of a socially learned response (Bandura, 1973, 1977, 1986; Skinner, 1971, 1974). In time, a general consensus has emerged, in which, as Brown (1987) notes, "most serious students of human violence recognize some mixture of innate predisposition (which may vary with individuals) and situational conditions" (pp. 8–9). Often, explanations of conflict in political science have suggested psychological factors as a key component. For example, the role of perception and misperception between the leaders of states, in causing or avoiding international conflict, has been described at length across historical crisis cases (Jervis, 1976; Lebow, 1981). Similarly, problems of successful crisis management, given leader psychology or organizational limitations as a factor in avoidance of war, have been discussed by a number of scholars (Allison & Zelikow, 1999; George, 1991). The dynamics and composition of policy-making groups themselves have been suggested to play a major role in averting or causing conflict (Janis, 1972; Janis & Mann, 1977). Finally, the personalities and characteristics of leaders have also been suggested to play a role in causing or preventing conflicts (Birt, 1993; Post, 1991; Stoessinger, 1985).

One of the earliest expositions of the causes of political violence is found in Thucydide's *History of the Peloponnesian War*, which chronicles the events surrounding the bloody conflict between the neighboring Greek city-states of Sparta and Athens, over 2,400 years ago.

Although an ancient Greek historian, Thucydides has often been described as the first realist, because of his attention to the anarchic, self-help nature of the ancient Greek international system; his emphasis upon how the Spartans and Athenians competed with one another in their pursuit of power, alliances, and influence (power politics); and in his clear depiction (captured in the Melian Debate) of the lack of morality in the affairs of states (might makes right). Hence, the famous statement by the Athenians to their weaker Melian neighbors, "the strong do what they will and the weak suffer what they must" (see Hans Morgenthau, 1948, for an overview of basic realist, power politics arguments). Yet, even though much of Thucydides's history clearly expresses realist, power politics notions of state behavior, including the notion that competition between states for power often leads to conflict, one could also say that Thucydides could also be considered one of the first political psychologists.

Thucydides, far from using only state characteristics or power motivations to explain the war, suggested (much as a modern-day political psychologist might) that the main spark igniting the bloody conflict between Sparta and Athens was fear, on the part of both sides, of one another: fear by the Spartans of what they perceived to be the growing power of Athens and its increasingly expansionistic policies; and fear by the Athenians of what they perceived to be a ruthless, militaristic power that was bent on competing with them for hegemony over all of Greece. During the councils of war, which followed on both sides, speeches by the leaders of Sparta and Athens were replete with immensely negative stereotypes and caricatures of each another, as well as strong **enemy images** (Cottam, 1994). Driven by these perceptions (and misperceptions) of each other, war became inevitable. Yet, the end result of this 23-year struggle was not supremacy over Greece, but the weakening of both combatants to such an extent that they were easily conquered by the Persians almost immediately afterwards. Objectively, if we were to speak the language of realists, the balance of power in that region of the world never would have made it in the broader interests of either Sparta nor Athens to go to war with one another. They needed to be allies and to pool their military power to offset the might of Persia, as they had in earlier conflicts. But, as Thucydides demonstrates, neither side was making such cooly rational calculations of the regional power balance. Instead, the psychology of fear and misperception were at work, leading both nations to a disastrous bloodbath. Indeed, as Thucydides makes plain, to ignore the psychological factors at work between Sparta and Athens would be to miss a crucial underlying cause of the war.

Similarly, the events leading up to the First World War (1914–1918) provide another powerful illustration of the importance of psychological variables in explaining conflict. Many factors contributed to the speed with which war engulfed Europe in the summer of 1914 (e.g., military alliances, great power competition over colonies and naval forces, etc.), but it is also clear that misperception by leaders played a major role (Farrar, 1988). Indeed, the Great War was one that was desired by none of the political leaders of the time. Certainly, the Austrians did not envision their dispute with Serbia igniting a world war, nor did the German Kaiser, when he (unwisely) gave support to his Austrian ally. Once again, fear played a major role among both political and military leaders of the time. All accepted that technological advancements in warfare, and the rapid mobilization capabilities provided by modern railway systems, had fundamentally altered the nature of warfare. Not only would a major war be so immensely destructive as to last, at best, 3 months (a widely held belief prior to 1914), but, more important, the state that succeeded in mobilizing (getting its armies organized and transported to the front lines) first would automatically be the victor (see Keegan, 1998; Tuchman, 1962).

In crisis management terms, this was a highly unstable security environment, analogous to a country during the Cold War having the capability of launching a completely disarming nuclear first-strike upon an opponent (Jervis, 1976; Levy, 1991). It gave policymakers precious little time to manage a crisis, nor did it allow for defensive moves (because these would be automatically perceived to be offensive by their opponents). In 1914, one needed a mobilized army at the front line to either defend yourself from attack or invade your neighbor. Offensive and defensive capability were indistinguishable from one another. As a result, even though statesmen on all sides tried to reassure one another that their mobilizations were purely for defensive purposes only, each fell into what Jervis (1976) later described as the **security dilemma**, a situation in which the actions taken by each state to increase its own security had the effect of simultaneously decreasing the security of its neighbors. Because the true motivations of their neighbors could not be determined with certainty, each state was left to make decisions based solely upon their beliefs about their neighbors' motivations and capabilities. By the end of August, Europe was in flames, in a conflict that would eventually claim over 15 million lives.

The Security Dilemma

The basic notion of the **security dilemma** is a simple one. Faced with what is perceived (either correctly or incorrectly) to be a threatening international security environment, national leaders take actions they perceive to be defensive ones (such as arms buildups, increased defense spending, fortification of borders, development of national missile defenses, etc.) to protect themselves from these external threats. Knowing that their own motivations are peaceful, these leaders tend to make the assumption that their true (peaceful) intentions are equally clear to all of their neighbors (Jervis, 1976). However, unlike the relatively unthreatening steps (at least to law-abiding neighbors) that a homeowner might take to enhance the security of their own house from burglars (such as installing alarms or better locks, putting bars on windows, or buying a guard dog), equivalent actions taken by states to enhance their security, vis-à-vis other states, require the building of more imposing militaries or defenses, which are actions that inevitably undermine the security of their neighbors.

The reason for this is that what distinguishes offensive and defensive weapons from one another are the motivations of their owners, not the basic characteristics of the arms themselves. Hence, the long-standing joke among security specialists that the true difference between an offensive and defensive weapon is which end of the barrel you are looking down. Indeed, the problem for policymakers, struggling to understand the psychology of their potential opponents (and their real policy intentions), is that they become trapped in a cycle of trying to divine intentions based solely upon visible indicators of behavior (i.e., size of militaries, where they were located, what political disputes would arise between them, etc.). Unfortunately, as Jervis (1976) ably points out with the notion of the security dilemma, in the real world of security, you cannot judge an opponent's true military intentions based solely upon their capabilities. Any military weapon—whether it is guns, tanks, planes, or nuclear weapons—can be employed either offensively or defensively (to attack a neighbor or to defend the homeland). The military strategy adopted determines how the characteristics of the weapons will be used, not vice versa. Weapons themselves are agnostic. Further, almost any action taken by a state for defensive purposes could also support offensive military strategies.

For example, NMD programs, which are sought to provide states with the ability to intercept and destroy an opponent's incoming missiles (thereby shielding their countries from attack), are often described as purely defensive, by their advocates. And clearly, some uses of NMD would be purely defensive (say, by a nonnuclear country without an offensive military, which sought only to prevent another country from attacking it with nuclear weapons in war). However, as other countries facing proposed NMD defenses have vehemently argued (as Russia and China have, against U.S. missile defense plans), a shield can also be offensive in nature. A country that suddenly became invulnerable to nuclear retaliation by other states could use that invulnerability to its own military advantage. It could launch a nuclear first strike of its own with impunity, or invade the other country militarily and fear no retaliation on their own nation. In this sense, an effective NMD would provide its owner with actual military superiority over all other states and would vastly increase its options across the board, for using both nuclear and conventional forces (because no retaliation would need to be considered). Thus, NMD can be both offensive and defensive. How it is used, not its characteristics, make it one or the other. Regardless of the true motivations of a country (which other states can never be absolutely certain of), the basic security reality is that, by strengthening their military postures, states obtain more offensive options, should they ever choose to become aggressors. In an international system characterized by anarchy, neighboring states must consider all of the possibilities behind their opponent's actions, and assume the worst (see Jervis, 1976; Richardson, 1960).

As a result, policymakers, pursuing what they believe to be purely defensive military buildups, often fail to understand how their actions are likely to be perceived (or misperceived) by neighboring states. Because defensively motivated policymakers know that their own motivations for their military buildups are peaceful, they sometimes assume (incorrectly) that these peaceful intentions are obvious and self-evident to all interested observers. Unfortunately, this is often not the case. For example, during the Cold War, both sides (the United States and the Soviet Union) saw the actions of the other in a threatening light. The formation of the great military alliances of the period—NATO in the West and the Warsaw Pact in the East—were seen by their creators as defensive in nature, but were viewed by their opponents as evidence of hostile intent and a desire to possibly launch an armed invasion. Similarly, Soviet military doctrine of the time held that, to defend against Western attack, one needed massive, numerically superior conventional forces that could offset issues of quality with sheer quantity—a strategy that had been employed effectively against the Germans in the Second World War (Legvold, 1988). However, for the West, the massive size of the Red Army, its forward deployment in Eastern Europe, and the buildup of such large numbers of tanks, artillery, combat aircraft, and so on were seen as clearly having offensive potential. The Cold War became a classic example of the security dilemma in action. Although we now know that neither side seriously contemplated invading the other during the Cold War, these motivations or intentions were not accurately perceived or understood by their opponents (see Gaddis, 1992, 1997).

Contributing to these problems of perception are issues of attribution, or how we tend to psychologically assign cause and effect relationships in our environment. For example, the **fundamental attribution error**, which, as we have seen in previous chapters, involves our tendency to attribute another person's behavior or actions to their dispositional qualities (their personalities, motivations, etc.), rather than to situational factors in the environment that may have caused the behavior (Heider, 1958). In the security dilemma example just described, U.S. policymakers during the Cold War tended to explain the Soviet Union's military buildup and forward deployment of forces in Eastern Europe by the dispositional qualities of Soviet leaders (i.e., Stalin or Khruschev's aggressive, expansionistic intentions toward Western Europe), and not by situational factors (such as the formation of NATO, concerns about another invasion from the West, etc.), which actually motivated the behavior.

A somewhat similar process of misattribution during the Cold War is described by Holsti's (1967, 1969) work describing the ways in which American policymakers perceived the behavior and motivations of their Soviet counterparts. For example, in describing the belief system of John Foster Dulles, who served as Dwight Eisenhower's secretary of state during the 1950s, Holsti observed that his worldview was characterized by an **inherent bad-faith** perspective of the Soviets. Simply stated, if Soviet behavior in the world was good (i.e., not threatening to U.S. interests), it was not because Soviet intentions were benign, but rather, their good behavior only resulted from overwhelming U.S. military strength. On the other hand, when Soviet behavior in the world was bad (i.e., threatening U.S. interests in Berlin or Cuba), this was a true reflection of their real policy intentions. American policymakers throughout the Cold War routinely shared this perspective on the Soviets (as did many Soviet policymakers of the United States). Further illustrations of this belief system include Paul Nitze's formulation of Soviet intentions, in NSC-68 (perhaps the most important U.S. foreign policy document of the Cold War) and Ronald Reagan's depiction of the Soviet Union as "the evil empire" and his "peace through strength" arguments of the 1980s, to justify the largest peacetime military buildup in American history.

Obviously, this belief system made it very difficult for either side to show good faith toward the other, since this would often be interpreted as further evidence supporting the effectiveness of pursuing a tough policy line toward them. It also allowed policymakers to effectively preserve their existing enemy images or negative stereotypes of one another, because the selective perception involved allowed them to discount any cooperative behavior by their opponents as coerced and focus upon the examples of negative behavior that better reflected their existing views of the other side.

The Cold War relationship between the United States and Soviet Union has also been described as being characterized by a **malignant (spiral) process of hostile interaction** (Deutsch, 1986). According to Deutsch (1986), the key elements contributing to the development and perpetuation of a protracted, malignant interaction process include

(1) an anarchic social situation, (2) a win–lose or competitive orientation, (3) inner conflicts (within each of the parties) that express themselves through external conflict, (4) cognitive rigidity, (5) misjudgments and misperceptions, (6) unwitting commitments, (7) self-fulfilling prophecies, (8) vicious escalating spirals, and (9) a gamesmanship orientation which turns the conflict away from issues of what in real life is being won or lost to an abstract conflict over images of power. (p. 131)

The malignant process escalates, as these elements interact with one another to gradually worsen ongoing conflicts, causing them to spiral toward more hostile interactions over time. Thus, according to Deutsch, the basic security dilemma problem for the superpowers, and their fear of becoming militarily inferior, created an anarchic social situation characterized by extreme competitiveness (a win–lose orientation) on their parts. As a result, gains in military capability by one side were viewed as threatening losses to the security of the other. Adding to this problem was the use of the external enemy to serve as justification for internal conflicts in both superpower societies (i.e., the need for Stalin's harsh rule at home or the need for internationalist policies in the United States). Cognitive rigidity by policymakers in how they viewed the other side's inherent bad-faith belief systems, and so on, led to misjudgments and misperceptions of opponents, unwitting commitments to rigid policy positions, and escalating spirals of conflict. The hostility and suspicion expressed toward the other side became a self-fulfilling prophecy, when that hostility was returned in kind (Deutsch, 1986).

The Psychology of Deterrence

During the Cold War, the superpowers sought to deter extreme threats to their national interests (e.g., invasions of their homelands or attacks upon vital allies) through nuclear deterrence—or the threat to retaliate for such aggression by using nuclear weapons. A simple definition of **deterrence** is the threat by one political actor to take actions in response to another actor's potential actions, which would make the costs (or losses) incurred far outweigh any possible benefits (or gains) obtained by the aggressor. Of course, definitions of deterrence vary across the literature. Schelling (1966, 1980), for example, defines *deterrence* as the use of threats to prevent someone from doing something (or starting something). Stein (1992), on the other hand, defines it as threatening punishment or denial, to prevent an adversary from taking unwanted action. Using a classic Cold War example to illustrate deterrence: Even if the Soviets could successfully invade and occupy Western Europe and obliterate the United States in a nuclear first strike, this country still had enough surviving forces to respond with a retaliatory nuclear attack that would utterly destroy the Soviet Union. Thus, no matter how great the potential gains were, the consequences (utter destruction of the home nation in retaliation) would far exceed any gains from the original aggression. As a result, once both superpowers possessed comparable abilities to attack and destroy the other with nuclear weapons, by the late 1960s, the famous mutual assured destruction (MAD) nuclear doctrine was established, recognizing this deterrent relationship.

But the most fundamental element to this deterrence formula has always been perceptual. Both sides during the Cold War recognized that the credibility of their nuclear retaliatory threats were only effective if the other side truly believed that they would really carry them out, if suitably provoked. In the final analysis, whether deterrence would fail or succeed depended not upon how many weapons each side possessed, but upon the perceptions each side possessed regarding the willingness of their opponents to really push the button. Thus, deterrence (whether nuclear or conventional) is, at its heart, a psychological relationship between the deterrer and the deterred. In order for deterrence to function successfully (e.g., prevent any aggression from taking place to begin with), the actor seeking to deter an opponent must be able to effectively communicate to them (and they must accurately perceive) that the deterrer has the physical capability to carry out a threat (nuclear weapons, survivable delivery systems, etc.) and that the threat has credibility (that the deterrer truly has the resolve [or willingness] to carry out their promised retaliation, no matter how horrific the consequences). If an opponent does not believe in the credibility of your threat, regardless of your real intentions, then you will not be able to effectively deter them. This is part of the inherent peril of deterrence— that it can unravel because of an opponents misperception of either your substantive military capabilities or the credibility of your threats to use these capabilities.

Consider the example of Saddam Hussein's calculations prior to the invasion of Kuwait. Although truly one of history's worst generals, even Hussein understood that the United States enjoyed vast, overwhelming military superiority over Iraq, in terms of numbers and quality of equipment. That much was no mystery to him. What he fundamentally misunderstood was the extent to which an immense technological gap had opened up between the U.S. armed forces and those of less advanced states. Indeed, this revolution in military affairs was not fully appreciated, even by U.S. analysts, until after the war was over (Biddle, 1998; Cohen, 1996; Freedman & Karsh, 1993; O'Hanlon, 2000). Yet, for Saddam, the calculation was never one of pure military capabilities. Rather, his calculations were governed by his perception (as it turned out, an incorrect perception) of the credibility of the U.S. threat to intervene in the region and reverse his invasion. Indeed, he told both U.S. officials and reporters, prior to the Gulf War, that, after Vietnam, Iraq only needed to have the ability to cause lots of American casualties, to deter the United States from becoming militarily involved in a conflict. Saddam believed that this country had no willingness to accept casualties and could never sustain substantial losses of troops, politically, at home. This perception is indicative of the **degenerate image** discussed in chapters 3 and 8. Recall that that is an image wherein a country of equal or greater power is seen as confused and lacking the will to respond to the actions of another country. The image was supported by previous actions by the United States, particularly in communications from the American ambassador that this country would not oppose his position on the dispute with Kuwait on the oil fields. In order to use that perceived lack of will on the part of the United States to their advantage, Hussein and his spokesmen spent much time making pronouncements to the world's press regarding the tens of thousands of body bags that would be required to send the Americans back home, if they attacked him. Once inside Kuwait, the Iraqi forces dug in and attempted to create for Coalition forces the choice of accepting his invasion or fighting a long, bloody war of attrition, like the one he had recently waged with Iran (Freedman & Karsh, 1993).[1] This degenerate image-based perception by Saddam of reality—both of actual U.S. credibility (our willingness to accept casualties or use force to reverse the Kuwaiti invasion) and actual U.S. military capabilities vis-á-vis the Iraqi forces in Kuwait (the technological gap)—made the Iraqi leader unwisely accept the risk (which he viewed as slight) that the United States would intervene in the Gulf and would be willing to pay the price, in blood, to reverse his invasion (Freedman & Karsh, 1993; Stein, 1992; Woodward, 1991). His perceptions of the situation mattered more than calculations of U.S. military capabilities (which he did not believe Washington would be able to fully exploit).

There exists tremendous debate and disagreement within the political science literature over how to test deterrence theory, with the center of the debate usually revolving around how differing camps of scholars have chosen to operationalize the concept or to interpret historical events (cf. Huth & Russett, 1984, 1988, 1990; Lebow & Stein, 1987, 1989, 1990). As Herring (1995) observes, regarding this debate, "Virtually all aspects of how to test deterrence and compellence theory are disputed" (p. 33). The use of historical cases purporting to represent successes or failures of deterrence, by these authors, has been problematic, to say the least, be- cause there are seldom universally accepted, objective interpretations of historical events or records of exactly what was on the minds of the policymakers during the crises (rather impor- tant, when motivation matters as much as it does for deterrence questions). Although it is be- yond the scope of this chapter to delve into these debates at length, there exist a number of ex- cellent overviews and critical analyses of these methodological debates (Harvey, 1997a, 1997b, 1997c, 1998; Herring, 1995). As Harvey (1997b) briefly explains:

> Case selection and coding immediate deterrence encounters remains a key area of diffi- culty for researchers who test deterrence theory using the dominant success–failure strategy. The approach recommends identifying cases of immediate deterrence, coding these cases as instances of success or failure, isolating conditions that were present or absent during failures, and, based on these differences, drawing conclusions about why and how deterrence works. The problem, as Huth and Russett acknowledge, is that a sin- gle crisis frequently encompasses several different types of interactions and out- comes. . . . Carefully separating the threat/counterthreat sequence that would allow the researcher to pinpoint those aspects of behavior that conform to a direct or extended, im- mediate deterrence or compellence military encounter is often difficult, if not impossi- ble, to accomplish with any degree of empirical precision, especially if the entire crisis is the unit of analysis. (p. 13)

Harvey (1997b) seeks to avoid some of the pitfalls of seeking to judge historical cases as a whole as deterrence successes or failures, based on a single dominant exchange, by employ- ing the **protracted crisis approach.** Explicitly rejecting the assumption that crises should be counted as a "single, dominant encounter," Harvey (1997b) argues that, much like the frames of a motion picture film, crises should be viewed as a long series of "separate and distinct de- terrence and compellence exchanges" (p. 13) running throughout the crisis, from the begin- ning until the end of any episode. As Harvey notes:

> Dissecting each crisis to reveal different encounters allows for multiple interpretations of any one foreign policy crisis and, therefore, can help to account for discrepancies

across existing case lists; it forces the researcher to specify the precise time frame and exact sequence within which the appropriately designated threats, counter-threats and responses are made. (p. 13)

In adopting this approach, Harvey follows in the tradition of George and Smoke (1974), who also argued for viewing deterrence cases as involving multiple exchanges in a protracted crisis. As a result, an individual case, such as Bosnia-Herzegovina (1993–1994), moves, from being a single case of one primary exchange between the parties, to one with 14 total exchanges between the parties (Harvey, 1997c). Indeed, much of the disagreement between Huth/Russett and Lebow/Stein centers upon what stage of a historical crisis they have focused upon for their analysis of deterrence failure or success—a problem that is eliminated through adoption of Harvey's more nuanced approach.

Of course, in order to determine whether or not an actor has been deterred from taking a specified action (or has been compelled to change course from an already adopted course of action), as the result of credible threats (military, economic, or political), one has to know the motivations of that actor. In other words, did they actually intend to take the course of action that is the subject of the deterrent or compellent action? You cannot deter an action that was not being considered by your opponent in the first place, nor can you judge an effort at deterrence or compellence as a success or failure, in the absence of information about your opponent's intentions. As many scholars have noted, it is the target actor's motivations, their calculations of costs–benefits, their ability to accurately perceive their environments (whether those are military or political ones), and their own particular judgments regarding the correlation of these elements, which must drive any discussion of deterrence or compellence success or failure (see George, 1991a,b; George & Smoke, 1974; Jervis, Lebow, & Stein, 1985; Schelling, 1966; Stein, 1992).

A good illustration of this point is found in Stein's (1992) analysis of U.S. deterrence and compellence attempts upon Iraq prior to the Gulf War of 1990–1991. Although the historical record provides a great deal of data to support any number of hypotheses regarding why deterrence or compellence efforts failed in this case, in the end, it is the motivations and calculations of Saddam Hussein that drive Stein's analysis of these efforts. Stein suggests three possibilities for the failure of U.S. deterrence and compellence efforts against Iraq: (1) that the U.S. failed to mount an effective strategy of deterrence in the period preceding the Kuwaiti invasion; (2) that Saddam Hussein systematically miscalculated the capabilities and resolve of the United States; or, finally, (3) that Saddam could not be deterred, regardless of the strategy employed (Stein, 1992). At the heart of the question, however, is the issue of Saddam Hussein's motives and intentions: Was he an "opportunity-driven aggressor" or a "vulnerable leader motivated by need"? (Stein, 1992, p. 155). Stein also points out that many of Saddam's strategic calculations prior to the Gulf War, which may have led him to discount the credibility of U.S. threats to use force (i.e., the likelihood of a major U.S. intervention, American willingness to take heavy casualties, the difficulties facing Arab leaders in maintaining public support for a war against another Arab state), were not necessarily irrational. Although traditional realists, such as Morgenthau (1948), would argue that imbalances of power between states are often a cause of war, Stein (1992) notes that "overwhelming local military superiority does not, however, necessarily lead to crisis and war unless the motive and the intention to use force are also present" (p. 156). In the case of the Gulf War, Stein makes a strong case that it is the psychology of Saddam Hussein (his motives, calculations, and perceptions of his environment) that, in the final analysis, determined the outcomes of all of the U.S. influence attempts.

Another important issue to consider when testing deterrence theory is how the analyst will view limited uses of force by one or both parties in a deterrence relationship. This touches upon the distinction between **general** and **immediate deterrence**. As Herring (1995) explains, "General deterrence is the use of a standing threat in order to prevent someone from seriously considering doing something, while immediate deterrence is the use of specific threats to prevent someone from doing something which is being seriously considered" (p. 18). Although any use of force could be argued to represent a failure of general deterrence, George and Smoke (1974) argue that limited force can be used to probe a general deterrence commitment, without compromising deterrence itself. For example, in Kashmir, India and Pakistan have had numerous crises and military clashes that have threatened to escalate into major wars, perhaps even nuclear ones, over the past 12 years. Yet, to argue that these brief, though intense, military incursions, or the periodic shelling that goes on along the borders, represents a failure of general deterrence misses the point that it is probably the fear of nuclear escalation that prevented these skirmishes from growing (Hagerty, 1995/1996, 1998). At most, such probes should be seen only as "a partial failure of immediate deterrence" (Herring, 1995, p. 26), and not failures of general deterrence.

Of course, the strongest critiques of deterrence theory have always had a psychological basis. In particular, critics have noted that the retaliatory threats required by deterrence often demand a state to make arguably irrational decisions (i.e., commit national suicide by launching a retaliatory nuclear strike upon an opponent, which would invite an equally devastating retaliation, in return, by the victim). One can easily make the argument that an opponent might be deterred by a state, if it promised nuclear retaliation in response to aggression (because the costs would outweigh the benefits), but it is equally the case that, for the state actually carrying out this threat, the costs would also outweigh the benefits. The need for states to make such a fundamentally irrational decision into a rational one has led security analysts to rely upon "meta-rational" solutions to game-theory approaches, in their search for a logic to support the credibility of some of the more extreme deterrent threats required of nuclear states.

For example, the game of **chicken** (see Figure 10.1) has often been used by scholars to represent the nature of the deterrence problem facing the superpowers during the Cold War (Brams, 1985; Freedman, 1981; Jervis, 1976). In that game, one imagines a long, deserted stretch of highway with two cars facing each other at opposite ends of the road. The object of chicken, predictably, is to get the other driver to "chicken out" first (i.e., swerve out of

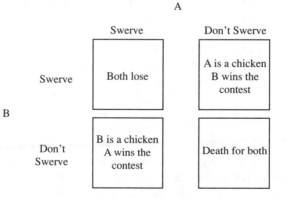

FIG. 10.1. The game of chicken. Each driver wants the other to believe that they will not swerve, thereby forcing the other to chicken out and swerve first. Whoever swerves first is a chicken. But the dilemma for both drivers is just that: Will the other really swerve first? If neither do, both die.

the way of your oncoming vehicle), while you continue to drive straight down the highway. Thus, both drivers (assuming they were not suicidal maniacs) would need to not only demonstrate their capability of causing a horrific, fatal accident by driving straight down the road as fast as possible, but would also need to somehow communicate the credibility of their threat to continue to do so (regardless of the consequences) to the opposing driver, in the hope of making him swerve out of the way first. Obviously, for both drivers, the rational solution is to swerve out of the way of the other car every time, because to actually carry out the threat would carry a cost greater than any conceivable benefit a victory might bring to the driver. However, if the drivers insist upon playing chicken (or for states to rely upon MAD nuclear doctrines for their security) and, for some reason, must play the game to win, then it becomes imperative for them to be able to make an irrational threat credible, because, if the threat is not credible, neither driver will swerve and both will die (Brams, 1985).

Making such a threat credible could be accomplished in a number of different ways. For instance, one driver might put the car on cruise control, throw the steering wheel out of the window, and crawl into the backseat to read a good (short) book. Seeing such behavior and recognizing it for what it was an **irrevocable commitment**—the other driver would have no further cause to doubt the credibility of his opponent's threat and would recognize that only he now had control over whether the cars crashed or not. At this point, the rational decision would be to swerve in the face of this irrevocable commitment by his opponent to this inherently irrational action (Powell, 1990). Similarly, countries have relied upon **the threat that leaves something to chance** to make irrational threats credible (Freedman, 1981; Powell, 1990; Schelling, 1966). In other words, even if you really do not believe your opponent would actually go through with a retaliatory strike that would result in their own self-destruction, these threats retain some credibility if your opponent could become dangerous (Rhodes, 1989) in the context of a crisis. Simply put, the country's leaders might not be able to control all of their military forces in the event of a war, especially if nuclear weapons began going off and interrupting command-and-control functions between the nation's leaders and its armed forces. As a result, the leaders would lose positive control over their forces and would lack the ability to prevent retaliation from occurring (Feaver, 1992–1993; Sagan, 1994).

During the Cold War, both superpowers adopted strategic postures that were roughly the equivalent to climbing into the backseat of the speeding vehicle in chicken. Subordinates (like submarine commanders) were given preauthorization to launch their weapons, in the event of permanently losing contact with the nation's leadership during a crisis. Similarly, both sides adopted "launch-on-warning" or "launch-on-impact" doctrines regarding nuclear weapons, in which subordinates would have authorization to retaliate upon evidence of imminent or current nuclear attack by an opponent. There was even consideration (although this was never adopted, except in the Hollywood film *Wargames*) of leaving the actual decision (and ability) to retaliate to computers, thereby removing humans from the decision loop entirely (see Freedman, 1981; Smoke, 1987). Although this last option would have come closest to the logic of throwing the steering wheel out of the window and curling up to read in the backseat, the earlier options also held with them (and increased) the possibility that an objectively irrational response could still occur, or that, even if the other country's leaders lacked the resolve to really push the button, they still might not be able to prevent their armed forces from retaliating, anyway, during an attack. And the greater the disruption of command-and-control as the result of an attack, or the greater the stress of an ongoing crisis between two nuclear-armed states, the greater the likelihood (or possibility) that the state could become *contingently unsafe* and respond irrationally to a provocation.

In addition, critics of reliance on deterrence for maintaining peace between nuclear states also note the many psychological or information-processing challenges that deterrence must master to function properly (Dunn, 1982; Feaver, 1992–1993; Feaver & Niou, 1996; Lebow & Stein, 1989, 1990; Sagan, 1994). For example, they observe that history is replete with cases in which decision makers have misperceived either the nature of their security environments (e.g., the Peleponnesian War, the First World War) or the intentions and motivations of their opponents (e.g., Chamberlain of Hitler at Munich, the superpowers of each other during the Cold War). Given the potential consequences of a breakdown in deterrence (nuclear war), these critics have argued that it was dangerous, given the enormous difficulties facing policymakers in seeking to rely on deterrence, to depend upon it to maintain the peace. Not only did deterrence require policymakers to rationally take irrational actions to support the strategy, but it also required them to accurately perceive their own (and their opponent's) capabilities and intentions and to be able to maintain positive control over their subordinates and arsenals during challenging crisis contexts. Further, by focusing principally on the use of threats, deterrence theory tended to ignore the role that rewards and concessions might play in defusing or preventing conflicts (Jervis, 1976). One possible consequence of relying upon threats, rather than on more positive inducements, is that it reinforces the perception of policymakers of the opposing state as being hostile or aggressive. As a result, **cognitive rigidity** among policymakers can exacerbate the tensions between states, as neutral or friendly behavior is ignored or reinterpreted to better fit a preexisting negative stereotype (Holsti, 1967; Jervis, 1976). Because foreign policy beliefs are highly resistant to change (George, 1980), once a particular image or stereotype of a neighboring state is adopted (e.g., as aggressive and likely to attack or as weak and unlikely to attack), **belief perseverance** will serve as a barrier either to the successful transmission of warnings of credible threats or to the gathering of information that diverges from the accepted belief systems of policymakers (Tetlock, McGuire, & Mitchell, 1991).

In contrast to deterrence theory, Jervis (1976) lays out a **spiral model** that incorporates many of the concerns that critics have about the assumptions of deterrence. Indeed, spiral theorists focus upon many of the same dynamics previously described by Deutsch's (1986) "The malignant spiral process of hostile interaction." As Jervis (1976) observes:

> If much of deterrence theory can be seen in terms of the game of Chicken, the spiral theorists are more impressed with the relevance of the Prisoner's Dilemma. . . . If each state pursues its narrow self-interest with a narrow conception of rationality, all states will be worse off than they would be if they cooperated. . . . A second point highlighted by the Prisoner's Dilemma is that cooperative arrangements are not likely to be reached through coercion. Threats and an adversary posture are likely to lead to counteractions with the ultimate result that both sides will be worse off than they were before. (p. 67; see Figure 10.2)

Thus, the emphasis of spiral theorists is upon reducing the degree to which rival states overestimate the hostility of one another, countering the dynamics of the security dilemma through confidence-building measures, and using concessions to both reduce tensions and induce a less hostile, aggressive perception of the state's intentions by neighbors. Jervis (1976) notes that the two theories contradict each other at every point:

> Policies that flow from deterrence theory (e.g., development of potent and flexible armed forces; a willingness to fight for issues of low intrinsic value; avoidance of any appearance of weakness) are just those that, according to the spiral model, are most apt to heighten tensions and create illusory incompatibility. And the behavior advocated by

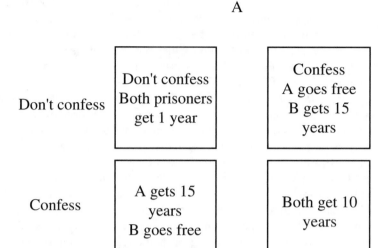

FIG. 10.2.   The prisoner's dilemma. In this classic game, two prisoners, A and B, accused of a crime, have the options of confessing or not confessing. If they maintain their alliance and neither confesses, both get short sentences. If each of them confesses, they each get a heavy sentence. But if one confesses and the other does not, the prisoner who confessed is rewarded with freedom, and the one who did not confess gets a severely heavy sentence. The dilemma for each prisoner is that, if they trust the other not to confess, their best option is to rat out their partner in crime.

the spiral theorists (attempts to reassure the other side of one's nonaggressiveness, the avoidance of provocations, the undertaking of unilateral initiatives) would, according to deterrence theory, be likely to lead an aggressor to doubt the state's willingness to resist. (p. 84)

Further, neither deterrence nor spiral theories have proven adequate to explain all historical cases of conflict or avoidance of conflict (Jervis, 1976). The outbreak of World War I, in 1914, is often used to illustrate spiral dynamics (e.g., misperception and distrust, enemy images, security dilemmas), but the experiences of Chamberlain with Hitler at Munich, in 1938 (e.g., use of concessions and diplomacy, avoidance of threats), runs contrary to its predictions. Similarly, deterrence theorists are much happier using the example of Munich's appeasement and the aggressive states of the 1930s, to illustrate the importance of not appearing weak to opponents through concessions and maintaining credible threat postures, than they are using the 1914 example, which illustrates the dangers to this approach. As Jervis (1976) observes, "given the histories of these two conflicts, it is not surprising that deterrence theories have little to say about World War I and that the spiral theorists rarely discuss the 1930s" (p. 95).

As the ongoing debates over deterrence effectiveness between Huth and Russett (1984, 1988, 1990) and Lebow and Stein (1987, 1989, 1990) have illustrated, proving that deterrence works, empirically, through examining past historical cases of deterrence successes and failures, is exceedingly difficult. Indeed, because successful deterrence would often be invisible, because it would prevent a state from ever taking an action, in the first place, that it believed would provoke retaliation, what would be visible in the historical record would generally be only deterrence failures that led to war, not successful examples of deterrence that maintained the peace. Despite decades of research and debate on the subject of deterrence, scholars still greatly dispute whether deterrence is generally successful or not, or what historical cases legitimately represent one or the other outcome. Indeed, the long peace of the Cold War and the absence of a World War III, between 1947 and 1991, are still hotly debated among scholars, who see it as either (1) a powerful example of how deterrence can maintain international peace and stability or (2) a case of extraordinary good luck, in which war was avoided for other reasons (see an excellent overview of this debate in Gjelstad & Njolstad, 1996).

The Effects of Problem Representation or Framing Upon Perception and Decision Making in the Security Context

How policymakers frame or represent (structure or assign meaning to) a given policy problem, option, or situation—in other words, how they perceive it, or see it as similar or dissimilar to previous events—can be critically important in determining how they will behave when making decisions in a security setting (see Sylvan & Voss, 1998; Tetlock & Belkin, 1996). At the simplest level, limitations on the ability of decision makers to accurately perceive the entirety of their policy environments (or the true range of options available to them in dealing with a given policy problem) may result in decisions being made that are based upon either a distorted or incomplete understanding of the situation (Jervis, 1976; Vertzberger, 1990). In security studies, for example, when assessing military balances of power, it is important to recognize that, although there is an *objective reality* regarding a nation's military capabilities (i.e., an actual number of tanks, aircraft, soldiers; specific qualitative characteristics of weapons systems that govern their performance on the battlefield; explicit military doctrines or strategies that will govern the use of a nation's armed forces in battle, etc.), it is how policymakers perceive their opponent's military forces and capabilities that will govern how they view them and the decisions they will make vis-à-vis that country.

Recall the earlier example of Saddam Hussein's calculations prior to the Gulf War, in which his misperceptions regarding his own military's abilities to create a war of attrition dilemma for American policymakers were coupled with his mistaken belief that the United States was unwilling to absorb large numbers of combat casualties, leading him to discount the credibility of American military threats over Kuwait (Stein, 1992). Similarly, there was an *objective military reality* in 1914 (at that point unknown to Europe's military leaders) regarding how military strategies emphasizing the "cult of the offensive" and infantry assaults would fare against the advent of the heavy machine gun, more precise and powerful artillery, and their use to defend fortified positions (Keegan, 1998; Tuchman, 1962), but decisions were made based upon policymakers' mistaken perceptions of reality (Snyder, 1984; Van Evera, 1984).

How policymakers frame their strategic environments can shape what they believe to be their options. For example, it was universally accepted military doctrine prior to 1914 that technological advances (quantified in terms of machine guns, numbers of divisions, ability to mobilize and transport these forces to the fronts using railroads, etc.) made modern war so destructive that it could only last a matter of months. Further, the first nation to fully deploy its forces, given this revolution in military technology, would automatically win (Keegan, 1998; Tuchman, 1962). This representation of the problem by decision makers contributed to their sense of a security dilemma and to failure to recognize a new military reality in which weapons technology had rendered the offensive strategy inferior to the defensive one.

To illustrate this point about how our subjective perceptions of the situation are not necessarily driven by objective reality, imagine that your professor advises your class that there is a giant pit in the floor in the middle of your classroom, filled with sharp iron spikes. With the room's lights on, and the warnings about its existence given, it is highly unlikely that students would inadvertently stumble into it. Thus, the objective reality is observable (students could see the pit), the credibility of the threat (that falling into the pit would cause serious, if not fatal, injury) is believable, and students' behavior is impacted (no one attempts shortcuts across the center of the room after class). However, if the lights are off and no warnings are given, then many students would likely fall into the pit. In neither case is the students' behavior irrational, and whether the light is on or off, the pit continues to exist. Simply put, individuals respond to the reality they perceive, and their behavior is unaffected by what they either do not believe to be true or do not observe directly. This illustrates the nature of the problem for policymakers in effectively communicating deterrent threats to their opponents (who subjectively perceive reality) and how powerful framing effects might be, once policymakers have accepted as truth a particular formulation of reality.

For example, a growing literature has focused upon how policymakers use of **analogical reasoning** to frame (or understand) policy problems and upon the kinds of policy options that might be appropriate to address their problem (Khong, 1992; May, 1973; Neustadt & May, 1986). An **analogy** is essentially a decision-making heuristic, or shorthand, in which policymakers see a current event or situation as similar to (or sharing many of the same characteristics as) a previous historical event. When U.S. policymakers, for instance, consider intervening militarily in almost any situation, whether it is sending the military to the Persian Gulf to liberate Kuwait after the Iraqi invasion, sending peacekeepers to Bosnia to keep the warring factions apart and to maintain regional stability, or even to engage in humanitarian relief efforts to prevent starvation in Somalia—the **Vietnam analogy** is frequently heard (Preston, 2001). This analogy suggests that any U.S. military intervention will likely result in the same outcome as did American intervention in Vietnam during the 1960s and 1970s: an open-ended commitment to a losing cause that will result in tremendous bloodshed for our troops and political unrest at home. To say that something will be "another Vietnam" is to essentially say, "We should not become involved because of how bad our experience in Vietnam was" and that we will be inviting a political disaster.

Of course, although the Vietnam analogy works against policymakers intervening militarily abroad, other analogies encourage such intervention. The **Munich analogy**, for example, argues that, if you do not stand up to an aggressor, and instead seek to appease them or make concessions to them in the hopes of keeping the peace, the end result will be to only encourage them to be even more aggressive and will likely bring on the very war you sought to avoid (Khong, 1992; Neustadt & May, 1986; May, 1973). Obviously, this analogy grew out of an earlier historical experience, that of British Prime Minister Neville Chamberlain's efforts at Munich, in 1938, to appease Adolf Hitler's territorial demands and to achieve "peace in our time," through these concessions. The result of Chamberlain's appeasement has been argued by many to have only emboldened Hitler more and to have encouraged further actions on his part (such as the invasion of the rest of Czechoslovakia in 1938 and Poland in 1939), which subsequently led to World War II.

Clearly, how policymakers perceive the situation, and what kind of analogies they use to understand the problems they face, have a tremendous impact upon the ultimate policy decisions for war or peace. As Khong (1992) illustrates in *Analogies at War*, President Lyndon Johnson and his advisers were influenced the most by the Munich analogy in their decision making on whether or not to intervene militarily in Vietnam in 1965. Seeing the North Vietnamese as aggressive expansionists in the Hitler mold, perhaps as mere surrogates for a general pattern of Soviet-led communist aggression worldwide (the dominant U.S. policy view, given containment policy), the choice was clear for Johnson. Intervening in Vietnam, they thought, was the only thing standing between maintaining regional stability and a row of falling dominoes throughout Southeast Asia, as country after country eventually would fall to continuing communist aggression after South Vietnam was conquered. Johnson chose to send more and more U.S. troops to Vietnam (Preston, 2001). Similarly, during the lead-up to the Gulf War, President George Bush frequently invoked the Munich analogy in explaining the need to send U.S. forces to oppose Saddam Hussein and to liberate Kuwait. In this case, the analogy suggested that Hussein would continue his aggression into Saudi Arabia and beyond, if left unchecked in Kuwait (Preston, 2001). In contrast, John F. Kennedy's use of the **Guns of August analogy,** during the Cuban Missile Crisis of 1962—an analogy based upon the experience of the events leading up to the outbreak of the First World War, a war which none of the policymakers desired or intended to occur—led him to be far more cautious and mindful of his actions during the tense days of that crisis (Preston, 2001; Schlesinger, 1965; Sorensen, 1965). In this case, one could argue that analogy served a war-avoidance function for Kennedy and sensitized him to how easily the crisis could spin out-of-control and into war.

That analogies are always gross simplifications of reality, and that seldom are two historical situations identical, is beside the point. Policymakers use analogies in their decision making, sometimes well and sometimes poorly, and their use can (as illustrated) often have significant consequences in terms of the ultimate decisions for war or peace (Neustadt & May, 1986).

Another growing body of framing literature in political science seeks to apply **prospect theory** to foreign policy decision making and security issues (Haas, 2001; Lebow and Stein, 1987; Levy, 1997; McDermott, 1998). Building upon a psychological model developed by Kahneman and Tversky (1979), prospect theory predicts that individuals will tend to be risk averse in the domain of gains and risk seeking in the domain of losses (Tetlock et al., 1991). Further, what determines whether something is considered to be a gain or a loss is determined relative to the original starting, or reference, point. In other words, "Change is evaluated relative to that position, but value itself derives from the difference between that starting, or reference, point and the amount of any positive or negative shift away from it" (McDermott, 1998, p. 28). As McDermott (1998) observes:

> In theoretical terms . . . people tend to be risk averse in the domain of gains and risk seeking in the domain of losses; this is the crux of prospect theory. In short, prospect theory predicts that domain affects risk propensity. . . . losing hurts more than a comparable gain pleases. . . . Loss aversion is exemplified by the endowment effect, whereby people value what they possess to a greater degree than they value an equally attractive alternative. This endowment bias makes equal trade unattractive. It also presents a bias toward the status quo in almost any negotiating context. (p. 29)

This determination of domain is inherently a subjective one, because individual policymakers may value certain outcomes (e.g., policy success, popularity, poll numbers) differently from one another, but prospect theory only needs to have knowledge of how policymakers perceive the domain (gains or losses), in order to predict their risk propensity (McDermott, 1998). In addition, prospect theory takes into account the fact that people assign different weights to the likelihood of certain probability outcomes. As McDermott (1998) observes, highly vivid, yet low-probability events (e.g., being in a plane crash) tend to be overweighted by people, but high- or medium-probability events (e.g., being in a car wreck) are subjectively underweighted:

> The classic examples of this are lotteries and insurance. In lotteries, people are willing to take a sure loss, however small, for the essentially nonexistent chance of a huge gain. In this way, people can be risk seeking in gains when the probability of gain is low. In insurance, people are willing to take a sure loss in the present to prevent the

small likelihood of a larger loss in the future. In this situation, people can be risk averse in losses when the probability of loss is small. In both these situations, expected utility models might not consider such behavior to be normative. However, prospect theory accounts for these discrepancies by noting the extreme (over)weight and attention that individuals give to small probabilities that potentially involve either huge gains (winning the lottery) or huge losses (losing your house in a fire). This phenomenon helps account for worst-case scenario planning. (pp. 31–32)

Translated to questions of international conflict and war, one would expect policymakers of nations to take far greater chances (and risk war far more often) to protect their current resources (e.g., national territory, economic relationships, etc.) than they would to gain additional resources beyond what they currently control. In other words, they would be expected to be risk averse in the domain of gains and risk acceptant in the domain of losses. For deterrence, this suggests that the credibility of a threat made by a nation faced with losing its national sovereignty, territory, or very existence, is far higher (and more believable) than threats made by states just seeking aggrandizement (more territory). Further, in crisis management terms, this suggests that the danger of war is greatest, and the risks likely to be taken by states are more extreme, when a crisis threatens the current resources of the state (the status quo). At the same time, prospect theory poses a serious challenge to traditional realist, power politics formulations of international politics (Morgenthau, 1948), because it questions its main assumptions about power-maximizing as the primary goal of states in their interactions with one another (McDermott, 1998). Instead, although states may seek to increase their own power resources when risks are low, they will focus first and foremost upon maintaining what they currently have (the status quo). Further, they will be less likely to go to war to obtain gains from other states when potential risks are high (be risk averse in the domain of gains), and they will be far more likely to go to war with other states when their own resources are threatened (be more risk acceptant in the domain of losses).

Accountability

Another interesting psychological concept that has implications for understanding international conflict is **accountability** (Tetlock, 1985). Specifically, accountability argues that political leaders will take greater risks, and will be more likely to engage in conflict, the more they lack accountability to a higher power (i.e., a ruling coalition, a voting public, a military junta). President Saddam Hussein of Iraq, for example, answered (and was accountable) to no one domestically, and he could essentially do as he liked in terms of foreign or domestic policy. Because there was no accountability internally, one would expect him to engage in much riskier, more conflictual behavior toward other nations (such as Kuwait) than we would of leaders of more democratic nations, who are more accountable to others (such as a voting public, Parliament or Congress, etc.). This basic notion of accountability underpins much of the current democratic peace argument—that democracies are inherently more peaceful (and less warlike) than autocracies—and is clearly useful in terms of understanding the psychology of international conflict (Hermann & Kegley, 1995).

Group Dynamics and Malfunctions of Process

Finally, malfunctions of group process or decision making under stress have often been suggested to increase the likelihood of bad decisions or conflict (Hermann, 1979; Janis, 1972; Janis & Mann, 1977). Perhaps the most familiar argument regarding such group malfunctions under stress has been that of Janis (1972) and his **groupthink** concept, presented in chapter 4. As noted there, Janis argues that governmental policy groups, particularly at high levels, tend to be smaller groups that, eventually develop a pattern of interactions among group members that emphasizes the maintenance of group cohesion, solidarity, and loyalty. Although not necessarily a bad thing, this emphasis upon group cohesion can lead to faulty group decision processes, or **group malfunctions**. These faulty processes, which become far more pronounced and prevalent during the high **stress** conditions of crises, can lead groups to become even more insular and to fall into patterns of decision making that increase the chances of conflict. As mentioned in chapter 4, the eight symptoms of groupthink listed by Janis (1972) are:

1. **The illusion of invulnerability**. Group members find a comfort zone within the group, because of the psychological belief that there is safety in numbers. Ultimate responsibility for group decisions or actions is dispersed among the entire group, making no one individual ultimately accountable for the outcomes. Janis notes that this leads to a tendency towards the **risky shift**, or pattern in which groups tend to take riskier decisions (and more chances) than do individuals.

2. **Rationalization**. Group members rationalize (or explain away) information or opinions that do not support the dominant preexisting beliefs held by the group members.

3. **Belief in the inherent morality of the group**. Group members share with one another the belief that they are making the best decisions possible, that they are trying to do the right thing, and that they have a solid moral compass.

4. **Active use of stereotypes**. Group members simplify reality and their information processing, through reliance upon use of stereotypes and other simplifying heuristics.

5. **Use of direct pressure on dissenters**. Group members pressure individual group members who may disagree with the dominant view of the group, to "not rock the boat" and to go along with the group.

6. **Self-censorship**. Dissenting group members, in time, cease to challenge or question the dominant group views, because of the application of direct pressure upon them and because of a concern for group cohesion.

7. **Use of mindguards**. Self-appointed individuals within the group seek to maintain the group's cohesion and morale by applying direct pressure to dissenters and by preventing access of information or views to the group that might challenge its existing beliefs.

8. **Illusion of unanimity**. Group members come to believe that everyone in the group agrees with the dominant group view and supports their policy decisions, because no one vocally objects. It is an illusion, because of the use of direct pressure and the self-censorship of group members, who may well disagree with the group, but lack the will to object.

Janis (1972) argues that these group malfunctions, leading to groupthink by senior decision-making groups, led to a number of historical **policy fiascoes** (or failures of policy). Examples of such fiascoes include U.S. naval leaders' decision making prior to Pearl Harbor, the Kennedy administration's decision making surrounding the Bay of Pigs, the decision by General Douglas MacArthur to approach the Yalu River during the Korean War (thereby provoking Chinese intervention), and the decision by the Johnson administration to intervene in Vietnam in 1965. That Janis identifies only cases of war, or resort to force, as policy fiascoes, in his book, illustrates his strong normative bias against war ('t Hart et al., 1997). However, regardless of the subjectivity of his overall analyses, Janis does make a useful point, in observing that the interactional and decision dynamics within groups can sometimes lead policymakers to war. A more detailed discussion of group dynamics is presented in chapter 4.

CONCLUSION

Throughout this chapter, numerous examples have been provided of how political psychological approaches have been applied, in political science to the study of international security and conflict, ranging from the security dilemma, to deterrence and prospect theories, to the impact of group dynamics. Obviously, this brief review merely scratches the surface of this wide-ranging security literature and is by no means intended to be exhaustive. Our task was not to replicate a national security textbook, but to provide students with a useful insight into how psychological approaches have been employed to study important political questions. Further, it should be noted that much of the literature discussed elsewhere in this textbook, such as the development of social identity, stereotypes, ethnic conflict, and so on can also be usefully applied to the study of international security and conflict. Indeed, psychological approaches have much to offer, as we continue to advance our understanding of this important subject.

KEY TERMS

Accountability
Analogy
Deterrence
Group malfunctions
Groupthink

Guns of August analogy
Munich analogy
Policy fiascoes
Protracted crisis
    approach

Prospect theory
Risky shift
Security dilemma
Vietnam analogy

Topics, Theories/Explanations, and Cases in Chapter 10

Topics	Theories/Explanations	Cases
Why war?	Psychology of fear and misperception	Peloponnesian War
	Security dilemma	World War I
Security dilemma	Fundamental attribution error	Cold War
	Inherent bad faith	
	Spiral process	
Psychology of deterrence	Cognitive rigidity	Cold War
	Belief perseverance	Iraq protracted crisis
	Spiral model	General and immediate deterrence
		Game of chicken
Problem representation	Framing	Vietnam analogy
	Analogical reasoning	Munich analogy
	Prospect theory	Guns of August analogy
Accountability	Group malfunctions Stress	
Groupthink	Eight symptoms of groupthink	

SUGGESTIONS FOR FURTHER READING

Overviews of the Security Literature

Haftendorn, H. (1991). The security puzzle: Theory-building and discipline-building in international security. *International Studies Quarterly, 35,* 3–17.

Krause, K., & Williams, M. C. (1996). Broadening the agenda of security studies: Politics and methods. *Mershon International Studies Review, 40,* 229–254.

Walt, S. M. (1991). The renaissance of security studies. *International Studies Quarterly, 35,* 211–239.

Rational-Choice or Game Theory Approaches

Brams, S. J. (1985). *Superpower games: Applying game theory to superpower conflict.* New Haven, CT: Yale University Press.

Walt, S. M. (1999). Rigor or rigor mortis? Rational choice and security studies. *International Security, 23,* 5–48.

Classic Treatments of Security or Deterrence

Brody, B. (1973). *War and politics.* New York: Macmillan.

Schelling, T. (1960). *The strategy of conflict.* London: Oxford University Press.

Mearsheimer, J. J. (1983). *Conventional deterrence.* Ithaca, NY: Cornell University Press.

Powell, R. (1990). *Nuclear deterrence theory: The search for credibility.* New York: Cambridge University Press.

Schelling, T. (1966). *Arms and influence.* New Haven, CT: Yale University Press.

ENDNOTE

1. See Mearsheimer (1983) for more on wars of attrition and other military strategies.

Glossary

achievement motive.   A person's concern with excellence and task accomplishment.

accountability.   To have one's actions be transparent and evaluated by authorities with the power to punish wrongdoing. Political leaders will take greater risks, and be more likely to engage in conflict, the more they lack accountability to a higher power.

affect.   A generic term for a whole range of preferences, evaluations, moods, and *emotions*.

affiliation intimacy motive.   Concern with establishing, maintaining, or restoring warm and friendly relationships with other persons or *groups*.

agenda setting.   When the media defines which issues need attention and in what form.

agreeableness.   A *Big Five* personality trait. It means a person is trusting, positive, and good-natured.

ally image.   A country or *group* perceived to be equal to the perceiver's country in terms of culture and capability, with good intentions, multiple groups in decision-making roles, and associated with threat or opportunity.

altruists.   People who help others and who speak out, despite a risk for their personal safety.

analogy.   A decision-making heuristic, or shorthand, in which policymakers see a current event or situation as similar to (or sharing many of the same characteristics as) a previous historical event.

assimilation effect.   When information similar to other information is perceived as even more similar than it objectively is.

associative networks.   *Knowledge structures* embedded in long-term memory, consisting of nodes linked to one another, forming a network of associations.

attitudes.   An enduring system of positive or negative *beliefs*, affective feelings and *emotions*, and action tendencies regarding attitude objects, that is, the entity being evaluated.

attribution theory.   A psychological theory that argues that people process information like naïve scientists; that is, they search for cause in the behavior of others.

authoritarian personality.   A personality type. Originally the type was said to contain the traits of conventionalism (rigid adherence to conventional values), submission to authority figures, authoritarian aggression (i.e., aggressive impulses toward those who are not conventional), anti-intraception (i.e., rejection of tenderness, imagination, subjectivity), superstition and *stereotype* (fatalistic belief in mystical determinants of the future, and rigid thinking), high value placed on power and toughness, destructiveness and cynicism, projectivity (i.e., the *projection* outward of unacceptable impulses), and an excessive concern with the sexual activity of others. In Altemeyer's (1996) reconceptualization, the type has three traits: authoritarian submission, authoritarian aggression, and conventionalism.

autokinetic effect.   A perceptual illusion that occurs when a single point of light in a darkened room appears to be moving.

availability heuristic.   When people predict the likelihood of something, based on the ease with which they can think of instances or examples of it.

avoidance of value trade-offs.   When people mistakenly believe that a policy that contributes to one value also contributes to several other values, even though there is no reason why the world should be constructed in such a neat and helpful manner.

balance.   A harmonious state in which the entities comprising the situation and the feelings about them fit together without stress.

barbarian image.   A country or *group* perceived to be superior in capability, inferior in culture, monolithic in decision making, and associated with extreme threat.

bargaining theory.   When coalitions form on the basis of considering expected payoffs.

belief system.   A clustering of *beliefs*.

beliefs.   Associations people create between an object and its attributes.

Big Five.   Core personality dimensions or traits: *neuroticism*, *extroversion*, *agreeableness*, *openness to experience*, and *conscientiousness*.

black and white model.   A model develop by Converse (1964), describing responses to *attitude* questions, which, for some people, remain very stable, but for others, the responses change in an apparently random pattern.

bolstering.   When multiple reasons occur for the correctness of a decision, based on information processing.

bystander phenomenon.   When people are part of a *group*, there is a *diffusion of responsibility*, and people feel less compelled to intervene and help.

christian identity.   An unusual reading of the Bible often adhered to by racist groups in America which maintains that White people, but not non-Whites, are descended from Adam and Eve. Non-Whites are deemed "mud people."

coercive power.   The capacity to punish those who do not comply with requests or demands.

cognition.   A collective term for the psychological processes involved in the acquisition, organization, and use of knowledge.

cognitive complexity.   Ability to differentiate the environment: Degree of differentiation a person shows in describing or discussing other people, places, policies, ideas, or things.

cognitive processes.   What happens in the mind while people move from observation of a stimulus to a response to that stimulus.

cognitive style.   The way a person gathers and processes information from his environment.

cohesion.   The factors that cause a *group* member to remain in the group.

collegial management style.   Emphasizes teamwork, shared responsibility, and problem solving within a *group*.

colonial image.   A country or *group* perceived as inferior in culture and capability, benign in intentions, monolithic in decision making, and associated with opportunity.

collective fences.   When individual members of a group avoid behaviors costly to them as individuals, resulting in harm to the group as a whole.

collective trap.   Behaviors that reward an individual *group* member can be harmful to the rest of the group, especially if engaged in by enough group members.

competitive management style.   Relatively unstructured information network, with leader placed in arbiter position among competing advisers with overlapping areas of authority.

conformity.   The tendency to change one's *beliefs* or behaviors, so that they are consistent with the standards set by the *group*.

conscientiousness.   A *Big Five* personality trait. It means a person is responsible, dependable, and goal-directed.

contact hypothesis.   The argument that increasing intergroup contact, exposing people to the complexity of *group* members, breaks down *stereotypes*.

contrast effect.   A social category serves as an anchor or central reference point for incoming information. When information is compared to that anchor and when it is different from expectations, the contrast effect makes it seem moreso.

core community nonnation-states.   Countries with a dominant ethnic or sectarian community, who believe that they are the primary nation embodied in the country and who identify with that nation in the strongest terms. In addition, that community tends to have great capability and control of the political system.

culture of terror.   An institutionalized system of permanent intimidation of the masses or subordinated communities by the elite, characterized by the use of torture, disappearances, and other forms of extrajudicial *death squad* killings as standard practice. A culture of terror establishes collective fear as a brutal means of social control. In these systems, there is a constant threat of *repression*, torture, and death for anyone who is actively critical of the political status quo.

death squads.   "Progovernment *groups* who engage in extrajudicial killings of people they define as enemies of the state" (Sluka, 2000, p. 141).

defense mechanisms.   *Unconscious* techniques used to distort reality and prevent people from feeling anxiety. They are also used to defend the *ego*.

degenerate image.   A country or *group* perceived as superior or equal in culture and capability, but lacking resolve and will. It is associated with perceptions of opportunity.

dehumanization.   A process in which a particular social *group* is regularly described as less than human, and therefore deserving of treatment one would not administer to a human being.

deindividuation.   This occurs when people attribute their behavior to the *group*'s behavior and thereby abandon individual responsibility for their own actions. There is a *diffusion of responsibility*.

denial.   A *defense mechanism* wherein people may deny reality (e.g., denying the country is going to war, despite the mobilization of troops) or may deny an impulse (e.g., proclaiming that you are not angry when you are).

deterrence.   The threat by one political actor to take actions in response to another actor's potential actions, which would make the costs (or losses) incurred far outweigh any possible benefits (or gains) obtained by the aggressor.

diffusion of responsibility.   When individuals feel no responsibility for their actions. It occurs when there is more than one person present in the situation to take all or some of the responsibility for the outcomes.

dissonance.   An aversive state that results when behavior is inconsistent with *attitudes*.

drunkard's search.   An informational shortcut named after the drunkard who lost his keys in the street and looks for them under the lamppost, because the light is better there, not because that is where he lost the keys. This is analogous to the use of information in political decisions when people reduce complicated issues and choices among candidates to simple comparisons, because that is easier.

ego.   The part of the personality that moderates between *id*, and its desire for pleasure, and the realities of the social world.

emotion.   A complex assortment of *affects*, beyond merely good feelings or bad, to include delight, serenity, anger, sadness, fear, and more.

empathy.   "An 'other-centered' *emotion* which is produced by observing another individual in need and taking that individual's perspective" (Rumble, 2003, p. 8; Batson, 1991).

enemy image.   The enemy is perceived as relatively equal in capability and culture. In its most extreme form, the diabolical enemy is seen as irrevocably aggressive in motivation, monolithic in decisional structure, and highly rational in decision making (to the point of being able to generate and orchestrate multiple complex conspiracies).

entiativity.   The extent to which a collection of people is perceived as a coherent entity.

escalation of commitment.   This occurs in situations in which some course of action has led to losses, but there is a possibility of achieving better outcomes by investing further time, money, or effort.

ethnocentrism.   The view of things in which one's own *group* is the center of everything and looks with contempt on outsiders.

expected payoffs.   Expectations based on *norms* of equity and equality and *group* members will appeal to whichever norm provides them with the largest payoff.

externals.   People who believe the external environment determines strongly what happens to them. They are more susceptible to authority. *Contrast* **internals**.

extremist.   A person who is excessive and inappropriately enthusiastic and/or inappropriately concerned with significant life purposes, implying a focused and highly personalized interpretation of the world. Politically, it is behavior that is strongly controlled by *ideology*, in which the influence of ideology is such that it excludes or attenuates other social, political, or personal forces that might be expected to control and influence behavior.

extroversion.   A *Big Five* personality trait. It means a person is outgoing, talkative, assertive, and likes to socialize.

formalistic management style.   Emphasis upon strict hierarchical, orderly decision structures.

forming.   The first stage of *group* formation. This stage is also referred to as the orientation stage, because prospective members are orienting themselves to the group.

fundamental attribution error.   Occurs when people attribute other people's behavior to internal, dispositional causes, rather than to situational causes.

fundamental interpersonal relations orientation (FIRO).   An explanation of how joining a *group* can fulfill psychological needs. According to this perspective, joining a group can satisfy three basic needs: **inclusion** (the desire to be part of a group), **control** (the need to organize an aspect of the group), and **affection** (the desire to establish positive relations with others). For individuals with these needs, joining a group offers them a way to fulfill these needs.

funnel of causality.   Distinguishes long-term factors that affect how Americans vote, (attachment to a party or *party identification* and *group* interests), from short-term factors, (currently important issues and candidates and their qualities).

genocide.   Actions designed to eliminate a *group* of people from the face of the earth.

Gresham's law of political information.   An informational shortcut wherein the use of a small amount of personal information about a candidate dominates a large amount of historical information of that candidates historical record.

group.   A collection of people who are perceived to belong together and who are dependent on one another.

group development.   The stages of growth and change that occur in a *group*, from its formation to its dissolution.

group malfunctions.   Faulty *group* decision processes.

group polarization.   The tendency for individuals' opinions to become more extreme after a *group* discussion than before the discussion.

groupthink.   Governmental policy *groups*, particularly at high levels, tend to be smaller groups that, in time, develop a pattern of interactions between group members, which emphasizes the maintenance of group cohesion, solidarity, and loyalty. This emphasis upon group cohesion can lead to faulty group decision processes, or *group malfunctions*.

Guns of August analogy.   An *analogy* based upon the experience of the events leading up to the outbreak of the First World War, a war that none of the policymakers desired or intended to have occur.

heuristic.   Mental shortcuts in processing information about others.

id.   The warehouse for all instincts and drives. The id follows the pleasure principle.

ideologue.   A person who knows what liberal and conservative values are, what positions on important political issues are liberal and conservative positions, which party represents liberal and which party represents conservative principles, and which candidates stand for which issues.

ideology.   A particularly elaborate, closely-woven, and far-ranging structure of *attitudes* and *beliefs*.

image.   A political psychology concept equivalent to a *stereotype* of a political *group* or country. Images contain information about a country's capabilities, culture, intentions, the kinds of decision-making groups (lots of people involved in decision making or only a few), and perceptions of threat or opportunity.

imperialist image.   A country or *group* perceived to be superior in capability, dominating in culture, exploitive in intentions, and associated with threat.

impression-based model of information processing.   The argument that, as information is acquired, it is used to enhance and update the *beliefs* about a candidate or party, and the specific details of the information are forgotten.

in-group.   *Groups* we belong to.

internals.   People who believe they have considerable control over their fate. They are more likely to resist authority. *Contrast* **externals**.

irridentism.   The desire to join together all parts of a national community within a single territorial state.

issue.   A dispute about public policy.

issue frames.   Alternative definitions, constructions, or depictions of a policy problem.

knowledge structures.   The mental organization of knowledge about political actors and issues.

levels of conceptualization.   A classification scheme of Americans' political sophistication, ranging from "*ideologues*," those who are very sophisticated, to "absence of issue content," those with very little knowledge of politics.

locus of control.   View of the world in which an individual does or does not perceive some degree of control over situations in which they are involved; whether government can influence what happens in or to a nation.

Maximalists.   Challengers to the *Michigan model*, who argue that people do not necessarily think linearly about politics, that *emotions* play a role as well, and that the average American is more politically sophisticated than the Michigan model maintains.

Michigan model.   A pioneering framework examining the political *attitudes* of Americans. The scholars of the Michigan school developed a model of American attitudes, in which it was assumed that Americans should have an integrated mental map of the political system, connecting candidates, parties, issues, and *groups* to ideological principles, in a consistent manner. Their research revealed that this is fairly rare in the American public.

minimal group paradigm.   Competition can occur, even when the stakes are only psychological, and among *groups* that are arbitrarily formed by experimenters with no real interaction or conflict.

minimum-power theory.   When coalition members expect payoffs that are directly proportional to their ability to turn a losing coalition into a winning one.

minimum-resource theory.   When *group* members form coalitions on the basis of equal input–equal output.

motives.   Those aspects of personality concerned with goals and goal-directed actions.

mujahedin.   Holy warriors who fought to get the Soviet Union out of Muslim Afghanistan.

multiethnic or multisectarian state.   A country with at least two ethnic *groups*, neither of which is capable of assimilating or absorbing the other nor of seceding and maintaining independence, where primary identity is with the ethnic group.

multinational states.   A country in which several *groups* of people, who think of themselves as separate nations and who actually have the capacity to establish viable independent states, live together in a single country.

Munich analogy.   If you do not stand up to an aggressor, and instead seek to appease them or make concessions to them in the hopes of keeping the peace, the end result will be to only encourage them to be even more aggressive and probably to bring on the very war you sought to avoid.

nation-state.   A state in which the average citizen has a primary identity with the national community, believes that community should be an independent state, and grants that community primary loyalty.

nationalism.   The *belief* that a *group* of people, or a community, belong together in an independent country, and a willingness to grant that community primary loyalty.

need for achievement.   A personality trait involving concern with excellence and task accomplishment.

need for affiliation intimacy.   A personality trait involving a concern for close relations with others.

need for power.   A personality trait involving a concern for impact and prestige.

neurotic anxiety.   A fear of being punished for doing something the *id* wants the person to do.

neuroticism.   A *Big Five* personality trait. It means that a person is anxious, has maladaptive coping abilities, and is prone to depression.

normal vote.   An election in which people voted according to their *party identification* and in which independents split evenly between the two parties.

norming.   The third stage of *group development*, a phase in which conflict is replaced with cohesion and feelings of unity.

norms.   Expectations about how all *group* members should behave in a group.

openness.   A *Big Five* personality characteristic. It means a person is proactive, independent, and tolerant of different viewpoints.

operational codes.   Constructs representing the overall *belief* systems of leaders about the world (i.e., how it works, what it is like, what kinds of actions are most likely to be successful, etc.).

orientation toward political conflict.   Relates to how open a president is to face-to-face disagreements and confrontations among his advisers.

out-group.   *Groups* that we do not belong to.

paramilitaries.   "Organizations that resort to the physical elimination of presumed auxiliaries of rebel groups and of individuals seen as subversive of the moral order. . . . They mostly operate through *death squads*" (Cubides, 2001, 129).

party identification.   An *attitude* regarding attachment to (identification with) a political party.

performing.   The fourth stage of *group development*. Performance usually only occurs when the groups mature and have successfully gone through the previous stages of development. Many groups do not reach the performing stage.

perspective-taking.   Involves empathizing with others, experiencing their perspective and the *emotions* that it generates in them.

phenomenal absolutism error.   When a judgment that the observer makes about the *group* is not perceived as a judgment about the group, but as an attribute of the group itself.

policy fiascoes.   Failures of policy.

politics-is-complicated model (also known as the **principled objection** model).   The argument that White Americans vary in the degree to which they blame the inequalities between the races on structural factors (such as the historical legacy of slavery and current system-wide discrimination), as opposed to individual factors (individual acts of *prejudice* and discrimination, rather than system-wide factors).

power motive.   Concern with establishing, maintaining, or restoring one's power, (i.e., one's impact, control, or influence over others).

prejudice.   A response to out-group members, based upon their membership in the group; a negative evaluative orientation toward a group and consequently an aversion to group members; an attribution of negative characteristics toward a group and its members that is incorrect; and, finally, consistency in the negative orientation toward the group and its members.

priming.   When the media points out to the public which elements of which issues are important.

prisoner's dilemma.   When participants cannot communicate with one another, yet the outcome of the game for each person is contingent on what the other person decides.

projection.   A defense mechanism attributing one's own objectionable impulses to another person, or projecting them onto another.

prospect theory.   Predicts that individuals will tend to be risk averse in the domain of gains and risk seeking in the domain of losses.

protracted crisis approach.   The perspective that a crisis should be viewed as a long series of separate and distinct *deterrence* and compellence exchanges running throughout the crisis from the beginning until the end of any episode.

psychoanalytic or psychodynamic theories.   Psychoanalytic theories assess the role of the *unconscious* in human behavior and the motives and drives that underlie behavior.

rationalization.   A defense mechanism wherein people reinterpret their own objectionable behavior to make it seem less objectionable.

reality principle.   According to the reality principle, the demands of the *id* will be blocked or channeled in accordance with reality, but also in accordance with the personality.

realistic conflict theory.   Proposal that intergroup *stereotyping* and derogation occurs as a result of competition for resources and competitive goals.

referent power.   Power a person possesses when others identify with that person, because they are similar to us or because we want to be like them.

representativeness heuristic.   A shortcut using probability expectations to make judgments about others.

repression.   A defense mechanism in which a person involuntarily eliminates an unpleasant memory.

reward power.   The ability to control the distribution of positive and negative reinforcers.

right-wing authoritarianism.   Submission to perceived authorities, particularly those in the establishment or established system of governance.

risky shift.   When *groups* tend to take riskier decisions (and more chances) than do individuals.

rogue image.   A country or *group* perceived as inferior in culture and capability, with monolithic decision making, and associated with threat.

roles.   Expectations about how a person ought to behave in a *group*.

scapegoat.   A *group* that is blamed for all of society's illnesses.

schema.   A cognitive structure that represents knowledge about a concept or type of stimulus, including its attributes and the relations among those attributes.

scientific method.   Four cyclical steps that researchers repeatedly execute as they try to understand and predict behavior: making observations, formulating tentative explanations, making further observations and experimenting, and refining and retesting explanations.

security dilemmas. Conflicts in which the efforts made by one state to defend itself are simultaneously seen as threatening by its opponents, even if those actions were not intended to be threatening.

sense of efficacy. A presidential stylistic variable involving presidents' confidence and interest in particular policy areas. Presidents give high priority to policy areas in which they have a strong sense of efficacy.

shared sovereignty strategies. An integration strategy in which an ethnic or racial *group* is given some degree of self-rule.

social causality. During hard times, the *groups* that people are particularly attracted to are those that provide an ideological blueprint for a better world and an enemy who must be destroyed to fulfill the *ideology*.

social-decision schemes. The process by which *groups* combine the preferences of all the members of the group, to arrive at a single group decision.

social dominance theory. Presents a social dominance orientation measure that differentiates those who prefer social *group* relations to be equal or hierarchical, and the extent to which people want their *in-group* to dominate *out-groups*.

social identity. The part of a person's self-concept that is determined by the *groups* to which the person belongs.

social identity theory. Explores the impact of *group* identity and desire for positive comparisons to other groups on behavior.

social justification. When a *group*'s poor treatment is justified.

social learning theory. The argument that children learn negative *attitudes* and discriminatory behavior from their parents, teachers, family, friends, and others, when they are rewarded for such behavior.

social loafing. The tendency of *group* members to work less hard when in a group than when working alone.

status. How power is distributed among members in a *group*.

stereotypes. *Beliefs* about the attributes of people in particular *groups* or social categories.

storming. The second stage of *group development*, which is characterized as one of conflict.

suicide bomber. When a person is willing to commit suicide in order to ensure maximum effectiveness in a terrorist attack.

superego. The moral arm or conscience of the personality.

symbolic racism. The argument that racism in American still exists, but is disguised as traditional American individualist values.

task–interpersonal emphasis. Relative emphasis in interactions with others on getting the task done versus focusing on feelings and needs of others.

terrorism. "In principle, terrorism is deliberate and systematic violence performed by small numbers of people, whereas communal violence is spontaneous, sporadic, and requires mass participation. The purpose of terrorism is to intimidate a watching popular audience by harming only a few, whereas *genocide* is the elimination of entire communities. Terrorism is meant to hurt, not to destroy. Terrorism is preeminently political and symbolic, whereas guerilla warfare is a military activity. Repressive terror from above is the action of those in power, whereas terrorism is a clandestine resistance to authority." (Crenshaw, 2001, p. 406)

third-party intervention. A party that helps to reduce conflict in a group, by serving various functions.

transactional leadership. When the leader approaches followers with an eye toward exchanging one valued thing for another.

transformational leadership. When leaders engage their followers in such a way that they raise each other to higher levels of motivation and morality.

three-stage model of group decision making. According to Bales and Strodtbeck (1951), *groups* proceed through three stages before eventually arriving at a decision: orientation, discussion, and decision making.

traits. Personality characteristics that are stable over time and in different situations. Traits produce predispositions to respond in thinking, feeling, or actions to people, events, and situations, in a particular way.

truth and reconciliation commission. An investigative commission designed to reveal the truths of political violence and to achieve some measure of reconciliation and forgiveness. It gathers evidence, determines *accountability*, and often recommends policies for the treatment of victims and perpetrators.

ultimate attribution error. The use of *prejudices* and preexisting *beliefs* in evaluation of others.

unconscious. A part of the mind that people are unaware of. Freud introduced the idea that the mind is like an iceberg. Only a small part of the iceberg is visible, floating above water. Around 90% is underwater and unobservable. Similarly, people are conscious of only a small part of the mind.

utilitarian integration strategy. A strategy to promote integration by satisfying the populations' needs. It requires removing any obstacles to equality of access to important political positions in the country.

values. Deeply held *beliefs* about what should be true, even if it is not currently true.

variable. Something that is thought to influence, or to be influenced by, something else.

Vietnam analogy. This analogy suggests that any U.S. military intervention will likely result in the same outcome as did American intervention in Vietnam during the 1960s and 1970s; an open-ended commitment to a losing cause that will result in tremendous bloodshed for our troops and political unrest at home.

REFERENCES

Abanes, R. (1996). *American militias: Rebellion, racism and religion*. Downers Grove, IL: InterVarsity.

Adam, H., & Moodley, K. (1993). South Africa: The opening of the apartheid mind. In J. McGarry & B. O'Leary (Eds.), *The politics of ethnic conflict regulation*. New York: Routledge.

Adorno, T., Frenkel-Brunswick, E., Levinson, D., & Sanford, P. (1950). *The authoritarian personality*. New York: Harper.

Aldag, R. J., & Fuller, S. R. (1993). Beyond fiasco: A reappraisal of the groupthink phenomenon and a new model of group decision processes. *Psychological Bulletin, 113*, 533–552.

Alexander, M. G., Brewer, M. B., & Herrmann, R. K. (1999). Images and affect: A functional analysis of out-group stereotypes. *Journal of Personality and Social Psychology, 77*, 78–93.

Allen, C. F., & Portis, J. (1992). *The comeback kid: The life and career of Bill Clinton*. New York: Birch Lane.

Allen, V. L., & Wilder, D. A. (1979). Group categorization and attribution of belief similarity. *Small Group Behavior, 10*, 73–80.

Allison, G. (1971). *Essence of decision: Explaining the Cuban Missile Crisis*. Boston: Little, Brown.

Allison, G. & Zelikow, P. (1999). *Essence of decision: Explaining the Cuban Missile Crisis*. New York: Longman.

Allport, G. (1937). *Personality: A psychological interpretation*. New York: Holt, Rinehart & Winston.

Allport, G. (1954). *The nature of prejudice*. Cambridge, MA: Addison-Wesley.

Allport, G. (1961). *Pattern and growth in personality*. New York: Holt, Rinehart & Winston.

Allport, G. (1968). *The person in psychology*. Boston: Beacon.

Altemeyer, B. (1981). *Right-wing authoritarianism*. Winnipeg, Canada: University of Manitoba Press.

Altemeyer, B. (1988). *Enemies of freedom: Understanding right-wing authoritarianism*. San Francisco: Jossey-Bass.

Altemeyer, B. (1996). *The authoritarian specter*. Cambridges, MA: Harvard University Press.

Altemeyer, B. (1998). The other "authoritarian personality." *Advances in Experimental and Social Psychology, 30*, 47–92.

Ambrose, S. E. (1990). *Eisenhower: Soldier and president*. New York: Simon & Schuster.

American Patriotic Network: (2002). *How dead are the Bill of Rights?* retrieved on June 18, 2002 from http://www.civil-liberties.com

American Psychiatric Association. (2000). *Diagnostic and statistical manual of mental disorders: DSM-IV-TR*. Washington, DC: Author.

Anderson, J. (1983). *The architecture of cognition*. Cambridge, MA: Harvard University Press.

Ansolabehere, S., Behr, R., & Inyengar, S. (1993). *The media game*. New York: Macmillan.

Aronson, E., & Mills, J. (1959). Effect of severity of initiation on liking for a group. *Journal of Abnormal and Social Psychology, 59*, 177–181.

Asch, S. E. (1955). Opinions and social pressure. *Scientific American, 19,* 31–35.

Asch, S. E. (1956). Studies of independence and conformity: A minority of one against a unanimous majority. *Psychological Monographs, 70* (Serial No. 416).

Ayers, R. W. (2000). A world flying apart? Violent nationalist conflict and the end of the cold war. *Journal of Peace Research, 37,* 105–117.

Bales, R. F. (1951). *Interaction process analysis.* Boston: Addison-Wesley.

Bales, R. F., & Strodtbeck, F. L. (1951). Phases in group problem solving. *Journal of Abnormal Social Psychology, 46,* 485–495.

Ball, G. W. (1982). *The past has another pattern.* New York: Norton.

Bandura, A. (1973). *Aggression: A social learning analysis.* Englewood Cliffs, NJ: Prentice Hall.

Bandura, A. (1977). *Social learning theory.* Englewood Cliffs, NJ: Prentice Hall.

Bandura, A. (1986). *Social foundations of thought and action: A social cognitive theory.* Englewood Cliffs, NJ: Prentice Hall.

Barber, J. D. (1972). *The presidential character: Predicting performance in the White House.* Englewood Cliffs: Prentice Hall.

Barilleaux, R. J. (1992). George Bush and the changing context of presidential leadership. In R. J. Barilleaux & M. W. Stuckey (Eds.), *Leadership and the Bush presidency: Prudence or drift in an era of change?* (pp. 3–23). Westport, CT: Praeger.

Barley, S. R., & Bechky, B. A. (1994). In the backrooms of science: The work of technicians in science labs. *Work and Occupations, 21,* 85–126.

Barlow, K. M., Taylor, D. M., & Lambert, W. E. (2000). Ethnicity in America and feeling "American." *Journal of Psychology, 134,* 581–600.

Baron, R. A. (1989). Applicant strategies during job interviews. In R. W. Eder & G. R. Ferris (Eds.), *The employment interview: Theory, research, and practice* (pp. 204–216). Newbury Park, CA: Sage.

Baron, R. S. (1986). Distraction-conflict theory: Progress and problems. In L. Berkowitz (Ed.), *Advances in experimental social psychology* (Vol. 19, pp. 1–40). New York: Academic.

Baron, R. S., Vandello, U. A., & Brunsman, B. (1996). The forgotten variable in conformity research: Impact of task importance on social influence. *Journal of Personality and Social Psychology, 71,* 915–927.

Barrera, M., Jr. (1986). Distinctions between social support concepts, measures, and models. *American Journal of Community Psychology, 14,* 413–422.

Bartels, L. (1996). Uninformed votes: Information effects in presidential elections. *American Journal of Political Science, 40,* 194–230.

Bartels, L. (2000). Partisanship and voting behavior, 1952–1996. *American Journal of Political Science, 44,* 35–50.

Bartle, J. (1998). Left-right position matters but does social class? Causal models of the 1992 British general election. *British Journal of Political Science, 28,* 501–529.

Barton, S. L., Duchon, D., & Dunegan, K. J. (1989). An empirical test of Staw and Ross's prescription for the management of escalation of commitment behavior in organizations. *Decision Science, 20,* 532–544.

Bass, B. M. (1955). Authoritarianism or acquiescence? *Journal of Abnormal and Social Psychology, 51,* 616–623.

Bassili, J. N., & Provencal, A. (1988). Perceiving minorities: A factor-analytic approach. *Personality and Social Psychology Bulletin, 14,* 5–15.

Bastien, D., & Hostager, T. (1998). Jazz as a process of organizational innovation. *Communication Research, 15,* 582–602.

Batson, C. D. (1975). Rational processing or rationalization? The effect of disconfirming information on a stated religious belief. *Journal of Personality and Social Psychology, 32,* 176–184.

Baumeister, R. F. (1997). *Evil: Inside human violence and cruelty.* New York: Freeman.

Bazerman, M. H., Beekun, R. I., & Schoorman, F. D. (1982). Performance evaluation in a dynamic context: A laboratory study of the impact of a prior commitment to the rates. *Journal of Applied Psychology, 67,* 873–876.

Bazerman, M. H., Giuliano, T., & Appelman, A. (1984). Escalation in individual and group decision making. *Organizational Behavior and Human Performance, 33,* 141–152.

Beal, D. J., O'Neal, E. C., Ong, J., & Ruscher, J. B. (2000). The ways and means of interracial aggression: Modern racists' use of covert retaliation. *Personality and Social Psychology Bulletin, 26,* 1225–1238.

Beck, A. (1999). *Prisoners of hate: The cognitive basis of anger, hostility and violence.* New York: HarperCollins.

Beck, P., Dalton, R., Greene, S., & Huckfeldt, R. (2002). The social calculus of voting: Interpersonal, media, and organizational influences on presidential choices. *American Political Science Review, 96,* 57–74.

Beeler, J. D. (1998). Effects of counter-explanation on escalation of commitment: An experimental assessment of individual and collective decisions. *Advances in accounting behavioral research, 1,* 85–99.

Beeler, J. D., & Hunton, J. E. (1997). The influence of compensation method and disclosure level of information search strategy and escalation of commitment. *Journal of Behavioral Decision Making, 10,* 77–91.

Begley, S. (2000, May 21). The roots of evil. *Newsweek, 137,* pp. 30–35.

Bennis, W. G., & Shepard, H. A. (1956). A theory of group development. *Human Relations, 9,* 415–437.

Bentler, P. M., & Speckart, G. (1981). Attitudes cause behaviors: A structural equation analysis. *Journal of Personality and Social Psychology, 40,* 226–238.

Berelson, B., Lazarsfeld, P., & McFee, W. (1954). *Voting: A study of opinion formation in a presidential campaign.* Chicago: Chicago University Press.

Berent, M., & Krosnick, J. (1995). The relation between political attitude importance and knowledge structure. In M. Lodge & K. McGraw (Eds.), *Political judgment: Structure and Process.* Ann Arbor: University of Michigan Press.

Berger, J., Rosenholtz, S. J., & Zelditch, M. (1980). Status organizing processes. *Annual Review of Sociology, 6,* 479–508.

Berkowitz, L. (1989). Frustration-aggression hypothesis: Examination and reformulation. *Psychological Bulletin, 106,* 59–73.

Berman, L. (1982). *Planning a tragedy: The Americanization of the war in Vietnam.* New York: Norton.

Berman, L. (1989). *Lyndon Johnson's war: The road to stalemate in Vietnam.* New York: Norton.

Berman, L., & Goldman, E. (1996). Clinton's foreign policy at midterm. In C. Campbell & B. A. Rockman (Eds.), *The Clinton Presidency: First appraisals.* Chatham, NJ: Chatham House.

Bernstein, R., & Munro, R. (1997). *The coming conflict with China.* New York: Knopf.

Berscheid, E. (1987). Emotion and Interpersonal communication. In M. Roloff & G. Miller (Eds.), *Interpersonal processes: New directions in communication research.* Thousand Oaks, CA: Sage.

Bert, W. (1997). *The reluctant superpower: United States' policy in Bosnia, 1991–1995.* London: Macmillan.

Bertram, B. C. R. (1978). Living in groups: Predators and prey. In P. G. Bateson & R. A. Hinde (Eds.), *Behavioral ecology: An evolutional approach*. London: Blackwell.

Bettenhausen, K., & Murnighan, J. K. (1991). The development of an intragroup norm and the effects of interpersonal structural challenges. *Administrative Science Quarterly, 36*, 20–35.

Biddle, S. (1998). The past as prologue: Assessing theories of future warfare. *Security Studies, 8*, 1–74.

Bieri, J. (1966). Cognitive complexity and personality development. In O. J. Harvey (Ed)., *Experience, structure and adaptability* (pp.13–37). New York: Springer.

Billig, M., & Tajfel, H. (1973). Social categorization and similiarity in intergroup behavior. *European Journal of Social Psychology, 3*, 27–52.

Billings-Yun, M. (1988). *Decision against war: Eisenhower and Dien Bien Phu, 1954*. New York: Columbia University Press.

Birt, R. (1993). Personality and foreign policy: The case of Stalin. *Political Psychology, 15*, 607–626.

Bizman, A., & Amir, Y. (1984). Integration and attitudes. In Y. Amir & S. Sharan (Eds.), *School desegregation*. Hillsdale, NJ: Lawrence Erlbaum Associates.

Blanton, S. L. (1996). Images in conflict: The case of Ronald Reagan and El Salvador. *International Studies Quarterly, 40*, 23–44.

Blascovich, J., Nash, R. F., & Ginsburg, G. P. (1978). Heart rate and competitive decision making. *Personality and Social Psychology Bulletin, 4*, 115–118.

Blass, T. (1991). Understanding behavior in the Milgram obedience experiment: The role of personality, situations, and their interactions. *Journal of Personality and Social Psychology, 60*, 398–413.

Bobo, L. (1983). Whites' opposition to busing: symbolic racism or realistic group conflict? *Journal of personality and social psychology, 45*, 1196–1210.

Bobo, L. (1988). Group conflict, prejudice, and the paradox of contemporary racial attitudes. In P. Katz & D. Taylor (Eds.), *Eliminating racism: Profiles in controversy*. New York: Plenum.

Bobo, L., & Smith, R. (1994). From Jim Crow racism to laissez-faire racism: An essay on the transformation of racial attitudes in America. In W. Katkin & A. Tyree (Eds.), *Beyond pluralism: Essays on the conceptions of groups and identities in America*. Stanford, CA: Stanford University Press.

Bond, C. F., Jr., & Titus, L. J. (1983). Social facilitation: A meta-analysis of 241 studies. *Psychological Bulletin, 94*, 265–292.

Bond, R., & Smith, P. B. (1996). Culture and conformity: A meta-analysis of studies using Asch's line judgment task. *Psychological Bulletin, 119*, 111–137.

Bone, P. (1999). *Rwanda: The Children's Return*. Retrieved September 20, 2000 from http://theage.com.au/news/agenews/pbrwanda.htm

Bowen, M. G. (1987). The escalation phenomenon reconsidered: Decision dilemmas or decision errors? *Academy of Management Review, 12*, 52–66.

Brams, S. J. (1985). *Superpower games: Applying game theory to superpower conflict*. New Haven, CT: Yale University Press.

Brauer, M., Judd, C. M., & Gliner, M. D. (1995). The effects of repeated expressions on attitude polarization during group discussions. *Journal of Personality and Social Psychology, 68*, 1014–1029.

Braungart, R. G., & Braungart, M. (1992). From protest to terrorism: The case of SDS and the Weathermen. In D. della Porta (Ed.), *Social movements and violence: Participation in underground organizations* (pp. 45–78). Greenwich, CT: JAI.

Brawley, L. R., Carron, A. V., & Widmeyer, W. N. (1988). Exploring the relationship between cohesion and group resistance to disruption. *Journal of Sport and Exercise Psychology, 10,* 199–213.

Brehm, J. W. (1976). Responses to loss of freedom: A theory of psychological reactance. In J. W. Thibaut, J. T. Spence, & R. C. Carson (Eds.), *Contemporary topics in social psychology* (pp. 51–78). Morristown, NJ: General Learning.

Brewer, M. B. (1979). Ingroup bias in the minimal intergroup situation: A cognitive-motivational analysis. *Psychological Bulletin, 86,* 307–324.

Brewer, M. B. (1988). A dual process model of impression formation. In T. Srull & R. Wyer (Eds.), *Advances in social cognition* (Vol. 1, pp. 1–36). Hillsdale, NJ: Lawrence Erlbaum Associates.

Brewer, M. B. (1991). The social self: On being the same and different at the same time. *Personality and Social Psychology Bulletin, 17,* 475–482.

Brewer, M. B., & Brown, R. J. (1998). Intergroup relations. In D. T. Gilbert, S. T. Fiske, & G. Lindzey (Eds.), *The handbook of social psychology* (4th ed., Vol. 2, pp. 554–594). New York: McGraw-Hill.

Brewer, M. B., & Kramer, R. M. (1986). Choice behavior in social dilemmas: Effects of social identity, group size, and decision framing. *Journal of Personality and Social Psychology, 50,* 543–547.

Brewer, M. B., & Miller, N. (1984). Beyond the contact hypothesis: Theoretical perspectives on desegregation. In N. Miller & M. Brewer (Eds.), *Groups in contact: The psychology of desegregation.* New York: Academic.

Brickner, M. A., Harkins, S. G., & Ostrom, T. M. (1986). Effects of personal involvement: Thought-provoking implications for social loafing. *Journal of Personality and Social Psychology, 51,* 763–770.

Brockner, J. (1992). The escalation of commitment to a failing course of action: Toward theoretical progress. *Academy of Management Review, 17,* 39–61.

Brockner, J., Rubin, J. Z., & Lang, E. (1981). Face-saving and entrapment. *Journal of Experimental Social Psychology, 17,* 68–79.

Brockner, J., Shaw, M. C., & Rubin, J. Z. (1979). Factors affecting withdrawal from an escalating conflict: Quitting before it's too late. *Journal of Experimental Social Psychology, 15,* 492–503.

Broder, J. (1999, July 28). Russian Primier warns U.S. against role as policeman. *New York Times,* p. A8.

Brodie, F. M. (1981). *Richard Nixon: The shaping of his character.* New York: Norton.

Brody, R. A., & Rothenberg, L. S. (1988). The instability of partisanship and analysis of the 1980 presidential election. *British Journal of Political Science, 18,* 445–465.

Brown, R. (1974). Further comment on the risky shift. *American Psychologist, 29,* 468–470.

Brown, R. P., Charnsangavej, T., Keough, K. A., Newman, M. L., & Rentfrow, P. (2000). Putting the "affirm" into affirmative action: Preferential selection and academic performance. *Journal of Personality and Social Psychology, 79,* 736–747.

Brown, S. (1987). *The causes and prevention of war.* New York: St. Martin's Press.

Brown, V., & Paulus, P. B. (1996). A simple dynamic model of social factors in group brainstorming. *Small Group Research, 27,* 91–114.

Browning, C. (1992). *Ordinary men: Resen police battalion 101 and the final solution in Poland.* New York: HarperCollins.

Browning, R. P., & Jacob, H. (1964). Power motivation and the political personality. *Public Opinion Quarterly, 28,* 75–90.

Bruni, F. (2003, April 11). What's in a name? For a Turkish youth, maybe jail. *New York Times,* p. A3.

Bullock, A., & Stallybrass, O. (1977). *The Harper dictionary of modern thought*. New York: Harper & Row.

Burke, J. P. (1992). *The institutional presidency*. Baltimore: John Hopkins University Press.

Burke, J. P., & Greenstein, F. I. (1991). *How presidents test reality: Decisions on Vietnam, 1954 and 1965*. New York: Russell Sage Foundation.

Burnett, D. G. (2001). *A trial by jury*. New York: Knopf.

Burns, J. M. (1978). *Leadership*. New York: Harper & Row.

Burns, J. M. (1992). The power of leadership. In A. Mughan & S. C. Patterson (Eds.), *Political leadership in democratic societies* (pp. 17–28). Chicago: Nelson-Hall.

Burnstein, E., & Vinokur, A. (1977). Persuasive arguments and social comparison as determinants of attitude polarization. *Journal of Experimental Social Psychology, 13*, 315–332.

Burton, J. (1990). *Conflict: Its resolution and prevention*. London: Macmillan.

Bushart, H. L., Craig, J., & Barnes, M. (1998). *Soldiers of God: White supremacists and their holy war for America*. New York: Pinnacle.

Butler, D. E., & Stokes, D. (1974). *Political change in Britain* (2nd ed.). New York: Macmillan.

Byers, R. S. (1972). The task/affect quotient. *Comparative Political Studies, 5*, 109–120.

Byers, R. S. (1973). Small group theory and shifting styles of political leadership. *Comparative Political Studies, 5*, 443–469.

Byman, D. (1998). The logic of ethnic terrorism. *Studies in Conflict and Terrorism, 21*, 149–169.

Byman, D. (2000). Forever enemies? The manipulation of ethnic identities to end ethnic wars. *Security Studies, 9*, 149–190.

Byrne, H., Stanley, W., & Garst, R. (2000). *Rescuing police reform: A challenge for the new Guatemalan government*. Washington, DC: Washington Office on Latin America.

Caldwell, D. F., & O'Reilly, C. A. (1982). Response to failure: The effects of choice and responsibility on impression management. *Academy of Management Journal, 25*, 121–136.

Califano, J. A., Jr. (1991). *The triumph and tragedy of Lyndon Johnson: The White House years*. New York: Simon & Schuster.

Call, C., & Barnett, M. (2000). Looking for a few good cops: Peacekeeping, peacebuilding, and CIVPOL. In T. T. Holm & E. B. Eide (Eds.), *Peacebuilding and police reform*. Portland: Frank Cass.

Camacho, L. M., & Paulus, P. B. (1995). The role of social anxiousness in group brainstorming. *Journal of Personality and Social Psychology, 68*, 1071–1080.

Campbell, A., Converse, P., Miller, W., & Stokes, D. (1960). *The American voter*. New York: Wiley.

Campbell, A., Converse, P., Miller, W., & Stokes, D. (1964). *The American voter: An abridgement*. New York: Wiley.

Campbell, C. S. (1986). *Managing the Presidency: Carter, Reagan, and the search for executive harmony*. Pittsburgh, PA: University of Pittsburgh Press.

Campbell, C. S. (1996). Management in a sandbox: Why the Clinton White House failed to cope with gridlock. In C. Campbell & B. A. Rochman (Eds.), *The Clinton Presidency first appraisals,* (pp. 51–87). Chatham, NJ: Chatham House.

Campbell, D. T. (1958). Common fate, similarity, and other indices of the status of aggregates of persons as social entities. *Behavioral Science, 3*, 14–25.

Cantril, H. (1967). A fresh look at the human design. In J. F. T. Bugental (Ed.), *Challenges of a humanistic psychology*. New York: McGraw-Hill.

Carmack, R. (1992). The story of Santa Cruz Quiché. In Robert Carmack (Ed.), *Harvest of violence: The Maya Indian and the Guatemalan crisis* (pp. 39–69). Norman, OK: University of Oklahoma Press.

Carmines, E., & Merriman, R. (1993). The changing American dilemma: Liberal values and racial policies. In P. Sniderman, P. Tetlock, & E. Carmines (Eds.), *Prejudice, politics and the American dilemma*. Stanfords, CA: Stanford University Press.

Carnegie Commission on Preventing Deadly Conflict. (1997). *Preventing deadly conflict: Final report*. New York: Carnegie Corporation of New York.

Carson, R. C. (1969). *Interaction concepts of personality*. Chicago: Aldine.

Cassels, A. (1975). *Fascism*. New York: Crowell.

Cattell, R. B. (1964). *Personality and social psychology*. San Diego, CA: Knapp.

Cattell, R. B. (1965). *The scientific analysis of personality*. Baltimore: Penguin.

Cattell, R. B., & Child, D. (1975). *Motivation and dynamic structure*. New York: Wiley.

Cialdini, R. B., & Trost, M. R. (1998). Social influence: Social norms, conformity, and compliance. In D. T. Gilbert, S. T. Fiske, & G. Lindzey (Eds.), *Handbook of social psychology*, (Vol. 2, pp. 151–192). Boston: McGraw-Hill.

Clark, R. D. (1990). Minority influence: The role of argument refutation of the majority position and social support for the minority position. *European Journal of Social Psychology, 20,* 489–497.

Clifford, C. (1991). *Counsel to the President*. New York: Random House.

Clift, E., & Cohn, B. (1993, November 22). President cliffhanger. *Newsweek*, 122, pp. 26–29.

Cohen, B. (1963). *The press and foreign policy*. Princeton, NJ: Princeton University Press.

Cohen, E. (1996). A revolution in warfare. *Foreign Affairs, 75,* 37–54.

Cohen, S. (2001). *States of denial: Knowing about atrocities and suffering*. Oxford, UK: Blackwell.

Conlon, E. J., & Parks, J. M. (1987). Information requests in the context of escalation. *Journal of Applied Psychology, 72,* 344–350.

Conover, P., & Feldman, S. (1991). Where is the schema? Critiques. *American Political Science Review, 85,* 1364–1369.

Conroy, J. (2000). *Unspeakable acts, ordinary people*. New York: Knopf.

Converse, P. E. (1964). The nature of belief systems in mass publics. In D. Apter (Ed.), *Ideology and its discontents*. New York: Free Press.

Converse, P. E. (1966). The concept of a normal vote. In A. Campbell, P. E. Converse, W. E. Miller, & D. Stokes (Eds.), *Elections and the political orders*. New York: Wiley.

Cook, M. (1977). The social skill model and interpersonal attraction. In S. Duck (Ed.), *Theory and practice in interpersonal attraction*. New York: Academic Press.

Corneille, O., Yzerbyt, V. Y., Rogier, A., & Buidin, G. (2001). Threat and the group attribution error: When threat illicits judgments of extremity and homogeneity. *Personality and Social Psychology Bulletin, 27,* 427–446.

Coser, L. A. (1956). *The functions of social conflict*. Glencoe, IL: Free Press.

Costa, P. T., & McCrae, R. (1985). *Revised NEO Personality Inventory (NEO PI-R) and NEO Five-Factor Inventory (NEO-FFI): Professional manual*. Odessa, FL: Psychological Assessment Resources.

Cottam, M. (1986). *Foreign policy decision making: The influence of cognition*. Boulders, CO: Westview.

Cottam, M. (1994). *Images and intervention*. Pittsburgh, PA: University of Pittsburgh Press.

Cottam, M., & Cottam R. (2001). *Nationalism and politics: The political behavior of nation states*. Boulder, CO: Lynne Rienner.

Cottam, M., Mahdasian, S., & Sarac, M. (2000, March). *The degenerate and the rogue: War in Kosovo*. Paper presented at the International Studies Association, Los Angeles.

Cottam, M., & Marenin, O. (1999). International cooperation in the war on drugs: Mexico and the United States. *Policing and Society, 9,* 209–240.

Cottam, R. (1977). *Foreign policy motivation*. Pittsburgh, PA: University of Pittsburgh Press.

Cottrell, N. B. (1972). Social facilitation. In C. G. McClintock (Ed.), *Experimental social psychology* (pp. 185–236). New York: Holt, Rinehart & Winston.

Cottrell, N. B., Wack, D. L., Sekerak, G. J., & Rittle, R. H. (1968). Social facilitation of dominant responses by the presence of an audience and the mere presence of others. *Journal of Personality and Social Psychology, 9,* 245–250.

Crabb, C. B., Jr., & Mulcahy, K. V. (1986). *Presidents and foreign policy making: From FDR to Reagan*. Baton Rouge: Louisiana State University Press.

Crenshaw, M. (2000). The psychology of terrorism: An agenda for the 21st century. *Political Psychology, 21, 405–420.*

Crnobrnja, M. (1994). *The Yugoslav drama*. Montreal: McGill-Queens University Press.

Cronin, T. E. (1980). *The state of the Presidency,* (2nd ed.). Boston: Little, Brown.

Cropanzano, R. (Ed.). (1993). *Justice in the workplace*. Hillsdale, NJ: Lawrence Erlbaum Associates.

Cubides, F. C. (2001). From private to public violence: The paramilitaries. In C. Berquist, R. Peñaranda, & G. Sánchez (Eds.), *Violence in Colombia, 1990–2000*. Wilmington, DE: Scholarly Resources.

Dallek, R. (1979). *Franklin D. Roosevelt and American foreign policy, 1932–1945*. New York: Oxford University Press.

Dallek, R. (1983). *The American style of foreign policy*. New York: Knopf.

Dasgupta, N., Banji, M. R., & Abelson, R. P. (1999). Group entiativity and group perception: Association between physical features and psychological judgment. *Journal of Personality and Social Psychology, 75,* 991–1005.

Davies, S. (1992). Introduction: Sowing the seeds of violence. In Robert Carmack (Ed.), *Harvest of violence: The Maya Indian and the Guatemalan crisis*. Norman, OK: University of Oklahoma Press.

Davis, W. L., & Phares, E. J. (1967). Internal-external control as a determinant of information-seeking in a social influence situation. *Journal of Personality, 35,* 547–561.

De Cataldo Neuberger, L., Valentini, T. (1996). *Women and terrorism*. New York: St. Martin's Press.

Delli Carpini, M. X., & Keeter, S. (1993). Measuring political knowledge: Putting first things first. *American Journal of Political Science, 37,* 1179–1206.

Delli Carpini, M. X., & Keeter, S. (1996). *What Americans know about politics and why it matters*. New Haven, CT: Yale University Press.

Denver, D. (1994). *Elections and voting behaviour in Britain*. London: Harvester Wheatsheaf.

Denver, D. (1998). The government that could do no right. In A. King, D. Denver, I. McLean, P. Norris, P. Norton, D. Sanders, et al. (Eds.), *The new labour triumphs: Britain at the polls*. Chatham, NJ: Chatham House.

Desportes, J. P., & Lemaine, J. M. (1988). The sizes of human groups: An analysis of their distributions. In D. Canter, J. C. Jesuino, L. Soczka, & G. M. Stephenson (Eds.), *Environmental social psychology* (pp. 57–65). Dordrecht, Netherlands: Kluwer.

Deutsch, M. (1969). Socially relevant science: Reflections on some studies of interpersonal conflict. *American Psychologist, 24,* 1076–1092.

Deutsch, M. (1973). *The resolution of conflict*. New Haven, CT: Yale University Press.

Deutsch, M. (1986). The malignant (spiral) process of hostile interaction. In R. K. White (Ed.), *Psychology and the prevention of nuclear war* (pp. 131–154). New York: New York University Press.

Deutscher, I. (1973). *What we say/what we do: Sentiments and acts*. Glenview IL: Scott, Foresman.

Devine, P. G., & Elliot, A. J. (1995). Are racial stereotypes really fading? The Princeton trilogy revisited. *Personality and Social Psychology Bulletin, 21,* 1139–1150.

Diamond, L. (1988). *Class, ethnicity, and democracy in Nigeria: The failure of the First Republic.* Syracuse, NY: Syracuse University Press.

Dickey, C. (2002, April 15). Inside Suicide Inc. *Newsweek, 139,* pp. 26–32.

Dicks, H. V. (1972). *Licensed mass murder: A socio-psychological study of some SS killers.* New York: Basic Books.

Diehl, M., & Stroebe, W. (1987). Productivity loss in brainstorming groups: Toward the solution of a riddle. *Journal of Personality and Social Psychology, 53,* 497–509.

Dietz-Uhler, B. (1996). The escalation of commitment in political decision-making groups: A social identity approach. *European Journal of Social Psychology, 26,* 611–629.

Dietz-Uhler, B. (1999). Defensive reactions to group-relevant information. *Group Processes and Intergroup Relations, 2,* 17–29.

Dillon, M. (1989). *The Shankill Butchers: A case study of mass murder.* London: Arrow Books.

Dion, K. L. (1979). Intergroup conflict and intragroup cohesion. In W. G. Austin & S. Worchel (Eds.), *The social psychology of intergroup relations* (pp. 211–224). Pacific Grove, CA: Brooks/Cole.

DiRenzo, G. J. (1974). Perspectives on personality and political behavior. In G. J. DiRenzo (Ed.), *Personality and politics.* Garden City, NY: Anchor.

Doder, D., & Branson, L. (1999). *Milosevic: Portrait of a tyrant.* New York: Free Press.

Doise, W. (1969). Intergroup relations and polarization of individual and collective judgments. *Journal of Personality and Social Psychology, 12,* 136–143.

Donley, R. E., & Winter, D. (1970). Measuring the motives of public officials at a distance: An exploratory study of American presidents. *Behavioral Science, 15,* 227–236.

Donovan, R. J. (1977). *Conflict and crisis: The presidency of Harry S. Truman, 1945–1948.* New York: Norton.

Donovan, R. J. (1982). *Tumultuous years: The presidency of Harry S. Truman, 1949–1953.* New York: Norton.

Dowd, M. (2001, July 4). The relaxation response. *The New York Times,* p. A1.

Dreben, E., Fiske, S., & Hastie, R. 1979. The dependence of item and evaluative information: Impression and recall order effects in behavior-based impression formation. *Journal of Personality and Social Psychology, 37,* 1758–1768.

Drew, E. (1994). *On the edge: The Clinton presidency.* New York: Simon & Schuster.

Driver, M. J. (1977). Individual differences as determinants of aggression in the inter-nation simulation. In M. G. Hermann (Ed.), *A psychological examination of political leaders* (pp. 337–353). New York: Free Press.

Duckitt, J. (1994). *The social psychology of prejudice.* Westport, CT: Praeger.

Duckitt J., & Mphuthing, T. (1998). Political power and race relations in South Africa: African attitudes before and after the transition. *Political Psychology, 19,* 809–832.

Dunn, L. A. (1982). *Controlling the bomb: Nuclear proliferation in the 1980s.* New Haven, CT: Yale University Press.

Dunn, T. (1996). *The militarization of the U.S.–Mexico Border, 1978–1992.* Austin: University of Texas, Center for Mexican American Studies.

Durand, V. M. (1985). Employee absenteeism: A selective review of antecedents and consequences. *Journal of Organizational Behavior Management, 7,* 135–167.

Durkheim, E. (1938/1966). *The rules of sociological method.* New York: Free Press.

Dyer, W. G. (1987). *Team building: Issues and alternatives* (2nd ed.). Reading, MA: Addison-Wesley.

Dyson, S. B. (2001) Drawing policy implications from the 'operational code' of a 'new' political actor: Russian President Vladimir Putin. *Policy Sciences, 34,* 329–346.

Eades, L. M. (1999). *The end of aparteid in South Africa.* Westport, CT: Greenwood.

Eagly, A. H., & Chaiken, S. (1998). Attitude structure and function. In D. T. Gilbert, S. T. Fiske, & G. Lindzey (Eds.), *The handbook of social psychology* (4th ed.). New York: McGraw-Hill.

Easton, D., & Dennis, J. (1969). *Children in the political system.* New York: McGraw-Hill.

Easton, D., & Dennis, J. (1973). Governing authorities. In J. Dennis (Ed.). *Socialization to politics.* New York: Wiley.

Edwards, J. A., Weary, G., von Hipple, W., & Jacobson, J. A. (2000). The effects of depression on impression formation: The role of trait and category diagnosticity. *Personality and Social Psychology Bulletin, 26,* 462–473.

Eiser, R. J., & Stroebe, W. (1972). *Categorization and social judgment.* New York: Academic.

Ellemers, N., Wilke, H., & van Kippenberg, A. (1993). Effects of the legitimacy of low group or individual status on individual and collective identity enhancement strategies. *Journal of Personality and Social Psychology, 64,* 766–778.

Elliott, M., & Cohn, B. (1994, March 28). A head for diplomacy?: Clinton: One year in, he's still struggling to get his mind around foreign policy. *Newsweek, 123,* pp. 28–29.

Elms, A. C., & Milgram, S. (1966). Personality characteristics associated with obedience and defiance toward authoritative command. *Journal of Experimental Research in Personality, 2,* 282–289.

Emerson, R. (1960). *From empire to nation.* Boston: Beacon.

Emmons, R. (1997). Motives and goals. In R. Hogan, J. Johnson, & S. Briggs (Eds.), *Handbook of personality psychology.* New York: Academic.

Engleberg, S., & Gordon, M. (1993, December 26). CIA fear N. Korea already has bomb. *San Jose Mercury News,* p. 1, 20.

Entman, R. (1993). Framing: Toward clarification of a fractured paradigm. *Journal of Communication, 43,* 293–300.

Epstein, S. (1979). The stability of behavior: I. On predicting most of the people most of the time. *Journal of Personality and Social psychology, 7,* 1097–1126.

Erikson, E. H. (1950). *Childhood and society.* New York: Norton.

Erikson, E. H. (1958). *Young Man Luther.* New York: Norton.

Erikson, E. H. (1969). *Gandhi's Truth.* New York: Norton.

Etheredge, L. S. (1978). *A world of men: The private sources of American foreign policy.* Cambridge, MA: MIT Press.

Ethridge, M. E., & Handelman, H. (1998). *Politics in a changing world.* New York: St. Martin's Press.

Ewen, R. (1998). *An introduction to theories of personality* (5th ed.). Mahwah, NJ: Lawrence Erlbaum Associates.

Eysenck, H. J. (1975). *The inequality of man.* San Diego, CA: Edits Publishers.

Eysenck, H. J. (1979). The conditioning model of neurosis. *Behavior and Brain Sciences, 2,* 155–199.

Ezekiel, R. (1996). *The racist mind: Portraits of American neo-Nazis.* New York: Penguin.

Falbo, T. (1977). The multidimensional scaling of power strategies. *Journal of Personality and Social Psychology, 35,* 537–548.

Farley, R. (1996). *The new American reality: Who we are, how we got here, and where we are going.* New York: Russell Sage Foundation.

Farrar, L. L. Jr., (1988). The limits of choice: July 1914 reconsidered. In M. Small & D. Singer (Eds.), *International war: An anthology,* (2nd ed. pp. 264–287). Homewood IL: Dorsey.

Fazio, R. H., & Williams, C. (1986). Attitude accessibility as a moderator of the attitude–perception and attitude–behavior relations: an investigation of the 1984 presidential election. *Journal of Personality and Social Psychology, 51,* 505–514.

Feaver, P. D. (1992–1993). Command and control in emerging nuclear nations. *International Security, 17,* 160–187

Feaver, P. D., & Niou, E. (1996). Managing nuclear proliferation: Condemn, strike, or assist? *International Studies Quarterly, 40,* 209–234.

Feldman, D. C. (1984). The development and enforcement of group norms. *Academy of Management Review, 9,* 47–53.

Festinger, L. (1950). Informal social communication. *Psychological Review, 57,* 271–282.

Festinger, L. (1954). A theory of social comparison processes. *Human Relations, 7,* 117–140.

Festinger, L. (1957). *A theory of cognitive dissonance.* Evanston, IL: Row, Peterson.

Festinger, L., Schachter, S., & Back, K. (1950). *Social pressures in informal groups.* New York: Harper.

Fijalkawski, J. (1996). Aggressive nationalism and immigration in Germany. In R. Caplan & J. Feffer (Eds.). *Europe's new nationalism: States and minorities in conflict.* Oxford, UK: Oxford University Press.

Fiorina, M. P. (1981). *Retrospective voting in American national elections.* New Haven, CT: Yale University Press.

Fishbein, M., & Ajzen, I. (1975). *Belief, attitude, intention, and behavior: An introduction to theory and research.* Reading, MA: Addison-Wesley.

Fishbein, M., & Ajzen, I. 1980. Predicting and understanding consumer behavior: attitude–behavior correspondence. In I. Ajzen & M. Fishbein (Eds.), *Understanding attitudes and predicting social behavior.* Englewood Cliffs, NJ: Prentice Hall.

Fisher, R. J. (1990). Needs theory, social identity and an eclectic model of conflict. In J. Burton (Ed.), *Conflict: Human needs theory.* New York: St. Martin's Press.

Fisher, R. J. (2001). Cyprus: The failure of mediation and the escalation of an identity-based conflict to an adversarial impasse. *Journal of Peace Research, 38,* 307–326.

Fiske, S. (1986). Schema-based versus piecemeal politics: A patchwork quilt, but not a blanket of evidence. In R. R. Lau & D. O. Sears (Eds.), *Political cognition.* Hillsdale, NJ: Lawrence Erlbaum Associates.

Fiske, S. (1998). Stereotyping, prejudice, and discrimination. In D. T. Gilbert, S. T. Fiske, & G. Lindzey (Eds.), *The handbook of social psychology* (4th ed., Vol. 2, pp. 357–411). New York: McGraw-Hill.

Fiske, S., & Pavelchak, M. (1986). Category-based vs. piecemeal-based affective responses: Developments in schema-triggered affect. In R. Sorrentino & E. Higgings (Eds.), *Handbook of motivation and cognition.* New York: Guilford.

Fiske, S., & Taylor, S. E. (1991). *Social cognition.* New York: McGraw-Hill.

Fodor, E. M. (1985). The power motive, group conflict, and physiological arousal. *Journal of Personality and Social Psychology, 49,* 1408–1415.

Fodor, E. M., & Farrow, D. L. (1979). The power motive as an influence on the use of power. *Journal of Personality and Social Psychology, 37,* 2091–2097.

Fodor, E. M., & Smith, T. (1982). The power motive as an influence on group decision making. *Journal of Personality and Social Psychology, 42,* 178–185.

Forsyth, D. R. (1990). *Group dynamics.* Pacific Grove, CA: Brooks/Cole.

Foschi, M., Warriner, G. K., & Hart, S. D. (1985). Standards, expectations, and interpersonal influence. *Social Psychology Quarterly, 48,* 108–117.

Fox, F., & Staw, B. M. (1979). The trapped administrator: The effects of job insecurity and policy resistance upon commitment to a course of action. *Administrative Science Quarterly, 24,* 449–471.

Franklin, C. H. (1992). Measurement and dynamics of party identification. *Political Behavior, 14,* 297–309.

Franklin, C. H., & Jackson, J. E. (1983). The dynamics of party identification. *American Political Science Review, 77,* 957–973.

Fredrickson, G. (1999). Models of American ethnic relations: A historical perspective. In D. Prentice and D. Miller (Eds.), *Cultural divides: Understanding and overcoming group conflict.* New York: Sage.

Freedman, J., & Fraser, S. (1966). Compliance without pressure: The foot-in-the-door technique. *Journal of Personality and Social Psychology, 4,* 195–202.

Freedman, L. (1981). *The evolution of nuclear strategy.* London: Macmillan.

Freedman, L., & Karsh, E. (1993). *The Gulf conflict, 1990–1991: Diplomacy and war in the new world order.* Princeton, NJ: Princeton University Press.

Freeman, A. (1999, June 11). Turkish Kurds endure conditions "just like Kosovo." *Globe and Mail,* p. A1.

French, J. R. P., & Raven, B. (1959). The bases of social power. In D. Cartwright (Ed.), *Studies in social power.* Ann Arbor, MI: Institute for Social Research.

Freud, S. (1950). *Beyond the pleasure principle,* (translated by C. J. Hubback) New York: Liveright. (Original work published 1920).

Freud, S. (1951). Letter to Albert Einstein, September 1932. In W. Ebenstein (Ed.), *Great political thinkers: Plato to the present* (pp. 804–810). New York: Rinehart.

Freud, S. (1962). *Civilization and its discontents* (translated by J. Skrachey). New York: Norton. (Original work published 1930).

Frey, D. (1986). Recent research on selective exposure to information. In L. Berkowitz (Ed.), *Advances in experimental social psychology* (Vol. 19, pp. 41–80). New York: Academic.

Freyre, G. (1956). *The masters and the slaves (casa-grande and senzala): A study in the development of Brazilian civilization* (S. Putnam, Trans.). New York: Knopf.

Friedland, N. (1976). Social influence via threats. *Journal of Experimental Social Psychology, 12,* 552–563.

Frijda, N. (1986). *The emotions.* Cambridge, UK: Cambridge University Press.

Fromm, E. (1941). *Escape from freedom.* New York: Holt, Rinehart, & Winston.

Fromm, E. (1955). *The sane society.* New York: Holt, Rinehart, & Winston.

Fromm, E. (1964). *The heart of man.* New York: Holt, Rinehart & Winston.

Frontline (1995). Special reports: Rwanda in crisis. Retrieved November 21, 2000 from http://www.pbs.org/wgbh/pages/frontline/shows/rwanda/reports/prunlerexcerpt.htm/

Frontline (1998). *Who Is Osama bin Laden and What Does He Want?* Retrieved from http://www.pbs.org/wgbh/pages/frontline/shows/binladen/who

Fuller, S. R., & Aldag, R. J. (1997). Challenging the mindguards: Moving small group analysis beyond groupthink. In B. Sundelius, P 't Hart, & E. Stern (Eds.), *Beyond groupthink: Group decision making in foreign policy.* Ann Arbor: University of Michigan Press.

Funk, C. (1999). Bringing the candidate into models of candidate evaluation. *The Journal of Politics, 61,* 700–720.

Gaddis, J. L. (1992). *The United States and the end of the Cold War: Implications, reconsiderations, provocations.* New York: Oxford University Press.

Gaddis, J. L. (1997). *We now know: Rethinking Cold War history.* New York: Oxford University Press.

Gaertner, S. L., & Dovidio, J. (1986). The aversive form of racism. In J. F. Dovidio & S. L. Gaertner (Eds.), *Prejudice, discrimination and racism* (pp. 61–89). Orlando, FL: Academic.

Gaertner, S. L., & Insko, C. (2000). Intergroup discrimination in the minimal group paradigm: Categorization, reciprocation, or fear? *Journal of Personality and Social Psychology, 79,* 77–94.

Gaertner, S. L., Mann, J., Murrell, A., & Dovidio, J. F. (1989). Reducing intergroup bias: The benefits of recategorization. *Journal of Personality and Social Psychology, 57,* 239–249.

Gaertner, S. L., Mann, J. A., Dovidio, J. F., Murrell, A. J., & Pomare, M. (1990). How does cooperation reduce intergroup bias? *Journal of Personality and Social Psychology, 59,* 692–704.

Galinsky, A., & Moskowitz, G. (2000). Perspective-taking: Decreasing stereotype expression, stereotype accessibility, and in-group favoritism. *Journal of Personality and Social Psychology, 78,* 708–724.

Gage, N., Leavitt, G., & Stone, G. (1957). The psychological meaning of acquiescence set for authoritarianism. *Journal of Abnormal and Social Psychology, 55,* 98–103.

Gallup Poll (2000, March 22). *One in Five Americans Unaware That Either Bush or Gore Is a Likely Presidential Nominee.* Retrieved August 16, 2001 from http://www.gallup.com

Gallup Poll (2001, July 24). *Gallup Poll Analysis-Majority of Americans Continue to Support Nuclear Missile Defense System.* Retrieved August 16, 2001 from http://www.gallup.com

Gamson, W. A. (1961). An experimental test of a theory of coalition formation. *American Sociological Review, 26,* 565–573.

Gamson, W. A. (1964). Experimental studies of coalition formation. In L. Berkowitz (Ed.), *Advances in experimental social psychology,* (Vol. 1, pp. 82–110). New York: Academic.

Geiger, S. W., Robertson, C. J., & Irwin, J. G. (1998). The impact of cultural values on escalation of commitment. *International Journal of Organizational Analysis, 6,* 165–176.

George, A. L. (1969). The 'operational code': A neglected approach to the study of political leaders and decision making. *International Studies Quarterly, 13,* 190–222.

George, A. L. (1979). The causal nexus between cognitive beliefs and decision making behavior: The 'operational code' belief system. In L. Falkowski (Ed.), *Psychological models in international politics* (pp. 95–123). Boulder, CO: Westview.

George, A. L. (1980). *Presidential decisionmaking in foreign policy: The effective use of information and advice.* Boulder, CO: Westview.

George, A. L. (1991a). *Forceful persuasion: An alternative to war.* Washington, DC: United States Institute of Peace.

George, A. L. (Ed.) (1991b). *Avoiding war: Problems of crisis management.* Boulder, CO: Westview.

George, A. L., & George, J. L. (1964). *Woodrow Wilson and Colonel House: A personality study.* New York: Dover.

George, A. L., & George, J. L. (1998). *Presidential personality and performance.* Boulder, CO: Westview.

George, A. L., & Hall, J. (2000). The warning-response problem and missed opportunities in preventive diplomacy. In B. Jentleson (Ed.), *Opportunities missed, opportunities seized: Preventive diplomacy in the post-cold war world.* New York: Rowman & Littlefield.

George, A. L., & Smoke, R. (1974). *Deterrence in American foreign policy.* New York: Columbia University Press.

George, A. L., & Stern, E. (2002). Harnessing conflict in foreign policy making: From devil's advocate to multiple advocacy. *Presidential Studies Quarterly, 32,* 484–508.

George, J., & Wilcox, L. (1996). *American extremists: Militias, supremacists, klansmen, communists and others.* New York: Prometheus Books.

Gerth, J. (1996, July 15). Unofficial best buddy to the President. *The New York Times*, pp. A1, A9.

Gifford, R., & O'Connor, B. (1987). The interpersonal circumplex as a behavior map. *Journal of Personality and Social Psychology, 52,* 1019–1026.

Gjelstad, J., & Njolstad, O. (Eds.) (1996). *Nuclear rivalry and international order*. London: Sage.

Glad, B. (1980). *Jimmy Carter: In search of the great White House*. New York: Norton.

Glad, B. (1983). Black-and-white thinking: Ronald Reagan's approach to foreign policy. *Political Psychology, 4,* 33–76.

Glad, B. (1989). Reagan's midlife crisis and the turn to the right. *Political Psychology, 10,* 593–624.

Glynn, C., Herbst S., O'Keefe, G., & Shapiro, R. (1999). *Public opinion*. Boulder, CO: Westview.

Goltz, S. M. (1992). A sequential learning analysis of decisions in organizations to escalate investments despite continuing costs or losses. *Journal of Applied Behavior Analysis, 25,* 561–574.

Gordon, M., & Sciolino, E. (1998, February 25). Fingerprints on Iraqi accord belong to Albright. *The New York Times*, pp. A1, A10.

Graber, D. (1984). *Processing the news: How people tame the information tide*. New York: Longman.

Graham-Brown, S., & Sauckur, Z. (1995). *The Kurds, a regional issue*. Retrieved March 5, 1996, from http://www.unhcr.ch/refworld/country/writenet

Gramzow, R. H., Gaertner, L., & Sedikides, C. (2001). Memory for in-group and out-group information in a minimal group context: The self as an information base. *Journal of Personality and Social Psychology, 80,* 188–205.

Green, D. P., Abelson, R. P., & Garnett, M. (1999). The distinctive political views of hate-crime perpetrators and white supremacists. In D. A. Prentice and D. T. Miller (Eds.), *Cultural divides: Understanding and overcoming group conflict*. New York: Sage.

Greenstein, F. I. (1969). *Personality and politics: Problems of evidence, inference, and conceptualization*. Chicago: Markham.

Greenstein, F. I. (1982). *The hidden-hand presidency: Eisenhower as leader*. New York: Basic Books.

Greenstein, F. I. (1988). *Leadership in the modern presidency*. Cambridge, MA: Harvard University Press.

Greenstein, F. I. (1995). Political style and political leadership: The case of Bill Clinton. In S. Renshon (Ed.), *The Clinton Presidency: Campaigning, governing, and the psychology of leadership* (pp. 137–148). Boulder, CO: Westview.

Greenstein, F. I. (2000). *The presidential difference: Leadership style from FDR to Clinton*. New York: Free Press.

Greer, C. R., and Stephens, G. K. (2001). Escalation of commitment: A comparison of differences between Mexican and U.S. decision-makers. *Journal of Management, 27,* 51–78.

Grieve, P. G., & Hogg, M. A. (1999). Subjective uncertainty and intergroup discrimination in the minimal group situation. *Personality and Social Psychology Bulletin, 25,* 926–940.

Griffith, J., & Greenlees, J. (1993). Group cohesion and unit versus individual deployment of U.S. Army reservists in Operation Desert Storm. *Psychological Reports, 73,* 272–274.

Groff, B. D., Baron, R. S., & Moore, D. L. (1983). Distraction, attentional conflict, and drive like behavior. *Journal of Experimental Social Psychology, 19,* 359–380.

Grosser, D. (1992). The dynamics of German reunification. In D. Grosser (Ed.), *German unification: The unexpected challenge* (pp. 1–20). Oxford, UK: Berg.

Gunter, M. (1990). *The Kurds in Turkey.* Boulder, CO: Westview.

Gurr, T. R. (1994). Peoples against states: Ethnopolitical conflict and the changing world system. *International Studies Quarterly, 38,* 347–377.

Haas, M. L. (2001). Prospect theory and the Cuban missile crisis. *International Studies Quarterly, 45,* 241–270.

Hackman, J. R., Brousseau, K. R., & Weiss, J. A. (1976). The interaction of task design and group performance strategies in determining group effectiveness. *Organizational Behavior and Human Performance, 16,* 350–365.

Hackman, J. R., & Lawler, E. (1971). Employee reactions to job characteristics. *Journal of Applied Psychology, 55,* 259–286.

Hackman, J. R., & Morris, C. G. (1975). Group tasks, group interaction process, and group performance effectiveness: A review and proposed integration. In L. Berkowitz (Ed.), *Advances in experimental social psychology,* (Vol. 8, pp. 47–99). New York: Academic.

Hagerty, D. T. (1995–1996). Nuclear deterrence in South Asia: The 1990 Indo-Pakistani crisis. *International Security, 20,* 79–115.

Hagerty, D. T. (1998). *The consequences of nuclear proliferation: Lessons from South Asia.* Cambridge, MA: MIT Press.

Hall, C., & Lindzey, G. (1970). *Theories of personality* (2nd ed.). New York: Wiley.

Hanchard, M. (1993). Movimento negro in Brazil. In K. Warren (Ed.), *The violence within: Cultural and political opposition in divided nations* (pp. 57–85). Boulder, CO: Westview.

Haney, P. J. (1997). *Organizing for foreign policy crises: Presidents, advisers, and the management of decision making.* Ann Arbor: University of Michigan Press.

Hantula, D. A. (1992). The basic importance of escalation. *Journal of Applied Behavior Analysis, 25,* 579–583.

Hardy, C., & Latane, B. (1986). Social loafing on a cheering task. *Social Science, 71,* 165–172.

Hargrove, E. C. (1988). *Jimmy Carter as president: Leadership and the politics of the public good.* Baton Rouge: Louisiana State University Press.

Haritos-Fatouros, M. (1988). The official torturer: A learning model for obedience to the authority of violence. *Journal of Applied Social Psychology, 18,* 1107–1120.

Harkins, S. G. (1987). Social loafing and social facilitation. *Journal of Experimental Social Psychology, 23,* 1–18.

Harkins, S. G., & Petty, R. E. (1982). Effects of task difficulty and task uniqueness on social loafing. *Journal of Personality and Social Psychology, 43,* 1214–1229.

Harper, N. L., & Askling, L. R. (1980). Group communication and quality of task solution in a media production organization. *Communication Monographs, 47,* 77–100.

Harris, J. F. (1997, January 20). Winning a second term; waiting for a second wind, *Washington Post National Weekly Edition,* A8.

Harvey, F. P. (1997a). *The future's back: Nuclear rivalry, deterrence theory, and crisis stability after the cold war.* Montreal: McGill-Queen's University Press.

Harvey, F. P. (1997b). Deterrence and compellence in protracted crises: Methodology and preliminary findings. *International Studies Notes, 22,* 12–23.

Harvey, F. P. (1997c). Deterrence and ethnic conflict: The case of Bosnia-Herzegovina, 1993–1994. *Security Studies, 6,* 181–210.

Harvey, F. P. (1998). Rigor mortis, or rigor, more tests: Necessity, sufficiency, and deterrence logic. *International Studies Quarterly, 42,* 675–707.

Harvey, P. H., & Greene, P. J. (1981). Group composition: An evolutionary perspective. In H. Kellerman (Ed.), *Group cohesion.* New York: Grune & Stratton.

Hastie, R. (1986). Review essay: Experimental evidence on group accuracy. In G. Owen & B. Gofman (Eds.), *Information pooling and group decision making* (pp. 129–157). Westport, CT: JAI.

Hastie, R., & Park, B. (1986). The relationship between memory and judgment depends upon whether the task is memory-based or on-line. *Psychological Review, 93,* 258–268.

Hastorf, A. H., & Cantril, H. (1954). They saw a game: A case study. *Journal of Abnormal and Social Psychology, 49,* 129–134.

Heider, F. (1946). Attitudes and cognitive organization. *Journal of Psychology, 21,* 107–112.

Heider, F. (1958). *The psychology of interpersonal relations.* New York: Wiley.

Hermann, M. G. (1976). Circumstances under which leader personality will affect foreign policy: Some propositions. In J. N. Rosenau (Ed.), *In search of global patterns* (pp. 326–333). New York: Free Press.

Hermann, M. G. (1979). Indicators of stress in policymakers during foreign policy crises. *Political Psychology, 1,* 27–46.

Hermann, M. G. (1980a). Assessing the personalities of Soviet politburo members. *Personality and Social Psychology Bulletin, 6,* 332–352.

Hermann, M. G. (1980b). Explaining foreign policy behavior using personal characteristics of political leaders. *International Studies Quarterly, 24,* 7–46.

Hermann, M. G. (1983). *Handbook for assessing personal characteristics and foreign policy orientations of political leaders.* Columbus, OH: Mershon Center Occasional Papers.

Hermann, M. G. (1984). Personality and foreign policy decision making: A study of 53 heads of government. In D. A. Sylvan & S. Chan (Eds.), *Foreign policy decision-making: perceptions, cognition, and artificial intelligence* (pp. 53–80). New York: Praeger.

Hermann, M. G. (1986). Ingredients of leadership. In M. G. Hermann (Ed.), *Political psychology: Contemporary problems and issues* (pp. 167–192). San Francisco: Jossey-Bass.

Hermann, M. G. (1987). Assessing the foreign policy role orientations of sub-Saharan African leaders. In S. Walker (Ed.), *Role theory and foreign policy analysis* (pp. 161–198). Durham, NC: Duke University Press.

Hermann, M. G. (1988). Hafes Al -Assad, President of Syria: A leadership profile. In B. Kellerman and J. Rubins (Eds.), *Leadership and negotiation in the Middle East* (pp. 70–95). New York: Praeger.

Hermann, M. G. (1989). Defining the Bush presidential style. *Mershon Center Memo.* Columbus, OH: The Ohio State University.

Hermann, M. G. (1995). Advice and advisers in the Clinton presidency: The impact of leadership style. In S. Renshon (Ed.), *The Clinton presidency: Campaigning, governing, and the psychology of leadership* (pp. 149–164). Boulder, CO: Westview.

Hermann, M. G. (1999a). *Assessing leadership style: A trait analysis.* Columbus, OH: Social-Science Automation.

Hermann, M. G. (1999b). *Leadership profile of Bill Clinton.* Columbus, OH: Social Science Automation.

Hermann, M. G. (2000). An appendum: Making empirical inferences about elite decision making politically relevant. *The Political Psychologist, 15,* 24–29.

Hermann, M. G. (2001). How decision units shape foreign policy: A theoretical framework. *International Studies Review, 3,* 47–82.

Hermann, M. G., & Kegley, C. W., Jr. (1995). Rethinking democracy and international peace: Perspectives from political psychology. *International Studies Quarterly, 39,* 511–533.

Hermann, M. G., & Preston, T. (1994). Presidents, advisers, and foreign policy: The effect of leadership style on executive arrangements. *Political Psychology, 15,* 75–96.

Hermann, M. G., & Preston. T. (1998). Presidents, leadership style, and the advisory process. In E. R. Wittkopf & J. M. McCormick (Eds.), *The domestic sources of American foreign policy: Insights and evidence* (pp. 351–368). Lanham, MD: Rowman & Littlefield.

Hermann, M. G., Preston, T., & Young, M. (1996, April 17). *Who leads can matter in foreign policymaking: A framework for leadership analysis.* Paper presented at the annual meeting of the International Studies Association, San Diego, CA.

Herr, P. (1986). Consequences of priming: Judgment and behavior. *Journal of Personality and Social Psychology, 40,* 843–861.

Herring, E. (1995). *Danger and opportunity: Explaining international crisis outcomes.* Manchester, UK: Manchester University Press.

Herrmann, R. (1985a). *Perceptions and behavior in Soviet foreign policy.* Pittsburgh, PA: University of Pittsburgh Press.

Herrmann, R. (1985b). Analyzing Soviet images of the United States. *Journal of Conflict Resolution, 29,* 665–697.

Herrmann, R. (1988). The empirical challenge of the cognitive revolution: A strategy for drawing inferences about perceptions. *International Studies Quarterly, 32,* 175–203.

Herrmann, R. (1991). The Soviet decision to withdraw from Afghanistan: Changing strategic and regional images. In R. Jervis & J. Snyder (Eds.), *Dominoes and bandwagons* (pp. 220–249). New York: Oxford.

Herrmann, R., Voss, J. F., Schooler, T.Y., & Ciarrochi, J. (1997). Images in international relations: An experimental test of cognitive schemata. *International Studies Quarterly, 41,* 403–433.

Hess, R., & Torney, J. (1967). *The development of political attitudes in children.* Chicago: Aldine.

Hewstone, M. (1989). Intergroup attribution: Some implications for the study of ethnic prejudice. In J. P. van Oudenhoven & T. Willemsen (Eds.), *Ethnic minorities: Social psychological perspectives.* Berwyn, PA: Swets North America.

Hewstone, M., & Brown, R. (Eds.), (1986). *Contact and conflict in intergroup encounters.* Oxford, UK: Basil Blackwell.

Hill, G. W. (1982). Group versus individual performance: Are N + 1 heads better than one? *Psychological Bulletin, 91,* 517–539.

Hiltrop, J. M., & Rubin, J. Z. (1982). Effect of intervention mode and conflict of interest on dispute resolution. *Journal of Personality and Social Psychology, 42,* 665–672.

Hirokawa, R. Y. (1980). A comparative analysis of communication patterns within effective and ineffective decision-making groups. *Communication Monographs, 47,* 312–321.

Hirt, E. R., & Markman, K. D. (1995). Multiple explanation: A consider-an-alternative strategy for debiasing judgments. *Personality and Social Psychology Bulletin, 69,* 1069–1086.

Hogg, M. A., & Abrams, D. (1988). *Social identifications: A social psychology of intergroup relations and group processes.* New York: Routledge.

Hogg, M. A., Turner, J. C., & Davidson, B. (1990). Polarized norms and social frames of reference: A test of the self-categorization theory of group polarization. *Basic and Applied Social Psychology, 11,* 77–100.

Holbrooke, R. (1999). *To end a war.* New York: Random House.

Hollander, E. P. (1985). Leadership and power. In G. Lindzey & E. Aronson (Eds.), *Handbook of social psychology* (Vol. 2, 3rd ed., pp. 485–537). New York: Random House.

Holsti, O. (1962). The belief system and national images: A case study. *Journal of Conflict Resolution, 6,* 244–252.

Holsti, O. (1967) Cognitive dynamics and images of the enemy. In R. Fagen (Ed.), *Enemies in politics* (pp. 25–96). Chicago: Rand McNally.

Holsti, O. (1969). The belief system and national images: A case study. In J. Rosenau (Ed.), *International politics and foreign policy*, (2nd ed., pp. 543–550). New York: Free Press.

Holsti, O. (1970). The 'operational code' approach to the study of political leaders: John Foster Dulles' philosophical and instrumental beliefs. *Canadian Journal of Political Science, 3*, 123–157.

Holsti, O. (1977). *The "operational code" as an approach to analysis of belief systems*. Final Report to the National Science Foundation.

Holtz, R., & Miller, N. (1985). Assumed similarity and opinion certainty. *Journal of Personality and Social Psychology, 48*, 890–898.

Horowitz, D. (1985). *Ethnic groups in conflict*. Berkeley: University of California Press.

House, R. J. (1990). Power and personality in complex organizations. In B. M. Staw and L. L. Cummings (Eds.), *Personality and organizational influence* (pp. 181–233). Greenwich, CT: JAI.

Howard, J. W., & Rothbart, M. (1980). Social categorization and memory for in-group and out-group behavior. *Journal of Personality and Social Psychology, 38*, 301–310.

Hoyt, P., & Garrison, J. (1997). Political manipulation within the small group: Foreign policy advisers in the Carter administration. In P. 't Hart, E. Stern, & B. Sundelius (Eds.), *Beyond groupthink: Political group dynamics and foreign policy-making* (pp. 249–274). Ann Arbor: University of Michigan Press.

Huckfeldt, R., Levine, J., Morgan, W., & Sprague, J. (1999). Accessibility and the political utility of partisan and ideological orientation. *American Journal of Political Science, 43*, 888–911.

Human Rights Watch. (1999, March). *Leave none to tell the story*: Retrieved 3/1/01 from http://www.hrw.org/reports/1999/rwanda

Human Rights Watch. (1999). *Human Rights Watch World Report 2000*. New York: Human Rights Watch.

Human Rights Watch. (2000). *Human Rights Watch World Report 2001*. New York: Human Rights watch.

Hunter, J. D. (1991). *Culture wars: The struggle to define America*. New York: Basic Books.

Huth, P., & Russett, B. (1984). What makes deterrence work?: Cases from 1900–1980. *World Politics, 36*, 496–526.

Huth, P., & Russett, B. (1988). Deterrence Failure and Crisis Escalation. *International Studies Quarterly, 32*, 29–45.

Huth, P., & Russett, B. (1990). Testing deterrence theory: Rigor makes a difference. *World Politics, 42*, 466–501.

Ihonvbere, J. O. (1994). *Nigeria: The politics of adjustment and democracy*. New Brunswick, NJ: Transaction.

Insko, C. A., & Schopler, J. (1987). Categorization, competition, and collectivity. In C. Hendrick (Ed.), *Group processes: Review of personality and social psychology* (Vol. 8, pp. 213–251). Newbury Park, CA: Sage.

Isaak, R. A. (1975). *Individuals and world politics*. North Scituate, MA: Duxbury.

Isen, A. (1993). Positive affect and decision making. In M. Lewis & I. Haviland (Eds.), *Handbook of Emotions* (pp. 261–277). New York: Guilford.

Isenberg, D. J. (1986). Group polarization: A critical review and meta-analysis. *Journal of Personality and Social Psychology, 50*, 1141–1151.

Iyengar, S. (1990). Shortcuts to political knowledge: The role of selective attention and accessibility. In J. Ferejohn & J. Kuklinski (Eds.), *Information and democratic processes* (pp. 160–185). Urbana, IL: University of Illinois Press.

Iyengar, S. (1991). *Is anyone responsible? How television frames political issues*. Chicago: University of Chicago Press.

Iyengar, S., & Kinder, D. (1987). *News that matters.* Chicago: University of Chicago Press.

Iyengar, S., Peters, M., & Kinder, D. (1982). Experimental demonstrations of the not-so-minimal political consequences of mass media. *American Political Science Review, 76,* 848–858.

Iyengar, S. Peters, M., Kinder, D., & Krosnick, J. (1984). The evening news and presidential elections. *Journal of Personality and Social Psychology, 46,* 778–787.

Izard, C. E. (1977). *Human emotions.* New York: Plenum.

Jackman, M. (1978). General and applied tolerance: Does education increase commitment to racial integration? *American Journal of Political Science. 22,* 302–324.

Jackson, A. (2001). *Images and police behavior: An analysis of police-community relations.* Unpublished doctoral dissertation, Washington State University, Pullman, WA.

Jackson, D., & Messick, S. (1957). A note on ethnocentrism and acquiescent response sets. *Journal of Abnormal and Social Psychology, 54,* 132–134.

Jacobs, L., & Shapiro, R. (1994). Issues, candidate image and priming: The use of private polls in Kennedy's 1960 presidential campaign. *American Political Science Review, 88,* 527–540.

James, H. (1989). *A German identity, 1770–1990.* London: Westfield & Nicolson.

James, J. A. (1951). A preliminary study of the size determinant in small group interaction. *American Sociological Review, 16,* 474–477.

Janes, L., & Olson, J. M. (2000). Jeer pressure: The behavioral effects of observing ridicule of others. *Personality and Social Psychology Bulletin, 26,* 474–485.

Janis, I. L. (1972). *Victims of groupthink.* Boston: Houghton Mifflin.

Janis, I. L. (1983). *Groupthink: Psychological studies of policy decisions and fiascoes* (2nd ed.). Boston: Houghton Mifflin.

Janis, I. L., & Mann, L. (1977). *Decision making: A psychological analysis of conflict, choice, and commitment.* New York: Free Press.

Jennings, M. K., & Niemi, R. (1974). *Families, schools and political learning.* Princeton, NJ: Princeton University Press.

Jentleson, B. (2000). Preventive diplomacy: A conceptual and analytical framework. In B. Jentleson (Ed.), *Opportunities missed, opportunities seized: Preventive diplomacy in the post–cold war world.* New York: Rowman & Littlefield.

Jervis, R. (1976). *Perception and misperception in international politics.* Princeton, NJ: Princeton University Press.

Jervis, R. (1995). The Drunkard's search. In S. Iyengar & W. McGuire (Eds.), *Explorations in political psychology* (pp. 338–360). Durham, NC: Duke University Press.

Jervis, R., Lebow, R. N., & Stein, J. (1985). *Psychology and deterrence.* Baltimore: John Hopkins University Press.

Johnson, M. P., & Ewens, W. (1971). Power relations and affective style as determinants of confidence in impression formation in a game situation. *Journal of Experimental Social Psychology, 7,* 98–110.

Johnson, R. T. (1974). *Managing the White House: An intimate study of the presidency.* New York: Harper & Row.

Jones, B., & Kavanagh, D. (1998). *British politics today* (6th ed.). Washington, DC: CQ Press.

Jones, C. O. (1988). *The trusteeship presidency: Jimmy Carter and the United States Congress.* Baton Rouge: Louisiana State University Press.

Jones, C. O. (1996). Campaigning to govern: The Clinton style. In C. Campbell & B. A. Rockman (Eds.), *The Clinton presidency: First appraisals.* Chatham, NJ: Chatham House.

Jones, E. E., & Davis, K. E. (1965). From acts to dispositions: The attribution process in person perception. In L. Berkowitz (Ed.), *Advances in experimental social psychology* (Vol. 2, pp. 220–266). New York: Academic.

Jones, E. E., & Harris, V. A. (1967). The attribution of attitudes. *Journal of Experimental Psychology, 3,* 1–24.

Judah, T. (2000). *Kosovo: War and revenge.* New Haven, CT. Yale University Press.

Judd, C. M., & Krosnick, J. A. (1989). The structural bases of consistency among political attitudes: Effects of political expertise and attitude importance. In A. R. Pratkanis, S. J. Breckler, & A. G. Greenwald (Eds.), *Attitude structure and function.* Hillsdale, NJ: Lawrence Erlbaum Associates, Inc.

Kaarbo, J. (1998). Power politics in foreign policy: The influence of bureaucratic minorities. *European Journal of International Relations, 4,* 67–97.

Kaarbo, J., & Beasley, R. (1998). A political perspective on minority influence and strategic group composition. In M. Neale, E. Mannix, & D. Gruenfeld (Eds.), *Research on groups and teams* (Vol. 1, pp. 125–147). Greenwich, CT: JAI.

Kaarbo, J., & Gruenfeld, D. (1998). The social psychology of inter- and intra-group conflict in governmental politics. *Mershon International Studies Review, 42,* 226–233.

Kaarbo, J., & Hermann, M. (1998). Leadership styles of prime ministers: How individual differences affect the foreign policy process. *Leadership Quarterly, 9,* 243–263.

Kahn, J. (2000, December 31). Bush filling cabinet with team of power-seasoned executives, *The New York Times* p. A1.

Kahneman, D. & Tversky, A. (1973). On the psychology of prediction. *Psychological Review, 80,* 237–251.

Kahneman, D., & Tversky, A. (1979). A Prospect theory: An analysis of decision under risk. *Econometrica, 47,* 263–291.

Kaid, L., & Chanslor, M. (1995). Changing candidate images: The effects of political advertising. In K. Hacker (Ed.), *Candidate images in presidential elections* (pp. 131–134). Westport, CT: Praeger.

Kaplan, A. (1981). The psychodynamics of terrorism. In Y. Alexander & J. Gleason (Eds.), *Behavioral and quantitative perspectives on terrorism.* New York: Pergamon.

Kaplan, J., & Weinberg, L. (1998). *The emergence of a Euro-American radical right.* New Brunswick, NJ: Rutgers University Press.

Karau, S. J., & Williams, K. D. (1993). Social loafing: A meta-analytic review and theoretical integration. *Journal of Personality and Social Psychology, 65,* 681–706.

Karazic, R. (1996, April 16). *State of Republic* [address]. Retrieved (May 26, 2002), from http://www.cdsp.neu.edu/info/students/marko/telegraf/telegraf2.html

Katz, D., & Stotland, E. (1959). A preliminary statement of a theory of attitude structure and change. In S. Koch (Ed.), *Psychology: A study of a science* (Vol. 3, pp. 423–475). New York: McGraw-Hill.

Kaufman, S. (2001). *Modern hatreds: The symbolic politics of ethnic war.* Ithaca, NY: Cornell University Press.

Kawakami, J., Dovidio, J. F., Moll, J., Hermson, S., & Russin, A. (2000). Just say no to stereotyping: Effect of training in the negation of stereotypic associations on stereotype activation. *Journal of Personality and Social Psychology, 78,* 871–888.

Kearns, D. (1976). *Lyndon Johnson and the American dream.* New York: Harper & Row.

Kecmanovic, D. (1996). *The mass psychology of ethnonationalism.* New York: Plenum.

Keegan, J. (1998). *The First World War.* New York: Vintage.

Kellerman, B. (1984). Leadership as a political act. In B. Kellerman, (Ed.), *Leadership: Multidisciplinary perspectives* (pp. 63–89). Englewood Cliffs, NJ: Prentice Hall.

Kellstedt, P. (2000). Media framing and the dynamics of racial policy preferences. *American Journal of Political Science, 44,* 239–255.

Kelley, H. H. (1967). Attribution theory in social psychology. In D. Levine (Ed.), *Nebraska symposium on motivation* (Vol. 15, pp. 192–240). Lincoln: University of Nebraska Press.

Kelman, H. C. (1958). Compliance, identification, and internalization: Three processes of attitude change. *Journal of Conflict Resolution, 2,* 51–60.

Kelman, H. C. (1961). Processes of opinion change. *Public Opinion Quarterly, 25,* 57–78.

Kelman, H. C. (1965). *International behavior: A social-psychological analysis.* New York: Holt, Rinehart & Winston.

Kelman, H. C. (1990). Applying a human needs perspective to the practice of conflict resolution: The Israeli-Palestinian case. In J. Burton (Ed.), *Conflict: Human needs theory* (pp. 283–297). New York: St. Martin's Press.

Kelman, H. C., & Hamilton, V. L. (1989). *Crimes of obedience.* New Haven: Yale University Press.

Keltner, D., & Robinson, R. J. (1997). Defending the status quo: Power and bias in social conflict. *Personality and Social Psychology Bulletin, 23,* 1066–1077.

Kernan, M. C., & Lord, R. G. (1989). The effects of explicit goals and specific feedback on escalation processes. *Journal of Applied Social Psychology, 19,* 1125–1143.

Kerr, N. L., & Bruun, S. E. (1981). Ringelmann revisited: Alternative explanations for the social loafing effect. *Personality and Social Psychology Bulletin, 7,* 224–231.

Kerr, N. L., & Bruun, S. E. (1983). Dispensibility of member effort and group motivation losses: Free-rider effects. *Journal of Personality and Social Psychology, 44,* 78–94.

Khong, Y. F. (1992). *Analogies at war: Korea, Munich, Dien Bien Phu, and the Vietnam decisions of 1965.* Princeton, NJ: Princeton University Press.

Kiesler, D. J. (1983). The 1982 interpersonal circle: A taxonomy for complementarity in human transactions. *Psychological Review, 90,* 185–214.

Kinder, D. (1986). Presidential character revisited. In R. Lau & D. Sears (Eds.), *Political cognition* (pp. 233–255). Hillsdale: Lawrence Erlbaum, Associates.

Kinder, D., & Mendelberg, T. (2000). Individualism reconsidered: Principles and prejudice in contemporary American opinion. In D. O. Sears, J. Sidanius, & L. Bobo (Eds.), *Racialized politics: the debate about racism in America.* Chicago: University of Chicago Press.

Kinder, D., & Sanders, L. (1996). *Divided by color: Racial politics and democratic ideals.* Chicago: University of Chicago Press.

Kinder, D., & Sears, D. (1981). Prejudice and politics: Symbolic racism versus racial threats to the good life. *Journal of Personality and Social Psychology, 40,* 414–431.

King, A. (1998). Why Labour won—at last. In A. King, D. Denver, I. McLean, P. Norris, P. Norton, D. Sanders, et al. (Eds.), *New Labour triumphs: Britain at the polls.* Chatham, NJ: Chatham House.

Kipnis, D. (1984). The use of power in organizations and in interpersonal settings. *Applied Social Psychology Annual, 5,* 179–210.

Klang, C. (1998, February 1). *Evil, filthy rotten conspiracy. The Idaho Observer.* Retrieved from http://proliberty.com on March 20, 2000.

Kleck, R. E. and Wheaton, J. (1967). Dogmatism and responses to opinion-consistent and opinion-inconsistent information. *Journal of Personality and Social Psychology, 5,* 249–252.

Kline, E. (1998). *ASF Chechnya Brief.* Retrieved March 16, 2001, from www.wdn.com/asf

Komorita, S. S., Hamilton, T. P., & Kravitz, D. A. (1984). Effects of alternatives in coalition bargaining. *Journal of Experimental Social Psychology, 20,* 116–136.

Komorita, S. S., & Miller, C. E. (1986). Bargaining strength as a function of coalition alternatives. *Journal of Personality and Social Psychology, 51,* 325–332.

Komorita, S. S., & Nagao, D. (1983). The functions of resources in coalition bargaining. *Journal of Personality and Social Psychology, 44,* 95–106.

Kluegel, J. & Bobo, L. (1993). Dimensions of whites' beliefs about the black-white socio-economic gap. In P. Sniderman, P. Tetlock, & E. Carmines (Eds.), *Prejudice, politics, and the American dilemma* (pp 127–147). Stanford, CA: Stanford University Press.

Kotter, J. P., & Lawrence, P. R. (1974). *Mayors in action.* New York: Wiley.

Kravitz, D. A. (1987). Size of smallest coalition as a source of power in coalition bargaining. *European Journal of Social Psychology, 17,* 1–21.

Kressel, N. (Ed.) (1993). *Political psychology: Classic and contemporary readings.* New York: Paragon House.

Kressel, N. (1996). *Mass hate: The global rise of genocide and terror.* New York: Plenum.

Krosnick, J. (1988). Attitude importance in social evaluation: A study of police preferences, presidential candidate evaluations, and voting behavior. *Journal of Personality and Social Psychology, 55,* 196–210.

Krosnick, J. (1989). Attitude importance and attitude accessibility. *Personality and Social Psychology Bulletin, 15,* 297–308.

Krosnick, J., & Kinder, J. (1990). Altering the foundations of support for the president. *American Political Science Review, 84,* 497–512.

Kuckfeldt, R., Levine, J., Morgan, W., & Sprague, J. (1999). Accessibility and the political utility of partisan and ideological orientations. *American Journal of Political Science, 43,* 888–911.

Kuklinski, J. H., Riggle, E., Ottati, V., Schwarz, N. & Wyer, R. (1991). The cognitive and affective bases of political tolerance judgments. *American Journal of Political Science, 35,* 1–27.

Kuklinski, J. H., Luskin, R. C., & Bolland, J. (1991). Where is the schema? Going beyond the "s" word in political psychology. *American Political Science Review, 85,* 1341–1355.

Kuntner, B., Wilkins, C., & Yarrow, P. R. (1952). Verbal attitudes and overt behavior involving racial prejudice. *Journal of Abnormal and Social Psychology, 47,* 649–652.

LaBaron, A. (1993). The creation of the modern Maya. In C. Young (Ed.), *The rising tide of cultural pluralism: The nation-state at bay?* Madison: University of Wisconsin Press.

Lake, A. (1994). Confronting Backlash states. *Foreign Affairs, 73,* 45–55.

Lambert, A. J., Burroughs, T., & Nguyen, T. (1999). Perceptions of risk and the buffering hypothesis: The role of just world beliefs and right-wing authoritarianism. *Personality and Social Psychology Bulletin, 25,* 643–656.

Lane, R. (1962). *Political ideology: Why the American common man believes what he does.* New York: Free Press.

Lane, R., & Sears, D. (1964). *Public opinion.* Englewood, NJ: Prentice Hall.

Langer, E. (1990, July 16). The American neo-Nazi movement today. *The Nation, 215,* 82–105.

La Pierre, R. T. (1934). Attitudes versus actions. *Social Forces, 13,* 230–237.

Laqueur, W. (1980). *The terrible secret: Suppression of the truth about Hitler's Final Solution.* Boston: Little, Brown.

Larson, A. (1968). *Eisenhower: The president nobody knew.* New York: Scribner's.

Lasswell, H. (1930). *Psychopathology and politics.* Chicago: University of Chicago Press.

Lasswell, H. (1948). *Power and personality.* New York: Norton.

Latane, B., & Darley, J. M. (1970). *The unresponsive bystander. Why doesn't he help?* New York: Appleton-Century-Crofts.

Latane, B., Williams, K. D., & Harkins, S. (1979). Many hands make light the work: The causes and consequences of social loafing. *Journal of Personality and Social Psychology, 37,* 822–832.

Lau, R. (1986). Political schemata, candidate evaluations and voting behavior. *American Journal of Political Science, 29,* 119–138.

Lau, R. (1995). Information search during an election campaign: Introducing a processing-tracing methodology for political scientists. In M. Lodge & K. McGraw (Eds.), *Political judgment: Structure and processes* (pp. 179–205) Ann Arbor: University of Michigan Press.

Lau, R., & Redlawsk, D. (1997). Voting correctly. *American Political Science Review, 91,* 585–598.

Laughlin, P. R. (1988). Collective induction: Group performance, social combination processes, and mutual majority and minority influence. *Journal of Personality and Social Psychology, 54,* 254–267.

Lavine, H. (2002). On-line versus memory-based process models. In K. Monroe (Ed.), *Political psychology* (pp. 225–247). Mahwah, NJ: Lawrence Erlbaum Associates.

Lawler, E. J. (1992). Affective attachments to nested groups: A choice-process theory. *American Sociological Review, 57,* 327–339.

I_._.ɪr, E. ɪ., & Thompson, M. E. (1978). Impact of a leader's responsibility for inequity on subordinate revolts. *Social Psychology Quarterly, 41,* 264–268.

Lazarsfeld, P., Berelson, B., & Gaudet, H. (1944). *The people's choice.* New York: Duell, Sloan & Pearce.

Lazarus, R. S. (1991). *Emotion and adaptation.* New York: Oxford University Press.

Leary, M. R. (1983). *Understanding social anxiety.* Newbury Park, CA: Sage.

Leatherwood, M. L., & Conlon, E. J. (1987). Diffusibility of blame: Effects on persistence in a project. *Academy of Management Review, 30,* 836–847.

LeBon, G. (1960). *The crowd: A study of the popular mind.* New York: Viking. (Original work published 1895).

Lebow, R. N. (1981). *Between peace and war: The nature of international crisis.* Baltimore: John Hopkins University Press.

Lebow, R. N., & Stein, J. G. (1987). Beyond deterrence. *Journal of Social Issues, 43,* 5–71.

Lebow, R. N. & Stein, J. G. (1989). Rational deterrence theory: I think, therefore I deter. *World Politics, 41,* 208–224.

Lebow, R. N., & Stein, J. G. (1990). Deterrence: The elusive dependent variable. *World Politics, 42,* 336–369.

Lee, M.A. (1997). *The beast reawakens.* New York: Routledge.

Leffler, A., Gillespie, D. L., & Conaty, J. C. (1982). The effects of status differentiation on nonverbal behavior. *Social Psychology Quarterly, 45,* 153–161.

Legvold, R. (1988). War, weapons, and Soviet foreign policy. In S. Bialer and M. Mandelbaum (Eds.), *Russia and American Foreign Policy* (pp. 97–132). Boulder, CO: Westview.

Leites, N. (1951). *The operational code of the politburo.* New York: McGraw-Hill.

Leites, N. (1953). *A study of bolshevism.* New York: Free Press.

Lerner, M. J., & Miller, D. T. (1978). Just world research and the attribution process: Looking back and ahead. *Psychological Bulletin, 85,* 1030–1051.

Levin, H., & Fleischmann, B. (1968). Childhood socialization. In E. Borgata & W. Lambert (Eds.), *Handbook of personality theory and research* (pp. 215–238). Chicago: Rand McNally.

Levin, J., & Levin, W.C. (1982). *The functions of prejudice and discrimination.* New York: Harper & Row.

Levin, S., & Sidanius, J. (1999). Social dominance and social identity in the United States and Israel: Ingroup favoritism or outgroup derogation? *Political Psychology, 20,* 99–126.

Levine, J. M., & Moreland, R. L. (1998). Small groups. In D.T. Gilbert, S.T. Fiske, G. Lindrey (Eds.)*The handbook of social psychology* (4th ed., pp. 415–469). New York: McGraw-Hill.

LeVine, R.A., & Campbell, D. T. (1972). *Ethnocentrism: Theories of conflict, ethnic attitudes and group behavior.* New York: Wiley.

Levy, J. (1991). The role of crisis management in the outbreak of World War I. In A. George (Ed.), *Avoiding War: Problems of crisis management* (pp. 62–102). Boulder, CO: Westview.

Levy, J. (1994). Learning and foreign policy: Sweeping a conceptual minefield. *International Organization, 48,* 279–312.

Levy, J. (1997). Prospect theory, rational choice, and international relations. *International Studies Quarterly, 41,* 87–112.

Lewin, K. (1935). *A dynamic theory of personality.* New York: McGraw-Hill.

Lewin, K., Lippitt, R., & White, R. (1939). Patterns of aggressive behavior in experimentally created "social climates." *Journal of Social Psychology, 10,* 271–299.

Lickel, B., Hamilton, D. L., Wieczorkowski, G., Lewis, A., Sherman, S. J., & Uhles, A. N. (2000). Varieties of groups and the perception of group entiativity. *Journal of Personality and Social Psychology, 78,* 223–246.

Lifton, R. J. (1986). *The Nazi doctors: Medical killing and the psychology of genocide.* New York: Basic Books.

Light, P. C. (1982). *The president's agenda: Domestic policy choice from Kennedy to Carter.* Baltimore: John Hopkins University Press.

Link, M., & Glad, B. (1994). Exploring the psychopolitical dynamics of advisory relations: The Carter administration's "crisis of confidence." *Political Psychology, 15,* 461–480.

Linville, P. (1982). Affective consequences as complexity regarding the self and others. In M. Clarke & S. Fiske (Eds.), *Affect and cognition.* Hillsdale, NJ: Lawrence Erlbaum Associates, Inc.

Linville, P., & Jones, E. (1980). Polarized appraisals of outgroup members. *Journal of Personality and Social Psychology, 38,* 698–703.

Lodge, H. C. (1976). *As it was: An inside view of politics and power in the '50s and '60s.* New York: Norton.

Lodge, M. (1995). Toward a procedural model of candidate evaluation. In M. Lodge & K. McGraw (Eds.), *Political judgment: Structure and processes* (pp. 111–139). Ann Arbor: University of Michigan Press.

Lodge, M., & Hamill, R. (1986). A partisan schema for political information processing. *American Journal of Political Science, 80,* 505–519.

Lodge, M., McGraw, K. M., & Stroh, P. (1989). An impression driven model of candidate evaluation. *American Political Science Review, 83,* 399–419.

Lodge, M., Steenbergen, M., & Brau, S. (1995). The responsive voter: Campaign information and the dynamics of candidate evaluation. *American Political Science Review, 89,* 309–326.

Lodge, M., & Stroh, P. (1995). Inside the mental voting booth. In S. Inyengar & W. McGuire (Eds.), *Explorations in political psychology* (pp. 225–263). Durham, NC: Duke University Press.

Loftus, E. (1979). *Eyewitness testimony.* Cambridge, MA: Harvard University Press.

Longman, H. R., & Park, B. 1986. The relationship between memory and judgment depends on whether the judgment task is memory-based or on-line. *Psychological Review, 93,* 258–268.

Lorenz, K. (1966). *On aggression.* New York: Harcourt, Brace, & World.

Lott, A. J., & Lott, B. E. (1965). Group cohesiveness as interpersonal attraction: A review of relationships with antecedent and consequent variables. *Psychological Bulletin, 64,* 259–309.

Loyd, A. (1999). *My war gone by, I miss it so.* New York: Penguin.

Luce, R. D., & Raiffa, H. (1957). *Games and decisions.* New York: Wiley.

Lund, M. (1996). *Preventing violent conflict: A strategy for preventive diplomacy.* Washington, DC: U.S. Institute of Peace Press.

Lund, M. (2000). Preventive diplomacy for Macedonia, 1992–1999: From containment to nation-building. In B. Jentleson (Ed.), *Opportunities missed, opportunities seized: Preventive diplomacy in the post-cold war world* (pp. 173–208). New York: Rowman & Littlefield.

Lyons, M. (1997). Presidential character revisited. *Political Psychology, 18,* 791–811.

Maccoby, E., Matthews, R., & Morton, A. (1954). Youth and political change. *Public Opinion Quarterly, 18,* 23–29.

Mackie, D. M. (1986). Social identification effects in group polarization. *Journal of Personality and Social Psychology, 50,* 720–728.

Mackie, D. M., Devos, T., & Smith, E. R. (2000). Intergroup emotions: Explaining offensive action tendencies in an intergroup context. *Journal of Personality and Social Psychology, 79,* 602–616.

Mackie, D. M., & Goethals, G. R. (1987). Individual and group goals. In C. Hendrick (Ed.), *Review of personality and social psychology* (Vol. 8, pp. 144–166). Newbury Park, CA: Sage.

Mackie, D., & Hamilton, D. (Eds.), (1993). *Affect, cognition and stereotyping: Interactive processes in group perception.* New York: Academic.

Maddi, S. R. (1996). *Personality theories: A comparative analysis.* (6th ed.). Washington, DC: Brooks/Cole.

Madigan, T. (2001). *The burning: Massacre, destruction, and the Tulsa race riot of 1921.* New York: St. Martin's Press.

Madsen, K. B. (1961). *Theories of motivation: A comparative study of modern theories of motivation* (2nd ed.). Cleveland, OH: Howard Allen.

Magnavita, J. (2002). *Theories of personality: Contemporary approaches to the science of personality.* New York: Wiley.

Mahncke, D. (1992). Reunification as an issue in German politics, 1949–1990. In D. Grosser (Ed.), *German unification: The unexpected challenge* (pp. 33–54). Oxford, UK: Berg.

Mani, R. (2000). Contextualizing police reform: Security, the rule of law and post-conflict peacebuilding. In E. B. Eide & T. T. Holm (Eds.), *Peacebuilding and police reform* (pp. 9–26). Portland,: Frank Cass.

Manis, M., Nelson, T., & Shedler, J. (1988). Stereotypes and social judgment: extremity, assimilation and contrast. *Journal of Personality and Social Psychology, 51,* 493–504.

Maraniss, D. (1995). *First in his class: A biography of Bill Clinton.* New York: Simon & Schuster.

Maraniss, D. (1998). *The Clinton enigma: A four-and-a-half-minute speech reveals this president's entire life.* New York: Simon & Schuster.

Marcus, G., & MacKuen, M. (1993). Anxiety, enthusiasm, and the vote: The emotional underpinnings of learning and involvement during presidential campaigns. *American Political Science Review, 87,* 672–685.

Marcus, G., Neuman, W. R., & MacKuen, M. (2000). *Affective intelligence and political judgment.* Chicago: University of Chicago Press.

Marks, M. L., Mirvis, P. H., Hackett, E. J., & Grady, J. F. (1986). Employee participation in a quality circle program: Impact on quality of work life, productivity, and absenteeism. *Journal of Applied Psychology, 71,* 61–69.

Markus, G. (1982). Political attitudes during an election year: A report on the 1980 NEW panel study. *American Political Science Review, 76,* 538–560.

Markus, G., & Converse, P. (1979). A dynamic simultaneous equation model of electoral choice. *American Political Science Review, 73,* 1055–1070.

Marques, J., Yeerbyt, V. Y. & Leyens, J. P. (1988). The "black sheep effect": Extremity of judgments towards in group members as a function of group identification. *European Journal of Social Psychology, 18,* 1–16.

Marques, J., Abrams, D., Paez, D., & Hogg, M. (2001). Social categorization, social identification, and rejection of deviant group members. In M. A. Hogg & S. Tindale (Eds.), *Blackwell handbook of social psychology: Group processes* (pp. 406–424). Malden, MA: Blackwell.

Martin, J. L. (2001). *The Authoritarian Personality*, 50 years later: What lessons are there for political psychology? *Political Psychology, 22,* 1–26.

Marx, A. (1998). *Making race and nation: A comparison of the United States, South Africa, and Brazil.* Cambridge, UK: Cambridge University Press.

Maslach, C., Stapp, J., & Santee, R. T. (1985). Individuation: Conceptual analysis and assessment. *Journal of Personality and Social Psychology, 49,* 729–738.

Maslow, A. (1954). *Motivation and personality.* New York: Harper & Row.

Mastors, E. (2000). Gerry Adams and the Northern Ireland peace process: A research note. *Political Psychology, 21,* 839–846.

Mattoso, K. M. de Queiros. (1986). *To be a slave in Brazil, 1550–1888.* New Brunswick, NJ: Rutgers University Press.

May, E. R. (1973). *Lessons of the past: The use and misuse of history in American foreign policy.* New York: Oxford University Press.

Mayer, W. (1996). In defense of negative campaigning. *Political Science Quarterly, 111,* 437–455.

Mazarr, M. J. (1995). *North Korea and the bomb: A case study in nonproliferation.* London: MacMillan.

Maznevski, M. L. (1994). Understanding our differences: Performance in decision-making groups with diverse members. *Human Relations, 47,* 531–552.

Mazur, A. (1985). A biosocial model of status in face-to-face groups. *Social Forces, 64,* 377–402.

Mbachu, D. (2000, October 19). Nigeria cracks down on ethnic violence. *The Washington Post,* p. 4.

Mbeki's letter to world leaders (2000, April 20). BBC News. Retrieved July 20, 2000 from http://www.bbc.co.uk/2/hi/africa/7204.48.stm

McCain, B. E. (1986). Commitment under conditions of persistent failure: Escalation and deescalation. *Journal of Applied Psychology, 71,* 280–284.

McClelland, D. C. (1975). *Power: The inner experience.* New York: Irvington.

McClelland, D. C. (1985). How motives, skills, and values determine what people do. *American Psychologist, 40,* 812–825.

McClelland, D. C., & Boyatzis, R. E. (1982). Leadership, motive pattern and long-term success in management. *Journal of Applied Psychology, 67,* 737–743.

McClosky, H., & Zaller, J. (1984). *The American ethos: Public attitudes toward capitalism and democracy.* Cambridge, MA: Harvard University Press.

McCombs, M., & Shaw, D. (1972). The agenda-setting function of the press. *Public Opinion Quarterly, 36,* 176–187.

McCrae, R. (1993). Moderated analyses of longitudinal personality stability. *Journal of Personality and Social Psychology, 65,* 577–585.

McCullough, D. (1992). *Truman.* New York: Simon & Schuster.

McDermott, R. (1998). *Risk-taking in international politics: Prospect theory in American foreign policy.* Ann Arbor: University of Michigan Press.

McGraw, K. (2000). Contributions of the cognitive approach to political psychology. *Political Psychology, 21,* 805–827.

McGraw, K., Lodge, M., & Stroh, P. (1990). On-line processing in candidate evaluation: The effects of issue order, issue importance, and sophistication. *Political Behavior, 12,* 41–58.

McGraw, K., & Steenbergen, M. (1995). Pictures in the head: Memory representations of political actors. In M. Lodge & K. M. McGraw (Eds.), *Political judgment: Structure and Process* (pp. 15–41). Ann Arbor: University of Michigan Press.

McLeod, P. L., & Lobel, S. A. (1992). The effects of ethnic diversity on idea generation in small groups. *Academy of Management Best Paper Proceedings, 22,* 227–231.

McNamara, R. S. (1995). *In retrospect: The tragedy and lessons of Vietnam.* New York: Random House.

McPherson, H. (1972). *A political education.* Boston: Little, Brown.

McVeigh Helped Speed Militias Demise. (2001, June 10). *The Idaho Spokesman Review,* p. A10.

Mearsheimer, J. J. (1983). *Conventional deterrence.* Ithaca, NY: Cornell University Press.

Meloen, J. (1994). A critical analysis of forty years of authoritarianism research: Did theory testing suffer from cold war attitudes? In R. F. Farnen (Ed.), *Nationalism, ethnicity, and identity* (pp. 127–165). New Brunswick, NJ: Transaction.

Mendelberg, T. (2001). *The race card: Campaign strategy, implicit messages, and the norm of equality.* Princeton, NJ: Princeton University Press.

Merelman, R. (1969). The development of political ideology: A framework for the analysis of political socialization. *American Political Science Review, 63,* 750–767.

Merelman, R. (1986). Revitalizing political socialization. In M. G. Hermann (Ed.), *Political psychology*, (pp. 279–319). San Francisco: Jossey-Bass.

Messe, L. A., Kerr, N. L., & Sattler, D. N. (1992). "But some animals are more equal than others": The supervisor as a privileged status in group contexts. In S. Worchel, W. Wood, & J. A. Simpson (Eds.), *Group process and productivity* (pp. 203–223). Newbury Park, CA: Sage.

Messick, D. M., & Brewer, M. B. (1983). Solving social dilemmas: A review. In L. Wheeler & P. Shaver (Eds.), *Review of personality and social psychology* (Vol. 4, pp. 11–44). Beverly Hills, CA: Sage.

Michaelsen, L. K., Watson, W. E., & Black, R. H. (1989). A realistic test of individual vs. group consensus decision making. *Journal of Applied Psychology, 74,* 834–839.

Michener, H. A., & Burt, M. R. (1975). Use of social influence under varying conditions of legitimacy. *Journal of Personality and Social Psychology, 32,* 398–407.

Michener, H. A., & Lawler, E. J. (1975). The endorsement of formal leaders: An integrative model. *Journal of Personality and Social Psychology, 31,* 216–223.

Milbank, D. (2001). *Smashmouth: Two years in the gutter with Al Gore and George W. Bush: Notes from the 2000 campaign trail.* New York: Basic Books.

Milburn, M. A. (1991). *Persuasion and politics: The social psychology of public opinion.* Pacific Grove, CA: Brooks-Cole/Wadsworth.

Milburn, M. A., & Conrad, S. D. (1996). *The politics of denial.* Cambridge, MA: MIT Press.

Milburn, M. A., Conrad, S. D., Sala, F., & Carberry, S. (1995). Childhood punishment, denial and political attitudes. *Political Psychology, 16,* 447–478.

Milburn, M. A., & McGrail, A. B. (1992). The dramatic presentation of news and its effects on cognitive complexity. *Political Psychology, 13,* 613–632.

Milgram, S. (1974). *Obedience to authority.* New York: Harper & Row.

Miller, A. (1983). *For your own good: Hidden cruelty in child rearing and the roots of violence.* Translated by Hildegarde and Huntor Hannum. New York: Farrar, Straus Giroux.

Miller, A., Wattenberg, M. P., & Malanchuk, O. (1986). Schematic assessments of presidential candidates. *American Political Science Review, 80,* 521–540.

Miller, C. E. (1980). Effects of payoffs on coalition formation: A test of three theories. *Social Psychology Quarterly, 43,* 154–164.

Miller, C. E., & Komorita, S. S. (1986). Changes in outcomes in coalition bargaining. *Journal of Personality and Social Psychology, 51,* 720–729.

Miller, J., & Krosnick, J. (1996). News media impact on the ingredients of presidential evaluations: A program of research on the priming hypothesis. In D. C. Mutz, P. Sniderman, & R. Brody (Eds.), *Political persuasion and attitude change.* Ann Arbor: University of Michigan Press.

Miller, J., & Krosnick, J. (2000). News media impact on the ingredients of presidential evaluations: Politically knowledgeable citizens are guided by a trusted source. *American Journal of Political Science, 44,* 295–309.

Miller, W., & Shanks, M. (1996). *The new American voter.* Cambridge, MA: Harvard University Press.

Minard, R. (1952). Race relationships in the Pocohontas coal field. *Journal of Social Issues, 8,* 29–44.

Minow, M. (1998). *Between vengeance and forgiveness: Facing history after genocide and mass violence.* Boston: Beacon.

Mischel, W. (1973). Toward a cognitive social learning reconceptualization of personality. *Psychological Review, 30,* 252–283.

Mitchell, A. (1995, August 17). Panetta's sure step in high-wire job. *The New York Times,* A16.

Mitchell, A., & Purdum, T. (1996, January 2). Clinton the conciliator finds his line in sand. *The New York Times,* A1, A8.

Molm, L. D. (1987). Extending power-dependence theory: Power processes and negative outcomes. In E. J. Lawler & B. Markovsky (Eds.), *Advances in group processes* (Vol. 4, pp. 171–198). Greenwich, CT: JAI.

Molm, L. D. (1988). The structure and use of power: A comparison of reward and punishment power. *Social Psychology Quarterly, 51,* 108–122.

Mongar, T. M. (1974). Personality and decision-making: John F. Kennedy in four crisis decisions. In G. J. DiRenzo (Ed.), *Personality and politics* (pp. 334–372). Garden City, NY: Doubleday-Anchor.

Monroe, K. R. (Ed.) (2002). *Political psychology.* Mahwah, NJ: Lawrence Erlbaum Associates, Inc.

Moon, H. (2001). The two faces of conscientiousness: Duty and achievement striving in escalation of commitment dilemmas. *Journal of Applied Psychology, 86,* 535–540.

Moreland, R. L. (1987). The formation of small groups. In C. Hendrick (Ed.), *Review of personality and social psychology,* Vol. 8, (pp. 80–110). Newbury Park, CA: Sage.

Morgenthau, H. J. (1948). *Politics among nations: The struggle for power and peace.* New York: Knopf.

Morris, D. (1997). *Behind the Oval Office: Winning the presidency in the nineties.* New York: Random House.

Morris, W. N., & Miller, R. S. (1975). The effects of consensus-breaking and consensus-preempting partners on reduction in conformity. *Journal of Experimental Social Psychology, 11,* 215–223.

Moscovici, S. (1985). Social influence and conformity. In G. Lindzey & E. Aronson (Eds.), *Handbook of social psychology* (3rd ed., Vol. 2, pp. 347–412). New York: Random House.

Mullen, B., & Copper, C. (1994). The relation between group cohesiveness and performance: An integration. *Psychological Bulletin, 115,* 210–227.

Mullen, B., Johnson, C., & Salas, E. (1991). Productivity loss in brainstorming groups: A meta-analytic interpretation. *Basic and Applied Social Psychology, 12,* 3–24.

Murmendy, A., Kessler, T., Kilnk, A., & Mielke, R. (1999). Strategies to cope with negative social identity: Predictions by social identity theory and relative deprivation theory. *Journal of Personality and Social Psychology, 76,* 229–245.

Mussweiler, T., Gabriel, S., & Bodenhausen, G. V. (2000). Shifting social identities as a strategy for reflecting threatening social comparisons. *Journal of Personality and Social Psychology, 79,* 398–409.

Myers, D. G. (1978). Polarizing effects of social comparison. *Journal of Experimental Social Psychology, 14,* 554–563.

Myers, D. G., & Lamm, H. (1976). The group polarization phenomenon. *Psychological Bulletin, 83,* 602–627.

Myrdal, G. (1944). *An American dillemma.* New York: McGraw-Hill.

Nelson, A. K. (1983). The 'top of the policy hill': President Eisenhower and the National Security Council. *Diplomatic History, 17,* 307–326.

Nelson, T., Clawson, R., & Oxley, Z. (1997). Media framing of a civil liberties conflict and its effect on tolerance. *American Political Science Review, 91,* 567–583.

Nelson, T., & Kinder, D. (1996). Issue frames and group-centrism in American public opinion. *Journal of Politics, 58,* 1055–1078.

Nelson, T., & Oxley, Z. (1999). Issue framing effects on belief importance and opinion. *Journal of Politics, 61,* 1040–1067.

Nemeth, C. J. (1986). Differential contributions of majority and minority influence. *Psychological Review, 93,* 23–32.

Nemeth, C. J., Connell, J. B., Rogers, J. D., & Brown, K. S. (2001). Improving decision making by means of dissent. *Journal of Applied Social Psychology, 31,* 45–58.

Neumann, W. R. (1986). *The paradox of mass politics.* Cambridge, MA: Harvard University Press.

Neustadt, R. E. (1990). *Presidential power and the modern presidents: The politics of leadership from Roosevelt to Reagan.* New York: Free Press.

Neustadt, R. E., & May, E. R. (1986). *Thinking in time: The uses of history for decision makers.* New York: Free Press.

Newcomb, T. M. (1943). *Personality and social change.* New York: Dryden.

Newcomb, T. M. (1960). Varieties of interpersonal attraction. In D. Cartwright & A. Zander (Eds.), *Group dynamics: Research and theory* (2nd ed., pp. 104–119). Evanston, IL: Row, Peterson.

Newcomb, T. M. (1961). *The acquaintance process.* New York: Holt, Rinehart & Winston.

Newcomb, T. M. (1979). Reciprocity of interpersonal attraction: A nonconfirmation of a plausible hypothesis. *Social Psychology Quarterly, 42,* 299–306.

Nie, N., Verba, S., & Petrocik, J. (1976). *The changing American voter.* Cambridge, MA: Harvard University Press.

Nieburg, H. L. (1969). *Political violence: The behavioral process.* New York: St. Martin's Press.

Niemi, R. (1973). Political socialization. In J. Knutson (Ed.). *Handbook of political psychology* (pp. 117–138). San Francisco: Jossey-Bass.

Niemi, R., & Hepburn, M. (1995). The rebirth of political socialization. *Perspectives on Political Science, 24,* 7–16.

Niemi, R., & Weisberg, H. (Eds.). (1993). *Controversies in voting behavior* (3rd ed.). Washington, DC: Congressional Quarterly.

Norris, P. (1997). *Electoral change since 1945.* Cambridge, MA: Blackwell.

Northcraft, G. B., & Neale, M. A. (1986). Opportunity costs and the framing of resource allocation decisions. *Organizational Behavior and Human Decision Processes, 37,* 348–356.

Northcraft, G. B., & Wolf, G. (1984). Dollars, sense, and sunk costs: A life-cycle model of resource allocation decisions. *Academy of Management Review, 9,* 225–234.

Nunn, C., Crockett, H., & Williams, J. A. (1978). *Tolerance for nonconformity.* San Francisco: Jossey-Bass.

Nutt, P. C. (1990). *Making tough decisions: Tactics for improving managerial decision making.* San Francisco: Jossey-Bass.

Nydegger, R. V. (1975). Information processing complexity and leadership status. *Journal of Experimental Social Psychology, 11,* 317–328.

O'Dell, J. W. (1968). Group size and emotional interaction. *Journal of Personality and Social Psychology, 8,* 75–78.

O'Hanlon, M. (2000). *Technological change and the future of warfare.* Washington, DC: Brookings Institute.

Oliner, S., & Oliner, P. (1988). *The altruistic personality: Rescuers of Jews in Nazi Europe.* New York: Free Press.

Olson, B. D., & Evans, D. L. (1999). The role of the big five personality dimensions in the direction and affective consequences of everyday social comparisons. *Personality and Social Psychology Bulletin, 25,* 1498–1508.

Olson, D. V. A., & Caddell, D. (1994). Generous congregations, generous givers: Congregational contexts that stimulate individual giving. *Review of Religious Research, 36,* 168–180.

Ortony, A., Clore, G., & Collins, A. (1988). *The cognitive structure of emotions.* Cambridge, UK: Cambridge University Press.

O'Toole, P. (2000, November 21). Hate-figure and hero. *BBC News.* Retrieved March 23, 2001 from http://www.bbc.co.uk/2/hi/europe/213964.stm

Ottati, V., & Wyer, R. (1990). The cognitive mediators of political choice: Toward a comprehensive model of political information processing. In J. Ferejohn & J. Kuklinski (Eds.), *Information and democratic processes* (pp. 186–215). Urbana, IL: University of Illinois Press.

Ottati, V.C., & Wyer, R.S. (1995). Affect and political judgement. In S. Iyengar & W. McGuire (Eds.), *Explorations in political psychology* (pp. 296–315). Durham NC: Duke University.

Oyovbaire, S. (1984). *Federalism in Nigeria.* New York: St. Martin's, Press.

Page, B. I., & Jones, C. C. (1979). Reciprocal effects of policy preferences, party loyalties, and the vote. *American Political Science Review, 73,* 1055–1070.

Park, J., & Banaji, M. R. (2000). Mood and heuristics: The influence of happy and sad states on sensitivity and bias in stereotyping. *Journal of Personality and Social Psychology, 78,* 1005–1023.

Patterson, M. L., & Schaeffer, R. E. (1977). Effects of size and sex composition on interaction distance, participation, and satisfaction in small groups. *Small Group Behavior, 8,* 433–442.

Patterson, T. (1993). *Out of order.* New York: Knopf.

Payin, E. A., & Popov, A. A. (1996). *Chechnya—From past to present* (RAND CF-129-CRES) Santa Monica, CA: RAND.

Pearlstein, R. M. (1991). *The mind of the political terrorist.* Wilmington, DE: Scholarly Resources.

Pearson, C. A. L. (1987). Participative goal setting as a strategy for improving performance and job satisfaction: A longitudinal evaluation with railway track maintenance groups. *Human Relations, 40,* 473–488.

Pearson, C. A. L. (1992). Autonomous work groups: An evaluation at an industrial site. *Human Relations, 45,* 905–936.

Peffley, M., & Hurwitz, J. (1998). Whites' stereotypes of Blacks: Sources and political consequences. In J. Hurwitz & M. Peffley (Eds.), *Perception and prejudice: Race and politics in
the United States*. New Haven, CT: Yale University Press.

Perera, V. (1993). *Unfinished conquest: The Guatemalan tragedy*. Berkeley: University of
California Press.

Perloff, R. M. (1993). *The dynamics of persuasion*. Hillsdale, NJ: Lawrence Erlbaum, Associates.

Perreault, S., & Bourhis, R. (1999). Ethnocentrism, social identification, and discrimination.
Personality and Social Psychology Bulletin. 25, 92–103.

Pervin, L. A., & John, O. (1997). *Personality: Theory and research* (7th ed.). New York: Wiley.

Peterson, S. (2000a, December 11). Heavy civilian toll in Chechnya's "unlimited violence."
Christian Science Monitor, p. A7.

Peterson, S. (2000b). *Me against my brother: At war in Somalia, Sudan, and Rwanda*. New
York: Routledge.

Pettigrew, T. (1979). The ultimate attribution error: Extending Allport's cognitive analysis of
prejudice. *Personality and Social Psychology Bulletin, 5*, 461–476.

Pettigrew, T., & Martin, J. (1989). Organizational inclusion of minority groups: A social psychological analysis. In J. P. van Oudenhoven and T. Willemsen (Eds.), *Ethnic minorities:
Social psychological perspectives* (pp. 169–200). Berwyn, PA: Swets North America.

Pettigrew, T., & Meertens, R. (1995). Subtle and blatant prejudice in western Europe.
European Journal of Social Psychology, 25, 57–76.

Petty, R. E., & Cacioppo, J. T. (1986). The elaboration likelihood model of persuasion. In
L. Berkowitz (Ed.), *Advances in experimental social psychology* Vol. 19, (pp. 123–205).
New York: Academic.

Pika, J. A. (1988). Management style and the White House. *Administration and Society, 20*,
3–29.

Plock, E. (1993). *East German–West German relations and the fall of the GDR*. Boulder, CO:
Westview.

Popkin, S. (1994). *The reasoning voter: Communication and persuasion in presidential
campaigns*. Chicago: University of Chicago Press.

Popper, M. (2000). The development of charismatic leaders. *Political Psychology, 21*,
729–744.

Porter, R. B. (1980). *Presidential decision making: The economic policy board*. Cambridge,
UK: Cambridge University Press.

Post, J. M. (1984). Notes on a psychodynamic theory of terrorist behavior. *Terrorism: An
International Journal, 7*, 241–256.

Post, J. M. (1987) "It's us against them": The group dynamics of political terrorism. *Terrorism: An International Journal, 10*, 23–35.

Post, J. M. (1986a). Narcissism and the charismatic leader–follower relationship. *Political
psychology, 7*, 675–687.

Post, J. M. (1986b). Hostilité, conformité, fraternité: The group dynamics of terrorist behavior. *International Journal of Group Psychotherapy, 36*, 211–224.

Post, J. M. (1990). Terrorist psycho-logic: Terrorist behavior as a product of psychological
forces. In W. Reich (Ed.), *Origins of terrorism: Psychologies, ideologies, theologies, states
of mind* (pp. 25–40). Cambridge, UK: Cambridge University Press.

Post, J. M. (1991). Saddam Hussein of Iraq: A political psychology profile. *Political Psychology, 12*, 279–289.

Post, J. M. (1993a). The defining moment of Saddam's life: A political psychology perspective on the leadership and decision making of Saddam Hussein during the Gulf Crisis. In

S. A. Renshon (Ed.), *The political psychology of the Gulf War: Leaders, publics, and the process of conflict*. Pittsburgh, PA: University of Pittsburgh Press.

Post, J. M. (1993b). Current concepts of the narcissistic personality: Implications for political psychology. *Political Psychology, 14,* 99–122.

Post, J. M. (2003). Leader personality assessments in support of government policy. In J. M. Post, (Ed.), *The psychological assessment of political leaders* (pp. 39–61). Ann Arbor: University of Michigan Press.

Powell, C. (1995). *My American journey*. New York: Random House.

Powell, R. (1990). *Nuclear deterrence theory: The search for credibility*. New York: Cambridge University Press.

Power, S. (2002). *"A problem from hell": America and the age of genocide*. New York: Basic Books.

Pratkanis, A. R. (1989). The cognitive representation of attitudes. In A. R. Pratkanis, S. J. Breckler, & A. G. Greenwald (Eds.), *Attitude structure and function* (pp. 71–98). Hillsdale, NJ: Lawrence Erlbaum Associates.

Pratkanis, A. R., & Greenwald, A. G. (1989). A sociocognitive model of attitude structure and function. In L. Berkowitz (Ed.). *Advances in experimental social psychology* (Vol. 22, pp. 245–285). New York: Academic Press.

Pratto, F., Sidanius, J., Stallworth, L., & Malle, B. (1994). Social dominance orientation: a personality variable predicting social and political attitudes. *Journal of personality and social psychology, 67,* 741–763.

Pressraham-Brown, S., & Sackur, Z. (1995). *The Middle East: The Kurds—A regional issue*. Retrieved April 17, 2001, from www.unhcr.ch/refworld/country/writenet/wrikurd.htm

Preston, T. (1996a). *The president and his inner circle: Leadership style and the advisory process in foreign policy making*. Unpublished doctoral dissertation, The Ohio State University, Columbus.

Preston, T. (1996b, November 15). *The president and his inner circle: A new theory of leadership style and advisory processes*. Paper presented at the Richard E. Newstadt Conference, Columbia University, New York.

Preston, T. (1997). 'Following the leader': The impact of U.S. presidential style upon advisory group dynamics, structure, and decision. In P. 't Hart, E. Stern, & B. Sundelius (Eds.), *Beyond groupthink: Political group dynamics and foreign policymaking* (pp. 191–248). Ann Arbor: University of Michigan Press.

Preston, T. (2001). *The president and his inner circle: Leadership style and the advisory process in foreign policy making*. New York: Columbia University Press.

Preston, T., & 't Hart, P. (1999). Understanding and evaluating bureaucratic politics: The nexus between political leaders and advisory systems. *Political Psychology, 20,* 49–98.

Preston, T., & Young, M. (1992, March 25). *An approach to understanding decision making: The Bush administration, the Gulf Crisis, management style, and world view*. Paper presented at International Studies Association Meeting, Atlanta, Georgia.

Pritchard, R. D., Jones, S. D., Roth, P. L., Stuebing, K. K., & Ekeberg, S. E. (1988). Effects of group feedback, goal setting, and incentives on organizational productivity. *Journal of Applied Psychology, 73,* 337–358.

Pruitt, D. G. (1998). Social conflict. In D. Gilbert, S. Fiske, & G. Lindzey (Eds.), *The handbook of social psychology* (4th ed., Vol. 2, pp. 470–503). New York: McGraw-Hill.

Pruitt, D. G., & Kimmel, M. J. (1977). Twenty years of experimental gaming: Critique, synthesis, and suggestions for the future. *Annual Review of Psychology, 28,* 363–392.

Pruitt, D. G., & Rubin, J. Z. (1986). *Social conflict: Escalation, stalemate, and settlement*. New York: Random House.

Purdum, T. S. (1996, August 29). The incumbent as an enigma: William Jefferson Clinton. *The New York Times*, pp. A1, A14.

Rabbie, J. M. (1991). A behavioral interaction model: Toward a social-psychological framework for studying terrorism. *Terrorism and Political Violence, 3*, 134–163.

Rabbie, J. M., & Wilkens, G. (1971). Intergroup competition and its effects on intragroup and intergroup relations. *European Journal of Social Psychology, 1*, 215–234.

Rabie, M. (1994). *Conflict resolution and ethnicity*. Westport, CT: Praeger.

Rabinowitz, J. L. (1999). Go with the flow or fight the power? The interactive effect of social dominance orientation and perceived injustice on support for the status quo. *Political Psychology, 20*, 1–24.

Raden, D. (1999). Is anti-Semitism currently part of an authoritarian attitude syndrome? *Political Psychology, 20*, 323–343.

Rahn, W., Aldrich, J., Borgida, E., & Sullivan, J. (1990). A social cognitive model of candidate appraisal. In J. Ferejohn & J. Kuklinski (Eds.), *Information and democratic process*, (pp. 136–159). Chicago: University of Chicago Press.

Ramboullet Agreement (1999) Retrieved June 19, 1999, from www.state.gov

Raven, B. H. (1965). Social influence and power. In I. D. Steiner & M. Fishbein (Eds.), *Current studies in social psychology* (pp. 371–382). New York: Holt, Rinehart, & Winston.

Reich, R. (1997). *Locked in the cabinet*. New York: Knopf.

Remington, R. (1996). The Yugoslav army: Trauma and transition. In C. Danopoulos & D. Zirker (Eds.), *Civil-military relations in the Soviet and Yugoslav successor states* (pp. 153–173) Boulders, CO: Westview.

Renshon S. A. (2003). Psychoanalytic assessments of character and performance in presidents and candidates: Some observations on theory and method. In J. M. Post (Ed.), *The psychological assessment of political leaders* (pp. 105–136). Ann Arbor: University of Michigan Press.

Renshon, S. A. (1996). *High hopes: The Clinton presidency and the politics of ambition*. New York: New York University Press.

Reyes-Quilodran, C. (2001). *The main factors that could determine the behavior of a torturer*. Unpublished master's thesis, Washington State University, Pullman, WA.

Rhodes, E. (1989). *Power and MADness: The logic of nuclear coercion*. New York: Columbia University Press.

Richards, J. M., & Gross, J. J. (1999). Composure at any cost? The cognitive consequences of emotion suppression. *Personality and Social Psychology Bulletin, 25*, 1033–1044.

Richardson, L. (1960). *Arms and insecurity*. Pittsburgh, PA: Boxwood Press.

Ridgeway, J. (1995). *Blood in the face* (2nd ed.) New York: Thunder's Mouth.

Rigby, A. (2001). *Justice and reconciliation after the violence*. Boulder, CO: Lynne Rienner.

Ringelmann, M. (1913). Research on animate sources of power: The work of man. *Annales de L'Institut National Agronomique, 12*(2), 1–40.

Robins, R. S., & Post, J. (1997). *Political paranoia: The psychopolitics of hatred*. New Haven, CT: Yale University Press.

Robinson, R., Keltner, D., Ward, A., & Ross, L. (1995). Actual versus assumed differences in construal: "Naive realism" in intergroup perception and conflict. *Journal of Personality and Social Psychology, 68*, 404–417.

Rockman, B. A. (1996). Leadership style and the Clinton Presidency. In C. Campbell & B. Rockman, (Eds.), *The Clinton presidency: First appraisals* (pp. 325–362). Chatham, NJ: Chatham House.

Rogers, R., & Prentice-Dunn, S. (1981). Deindividuation and anger-mediated interracial aggression: Unmasking regressive racism. *Journal of Personality and Social Psychology, 41*, 63–73.

Rogow, A. (1963). *James Forrestal: A study in personality, politics, and policy*. New York: Macmillan.

Rokeach, M. (1954). The nature and meaning of dogmatism. *Psychological Review, 61,* 194–204.

Rokeach, M. (1973). *The nature of human values*. New York: Free Press.

Romano, L. (2000, May 2). An enigma awaits death. *The Washington Post,* pp. A1, A3.

Rosch, E. (1978). Principles of categorization. In E. Rosch & B. Lloyd (Eds.), *Cognition and categorization* (pp. 27–38). Hillsdale, NJ: Lawrence Erlbaum, Associates.

Rosenberg, T. (1992). *Children of Cain: Violence and the violent in Latin America*. New York: Penguin.

Ross, J. (1994). The psychological causes of oppositional political terrorism: Toward an integration of findings. *International Journal of Group Tensions, 24,* 157–185.

Ross, J., & Staw, B. M. (1986). Expo 86: An escalation prototype. *Administrative Science Quarterly, 31,* 274–297.

Ross, L. (1977). The intuitive psychologist and his shortcomings: Distortions in the attribution process. In L. Berkowitz (Ed.), *Advances in experimental social psychology* (Vol. 10, pp. 174–221). New York: Academic.

Rothbart, M., & Johns, O. (1993). Intergroup relations and stereotype change: A social-cognitive analysis and some longitudinal findings. In P. Sniderman, P. Tetlock, & E. Carmines (Eds.), *Prejudice, politics, and the American dilemma* (pp. 32–59). Stanford, CA: Stanford University Press.

Rothchild, D., Olorunsola, V. A. (1983). *States versus ethnic claims: African policy dilemmas*. Boulder, CO: Westview.

Rothman, J., & Olson, M. L. (2001). From interests to identities: Towards a new emphasis on interactive conflict resolution. *Journal of Peace Research, 38,* 289–305.

Rothschild, J. (1981). *Ethnopolitics: A conceptual framework*. New York: Columbia University Press.

Rotter, J. B. (1966). Generalized expectancies for internal versus external control of reinforcement. *Psychological Monographs: General and Applied, 80,* 609–633.

Rowe, A. J., & Mason, R. O. (1987). *Managing with style: A guide to understanding, assessing, and improving decision making*. San Francisco: Jossey-Bass.

Rubenstein, C. M., & Shaver, P. (1980). Loneliness in two northeastern cities. In J. Hartog & R. Audy (Eds.), *The anatomy of loneliness*. New York: International Universities Press.

Rubin, J. Z., & Brockner, J. (1975). Factors affecting entrapment in waiting situations: The Rosencrantz and Guildenstern effect. *Journal of Personality and Social Psychology, 31,* 1054–1063.

Ruby, C. (2002). Are terrorists mentally deranged? *Analyses of Social Issues and Public Policy, 23,* 15–26.

Ruder, M. K., & Gill, D. L. (1982). Immediate effects of win–loss on perceptions of cohesion in intramural and intercollegiate volleyball teams. *Journal of Sport Psychology, 4,* 227–234.

Rumble, A. (2003). *Empathy induced cooperation and social dilemmas: An investigation into the influence of attribution type*. Unpublished doctoral dissertation, Washington State University, Pullman, WA.

Rummel, R. J. (1994a). *Death by government*. New Brunswick, NJ: Transaction Books.

Rusk, D. (1990). *As I saw it*. New York: Norton.

Russell, D., Peplau, L. A., & Cutrona, C. E. (1980). The revised UCLA Loneliness Scale: Concurrent and discriminant validity evidence. *Journal of Personality and Social Psychology, 39,* 472–480.

Sabato, L. (1991). *Feeding frenzy: How attack journalism has transformed American politics.* New York: Free Press.

Sabini, J. P., & Silver, M. (1993). Destroying the innocent with a clear conscience: A sociopsychology of the Holocaust. In N. Kressel (Ed.), *Political psychology: Classic and contemporary readings* (pp. 192–217). New York: Paragon House.

Sagan, S. D. (1994). The perils of proliferation: Organization theory, deterrence theory, and the spread of nuclear weapons. *International Security, 18,* 66–107.

Sanders, D. & Seyd, P. (Eds.), *New Labour triumphs: Britain at the polls.* Chatham, NJ: Chatham House.

Satterfield, J. M. (1998). Cognitive-affective states predict military and political aggression and risk taking. *Journal of Conflict Resolution, 42,* 667–690.

Scalapino, R. (1999). The People's Republic of China at fifty. *The National Bureau of Asian Research 10*(4): 1–13. Retrieved November 15, 2000 from http://www.taiwansecurity.org

Schafer, M. (1997). Images and policy preferences. *Political Psychology, 18,* 813–827.

Schafer, M., & Crichlow, S. (2000). Bill Clinton's operational code: Assessing source material bias. *Political Psychology, 21,* 559–571.

Schelling, T. (1966). *Arms and influence.* New Haven, CT: Yale University Press.

Schelling, T. (1980). *The strategy of conflict* (2nd ed.). Cambridge, MA: Harvard University Press.

Schimmack, U., Oishi, S., Diener, E. & Suh, E. (2000). Facets of affective experiences: A framework for investigations of trait affect. *Personality and Social Psychology Bulletin, 26,* 655–668.

Schirmer, J. (1998). *The Guatemalan military project: A violence called democracy.* Philadelphia: University of Pennsylvania Press.

Schlesinger, A. M., Jr. (1965). *A thousand days: John F. Kennedy in the White House.* Boston: Houghton Mifflin.

Schöpflin, G. (1993). The rise and fall of Yugoslavia. In J. McGarry & B. O'Leary (Eds.), *The politics of ethnic conflict* (pp. 172–203). New York: Routledge.

Schroder, H., Driver, M., & Streufert, S. (1967). *Human information processing.* New York: Holt, Rinehart, & Winston.

Schuman, H., Steeh, C., Bobo, L., & Krysan, M. (1997). *Racial attitudes in America: Trends and interpretations.* Cambridge, MA: Harvard University Press.

Schultz, D. (1981). *Theories of personality* (2nd ed.). Monterey, CA: Brooks/Cole.

Schutz, W. C. (1958). *FIRO: A three-dimensional theory of interpersonal behavior.* New York: Rinehart.

Sciolino, E., & Purdum, T. (1995, February 19). Gore is no typical vice president in the shadows: He carves out a niche as trouble-shooter and close adviser. *The New York Times,* pp. A1, A16.

Scott, J. P. (1969). Biological basis of human warfare: An interdisciplinary problem. In M. Sherif & C.W. Sherif (Eds.), *Interdisciplinary relationships in the social sciences* (pp. 121–136). Chicago: Aldine.

Scott, J. P. (1981). Biological and psychological bases of social attachment. In H. Kellerman (Ed.), *Group cohesion: Theoretical and clinical perspectives* (pp. 206–224). New York: Grune & Stratton.

Scott, W. A. (1963). Cognitive complexity and cognitive balance. *Sociometry, 26,* 66–74.

Searle-White, J. (2001). *The psychology of nationalism.* New York: Palgrave.

Sears, D. O. (1975). Political socialization. In F. Greenstein & N. W. Polsby (Eds.), *Handbook of political science* (Vol. 2, pp. 93–153) Reading, MA: Addison-Wesley.

Sears, D. O. (1993). Symbolic politics: a socio-psychological theory. In S. Iyengar & W. McGuire (Eds.), *Explorations in political psychology* (pp. 113–149). Durham, NC: Duke University Press.

Sears, D. O., Henry, P. J., & Kosterman, R. (2000). Egalitarian values and contemporary racial politics. In D. O. Sears, J. Sidanius, & L. Bobo (Eds.), *Racialized politics: The debate about racism in America* (pp. 75–117). Chicago: University of Chicago Press.

Sears, D. O., Hetts, J., Sidanius, J., & Bobo, L. (2000). Race in American politics. In D. O. Sears, J. Sidanius, and L. Bobo (Eds.), *Racialized politics: The debate about racism in America* (pp. 1–43).

Sears, D. O., & Kinder, D. (1971). Racial tensions and voting in Los Angeles. In W. Hirsch (Ed.), *Los Angeles: Viability and prospects for metropolitan leadership*. New York: Praeger.

Sears, D. O., Sidanius, J. & L. Bobo (Eds.) (2000). *Racialized politics: The debate about racism in America*. Chicago: University of Chicago Press.

Seashore, S. E. (1954). *Group cohesiveness in the industrial work group*. Ann Arbor, MI: Institute for Social Research.

Sechrist, G. B., & Stangor, C. (2001). Perceived consensus influences intergroup behavior and stereotype accessibility. *Journal of Personality and Social Psychology, 80,* 645–654.

Seyd, P. (1998). Tony Blair and New Labour. In A. King, D. Denver, I. McLean, P. Norris, & D. Sanders, & P. Seyd (Eds.), *New Labour Triumphs: Britain at the Polls* (pp. 49–73). Chatham, NJ: Chatham House.

Shakur, S. (1993). *Monster: The autobiography of an L.A. gang member*. New York: Penguin.

Shapiro, R., Kumar, M., & Jacobs, L. (Eds.) (2000). *Presidential power: Forging the presidency for the 21st century*. New York: Columbia University Press.

Shapley, L. S. (1953). A value for n-person games. In H. W. Kuhn & A. W. Tucker (Eds.), *Contributions to the theory of games* (Vol. 2, pp. 53–65). Princeton, NJ: Princeton University Press.

Shaw, J. I., & Condelli, L. (1986). Effects of compliance outcome and basis of power on the powerholder–target relationship. *Personality and Social Psychology Bulletin, 12,* 236–246.

Shaw, M. E. (1981). *Group dynamics: The psychology of small group behavior* (3rd ed.). New York: McGraw-Hill.

Shaw, R. P., & Wong, Y. (1989). *Genetic seeds of warfare: Evolution, nationalism and patriotism*. Boston: Unwin Hyman.

Sherif, C.W., Sherif, M., & Nebergall, R. E. (1965). *Attitude and attitude change: The social judgment–involvement approach*. Philadelphia: Saunders.

Sherif, M. (1936). *The psychology of social norms*. New York: Harper & Row.

Sherif, M. (1966). *In common predicament: Social psychology of intergroup conflict and cooperation*. Boston: Houghton Mifflin.

Sherif, M. (1967). *Group conflict and cooperation*. London: Routledge & Kegan Paul.

Sherif, M., Harvey, D. J., White, B. J., Hood, W. R., & Sherif, C. W. (1961). *The Robbers' cave experiment*. Norman, OK: Institute of Group Relations.

Sherif, M., & Hovland, C. I. (1961). *Social judgment: Assimilation and contrast effects in communication and attitude change*. New Haven, CT: Yale University Press.

Sherif, M., & Sherif, C.W. (1979). Research on intergroup relations. In W. G. Austin & S. Worchel (Eds.), *The social psychology of intergroup relations* (pp. 24–29). Glencoe, IL: Free Press.

Shils, E. (1954). Authoritarianism: Right and left. In R. Christie & M Jahoda (Eds.), *Studies in the scope and method of "the authoritarian personality"* (pp. 24–49). Glencoe, IL: Free Press.

Shimko, K. (1991). *Images and arms control*. Ann Arbor: University of Michigan.

Shipler, D. 1997. *A country of strangers: Blacks and whites in America*. New York: Knopf.

Shiraev, E., & Zubok, V. (2000). *Russian anti-Americanism from Stalin to Putin*. New York: St. Martin's Press.

Shively, W. P. (1999). *Power and choice*. Boston: McGraw-Hill.

Sidanius, J. (1993). The psychology of group conflict and the dynamics of oppression: A social dominance perspective. In S. Inyengar & W. McGuire (Eds.), *Explorations in political psychology*. Durham, NC: Duke University Press.

Sidanius, J., & Pratto, F. (1993). The dynamics of social dominance and the inevitability of oppression. In P. Snidermand & P. Tetlock (Eds.), *Prejudice, politics, and race in America today*. Stanford, CA: Stanford University Press.

Sidanius, J., & Pratto, F. (1999). *Social dominance: An intergroup theory of social hierarchy and oppression*. New York: Cambridge University Press.

Sidanius, J., Singh, P., Hetts, J., & Federico, C. (2000). It's not affirmative action, it's the Blacks. In D. O. Sears, J. Sidanius, & L. Bobo (Eds.), *Racialized politics: The debate about racism in America*. Chicago: University of Chicago Press.

Sigal, L. (1998). *Disarming strangers: Nuclear diplomacy with North Korea*. Princeton, NJ: Princeton University Press.

Sigel, R. (1995). New directions for political socialization research: Thoughts and suggestions. *Perspectives on Political Science, 24*, 17–33.

Silber, L., & Little, A. (1996). *Yugoslavia: Death of a nation*. New York: Penguin.

Silke, A. (1998). Chesire-cat logic: The recurring theme of terrorist abnormality in psychological research. *Psychology, Crime, and Law, 4*, 51–69.

Simonton, D. K. (1988). Presidential style: Personality, biography, and performance. *Journal of Personality and Social Psychology, 55*, 928–936.

Simpson, C. (2000a, March 3). Accusations over Rwanda plane crash. *BBC News*. Retrieved August 8, 2000 from http://www.bbc.co.uk/1/hi/world/africa/6648.stm

Simpson, C. (2000b, November 14). Quiet soldier who runs Rwanda. *BBC News*. Retrieved August 8, 2000 from http://www.bbc.co.uk/2/hi/africa/689405.stm

Sinclair, L., & Kunda, Z. (1999). Reactions to a black professional: Motivated inhibition and activation of conflicting stereotypes. *Journal of Personality and Social Psychology, 77*, 885–904.

Skinner, B. L. (1971). *Beyond freedom and dignity*. New York: Knopf.

Skinner, B. L. (1974). *About behaviorism*. New York: Knopf.

Skovertz, J. (1988). Models of participation in status-differentiated groups. *Social Psychology Quarterly, 51*, 43–57.

Sluka, J. A. (2000a). Introduction: State terror and anthropology. In J. A. Sluka (Ed.), *Death squad: The anthropology of state terror*. Philadelphia: University of Pennsylvania Press.

Sluka, J. A. (2000b). For God and Ulster: The culture of terror and loyalist death squads in Northern Ireland. In J. A. Sluka (Ed.), *Death squad: The anthropology of state terror* (pp. 127–157). Philadelphia: University of Pennsylvania Press.

Smith, A. (1981). *The ethnic revival*. Cambridge, UK: Cambridge University Press.

Smith, C. P., Atkinson, J. W., McClelland, D. C., & Veroff, J. (Eds.). (1992). *Motivation and personality: Handbook of thematic content analysis*. Cambridge, UK: Cambridge University Press.

Smith, E. (1989). *The unchanging American voter*. Berkeley: University of California Press.

Smith, E. (1993). Social identity and social emotions: Toward new conceptualizations of prejudice. In D. M. Mackie & D. L. Hamilton (Eds.), *Affect, cognition and stereotyping: Interactive processes in group perception* (pp. 297–315). San Diego, CA: Academic.

Smith, E. (1999). The effects of investments in the social capital of youth on political and civic behavior in young adulthood. A longitudinal analysis. *Political Psychology, 20*, 553–580. context of the Arab–Israeli conflict. *Political Psychology, 20*, 581–591.

Smith, H. K. (1988). *The power game: How Washington works*. New York: Ballantine.

Smoke, R. (1987). *National security and the nuclear dilemma* (2nd ed.). New York: Random House.

Sniderman, P., Brody, R., & Tetlock, P. (1991). *Reasoning and choice: Explorations in political psychology*. Cambridges, UK: Cambridge University Press.

Sniderman, P., & Carmines, E. (1997). *Reaching beyond race*. Cambridge, MA: Harvard University Press.

Sniderman, P., Crosby, G., & Howell, W. (2000). The politics of race. In D. O. Sears, J. Sidanius, & L. Bobo (Eds.). (2000). *Racialized politics: The debate about racism in America* (pp. 236–278) Chicago: University of Chicago Press.

Sniderman, P., Glaser, J., & Griffin, R. (1990). Information and electoral choice. In J. Ferejohn & J. Kuklinski (Eds.), *Information and democratic processes* (pp. 117–135). Urbana, IL: University of Illinois Press.

Sniderman, P., & Hagen, M. (1985). *Race and inequality: A study in American values*. Chatham, NJ: Chatham House.

Sniderman, P., & Piazza, T. (1993). *The scar of race*. Cambridge, MA: Harvard University Press.

Sniderman, P., Piazza, T., & Harvey, H. (1998). Prejudice and politics: An intellectual biography of a research project. In J. Hurwitz & M. Peffley (Eds.), *Perception and prejudice: Race and politics in the United States* (pp. 17–34). New Haven, CT: Yale University Press.

Sniderman, P., & Tetlock, P. (1986) Reflections on American racism. *Journal of Social Issues, 42*, 173–187.

Snyder, J. L. (1984). *The ideology of the offensive: Military decision making and the disasters of 1914*. Ithaca, NY: Cornell University Press.

Snyder, M. (1987). *Public appearances/private realities: The psychology of self-monitoring*. New York: Freeman.

Sorensen, T. C. (1965). *Kennedy*. New York: Harper & Row.

Spink, K. S., & Carron, A. V. (1992). Group cohesion and adherence in exercise classes. *Journal of Sport and Exercise Psychology, 14*, 78–86.

Sprinzak, E. (2000, September/October). Rational fanatics. *Foreign Policy 133*, 66–73.

Srull, T., & Wyer, R. (1989). Person memory and judgment. *Psychological Review, 96*, 58–83.

Stangor, C., Sechrist, G. B., & Jost, J. T. (2001). Changing racial beliefs by providing consensus information. *Personality and Social Psychology Bulleting, 27*, 486–495.

Stassen, H., & Houts, M. (1990). *Eisenhower: Turning the world toward peace*. St. Paul, MN: Merrill/Magnus.

Stasser, G., Kerr, N. L., & Davis, J. H. (1989). Influence processes and consensus models in decision-making groups. In P. B. Paulus (Ed.), *Psychology of group influence* (2nd ed., pp. 279–326). Hillsdale, NJ: Lawrence Erlbaum Associates.

Stasser, G., & Titus, W. (1987). Effects of information load and percentage of shared information on the dissemination of unshared information during group discussion. *Journal of Personality and Social Psychology, 53*, 81–93.

Staub, E. (1989). *The roots of evil: The origins of genocide and other group violence*. Cambridge, UK: Cambridge University Press.

Staub, E. (1999). The roots of evil: Social conditions, culture, personality and basic human needs. *Personality and Social Psychology Review, 3*, 179–192.

Staub, E. (2000). Genocide and mass killing: Origins, prevention, healing and reconciliation. *Political Psychology, 21*, 367–382.

Staw, B. M. (1976). Knee deep in the Big Muddy: A study of escalating commitment to a chosen course of action. *Organizational Behavior and Human Performance, 16*, 27–44.

Staw, B. M., & Fox, F. V. (1977). Escalation: The determinants of commitment to a chosen course of action. *Human Relations, 30*, 431–450.

Staw, B. M., & Ross, J. (1987). Behavior in escalation situations: Antecedents, prototypes, and solutions. *Research in Organizational Behavior, 9,* 39–78.

Staw, B. M., & Ross, J. (1989). Understanding behavior in escalation situations. *Science, 246,* 216–220.

Steel, R. (1969, March 13). Endgame. *New York Review of Books, 12,* 15–22.

Stein, J .G. (1992). Deterrence and compellence in the Gulf, 1990–91: A failed or impossible task? *International Security, 17,* 147–179.

Stein, N., Trabasso, T., & Liwag, M. (1993). The representation and organization of emotional experience: Unfolding the emotion episode. In M. Lewis & J. Haviland (Eds.), *Handbook of emotions* (pp. 279–300). New York: Guilford.

Steiner, I. D. (1972). *Group process and productivity.* New York: Academic.

Steinert, M. (1977). *Hitler's war and the Germans: Public mood and attitude during the Second World War.* Athens, OH: Ohio University Press.

Stephan, W., & Stephan, C. (1993). Cognition and affect in stereotyping: Parallel interactive networks. In D. Mackie & D. Hamilton (Eds.), *Affect, cognition, and stereotyping: Interactive processes in group perception.* New York: Academic.

Stephanopoulos, G. (1999). *All too human: A political education.* Boston: Little, Brown.

Stern, E. (1997). Probing the plausibility of newgroup syndrome: Kennedy and the Bay of Pigs. In P. 't Hart, E. Stern, & B. Sundelius (Eds.), *Beyond groupthink: Political group dynamics and foreign policy making* (pp. 153–189). Ann Arbor: University of Michigan Press.

Stern, E., & Sundelius, B. (1994). The essence of groupthink. *Mershon International Studies Review, 1,* 101–108.

Stern, E., & Sundelius, B. (1997). Understanding small group decisions in foreign policy: Process diagnosis and research procedure. In P. 't Hart, E. Stern, & B. Sundelius, (Eds.), *Beyond groupthink: Political group dynamics and foreign policy making* (pp. 123–150). Ann Arbor: University of Michigan Press.

Stewart, P. D., Hermann, M. G., & Hermann, C. F. (1989). Modeling the 1973 Soviet decision to support Egypt. *American Political Science Review, 83,* 35–59.

Stimson, J. A. (1975). Belief systems: Constraint, complexity, and the 1972 election. *American Journal of Political Science, 20,* 393–417.

Stoessinger, J. G. (1985). *Why nations go to war.* New York: St. Martin's Press.

Stroessner, S., & Mackie, D. (1993). Affect and perceived group variability: Implications for stereotyping and prejudice. In D. Mackie & D. Hamilton (Eds.), *Affect, cognition and stereotyping: Interactive processes in group perception* (pp. 63–86). New York: Academic.

Stogdill, R. M., & Bass, B. M. (1981). *Stogdill's handbook of leadership: A survey of theory and research.* New York: Free Press.

Stokes, D. (1963). Spatial models of party competition. *American Political Science Review, 57,* 368–377.

Stoll, D. (1992). Evangelicals, guerrillas, and the army: The Ixtil triangle under Ríos Montt. In R. Carmack (Ed.), *Harvest of violence: The Maya Indian and the Guatemalan crisis* (pp. 109–116). Norman, OK: University of Oklahoma Press.

Stone, W., & Schaffner, P. (1988). *The psychology of politics.* New York: Springer-Verlag.

Stoner, J. A. F. (1961). *A comparison of individual and group decisions involving risk.* Unpublished master's thesis, Massachusetts Institute of Technology, Cambrige, MA.

Stouffer, S. (1955). *Communism, conformity, and civil liberties.* New York: Doubleday.

Stuart, D., & Starr, H. (1981). The 'inherent bad faith model' reconsidered: Dulles, Kennedy, and Kissinger. *Political Psychology, 3,* 1–33.

Suedfeld, P., & Rank, A. D. (1976). Revolutionary leaders: Long-term success as a function of changes in conceptual complexity. *Journal of Personality and Social Psychology, 34,* 169–178.

Suedfeld, P., & Tetlock, P. (1977). Integrative complexity of communication in international crisis. *Journal of Conflict Resolution, 21*, 169–184.

Sullivan, J., Piereson, J., & Marcus, G. (1979). An alternative conceptualization of political tolerance: Illusory increases, 1950's–1970's. *American Political Science Review, 73*, 781–794.

Sullivan, J., Piereson, H., & Marcus, G. (1982). *Political tolerance and American democracy.* Chicago: University of Chicago Press.

Sumner, W. G. (1906). *Folkways.* Boston: Ginn.

Swim, J. K., & Miller, D. (1999). White guilt: Its antecedents and consequences for attitudes toward affirmative action. *Personality and Social Psychology Bulletin, 25*, 500–514.

Sylvan, D., & Voss. J. (Eds.) (1998). *Problem representation in foreign policy decision making.* Cambridge, UK: Cambridge University Press.

Tajfel, H. (1970). Experiments in intergroup discrimination. *Scientific American, 223*, 96–102.

Tajfel, H. (1978). Social categorization, social identity, and social comparison. In H. Tajfel (Ed.), *Differentiation between social groups: Studies in the social psychology of intergroup relations* (pp. 61–76). New York: Academic.

Tajfel, H. (1982). *Human groups and social categories.* Cambridge, UK: Cambridge University Press.

Tajfel, H., & Billig, M. (1974). Familiarity and categorization in intergroup behavior. *Journal of Experimental Social Psychology, 10*, 159–170.

Tajfel, H., Billig, M. G., Bundy, R. P., & Flament, C. (1971). Social categorization and intergroup behavior. *European Journal of Social Psychology, 1*, 149-178.

Tajfel, H., & Forgas, J. (1981). Social categorization: Cognition, values and groups. In J. Forgas (Ed.), *Social cognition: Perspectives on everyday understanding* (pp. 113–140). London: Academic.

Tajfel, H., & Turner, J.C. (1979). An integrative theory of intergroup conflict. In W. G. Austin & S. Worchel (Eds.), *The social psychology of intergroup relations* (pp. 33–48). Monterey, CA: Brooks/Cole.

Tajfel, H., & Turner, J. C. (1986). The social identity theory of intergroup behavior. In S. Worchel & W. G. Austin (Eds.), *Psychology of intergroup relations* (pp. 7–24). Chicago: Nelson-Hall.

Talbot, C. (2000, December 23). Rwanda on the offensive in Congo war. *Washington Post.*

Tannenbaum, F. (1947). *Slave and citizen: The Negro in the Americas.* New York: Knopf.

Taylor, D. W., Berry, P. C., & Block, C. H. (1958). Does group participation when using brainstorming facilitate or inhibit creative thinking? *Administrative Science Quarterly, 3*, 23–47.

Taylor, M. (1991). *The fanatics: A behavioral approach to political violence.* London: Bassey's.

Taylor, M., & Quale, E. (1994). *Terrorist lives.* London: Bassey's.

Taylor, S. E., & Crocker, J. (1981). Schematic bases of social information processing. In T. Higgins, C. P. Herman, & M. P. Zanna (Eds.), *Social Cognition: The Ontario Symposium.* (Vol. 1, pp. 89–134). Hillsdale, NJ: Lawrence Erlbaum Associates.

Taysi, T., & Preston, T. (2001). The personality and leadership style of President Khatami: Implications for the future of Iranian political reform. In O. Feldman & L. O. Valenty (Eds.), *Profiling political leaders: Cross-cultural studies of personality and behavior* (pp. 57–77). Westport, CT: Praeger.

Teens Sharper on Bart than Neust (1998, September 6). *Idaho Spokesman Review*, p. A6.

Teger, A. (1980). *Too much invested to quit.* New York: Pergamon.

Tepperman, J. (2002). Truth and consequences. *Foreign Affairs, 81*, 128–145.

Tetlock, P. (1983). Integrative complexity of American and Soviet foreign policy rhetorics: A time-series analysis. *Journal of Personality and Social Psychology, 49,* 565–585.

Tetlock, P. (1985). Accountability: The neglected social context of judgment and choice. In B. M. Staw & L. Cummings (Eds.), *Research in Organizational Behavior,* (Vol. 7, pp. 297–332). Greenwich, CT: JAI Press.

Tetlock, P., & Belkin, A (Eds.) (1996). *Counterfactual thought experiments in world politics: Logical, methodological, and psychological perspectives.* Princeton, NJ: Princeton University Press.

Tetlock, P., & Kim, J. I. (1987). Accountability and judgment processes in a personality prediction task. *Journal of Personality and Social Psychology, 52,* 700–709.

Tetlock, P., McGuire, C., & Mitchell, G. (1991). Psychological perspectives on nuclear deterrence. *Annual Review of Psychology, 42,* 239–276.

Tetlock, P. E., Peterson, R. S., McGuire, C., Chang, S., & Feld, P. (1992). Assessing political group dynamics: A test of the groupthink model. *Journal of Personality and Social Psychology, 63,* 403–425.

Tetlock, P. E., & Tyler, A. (1996). Churchills cognitive and rhetorical style: The debates over Nazi intentions and self-government for India. *Political Psychology, 17,* 149-170.

't Hart, P. (1994) *Groupthink in government: A study of small groups and policy failure.* Baltimore: Johns Hopkins University Press. (Original work published 1990).

't Hart, P. (1997). From analysis to reform of policymaking groups. In P. 't Hart, E. Stern, & B. Sundelius (Eds.), *Beyond groupthink: Political group dynamics and foreign policymaking* (pp. 3–33). Ann Arbor: University of Michigan Press.

't Hart, P., Stern, E. K., & Sundelius, B. (1997). *Beyond groupthink: Political group dynamics and foreign policy-making.* Ann Arbor: University of Michigan Press.

Thomas, R. (1996). History, religion, and national identity. In R. Thomas & H. R. Friman (Eds.), *The south Slav conflict: History, religion, ethnicity, and nationalism.* New York: Garland.

Tibon, S., & Blumberg, H. (1999). Authoritarianism and political socialization in the context of the Arab-Israeli conflict. *Political Psychology, 20,* 581–591.

Towles-Schwen, T., & Fazio, R. H. (2001). On the origins of racial attitudes: Correlates of childhood experiences. *Personality and Social Psychology Bulletin, 27,* 162–175.

Triplett, N. (1898). The dynamogenic factors in peacemaking and competition. *American Journal of Psychology, 9,* 507–533.

Trost, M. R., Maass, A., & Kendrick, D. T. (1992). Minority influence: Personal relevance biases cognitive processes and reverses private acceptance. *Journal of Experimental Social Psychology, 28,* 234–254.

Tuchman, B. (1962). *The guns of August.* New York: Macmillan.

Tucker, R. C. (1968). The theory of charismatic leadership. *Daedalus, 97,* 731–756.

Tucker, R.C. (1970). The theory of charismatic leadership. In D. A. Rustow (Ed.), *Philosophers and kings: Studies in leadership.* New York: Braziller.

Tuckman, B. W. (1965). Developmental sequence in small groups. *Psychological Bulletin, 63,* 384–399.

Tuckman, B. W., & Jensen, M. A. C. (1977). Stages of small-group development revisited. *Group and Organization Studies, 2,* 419–427.

Turkish troops pursue Kurds (2000, April,) *BBC News.* Retrieved February 8, 2001 from http://www.bbc.co.uk/hi/english/world/middle east/news id_698000/698205.stm

Turner, J. C. (1986). Social categorization and social discrimination in the minimal group paradigm. In H. Tajfel (Ed.), *Differentiation between social groups: Studies in the social psychology of intergroup relations* (pp. 235–250). New York: Academic.

Turner, J. C., & Brown, R. (1986). Social status, cognitive alternatives and intergroup relations. In H. Tajfel (Ed.), *Differentiation between social groups: Studies in the social psychology of intergroup relations* (pp. 201–234). New York: Academic.

Turner, R. (1978). The role and the person. *American Journal of Sociology, 84*, 1–23.

Tversky, A., & Kahneman, D. (1982). Judgment under uncertainty: Heuristics and biases. Cambridge, UK: Cambridge University Press.

Tversky, A., & Kahneman, D. (1986). Rational choice and the framing of decisions. *Journal of Business, 59*, S251–S278.

Ulman, R. B., & Abse, D. W. (1983). The group psychology of madness: Jonestown. *Political Psychology, 4*, 637–661.

United States Census Bureau. (1998). Retrieved July 26, 2001, from http://www.census.gov/prod/3/98pubs/98statab

United States Department of State (1999). *Overview of state-sponsored terrorism.* Retrieved September 11, 2001 from www.state.gov/www/global/terrorism/1999Report/sponsor.html

van den Broek, A. (1999). Does differential cohort socialization matter? The impact of cohort replacement and the presence of rnetergenerational differences in the Netherlands. *Political Psychology, 20*, 501–523.

van den Heuvel, H., & Meertens, R. (1989). The culture assimilator: Is it possible to improve interethnic relations by emphasizing ethnic differences? In J. P. van Oudenhoven & T. Willemsen (Eds.), *Ethnic minorities: Social psychological perspectives* (pp. 221–236). Berwyn, PA: Swets North America.

van Egeren, L. F. (1979). Cardiovascular changes during social competition in a mixed-motive game. *Journal of Personality and Social Psychology, 37*, 858–864.

Van Evera, S. (1984). The cult of the offensive and the origins of the First World War. *International Security, 9*, 58–107.

van Knippenberg, A., & Ellemers, N. (1990). Social identity and intergroup differentiation processes. In W. Stroebe & M. Hewstone (Eds.), *European Review of Social Psychology* (Vol. 1, pp. 137–169). Chichester: Wiley.

van Oudenhoven, J. P. (1989). Improving interethnic relationships: How effective is cooperation? In J. P. van Oudenhoven & T. Willemsen (Eds.), *Ethnic minorities: Social psychological perspectives* (pp. 201–220). Berwyn, PA: Swets North America.

Vertzberger, Y. (1990). *The world in their minds: Information processing, cognition, and perception in foreign policy decisionmaking.* Stanford, CA: Stanford University Press.

Vertzberger, Y. (1997). Collective risk-taking: The decision-making group. In P. 't Hart, E. Stern, & B. Sundelius (Eds.), *Beyond groupthink: Political group dynamics and foreign policy-making* (pp. 275–308). Ann Arbor: University of Michigan Press.

Volkan, V. (1980). Narcissistic personality organization and reparative leadership. *International Journal of Group Psychotherapy, 30*, 131–152.

Volpato, C., Maass, A., Mucchi-Faina, A., & Vitti, E. (1990). Minority influence and social categorization. *European Journal of Social Psychology, 20*, 119–132.

Waite, R. G. L. (1977). *The psychopathic god: Adolph Hitler.* New York: Basic Books.

Walker, A. M., & Sorrentino, R. M. (2000) Control motivation and uncertainty: Information processing or avoidance in moderate depressives and nondepressives. *Personality and Social Psychology Bulletin, 26*, 436–451.

Walker, S. (1977). The interface between beliefs and behavior: Henry Kissinger's operational code and the Vietnam War. *Journal of Conflict Resolution, 21*, 129–167.

Walker, S. (1983). The motivational foundations of political belief systems: A re-analysis of the operational code construct. *International Studies Quarterly, 27*, 179–202.

Walker, S. (1995). Psychodynamic processes and framing effects in foreign policy decision-making: Woodrow Wilson's operational code. *Political Psychology, 16,* 697–718.

Walker, S., & Falkowski, L. (1984). The operational codes of U.S. presidents and secretaries of state: Motivational foundations and behavioral consequences. *Political Psychology, 5,* 237–266.

Walker, S., & Schafer, M. (2000). The political universe of Lyndon B. Johnson and his advisers: Diagnostic and strategic propensities in their operational codes. *Political Psychology, 21,* 529–543.

Walker, S., Schafer, M., & Young, M. (1998). Systematic procedures for operational code analysis: Measuring and modeling Jimmy Carter's operational code. *International Studies Quarterly, 42,* 175–190.

Wallach, M. A., Kogan, N., & Bem, D. J. (1962). Group influence on individual risk taking. *Journal of Abnormal and Social Psychology, 65,* 75–86.

Wallace, M. D., & Suedfeld, P. (1988). Leadership performance in crisis: The longevity–complexity link. *International Studies Quarterly, 32,* 439–452.

Wallace, M.D., Suedfeld, P., & Thachuk, K. A. (1996). Failed leader or successful peacemaker? Crisis behavior, and the cognitive processes of Mikhail Sergeyevitch Gorbachev. *Political Psychology, 17,* 453–472.

Warren, K. (1993). Interpreting *La Violencia* in Guatemala: Shapes of Mayan silence and resistance. In K. Warren (Ed.), *The violence within: Cultural and political opposition in divided nations* (pp. 1–23). Boulder, CO: Westview.

Watson, J. (1994). The Clinton White House. *Presidential Studies Quarterly, 23,* 429–436.

Watson, W. E., Michaelsen, L. K., & Sharp, W. (1991). Member competence, group interaction, and group decision making: A longitudinal study. *Journal of Applied Psychology, 76,* 803–809.

Watts, M. (1999). Are there typical age curves in political behavior? The "age invariance" hypothesis and political socialization. *Political Psychology, 20,* 477–499.

Webber, M. (1996). *The international politics of Russia and the successor states.* Manchester, UK: Manchester University Press.

Weiner, B. (1986). *An attribution theory of motivation and emotion.* New York: Springer-Verlag.

Weintraub, W. (1981). *Verbal behavior: Adaptation and psychopathology.* New York: Springer.

Weintraub, W. (1986). Personality profiles of American presidents as revealed in their public statements: The presidential news conferences of Jimmy Carter and Ronald Reagan. *Political Psychology, 7,* 285–295.

Weintraub, W. (1989). *Verbal behavior in everyday life.* New York: Springer.

Weir, F. (2000, May 24). Taming Chechnya, Russia too. *Christian Science Monitor,* pp. A1, A5

Westholm, A. (1999). The perceptual pathway: Tracing the mechanisms of political value transfer across generations. *Political Psychology, 20,* 525–551.

White, R. K. (1968). *Nobody wanted war: Misperception in Vietnam and other wars.* Garden City, NY: Doubleday.

White, R. K. (1977). Misperception in the Arab-Israeli conflict. *Journal of Social Issues, 33,* 190–221.

Whitley, B. E., Jr. (1999). Right-wing authoritarianism, social dominance orientation, and prejudice. *Journal of Personality and Social Psychology, 77,* 126–134.

Whitney, K., Sagrestano, L. M., & Maslach, C. (1994). Establishing the impact of individuation. *Journal of Personality and Social Psychology, 66,* 1140–1153.

Whyte, G. (1986). Escalating commitment to a course of action: A reinterpretation. *Academy of Management Review, 11,* 311–321.

Whyte, W. F. (1943). *Street corner society.* Chicago: University of Chicago Press.

Wicklund, R. A., Cooper, J., & Linder, D. (1967). Effects of expected effort on attitude change prior to exposure. *Journal of Experimental Social Psychology, 3,* 41–78.

Widmeyer, W. N., Brawley, L. R., & Carron, A. V. (1990). The effects of group size in sport. *Journal of Sport and Exercise Psychology, 12,* 177–190.

Wilder, D. A., & Shapiro, P. N. (1984). Role of outgroup cues in determining social identity. *Journal of Personality and Social Psychology, 47,* 342–348.

Wilson, E. O. (1978). *On human nature.* Cambridge, MA: Harvard University Press.

Wilson, S. (2001a, April 17) Colombian right's 'cleaning' campaign. *The Washington Post,* p. A11

Wilson, S. (2001b, April 21). Colombian massacre large, brutal. *The Washington Post,* p. A14

Winter, D. G. (1973). *The power motive.* New York: Free Press.

Winter, D. G. (1980). Measuring the motive patterns of Southern African political leaders at a distance. *Political Psychology, 2,* 75–85.

Winter, D. G. (1987). Leader appeal, leader performance, and the motive profiles of leaders and followers: A study of American presidents and elections. *Journal of Personality and Social Psychology, 52,* 196–202.

Winter, D. G. (2003). Assessing leaders' personalities: A historic survey of academic research studies. In J. D. Post (Ed.), *The psychological assessment of political leaders* (pp. 11–38). Ann Arbor: University of Michigan Press.

Winter, D. G., & Carlson, L. A. (1988). Using motive scores in the psychobiographical study of an individual: The case of Richard Nixon. *Journal of Personality, 56,* 75–103.

Winter, D. G., Hermann, M. G., Weintraub, W., and Walker, S. G. (1991). The personalities of Bush and Gorbachev measured at a distance: Procedures, portraits, and policy. *Political Psychology, 12,* 215–245.

Winter, D. G., & Stewart, A. J. (1977). Content analysis as a technique for assessing political leaders. In M. G. Hermann (Ed.), *A psychological examination of political leaders* (pp. 21–61). New York: Free Press.

Wittenbaum, G., & Stasser, G. (1996). Management of information in small groups. In J. Nye & A. Bower (Eds.), *What's social about social cognition?* Thousand Oaks, CA: Sage.

Wolfenstein, E. V. (1971). *The revolutionary personality.* Princeton, NJ: Princeton University Press.

Wood, W., Lundgren, S., Ouellette, J. A., Busceme, S., & Blackstone, T. (1994). Minority influence: A meta-analytic review of social influence processes. *Psychological Bulletin, 115,* 323–345.

Woodward, B. (1991). *The commanders.* New York: Simon & Schuster.

Woodward, B. (1996). *The choice.* New York: Simon & Schuster.

Woodward, S. (1995). *Balkan tragedy: Chaos and dissolution after the cold war.* Washington, DC: Brookings Institute.

Woodward, S. (2000). Costly disinterest: Missed opportunities for preventive diplomacy in Croatia and Bosnia and Herzegovina, 1985–1991. In B. Jentleson (Ed.), *Opportunities missed, opportunities seized: Preventive diplomacy in the post-cold war world.* New York: Rowman & Littlefield.

Worchel, S., & Brehm, J. W. (1971). Direct and implied social restoration of freedom. *Journal of Personality and Social Psychology, 18,* 294–304.

Wyer R.S., & Ottati, V. (1995). Political information processing. In S. Inyengar & W. McGuire (Eds.), *Explorations in political psychology* (pp. 264–295). Durham, NC: Duke University Press.

Yinger, J. M. (1994). *Ethnicity: Source of strength? Source of conflict?* Albany: State University of New York Press.

Young, C. (1976). *The politics of cultural pluralism.* Madison: University of Wisconsin Press.

Young, C. (1983). Comparative claims to political sovereignty: Biafra, Katanga, Eritrea. In D. Rothchild & V. Olorunsola (Eds.), *State versus ethnic claims: African policy dilemmas* (pp. 199–232). Boulder, CO: Westview Press.

Zaccaro, S. J. (1984). Social loafing: The role of attractiveness. *Personality and Social Psychology Bulletin, 10,* 99–106.

Zajonc, R. B. (1965). Social facilitation. *Science, 149,* 269–274.

Zajonc, R. B. (1980a). Feeling and thinking: Preferences need no inferences. *American Psychologist, 39,* 139–151.

Zajonc, R. B. (1980b). Compresence. In P. B. Paulus (Ed.), *Psychology of group influence* (pp. 35–60). Hillsdale, NJ: Lawrence Erlbaum Associates.

Zaller, J. R. (1992). *The nature and origins of mass opinion.* New York: Cambridge University Press.

Zander, A. (1985). *The purposes of groups and organizations.* San Francisco: Jossey-Bass.

Zenger, T. R., & Lawrence, B. S. (1989). Organizational demography: The differential effects of age and tenure distributions on technical communication. *Academy of Management Journal, 32,* 353–376.

Zhao, S. (2000). Chinese nationalism and its international orientations. *Political Science Quarterly, 115,* 1–33.

Ziller, R. C., Stone, W. F., Jackson, R. M., & Terbovic, N. J. (1977). Self-other orientations and political behavior. In M. G. Hermann (Ed.), *A psychological examination of political leaders* (pp. 337–353). New York: Free Press.

Zurcher, L. A., Jr. (1969). Stages of development in poverty program neighborhood action committees. *Journal of Applied Behavioral Science, 15,* 223–258.

Author Index

Subject Index